Lecture Notes in Computer Science   4903

Commenced Publication in 1973
Founding and Former Series Editors:
Gerhard Goos, Juris Hartmanis, and Jan van Leeuwen

Editorial Board

T0223160

Shin'ichi Satoh Frank Nack Minoru Etoh (Eds.)

Advances in Multimedia Modeling

14th International Multimedia
Modeling Conference, MMM 2008
Kyoto, Japan, January 9-11, 2008
Proceedings

 Springer

Volume Editors

Shin'ichi Satoh
National Institute of Informatics
Digital Content and Media Sciences Research Division
2-1-2 Hitotsubashi, Chiyoda-ku, Tokyo 101-8430, Japan
E-mail: satoh@nii.ac.jp

Frank Nack
University of Amsterdam
Human-Computer Studies Laboratory (HCS), Institute for Informatics
Kruislaan 419, 1098 VA Amsterdam, The Netherlands
E-mail: Frank.Nack@cwi.nl

Minoru Etoh
NTT DoCoMo Research Laboratories
3-5 Hikarionoka, Yokosuka 239-8536, Japan
E-mail: etoh@ieee.org

Library of Congress Control Number: 2007941600

CR Subject Classification (1998): H.5.1, H.5, I.4, H.2.4, I.3, H.3-4, E.4

LNCS Sublibrary: SL 3 – Information Systems and Application, incl. Internet/Web
and HCI

ISSN   0302-9743
ISBN-10   3-540-77407-6 Springer Berlin Heidelberg New York
ISBN-13   978-3-540-77407-5 Springer Berlin Heidelberg New York

Springer is a part of Springer Science+Business Media

springer.com

© Springer-Verlag Berlin Heidelberg 2008
Printed in Germany

Typesetting: Camera-ready by author, data conversion by Scientific Publishing Services, Chennai, India
Printed on acid-free paper   SPIN: 12208562   06/3180   5 4 3 2 1 0

Preface

Welcome to the 14th International Multimedia Modeling Conference (MMM2008), held January 9–11, 2008 at Kyoto University, Kyoto, Japan. MMM is a leading international conference for researchers and industry practitioners to share their new ideas, original research results and practical development experiences from all multimedia related areas.

It was a great honor to have MMM2008, one of the most long-standing multimedia conferences, at one of the most beautiful and historically important Japanese cities. Kyoto was an ancient capital of Japan, and was and still is at the heart of Japanese culture and history. Kyoto in winter may distinctively offer the sober atmosphere of an ink painting. You can enjoy old shrines and temples which are designated as World Heritage Sites. The conference venue was the Clock Tower Centennial Hall in Kyoto University, which is one of the oldest universities in Japan.

MMM2008 featured a comprehensive program including three keynote talks, six oral presentation sessions, and two poster and demo sessions. The 133 submissions included a large number of high-quality papers in multimedia content analysis, multimedia signal processing and communications, and multimedia applications and services. We thank our 137 Technical Program Committee members and reviewers who spent many hours reviewing papers and providing valuable feedback to the authors. Based on the 3 or 4 reviews per paper the Program Chairs decided to accept only 23 as oral papers and 24 as poster papers, where each type of presentation could in addition present the work as a demo. The acceptance rate of 36% follows the MMM tradition of fulfilling fruitful discussions throughout the conference. Additionally, three paper awards were chosen: the Best Paper Award, the Best Student Paper Award, and the Best Poster Award.

The technical program is an important aspect but only provides its full impact if surrounded by challenging keynotes. We are pleased with and thankful to our keynote speakers, Tsuhan Chen, Shigeo Morishima and Tat-Seng Chua, for having accepted to present at MMM2008.

We are also heavily indebted to many individuals for their significant contribution. We thank the MMM Steering Committee for their invaluabe input and guidance in crucial decisions. We wish to acknowledge and express our deepest appreciation to the Organizing Co-chairs, Yuichi Nakamura and Ichiro Ide, the Finance Chair, Shigeyuki Sakazawa, the Publication Co-chairs, Toshihiko Yamasaki and Hiroshi Mo, the Publicity and Sponsorship Chair, Naoko, and Nitta, and the Local Arrangement Committee and Conference Management services. Without their efforts and enthusiasm, MMM2008 would not have been made a reality.

We gratefully thank the Media Center, Kyoto University, the Support Center for Advanced Telecommunications Technology Research Foundation (SCAT), International Communications Foundation (ICF) and the Telecommunications Advancement Foundation (TAF) for their generous support of MMM2008, which made several key aspects of the conference possible.

Finally, we wish to appreciatively thank all Committee members, reviewers, session Chairs, student volunteers and supporters. Their contributions cannot be measured in words.

January 2008

Kiyoharu Aizawa
Noboru Babaguchi
Shin'ichi Satoh
Frank Nack
Minoru Etoh

MMM2008 Organization

Organizing Committee

General Co-chairs	Kiyoharu Aizawa
	University of Tokyo, Japan
	Noboru Babaguchi
	Osaka University, Japan
Program Co-chairs	Shin'ichi Satoh
	National Institute of Informatics, Japan
	Frank Nack
	University of Amsterdam, The Netherlands
	Minoru Etoh
	NTT DoCoMo Research Laboratories, Japan
Organizing Co-chairs	Yuichi Nakamura
	Kyoto University, Japan
	Ichiro Ide
	Nagoya University, Japan
Finance Chair	Shigeyuki Sakazawa
	KDDI R&D Laboratories, Japan
Publication Co-chairs	Toshihiko Yamasaki
	University of Tokyo, Japan
	Hiroshi Mo
	National Institute of Informatics, Japan
Publicity and Sponsorship Chair	Naoko Nitta
	Osaka University, Japan
Asian Liaisons	Yi-Ping Phoebe Chen
	Deakin University, Australia
	Tat-Seng Chua
	National University of Singapore, Singapore
	Yo-Sung Ho
	Gwangju Institute of Science and Technology, Korea
	Wei-Ying Ma
	Microsoft Research Asia, China
USA Liaison	Shih-Fu Chang
	Columbia University, USA
European Liaison	Nicu Sebe
	University of Amsterdam, The Netherlands

Steering Committee

Yi-Ping Phoebe Chen
  Deakin University, Australia
Tat-Seng Chua
  National University of Singapore, Singapore
Tosiyasu L. Kunii
  Kanazawa Institute of Technology, Japan
Wei-Ying Ma
  Microsoft Research Asia, China
Nadia Magnenat-Thalmann
  University of Geneva, Switzerland
Patrick Senac
  ENSICA, France

Program Committee

Brett Adams
  Curtin University of Technology,
  Australia
Laurent Amsaleg
  IRISA-CNRS, France
Elisabeth Andre
  University of Augsburg, Germany
Yasuo Ariki
  Kobe University, Japan
Lora Aroyo
  Free University Amsterdam,
  The Netherlands
Selin Aviyente
  Michigan State University, USA
Brian Bailey
  University of Illinois, USA
Selim Balcisoy
  Sabanci University, Turkey
Claus Bauer
  Dolby Laboratories, USA
Stefano Bocconi
  Università degli Studi di Torino,
  Italy
Susanne Boll
  University of Oldenburg, Germany
Kevin Brooks
  Motorola, USA

Lekha Chaisorn
  Institute for Infocomm Research,
  Singapore
Tat-Jen Cham
  Nanyang Technological University,
  Singapore
Edward Chang
  University of California, USA
Lap-Pui Chau
  Nanyang Technological University,
  Singapore
Yi-Shin Chen
  National Tsing Hua University,
  Taiwan
Gene Cheung
  HP Labs, Japan
Liang-Tien Chia
  Nanyang Technological University,
  Singapore
Tat-Seng Chua
  National University of Singapore,
  Singapore
Jean-Pierre Courtiat
  Gmail, USA
Michel Crucianu
  Conservatoire National des Arts et
  Métiers, France

Alberto Del Bimbo
 University of Florence, Italy
Zoran Dimitrijevic
 Google, USA
Ajay Divakaran
 MERL, USA
Chabane Djeraba
 University of Sciences and
 Technologies of Lille, France
Chitra Dorai
 IBM T.J. Watson Research Center,
 USA
Jean-Luc Dugelay
 Institut Eurecom, France
Touradj Ebrahimi
 EPFL, Switzerland
Jianping Fan
 University of North Carolina, USA
Marin Ferecatu
 INRIA, France
Pascal Frossard
 Swiss Federal Institute of
 Technology - EPFL, Switzerland
Borko Furht
 Florida Atlantic University, USA
Joost Geurts
 INRIA, France
Forouzan Golshani
 Wright State University, USA
Yihong Gong
 NEC Labs America, USA
Andrew Gordon
 University of Southern California,
 USA
Valerie Gouet
 Conservatoire National des Arts et
 Métiers, France
Patrick Gros
 INRIA, France
William Grosky
 University of Michigan, USA
Zhenghui Gu
 Institute for Infocomm Research,
 Singapore

Mario Gutiérrez
 ITESM Campus Toluca, Mexico
Huang Haibin
 Institute for Infocomm Research,
 Singapore
Seiichiro Hangai
 Tokyo University of Science, Japan
Alan Hanjalic
 Delft University of Technology,
 The Netherlands
Madoka Hasegawa
 Utsunomiya Univeristy, Japan
Miki Haseyama
 Hokkaido University, Japan
Alexander Hauptmann
 Carnegie Mellon University, USA
Laura Hollink
 VU University Amsterdam,
 The Netherlands
Youn-Sik Hong
 University of Incheon, Korea
Xian-Sheng Hua
 Microsoft Research Asia, China
Weimin Huang
 Institute for Infocomm Research,
 Singapore
Benoit Huet
 Institut Eurecom, France
Jane Hunter
 University of Queensland, Australia
Alejandro Jaimes
 IDIAP, Switzerland
Alexis Joly
 INRIA, France
Björn Jónsson
 Reykjavik University, Iceland
James Joshi
 University of Pittsburgh, USA
Yoshinari Kameda
 University of Tsukuba, Japan
Mohan Kankanhalli
 National University of Singapore,
 Singapore

Jiro Katto
   Waseda University, Japan
Andruid Kerne
   Texas A&M Interface Ecology Lab,
   USA
Seon Kim
   University of Denver, USA
Asanobu Kitamoto
   National Institute of Informatics,
   Japan
Kazuya Kodama
   National Institute of Informatics,
   Japan
Duy-Dinh Le
   National Institute of Informatics,
   Japan
Clement Leung
   University of Victoria, Australia
Michael Lew
   Leiden University,
   The Netherlands
Mingjing Li
   Microsoft Research Asia, China
Qing Li
   City University of Hong Kong,
   Hong Kong
Te Li
   Institute for Infocomm Research,
   Singapore
Zhengguo Li
   Institute for Infocomm Research,
   Singapore
Rainer Lienhart
   University of Augsburg, Germany
Joo-Hwee Lim
   Institute for Infocomm Research,
   Singapore
Chia-Wen Lin
   National Chung-Cheng University,
   Taiwan
Weisi Lin
   Nanyang Technological University,
   Singapore
Craig Lindley
   HGO Visby, Sweden

Zhu Liu
   AT&T Laboratories, USA
Guojun Lu
   Monash University, Australia
Zhongkang Lu
   Institute for Infocomm Research,
   Singapore
Nadia Magnenat-Thalmann
   Miralab, Switzerland
Jean Martinet
   National Institute of Informatics,
   Japan
Tao Mei
   Microsoft Research Asia, China
Bernard Merialdo
   Institut Eurecom, France
Hisashi Miyamori
   NICT, Japan
Masayuki Mukunoki
   Hiroshima City University, Japan
Yasuyuki Nakajima
   KDDI Labs, Japan
P. Narayanan
   International Institute of
   Information Technology, India
Chong-Wah Ngo
   City University of Hong Kong,
   Hong Kong
Laurence Noel
   Mondeca, France
Wei Tsang Ooi
   National University of Singapore,
   Singapore
Vincent Oria
   NJIT, USA
Kazuhiro Otsuka
   NTT, Japan
Yannick Prié
   Université Claude Bernard Lyon 1,
   France
Matthias Rauterberg
   Technical University Eindhoven,
   The Netherlands
Lloyd Rutledge
   CWI, The Netherlands

Andrew Salway
  Burton Bradstock Research Labs,
  UK
Patrick Schmitz
  Ludicrum Enterprises, USA
Claudia Schremmer
  CSIRO Australia, Australia
Nicu Sebe
  University of Amsterdam,
  The Netherlands
Ishwar Sethi
  Oakland University, USA
Timothy Shih
  Tamkang University, Taiwan
Koichi Shinoda
  Tokyo Institute of Technology,
  Japan
Cees Snoek
  University of Amsterdam,
  The Netherlands
Ronggong Song
  National Research Council Canada,
  Canada
Ola Stockfelt
  Göteborg University, Sweden
Qibin Sun
  Institute for Infocomm Research,
  Singapore
Hari Sundaram
  Arizona State Univeristy, USA
Audrey Tam
  RMIT University, Australia
Wai-tian Tan
  Hewlett-Packard, USA
Kiyoshi Tanaka
  Shinshu University, Japan
Taro Tezuka
  Kyoto University, Japan
Daniel Thalmann
  EPFL, Switzerland
Jo-Yew Tham
  Institute for Infocomm Research,
  Singapore
George Tzanetakis
  University of Victoria, Canada

Shingo Uchihashi
  Fuji Xerox Co. Ltd., Japan
Mihaela van der Schaar
  University of California at
  Los Angeles, USA
Svetha Venkatesh
  Curtin University of Technology,
  Australia
Benjamin Wah
  University of Illinois, USA
Marcel Worring
  University of Amsterdam,
  The Netherlands
Feng Wu
  Microsoft Research Asia, China
Jiankang Wu
  Institute for Infocomm Research,
  Singapore
Shiqian Wu
  Institute for Infocomm Research,
  Singapore
Changsheng Xu
  Institute for Infocomm Research,
  Singapore
Nobuyuki Yagi
  NHK Science and Technical
  Research Laboratories, Japan
Keiji Yanai
  University of Electro-Communications,
  Japan
Xiaokang Yang
  Shanghai Jaoton University, China
Susu Yao
  Institute for Infocomm Research,
  Singapore
Yoshiyuki Yashima
  NTT Corporation, Japan
Rongshan Yu
  Dolby Laboratories, USA
Avideh Zakhor
  University of California at Berkeley,
  USA
Zhongfei Zhang
  State University of New York at
  Binghamton, USA

Haifeng Zheng
  Fuzhou University, China
Bin Zhu
  Microsoft Research China, China

Yongwei Zhu
  Institute for Infocomm Research,
  Singapore
Roger Zimmermann
  University of Southern California,
  USA

Additional Reviewers

Rachid Benmokhtar
  Eurecom Institute, France
Marco Bertini
  University of Florence, Italy
Nouha Bouteldja
  Conservatoire National des Arts et
  Métiers, France
Duan-Yu Chen
  Academia Sinica, Taiwan
Eric Galmar
  Eurecom Institute, France
Shuqiang Jiang
  Chinese Academy of Sciences, China
Dan Jurca
  EPFL, Switzerland
Francisco Jose Silva Mata
  Centro de Aplicaciones de
  Tecnologías de Avanzada, Italy
Simon Moncrieff
  Curtin University, Australia
Antonio Ortega
  University of Southern California,
  USA
Marco Paleari
  Eurecom Institute, France

Guo-Jun Qi
  University of Science and
  Technology of China, China
Philipp Sandhaus
  Oldenburg R&D Institute for
  Information Technology Tools and
  Systems, Germany
Tele Tan
  Curtin University, Australia
Jinhui Tang
  University of Science and
  Technology of China, China
Ivana Tosic
  EPFL, Switzerland
Ba Tu Truong
  Curtin University, Australia
Jinjun Wang
  NEC Laboratories America, Inc.,
  USA
Meng Wang
  University of Science and
  Technology of China, China
Yan-Tao Zheng
  National University of Singapore,
  Singapore

Local Arrangements Committee

Masaaki Iiyama
  Kyoto University, Japan
Takuya Funatomi
  Kyoto University, Japan
Motoyuki Ozeki
  Kyoto University, Japan
Takahiro Koizumi
  Kyoto University, Japan

Other Contributors

Web Site Design	Lina
	Nagoya University, Japan
Program Brochure Design	Tomokazu Takahashi
	JSPS/Nagoya University, Japan
Official Travel Agent	JTB Western Japan Corp., Kyoto Branch

Table of Contents

Media Understanding

A Novel Approach for Filtering Junk Images from Google Search
Results 1
    Yuli Gao, Jianping Fan, Hangzai Luo, and Shin'ichi Satoh

Object-Based Image Retrieval Beyond Visual Appearances 13
    Yan-Tao Zheng, Shi-Yong Neo, Tat-Seng Chua, and Qi Tian

MILC^2: A Multi-Layer Multi-Instance Learning Approach to Video
Concept Detection 24
    *Zhiwei Gu, Tao Mei, Jinhui Tang, Xiuqing Wu, and
    Xian-Sheng Hua*

Poster I

An Implicit Active Contour Model for Feature Regions and Lines 35
    Ho-Ryong Jung and Moon-Ryul Jung

New Approach for Hierarchical Classifier Training and Multi-level
Image Annotation 45
    Jianping Fan, Yuli Gao, Hangzai Luo, and Shin'ichi Satoh

Extracting Text Information for Content-Based Video Retrieval 58
    Lei Xu and Kongqiao Wang

Real-Time Video Surveillance Based on Combining Foreground
Extraction and Human Detection 70
    Hui-Chi Zeng, Szu-Hao Huang, and Shang-Hong Lai

Detecting and Clustering Multiple Takes of One Scene 80
    Werner Bailer, Felix Lee, and Georg Thallinger

An Images-Based 3D Model Retrieval Approach 90
    *Yuehong Wang, Rujie Liu, Takayuki Baba, Yusuke Uehara,
    Daiki Masumoto, and Shigemi Nagata*

'Oh Web Image, Where Art Thou?' 101
    Dirk Ahlers and Susanne Boll

Complementary Variance Energy for Fingerprint Segmentation 113
    Z. Hou, W.Y. Yau, N.L. Than, and W. Tang

Similarity Search in Multimedia Time Series Data Using
Amplitude-Level Features 123
   Johannes Aßfalg, Hans-Peter Kriegel, Peer Kröger, Peter Kunath,
   Alexey Pryakhin, and Matthias Renz

Sound Source Localization with Non-calibrated Microphones 134
   Tomoyuki Kobayashi, Yoshinari Kameda, and Yuichi Ohta

PriSurv: Privacy Protected Video Surveillance System Using Adaptive
Visual Abstraction 144
   Kenta Chinomi, Naoko Nitta, Yoshimichi Ito, and Noboru Babaguchi

Distribution-Based Similarity for Multi-represented Multimedia
Objects 155
   Hans-Peter Kriegel, Peter Kunath, Alexey Pryakhin, and
   Matthias Schubert

Creative Media

A Multimodal Input Device for Music Authoring for Children 165
   Yasushi Akiyama and Sageev Oore

Free-Shaped Video Collage 175
   Bo Yang, Tao Mei, Li-Feng Sun, Shi-Qiang Yang, and
   Xian-Sheng Hua

Aesthetics-Based Automatic Home Video Skimming System 186
   Wei-Ting Peng, Yueh-Hsuan Chiang, Wei-Ta Chu, Wei-Jia Huang,
   Wei-Lun Chang, Po-Chung Huang, and Yi-Ping Hung

Using Fuzzy Lists for Playlist Management 198
   François Deliège and Torben Bach Pedersen

Visual Content Representation

Tagging Video Contents with Positive/Negative Interest Based on
User's Facial Expression 210
   Masanori Miyahara, Masaki Aoki, Tetsuya Takiguchi, and
   Yasuo Ariki

Snap2Play: A Mixed-Reality Game Based on Scene Identification 220
   Tat-Jun Chin, Yilun You, Celine Coutrix, Joo-Hwee Lim,
   Jean-Pierre Chevallet, and Laurence Nigay

Real-Time Multi-view Object Tracking in Mediated Environments 230
   Huan Jin, Gang Qian, and David Birchfield

Reconstruct 3D Human Motion from Monocular Video Using Motion
Library   242
  *Wenzhong Wang, Xianjie Qiu, Zhaoqi Wang, Rongrong Wang, and
  Jintao Li*

Poster II

Appropriate Segment Extraction from Shots Based on Temporal
Patterns of Example Videos   253
  Yousuke Kurihara, Naoko Nitta, and Noboru Babaguchi

Fast Segmentation of H.264/AVC Bitstreams for On-Demand Video
Summarization   265
  Klaus Schöffmann and Laszlo Böszörmenyi

Blurred Image Detection and Classification   277
  Ping Hsu and Bing-Yu Chen

Cross-Lingual Retrieval of Identical News Events by Near-Duplicate
Video Segment Detection   287
  Akira Ogawa, Tomokazu Takahashi, Ichiro Ide, and Hiroshi Murase

Web Image Gathering with a Part-Based Object Recognition
Method   297
  Keiji Yanai

A Query Language Combining Object Features and Semantic Events
for Surveillance Video Retrieval   307
  *Thi-Lan Le, Monique Thonnat, Alain Boucher, and
  François Brémond*

Semantic Quantization of 3D Human Motion Capture Data Through
Spatial-Temporal Feature Extraction   318
  Yohan Jin and B. Prabhakaran

Fast Intermode Decision Via Statistical Learning for H.264
Video Coding   329
  Wei-Hau Pan, Chen-Kuo Chiang, and Shang-Hong Lai

A Novel Motion Estimation Method Based on Normalized Cross
Correlation for Video Compression   338
  Shou-Der Wei, Wei-Hau Pan, and Shang-Hong Lai

Curved Ray-Casting for Displacement Mapping in the GPU   348
  Kyung-Gun Na and Moon-Ryul Jung

Emotion-Based Music Visualization Using Photos   358
  *Chin-Han Chen, Ming-Fang Weng, Shyh-Kang Jeng, and
  Yung-Yu Chuang*

LightCollabo: Distant Collaboration Support System for
Manufacturers   369
    Tetsuo Iyoda, Tsutomu Abe, Kiwame Tokai, Shoji Sakamoto,
    Jun Shingu, Hiroko Onuki, Meng Shi, and Shingo Uchihashi

Video Codec

Accurate Identifying Method of JPEG2000 Images for Digital
Cinema   380
    Takahiro Fukuhara, Kazuhisa Hosaka, and Hitoshi Kiya

Optimization of Spatial Error Concealment for H.264 Featuring Low
Complexity   391
    Shih-Chia Huang and Sy-Yen Kuo

Temporal Error Concealment for H.264 Using Optimum Regression
Plane   402
    Shih-Chia Huang and Sy-Yen Kuo

Transform Domain Wyner-Ziv Codec Based on Turbo Trellis Codes
Modulation   413
    J.L. Martínez, W.A.R.J. Weerakkody, P. Cuenca, F. Quiles, and
    W.A.C. Fernando

Media Retrieval

Selective Sampling Based on Dynamic Certainty Propagation for Image
Retrieval   425
    Xiaoyu Zhang, Jian Cheng, Hanqing Lu, and Songde Ma

Local Radon Transform and Earth Mover's Distances for Content-Based
Image Retrieval   436
    Wei Xiong, S.H. Ong, Weiping Lee, and Kelvin Foong

Content Based Querying and Searching for 3D Human Motions   446
    Manoj M. Pawar, Gaurav N. Pradhan, Kang Zhang, and
    Balakrishnan Prabhakaran

Bi-modal Conceptual Indexing for Medical Image Retrieval   456
    Joo-Hwee Lim, Jean-Pierre Chevallet, Diem Thi Hoang Le, and
    Hanlin Goh

Audio and Music

Audio Analysis for Multimedia Retrieval from a Ubiquitous Home   466
    Gamhewage C. de Silva, Toshihiko Yamasaki, and Kiyoharu Aizawa

Effectiveness of Signal Segmentation for Music Content
Representation 477
  Namunu C. Maddage, Mohan S. Kankanhalli, and Haizhou Li

Probabilistic Estimation of a Novel Music Emotion Model............. 487
  Tien-Lin Wu and Shyh-Kang Jeng

Acoustic OFDM: Embedding High Bit-Rate Data in Audio............ 498
  *Hosei Matsuoka, Yusuke Nakashima, Takeshi Yoshimura, and
  Toshiro Kawahara*

Author Index 509

A Novel Approach for Filtering Junk Images from Google Search Results

Yuli Gao[1], Jianping Fan[1,*], Hangzai Luo[1], and Shin'ichi Satoh[2]

[1] Department of Computer Science, UNC-Charlott, USA
{jfan,ygao,hluo}@uncc.edu
[2] National Institute of Informatics, Tokyo, Japan
satoh@nii.ac.jp

Abstract. Keyword-based image search engines such as Google Images are now very popular for accessing large amount of images on the Internet. Because only the text information that are directly or indirectly linked to the images are used for image indexing and retrieval, most existing image search engines such as Google Images may return large amount of junk images which are irrelevant to the given queries. To filter out the junk images from Google Images, we have developed a kernel-based image clustering technique to partition the images returned by Google Images into multiple visually-similar clusters. In addition, users are allowed to input their feedbacks for updating the underlying kernels to achieve more accurate characterization of the diversity of visual similarities between the images. To help users assess the goodness of image kernels and the relevance between the returned images, a novel framework is developed to achieve more intuitive visualization of large amount of returned images according to their visual similarity. Experiments on diverse queries on Google Images have shown that our proposed algorithm can filter out the junk images effectively. Online demo is also released for public evaluation at: *http://www.cs.uncc.edu/~jfan/google_demo/*.

Keywords: Junk image filtering, similarity-preserving image projection.

1 Introduction

As online image sharing and personal journalism become more and more popular, there is an urgent need to develop more effective image search engines, so that users can successfully retrieve large amount of images on the Internet. Text-based image search engines such as Google Images have achieved great success on exploiting text information to index and retrieve large-scale online image collections. Even Google has the most powerful text search engine in the world, Google Images is still unsatisfactory because of the relatively low precision rate of the top ranked images [6-10]. One of the major reasons for this phenomena is due to the fact that Google simplifies the image search problem as a purely text-based search problem, and the underlying assumption is that the image semantics are directly related to the text terms extracted from the associated documents. Unfortunately, such oversimplified online image indexing approach has completely ignored that the linkages between the image semantics and the text

---

* Correspondence Author.

S. Satoh, F. Nack, and M. Etoh (Eds.): MMM 2008, LNCS 4903, pp. 1–12, 2008.

terms (that can be extracted from the associated text documents) may not be one-to-one correspondence, but they could be one-to-many, many-to-one, or many-to-many relationships, or even there is no exact correspondence between the image semantics and the associated text terms. This is the major reason why Google Images may return large amount of junk images which are irrelevant to the given keyword-based queries. In addition, a lot of real world settings, such as photo-sharing websites, may only be able to provide biased and noisy text taggings which may further mislead the text-based image search engines such as Google Images. Therefore, there is an urgent need to develop new algorithms to support junk image filtering from Google Images [6-10].

With the increasing computional power of modern computers, it is possible to incorporate image analysis algorithms into the text-based image search engines such as Google Images without degrading their response speed significantly. Recent advance in computer vision and multimedia computing can also allow us to take advantages of the rich visual information (embedded in the images) for image semantics interpretation. Some pioneer works have been proposed to improve Google Images [6-10].

By integrating multi-modal information (visual similarity, associated text, and users' feedbacks) for image semantics interpretation, we have developed a novel framework to filter out the junk images from Google Images. Our scheme takes the following major steps for junk image filtering: (a) Google Images is first performed to obtain large amount of images returned for a given text-based query; (b) Our feature extraction algorithm is then performed to extract both the global and local visual features for image similarity characterization; (c) The diverse visual similarities between the images are characterized jointly by using multiple kernels and the returned images are partitioned into multiple clusters according to their kernel-based visual similarities; (d) A hyperbolic visualization algorithm is developed to achieve more understandable assessment of the relevance between the returned images and the users' real query intentions; (e) If necessary, users can involve to select few relevant images or junk images and such users' feedbacks are automatically transformed to update the kernels for image similarity characterization; (f) The updated kernel is further used to create a new presentation of the returned images adaptively according to the users' personal preferences.

2   Image Content Representation

The visual properties of the images are very important for users to assess the relevance between the images returned by keyword-based queries and their real query intentions [1-2]. Unfortunately, Google Images has fully ignored such important characteristics of the images. In this paper, we have developed a new framework to seamlessly integrate keyword-based image search with traditional content-based image search. To avoid the pitfalls of image segmentation tools, image segmentation is not performed for feature extraction. To characterize the diverse visual properties of images efficiently and effectively, both the global visual features and the local visual features are extracted for image similarity characterization. The global visual features such as color histogram can provide the global image statistics and the general perceptual properties of entire images [11]. On the other hand, the local visual features via wavelet image transformation can characterize the most significant information of the underlying image structures effectively [12].

To filter out the junk images from Google Images, the basic question is to define more suitable similarity functions to accurately characterize the diverse visual similarities between the images returned by the keyword-based queries. Recently, the use of kernel functions for data similarity characterization plays an important role in the statistical learning framework, where the kernel functions may satisfy some mathematical requirements and possibly capture some domain knowledge.

In this paper, we have proposed two basic image descriptors to characterize various visual and geometrical properties of images [11-12]: (a) global color histogram; (b) texture histogram via wavelet filter bank. The diverse visual similarities between the images can be characterized more effectively and efficiently by using a linear combination of their basic image kernels (i.e., mixture-of-kernels):

$$\hat{K}(x, y) = \sum_{i=1}^{\kappa} \alpha_i K_i(x, y), \qquad \sum_{i=1}^{\kappa} \alpha_i = 1 \tag{1}$$

where $\alpha_i \geq 0$ is the importance factor for the ith basic image kernel $K_i(x, y)$ for image similarity characterization. The rules for multiple kernel combination (i.e., the selection of the values for the importance factors α) depend on two key issues: (a) The relative importance of various visual features for image similarity characterization; (b) The users' preference. In this paper, we have developed an iterative algorithm to determine the values of the importance factors by seamlessly integrating both the importance of visual features and the users' preferences.

3   Kernel-Based Image Clustering

The images returned by the same keyword-based search are automatically partitioned into multiple clusters according to their kernel-based visual similarities. Our kernel-based image clustering algorithm is able to obtain the most significant global distribution structures of the returned images. Through using multiple kernels for diverse image similarity characterization, our kernel-based image clustering algorithm is able to handle high-dimensional visual features effectively.

The optimal partition of the returned images is obtained by minimizing the trace of the within-cluster scatter matrix, S_w^ϕ. The scatter matrix is given by:

$$S_w^\phi = \frac{1}{N} \sum_{l=1}^{\tau} \sum_{i=1}^{N} \beta_{li} \left(\hat{K}(x_i, x_j) - \frac{1}{N_l} \sum_{j=1}^{N} \beta_{lj} \hat{K}(x_i, x_j) \right) \tag{2}$$

where $\hat{K}(\cdot \cdot)$ is the mixture kernel function, N is the number of returned images and τ is the number of clusters, N_l is the number of images in the lth cluster. Searching the optimal values of the elements β_{li} that minimizes the expression of the trace can be achieved effectively by an iterative procedure. One major problem for kernel-based image clustering is that it may require huge memory space to store the kernel matrix when large amount of images come into view. Some pioneer works have been done for reducing the memory cost, such as Chunking, Sequential Minimal Optimization (SMO), SVM^{light}, and Mixture of Experts. One common shortage for these decomposition-based approaches is that global optimization is not performed.

Rather than following these decomposition-based approaches, we have developed a new algorithm for reducing the memory cost by seamlessly integrating parallel computing with global decision optimization. Our new algorithm takes the following key steps: (a) Users are allowed to define the maximum number of returned images which they want to see and assess, and thus it can reduce the memory cost significantly. In addition, the returned images are partitioned into multiple smaller subsets. (b) Our kernel-based image clustering algorithm is then performed on all these smaller image subsets to obtain a within-subset partition of the images according to their diverse visual similarities. (c) The support vectors for each image subset are validated by other image subsets through testing Karush-Kuhn-Tucker (KKT) conditions. The support vectors, which violate the KKT conditions, are integrated to update the decision boundaries for the corresponding image subset incrementally. This process is repeated until the global optimum is reached and an optimal partition of large amount of images under the same image topic can be obtained accurately.

Our kernel-based image clustering algorithm has the following advantages: (1) It can seamlessly integrate multiple kernels to characterize the diverse visual similarities between the images more accurately. Thus it can provide a good insight of large amount of images by determining their global distribution structures (i.e., image clusters and their distributions) accurately, and such global image distribution structures can further be integrated to achieve more effective image visualization for query result assessment. (2) Only the most representative images (which are the support vectors) are stored and validated by other image subsets, thus it may request far less memory space. The redundant images (which are non-support vectors) are eliminated early, thus it can significantly accelerate kernel-based image clustering. (3) Because the support vectors for each subset are validated by other subsets, our algorithm can handle the outliers and noise effectively and it can generate more robust clustering results.

4   Kernel Selection for Similarity-Preserving Image Projection

When the majority of the images returned by Google Images are relevant to the given keyword-based query, there should be an intrinsic clustering structure within the corresponding kernel matrix, i.e., the kernel matrix would be in the form of a perturbed block-diagonal matrix, where each block corresponds to one certain visual category, and other entries of the kernel matrix (which corresponds to outliers or wrong returns) are close to zero.

Based on this understanding, it seems reasonable to apply some meaningful "clusterness" measurement, such as the sum of square within-cluster distances, to estimate the relative importance between various basic image kernels, and such clusterness measurement can further be used as the criteria for kernel selection. However, this naive approach may actually yield a faulty decision due to the following reasons: (a) *The majority assumption may not hold true*. In the study conducted by Fergus et al. [6-7], it is reported that, among the images returned by Google Images, contains more "junk images" than "good images" for more than half of the queries they studied. (b) *A high "clusterness" measurement may not directly imply a good kernel matrix*, i.e., the reverse statement about the clusterness of the kernel matrix is not true. A trivial kernel matrix, with one in all its entries, may always yield the best clusterness score for all the queries. However, such trivial kernel matrix is certainly meaningless in revealing the true clustering structure. (c) *The text-based search engines unavoidably suffer from the problem of semantic ambiguity*. When users submit a query via keyword, the text-based image search engines such as Google Images may not know a priori which word sense corresponds to the user's request. Therefore, even the ideal kernel matrix may be available, the text-based search engines can not possibly know which image clusters are most relevant to the users' real needs.

Because the systems may not know the real needs of users (i.e., which image cluster is relevant or which image cluster is irrelevant to a given keyword-based query), it is very hard to define the suitable criteria to evaluate the goodness of the kernel matrix and achieve automatic kernel selection for junk image filtering, i.e., without users' inputs, it is very hard if not impossible to identify which image clusters correspond to the junk images. One potential solution for these difficulties is to allow users to interactively provide additional information for junk image filtering. Obviously, it is worth noting that such interaction should not bring huge burden on the users.

In order to capture users' feedbacks for junk image filtering, it is very important to enable similarity-based visualization of large amount of images returned by Google Images, so that users can quickly judge the relevance of an image with their real query intentions. It is well-known that the diverse visual similarities between the images can be characterized more effectively and efficiently by using different types of visual features and different types of kernels. Therefore, different types of these basic image kernels may play different roles on characterizing the similarity of the returned images from Google Images, and the optimal kernel for image similarity characterization can be approximated more effectively by using a linear combination of these basic image kernels with different importances. Obviously, such optimal combination of these basic image kernels for image similarity characterization also depends on users' preference.

To allow users to assess the relevance between the returned images and their real query intentions, it is very important to achieve similarity-based visualization of large amount of returned images by selecting an optimal combination of the basic image kernels. Instead of targeting on finding an optimal combination of these basic image kernels at the beginning, we have developed an iterative approach by starting from a single but most suitable basic image kernel for generating the image clusters and creating the hyperbolic visualization of the returned images, and the user's feedbacks are then integrated for obtaining the most accurate combination of the basic image kernels iteratively.

We adopt a semi-supervised paradigm for kernel combination and selection, where the most suitable basic image kernel is first used to generate the visually-similar image clusters and create the similarity-based visualization of the returned images. The users are then allowed to choose a couple of relevant/junk images. Such users' feedbacks are then transformed and integrated for updating the underlying image kernels incrementally, re-clustering the returned images and creating new presentation and visualization of the returned images. Through such iterative procedure, the most suitable image kernels can be selected and be combined to effectively characterize the diverse image similarities and filter out the junk images from Google Images.

To select the most suitable image kernel to start this iterative procedure, the S measure is used. For a given basic image kernel K, it can be turned into a distance matrix D, where the distance $D(x, y)$ between two images with the visual features x and y is given by:

$$D(x,y) = \parallel \phi(x) - \phi(y) \parallel = \sqrt{\hat{K}(x,x) + \hat{K}(z,z) - 2\hat{K}(x,z)} \tag{3}$$

where we use $\phi(x)$ to denote the implicit feature space of the image with the visual features x. We then rank all of these basic image kernels by their S scores, which is defined as:

$$S = \frac{\sum_{i=1}^{m} \sum_{j=i+1}^{m} D(x_i, x_j) - \sum_{i=1}^{m} \sum_{j=1}^{n} D(x_i, y_j)}{median(D)} \tag{4}$$

where $median(D)$ gives the median distance between all the pair-distances among all the image samples. $\{x_i | i = 1, \cdots, m\}$ and $\{y_j | j = 1, \cdots, n \ (m + n \geq 2)\}$ are the image pairs. Intuitively, S measure gives the favor of the basic image kernels which may have higher similarity between the relevant image pairs and lower similarity between the irrelevant image pairs. The smaller the S score, the better characterization of the image similarity. Therefore, the basic image kernel with the lowest S score is first selected as the ideal kernel to achieve an initial partition (clustering) of large amount of images returned by Google Images, and create an initial hyperbolic visualization of the returned images according to their kernel-based visual similarity, so that the users can easily assess the relevance between the returned images and their query intentions. In addition, the users can input their feedbacks interactively according to their personal preferences.

To preserve the similarity relationships between the returned images, the images returned by Google Images are projected to a 2D hyperbolic coordinate by using Kernel Principle Component Analysis (KPCA) according to the selected basic image kernel [13]. The kernel PCA is obtained by solving the eigenvalue equation:

$$Kv = \lambda M v \tag{5}$$

where $\lambda = [\lambda_1, \cdots, \lambda_M]$ denotes the eigenvalues and $v = [\vec{v_1}, \cdots, \vec{v_M}]$ denotes the corresponding complete set of eigenvectors, M is the number of the returned images, K is a kernel matrix.

The optimal KPCA-based image projection can be obtained by:

$$min \left\{ \sum_{i=1}^{M} \sum_{j=1}^{M} |\hat{K}(x_i, x_j) - d(x_i', x_j')|^2 \right\} \tag{6}$$

$$x_i' = \sum_{l=1}^{M} \alpha_l \hat{K}(x, x_l), \quad x_j' = \sum_{l=1}^{M} \alpha_l \hat{K}(x_l, x_j)$$

where $\hat{K}(x_i, x_j)$ is the original kernel-based similarity distance between the images with the visual features x_i and x_j, $d(x_i', x_j')$ is their location distance on the display unit disk by using kernel PCA to achieve similarity-preserving image projection. Thus the visually-similar images (i.e., images with smaller kernel-based similarity distances) can be visualized closely on the display unit disk. The suitable kernels for similarity-preserving image projection can be chosen automatically to make the most representative images from different clusters to be spatially distinct.

Our mixture-kernel function can characterize the diverse visual similarities between the images more accurately than the weighted distance functions used in multi-dimensional scaling (MDS), thus our KPCA-based projection framework can achieve better similarity-based image visualization than the MDS-based projection approaches. Therefore, KPCA-based image projection algorithm can preserve the similarity relationships between the images effectively.

5   Hyperbolic Image Visualization for Hypothesis Assessment

After such similarity-based image projection is obtained by using KPCA, Poincaré disk model [15] is used to map the returned images from their feature space (i.e., images which are represented by their visual features) onto a 2D display coordinate. Poincaré disk model maps the entire Euclidean space into an open unit circle, and produces a non-uniform mapping of the Euclidean distance to the hyperbolic space.

Formally, if let ρ be the hyperbolic distance and r be the Euclidean distance, of one certain image A to the center of the unit circle, the relationship between their derivative is described by:

$$d\rho = \frac{2}{1 - r^2} \cdot dr \tag{7}$$

Intuitively, this projection makes a unit Euclidean distance correspond to a longer hyperbolic distance as it approaches the rim of the unit circle. In other words, if the images are of fixed size, they would appear larger when they are closer to the origin of the unit circle and smaller when they are further away. This property makes it very suitable for visualizing large amount of images because the non-uniformity distance mapping creates an emphasis for the images which are in current focus, while de-emphasizing those images that are further form the focus point.

In practice, it is often difficult to achieve an optimal kernel at the first guess. Therefore, it is desirable to allow users to provide feedbacks to the system, e.g., how closely the current image layouts correspond to their real needs. On the other hand, it is also very important to guarantee that the system can capture such users' feedbacks effectively and transform them for updating the underlying kernel matrix and creating new presentation and visualization of large amount of returned images.

In this paper, we have explored the usage of *pair-wise* constraints which can be obtained from users' feedbacks automatically. In order to incorporate the users' feedbacks for improving kernel-based image clustering and projection, we have proposed an iterative algorithm that can directly translate the constraints (derived from the relevant and junk images given by the users) into the kernel transformation of input space (feature space) to generate more accurate kernels for image clustering and projection.

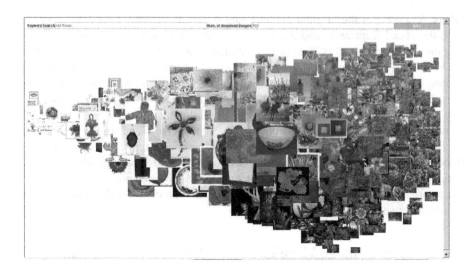

Fig. 1. Our online system for filtering junk images from Google Images, where the keyword "red flower" is used for Google image search and most junk images are projected on the left side

One naive method is to generalize the vector-based kernel by introducing a weight $w = (w_1, w_2, ..., w_N)$ on each feature dimension of the input vector space, i.e., $\phi(x) = (w_1 x_1, w_2 x_2, ..., w_N x_N)$. Suppose we encode the pair-wise constraints between two sets of feature vectors x, y in a constraint matrix $\mathbf{C}$, where $C(x, y) = 1$ for must-link image pairs (relevant image pairs); -1 for cannot-link image pairs (junk image pairs); 0 for non-constrained image pairs (image pairs which are not selected by the users), the weight w can then be updated as:

$$\widehat{w_i} = w_i \cdot e^{-\gamma \|x_i - y_i\| \cdot c(x,y)} \tag{8}$$

where γ is a learning rate specifiable by the users. This reweighing process corresponds to a dimension-wise rescaling of the input space such that the must-link image pairs can be *close* (in the form of norm distance) to each others, and the cannot-link image pairs are far apart. The resulting weight w also has an intuitive interpretation: dimensions associated with large weights are more discriminant. For example, when the feature vectors are represented as the color histogram, large weight for a certain dimension (color bin) means that the proportion of the image area associated with this quantized color play more important role on characterizing the image similarity. If we have m constraints to satisfy, the original input space can be transformed by a sequence of localized functions $f^1, f^2, \cdots, f^m$ and the final transformation of the input space is given by $\phi(x) = f^m(f^{m-1}(...f^2(f^1(x))))$.

However, the major limitation of this simple dimension-wise rescaling algorithm is that the scale factor along the full range of the respective dimension is uniform. If there exists the same rescaling demand on this dimension from both the must-link constraints and the cannot-link constraints, the rescaling would be cancelled.

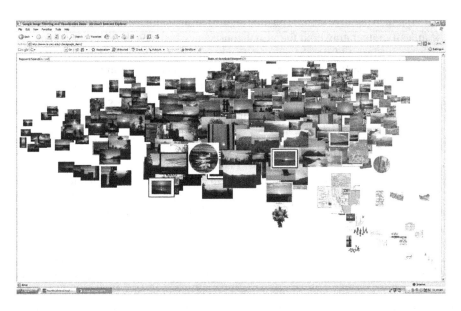

Fig. 2. Our online system for filtering junk images from Google Images, where the keyword "sunset" is used for Google image search and most junk images are projected on the right-bottom corner

To address this conflict, we have introduced two operators: ***shrinkage*** and ***expansion***, whose rescaling effects are limited to a local neighborhood. In this work, we use a piecewise linear function to achieve localized expansion and shrinkage. Obviously, other localized functions may also be applicable.

As indicated above, the transformation is now in the form of $f^k(\overrightarrow{x}) = (f_1(x_1), f_2(x_2), \cdots, f_N(x_N))$, where $f_i(x_i)$, $i = 1, \cdots, N$ are non-linear functions with localized transformations, and $\overrightarrow{x} = \{x_1, \cdots, x_N\}$ is N-dimensional feature vector. Given a pair of vectors u, v, the ith component of the transformation is to be updated as:

$$f_i(x_i) = \begin{cases} x_i & x_i < u_i \\ a \cdot (x_i - u_i) + u_i & x_i \in [u_i, v_i] \\ x_i + (a - 1) \cdot (v_i - u_i) & x_i > v_i \end{cases} \tag{9}$$

where $v_i > u_i$, a is a constant term that satisfies: $a > 1$ for expansion operation, and $0 < a < 1$ for shrinkage operation. We set $a = \frac{1}{\gamma}$ for the must-link constraints and $a = \gamma$ for the cannot-link constraints, where $\gamma > 1$ reflects the learning rate. This constrained rescaling is used in the hyperbolic visualization, which is iteratively rescaled until the best kernel for junk image filtering according to the users' personal preferences.

Although this rescaling is done piece-wise linearly in the input space, it can be a non-linear mapping in the feature space if non-linear kernels such as RBF are used. It can be proved that the new kernel satisfies Mercer's conditions because $\widehat{K}(x, y) = K(\phi(x), \phi(y))$, where $\phi(x) : R^N \longrightarrow R^N$.

Through such iterative kernel updating algorithm, an optimal kernel matrix is obtianed by seamlessly integrating both the visual consistency between the relevant images and the constraints derived from the user feedbacks, and our kernel-based image clustering algorithm is then performed to partition the returned images into multiple visual categories. The image cluster that is selected as the relevant images is returned to the user as the final result. Images in this cluster are then ranked in an ascending order according to their kernel-based similarity distances with the images that are selected by the users.

6 System Evaluation

For a given text-based image query, our system can automatically generate 2D hyperbolic visualization of the returned images according to their diverse kernel-based visual similarities. In Figs. 1, 2 and 3, the junk image filtering results for several keyword-based Google searches are given. From these experimental results, one can observe that our proposed system can filter out the junk images effectively. In addition, users are allowed to provide the must-link and the cannot-link constraints by clicking the relevant images and the junk images. Such constraints given by the users are automatically incorporated to update the underlying image kernels, generate new clustering and create new presentation and visualization of the returned images as shown in Fig. 4. One can observe that most junk images are filtered out after the first run of feedback. In order to invite more people to participate for evaluating our junk image filtering system, we have released our system at: ***http://www.cs.uncc.edu/~jfan/google_demo/*** .

To evaluate the effectiveness of our proposed algorithms for kernel selection and updating, the accuracy of the undlerying image clustering kernel is calculated for each user-system interaction. Given the *confusion matrix C* for image clustering, the accuracy is defined as:

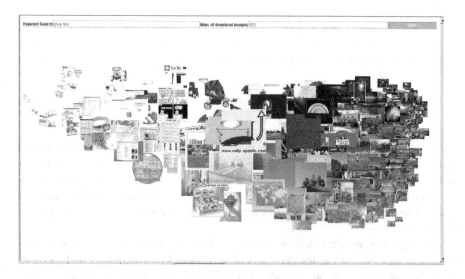

Fig. 3. Our online system for filtering junk images from Google Images, where the keyword "blue sky" is used for Google image search and most junk images are projected on the left side

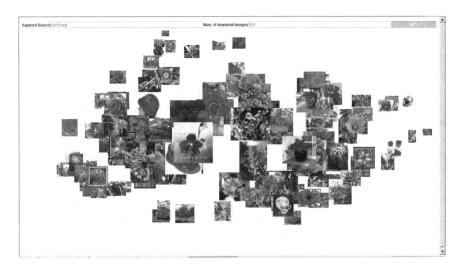

Fig. 4. The filtering results for the keyword-based search "red flower", the images, which boubdaries are in red color, are selected as the relevant images by users.

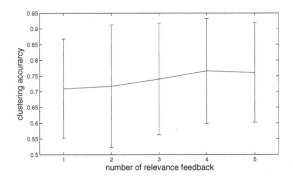

Fig. 5. Clustering accuracy as a function of the number of feedbacks provided by users. The solid line represents the average clustering accuracy while the error bar shows the standard deviation over all 500 queries.

$$Accurarcy = \frac{\sum_{i=1}^{c} C(i,i)}{\sum_{i=1}^{c} \sum_{j=1}^{c} C(i,j)} \tag{10}$$

where $c = 2$ is the number of clusters (i.e. relevant *versus* junk clusters). As shown in Fig. 5, the performance of our kernel-based image clustering algorithm generally increases with the number of constraints provided by the users, but it becomes stable after 4 iterations. On average, our kernel-based image clustering algorithm can achieve over 75% accuracy after filtering the junk images from Google Images. Compared to the original 58% average accuracy of Google Images, our proposed junk image filtering algorithm can achieve a significant improvement.

7   Conclusions

In this paper, we have presented an interactive kernel learning algorithm to filter out the junk images from Google Images or a similar image search engine. The interaction between users and the system can be done quickly and effectively through a hyperbolic visualization tool based on Poincaré disk model. Supplied with user-given constraints, our kernel learning algorithm can incrementally update the underlying hypotheses (margin between the relevant images and the junk images) to approximate the underlying image relevance more effectively and efficiently, and the returned images are then partitioned into multiple visual categories according to the learned kernel matrix automatically. We have tested our kernel learning algorithm and the relevance feedback mechanism on a variety of queries which are submitted to Google Images. Experiments have shown good results as to the effectiveness of this system. This work shows how a straightforward interactive visualization tool coupled tightly with image clustering methods and designed carefully so that the complex image clustering results are presented to the user in an understandable manner can greatly improve and generalize the quality of image filtering.

References

1. Fan, J., Gao, Y., Luo, H.: Multi-level annotation of natural scenes using dominant image compounds and semantic concepts. ACM Multimedia (2004)
2. Smeulders, A.W.M., Worring, M., Santini, S., Gupta, A., Jain, R.: Content-based image retrieval at the end of the early years. IEEE Trans. on PAMI (2000)
3. He, X., Ma, W.-Y., King, O., Li, M., Zhang, H.J.: Learning and inferring a semantic space from user's relevance feedback. ACM Multimedia (2002)
4. Tong, S., Chang, E.Y.: Support vector machine active learning for image retrieval. ACM Multimedia, 107–118 (2001)
5. Rui, Y., Huang, T.S., Ortega, M., Mehrotra, S.: Relevance Feedback: A power tool in interactive content-based image retrieval. IEEE Trans. on CSVT 8(5), 644–655 (1998)
6. Fergus, R., Perona, P., Zisserman, A.: A Visual Category Filter for Google Images. In: Pajdla, T., Matas, J(G.) (eds.) ECCV 2004. LNCS, vol. 3024, Springer, Heidelberg (2004)
7. Fergus, R., Fei-Fei, L., Oerona, P., Zisserman, A.: Learning object categories from Google's image search. In: IEEE CVPR (2006)
8. Cai, D., He, X., Li, Z., Ma, W.-Y., Wen, J.-R.: Hierarchical clustering of WWW image search results using visual, textual, and link information. ACM Multimedia (2004)
9. Wang, X.-J., Ma, W.-Y., Xue, G.-R., Li, X.: Multi-modal similarity propagation and its application for web image retrieval. ACM Multimedia (2004)
10. Gao, B., Liu, T.-Y., Qin, T., Zhang, X., Cheng, Q.-S., Ma, W.-Y.: Web image clustering by consistent utilization of visual features and surrounding texts. ACM Multimedia (2005)
11. Ma, W.-Y., Manjunath, B.S.: Texture features and learning similarity. IEEE CVPR, 425–430 (1996)
12. Fan, J., Gao, Y., Luo, H., Satoh, S.: New approach for hierarchical classifier training and multi-level image annotation. In: Satoh, S., Nack, F., Etoh, M. (eds.) MMM 2008. LNCS, vol. 4903, pp. 1–12. Springer, Heidelberg (2008)
13. Schölkopf, B., Smola, A.J., Müller, K.-R.: Kernel principal component analysis. Neural Computation 10(5), 1299–1319 (1998)
14. Vendrig, J., Worring, M., Smeulders, A.W.M.: Filter image browsing: Interactive image retrieval by using database overviews. Multimedia Tools and Applications 15, 83–103 (2001)
15. Fan, J., Gao, Y., Luo, H.: Hierarchical classification for automatic image annotation. ACM SIGIR (2007)

Object-Based Image Retrieval Beyond Visual Appearances

Yan-Tao Zheng[1], Shi-Yong Neo[1], Tat-Seng Chua[1], and Qi Tian[2]

[1] National University of Singapore, 3 Science Dr, Singapore 117543
[2] Institute for Infocomm Research (I2R), 21 Heng Mui Keng Terrace, Singapore 119613
{yantaozheng,neoshiyo,chuats}@comp.nus.edu.sg,
tian@i2r.a-star.edu.sg

Abstract. The performance of object-based image retrieval systems remains unsatisfactory, as it relies highly on visual similarity and regularity among images of same semantic class. In order to retrieve images beyond their visual appearances, we propose a novel image presentation, i.e. bag of visual synset. A visual synset is defined as a probabilistic relevance-consistent cluster of visual words (quantized vectors of region descriptors such as SIFT), in which the member visual words w induce similar semantic inference $P(c|w)$ towards the image class c. The visual synset can be obtained by finding an optimal distributional clustering of visual words, based on Information Bottleneck principle. The testing on Caltech-256 datasets shows that by fusing the visual words in a relevance consistent way, the visual synset can partially bridge visual differences of images of same class and deliver satisfactory retrieval of relevant images with different visual appearances.

Keywords: image retrieval and representation. Bag of visual synsets.

1 Introduction

As the amount of digital images has been increasing explosively, the image retrieval based on their visual content has spurted much research attention. Here, we narrow down our focus to object-based image retrieval (OBIR), which aims to retrieve images l containing salient object of same semantic class c as the given example query image q from a image collection $L = \{l_i\}_{i=1}^{n}$ of semantic classes $C = \{c_i\}_{i=1}^{m}$. Recently, the region-based representation for image retrieval [1-3, 10] has shown much superiority over traditional global features, as one single image feature computed over the entire image are not sufficient to represent important local characteristics of objects. Specifically, the bag-of-words image representation has drawn much attention, as it tends to code the local visual characteristics towards object level, which is closer to the perception of human visual systems [1]. Analogous to document representation in terms of words in text literature, the bag-of-words approach models an image as a bag of visual words, which are formed by vector quantization of local region descriptors, such as Scale Invariant Feature Transform

S. Satoh, F. Nack, and M. Etoh (Eds.): MMM 2008, LNCS 4903, pp. 13–23, 2008.

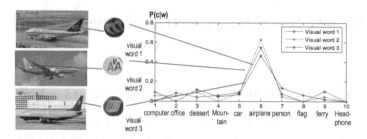

Fig. 1. Examples of visual synset that clusters three visual words with similar $P(c_i \mid w)$. (Note that visual synset does not necessarily correspond to semantic component of an object).

(SIFT) [8]. This part-based image representation allows for robustness against partial occlusions, clutter and varying object appearances caused by changes in pose, image capturing conditions, scale, translation and so on [3].

Though various systems [1-3, 10] have shown the superiority of part-based image representation, the bag of words approach is still feeble to deliver satisfactory image retrieval. The reason is obvious. As the bag of words image representation is isolated primitive low level visual feature, its retrieval performance relies highly on the visual similarity and regularity of objects of same semantic class. However, as the objects of same semantic class can have arbitrarily different shapes and visual appearances, the visual similarity, or equivalently the topological proximity of images in the visual feature space, might not necessarily imply the semantic relevance. These wide visual appearance diversities of objects result in the lack of regularity and coincidence between visual data in images and human semantic interpretations, and consequently, enfeeble the low level visual features, such as bag-of-words, to deliver satisfactory image retrieval.

In order to retrieve relevant images with different visual appearances, a higher level visual content unit is strongly demanded. We observe that due to visual heterogeneity and distinctiveness of objects, a considerable number of visual words are highly distinctive, intrinsic and indicative to certain classes. For example of airline logos in airplane images shown in Figure 1, these visual words tend to share similar object class probability distributions $P(c_i \mid w)$ that are salient and peaky around its belonging class, i.e. 'airplane'. If we cluster these visual words into one visual content unit, this unit shall possess similar class probability distribution and distinctiveness towards class 'airplane'. Meanwhile, it can partially bridge the visual differences among these visually disparate airplane images. Inspired by this observation, we define a novel visual content unit, *visual synset*, as a probabilistic concept or a relevance-consistent cluster of visual words, in which the member visual words w induce similar semantic inferences, i.e. the probability distributions $P(c_i \mid w)$ over the target semantic classes $C = \{c_i\}_{i=1}^{m}$ in the image database.

Compared to previous visual features, the visual synset can provide a means to connect objects of same class but with different visual appearances (visual words), and therefore, it can reasonably mitigate the semantic gap problem. Moreover, compared to bag-of-words (BoW) approach, the bag of visual synsets (BoVS) provides a more compact image representation that can alleviate the statistical sparseness problem, and meanwhile, enable computational efficiency and scalability. As the visual synset is built on top of bag of visual words, it also inherits all the advantages of bag of visual words, such as robustness to occlusion, cluster, scale changes, etc.

The main contribution of our work is: we propose a novel image feature, *visual synset*, to enable object-based image retrieval system to retrieve object images of same semantic class but different visual appearances.

2 Related Work

Liu el. at. [15] have provided a thorough survey on the literature of image retrieval systems, such as QUIB [4], BlobWorld [2], SIMPLcity [7], visualSEEK [6], Virage [5] and Viper [10], etc. The image representation for previous image retrieval systems can be generally classified into 2 types: (1) image-based or grid-based global features like color, color moment, shape or texture histogram over the whole image or grid [4] and (2) bag of visual words extracted from segmented image regions, salient keypoints and blobs [1-3, 6, 10]. The main drawback of global features is their sensitivity to scale, pose and lighting condition changes, clutter and occlusions. On the other hand, the part-based bag of visual words approach is more robust, as it describes an image based on the statistics of local region descriptors (visual words). One disadvantage of bag-of-words approach is that it neglects the geometric and spatial inter-relation between visual words. To address this issue, Zheng el at. [3] proposed to represent images in terms of visual phrases, which are pairs (bigram) of spatially adjacent visual words. Nevertheless, all of the aforementioned image representations are isolated low level visual features and usually are too primitive to model the images semantics, as their effectiveness depends highly on the visual similarity and regularity of objects of same class. Different from all previous retrieval systems, our proposed system aims to retrieve object images of different visual appearances but same semantic class.

3 Framework

As shown in Figure 2, the framework of the proposed system consists of two phases. Phase 1 can be considered as a standard bag-of-words (BoW) approach. Phase 2 is the approach of bag of visual synsets (BoVS) on top of the BoW approach. In phase 1, the region sampling based on extremal scale saliency [11] is applied on gray scale images to extract local regions. For each region, a 128D SIFT descriptor is computed. The vector quantization on SIFT descriptors is then performed to construct visual vocabulary by exploiting hierarchical k-means clustering. The output of phase 1 is the image representations in terms of visual word vectors. Details of phase 1 will be introduced in Section 3.1.

Phase 2 first takes a small set of labeled images from each class as training dataset to select a set of highly informative and distinctive visual words based on Information Gain criteria [14]. It then takes the joint probabilities of visual words and image

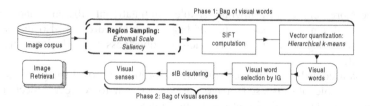

Fig. 2. The overall framework of proposed image retrieval system

classes (estimated from the labeled training set) as input to perform sequential Information Bottleneck (sIB) clustering algorithm [13] to group visual words with similar class probability distributions into visual synsets. According to the clustering assignment relation between visual words and visual synsets, phase 2 outputs the image representation in terms of vectors of visual synsets. Details of phase 2 will be introduced in Section 4.

3.1 Region Sampling Based on Extremal Scale-Saliency

We exploit the extremal scale saliency [11] based region sampling strategy for visual word construction in Phase 1. In fact, many region sampling algorithms are applicable here, e.g. keypoint detection like Lapacian of Gaussian, image segmentation, blobs of homogeneous regions, etc. The reason for utilizing extremal scale saliency [11] for region sampling is that we want to take the sampling of most repeatable image regions as the basis for visual word generation. This is to mitigate the statistical sparseness issue in BoW image representation, as the BoW image feature is usually a sparse vector with high dimensionality. We further argue that the repeatability of local regions of different images relies on the spatially integral similarity of the regions. Therefore, rather than using keypoint detection or image segmentation, we sample local regions by choosing the ones with extremal global saliency over the entire region.

In the scale-saliency algorithm [11], a region (circle) is determined by a point x in the image and its scale (radius). The scale-saliency algorithm defines the region's global saliency H_{d,R_x} in terms of the region's local signal complexity or unpredictability by exploiting the Shannon Entropy of local attributes as below:

$$H_{d,R_x} = -\sum P_{D,R_x}(d_i) \log_2 P_{D,R_x}(d_i) \tag{1}$$

where R_x is the local region of point x, D is the local attribute vector with values $d_1,...,d_r$, $P_{D,R_x}(d_i)$ is the probability of D taking the value d_i and H_{d,R_x} is the local entropy or saliency of region R_x. We select D as the color intensity histogram of local regions for efficiency purpose. Therefore, the regions with flatter intensity histogram distributions, namely more diverse color patterns, tend to have higher signal complexity and thus higher entropy and saliency.

We select regions with extremal saliency on two dimensions. First for each point, the maximal and minimal saliency and their respective scales (regions) are selected; this leads to two scale-saliency maps *SMapmin* and *SMapmax*. Second, rather than clustering points with similar spatial locations and saliency together as in [11] , we spatially detect the local extremal of saliency maps (minimal for *SMapmin* and maximal for *SMapmax*) by using Difference of Gaussian function

$$D(x,\sigma) = (G(x,k\sigma) * G(x,\sigma)) * SMap(x) \qquad (2)$$

where $D(x,\sigma)$ is the difference-of-Gaussian saliency of point x, $SMap(x)$ is the saliency value for point x, k is the multiplicative factor, σ is the blur factor and $G(x,\sigma) = (2\pi\sigma)^{-2} e^{-x^2/\sigma^2}$.

The result of DoG function is effectively a new saliency map $D(x,\sigma)$ whose values are the differences between two blurred saliency maps with different sharpness (σ). If $D(x,\sigma)$ is larger or smaller than all its 8 spatial neighbors, the local region specified by x and its scale is deemed to be the local extremal (maximal or minimal) in its surrounding neighborhood and will be selected for subsequent visual word generation. Intuitively, the selected extremal regions are regions with either largest color pattern diversity or smallest diversity, like homogenous color regions, in the neighborhood.

4   Image Retrieval Based on Bag of Visual Synsets

4.1   Visual Synset: A Semantic-Consistent Cluster of Visual Words

The *visual synset* is defined as a probabilistic concept or a semantic-consistent cluster of visual words. Rigorously speaking, a visual word does not have any semantic meaning alone, as existing region sampling algorithms, like image segmentation, are not able to make sampled regions precisely corresponding to semantic components of objects. Rather than in a conceptual manner, we define the 'semantic' of a visual word probabilistically. Given object classes $C = \{c_i\}_{i=1}^m$, the 'semantic' of a visual word w is defined as its contribution to the classification of its belonging image, namely how much w votes for each of the classes. As shown in Figure 1, the 'semantic' of a visual word can be approximately measured by $P(c|w)$, the semantic inference of visual word w towards object class c. We cluster the semantic-consistent visual words together into *visual synsets*, in the way that the member visual words might have different visual appearances but similar semantic inferences. The rational here is that a considerable number of visual words are of low frequency and highly intrinsic and indicative to certain classes, due to the distinctive visual appearances of objects. These visual words tend to have similar probability distribution $P(c|w)$, which peaks around its belonging classes. By grouping these highly distinctive and informative visual words into visual synsets, the visual differences of objects from the same class can be partially bridged. For example in Figure 3, two types of visually different regions (visual words) of airline logos can be grouped into one visual synset, based on their image class probability distribution. Consequently, the two sets of visually different airplane images will have some commonality in the feature space now.

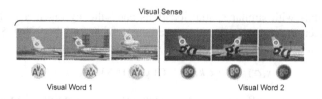

Fig. 3. A example of visual synset grouping two visual words representing two airline logos

4.2 Visual Synset Generation

4.2.1 Information Bottleneck (IB) Principle

By formulating visual synset construction as a task of visual word clustering based on their object class probability distributions, the issue now is reduced to how to measure the 'right' distance between these distributions, namely the similarity metric in clustering. The Information Bottleneck (IB) principle [12][13] provides a reasonable solution to address this issue. Given the joint distribution $P(w, c)$ of the visual words w and image classes c, the goal of IB principle is to construct the optimal compact representation of w, namely the visual synset clusters s, such that s preserves as much information about c as possible. In particular, the IB principle is reduced to the following Lagrangian optimization problem to maximize

$$L[P(s \mid c)] = I(S;C) - \beta I(W;S) \tag{4}$$

with respect to $P(s|c)$ and subject to the Markov condition $S \leftarrow W \leftarrow C$. The mutual information $I(S;C)$ is the statistical measure of information that visual synset variable S contains about object class C and defined as

$$I(S;C) = \sum_{s \in S, c \in C} P(c,s) \log \frac{P(c,s)}{P(s)P(c)} = \sum_{s \in S, c \in C} P(s)P(c \mid s) \log \frac{P(c \mid s)}{P(c)} \tag{5}$$

The term $\beta I(W; S)$ in Eq. 4 measures the information loss in clustering w into s. Intuitively, Eq. 4 aims to compress (cluster) the visual words into visual synsets through a compact bottleneck under the constraint that this compression maintains as much information about the object classes as possible, and meanwhile, keep the information loss in the compression (clustering) as small as possible.

4.2.2 Sequential IB (sIB) Clustering

We adopt the sequential Information Bottleneck (sIB) clustering algorithm to generate the optimal visual synset clusters in our approach, as it is reported to outperform other IB clustering implementations [13]. The target principled function that sIB algorithm exploits to guide the clustering process is $F(S) = L[P(s \mid c)]$ as in Eq. 4. The input of sIB algorithm are visual synset cluster cardinality |S|, and joint probability $P(w,c) = N_w(c)/N$, where $N_w(c)$ is the document frequency of visual word w in image class c, and N is the total number of visual word occurences. The sIB starts with some initial random clustering $S = \{s_1, s_2, ..., s_K\}$ on W. Similar to k-means clustering algorithm, at each iteration, sIB takes some $w \in W$ from its current cluster $s(w)$ and reassigns it to another cluster s^{new} such that the cost (or information loss) of merging w into s^{new} is minimum. Specifically, the merging cost $d_F(w, s^{new})$ is defined as (cf. [28] for more details):

$$d_F(w, s^{new}) = (P(w) + P(s)) \cdot JS(P(c \mid w), P(c \mid s)) \tag{6}$$

where $JS(x, y) =$ is the *Jensen-Shannon* divergence.

The convergence speed of sIB clustering depends on threshold ε. The clustering is deemed to be converged, if the number of cluster assignment changes in the loop is less than $\varepsilon \mid W \mid$. In order to avoid being trapped in local optima, several runs of clustering with different random initialization are repeated and the run with the highest target function $F(S)$ is chosen. Note that sIB utilized here is a "hard" clustering process, in which $P(s \mid w)$ is deterministic and one visual word belongs to only one visual synset.

4.2.3 Visual Word Selection for sIB Clustering

It is necessary to select discriminative and informative visual words for sIB clustering, as the indistinctive visual words usually have high frequencies and flat and non-salient image probability distributions, which will dominate the clustering process and lead to undiscriminating visual word clusters (visual synsets). We select a portion of most distinctive visual words to construct visual synsets based on the generic Information Gain (IG) criteria as below [14]:

$$IG(c; w) = -\sum_{i=1}^{m} P(c_i) \log(P(c_i))$$
$$+ P(w) \sum_{i=1}^{m} P(c_i \mid w) \log(P(c_i \mid w)) + P(w) \sum_{i=1}^{m} P(c_i \mid \overline{w}) \log(P(c_i \mid \overline{w})) \tag{7}$$

Intuitively, the higher value of $IG(c; w)$ means that c is more certain given the value of w. The visual words with high IG are usually distinctive and with low frequency and a peak and salient class probability distribution.

4.3 Image Retrieval, Indexing and Similarity Measure

With images represented by visual synsets, we index them by exploiting the inverted file scheme [16], due to its simplicity, efficiency and practical effectiveness. The similarity measure adopted here is the L-norm distance defined as below:

$$Sim(I_Q, I_D) = (\sum_i \mid v_i(I_Q) - v_i(I_D) \mid^l)^{1/l} \tag{8}$$

where I_Q is the query image, I_D is an image in the database, v_i is the ith dimension of image feature vector and l is set to 2 in the experiments. In retrieval, all the candidate answer images are ranked by its similarity value with the query image.

5   Experiments and Discussion

5.1   Testing Dataset and Experimental Setup

We exploit the Caltech-256 dataset [17] to evaluate the proposed system. The Caltech-256 dataset contains 257 image categories and a total of 30607 images. We randomly select 5 images from each class or a total of $257 \times 5 = 1285$ images as query images. The evaluation criteria utilized here is the mean average precision (MAP), which combines the precision, recall and ranking factors.

In the phase of region sampling, each image gives 1k to 3k sampled regions. In the phase of visual vocabulary construction, we perform hierarchical k-means clustering on approximately 0.8 million SIFT descriptors from 500 images. By setting the depth of clustering to 12 and the number of clusters per clustering to 2, we obtain $2^{12} = 4096$ primitive visual words in total. We then construct five sets of visual word codebooks with size K_W of 500, 1000, 2000 and 4000 respectively by using IG feature selection.

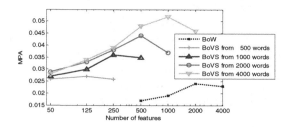

Fig. 4. MAPs of BoVS and BoW runs

For each visual codebook, we generate a number of visual synset sets by setting the number of visual synsets K_S to 50, 125, 250, 500, 1000 and 2000, with the condition $K_S < K_W$. For example, for the BoW with 1000 visual words, we will generate the BoVS with 50, 125, 250 and 500 visual synsets respectively. As the visual synset is a result of supervised learning, we select 30 images per class as the training set.

5.2   Image Retrieval on Caltech-256

We first perform image retrievals based on BoW with different number visual words K_W and BoVS with different number of visual synsets K_S generated from different BoW codebooks. Figure 4 displays the MAP of image retrievals of various runs. From Figure 4, we observe that with proper choice of K_S and BoW codebook, the BoVS delivers much superior performance over BoW. In particular, best run of BoVS with K_S =1000 generated from BoW with K_W = 4000 gives a MAP of 0.052. In average, this run returns 3.78 and 5.16 correct answer images in top 10 and 20 retrieved list respectively. Figure 5 illustrates the MAP for individual classes in this run. The first 3 classes with highest MAP in this run are 'leopards', 'motorbike' and 'face'. We attribute the MAP improvements by BoVS to the fact that the BoVS retrieves some relevant images with different visual appearances from query images, while the BoW

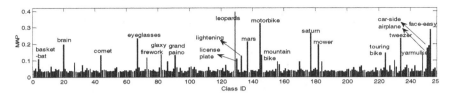

Fig. 5. MAP of classes of Cal-tech 256 with class names displayed when MAP > 0.1

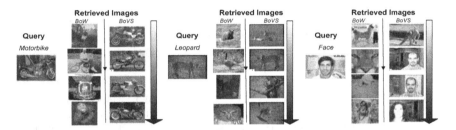

Fig. 6. Examples of retrieved images ranked from top to down

relies solely on local visual similarity. Figure 6 shows some retrieval examples of these classes by BoW and BoVS respectively. As shown, the relevant images retrieved by BoVS are visually disparate, while the images retrieved by BoW present local visual similarities with query images (like red texture of motorbike body and red regions of retrieved images). The retrieval via visual similarity can be easily spoiled by large intra-class visual variation, as images of same class can be fairly distinctive from each other. On the other hand, the BoVS utilizes such distinctiveness to group visual word with consistent relevance into visual synsets and link visually different images of same class to enhance retrieval performance. Besides superior performance, the BoVS also gives a more compact image representation. For example, the BoVS with K_S = 500 deliver reasonably satisfactory and much superior the retrieval efficiency and scalability, as the computational cost per retrieval is highly related to the dimensionality of image features.

From Figure 4, we also observe that too large or small number of visual synsets K_S does not raise to optimal MAP and the BoVS with K_S between 1/4 and 1/2 of BoW codebook size K_W usually gives optimal performances. This is because clustering visual words into visual synsets is a process of data compression (compressing several visual words into one visual synset). Too small K_S (large compression ratio) will force visual words with inconsistent relevance into one visual synset and result in non-distinctive visual synsets that loses relevant information about image classes, while too large K_S (small compression ratio) might lead to a sparse and non-coherent image distribution in visual synset feature space.

Next, we compare the performance of BoVS with visual phrase approach [3]. The best run of BoW with K_W = 2000 gives a MAP of 0.024, while the visual phrase (generated from the best run of BoW above) delivers a MAP of 0.028. Though the visual phrase delivers slightly better retrieval than BoW by incorporating spatial

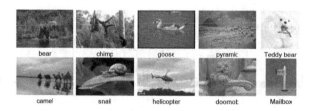

Fig. 7. Example image of classes in which BoW or visual phrase outperform BoVS

information, yet its performance is still not comparable to the 0.052 MAP of best BoVS run. This is because the visual phrase is also low level visual features and only able to retrieve visually similar images. However, after a detailed comparison, we find that 14 classes have BoW or visual phrase delivering better retrieval performance than BoVS. Figure 7 shows some example images from these classes. With close examination, we find that the images of these classes are not visually distinctive from images of other classes, either due to their cluttered backgrounds or "neutral" textures of objects. This leads to the lack of visual words distinctive to these classes. Consequently, these non-distinctive visual words might be clustered together with visual words from images of other classes and resulted non-distinctive visual synsets that effectively link images of different classes together.

6 Conclusion and Future Work

We have presented an object-based image retrieval system based on a novel image representation, bag of visual synsets. The visual synset is defined as a probabilistic concept or a semantic-consistent cluster of visual words. By exploiting the distributional clustering based on Information Bottleneck principle, the visual synset groups visual words with similar $P(c_i \mid w)$, i.e. distinctiveness towards object classes, to partially bridge the visual differences of objects from same semantic class. The experiments showed that the proposed image retrieval system can reasonably retrieve object images of the same semantic class but visually disparate to the query images.

Several open issues remain. First, the visual synset does not incorporate spatial inter-relation among visual words, which is an important characteristic for many object classes. Second, the proposed system does not include any relevance feedback mechanism, which is reported to be effective in improving retrieval performance.

References

1. Jing, F., Li, M., Zhang, L., Zhang, H.-J., Zhang, B.: Learning in region-based image retrieval. In: Proceedings of Conference on Image and Video Retrieval, pp. 206–215 (2003)
2. Carson, C., Belongie, S., Greenspan, H., Malik, J.: Blobworld: Image Segmentation Using Expectation-Maximization and Its Application to Image Querying. IEEE Transactions on Pattern Analysis and Machine Intelligence 24(8), 1026–1038 (2002)
3. Zheng, Q.-F., Wang, W.-Q., Gao, W.: Effective and efficient object-based image retrieval using visual phrases. In: Proceedings of ACM international conference on Multimedia, Santa Barbara, CA, USA, pp. 77–80 (2006)

4. Faloutsos, C., Barber, R., Flickner, M., Hafner, J., Niblack, W., Petkovic, D., Equitz, W.: Efficient and effective querying by image content. Journal of Intelligent Information Systems 3(3-4), 231–262 (1994)

5. Gupta, A.H., Jain, R.: Visual information retrieval. Communications of the ACM 40(5), 70–79 (1997)

6. Smith, J.R., Chang, S.-F.: VisualSEEk: a fully automated content-based image query system. In: Proceedings of ACM conference on Multimedia, Boston, U.S, pp. 87–98 (November 1996)

7. Wang, J.Z., Li, J., Wiederhold, G.: SIMPLIcity: Semantics-Sensitive Integrated Matching for Picture Libraries. IEEE Transactions on Pattern Analysis and Machine Intelligence 23(9), 947–963 (2001)

8. Lowe, D.: Distinctive image features from scale-invariant keypoints. International Journal of Computer Vision 20, 91–110 (2003)

9. Bekkerman, R., El-Yaniv, R., Tishby, N., Winter, Y.: Distributional word clusters vs. words for text categorization. Journal of Machine Learning Research g 3, 1183–1208 (2003)

10. Squire, D., Muller, W., Muller, H., Pun, T.: Content-based visual query of image databases: inspirations from text retrieval. Pattern Recognition Letters 21, 1193–1198 (2000)

11. Kadir, T., Brady, M.: Saliency, scale and image description. International Journal of Computer Vision 45(2), 83–105 (2001)

12. Bekkerman, R., El-Yaniv, R., Tishby, N., Winter, Y.: Distributional word clusters vs. words for text categorization. Journal of Machine Learning Research

13. Slonim, N., Friedman, N., Tishby, N.: Agglomerative multivariate information bottleneck. In: Advances in Neural Information Processing Systems (NIPS) (2001)

14. Yang, Y., Pedersen, J.O.: A comparative study on feature selection in text categorization. In: Proceedings of ICML, Nashville, US, pp. 412–420 (1997)

15. Liu, Y., Zhang, D., Lu, G., Ma, W.-Y.: A survey of content-based image retrieval with high-level semantics. Pattern Recognition 40(1), 262–282 (2007)

16. Witten, I.H., Moffat, A., Bell, T.C.: Managing gigabytes: compressing and indexing documents and images. Morgan Kaufmann Publishers Inc, San Francisco (1999)

17. Griffin, G., Holub, A., Perona, P.: The Caltech-256, Caltech Technical Report

MILC²: A Multi-Layer Multi-Instance Learning Approach to Video Concept Detection[*]

Zhiwei Gu[1], Tao Mei[2], Jinhui Tang[1], Xiuqing Wu[1], and Xian-Sheng Hua[2]

[1] Department of Electronic Engineering and Information Science,
University of Science and Technology of China, Hefei, 230027 China
{guzhiwei,jhtang}@mail.ustc.edu.cn, wuxq@ustc.edu.cn
[2] Microsoft Research Asia, Beijing, 100080 China
{tmei,xshua}@microsoft.com

Abstract. Video is a kind of structured data with multi-layer (ML) information, e.g., a shot is consisted of three layers including *shot, keyframe*, and *region*. Moreover, multi-instance (MI) relation is embedded along the consecutive layers. Both the ML structure and MI relation are essential for video concept detection. The previous work [5] dealt with ML structure and MI relation by constructing a MLMI kernel in which each layer is assumed to have equal contribution. However, such equal weighting technique cannot well model MI relation or handle *ambiguity propagation* problem, *i.e.*, the propagation of uncertainty of sub-layer label through multiple layers, as it has been proved that different layers have different contributions to the kernel. In this paper, we propose a novel algorithm named MILC² (Multi-Layer Multi-Instance Learning with Inter-layer Consistency Constraint.) to tackle the ambiguity propagation problem, in which an inter-layer consistency constraint is explicitly introduced to measure the disagreement of inter-layers, and thus the MI relation is better modeled. This learning task is formulated in a regularization framework with three components including *hyper-bag* prediction error, inter-layer inconsistency measure, and classifier complexity. We apply the proposed MILC² to video concept detection over TRECVID 2005 development corpus, and report better performance than both standard Support Vector Machine based and MLMI kernel methods.

1 Introduction

With explosive spread of video data, semantic content based video retrieval has been a challenging topic in multimedia research community. To deal with this issue, a set of concepts are predefined, e.g. 39 concepts in TRECVID benchmark [1] and 834 ones in LSCOM base [8], individual models are then learned to characterize these concepts, and concept detection is adopted as an intermediate step towards semantic understanding.

---

[*] This work was performed when the first author visited Microsoft Research Asia as an intern.

S. Satoh, F. Nack, and M. Etoh (Eds.): MMM 2008, LNCS 4903, pp. 24–34, 2008.
© Springer-Verlag Berlin Heidelberg 2008

We consider video as a multi-layer multi-instance (MLMI) setting [5]. An ideal concept detector should model both the multi-layer structure and the inherent multi-instance relation simultaneously. By multi-layer (ML), we indicate that video is constructed by multiple layer information, for example in Figure 1, a shot is composed of *shot*, *key-frame* and *region* layers. By multi-instance (MI), each sample has multiple "bag-instance" correspondences: a sample is regarded as a "*hyper-bag*," in which several *bags* are embedded along the multiple layers, and each bag can also be viewed as an *instance*. For example in the three-layer structure shown in Figure 1, a key-frame can be regarded as a *bag* of regions and also an *instance* of the shot. The *hyper-bag* is indicated as positive even if only one of its sub-layer instances falls within the concept, and indicated as negative only if all the sub-layer instances in it are negative. In the literature, most video concept detection methods focus on learning from feature vector in frame layer [1][9][12], they seldom utilize the multi-layer structure information. On the other hand, multi-instance relation is widely investigated in content-based image retrieval [7][2], in which single layer multi-instance relation is considered, while the multiple "bag-instance" correspondences are rarely studied. In our previous work [5], we proposed a multi-layer multi-instance kernel to exploit both aspects, the MLMI kernel captures the structure information by sufficiently enumerating all the sub-structures of each layer, and implicitly represents multi-instance relations by *max* function approximation. In [11], a multi-instance kernel is defined as the sum of instance kernels with uniform weighting. However, this MI kernel has not solved the multi-instance learning problem as the uniform weighting of instances does not accord with the multi-instance definition. In [6] they indicated that different instances in the same bag should have different contributions to the kernel. Similar to MI kernel, in MLMI kernel [5], both instances and layers make equal contributions, and it faces similar problems aforementioned. Actually, the contribution of instances to each layer and the contribution of sub-layers to the *hyper-bag* are with different weights. On the other hand, in MLMI setting, the learning algorithm is only given weak label to the target concept: the label is determined on the *hyper-bags* (*i.e.*, shots in the above example) without seeing the individual sub-layer labeling, the only instruction to the sub-layer labeling is implicitly given through the MI relation. Due to multi-layer extension, the ambiguity in MI setting will propagate layer by layer, we define such phenomena as *ambiguity propagation*, and appropriate modeling the MI relation is of vital importance addressing the problem.

In this paper, we propose a novel algorithm named MILC^2 [1] to explicitly model the multi-instance relations through layers and solve the *ambiguity propagation* problem. MILC^2 tackles the MLMI learning problem by reformulating the objective function with an explicit inter-layer consistency constraint. In the sense of MI relation, the maximal predictions of sub-layers should be consistent with the *hyper-bag* prediction, and the inter-layer consistency constraint penalizes the disagreement of predictions across different layers. Eventually, the concept

---

[1] **Multi-Layer Multi-Instance Learning** with **Inter-layer Consistency Constraint**, M, I, L, C appeared twice, and pronounced as [milk skwɛə].

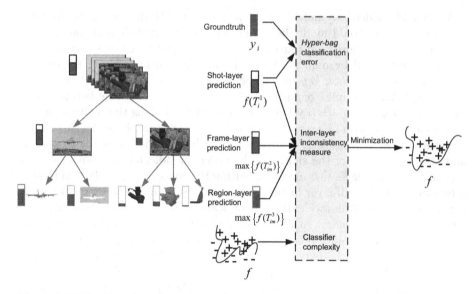

Fig. 1. MLMI setting in video concept detection and the proposed MILC^2 algorithm. A video shot is represented as three layers (*i.e.*, *shot*, *key-frame*, and *region*). The top row denotes the ground truth of shot for underline concept (*airplane*); on the left of the images are the predictions of the nodes. The inter-layer inconsistency measure explicitly expresses the multi-instance relations through layers.

detection learner is built up by minimizing three components, i.e., *hyper-bags'* prediction error, inter-layer inconsistency measure, and the classifier complexity, in a regularization framework. Figure 1 shows the main idea of the proposed algorithm. In the leftmost, a three-layer ML structure is illustrated, and red bottles representing predictions of nodes in the layers are shown on the left of the images, a full red bottle means "positive" and an empty bottle denote "negative." On the right, the three components of object function in MILC^2 are explained. Experiments on TRECVID 2005 corpus show that the MILC^2 algorithm performs better than the standard Support Vector Machine based approaches and the MLMI kernel method [5].

The rest of this paper is organized as follows. Section 2 gives the proposed algorithm, including the MLMI kernel and the MILC^2 approach. Section 3 provides the implementation issues for solving MILC^2 by CCCP. Section 4 presents the experimental results. Finally, concludes in Section 5 with some outlooks in the future.

2   The Proposed MILC^2 Algorithm

2.1   A MLMI Kernel

In MLMI setting, each sample can be viewed as an L-layer rooted tree. A rooted tree is a connected acyclic directed graph in which each node is connected by a unique path from a designated node called the root. L is the maximal length of the unique path from the root to nodes. Each node in the tree denotes a pattern of certain granularity. As shown in Figure 1, it is a three layer tree consisting of, from root to bottom, *shot*, *key-frame*, and *region*, where the granularity of descriptors of each layer increases with more detailed information of the samples. According to the multi-layer structure, we aim at capturing the structure information by sufficiently enumerate all the sub-structures of each layer.

Given an L-layer rooted tree $\mathbf{T}$, denote $N = \{n_i\}_{i=1}^{|N|}$ be the node set in $\mathbf{T}$, $|N|$ is the number of nodes. Let $\mathbf{S}$ be the sub-tree set, we denote s_i be the sub-trees whose parent is n_i, $s_i = \{s | s \in S \wedge parent(s) = n_i\} \in pow(S)$, $pow(S)$ refers to the power set of $\mathbf{S}$; besides, we have the bijection mapping $n_i \rightarrow s_i$. For each node $n_i \in N$, we define "node pattern" of n_i to be all the information associated with n_i, which is composed of three elements: layer info ℓ_i, descriptor f_i and sub-trees rooted at n_i (or s_i), denoted in the triplet form $\hat{n}_i =< \ell_i, f_i, s_i >$. Hence, $\mathbf{T}$ is expanded to the node pattern set $\{\hat{n}_i\}_{i=1}^{|N|}$. Figure 2 is a simple illustration of the expanded node pattern set, on the left, is the node pattern of the root, some sub-trees are figured out in dotted box. We construct the kernel of trees by the expanded node pattern set according to convolution kernel as follows,

$$k_{MLMI}(T, T') = \sum_{\hat{n} \in \hat{N}, \hat{n}' \in \hat{N}'} k_{\hat{N}}(\hat{n}, \hat{n}') \tag{1}$$

in which $k_{\hat{N}}$ is a kernel on the triplet space, note that $\hat{n}$ is composed of three elements, we construct the kernel by tensor product operation $(K_1 \otimes K_2((x, u), (y, v)) = K_1(x, y) \times K_2(u, v))$.

$$k_{\hat{N}}(\hat{n}, \hat{n}') = k_{\delta}(\ell_n, \ell_n') \times k_f(f_n, f_n') \times k_{st}(s_n, s_n') \tag{2}$$

where $k_{\delta}(x, y) = \delta_{x,y}$ is the matching kernel, k_f is a kernel on the feature space. k_{st} is kernel of sub-trees sets,

$$k_{st}(s_n, s_n') = \sum_{\hat{c} \in s_n, \hat{c}' \in s_n'} k_{\hat{N}}(\hat{c}, \hat{c}') \tag{3}$$

For leaf nodes when $s_n, s_n' = \emptyset, k_{st}$ set to be 1.

From the MLMI kernel definition, we find that the kernel between two trees is the combination of kernels defined on node patterns of homogene ous layers, and the node pattern kernel is built by their intrinsic structure utilizing the rich context and implicitly embedded multiple instance relations. It is worthy noting that, the kernel is semi-positive definite for trees on both the same and different layers, e.g. it is semi-positive definite for measuring the similarities between *shot-shot*, *shot-frame*, *shot-region* or *frame-region*, and so on. With the MLMI kernel, any kernel machines such as Support Vector Machine (SVM) could be used to the concept detection task.

2.2 MILC² Approach

Given dataset $\{(T_i, y_i)\}_{i=1}^{N^1}$, where $T_i \in \mathcal{T}$ is an L-layer rooted tree defined in section 2.1 representing the *hyper-bags*, $y_i \in \text{IR}$ is the label of T_i, N^1 is the

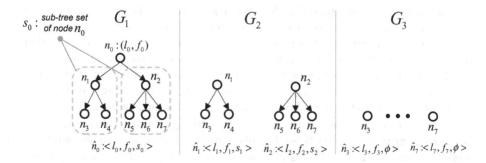

Fig. 2. The expanded node pattern set of a three layer MLMI setting, G_l denotes the node patterns in the lth layer

number of training *hyper-bags*. The objective is to learn a function $f(T) : T \mapsto$ IR from structured input space T to response values in IR. Without loss of generality, we re-index the overall nodes of training set into

$$\mathcal{I} : \left\{ T_1, \ldots, T_{N^1}, T_{11}^2, \ldots, T_{N^1 N_{N^1}^1}^2, \ldots, T_{11}^L, \ldots, T_{N^1 N_{N^1}^L}^L \right\}$$

where T_{im}^l denotes the mth sub-structure in l^{th} layer for hyper-bag i, and N_i^l is the number of sub-structures in l^{th} layer for hyper-bag i.

Recall that in standard SVM, features are firstly mapped to a high dimensional space (most probably infinite), a linear function in the mapped space is then learnt by minimizing both expected risk of training samples and the complexity of classifier. Once the kernel between the *hyper-bags* is determined, it is sufficient to learn a classifier by the standard SVM as in [5]. However, as aforementioned, in MLMI kernel the multi-instance relation is implicitly modeled, it is weak expressing the multi-instance relation essence, and cannot solve the *ambiguity propagation* problem smoothly. On the other hand, keeping the coherence of different layers in multi-instance manner could help deal with incorrectly labeled noisy data, and learn the hyper-plane more effectively. Accordingly, it is desirable to utilize the kernel between sub-structures for MLMI learning, and additional explicit constraint reflecting multi-instance relation and inter-layer consistency is necessary, Furthermore, since the MLMI kernel is valid across layers, ,it is easy to predict the response of sub-structures.

Let $\mathcal{H}$ be the Reproducing Kernel Hilbert Space (RKHS) of function $f(T)$. Denote $|f|_{\mathcal{H}}^2$ be the RKHS norm of f. The optimization problem of MLMI learning is formulated as

$$\min_{f \in \mathcal{H}} \frac{1}{2} |f|_{\mathcal{H}}^2 + \sum_{i=1}^{N^1} V\left(y_i, f(T_i), \left\{ f(T_{im}^l) \right\}_{m,l} | m = 1, \ldots, N_i^l; l = 2, \ldots, L \right) \quad (4)$$

in which the first item is the complexity of classifier and the second one refers to the expected risk of the MLMI samples, including the prediction error of *hyper-bags*, and the inconsistent measure between the *hyper-bags* and its sub-layers:

$$V\left(y_i, f(T_i), \{f(T_{im}^l)\}_{m,l}\right) = \lambda_1 V_1(y_i, f(T_i)) + \sum_{l=2}^{L} \lambda_l V_l\left(f(T_i), \{f(T_{im}^l)\}_m\right) \quad (5)$$

where $V_1(y_i, f(T_i))$ is a Hinge loss function. $V_l\left(f(T_i), \{f(T_{im}^l)\}_m\right)$ is an inter-layer inconsistency loss function measuring the disagreement between l^{th} sub-layer and the *hyper-bag*. Regularization constants , λ_1, λ_l determine the trade-off between them. To be specific, standard SVM just use the expected risk of *hyper-bags* (i.e., the first item in Eq.(5), but missed the risk of the very structure which is essential in modeling the MI relations (i.e., the second item in Eq.(5)).

As a result, the MLMI learning task is to solve the quadratic concave-convex optimization problem:

$$\min_{f \in \mathcal{H}} \frac{1}{2}|f|_{\mathcal{H}}^2 + \sum_{i=1}^{N^1} \lambda_1 V_1\left(y_i, f(T_i)\right) + \sum_{i=1}^{N^1} \sum_{l=2}^{L} \lambda_l V_l\left(f(T_i), \{f(T_{im}^l)\}_m\right) \quad (6)$$

As positive *hyper-bags* are labeled as $+1$, and negative ones being -1, by multi-instance relationship, the prediction of *hyper-bag* $f(T_i)$ should be consistent with the maximal prediction of its lth sub-layer $\max_{m=1,\dots,N^l}\{f(T_{im}^l)\}$. Various loss functions could be designed for V_l. In this paper, we consider using L_1 loss for simplicity.

$$V_l\left(f(T_i), \{f(T_{im}^l\}_{m,l}\right) = \left|f(T_i) - \max_{m=1,\dots,N^1} f(T_{im}^l)\right| \quad (7)$$

3   Solving MILC² by CCCP

We now rewrite the optimization function (6) as a constrained minimization problem by introducing slack variables, as shown in Eq.(8),

$$\min_{f \in \mathcal{H}, \delta_1, \delta_l, \delta_l^*, l=2,\dots,L} \frac{1}{2}|f|_{\mathcal{H}}^2 + \lambda_1 \delta_1^T \mathbf{1} + \sum_{l=2}^{L} \lambda_l \left(\delta_l^T \mathbf{1} + \delta_l^{*T} \mathbf{1}\right) \quad (8)$$

$$s.t. \begin{cases} 1 - y_i f(T_i) \le \delta_{1i}, & i = 1, \dots, N^1; \\ f(T_i) - \max_{m=1,\dots,N^1} f(T_{im}^l) \le \delta_{li}, & i = 1, \dots, N^1, l = 2, \dots, L; \\ \max_{m=1,\dots,N^1} f(T_{im}^l) - f(T_i) \le \delta_{li}^*, & i = 1, \dots, N^1, l = 2, \dots, L; \\ 0 \le \delta_{1i}, 0 \le \delta_{li}, 0 \le \delta_{li}^*, & i = 1, \dots, N^1, l = 2, \dots, L; \end{cases}$$

where $\delta_1 = [\delta_{11}, \delta_{12}, \dots, \delta_{1N^1}]^T$ are slack variables for the prediction errors on the *hyper-bags*, $\delta_l = [\delta_{l1}, \delta_{l2}, \dots, \delta_{lN^1}]^T$ and $\delta_l^* = [\delta_{l1}^*, \delta_{l2}^*, \dots, \delta_{lN^1}^*]^T$ are slack variables for the prediction inconsistency between l^{th} layer and the root layer, and $\mathbf{1} = [1, 1, \dots, 1]^T$ is vectors of 1's.

Let f be a linear function in the mapped high dimensional space $f(x) = W^T\phi(x) + b$, where $\phi(\cdot)$ is the mapping function. Ignore b in $|f|_{\mathcal{H}}^2$ as in SVM, and substitute f to Eq.(8), we have

$$\min_{W,b,\delta_1,\delta_l,\delta_l^*,l=2,...,L} \frac{1}{2}W^TW + \lambda_1\delta_1^T\mathbf{1} + \sum_{l=2}^{L}\lambda_l\left(\delta_l^T\mathbf{1} + \delta_l^{*T}\mathbf{1}\right) \tag{9}$$

$$s.t. \begin{cases} 1 - y_i(W^T\phi(T_i) + b) \le \delta_{1i}, & i = 1,...,N^1; \\ W^T\phi(T_i) - \max_{m=1,...,N^1}\{W^T\phi(T_{im}^l)\} \le \delta_{li}, i = 1,...,N^1, l = 2,...,L; \\ \max_{m=1,...,N^1}\{W^T\phi(T_{im}^l)\} - W^T\phi(T_i) \le \delta_{li}^*, i = 1,...,N^1, l = 2,...,L; \\ 0 \le \delta_{1i}, 0 \le \delta_{li}, 0 \le \delta_{li}^*, & i = 1,...,N^1, l = 2,...,L; \end{cases}$$

Note that the second and third constraints in Eq.(9) are non-linear concave-convex inequalities, and all the others are linear constraints; therefore, the *constrained concave-convex procedure* (CCCP) [10] is well suited to solve this optimization problem. Similar to [3], we use the sub-gradient of *max* function,

$$\partial\left(\max_{m=1,...,N^1}\{W^T\phi(T_{im}^l)\}\right) = \sum_{m=1}^{N^l}\beta_{im}^l\phi(T_{im}^l) \tag{10}$$

and

$$\beta_{im}^l = \begin{cases} 1/R, & W^T\phi(T_{im}^l) = \max_r\{W^T\phi(T_{ir}^l)\}; \\ 0, & otherwise. \end{cases} \tag{11}$$

R is the number of sub-structures with maximal response.

Now, Eq.(9) can be solved in an iterative fashion by fixing W and β in turn until W converges. When fixing W, solves Eq.(11), and when fixing β, solves

$$\min_{W,b,\delta_1,\delta_l,\delta_l^*,l=2,...,L} \frac{1}{2}W^TW + \lambda_1\delta_1^T\mathbf{1} + \sum_{l=2}^{L}\lambda_l\left(\delta_l^T\mathbf{1} + \delta_l^{*T}\mathbf{1}\right) \tag{12}$$

$$s.t. \begin{cases} 1 - y_i(W^T\phi(T_i) + b) \le \delta_{1i}, & i = 1,...,N^1; \\ W^T\phi(T_i) - \sum_{m=1}^{N^1}\beta_{im}^l W^T\phi(T_{im}^l) \le \delta_{li}, i = 1,...,N^1, l = 2,...,L; \\ \sum_{m=1}^{N^1}\beta_{im}^l W^T\phi(T_{im}^l) - W^T\phi(T_i) \le \delta_{li}^*, i = 1,...,N^1, l = 2,...,L; \\ 0 \le \delta_{1i}, 0 \le \delta_{li}, 0 \le \delta_{li}^*, & i = 1,...,N^1, l = 2,...,L; \end{cases}$$

However, we cannot solve Eq. (12) directly since W lies in the mapped feature space which usually goes infinite. Instead, we get rid of the explicit usage of W by forming the dual optimization problem. We introduce Lagrange multipliers $\alpha = [\alpha_1^1,...,\alpha_{N^1}^1,\alpha_1^2,...,\alpha_{N^1}^2,\alpha_1^{*2},...,\alpha_{N^1}^{*2},\alpha_1^L,...,\alpha_{N^1}^L,\alpha_1^{*L},...,\alpha_{N^1}^{*L}]^T$ in the above constraints and get the following dual formulation according to Karush-Kuhn-Tucker (KKT) theorem:

$$\min_\alpha\left\{\frac{1}{2}\alpha^TQ\alpha + p^T\alpha\right\} \tag{13}$$

$$s.t. \begin{cases} Y^T\alpha = 0; \\ 0 \le \alpha \le \Lambda. \end{cases}$$

and the equality $W = \sum_{i=1}^{\mathcal{N}} (A\alpha)_i \times \phi(\mathcal{I}(i))$ in which, α, p, Y, Λ are $\mathfrak{M} = (2L-1)N^1$ dimensional vectors, with entrances

$$p_i = \begin{cases} -1 & 1 \leq i \leq N^1; \\ 0 & otherwise \end{cases} \qquad Y_i = \begin{cases} y_i & 1 \leq i \leq N^1; \\ 0 & otherwise; \end{cases}$$

$$\Lambda_i = \begin{cases} \lambda_1 & 1 \leq i \leq N^1; \\ \lambda_l & (2l-3)N^1 + 1 \leq i \leq (2l-1)N^l; l = 2, \ldots, L; \end{cases}$$

$Q = A^T K A$ is the Gram matrix with K being kernel matrix, and A being a sparse matrix of $\mathfrak{N} \times \mathfrak{M}$, where $\mathfrak{N} = |\mathcal{I}|$ is the overall number of nodes in training set, $\mathfrak{M}$ is the dimension of α. Intuitively, A could be regarded as a multi-instance transform matrix representing the proposed additional inter-layer consistency constraint to the hyper-plane, in standard SVM, A is the identity matrix.

$$A_{IJ} = \begin{cases} y_I & I, J \in [1, N^1]; \\ -1 & I \in [1, N^1], J \in [(2l-3)N^1 + 1, (2l-2)N^1]; 2 \leq l \leq L; \\ 1 & I \in [1, N^1], J \in [(2l-2)N^1 + 1, (2l-1)N^1]; 2 \leq l \leq L; \\ \beta_I & I \notin [1, N^1], J \in [(2l-3)N^1 + 1, (2l-2)N^1]; l \text{ is the layer of node } \mathcal{I}(I); \\ -\beta_I & I \notin [1, N^1], J \in [(2l-2)N^1 + 1, (2l-1)N^1]; l \text{ is the layer of node } \mathcal{I}(I); \\ 0 & otherwise. \end{cases}$$

(14)

in which, β_I is the coefficient of node $\mathcal{I}(I)$ in Eq.(10).

Eventually, the soft decision function learnt is

$$f(x) = W^T \phi(x) + b = \left(\sum_{i=1}^{\mathcal{N}} (A\alpha)_i \times \phi(\mathcal{I}(i)) \right)^T \phi(x) + b = k^T(x)A\alpha + b \quad (15)$$

4   Experiment

To evaluate the performance, we conduct the experiments for shot level concept detection on the benchmark TRECVID 2005 development corpus [13]. This dataset contains about 80 hours news from 13 international TV programs in Arabic, English and Chinese. After shot boundary detection, 43,907 shots are segmented in development set. Then 50% (i.e., 21,950 shots) is selected as training data and the rest 50% (i.e., 21,957 shots) to test performance. In training set, 70% (i.e., 15,365 shots) is used for training and 30% (i.e., 6,585 shots) to validate the learned model. All sets are selected according to the video and shot ID sequentially. To assemble the multi-layer structure, the key frames of sub-shots provided by TRECVID organizer are used to form the frame layer, and each key frame is segmented into regions by JSEG method [4], then filter out regions less than 4% so as to get the region layer. Finally, the constructed MLMI setting contains 1.5 key frames per shot and five regions per key frame on average. Thereafter, several low-level feature extractors are adopted on shot, frame and region layer, respectively. In our experiment, 42 dimensional features including first three order moments of global motion (6-dim) and motion activity (8-dim) are extracted for shots; 225 dimensional block-wise color moments in Lab color space for key frames and 48 dimensional features with color correlogram, color moment, region size, wavelet texture and shape for regions. There are about 150,000 nodes in the whole training set, thus the computational cost is extremely high. In addition, the positive and negative samples are extremely unbalanced in the training set. We use down-sample scheme to deal with such problems, in the experiment, 10% negative samples and all positive ones are selected instead.

We use the following 10 concepts which are defined and adopted in TRECVID 2005 high-level feature extraction task for evaluation, i.e. *building, car, explosion fire, flag-US, maps, mountain, prisoner, sports, walking running* and *waterscape waterfront*. We use *Average Precision* (AP) to be performance metric which is applied officially in TRECVID task evaluations. The average AP over the 10 concepts is used to evaluate the overall performance, named *mean average precision* (MAP).

We compare the proposed method with SVM on single layer (SVM_SL), SVM on multi-layer (SVM_ML) and MLMI kernel based SVM method. In SVM_SL, the 225 dimensional frame layer feature is used solely, training procedure is built upon the frame level and testing on shot level as most widely used in TRECVID participants; while in SVM_ML, the multi-layer structure is taken into account and frame/region features are combined to shot layer. For MLMI kernel and MILC^2 methods, we choose RBF kernel for k_f in Eq.(2), so that $k_f(f_n, f'_n) = \exp((|f_n - f'_n|^2/2\sigma^2)$. Several parameters, i.e. σ and λ_1 in MLMI kernel, σ, λ_1 and λ_l in MILC^2 need to be specified, here we simply set $\lambda_2 = \lambda_3 = \ldots = \lambda_L$, and grid search is conducted by setting varying from 1 to 15 with step 2, λ_1 values $\{2^{-2}, 2^{-1}, \ldots, 2^5\}$ and λ_l values $\{10^{-3}, 10^{-2}, 10^{-1}, 1\}$. In the same manner, parameters of SVM_SL and SVM_ML are both set to be nearly optimal by grid search.

Figure 3 shows the AP and MAP results for the ten concepts with the top ranked 2000 shots returned. For *prisoner*, the positive training sample is extremely few and all detectors perform badly. For *building* and *car*, the methods using multi-layer information, i.e., SVM_ML, MLMI Kernel and MILC^2 method have worse results compared to SVM_SL, which indicates that the shot and region features weaken the separability of the problem. It reveals that MILC^2 works well on most concepts [2]. Compared to SVM_SL method, five out of ten concepts achieve better performance, two are degraded, and the rest three (i.e., *flag-US, mountain,* and *prisoner*) have close average precision. MILC^2 reports better performance than MLMI Kernel method for all concepts and outperforms SVM_ML on eight concepts except *mountain* and *prisoner*. On average, MILC^2 achieves the best performance, which obtains a MAP of 0.1648, showing 22.8% improvement over SVM_SL (0.1342), 19.23% over SVM_ML (0.1382) and 8.69% over MLMI Kernel method (0.1468), respectively.

---

[2] As 10% down-sampling for negative shots, training data is extremely insufficient for SVM to gain MAP reported in some TRECVID reports [1]. However, the relative comparisons can also show the advantages of the proposed method.

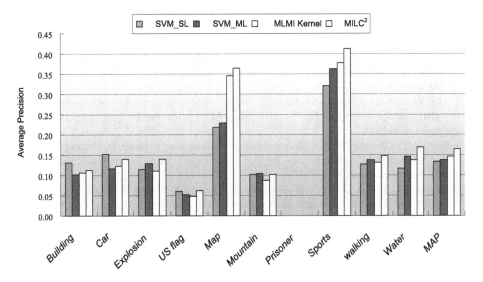

Fig. 3. Average precision (AP) and MAP of ten concepts by SVM_SL, SVM_ML, MLMI kernel and MILC^2 methods on TRECVID 2005 benchmark

5   Conclusion and Future Works

In this paper, multi-layer multi-instance (MLMI) learning, a new instance of structure learning is extensively analyzed. In MLMI learning, multi-layer structure and the "bag-instance" relation across layers are the most important two features distinguishing from general structure learning and multi-instance learning. To tackle MLMI learning task, we propose a novel algorithm named MILC^2. In MILC^2, an additional constraint penalizing the disagreement of inter-layer predictions is explicitly introduced to fit the MI relation. With this explicit constraint, MILC^2 solves the ambiguity propagation problem, which cannot be actually handled in MLMI kernel approach. The experimental results on TRECVID 2005 benchmark have shown that by leveraging the inter-layer consistency constraint, MILC^2 achieves better performance than standard SVM based approaches and the MLMI kernel method. Future works will be focused on reducing the computational complexity, and mining the instance labeling with instance relations imported.

References

1. TRECVID: TREC Video Retrieval Evaluation.
   `http://www-nlpir.nist.gov/projects/TRECVID`
2. Chen, Y., Bi, J., Wang, J.Z.: MILES: Multiple-instance learning via embedded instance selection. IEEE Trans. on Pattern Analysis and Machine Intelligence 28(12), 1931–1947 (2006)

3. Cheung, P.-M., Kwok, J.T.: A regularization framework for multiple-instance learning. In: Proceedings of International Conference on Machine Learning, pp. 193–200. ACM Press, New York (2006)
4. Deng, Y., Manjunath, B.S.: Unsupervised segmentation of color-texture regions in images and video. IEEE Trans. on Pattern Analysis and Machine Intelligence 23(8), 800–810 (2001)
5. Gu, Z., Mei, T., Hua, X.-S., Tang, J., Wu, X.: Multi-layer multi-instance kernel for video concept detection. In: Proceedings of ACM Multimedia, Augsburg, Germany (September 2007)
6. Kwok, J., Cheung, P.-M.: Marginalized multi-instance kernels. In: Proceedings of International Joint Conference on Artificial Intelligence, Hyderabad, India, pp. 901–906 (January 2007)
7. Maron, O., Ratan, A.L.: Multiple-instance learning for natural scene classification. In: Proceedings of International Conference on Machine Learning, pp. 341–349. Morgan Kaufmann, San Francisco (1998)
8. Naphade, M., Smith, J.R., Tesic, J., Chang, S.-F., Hsu, W., Kennedy, L., Hauptmann, A., Curtis, J.: Large-scale concept ontology for multimedia. IEEE MultiMedia 13(3), 86–91 (2006)
9. Qi, G.-J., Hua, X.-S., Rui, Y., Tang, J., Mei, T., Zhang, H.-J.: Correlative multi-label video annotation. In: Proceedings of ACM Multimedia, Augsburg, Germany (September 2007)
10. Smola, A., Vishwanathan, S., Hofmann, T.: Kernel methods for missing variables. In: Proceedings of International Workshop on Artificial Intelligence and Statistics, Barbados (2005)
11. Gartner, T., Flach, P.A., Kowalczyk, A., Smola, A.J.: Multi-instance kernels. In: Proceedings of International Conference on Machine Learning, pp. 179–186. Morgan Kaufmann, San Francisco (2002)
12. Yan, R., Naphade, M.: Semi-supervised cross feature learning for semantic concept detection in video. In: Proceedings of IEEE Computer Society Conference on Computer Vision and Pattern Recognition (2005)
13. Smeaton, A.F., Over, P., Kraaij, W.: Evaluation Campaigns and TRECVID. In: Proceedings of ACM SIGMM International Workshop on Multimedia Information Retrieval (2006)

An Implicit Active Contour Model for Feature Regions and Lines

Ho-Ryong Jung and Moon-Ryul Jung

Department of Media Technology
School of Media, Sogang Univ., Korea

Abstract. We present a level-set based implicit active contour method which can detect innermost homogeneous regions which are often considered feature regions or lines depending on the width of the regions. The curve evolution algorithm is derived from optimization of energy defined for the evolving curves. The energy has basically three terms: the first is the energy of the regions inside the curves, the second the energy of the bands inside the curves, and the third the energy of the bands outside the curves. If the band width is small, the total energy is minimized when the evolving curves lie at the boundaries of the innermost homogeneous regions, and the regions inside the curves are considered feature regions. Our method contrasts with the Chan-Vese model, which does not have the notion of innermost homogeneous regions but tries to find the curves such that the regions inside and outside them are both homogeneous. Our model approaches Chan-Vese model as the band width is increased, and is equivalent to Chan-Vese model when the band width is sufficiently large, so that all points inside/outside the curves lie within the bands inside/outside the curves, respectively.

Keywords: active contours, level-set, local band, features, thin regions.

1 Introduction

Active contour models are successful methods in field of image segmentation. The basic idea in active contour models is to evolve an initial curve, from a given image, in order to detect objects in that image. In recent years, active contour models are given more power by employing level set methods invented by Osher and Sethian [1]. The level-set formulation of active contour models are called implicit active contour models because the evolving curves are represented implicitly as the zero of the level-set function.

Active contour models are classified as edge-based models and region-based models. Edge-based models [2,3] make the evolving curves stopped by using an edge function defined in terms of the gradient of the image intensity. This method has disadvantages when the image has uncertain edges. Region-based models [4] try to find regions which are homogeneous, and the edges are obtained as the boundaries of the discovered regions. They are efficient when objet boundaries are weak, because they do not use use image gradient. But the Chan-Vese model

S. Satoh, F. Nack, and M. Etoh (Eds.): MMM 2008, LNCS 4903, pp. 35–44, 2008.
© Springer-Verlag Berlin Heidelberg 2008

[4] is not good at detecting thin regions, because it simply divides the whole image into the inner parts and the outer parts.

Recently, an implicit active contour model (Li model [5]) was proposed, which is able to correctly detect regions from images that have inhomogeneous intensities, in contrast to the Chan-Vese model [4]. The Li model considers a collection of overlapping local homogeneous regions as a meaningful region.

In addition, the Li model gets rid of re-initialization of the level-set function by incorporating a penalty term into the energy function, which keeps the level-set function from deviating from the distance function. But all these models are not suitable for detecting innermost homogeneous regions. For example, the roads of a map are thin homogeneous regions considered as feature lines, as shown in Figure 1. The white interior thin regions of CT image are also feature need to be detected, as shown in Figure 1. So, this paper proposes a novel active contour for detecting thin homogeneous regions. In our model, the initial contour is easy to locate, because it is placed to include everything in the given image.

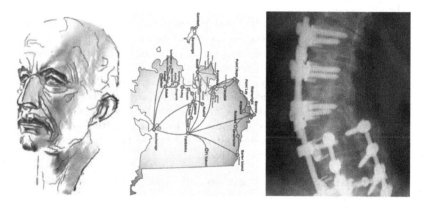

Fig. 1. The images with various feature lines and regions. Here "feature lines" are thin feature regions which look like lines. **Left** : Feature lines on the face ([9]). **Middle:** Feature lines on the map **Right**: Feature regions on the Neck replacement CT image.

2   Description of the Model

2.1   Background

The energy of the Chan-Vese model [4] is defined as follows:

$$F(\phi, c_1, c_2) = \lambda_1 \int_{\Omega} |u_0 - c_1|^2 H(\phi)dxdy \tag{1}$$

$$+\lambda_2 \int_{\Omega} |u_0 - c_2|^2 (1 - H(\phi))dxdy + \mu \int_{\Omega} \delta(\phi)|\nabla \phi|$$

Here $\phi(x)$ is the level-set function such that the $x's$ for which ϕ is positive is the inside regions and the $x's$ for which ϕ is negative is the outside regions. The Heaviside function H is defined by

$$H(x) = \begin{cases} 1, if \ x \geq 0 \\ 0, if \ x < 0 \end{cases} \tag{2}$$

So, the first and second terms in the right hand side of equation (1) refers to the energy of the inside regions and of the outside regions, respectively. c_1 and c_2 are constant densities (yet unknown), which represent the intensities of the regions inside and outside the curve C, and $\mu > 0$, $\nu > 0$, $\lambda_1, \lambda_2 > 0$ are parameters. The third term on the right hand side of equation (1) is the length of the evolving curves, as shown in equation 3.

$$length\{x|\phi(x) = 0\} = \int_{\Omega} |\nabla H(\phi)| = \int_{\Omega} \delta(\phi)|\nabla \phi| \tag{3}$$

Minimizing energy function $F(\phi, c1, c2)$ requires the partial derivative of F with respect to $c1$ and $c2$ to be zero. It in turn requires c_1 to be the average of u_0 inside the curves and c_2 to be the average of u_0 outside the curves.

Li et al. [5] proposed a novel model for detecting regions more accurately than does the Chan-Vese model. The Li model defines the homogeneity of a region by the sum of the homogeneities of overlapping local regions.

The difference between the Chan-Vese model and the Li model is illustrated in Figure 2. The Chan-Vese model has a tendency not to detect a region whose intensity changes gradually. The Li model evaluates the homogeneity of regions locally, so that a region can be considered meaningful if its overlapping local regions are homogeneous. Hence, for example, in the second image of Figure 2, the Chan-Vese model does not regard as meaningful a region whose intensity increases toward the center of the region. In contrast, the Li model finds the contour right at the boundary of such a region.

But both models are not capable of detecting thin homogeneous regions which are often considered feature curves. Figure 1 shows such examples.

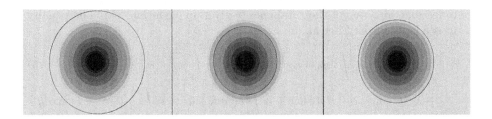

Fig. 2. Comparison between the Chan-Vese model and the Li model. **Left** : Initial contour. **Middle**: Chan-Vese Model: The contour does not lie at the boundary of the region whose intensity increases toward the center. **Right**: Li Model: The contour lies exactly at the boundary of the region whose intensity increases toward the center.

2.2   Energy Function of the Model

The energy function of our model is given by equation (4).

$$F(\phi, c_0, c_1, c_2) = \xi F_0(\phi, c_0) + \lambda_1 F_1(\phi, c_1) + \lambda_2 F_2(\phi, c_2) \tag{4}$$

$$= \xi \int_\Omega |u_0 - c_0|^2 H(\phi) dx + \lambda_1 \int_\Omega |u_0 - c_1|^2 H_1(\phi) dx$$

$$+ \lambda_2 \int_\Omega |u_0 - c_2|^2 H_2(\phi) dx$$

Here c_0 represents the intensity of the regions inside the evolving curves. c_1 and c_2 represent the intensity of the bands inside of the evolving curves and of the bands outside of the evolving curves, respectively. Functions H_1 and H_2 are defined by equation (5).

$$H_1(\phi(x)) = \begin{cases} 1 & \text{if} \quad 0 \le \phi(x) \le d_1 \\ 0 & \text{if} \quad \phi(x) < 0 \text{ or } \phi(x) > d_1 \end{cases}$$

$$H_2(\phi(x)) = \begin{cases} 1 & \text{if} \quad -d_2 \le \phi(x) \le 0 \\ 0 & \text{if} \quad \phi(x) < -d_2 \text{ or } \phi(x) > 0 \end{cases}$$

d_1, d_2 are the inside and outside band widths, respectively. d_1 is the value of the level-set function such that the points whose levels are less than d_1 belongs to the inside band. d_2 is similarly defined. The band widths are the parameter controlled by the user.

The first energy term F_0 demands that the regions of the desirable contours be homogeneous as much as possible. The first term forces the initial contour to contract toward the thin regions. However, the first term is not sufficient to detect innermost homogeneous regions. It can reach a local minimum where the contours lie within small margins of the boundaries of innermost regions. What we want is the situation where the contours lie exactly at the boundaries of innermost homogeneous regions. To help achieve this condition, we demand that the thin bands inside and outside the curves be homogeneous. We can achieve this condition by requiring inside and outside bans to be homogeneous as much as possible. These requirements are reflected by the second and third terms F_1 and F_2. By adding the length term and the penalty term for the violation of the distance function, we get the total energy given by equation (5). The penalty term is adopted from Li et al. [5].

$$F(\phi, c_0, c_1, c_2) = \xi \int_\Omega |u_0 - c_0|^2 H(\phi) dx + \lambda_1 \int_\Omega |u_0 - c_1|^2 H_1(\phi) dx \tag{5}$$

$$+ \lambda_2 \int_\Omega |u_0 - c_2|^2 H_2(\phi) dx + \mu \int_\Omega \delta(\phi) |\nabla \phi| dx + \nu \int_\Omega \frac{1}{2} (|\nabla \phi| - 1)^2 dx dy$$

When the user decreases the inside band widths d_1 and d_2, it means that the user wants to detect thin homogeneous regions as meaningful regions. According to equations (5) and (2), function H_1 is equivalent to H if the positive level-set values are all less than d_1. By similar reasoning, $H_2(\phi(x))$ is equivalent to

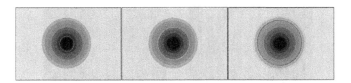

Fig. 3. The smaller the band width, the more homogeneous the detected region. Our experiments set the band widths to 3 to 5 pixels. **Left** : band size $(d_1 = d_2) = 3$. **Middle**: band size $= 100$. **Right** : band size $= 250$: the same result as the Chan-Vese model (See Figure 2).

$(1 - H(\phi(x)))$, if the outside band width d_2 is sufficiently large. Hence as the band widths increase, our model approaches the Chan-Vese model, and is equivalent to the Chan-Vese model, when the band widths are sufficiently large. See Figure 3 for the effect of the band widths.

2.3   Deriving the Level-Set Function Evolution Equation

A necessary condition for (ϕ, c_0, c_1, c_2) to be a local minimum for the energy functional (5) is given by equation (6).

$$c_0(\phi) = \frac{\int_\Omega u_0 H(\phi) dx}{\int_\Omega H(\phi(x)) dx}$$

$$c_1(\phi) = \frac{\int_\Omega u_0 H_1(\phi) dx}{\int_\Omega H_1(\phi(x)) dx} \qquad c_2(\phi) = \frac{\int_\Omega u_0 H_2(\phi) dx}{\int_\Omega H_2(\phi(x)) dx}$$

$$\frac{\partial F}{\partial \phi} = \xi\delta(\phi)(u_0 - c_0)^2 + \lambda_1\delta_1(\phi)(u_0 - c_1)^2 - \lambda_2\delta_2(\phi)(u_0 - c_2)^2 \qquad (6)$$

$$- \mu\delta(\phi)div(\frac{\nabla\phi}{|\nabla\phi|}) - \nu(\nabla^2\phi - div(\frac{\nabla\phi}{|\nabla\phi|})) = 0$$

Here $\delta(\phi)$ is a derivative of H with respect to ϕ, and it is a Dirac delta function whose peak is at $\phi = 0$. $\delta_1(\phi)$ is a sort of delta function with two peaks at $\phi = 0$ and $\phi = d_1$. Similarly $\delta_2(\phi)$ has two peaks at $\phi = 0$ and $\phi = -d_2$. The condition $\frac{\partial F}{\partial \phi} = 0$ can be achieved by solving the following evolution equation for ϕ:

$$\frac{\partial\phi}{\partial t} = -\frac{\partial F}{\partial \phi} = -\xi\delta(\phi)(u_0 - c_0)^2 - \lambda_1\delta_1(\phi)(u_0 - c_1)^2 \qquad (7)$$

$$+\lambda_2\delta_2(\phi)(u_0 - c_2)^2 + \mu\delta(\phi)div(\frac{\nabla\phi}{|\nabla\phi|}) + \nu(\nabla^2\phi - div(\frac{\nabla\phi}{|\nabla\phi|}))$$

In practice, we use regularized versions of the functions δ, δ_1, δ_2, H_1, H_2, denoted by δ_ϵ, etc., as shown in equation (8). The regularized versions of these functions cause the evolving level set function $\phi(x)$ to change at points x away from the contours, and it helps alleviating the problem of local minimum [4].

Fig. 4. Detecting the innermost region from the image, starting from the large initial contour($\mu = 1.0, \nu = 0, \lambda_1 = \lambda_2 = 1.0, \xi = 5$)

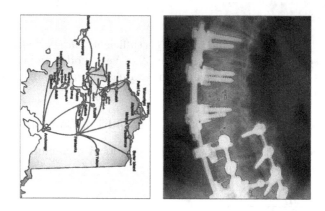

Fig. 5. Detecting the road lines from the map (left)($\mu = 1.0, \nu = 0, \lambda_1 = \lambda_2 = 1.0, \xi = 3$), and innermost regions from the CT image (right)($\mu = 1.0, \nu = 0, \lambda_1 = \lambda_2 = 1.0, \xi = 5$)

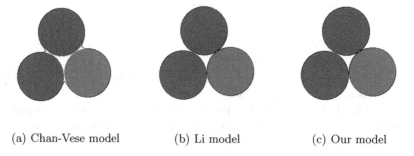

(a) Chan-Vese model   (b) Li model   (c) Our model

Fig. 6. (a-c): Both Li and our models detect three separate regions with different intensities, whereas Chan-Vese model does not

$$H_\epsilon(x) = \frac{1}{2}[1 + \frac{2}{\pi}\arctan(\frac{x}{\epsilon})] \quad \delta_\epsilon(x) = \frac{1}{\pi}\frac{\epsilon}{\epsilon^2 + x^2}$$

$$\delta_{1,\epsilon}(x) = \begin{cases} \delta_\epsilon(x) & \text{if } x \le \frac{d_1}{2} \\ \delta_\epsilon(x - d_1) & \text{if } x > \frac{d_1}{2} \end{cases} \quad \delta_{2,\epsilon}(x) = \begin{cases} \delta_\epsilon(x + d_2) & \text{if } x \le \frac{-d_2}{2} \\ \delta_\epsilon(x) & \text{if } x > \frac{-d_2}{2} \end{cases} \quad (8)$$

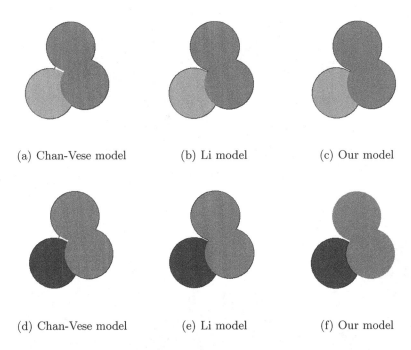

(a) Chan-Vese model   (b) Li model   (c) Our model

(d) Chan-Vese model   (e) Li model   (f) Our model

Fig. 7. **(a-c)**: The image has three overlapping regions whose intensities are similar (though the color images are shown, only the intensities are used). Both Li and our models detect a region which is the union of three overlapping regions, whereas Chan-Vese model does not. **(d-f)**: The image has three overlapping regions which as a region is not homogeneous. Our model detects one of the regions which is homogeneous and whose outside band is homogeneous. But both Chan-Vese and Li models do not.

Fig. 8. (Right) Thin regions are considered skeletons. (Left) Our model detects skeletons (the blue regions $\mu = 1.0, \nu = 0, \lambda_1 = \lambda_2 = 1.0, \xi = 2.5$).

The partial differential equation in (7) is implemented by the finite difference method as used by Chan and Vese [4].

Fig. 9. Various kinds of "innermost" regions detected by changing the parameter ξ. **Left** : $\xi = 0.5$: the boundary of the shirt is detected. **Right** : $\xi = 2$: the boundary of the horse is detected.

Fig. 10. Detecting the innermost homogeneous regions from a noisy image($\mu = 1.0$, $\nu = 0, \lambda_1 = \lambda_2 = 1.0, \xi = 4.5$)

3   Experiments

We used round-shaped and large initial contours in all the experiments. We used the same parameters of $\mu = 1.0, \nu = 0, \lambda_1 = \lambda_2 = 1.0$ for all images in this paper, except for ξ. See Figures 6 and 7 for comparison between the Chan-Vese model, the Li model, and our model. Figure 4 shows a simple case of images where the intensities change gradually. We detect the thin white region. With a large initial contour containing all the objects, the previous level-set active contour models can not detect the innermost thin region which looks like feature curves. They can only detect outer feature curves. In some cases the innermost regions are skeletons in objects. For example, see Figure 8 (left). In general, interior feature curves can be detected by skeletonization algorithms([10], [11]) once meaningful regions are detected. But our method directly detects thin regions which look like skeletons, as shown in Figure 8 (right). The image in Figure 4 has five regions. The previous level set active contour models can detect various feature regions by placing the initial contours at various locations. But starting from the initial contour containing everything in the image, we can detect various kinds of regions by changing the ξ parameter, which weighs the importance of the homogeneity of the region inside the curves. See Figure 9 for an example. Figure 10 shows that innermost homogeneous regions are detected from noisy images. The video[1] associated with the paper demonstrates the detecting process of feature regions for Figure 3, Figure 5, and Figure 10.

4 Conclusions

We generalized the Chan-Vese implicit region-based active contour model, so that innermost homogeneous regions in the input image can be detected. This capability is important because such regions are often considered feature regions. They are often considered feature lines when they are thin. In some cases we can use this model to detect skeletal features of an image. The curve evolution algorithm is derived from optimization of energy defined for the evolving curves. We demand that the curves lie at the boundaries of the innermost homogeneous regions. To help achieve this condition, we require that the regions inside the curves be homogeneous as far as possible, and the bands inside and outside the curves be homogeneous. If the band width is small, the energy is minimized when the evolving curves lie at the boundaries of the innermost homogeneous regions. Our method contrasts with the Chan-Vese model, which finds the curves such that the regions inside and outside them are both homogeneous. Our model approaches Chan-Vese model as the band width is increased, and is equivalent to Chan-Vese model when the band width is sufficiently large. By introducing the notion of band and controlling its size, we have been able to detect more meaningful regions than the Chan-Vese model allows.

Acknowledgements

This work has been supported by the Korea Culture and Content Agency (KOCCA) for two years.

References

1. Osher, S., Sethian, J.A.: Fronts propagating with curvature dependent speed: algorithms based on Hamilton-Jacobi for mulations. J.comp.Phys. 79, 12–49 (1988)
2. Kass, M., Witkin, A., Terzopoulos, D.: Snakes: Active contour models. International Journal of Computer Vision 1, 321–331 (1988)

---

[1] The video file is available at our site
ftp://163.239.125.107/moon/MMM08/video.avi

3. Blake, A., Isard, M.: Active contours, pp. 25–37. Springer, Heidelberg (1988)
4. Chan, T., Vese, L.: Active contours without edges. IEEE Trans. Imag. Proc. 10(2), 266–277 (2001)
5. Li., C., Kao, C.-Y., Gore, J.C., Ding, Z.: Implicit Active Contours Driven by Local Binary Fitting Energy. In: CVPR (2007)
6. Li., C., Xu, C., Gui, C., Fox, M.D.: Level Set Evolution Without Re-initialization: A New Variational Formulation. In: CVPR (2005)
7. Osher, S.: Level Set Methods and Dynamic Implicit Surfaces. Springer, New York (2002)
8. Zhao, H., Chan, T., Merriman, B., Osher, S.: A variational level set approach to multiphase motion. Journal of Computational Physics. 127(1) (1996)
9. Yutaka, O., Alexander, B., Hans-Peter, S.: Ridge-Valley Lines on Meshes via Implicit Surface Fitting. In: International Conference on Computer Graphics and Interactive Techniques archive ACM SIGGRAPH (2004)
10. Kalles, D., Morris, D.: A novel fast and reliable thinning algorithm. Image and Vision Computing 11(9), 588–603 (1993)
11. Remy, E., Thiel, E.: "Exact medial axis with euclidean distance. Image and Vision Computing 23, 167–175 (2005)

New Approach for Hierarchical Classifier Training and Multi-level Image Annotation

Jianping Fan[1,*], Yuli Gao[1], Hangzai Luo[1], and Shin'ichi Satoh[2]

[1] Dept. of Computer Science, UNC-Charlott, USA
{jfan,ygao,hluo}@uncc.edu
[2] National Institute of Informatics, Tokyo, Japan
satoh@nii.ac.jp

Abstract. In this paper, we have proposed a novel algorithm to achieve automatic multi-level image annotation by incorporating concept ontology and multi-task learning for hierarchical image classifier training. To achieve more reliable image classifier training in high-dimensional heterogeneous feature space, a new algorithm is proposed by incorporating multiple kernels for diverse image similarity characterization, and a *multiple kernel learning* algorithm is developed to train the SVM classifiers for the atomic image concepts at the first level of the concept ontology. To enable automatic multi-level image annotation, a novel *hierarchical boosting* algorithm is proposed by incorporating *concept ontology* and *multi-task learning* to achieve hierarchical image classifier training.

Keywords: Multi-task learning, concept ontology, image annotation.

1 Introduction

Image classification becomes increasingly important and necessary to support automatic image annotation, so that searching from large-scale image collections can be made more intuitively by using the adequate keywords [1-2]. However, the performance of image classifiers largely depends on three inter-related issues: (1) representative visual features for characterizing diverse visual properties of images; (2) suitable functions for image similarity characterization; (3) effective algorithms for image classifier training.

To address the first issue, the underlying visual features should be able to represent both the global and local visual properties of images effectively and efficiently [6-7]. To address the second issue, the underlying similarity functions should be able to characterize the diverse image similarity accurately [8-11]. To address the third issue, robust techniques for image classifier training are needed to bridge the semantic gap successfully. In addition, one single image may contain multiple levels of semantics [3-5], thus supporting hierarchical image classification plays an important role on achieving more sufficient image annotations for retrieval purposes.

When large-scale image collections come into view, more effective algorithms are strongly expected for learning the classifiers for large amount of image concepts by addressing the following issues: (a) *How to exploit the inter-concept correlations for*

---

* Correspondence author.

S. Satoh, F. Nack, and M. Etoh (Eds.): MMM 2008, LNCS 4903, pp. 45–57, 2008.
© Springer-Verlag Berlin Heidelberg 2008

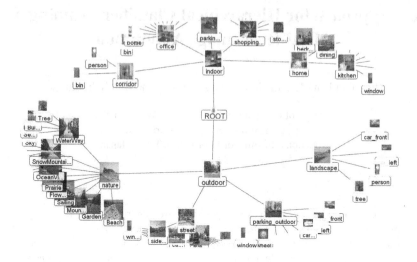

Fig. 1. Our concept ontology for image concept organization and image annotation

reducing the cost for learning large amount of image classifiers? The image concepts are dependent and such dependencies (inter-concept correlations) can be exploited for improving image classifier training and reducing the training cost significantly [8-11]. However, if such inter-concept correlations are simply exploited for hierarchical image classifier training, the classification errors will be transmitted among the relevant image classifiers (i.e., inter-concept error transmission) [9]. (b) *How to handle the problem of huge intra-concept diversity on visual properties*? One challenging problem for image classification is that the semantically-similar images (i.e., images belong to the same image concept) may have huge diversity on their visual properties, and thus it is very hard to use one single type of similarity function to characterize the diverse visual similarities between the images effectively. (c) *How to address the problem of huge inter-concept similarity on visual properties effectively*? The image concepts are dependent and may share some common visual properties [11], especially when they are the sibling children concepts under the same parent concept. For example, "garden", "beach", "sunset", "flower view", "mountain view", "ocean view", share some common visual properties and they can be treated as the sibling children concepts for the high-level image concept "nature scene". To enhance the discrimination power of the image classifiers, it is very important to develop more effective algorithms for handling the problem of inter-concept similarity on visual properties.

In this paper, we have developed a new framework for achieving automatic multi-level image annotation. The major components of our new framework include: (a) To capture the diverse visual properties of the images more accurately, both the local visual features and the global visual features are extracted for image similarity characterization. (b) To handle the problem of huge intra-concept diveristy on visual properties, multiple types of kernel functions are seamlessly integrated to characterize the diverse visual similarities between the images more effectively. (c) To address the problem of huge inter-concept similarity on visual properties, a novel hierarchical boosting algorithm is proposed by incorporating concept ontology and multi-task learning to exploit the inter-concept correlations for hierarchical image classifier training.

2   Concept Ontology Construction

As mentioned above, classifying large-scale images into the most relevant image concepts at different semantic levels is one promising solution to enable automatic multi-level image annotation. Supporting multi-level image annotation can further provide users with more flexibility to specify their queries via sufficient keywords at different semantic levels. Motivated by this observation, we have developed a novel scheme for *concept ontology* construction. On the concept ontology, each node represents one image concept at certain semantic level. The concept nodes at the first level of the concept ontology are defined as ***atomic image concepts***, which are used to represent the image concepts with the most specific subjects and smaller intra-concept variations on visual properties. They can further be assigned to the most relevant image concepts at the higher level of the concept ontology, which are used to interpret more general subjects of image contents with larger intra-concept variations on visual properties.

Each image in our training set is associated with the users' annotations of the underlying image semantics, and thus the keywords that are relevant to the image semantics (text terms for image semantics interpretation) are identified automatically by using standard text analysis techniques. Because multiple keywords may have the same word sense, Latent Semantic Analysis (LSA) is used to integrate the similar image topics. The results of LSA are the fuzzy clusters of the keywords with the same word sense.

The contextual relationships between the image concepts consists of two parts: (a) semantic similarity; (b) visual similarity. Unfortunately, most existing techniques completely ignore the inter-concept visual similarity for concept ontology construction, thus they cannot directly be extended to construct the concept ontology for organizing large amount of image concepts [11]. In this paper, both the semantic similarity and the visual similarity between the image concepts are seamlessly integrated to determine their inter-concept associations:

$$\varphi(C_i, C_j) = -\nu \cdot \log \frac{l(C_i, C_j)}{2D} + \omega \cdot \gamma(C_i, C_j), \qquad \nu + \omega = 1 \qquad (1)$$

where the first part denotes the semantic similarity between the image concepts C_j and C_i, the second part indicates their visual similarity according to the similarity between their image distributions, $l(C_i, C_j)$ is the length of the shortest path between C_i and C_j by searching the relevant keywords from WordNet [11], D is the maximum depth of WordNet, $\gamma(C_i, C_j)$ is the visual similarity between the images under C_i and C_j. Kullback-Leibler (KL) divergence between their image distributions is used to characterize the visual similarity between the image concepts C_i and C_j in the high-dimensional feature space. The concept ontology for our test data set is shown in Fig. 1.

3 Kernel-Based Image Similarity Characterization

To characterize the diverse visual properties of images efficiently and effectively, both the global visual features and the local visual features are extracted for image similarity characterization [6-7]. The global visual features such as color histogram can provide the global visual properties of entire images [6], but they may not be able to accurately capture the object information within the images. On the other hand, the local visual features such as SIFT (scale invariant feature transform) features can allow object detection from the cluttered backgrounds [7]. In our current implementations, the global visual features consist of 16-bin color histogram. As shown in Fig. 2, the localized operators, such as Gabor wavelet and difference-of-Gaussian filters, are performed to extract the local visual features for image similarity characterization. From these experimental results, one can observe that our localized operators can extract the principal visual properties of the relevant salient image components effectively. The local visual features consist of 62-dimensional texture features from Gabor filter banks, and a number of keypoints and their SIFT features.

To bridge the semantic gap, the basic question is to define more suitable similarity functions to accurately characterize the diverse visual similarities between the images. We have defined three *basic image kernels* to characterize the diverse visual similarities between the images based on "dense" (global visual features) or "sparse" (local visual features) image descriptors. The advantage of dense descriptors (global visual features) is their computational efficiency and their invariance to spatial relocation of objects. However, if the objects are salient in the image, sparse methods tend to offer better characterization of image similarity because they are more capable of detecting "interesting" regions/points and can deal with object cluttering and occlusions effectively.

We have incorporated three basic image kernels to characterize the diverse visual similarities between the images, and a linear combination of these basic image kernels can further form a family of various kernels to achieve more accurate characterization of the diverse image similarities. In this paper, we focus on three feature descriptors: (a) global color histogram; (b) texture histogram from wavelet filter bank; (c) local invariant feature point set. The first two descriptors are computed from every pixel of entire image; while the third descriptor is computed from small localized interesting image patches.

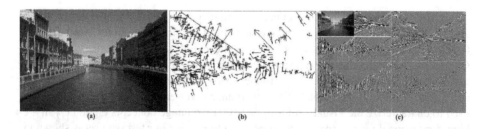

Fig. 2. Local visual feature extraction for image similarity characterization: (a) original images; (b) key points and SIFT vectors; (c) wavelet transformation

We quantize the color histogram uniformly into 16 bins and adopt the χ^2 kernel function and it is a Mercer kernel. Given two color histograms u and v with equal length (16 bins), their χ^2 statistical similarity is defined as :

$$\chi^2(u,v) = \frac{1}{2} \sum_{i=1}^{16} \frac{(u_i - v_i)^2}{u_i + v_i} \tag{2}$$

where u_i and v_i are the corresponding color bins from two color histograms u and v. The kernel function $K(u,v)$, which is used to characterize the similarity between these two color histograms, is defined as:

$$K(u,v) = e^{-\chi^2(u,v)/\sigma} \tag{3}$$

where σ is set to be the mean value of the χ^2 distances between all the image pairs in our experiments.

To capture image textures, we apply a bank of wavelet filters on each image as shown in Fig. 2(c), where the image textures are represented by histogramming the outputs of the filtered channels. Particularly, we apply two types of filters to extract different edge information and corner information: (a) Gabor filters at 6 orientations and 3 scales; (b) Difference of Gaussian (DoG) at four different scales.

Suppose there are m filtered responses for each image, we estimate the empirical distribution of the filtered responses by building a m-bin histogram $\{h_i | i = 1, \cdots, m\}$, where h_i is the filtered response for the ith channel. The kernel function $K(x,y)$ for the wavelet filter banks between two images x and y is then defined as:

$$K(x,y) = e^{-\sum_{i=1}^{m} \chi_i^2(h_i(x), h_i(y))/\sigma_i} \tag{4}$$

where $\chi_i^2(h_i(x), h_i(y))$ is the χ^2 distance between the two histograms $h_i(x)$ and $h_i(y)$ obtained from the ith filtering channel of the respective images.

The kernel function $K(x,y)$ can be decomposed as a product of component kernels $e^{-\chi_i^2(h_i(x), h_i(y))/\sigma_i}$:

$$K(x,y) = \prod_{i=1}^{m} e^{-\chi_i^2(h_i(x), h_i(y))/\sigma_i} \tag{5}$$

where each component kernel $e^{-\chi_i^2(h_i(x), h_i(y))/\sigma_i}$ satisfies Mercer's conditions. Therefore, the kernel function $K(x,y)$ also satisfies Mercer's conditions.

In this paper, we have employed difference of Gaussian (DoG) as the key point detector and SIFT features as the descriptors because of their distinctiveness and success in object detection [7]. For two images, their key point sets Q and P may have different numbers of key points: M_Q and N_p. Based on this observation, the Earth Mover's distance (EMD) between these two key point sets is then defined as:

$$D(Q,P) = \frac{\sum_{i=1}^{M_Q} \sum_{j=1}^{N_P} \beta_{ij} d(q_i, p_j)}{\sum_{i=1}^{M_Q} \sum_{j=1}^{N_P} \beta_{ij}} \tag{6}$$

where β_{ij} is an importance factor that can be determined automatically by solving a linear programming problem, and $d(q_i, p_j)$ is the ground distance function between two random key points q_i and p_j from Q and P.

To incorporate the EMD distance into our kernel-based image similarity characterization framework, we can extend Gaussian kernels as:

$$K(Q, P) = e^{-D(Q,P)/\gamma} \tag{7}$$

where γ is set as the mean value of $D(Q, P)$ of the image pairs in our experiments.

Using multiple kernels to approximate the diverse image similarities in the high-dimensional heterogeneous feature space can provide the following significant benefits: (a) *Kernel Function Selection:* Because the high-dimensional feature space is heterogeneous, using multiple kernel functions is able to achieve more accurate approximation of the diverse visual similarities between the images. To achieve more accurate approximation of the diverse visual similarities between the images, different kernels should be used for different types of visual features because their statistical properties are very different. Unfortunately, most existing machine learning tools concentrate on using an uniform kernel for various types of visual features and fully ignore the heterogeneity of their statistical properties. (b) *Training Sample Size Reduction and Classifier Generalization:* Learning SVM image classifiers in the high-dimensional heterogeneous feature space requires large amount of training images that exponentially increase with the feature dimensions. On the other hand, learning from limited training images could result in higher generalization error rate. Because the feature dimensions for each basic kernel function is relatively low, using multiple kernel functions to approximate the diverse image similarity can reduce the size of training images significantly and generalize the image classifiers effectively from a limited number of training images. (c) *Training Complexity Reduction:* The standard techniques for SVM classifier training have $O(n^3)$ time complexity and $O(n^2)$ space complexity, where n is the number of training images. Incorporating multiple kernel functions to jointly approximate the diverse image similarities can significantly reduce the cost for SVM image classifier training because smaller size of training images are required.

4 Hierarchical Image Classifier Training

We have proposed a bottom-up scheme to incorporate concept ontology and multi-task learning for enhancing hierarchical image classifier training.

4.1 Multiple Kernel Learning for Atomic Image Concept Detection

It is well-known that the diverse visual similarities between the images can be characterized more effectively and efficiently by using different types of visual features. For a given atomic image concept C_j at the first level of the concept ontology, its SVM classifier can be learned by a mixture of the basic image kernels (i.e., mixture-of-kernels):

$$\hat{K}(x, y) = \sum_{k=1}^{\kappa_j} \alpha_k K_k(x, y), \qquad \sum_{k=1}^{\kappa_j} \alpha_k = 1 \tag{8}$$

where $\alpha_k \geq 0$ is the importance factor for the kth basic image kernel $K_k(x, y)$ for image similarity characterization, κ_j is the total number of the basic image kernels. The importance factor α_k can be determined automatically from the training images.

Given a set of labeled training images $\Omega_{C_j} = \{X_l, Y_l | l = 1, \cdots, N\}$, the SVM classifier for the given atomic image concept C_j is then defined as:

$$f_{C_j}(X) = sign\left(\sum_{l=1}^{N} \beta_l Y_l \hat{K}(X_l, X) + b\right) \tag{9}$$

In the above multiple kernel learning problem, the visual features for the training image X_l are translated via κ_j kernel mappings: $\Phi(X) \mapsto \Re^{D_k}$, $k = 1, \cdots, \kappa_j$, from the original feature space into κ_j kernel spaces $(\Phi_i(X_l), \cdots, \Phi_{\kappa_j}(X_l))$, where D_k denotes the dimensionality of the kth feature subspace. The SVM classifier $f_{C_j}(X)$ can be obtained by:

$$min \; \frac{1}{2}\left(\sum_{k=1}^{\kappa_j} \|w_k\|_2\right)^2 + \lambda \sum_{l=1}^{N} \xi_l \tag{10}$$

subject to:

$$\forall_{l=1}^{N} : \xi_l \geq 0, \; Y_l\left(\sum_{k=1}^{\kappa_j}\langle w_k, \Phi_k(X_l)\rangle + b\right) \geq 1 - \xi_l$$

where λ is the penalty parameter between the training error rate and the regularization term. The dual problem for Eq. (10) is defined as:

$$min \; \gamma - \sum_{l=1}^{N} \beta_l \tag{11}$$

subject to:

$$\forall_{k=1}^{\kappa_j} : 0 \leq \beta \leq \lambda, \; \sum_{l=1}^{N} \beta_l Y_l = 0, \; \frac{1}{2}\sum_{l,m=1}^{N} \beta_l \beta_m Y_l Y_m K_k(X_l, X_m) \leq \gamma$$

where the kth kernel $K_k(X_l, X_m) = \langle \Phi_k(X_l), \Phi_k(X_m)\rangle$. By using multiple kernels for diverse image similarity characterization, the huge intra-concept diversity of visual properties can be handled more effectively.

4.2 Hierarchical Boosting for High-Level Image Concept Detection

Because of the inherent complexity of the task, automatic detection of the high-level image concepts with larger intra-concept variations of visual principles is still beyond the ability of the state-of-the-art techniques. Because the image concepts are dependent and such dependencies can be characterized effectively by the concept ontology, thus what is already learned for one certain image concept can be transfered to enhance the classifier training for its parent image concept and its sibling image concepts under the same parent node. Therefore, isolating the image concepts and learning their classifiers independently are not appropriate. Multi-task learning is one promising solution to this problem [12-15], but the success of multi-task learning largely depends on the relatedness of multiple tasks.

Based on these observations, we have developed a novel ***hierarchical boosting*** scheme that is able to combine the classifiers trained under different tasks to boost an ensemble classifier for a new image classification task. First, the concept ontology is used to identify the related tasks, e.g., multiple tasks for training the classifiers of the sibling image concepts under the same parent node are strongly related. Second, such task relatedness is used to determine the transferable knowledge and common features among the classifiers for the sibling image concepts to generalize their classifiers significantly from fewer training images. Because the classifiers for the sibling image concepts under the same parent node are used to characterize both their individual visual properties and the common visual properties for their parent node, they can compensate each other and their outputs are strongly correlated according to the new task (i.e., learning a bias classifier for their parent node).

To integrate multi-task learning for SVM image classifier training, a *common regularization term* W_0 of the SVM image classifiers is used to represent and quantify the transferable knowledge and common features among the SVM image classifiers for the sibling image concepts under the same parent node. The classifier for the atomic image concept C_j can be defined as:

$$f_{C_j}(X) = W_j^T X + b = (W_0 + V_j)^T X + b \qquad (12)$$

where W_0 is the common regularization term shared among the classifiers for the sibling atomic image concepts under the same parent node C_k, and V_j is the specific regularization term for the classifier of the atomic image concept C_j.

Given the labeled training images for L sibling atomic image concepts under the same parent node C_k: $\Omega = \{X_{ij}, Y_{ij} | i = 1, \cdots, N; j = 1, \cdots, L\}$, the margin maximization procedure is then transformed into the following joint optimization problem:

$$min \left\{ \sum_{j=1}^{L} \sum_{i=1}^{N} \xi_{ij} + \beta \sum_{j=1}^{L} \|W_0 + V_j\|^2 \right\} \qquad (13)$$

subject to:

$$\forall_{i=1}^{N} \forall_{j=1}^{L} : Y_{ij}(W_0 + V_j) \cdot X_{ij} + b \geq 1 - \xi_{ij}, \quad \xi_{ij} \geq 0$$

where $\xi_{ij} \geq 0$ represents the training error rate, L is the total number of atomic image concepts under the same parent node C_k, β is the positive regularization parameter. Thus the optimal classifier for C_j can be determined as:

$$f_{C_j}(X) = \sum_{j=1}^{L} \sum_{i=1}^{N} \alpha_{ij} Y_{ij} \hat{K}(X_{ij}, X) + \sum_{i=1}^{N} \beta_j Y_{ij} \hat{K}(X_{ij}, X) \qquad (14)$$

where the first part is used to characterize the common visual properties shared among these L sibling atomic image concepts under the same parent node C_k, the second part is used to characterize the invidual visual properties for the particular atomic image concept C_j, $\hat{K}(\cdot, \cdot)$ is the underlying mixture kernel.

The common regularization term W_0 for the sibling atomic image concepts is used to represent their common visual properties, and thus it is further treated as a prior regularization term to bias the SVM classifier for their parent node C_k. Setting such prior regularization term can exploit the output correlations between the SVM classifiers for the sibling atomic image concepts according to the new task, but also reduce the cost significantly for training a *bias classifier* for their parent node C_k. Based on such prior regularization term, the *bias classifier* for their parent node C_k can be learned more effectively by using few new training images. Thus the bias classifier for their parent node C_k is determined by minimizing:

$$min\left\{\frac{1}{2}\|W - W_0\|^2 + \alpha\sum_{l=1}^{m}[1 - Y_l(W^T \cdot X_l + b)]\right\} \tag{15}$$

where W_0 is the common regularization term for the sibling atomic image concepts under C_k, $\{X_l, Y_l | l = 1, \cdots, m\}$ are the new training images for learning the biased classifier for C_k.

Our System Annotations		
beach, nature, outdoor,cloudy sky, water, sand field	sunset, nature, outdoor, cloudy sky, sun, water	sidewalk, street, outdoor, building, tree, pedestrian
User Annotations		
beach, Savanna	sunset, beach, sky	sidewalk,New York

Fig. 3. Multi-level image annotation results both at the object level and at multiple concept levels

To learn the ensemble classifier for the given second-level image concept C_k, a novel **hierarchical boosting** scheme is developed by combining its bias classifier with the classifiers for its children image concepts. For the given second-level image concept C_k, the final prediction of its ensemble classifier can be obtained by a *logistic boosting* of the predictions of its bias classifier and the L classifiers for its L children image concepts.

$$H_{C_k}(X) = \sum_{h=1}^{L+1} p_h(X)f_{C_h}(X) \tag{16}$$

where $p_h(X)$ is the posterior distribution of the hth classifier $f_{C_h}(X)$ to be combined, and $p_h(X)$ is determined by:

$$p_h(X) = \frac{exp(f_{C_h}(X))}{\sum_{h=1}^{L+1} exp(f_{C_h}(X))} \qquad (17)$$

Our hierarchical boosting algorithm can provide the following benefits: (a) A new approach is developed for modeling the inter-task correlations by using a common predictive structure between multiple SVM image classifiers, and thus our hierarchical boosting algorithm can dramatically reduce the cost for achieving multi-task learning and significantly generalize the classifiers from fewer training images. For each image concept, incorporating the training images from other sibling image concepts for classifier training (via multi-task learning) can significantly enhance its discrimination power, especially when the available training images may not be representative for large amounts of unseen test images. (b) By exploiting the inter-concept correlations between the sibling image concepts to learn a bias classifier for their parent concept (which is able to characterize their common visual properties), our hierarchical boosting algorithm can handle the problem of huge inter-concept similarity on visual properties effectively. (c) Our hierarchical boosting algorithm is able to combine the classifiers trained for different tasks, leverage their individual strengths, and boost their performance significantly. The classifiers for the high-level image concepts are able to characterize both the common visual properties shared between their sibling children image concepts and their individual visual properties, thus our hierarchical boosting algorithm can provide more effective solution for hierarchical image classification.

5   Multi-level Image Annotation

We have integrated two innovative solutions seamlessly to address the inter-level error transmission problem: (1) enhancing the classifiers for the image concepts at the higher levels of the concept ontology, so that they can have higher discrimination power; (2) integrating a A^* *search algorithm* that is able to detect such misclassification path early and take appropriate actions for automatic error recovery [16]. An *overall probability* is calculated to determine the best path for hierarchical image classification. For a given test image, an optimal classification path should provide maximum value of the overall probability among all the possible classification paths. The overall probability $p(C_k)$ for one certain classification path (from one certain higher level image concept C_k to the relevant lower level image concept C_j) is defined as [16]:

$$p(C_k) = h(C_k) + g(C_j) \qquad (18)$$

where $h(C_k)$ is the posterior probability for the given test image to be classified into the current image concept C_k at the higher level of the concept ontology, $g(C_j)$ is the maximum posterior probability for the given test images to be classified into the most relevant child concept node C_j. Thus the classification path with the maximum value of overall probability for the given test image is selected. By using the overall probability, it is able for us to detect the incorrect classification path early and take appropriate actions for automatic error recovery. Our experimental results on hierarchical image classification and multi-level annotation are given in Fig. 3.

6   Algorithm Evaluation

In our current image set, we have 56,800 images: 2,800 images for natural scenes from Corel database, 25,000 images from MIT LabelMe, and 38,000 images from Google Image search engine. 37,800 images are labeled as the training set for learning the classifiers of 148 image concepts at 4 different semantic levels as shown in Fig. 1, 28,000 labeled images *which are not used for image classifier training* are treated as the test set for evaluating our hierarchical image classifiers. For each atomic image concept, 125 images are labeled as the training samples to learn the relevant SVM image classifier. In addition, the training images for these atomic image concepts are integrated as the training images for their parent nodes hierarchically. For each higher-level image concepts, 50 images are labeled as the new training samples to learn their bias classifiers. The visual features for image content representation include 16-D color histogram, 62-D wavelet-based textture features and 128-D interest points.

The *benchmark metric* for classifier evaluation includes *precision* ρ and *recall* ϱ. They are defined as:

$$\rho = \frac{\vartheta}{\vartheta + \xi}, \qquad \varrho = \frac{\vartheta}{\vartheta + \nu} \qquad (19)$$

where ϑ is the set of true positive images that are related to the corresponding image concept and are classified correctly, ξ is the set of true negative images that are irrelevant to the corresponding image concept and are classified incorrectly, and ν is the set of false positive images that are related to the corresponding image concept but are misclassified.

For the same image classification task under the same conditions (i.e., same set of visual features and same size of training images), our algorithm evaluation works focus on comparing our algorithms for multiple kernel learning and hierarchical boosting with the relevant techniques. Our proposed multiple kernel learning algorithm can achieve more effective SVM image classifier training as compared with traditional SVM classifier training techniques. As shown in Fig. 4, one can observe that our multiple kernel learning algorithm can significantly outperform the single-kernel learning techniques.

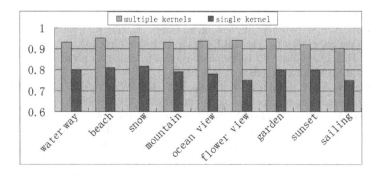

Fig. 4. The comparison results between our multiple kernel learning algorithm and single kernel learning technique

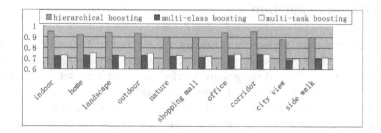

Fig. 5. The comparison results between our hierarchical boosting algorithm, multi-class boosting and multi-task boosting for the high-level image concepts

Our hierarchical boosting algorithm can significantly outperform the traditional techniques such as multi-class boosting and multi-task boosting [12-13]. As shown in Fig. 5, one can find that our hierarchical boosting algorithm can significantly outperform the traditional techniques such as multi-class boosting and multi-task boosting, especially for the image concepts on the higher levels of the concept ontology.

7 Conclusions

In this paper, we have proposed a novel algorithm for achieving automatic multi-level image annotation via hierarchical classification. To achieve more reliable image classifier training in high-dimensional heterogeneous feature space, a novel multiple kernel learning algorithm is proposed for training the SVM classifiers for the atomic image concepts. A hierarchical boosting algorithm is proposed by incorporating concept ontology and multi-task learning to achieve hierarchical image classifier training. Our experiments on large-scale image collections have also obtained very positive results.

References

1. Fan, J., Gao, Y., Luo, H.: Multi-level annotation of natural scenes using dominant image compounds and semantic concepts. ACM Multimedia (2004)
2. Smeulders, A.W.M., Worring, M., Santini, S., Gupta, A., Jain, R.: Content-based image retrieval at the end of the early years. IEEE Trans. on PAMI (2000)
3. Lim, J., Tian, Q., Mulhem, P.: Home photo content modeling for personalized event-based retrieval. IEEE Multimedia (2003)
4. Naphade, M., Smith, J.R., Tesic, J., Chang, S.-F., Hsu, W., Kennedy, L., Hauptmann, A., Curtis, J.: Large-scale concept ontology for multimedia. IEEE Multimedia (2006)
5. Yelizaveta, M., Chua, T.-S., Jain, R.: Semi-supervised annotation of brushwork in paintings domain using serial combinations of multiple experts. ACM Multimedia (2006)
6. Ma, W.-Y., Manjunath, B.S.: Texture features and learning similarity. In: IEEE CVPR, pp. 425–430 (1996)
7. Lowe, D.: Distinctive Image Features from Scale Invariant Keypoints. Intl Journal of Computer Vision 60, 91–110 (2004)
8. Li, J., Wang, J.Z.: Automatic Linguistic Indexing of Pictures by a Statistical Modeling Approach. IEEE Trans. on PAMI 25(9), 1075–1088 (2003)

 9. Fan, J., Luo, H., Gao, Y., Hacid, M.-S.: Mining image databases on semantics via statistical learning. In: ACM SIGKDD (2005)
10. Barnard, K., Forsyth, D.: Learning the semantics of words and pictures. In: IEEE ICCV, pp. 408–415 (2001)
11. Fan, J., Gao, Y., Luo, H.: Hierarchical classification for automatic image annotation. In: ACM SIGIR (2007)
12. Friedman, J., Hastie, T., Tibshirani, R.: Additive logistic regression: a statistical view of boosting. Annals of Statistics 28(2), 337–374 (2000)
13. Torralba, A., Murphy, K.P., Freeman, W.T.: Sharing features: efficient boosting procedures for multiclass object detection. In: IEEE CVPR (2004)
14. Yu, K., Schwaighofor, A., Tresp, V., Ma, W.-Y., Zhang, H.J.: Collaborative ensemble learning: Combining content-based information filtering via hierarchical Bayes. In: Proc. of Intl. Conf. on Uncertainty in Artificial Intelligence (UAI) (2003)
15. Shi, R., Chua, T.-S., Lee, C.-H., Gao, S.: Bayesian learning of hierarchical multinomial mixture models of concepts for automatic image annotation. In: Sundaram, H., Naphade, M., Smith, J.R., Rui, Y. (eds.) CIVR 2006. LNCS, vol. 4071, Springer, Heidelberg (2006)
16. Knuth, D.E.: The Art of Computer Programming. In: Sorting and Searching, vol. 3, Addison-Wesley, Reading (1978)

Extracting Text Information for Content-Based Video Retrieval

Lei Xu[1,2] and Kongqiao Wang[1]

[1] System Research Center, Beijing, Nokia Research Center
[2] Beijing University of Posts and Telecommunications

Abstract. In this paper we present a novel video text detection and segmentation system. In the detection stage, we utilize edge density feature, pyramid strategy and some weak rules to search for text regions, so that high detection rate can be achieved. Meanwhile, to eliminate the false alarms and improve the precision rate, a multilevel verification strategy is adopted. In the segmentation stage, a precise polarity estimation algorithm is firstly provided. Then, multiple frames containing the same text are integrated to enhance the contrast between text and background. Finally, a novel connected components based binarization algorithm is proposed to improve the recognition rate. Experimental results show the superior performance of the proposed system.

1 Introduction

While content-based video retrieval [1] has been on the agenda of researchers for more that a decade, availability of such systems remains limited. An outstanding issue for such systems is how to automatically extract the human level concepts and then use them from video annotation and indexing.

Text embedded in image and video is a special kind of visual object. Through the combination of a finite set of characters (several dozens for English and 6.8K for Chinese), text can easily express abundant information highly related to the video content. Therefore, although on-screen text can not represent all the semantic information of video, text detection/segmentation plus optical character recognition (OCR) is still a straightforward way to extract the semantic information for video annotation and retrieval. However, various languages, fonts, sizes, alignments, and more seriously, the complex backgrounds, make the problem of automatic text detection, segmentation and recognition extremely challenging.

The task of text detection is to localize the possible text regions in images or video frames. Current approaches can be classified into four categories. The first category is texture-based method. High-frequency wavelet coefficients [2], Gabor filter [3] and high-level central moments [4] have been employed as texture descriptors, while k-means clustering [2], neural network [3] and SVM [4] are often utilized for texture classification. The second category is color-based method [5]. The number of colors in the image is firstly reduced and the text regions can be detected in each color plane. The third category is edge-based method [6]. The connected component analysis (CCA) is conducted on the edge images to search for the text regions. The last category utilizes multiple-frame information for video text detection. For example, Wang et al [7] first

S. Satoh, F. Nack, and M. Etoh (Eds.): MMM 2008, LNCS 4903, pp. 58–69, 2008.

conduct MIN and MAX operation on a set of consecutive frames and then detect the text regions in the integrated images.

Many OCR techniques are designed for images where the color of text is clearly different from that of background. However, unlike scanned document images, video frames often possess very complex color distribution. Therefore text segmentation is adopted and serves as an intermediate stage linking detection and recognition. Shortly, its task is to divide the character strokes from the background. For example, adaptive binarization [8] can deal with complex background by calculating a local threshold for each pixel. Multiple frame integration is another type of methods for this purpose. It integrates different video frames which contain the same text, so that the contrast between text and background can be enhanced [9][10].

Although the above methods are rather effective, however, there are still some drawbacks which may prevent these techniques from practical applications. First, it is difficult to find a discriminative feature which can distinguish text from nontext perfectly, such that there may be many false alarms in the results. Second, the complex backgrounds in the text regions will deteriorate the performance of character recognition. To overcome these problems, we present a novel video text detection and segmentation system. The flowchart of this system is shown in figure 1.

In order to improve the detection performance, the system adopt a three-level verification strategy to eliminate the false alarms: (1) Connected component analysis is conducted and many false alarms are removed using geometrical constraints; (2) Local binary pattern (LBP), χ^2 distance and minimum classification error (MCE) criterion are

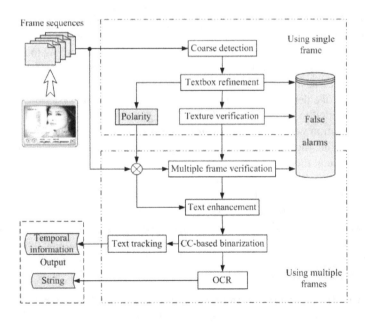

Fig. 1. The flowchart of the proposed video text detection and extraction system

employed to build a powerful texture classifier; (3) Temporal constraints are inflicted so that false alarms caused by short-term background objects can be eliminated.

To further improve the segmentation performance, a precise polarity estimation algorithm is first provided. Then based on the polarity, a multiple frame integration algorithm is conducted to enhance the contrast between text and background. Finally, we propose a novel connected component based binarization algorithm for better noise removal. Section 2 will introduce the main function modules of the system, and section 3 will analyze the experimental results. Section 4 is the conclusion of this paper.

2   Proposed System

2.1   Coarse-to-Fine Detection

From the viewpoint of texture analysis, the edge density in text region caused by character strokes is usually higher than that in background region, as is shown in figure 2(b). By exploiting this fact, given a input frame F, we calculate its binary edge image E and build a new empty image G with the same size. Then E is scanned by a sliding window. If the number of edge pixels in a window is larger than a threshold θ, all edge pixels in this window are copy to same position in G. After this operation, the result of figure 2(a) is figure 2(c). Since text may be aligned vertically, the scanning should be conducted using windows with different size.

Ideally, G should only contain stroke edges after the scanning has been finished. Note that there are many isolate strokes in Chinese and Japanese, and some stroke edge may be broken due to image degradation, such as low resolution. Therefore, we implement morphological close operation on G before labeling the connected components [11]. Finally, the candidate components are grouped together according to a set of geometrical constraints such as horizontal collinearity. The minimal bounding box of each group is regarded as a textbox.

Note that stroke density varies greatly due to different writing systems and fonts, so it is recommended to choose a slightly low θ to guarantee high detection rate. However, such selection will immediately cause a mass of false alarms, and as a result, it is necessary to refine the detected textboxes. To circumvent this difficulty, we present the textbox refinement module, as is listed in algorithm 1.

Another important aspect which motivates textbox refinement module is to determine the polarity of each textbox. Precise polarity estimation will greatly improve the performance of text segmentation. For example, we can see that figure 2(a) contains captions with different colors. Therefore, if the system automatically determines the polarity of each caption, the appropriate approach will be chosen so that better segmentation performance can be expected. Before detailed description of algorithm 1, we first define the polarity of textbox.

Definition 1. *The polarity of a textbox T is denoted by $P(T)$. We shall say that $P(T) = 0$ means that the characters in T are dark on a light background, while $P(T) = 1$ just the opposite.*

Fig. 2. Coarse detection: (a) is the input frame F; (b) is the edge image E; (c) is the resulted G after scanning E with a 39×19 window

---

Algorithm 1. Textbox refinement

Input: textbox T
Output: $P(T)$ /*$P(T) = -1$ means that T is a false alarm*/

1: T is firstly enlarged to some extent, such that potential text will be entirely enclosed by T's boundary. (e.g. the vertical boundaries move $h/5$ outward and horizontal boundaries move h outward in this paper, where h is height of T)
2: The enlarged T is binarized and we get an binary image B. Meanwhile, we conduct NOT operation on B and get another binary image $\bar{B}$.
3: The connected components in B and $\bar{B}$ are labeled. The components touching T's boundary or having large size are removed.
4: Without losing any generality, we at this moment suppose that text is black. Now we can verify whether B or $\bar{B}$ contains black text via the criteria in [12,8]. Here, $Is(B) = 1$ means that B contains black text, while $Is(B) = 0$ just the opposite.
5: **if** $Is(B) == 0$ and $Is(\bar{B}) == 0$ **then**
6:      return -1;
7: **else if** $Is(B) == 1$ and $Is(\bar{B}) == 0$ **then**
8:      return 0;
9: **else if** $Is(B) == 0$ and $Is(\bar{B}) == 1$ **then**
10:     return 1;
11: **else**
12:     A new image L with the same size of T is built and all pixels in L are initially set 255 (white). If component c_i in B and component c_j in $\bar{B}$ have similar size and position, we copy c_i and c_j to L. The pixels from B are set 0 (black), while the pixels from $\bar{B}$ are set 128 (gray).
13:     **if** there are more black outer contour points than gray ones in L **then**
14:         return 1;
15:     **else**
16:         return 0;
17:     **end if**
18: **end if**

After textbox refinement is finished, we can utilize the refined B (or $\bar{B}$, depending on T's polarity) to update T's boundary, such that T will fit the actual text region.

To further clarify the procedure of textbox refinement, we provide two examples. The first example is utilized to illustrate line 1-10 of algorithm 1. Figure 3(a) is the

Fig. 3. An example of polarity estimation: (a) is the input T; (b) and (c) correspond to B and $\bar{B}$ in line 2; (d) and (e) correspond to B and $\bar{B}$ in line 4

original textbox image, while (b) and (c) are binarization results corresponding to different polarity, respectively. After the operation in line 3 we get (d) and (e). Herein we can easily conclude that there is no text in 3(d) via the criteria in line 4, and consequently the polarity of figure 3(a) equals 1.

Figure 4 is the other example to illustrate line 11-17 of algorithm 1. These operation are activated only for *outline* characters such as figure 4 (a). Figure 4 (b) and (c) are results after line 3. We can find $Is(B) = Is(\bar{B}) = 1$ because there are regularly-aligned components in both (b) and (c). Herein the system will determine the polarity through the number of outer contour points. In this paper, an outer contour point in line 13 is defined as:

Definition 2. *A black pixel or a gray pixel in L is called an outer contour point, if there is at least one white pixel in its 3×3 neighborhood.*

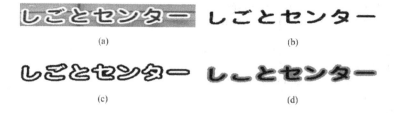

Fig. 4. Polarity estimation through outer contour points: (a) is the original textbox image; (b) and (c) are results after connected component analysis; (d) is the new image L where outer contour points can be counted

To handle text with various size, the procedure of coarse detection should be repeated in image pyramid. The textboxes detected in different levels of the pyramid are mapped to the original image size. Note that the same text region may be detected in multiple levels simultaneously, so the highly overlapped ones should be merged.

2.2 Texture Verification Using LBP

Although the textbox refinement module can improve the precision rate to some extent via empirical rules, however, it cannot eliminate false alarms which also possess regularly-aligned connected components. In order to solve this problem, a particular

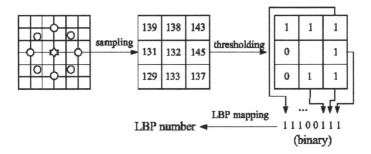

Fig. 5. Calculation of local binary pattern

texture verification (TV) module is employed. Namely, we first build a discriminative texture classifier (text versus nontext) and then each detected textbox can be verified by this classifier. Any textbox belonging to the nontext class is regarded as false alarm and should be abandoned.

The local binary pattern (LBP), which has shown superior performance for face detection and recognition [13,14], is adopted as the texture descriptor. The core idea of LBP is to threshold a local neighborhood by the center pixel value. Each threshold result is mapped as a LBP number and assigned to the center pixel. The histogram of the LBP numbers throughout the image eventually forms the desired feature vector. According to preliminary experiments, we choose the 59-dimensional LBP_{82}^{u2} operator [13].

Normalization is necessary due to different textbox size. The height of a horizontal textbox or the width of a vertical textbox is rescaled to 25, while maintaining the width/height ratio. Furthermore, each feature vector $v = \{v_1, \cdots, v_{59}\}$ is linearly normalized such that $\sum v_i = C$, where C is a constant.

The nearest prototype classifier (NPC) and χ^2 distance [13]

$$d(u, v) = \sum_{i=1}^{59} \frac{(u_i - v_i)^2}{u_i + v_i}$$

are employed for texture classification. All the training samples are collected manually and the prototype set $\{(w_i, c_i) | 1 \leq i \leq P\}$ is initialized via k-means clustering, where w_i is prototype vector and $c_i \in \{0, 1\}$ is its class label. These prototypes can be iteratively optimized through minimum classification error (MCE) criterion[15]. More specifically, given a labeled sample (x_t, y_t), we first find two prototypes w_k and w_l

$$k = \arg \min_{i, \, c_i = y_t} d(x_t, w_i)$$

$$l = \arg \min_{i, \, c_i \neq y_t} d(x_t, w_i)$$

and then update them using the following equations:

$$w_{ki}(t + 1) = w_k(t) + L'(t) d_l \frac{w_{ki} + 3x_{ti}}{(w_{ki} + x_{ti})^2} (x_{ti} - w_{ki}) \quad i = 1, \cdots, 59 \quad (1)$$

$$w_{li}(t+1) = w_l(t) - L'(t)d_k \frac{w_{li} + 3x_{ti}}{(w_{li} + x_{ti})^2}(x_{ti} - w_{li}) \quad i = 1, \cdots, 59 \qquad (2)$$

where

$$L(x_t) = \frac{1}{1 + e^{-\xi(d_k - d_l)}} \qquad (3)$$

$$L'(t) = 2\alpha \frac{L(x_t)(1 - L(x_t))}{(d_k + d_l)^2} \qquad (4)$$

In the above, the positive number ξ increases as training proceeds.

2.3 Multiple Frame Integration

We have noted that superimposed video text always last one second or more to guarantee the readability. In addition, we can also suppose that on most occasions a text line possesses fixed color and size during their existence. Such properties will easily facilitate the task of text detection and segmentation from three angles - textbox verification, text enhancement and text tracking.

The key issue for multiple frame integration is to determine whether two different textboxes contain exactly the same text. In [9], only the location information is adopted for decision. However, if the system only processes some representative frames or there are moving text in the video, location information becomes insufficient. In this paper, besides location, size and polarity, the intermediate results in line 3 of algorithm 1 are utilized for decision. More specially, for textboxes T_1 and T_2, we calculate the difference between corresponding B_1 and B_2 (or $\bar{B}_1$ and $\bar{B}_2$, depending on T_1's polarity). If the difference does not exceed certain threshold, we think that T_1 and T_2 belong to the same video caption.

Multiple frame verification (MFV). Simple temporal constraints can be inflicted on the detected textboxes to eliminate false alarms caused by short-term background objects. Suppose the single-frame-based detection has been finished. Then, for any textbox T (detected in F_n), the system can determine a series of consecutive frames $\Phi = \{F_m, \cdots, F_n, \cdots, F_l\}$, such that each frame in Φ owns a detected textbox that contains the same text with T. Here, interval $[m, l]$ can be approximately regarded as the duration of certain text line (or certain background object). Based on the high recall rate of coarse detection, T should be accepted as a valid result if and only if $l - m > \delta$, where δ is a predefined threshold.

Multiple frame text enhancement (MFTE). From the viewpoint of content-based video retrieval, providing recognition results for each frame is unnecessary. So it is feasible to integrate multiple image regions to enhance the contrast between character strokes and nearby backgrounds. In our work, based on the precise polarity estimation algorithm, we simply employ the MIN and MAX operation for text enhancement. First, the detected textboxes are divided into different groups, such that the textboxes in each group will contain the same text. Second, for a group whose polarity equals 0, we conduct MAX operation on all the grayscale textbox images belonging to the group. As for a group with polarity 1, MIN operation is conducted. Herein we call the integrated image *text line*. Figure 6 shows the effect of multiple frame text enhancement. We can find that the backgrounds are weakened more or less in the text lines compared with corresponding textboxes, which will be beneficial for the following binarization and recognition.

(a)

(b)

(c)

(d)

Fig. 6. Multiple frame text enhancement: (a) and (c) are textboxes with $p = 0$ and $p = 1$, respectively; (b) and (d) are corresponding results

Text tracking. Providing the precise duration information for each caption is very important for video retrieval system. However, since the coarse detection module can not ensure a recall rate of 100%, an additional text tracking module is necessary. The basic operation for text tracking is still image difference, which has been employed in the module of MFV. Note that the benchmark image for each text line is the corresponding integrated text line obtained from the module of MFTE.

2.4   Connected-Component-Based Binarization

The integrated text images should be binarized before sent to the OCR engine. Unlike the condition of scanned document images, a most challenging issue confronting video text images is that character strokes often possess similar color with the nearby background. Such instance is shown as figure 4 (a). Under this circumstance, it is hard to filter all background noises just by means of color (or grayscale) information. For example, the binarization results of figure 7(a) through globe OTSU's method [16] and adaptive BST method [17] are shown in figure 7 (b) and (c), respectively.

To solve this problem, we provide the CC-based binarization (CCBB) method, which is listed as algorithm 2. Through the collaboration of intensity information and local CC-based geometrical information, better segmentation performance can be achieved. On the one hand, we utilize the most character-like components to precisely estimate the gray value of the strokes. On the other hand, noise components can be filtered according to certain empirical rules. Figure 7(d) is the binarization result of figure 7(a) through CCBB. We can see that most background noise have been removed.

3   Experimental Results and Analysis

We perform experiments on two news videos with resolution 720×480. The corresponding video length is 15'35" and 32'32", respectively. Since each caption in these videos lasts at least 3 seconds, to make the system computationally efficient, only one frame from every 10 consecutive frames is picked up for further processing. Herein we get 2805 and 5852 frames for each video, respectively.

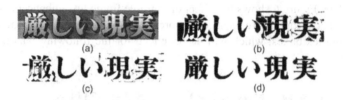

(a)

(b)

(c)

(d)

Fig. 7. Comparison of different binarization methods: (a) is the original image; (b) is result through OTSU's method; (c) is result through BST method; (d) is result through proposed method

---

Algorithm 2. Connected-component-based binarization

Input: grayscale integrated text image I
Output: binary text image R

1: I is binarized via common binarization methods (OTSU's method is employed in this paper) and we get the initial R.
2: **if** $P(I) == 1$ **then**
3:     $R = \bar{R}$;
4: **end if**
5: The connected components in R are labeled.
6: The components touching R's boundary or having large size are removed.
7: Among the remaining components, we choose those with large size and draw the histogram (using the pixels' original grayscale value in I).
8: In the histogram we choose two threshold T_1 and T_2, such that

$$\sum_{T_1 \leq x \leq 255} h(x) \approx \alpha N, \qquad \sum_{0 < x \leq T_2} h(x) \approx \alpha N$$

where N is the total number of pixels in the histogram and $\alpha \in [0.6, 0.9]$.
9: **for all** remaining component C_i in R **do**
10:     Calculate

$$M_i = \sum_{(j,k) \in C_i} Mid(I(j,k))$$

where $Mid(x)$ equals 1 if $T_1 \leq x \leq T_2$ or 0 otherwise. (j,k) is pixel coordinate.
11:     **if** $M_i < \beta \cdot N_i$ (N_i denotes the number of pixels in C_i, $\beta = 0.5$ in this paper) **then**
12:         Remove C_i;
13:     **end if**
14: **end for**
15: return R

The character size ranges from 22×22 to 110×110 in these two videos. The size of sliding window should be decided based on the smallest character size. According to our experimental results, we select 39×19 sliding window for horizontal captions and 19×39 one for vertical captions in the coarse detection stage. Furthermore, a 4-level image pyramid with scales [1,0.7,0.4,0.25] is adopted to detect the captions with larger size.

We utilize the recall rate (RR) and precision rate (PR) to evaluate the detection performance of our system. The recall rate is the ratio between the number of correctly

Table 1. Results of text detection and verification (%)

	Total textbox	Coarse		Fine		TV		MFV	
		RR	PR	RR	PR	RR	PR	RR	PR
video 1	7270	98.67	64.32	98.58	95.27	97.96	97.46	97.08	99.12
video 2	15028	98.21	62.28	98.06	94.14	96.87	96.03	96.12	98.33

Fig. 8. Some text detection/segmentation results

Table 2. The comparison of recognition rate for different methods

	Text lines	Characters	Detection rate	Recognition rate		
				None	MFI	MFI + CCBB
video 1	163	1542	99.09%	53.21%	83.05%	95.75%
video 2	330	2960	97.40%	58.04%	79.31%	95.53%

detected textboxes and the total number of textboxes, while the precision rate is the ratio between the number of correctly detected textboxes and the number of detected textboxes. Because a 3-level verification strategy is utilized in the stage of text detection, we count the detection results for each associated module, such that we can see their respective contributions. Table 1 lists the corresponding results. We can see that the multistage verification strategy improves the precision rate to a great extent while maintaining the high recall rate.

Textbox polarity acts as an important intermediate result in our system. We randomly select 1000 textboxes to evaluate the performance of our polarity estimation algorithm. According to the experimental results, there are only 3 errors for polarity estimation. Furthermore, we find that for about 83% of these textboxes, polarity is determined before line 11 of algorithm 1.

There is no commonly accepted methods to evaluate the text segmentation performance. Since the segmented results are directly recognized by the OCR engine, we simply employ the recognition rate instead. Furthermore, to see the effect of proposed multiple frame integration (MFI) and binarization algorithm, we also compare the recognition rate under different situations. These results are listed in table 2.

In table 2, *None* means that we directly binarize the detected textboxes through adaptive BST method. Because one video caption corresponds to a group of textboxes, the recognition rate for *None* is the average value of 3 textboxes for each caption. *MFI* means we binarize the integrated text lines through BST method. *MFI + CCBB* means that we binarize the integrated text lines through proposed CCBB. For *MFI* and *MFI + CCBB*, only one recognition result is got for each caption. From table 2 we can see that the collaboration of MFI and CCBB has greatly improved the overall recognition. The detection and segmentation results of some representative frames are listed in figure 8.

4   Conclusion

In this paper, we propose a novel video text detection/segmentation system. The main contribution of this paper is as follows. (1) A multistage verification strategy is proposed to improve the precision rate of the detection. (2) A precise polarity estimation algorithm is proposed so that effective multiple frame integration becomes available. (3) A CC-based binarization algorithm is provided to improve the overall recognition rate.

We perform experiments on two news videos and achieve the recognition rate of 95.75% and 95.53%, respectively. The correctly recognized text will provide abundant and precise information to facilitate the task of content-based video retrieval.

However, on-screen text can not present all semantic information of the current video. Therefore, text information should collaborate with other visual and audio information to provide more accurate information for content-based video retrieval.

Acknowledgement

The authors would like to thank Prof. Baihua Xiao, Dr. Jinqiao Wang and Dr. Jingchao Zhou for their suggestions. The authors also thank the anonymous reviewers for their helpful comments.

References

1. Aslandogan, Y., Yu, C.T.: Techniques and Systems for Image and Video Retrieval. IEEE Transactions on Knowledge and Data Engineering 11(1), 56–63 (1999)
2. Gllavata, J., Ewerth, R., Freisleben, B.: Text Detection in Images Based on Unsupervised Classification of High-frequency Wavelet Coefficients. In: Proceedings of 17th International Conference on Pattern Recognition, vol. 1, pp. 425–428 (2004)
3. Tekinalp, S., Alatan, A.: Utilization of Texture, Contrast and Color Homogeneity for Detecting and Recognizing Text from Video Frames. In: Proceedings of 2003 International Conference on Image Processing, vol. 2, pp. 505–508 (2003)
4. Kim, K., Byun, H., Song, Y., Choi, Y., Chi, S., Kim, K., Chung, Y.: Scene Text Extraction in Natural Scene Images Using Hierarchical Feature Combining and Verification. In: Proceedings of 17th International Conference on Pattern Recognition, vol. 2, pp. 679–682 (2004)
5. Wang, K., Kangas, J.A.: Character Location in Scene Images from Digital Camera. Pattern Recognition 36(10), 2287–2299 (2003)
6. Cai, M., Song, J., Lyu, M.R.: A New Approach for Video Text Detection. In: Proceedings of 2002 International Conference on Image Processing, vol. 1, pp. 117–120 (2002)

7. Wang, R., Jin, W., Wu, L.: A Novel Video Caption Detection Approach Using Multi-frame Integration. In: Proceedings of 17th International Conference on Pattern Recognition, vol. 1, pp. 449–452 (2004)

8. Wolf, C., Jolion, J.: Extraction and Recognition of Artificial Text in Multimedia Documents. Pattern Analysis and Application 6(4), 309–326 (2003)

9. Hua, X.S., Yin, P., Zhang, H.J.: Efficient Video Text Recognition Using Multiple Frame Integration. In: Proceedings of 2002 International Conference on Image Processing, vol. 2, pp. 397–400 (2002)

10. Lienhart, R., Wernicke, A.: Localizing and Segmenting Text in Images and Videos. IEEE Transactions on Circuits and Systems for Video Technology 12(4), 256–268 (2002)

11. Hasan, Y.M., Karam, L.J.: Morphological Text Extraction from Images. IEEE Transaction on Image Processing 9(11), 1978–1983 (2000)

12. Strouthopoulos, C., Papamarkos, N., Atsalakis, A.: Text Extraction in Complex Color Documents. Pattern Recognition 35(8), 1743–1758 (2002)

13. Ahonen, T., Hadid, A., Pietikinen, M.: Face Recognition with Local Binary Patterns. In: Pajdla, T., Matas, J(G.) (eds.) ECCV 2004. LNCS, vol. 3021, pp. 469–481. Springer, Heidelberg (2004)

14. Hadid, A., Pietikainen, M., Ahonen, T.: A Discriminative Feature Space for Detecting and Recognizing Faces. In: Proceedings of the 2004 IEEE Conference on Computer Vision and Pattern Recognition, vol. 2, pp. 797–804 (2004)

15. Jung, B.H., Katagiri, S.: Discriminative Learning for Minimum Error Classification. IEEE Transaction on Signal Processing 40(12), 3043–3054 (1992)

16. Otsu, N.: A Threshold Selection Method from Gray-level Histograms. Man and Cybernetics 9(1), 62–66 (1979)

17. Seeger, M., Dance, C.: Binarising Camera Images for OCR. In: Proceedings of the 6th International Conference on Document Analysis and Recognition, vol. 1, pp. 54–58 (2001)

Real-Time Video Surveillance Based on Combining Foreground Extraction and Human Detection

Hui-Chi Zeng, Szu-Hao Huang, and Shang-Hong Lai

Department of Computer Science, National Tsing Hua University, Hsinchu, Taiwan
lai@cs.nthu.edu.tw

Abstract. In this paper, we present an adaptive foreground object extraction algorithm for real-time video surveillance, in conjunction with a human detection technique applied in the extracted foreground regions by using AdaBoost learning algorithm and Histograms of Oriented Gradient (HOG) descriptors. Furthermore, a RANSAC-based temporal tracking algorithm is also applied to refine and trace the detected human windows in order to increase the detection accuracy and reduce the false alarm rate. The traditional background subtraction technique usually cannot work well for situations with lighting variations in the scene. The proposed algorithm employs a two-stage foreground/background classification procedure to perform background subtraction and remove the undesirable subtraction results due to shadow, automatic white balance, and sudden illumination change. Experimental results on some real surveillance video are shown to demonstrate the good performance of the proposed adaptive foreground extraction algorithm under a variety of different environments with lighting variations and human detection system.

Keywords: Surveillance, background subtraction, foreground extraction, lighting variation, human detection, RANSAC.

1 Introduction

A primary problem in video surveillance is to detect the foreground objects, and background subtraction is the most fundamental and common approach for this problem. In recent years, several different background subtraction techniques have been presented. Tuzel et al. [3] used a Bayesian approach to background modeling, and defined each pixel as a mixture of multivariate Gaussian distributions. Stauffer and Grimson [1] proposed to use a mixture of Gaussian functions to model the intensity distribution of each background pixel, and the background model can be gradually adapted to the temporal intensity changes.

After background subtraction, the subtracted non-background pixels may include the foreground objects and background pixels with lighting changes. Some shadow detection methods have been proposed in the past. Elgammal et al. [2] used the chromaticity coordinates r, g and the ratio of the lighting descent information for shadow detection. Tian et al. [4] presented a normalized cross-correlation algorithm

S. Satoh, F. Nack, and M. Etoh (Eds.): MMM 2008, LNCS 4903, pp. 70–79, 2008.

for shadow removal, but it is time-consuming and can not work well for homogeneous regions.

Human detection is an important application for surveillance system, and this challenging task needs a robust classifier in conjunction with a set of representative features. In recent years, many different learning algorithms, such as eigen-space analysis, neural network, support vector machine, and AdaBoost [5][6], have been proposed to solve the object detection problem in different applications.

Many features for human detection have been proposed. Viola et al. [7] used Adaboost and Haar-like wavelet to detect pedestrians. Dalal et al. [8] proposed the Histograms of Oriented Gradient (HOG) descriptors for human detection in order to be insensitive to color and brightness.

Temporal information can be utilized as an additional cue for temporal object tracking or refining the object detection results. Zhou and Hoang [9] performed appearance-based tracking by comparing the current histogram with the reference histogram. Hussein et al. [10] modeled the intensity values of each pixel as a time varying mixture of three Gaussian components for tracking.

The flowchart of proposed method is shown in Figure 1. In this paper, we propose a two-stage foreground/background segmentation algorithm that first performs background subtraction and removes the undesirable subtraction results due to shadow, automatic white balance, and sudden illumination change. In the second phase of the proposed video surveillance system, we use the Histograms of Oriented Gradient (HOG) features in conjunction with the AdaBoost classifier for human detection. Finally, a RANSAC-based temporal integration scheme is applied to refine the human detection results for each frame.

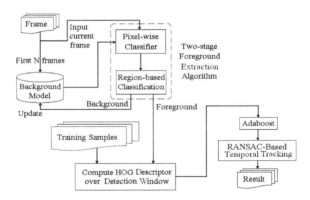

Fig. 1. The flowchart of the proposed human detection system

2 Two-Stage Foreground Extraction Algorithm

The light change includes brightening and darkening, which may be due to illumination changes, shadowing or white balance. For both cases, the influence is not on some individual independent pixels, but on a semi-transparent and gradually growing region. In the chromaticity coordinates, a pixel caused by the light change is considered unaffected. Let the red, green, and blue values of a pixel be R, G, and B. The chromaticity coordinates of the pixel, r, g, and b, are

$$r = \frac{R}{R+G+B}, g = \frac{G}{R+G+B}, b = \frac{B}{R+G+B}, \qquad (1)$$

and $r + g + b = 1$. Let the chromaticity coordinates of the background model of a pixel be r_b, g_b, and b_b and those of the observed pixel value be r_o, g_o, and b_o. If there is no foreground object, these three pairs should be very similar. However, the chromaticity coordinates of the pixels in the dark area can vary a lot even the lighting condition changes slightly in the RGB space since the value $R+G+B$ in equation (1) is small. Thus, we employ a two-stage algorithm to alleviate the problem due to lighting changes.

Firstly, a pre-learned classifier is used to pixel-wisely perform the background subtraction process and remove the background pixels which are under slight light changes, such as automatic white balance or indoor shadow diffusion. This is accomplished by using exponential functions of the background intensity to distinguish the relative chromaticity changes due to lighting changes or foreground objects [11].

Secondly, the remaining pixels are segmented into regions by using a single pass neighborhood connectivity algorithm [12] according to the gain, that is the ratio between the light change and the corresponding background value, given by

$$gain = \frac{I_o - I_b}{I_b}, \qquad (2)$$

where I_b is the corresponding background intensity value and I_o is the observed pixel intensity value. Then, the distributions of r_o and g_o of each region are compared with their corresponding background distributions of r_b and g_b to determine if the region is foreground or background with lighting changes by using the Bhattacharyya Distance as the measure, given by

$$D_{bhat}(P,Q) = \sum_{i=1}^{n} \sqrt{p_i q_i}, \qquad (3)$$

where $P = \{p_1,...,p_n\}$ and $Q = \{q_1,...,q_n\}$ are two n-dimension distributions. In addition, the average absolute $gain$ in the region, denoted by $|\overline{gain}|$, is also taken into the classification to account for the lighting variation information. Here, the variation of the intensity in the background region due to light changes is assumed to be not too large. Thus, a background region should satisfy the following conditions:

$$D_{bhat}\left(\overline{r_o}, \overline{r_b}\right) > T_r, \ D_{bhat}\left(\overline{g_o}, \overline{g_b}\right) > T_g, \ |\overline{gain}| < T_{gain}, \qquad (4)$$

where T_r, T_g and T_{gain} are the thresholds that are empirically determined.

For background modeling, the first N frames of the input sequence are used to train the initial background model. We employ the K-means clustering to find out the persistence appearance of each pixel. For this reason, we can build an accurate initial background model even if there are some foreground objects moving during the first

N frames. The history of each pixel, $\{X_1,...,X_N\}$, is modeled by three independent Gaussian distributions, and X is the color value, i.e. $X=\{X^R,X^G,X^B\}$. Foreground pixels are the pixels that are more than 2.5 times the standard deviations away from any of the three Gaussians. For a pixel value X_t, the update equations of the mean value, μ_t, and the variance, σ_t^2, at time t are given as follows:

$$\mu_t = (1-\rho)\mu_{t-1} + \rho X_t,$$
$$\sigma_t^2 = (1-\rho)\sigma_{t-1}^2 + \rho(X_t - \mu_t)^T(X_t - \mu_t),$$
(5)

where ρ is the update rate and its value is between 0 and 1.

3 Human Detection

After the previous steps, we can generate a foreground map. Then a sliding window with varying sizes searches over the extracted foreground regions, and we only apply human detection on the windows that contain certain enough percentages of foreground pixels. The human detector is accomplished by using AdaBoost [6] and HOG descriptors [8]. The training data sets used for training the AdaBoost detector are the well-established MIT [9] and INRIA [8] pedestrian databases. We also collect some patches with varying sizes sampled from the background, which are obtained in the previous step, as the negative training samples.

Dalal et al. [8] proposed HOG descriptor for human detection. First, the weight histograms of gradient orientations of the input image are computed, and then the HOG feature over the entire detection window is collected to be a descriptor of this detection window, while a normalization step within each block is performed to account for brightness and contrast changes. We refer to [8] for the details.

For the foreground map, a sliding window with size ranging from 25x50 to 50x100 and the incremental steps chosen as 5 for width and 10 for height is applied to search over the extracted foreground regions, and the windows with the foreground pixel density more than a certain percentage are considered further for human detection. These windows are divided into 5x10 cells. The histogram of gradient orientations is quantified into 8 bins in the range 0°-180°. The histograms for all the blocks are concatenated as a feature vector. Finally, this feature vector is normalized by its L_2 norm as follows:

$$v \rightarrow v / \sqrt{\|v\|_2^2 + \varepsilon^2},$$
(6)

where v is the un-normalized descriptor vector, $\|v\|_2$ is its 2-norm, and ε is a small positive constant to avoid dividing by zero.

In order to speed up the human detection, we compute the orientation from the gradients in the whole image before the search window runs over it. In addition, we build 8 integral images for the eight orientation fields with each for one quantized orientation level to compute the orientation histograms for each partitioned block rapidly. The same technique is also applied to compute the total number of foreground pixels for a block from the corresponding block in the foreground map.

4 RANSAC-Based Temporal Tracking

After the human detection step, the temporal information is used to further refine the human detection result, reduce the false alarms and recover the missed detection. The RANSAC-based temporal tracking algorithm is shown in Algorithm 1.

4.1 Track Estimation

Firstly, for the input N frames containing many human detection windows, we firstly divide them into three equal intervals along the time axis, i.e. N_1, N_2, and N_3. Then, three windows are randomly selected, W_1 from N_1, W_2 from N_2, and W_3 from N_3, to decide a spatial-temporal track, and the color distributions of the three picked windows should be similar, i.e.

$$D_{bhat}\left(D_{w_1}, D_{w_2}\right) > T_D , D_{bhat}\left(D_{w_2}, D_{w_3}\right) > T_D , D_{bhat}\left(D_{w_1}, D_{w_3}\right) > T_D , \qquad (7)$$

where D_i is the color distribution of window i and T_D is a threshold. Note that the color distribution D is a combined distribution which is a concatenation of the distributions of color component R, G, and B. If one picked window is at frame t_1 and the other is at frame t_2, the path between these two picked windows can be as approximated by a straight line. This assumption is reasonable if the interval between frame t_1 and frame t_2 is small, since a small interval of a curve can be well approximated by a straight line. Therefore, for an input long sequence, it can be divided into several shorter intervals, and each interval contains N frames. Then the RANSAC-based temporal tracking technique is performed on each interval. Finally the combination of the results of all intervals is the final RANSAC-based temporal tracking result of the input long sequence.

4.2 Voting

After the path is decided by three picked windows, a voting process is applied to check if the path is correct. The human detection windows are used to vote on this track according to the distance between the center position of the voting window and the estimated position of the track, and the similarity between the color distributions of the voting window and of any of the three picked windows. The similarity measurement is according to the equation (3). Therefore, a voting window W of frame t will vote for a spatial-temporal track C estimated by three picked windows, W_1, W_2, and W_3, if the following two conditions are satisfied:

$$D_{bhat}\left(D_w, D_{w_1}\right) > T_D \text{ or } D_{bhat}\left(D_w, D_{w_2}\right) > T_D \text{ or } D_{bhat}\left(D_w, D_{w_3}\right) > T_D \qquad (8)$$

Input : S_{hdw} : The set of the human detection results. Total M detection windows
in N frames, $\{(x_1,y_1,D_1),...,(x_M,y_M,D_M)\}$, where (x,y) is the center
and D is the color R,G,B distributions of the window.

S_{track} : The set of candidate successful tracks.

Initialize: Divide the N frames into 3 equal parts in time axis, N_1,N_2,N_3.

iteration1 $\leftarrow$ 0.   iteration2 $\leftarrow$ 0.

Algorithm:

repeat
1. $S_{track} \leftarrow \phi$.
2.   **repeat**
3.   Randomly pick three similar detection windows in S_{hdw}. One from N_1, one from N_2, and one from N_3.
4.   Use the centers of these three picked windows to fit an estimated spatial-temporal track C: C $\leftarrow \phi$.
5.   score $\leftarrow$ 0.
6.   **for** each frame, t = 1,2,...,N.
7.   Voting: **if** the center of a window W in S_{hdw} is near the position estimated by C in frame t and the color distribution in W is similar to that of any of the three picked windows
8.   C $\leftarrow$ C $\cup$ W.
9.   score $\leftarrow$ score + 1.
10.   **end if**
11.   **end for**
12.   **if** score > T_s
13.   C is a candidate successful track, $S_{track} \leftarrow S_{track} \cup$ C.
14.   **end if**
15.   iteration2 $\leftarrow$ iteration2 + 1.
16.   **until** iteration2 > T_2
17.   The highest-score track C_s in S_{track} is chosen as a successful track.
18.   Recover the missed detections of C_s in some frames.
19.   Remove the detection windows in C_s from S_{hdw}.
20.   iteration1 $\leftarrow$ iteration1 + 1.
until iteration1 > T_1 || the number of frames containing detection windows < T_s

Algorithm 1. RANSAC-based Temporal Tracking Algorithm

and

$$\sqrt{(x_w - x_c)+(y_w - y_c)} < T_c , \qquad (9)$$

where D_i is the color distribution of window i , T_D and T_c are the thresholds, (x_w,y_w) is the center of the window W, and (x_c,y_c) is the position of the path C at frame t. Although there may be many detection windows in a frame, at most one window may belong to the track. It is unreasonable that two or more human detection windows belong to the same path of a person in one frame. In other words, a frame has at most one vote for the track. Finally if the vote of the N frames exceeds a threshold, the track will be considered a valid one.

4.3 Missed Detection Recovery

The above procedure of random sampling and voting is repeated for a number of times, and finally the highest-score track is chosen as a successful track. Then the missed detections in some frames of the track will be recovered, and the detection windows voting for the successful track are assigned to it and they will not participate in the later voting again. The size of the recovered window is considered the same as the size of the closest detection window that in the same path, because the window size should not change too much between the neighboring frames. If the number of the frames containing detection windows is enough or the number of the iteration does not exceed a threshold yet, the above-mentioned steps will be repeated to find the next successful track.

5 Experiments Results

The proposed foreground extraction method is used for real-time video surveillance on a static web camera, and its execution time is about 24 frames per second for color images of size 320×240 pixels running on a PC with a 3GHz Pentium IV CPU.

An initial background model is constructed from video of 5-second length. Our experiments show that the proposed robust foreground extraction works well for a variety of environments with the same parameter setting.

5.1 Variety of Environments

The tested video sequences include different environments, and the proposed background segmentation algorithm and human detector provide satisfactory results in real-time. Some results are depicted in Figure 2.

Outdoor: The 1st row in Figure 2 is a PETS 2001 sequence with quick light change of sunshine (the right and bottom sides), and the 2nd column is an IPPR contest testing data 'Data3'.

Indoor and auto white balance: The 3rd and 4th columns of Figure 2 are the IBM research sequence and the IPPR contest testing video 'Data2', respectively, with automatic white balance. For indoor surveillance system, one of the major challenges is the influence of automatic white balance. As the result shows, our method can overcome the problem very well.

Turning on/off light: The 5rd row of Figure 2 is our own testing sequence with light turning off in the left side, and the small blobs at left side are caused by the noise and the movement of humans in the background. By using the region-based classification, the problem with stronger light variation, such as this case, can be handled correctly.

5.2 Accuracy

We evaluated the accuracy of our proposed foreground extraction method on 3 test videos, i.e. 'Data1', 'Data2' and 'Data3', with ground truth. Each video sequence

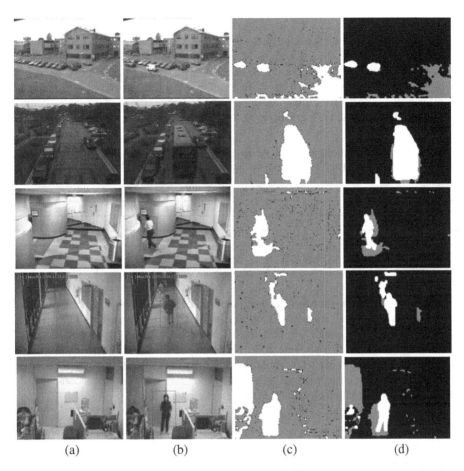

(a)   (b)   (c)   (d)

Fig. 2. The top two rows and bottom three ones are the classified results on outdoor and indoor environments, respectively. (a) The background image. (b) The current frame and the result of human detection. (c) The result of the pixel-wise classifier. The gray pixels are the background with lighting changes classified by the pixel-wise classifier, and the white pixels are the classified foreground region. (d) The result after the region-based classification. The gray pixels are the region similar to the background, and the white pixels are the foreground object.

contains 150 frames of size 320×240 pixels. 'Data1' and 'Data2' are the indoor surveillance videos with indoor diffusion shadow, serious automatic white balance, and the foreground objects with colors similar to the background. 'Data3' is a general outdoor video with some pedestrians, cars and shadows caused by these moving foreground objects.

Table 1 shows the comparison of accuracy by using the proposed algorithm and the other 3 methods on these 3 test video sequences. The accuracy is computed as the percentage of correctly classified pixels for the entire video sequence. The first method is the GMMs[1] without any lighting variation removal. The second method is to apply three non-adaptive thresholds to extract the foreground after GMM-based background subtraction [1]. These three non-adaptive thresholds were decided from the tail heights of the exponential function curves for the pixel-wise classifier. The third method is to use the normalized cross-correlation (NCC) at each pixel of the foreground region between current frame and the background image after the background subtraction [6]. It is evident from Table 1 that the proposed algorithm significantly outperforms the other methods and provides very accurate foreground/background segmentation results.

Table 1. The accuracy comparison of the proposed foreground extraction algorithm and the other 3 methods, including GMM [1], thresholding, and NCC[6], on 3 IPPR contest test sequences

	Data1	Data2	Data3	Average
GMM	56.7%	51.2%	98.6%	68.8%
Thresholding	92.2%	92.6%	98.8%	94.5%
NCC	95.8%	95.5%	99.0%	96.8%
Proposed foreground extraction method	99.3%	99.3%	99.7%	99.4%

The accuracy of our human detection is evaluated on four test sequences obtained from CAVIAR website[1]; namely, 'EnterExitCrossingPaths2cor' containing 481 frames, 'TwoLeaveShop2cor' containing 600 frames, 'OneStopNoEnter1cor' containing 725 frames, and 'OneLeaveShopReenter2cor' containing 560 frames. There are some cases with occlusion, foreground with similar color to the background, and people walking shoulder to shoulder in these four sequences. Table 2 summarizes the accuracy of the proposed human detection algorithm on these video sequences.

Table 2. The accuracy of the proposed human detection and tracking algorithm tested on 4 CAVIAR test sequences

	Hit rate	False alarm per frame
'EnterExitCrossingPaths2cor'(481 frames)	89.7%	0.004
'TwoLeaveShop2cor' (600 frames)	98.7%	0.04
'OneStopNoEnter1cor' (725 frames)	87.3%	0.067
'OneLeaveShopReenter2cor' (560 frames)	88.5%	0.12

The ground truth for these sequences can be downloaded in the CAVIAR website[1], and the information contains the coordinates, height, and width of the labeled human windows. If the overlapping area of the detected human window and the labeled one exceeds 60%, the detected human window is considered a hit one. The labeled human windows which are too small or incomplete will not be included in this accuracy assessment. The hit rate is the ratio of the number of the detected hit windows to the number of the labeled windows.

---

[1] http://groups.inf.ed.ac.uk/vision/CAVIAR/CAVIARDATA1/

6 Conclusions

In this paper, we presented a robust foreground object extraction algorithm and a human tracking algorithm for real-time video surveillance with lighting variations. The proposed two-stage foreground extraction algorithm performs background subtraction and removes the undesirable subtraction results due to lighting variations. Then we detect human from the extracted foreground regions by using the AdaBoost classifier in conjunction with the HoG descriptors. Finally, the RANSAC-based temporal tracking algorithm is utilized to refine and trace the detected human windows in order to increase the detection accuracy and reduce the false alarm rate. Experimental results show the proposed integrated algorithm can robustly detect humans from video with different types of lighting variation under different surveillance environments.

References

1. Stauffer, C., Grimson, W.E.L.: Adaptive background mixture models for real-time tracking. CVRP II, 246–252 (1999)
2. Elgammal, A., Harwood, D., Davis, L.: Non-parametric model for background subtraction. ECCV II, 751–767 (2000)
3. Tuzel, O., Porikli, F., Meer, P.: A bayesian approach to background modeling. MVIV III, 58 (2005)
4. Tian, Y.L., Lu, M., Hampapur, A.: Robust and efficient foreground analysis for real-time video surveillance. CVPR I, 1182–1187 (2005)
5. Freund, Y., Schapire, R.E.: A decision-theoretic generalization of on-line learning and an application to boosting. In: Computational Learning Theory, Eurocolt, pp. 23–37 (1995)
6. Viola, P., Jones, M.: Roust real-time face detection. IJCV 57, 137–154 (2004)
7. Viola, P., Jones, M.J., Snow, D.: Detecting pedestrians using patterns of motion and appearance. In: Proc. ICCV, vol. 1, pp. 734–741 (2003)
8. Dalal, N., Triggs, B.: Histograms of oriented gradients for human detection. In: Proc. IEEE Conf. Computer Vision Pattern Recognition, pp. 886–893 (2005)
9. Zhou, J., Hoang, J.: Real time robust human detection and tracking system. In: Proc. IEEE Conf. Computer Vision Pattern Recognition, p. 149.
10. Hussein, M., Almageed, W.A., Ran, Y., Davis, L.: Real-time human detection, tracking, and verification in uncontrolled camera motion environments. In: Proc. ICVS, p. 56 (2006)
11. Zeng, H.C., Lai, S.H.: Adaptive foreground object extraction for real-time video surveillance with lighting variations. In: Proc. ICASSP (2007)
12. Haralick, R., Shapiro, L.: Computer and robot vision 1. Addison Wesley, Reading (1992)

Detecting and Clustering Multiple Takes of One Scene

Werner Bailer, Felix Lee, and Georg Thallinger

JOANNEUM RESEARCH Forschungsgesellschaft mbH,
Institute of Information Systems & Information Management,
Steyrergasse 17, 8010 Graz, Austria
firstName.lastName@joanneum.at

Abstract. In applications such as video post-production users are confronted with large amounts of redundant unedited raw material, called rushes. Viewing and organizing this material are crucial but time consuming tasks. Typically multiple but slightly different takes of the same scene can be found in the rushes video. We propose a method for detecting and clustering takes of one scene shot from the same or very similar camera positions. It uses a variant of the LCSS algorithm to find matching subsequences in sequences of visual features extracted from the source video. Hierarchical clustering is used to group the takes of one scene. The approach is evaluated in terms of correctly assigned takes using manually annotated ground truth.

1   Introduction

In film and video production usually large amounts of raw material ("rushes") are shot and only a small fraction of this material is used in the final edited content. The reason for shooting that amount of material is that the same scene is often shot from different camera positions and several alternative takes for each of them are recorded, partly because of mistakes of the actors or technical failures, partly to experiment with different artistic options. The action performed in each of these takes is similar, but not identical, e.g. has omissions and insertions.

The result of this practice in production is that users dealing with rushes have to handle large amounts of audiovisual material which makes viewing and navigation difficult. Our work is motivated by two application areas where this problem exists. One is post-production of audiovisual content, where editors need to view and organize the material in order to select the best takes to be used (the ratio between the playtime of the rushes and that of the edited content is often 30:1). The other application area is documentation of audiovisual archives. While edited content is well documented (at least in larger broadcast archives) and thus reusable, raw material is in most cases not documented due to the amount of material and its redundancy [7]. In both applications, identifying the takes belonging to the same scene and grouping them could significantly increase the efficiency of the work.

In this paper we deal with the problem of identifying and grouping multiple takes of the same scene. In general the different takes of one scene may be shot

S. Satoh, F. Nack, and M. Etoh (Eds.): MMM 2008, LNCS 4903, pp. 80–89, 2008.

Fig. 1. Example of takes of the same scene: The upper row shows keyframes of the first take, the lower of the second take of one scene. Images taken from BBC 2007 rushes video data set.

from different camera positions. We restrict our work to the problem of takes shot from the same or very similar camera positions. Nonetheless the content between the different takes may vary, as actors and objects move differently or there are insertions and omissions in the action being performed. In addition there are takes that stop earlier (mostly due to mistakes) or start in the middle of the scene ("pickups"). The algorithm for detecting and grouping retakes has to deal with this variability.

Related research areas are the detection of similar video sequences and near-duplicates. There are many approaches for dealing with similarity matching of video clips, many of them applying still image features for clustering key frames of video sequences. Some of these approaches use more video oriented features such as sequences of key frames and camera motion [19] or motion trajectories [4]. However, while the feature extraction and matching approaches proposed in these papers are relevant for our problem, the implementation of similarity matching approaches usually finds all similar content, including takes of other similar scenes and not just those of the same scene. If clustering of takes has to be performed on a large set of material, similarity matching can be used as a preprocessing step to find candidates of related takes.

The most prominent application for near-duplicate detection is finding illegal copies of video content (cf. [11,10]). A related problem is the identification of known unwanted content in public access video databases [6]. These applications are based on the following assumptions: (i) the actual content of the videos to be matched is identical, (ii) partial matches need to be identified and (iii) the system is robust against a number of distortions, such as changes of sampling parameters, noise, encoding artifacts, cropping, change of aspect ratio etc. The first assumption does not hold for take clustering, while robustness to distortions is only necessary to a very limited degree in our application, as the content to be matched is captured and processed under very similar conditions. Another application of near-duplicate detection is topic tracking of news stories. Some approaches work on a story level and use features such as speech transcripts that are often not available in rushes [12]. Other approaches work on matching

sequences of key frames, tolerating gaps and insertions [9], which comes closer
to the requirements of our application.

The rest of this paper is organized as follows: Section 2 presents a novel algorithm for identifying similar takes based on the Longest Common Subsequence
(LCSS) model [5] and clustering them. In Section 3 we describe the evaluation
methodology used and present the results of evaluation on the TRECVID 2007
BBC rushes data set [15]. Section 4 concludes the discussion and outlines future
work.

2   Algorithm for Clustering of Takes

2.1   Problem Formulation

We can describe the problem of detecting multiple takes of the same scene as
follows: Let $P = \{p_k | k = 1..N\}$ be the set of parts of a video or a set of videos,
where a part is a shot or a subshot. Identify the set S of scenes, where for each
scene $s \in S$ there exists a set $T_s = \{t_1, \ldots, t_M\}$ of one or more takes. Each take
spans a full part p or a fraction of it: $t_i \subseteq p_k, t_i \in T_s, p_k \in P$. Each take can only
be assigned to one scene, i.e. $T_{s_i} \cap T_{s_j} = \{\}, \forall s_i, s_j \in S, i \neq j$.

The takes in one set are similar in terms of a certain distance function (using
the threshold θ_{sim} for the maximum distance) and sufficiently long (minimum
length θ_{len}, thus e.g. a few similar frames do not constitute a take):

$$T_s = \{t_i | \text{dist}(t_i, t_j) \leq \theta_{sim} \wedge |t_i| > \theta_{len}, \ i, j = 1 \ldots M\},$$

The distance function used is described in detail in Section 2.4.

2.2   Algorithm Overview

The first step is to split the input video into parts p and to extract the sequence
of features A_{p_k} for each part p_k. This feature sequence consists of elements
$a^i_{p_k, j}$, where i indicates the feature and j the position in the sequence. The
segmentation of the input video into parts and the extraction of features is
described in Section 2.3.

In order to detect which parts contain takes of the same scene, pair-wise
matching of the parts is performed. The LCSS algorithm described in Section 2.4
is applied to each pair $(p_u, p_v) \in P$, yielding a set of candidate subsequences
C_{p_u, p_v}. As some of them may overlap, sequences contained in others are removed
and overlapping matches are merged. Thus only the non-overlapping and non-
connected subsequences C'_{p_u, p_v} remain as candidate sequences for each pair of
parts. The next step is to cluster these candidate sequences into sets of similar
takes. This is described in detail in Section 2.5.

Finally, for each of the takes a sequence of relevance values over time is calculated. The relevance values are determined from the number of matches between
a take and other takes in the same scene. This information can be used to select
representative clips for the takes of a scene.

2.3   Feature Extraction

The first task is to segment the input video into parts. As a starting point, shot boundary detection is used to determine the set of shots, which is used as the initial set of parts. Only hard cut detection is performed: A linear SVM is used taking frame differences of three consecutive frames as input. The SVM is implemented through LIBSVM [3]. To train the SVM classifier, ground truth from the TRECVID 2006 shot boundary detection task [16] has been used.

For the set of initial parts, a feature sequence A_{p_k} is extracted for each part p_k as follows. In order to reduce the processing time and the length of the sequences to be matched, the set of features is only extracted every n^{th} frame (in our experiments, we use $n = 10$). The maximum offset between two elements of the feature sequences to be matched is thus $n/2$ frames. For these frames, the MPEG-7 descriptors ColorLayout and EdgeHistogram [13] are extracted. From the ColorLayout descriptor, the DC and the first two AC coefficients of each channel are used. The visual activity is calculated as the pixel difference of two consecutive frames and averaged over n frames. An element of the feature sequence is thus given as:

$$a_{p_k,j} = (ColorLayout_1, ..., ColorLayout_9, EdgeHistogram_1, ..., EdgeHistogram_{80}, VisualActivity)^T.$$

In many cases a shot contains exactly one take, however, there are shots containing several takes. Ideally, shots should be split at the take boundaries, e.g. at the point where the clapper board is shown or when someone shouts "action". Due to the lack of classifiers for these events we split shots at short-term peak values of the visual activity – computed during feature extraction – that are sufficiently distant from shot boundaries. The result is the final set of parts that is used as input for the subsequent steps of the algorithm. Our approach is intended to split the shot at the points where the clapper board is shown and removed, the camera is significantly moved or where production staff moves close in front of the camera. As we only split at high activities with a very short duration, most normal action – even fast one – does not cause a split. There are however false positives caused by abrupt strong movements of actors or objects.

2.4   LCSS Algorithm

In order to determine the similarity of parts, we need to identify subsequences of these parts that are sufficiently long and similar, accepting gaps and insertions. The problem is converted into identifying similar subsequences in the feature sequences of the parts. We need to find an appropriate similarity measure between two such feature sequences. Evaluation of similarity measures for object trajectories [18] has shown that the extension of the Longest Common Subsequence (LCSS) model proposed in [17] provides the best performance.

The authors of [17] introduce two thresholds: a real number ϵ that defines the matching threshold between the non-discrete elements of the sequences and an integer δ that defines the maximum offset in the positions to be matched.

In order to adapt the LCSS algorithm to our problem, we make the following modifications. As each element of the sequence is a multidimensional feature vector, we define a vector $\theta_{sim} = \{\epsilon_i\}$, that contains the matching thresholds for all features. Similarly, we introduce a vector $W = \{w_i\}$ representing the relative weights ($\sum_i w_i = 1$) of the features. The distance between two elements at positions j_1 and j_2 of the sequences A_{p_u} and A_{p_v} is then given as

$$\text{dist}(a_{p_u,j_1}, a_{p_v,j_2}) = \sum_i w_i \cdot \text{E}(a^i_{p_u,j_1}, a^i_{p_v,j_2}, \epsilon_i),$$

$$\text{E}(a^i_{p_u,j_1}, a^i_{p_v,j_2}, \epsilon_i) = \begin{cases} 1, & \text{if } \text{dist}_i(a^i_{p_u,j_1}, a^i_{p_v,j_2}) > \epsilon_i; \\ \text{dist}_i(a^i_{p_u,j_1}, a^i_{p_v,j_2}), & \text{otherwise}, \end{cases}$$

where dist_i is the feature specific distance function. The distance functions for ColorLayout and EdgeHistogram are those proposed in [14], the distance for visual activity is the L1-norm. The offset δ introduced in [17] is not relevant for our problem, as the matching subsequences can be anywhere in the parts. Instead, we introduce the maximum gap size γ of the subsequence. Note that the longest common subsequence does not necessarily fulfill the condition of having only gaps $\leq \gamma$, so instead of just finding the LCSS we are interested in finding all sufficiently long sequences (length $> \theta_{len}$) with gaps no longer than γ.

Our implementation of the LCSS algorithm is based on the one described in [5]. We compute the table containing the lengths for the subsequence matches (the "c table"). Instead of just reading the one optimal solution (starting in the lower right corner of the table) we follow all paths that end at a length greater than θ_{len} (for an example see Figure 2). The search is recursive and stops when either the start of the matching subsequence is reached or when the gap between two subsequent matches exceeds γ. The result is a set of (partly overlapping) matching subsequences (take candidates) $C_{p_u,p_v} = \{c_i\}$ between two parts p_u and p_v of the video.

2.5   Clustering Takes

Before the takes can be clustered it is necessary to identify the set of distinct sequences. Matches between a take candidate and take candidates from different parts may still contain partly or fully overlapping sequences. For example, the sequence [01:20:03 – 01:22:05] from part p_1 could match sequence [03:14:21 – 03:16:15] from part p_2, while sequence [03:15:00 – 03:16:18] from part p_2 matches sequence [10:50:24 – 10:52:15] from part p_3. Thus the first step is to collate these sequences, replacing all sequences that are contained within other sequences by the longer ones. A tolerance of 15 frames is used when determining if a sequence is contained within another. In our example the matching sequence in p_2 is [03:14:21 – 03:16:18].

The remaining sequences represent takes t which are to be clustered into sets of takes T_s of the same scene s. Hierarchical clustering using a single-linkage

	2.3	4.7	1.2	3.3	2.2	1.4
1.3	0	0	1	1	1	1
2.5	1	1	1	1	2	2
3.4	0	1	1	2	2	2
2.4	1	1	1	2	3	3
4.6	1	2	2	2	3	3
1.5	1	2	3	3	3	4
2.6	1	2	3	3	4	4

Fig. 2. Simplified example of the c table of LCSS matching (adopted from [5]). The values of the one dimensional feature sequences (shown at the top and on the left) are matched with thresholds $\theta_{sim} = 0.5$ and $\theta_{len} = 3$. The LCSS algorithm yields the sequence shown with emphasized border as the longest match. However, if we require a maximum gap $\gamma \leq 1$, this sequence is not a valid result, as there is a gap of two between the first two matching elements. Instead the sequences shown in gray are considered, which are results of the same length that additionally satisfy the gap constraint.

algorithm [8] is performed. The distance function between two clusters T_{s_i} and T_{s_j} is based on the longest common subsequence between their takes:

$$d(T_{s_i}, T_{s_j}) = \begin{cases} 1, & \text{if } |T_{s_i}| > 1 \wedge |T_{s_j}| > 1; \\ 1 - \max_{t \in T_{s_i}, t' \in T_{s_j}} \text{LCSS}_0(t, t'), & \text{otherwise,} \end{cases}$$

where LCSS_0 is the LCSS normalized by the lengths of the parts. This distance function prevents takes from distinct but similar scenes being clustered before less similar takes of the same scene. Clustering stops when the cutoff similarity is reached, which is given by the minimum length θ_{len} of a matching subsequence. The result of clustering is the set of scenes S.

3 Evaluation

3.1 Data Set and Ground Truth

The proposed algorithm has been evaluated on a subset of the TRECVID 2007 BBC rushes test data set [15]. The subset consists of six randomly selected videos out of this data set (in total 3 hours). For this subset ground truth has been manually annotated by identifying the set of scenes and the takes of each scene. All takes of a scene have been shot from the same camera position. No discrimination between complete and partial takes has been made. Shots of the video containing only test patters such as color bars or monochrome frames have been excluded from the test data.

The following parameters are used for evaluation. The minimum length θ_{len} is 30 frames, the gap size γ is 7 frames (the videos in the test have a frame rate of 25). For similarity matching the following thresholds and weights are used (the sequence of the features is ColorLayout, EdgeHistogram, VisualActivity): $\theta_{sim} = (0.03, 0.03, 0.03)^T$, $W = (0.5, 0.2, 0.3)^T$.

3.2   Methodology

For evaluation the number of takes correctly and falsely assigned to one scene (including partial takes) is counted. The exact temporal extent of the identified takes as well as the alignment of partial takes is not taken into account. Firstly this would have enormously increased the effort for creating the ground truth and secondly the correct temporal extent is difficult to define in many cases.

The input to the evaluation for one video are the set of scenes S' as defined by the ground truth and the set of scenes S resulting from the algorithm. As the sets may be defined differently and may also have different order, the first step is to align the scenes. This is done by assigning each result scene s to that scene s' of the ground truth, for which the overlap between the takes of the scenes is maximal:

$$\text{matching\_scene}(s, S') = \underset{s' \in S'}{\operatorname{argmax}} \sum_i \sum_j \text{overlap}(t_i, t'_j),\ t_i \in T_s,\ t'_j \in T'_s$$

where overlap calculates the temporal overlap between the takes in frames. Additionally a scene from the ground truth s' may only be assigned to at most one result scene s. After this step there may be unassigned scenes: the takes of an unassigned scene s are counted as false positives, the takes of an unassigned scene s' are counted as false negatives.

Once the scenes have been assigned, the number of temporally overlapping takes is counted. If a take of the ground truth overlaps with more than one take of the result, only a single overlap is counted. From the sum of correct overlaps of all clusters, precision and recall are calculated as follows:

$$precision = \frac{\sum_{s \in S} \text{nr\_overlaps}(s, \text{matching\_scene}(s, S'))}{\sum_{s \in S} |s|}$$

$$recall = \frac{\sum_{s \in S} \text{nr\_overlaps}(s, \text{matching\_scene}(s, S'))}{\sum_{s' \in S'} |s'|}$$

3.3   Results

Table 1 shows the evaluation results on the test set. In general the results are promising. In all but one case, precision is equal to or higher than recall. This means that the similarity between the feature sequences of takes (controlled by the threshold θ_{sim}) has been quite strictly enforced. As a result, takes in which the performed action diverges more have been grouped into separate scenes.

When analyzing the differences between the videos in the test set, it can be seen that the precision values are more uniformly distributed than the recall values (also supported by the respective differences between the mean and the median of the two measures).

Table 1. Number of scenes and takes in the test set and precision and recall results

Video	Nr. of scenes		Nr. of takes		Precision	Recall
	ground truth	detected	ground truth	detected		
MRS07063	6	4	26	17	0.7647	0.5000
MRS025913	8	9	28	28	0.8571	0.8571
MRS044731	7	9	34	31	0.5484	0.5000
MRS144760	6	5	24	26	0.8077	0.8750
MRS157475	8	8	36	32	0.6875	0.5903
MS216210	7	10	26	21	0.6190	0.5000
Mean	7.00	7.50	29.00	25.83	0.7141	0.6405
Median	7.00	8.50	27.00	27.00	0.7261	0.5556

The three videos with the lowest recall scores have similar kind of content: They contain dialog scenes with little action and all scenes have been shot in the same room. Thus the difference in visual appearance and activity between the scenes is very small (sometimes smaller than within takes of the same scene), so that takes are falsely assigned. Two of these three videos also have the lowest precision scores.

The noticeable difference between the two videos with the highest recall scores and the others is that the correct or a slightly higher number of takes has been found in these videos. This means that the lower recall scores are caused by mistakes in the segmentation of the input video into parts. There are parts that contain more than one take. Although these parts are correctly clustered, they are treated as single takes, thus missing the others contained in the same segment.

4   Conclusion and Future Work

We have presented an approach for identifying multiple takes of the same scene shot from the same or similar camera positions. The approach is based on matching sequences of extracted features (color and texture features of regularly sampled frames, visual activity) with a novel variant of the LCSS algorithm. Matching sequences are considered as take candidates and clustered by similarity in order to group them by scene.

The evaluation of our algorithm shows in general quite encouraging results, with precision being clearly better than recall. The lower recall scores are in many cases caused by insufficient segmentation of the input video, i.e. several takes are treated as one part. The strategy for splitting shots into potential takes could be improved by using features more targeted at the usual production scenario, such as training a classifier for clapper boards or analyzing the audio signal (long silence, clapper board sound, spotting the word "action"). This could improve the recall score in cases where sequence matching already performs well.

Another group of videos with lower precision and recall values are those containing a number of scenes with little action and shot at the same location (e.g. several dialog scenes in one room). The problem here is that takes of different scenes are more similar in terms of the visual features we are using than takes from the following or previous ones. As a consequence, takes are incorrectly assigned, thus reducing both precision and recall scores. A possible solution would be to use more advanced features as input for sequence matching, such as localized motion activity, object trajectories or alignment of words in the speech to text transcript. As a further step, it would also be interesting to have a second clustering step grouping take clusters showing the same action, but shot from different camera positions.

Detection and clustering of multiple takes of one scene is a useful tool in post-production and audiovisual archiving. An earlier version of the approach presented here has been used for creating skims of rushes video by eliminating the redundancy stemming from retakes [1]. It will also be integrated as a cluster criterion in the interactive video browsing tool described in [2].

Acknowledgments

The research leading to this paper was partially supported by the European Commission under the contracts FP6-045032, "Search Environments for Media – SEMEDIA" (http://www.semedia.org), IST-2-511316-IP, "IP-RACINE – Integrated Project Research Area Cinema" (http://www.ipracine.org) and FP6-027026, "Knowledge Space of semantic inference for automatic annotation and retrieval of multimedia content – K-Space" (http://www.k-space.eu).

BBC 2007 Rushes video is copyrighted. The BBC 2007 Rushes video used in this work is provided for research purposes by the BBC through the TREC Information Retrieval Research Collection.

References

1. Bailer, W., Lee, F., Thallinger, G.: Skimming rushes video using retake detection. In: TVS 2007. Proceedings of the TRECVID Workshop on Video Summarization, pp. 60–64. ACM Press, New York (September 2007)
2. Bailer, W., Thallinger, G.: A framework for multimedia content abstraction and its application to rushes exploration. In: Proceedings of ACM International Conference on Image and Video Retrieval, Amsterdam, NL (July 2007)
3. Chang, C.-C., Lin, C.-J.: LIBSVM: a library for support vector machines, Software (2001), http://www.csie.ntu.edu.tw/~cjlin/libsvm
4. Chang, S.-F., Chen, W., Meng, H., Sundaram, H., Zhong, D.: VideoQ: an automated content based video search system using visual cues. In: MULTIMEDIA 1997: Proceedings of the fifth ACM international conference on Multimedia, pp. 313–324. ACM Press, New York (1997)
5. Cormen, T.H., Leiserson, C.E., Rivest, R.L., Stein, C.: Introduction to Algorithms, 2nd edn. The MIT Press, Cambridge (2001)
6. Covell, M., Baluja, S., Fink, M.: Advertisement detection and replacement using acoustic and visual repetition. In: IEEE Workshop on Multimedia Signal Processing, pp. 461–466 (October 2006)

7. Delaney, B., Hoomans, B.: Preservation and Digitisation Plans: Overview and Analysis, PrestoSpace Deliverable 2.1 User Requirements Final Report (2004), http://www.prestospace.org/project/deliverables/D2-1_User_Requirements_Final_Report.pdf

8. Duda, R.O., Hart, P.E., Stork, D.G.: Pattern Classification. Wiley, Chichester (2000)

9. Duygulu, P., Pan, J.-Y., Forsyth, D.A.: Towards auto-documentary: tracking the evolution of news stories. In: MULTIMEDIA 2004: Proceedings of the 12th annual ACM international conference on Multimedia, pp. 820–827. ACM Press, New York (2004)

10. Hampapur, A., Bolle, R.M.: Comparison of distance measures for video copy detection. In: IEEE International Conference on Multimedia and Expo, pp. 737–740 (August 2001)

11. Hampapur, A., Hyun, K., Bolle, R.M.: In: Yeung, M.M., Li, C.-S., Lienhart, R.W. (eds.) Storage and Retrieval for Media Databases 2002. Society of Photo-Optical Instrumentation Engineers (SPIE) Conference, vol. 4676, pp. 194–201 (2001)

12. Hsu, W., Chang, S.-F.: Topic tracking across broadcast news videos with visual duplicates and semantic concepts. In: International Conference on Image Processing (ICIP) (October 2006)

13. MPEG-7. Information Technology—Multimedia Content Description Interface: Part 3: Visual. ISO/IEC 15938-3 (2001)

14. MPEG-7. Information Technology—Multimedia Content Description Interface: Part 8: Extraction and Use of MPEG-7 Descriptions. ISO/IEC 15938-8 (2001)

15. Over, P., Smeaton, A.F., Kelly, P.: The TRECVID 2007 BBC rushes summarization evaluation pilot. In: TVS 2007. Proceedings of the TRECVID Workshop on Video Summarization, pp. 1–15. ACM Press, New York (September 2007)

16. Alan, F., Smeaton, A.F., Over, P.: TRECVID 2006: Shot boundary detection task overview. In: Proceedings of the TRECVID Workshop (November 2006)

17. Vlachos, M., Kollios, G., Gunopoulos, D.: Discovering similar multidimensional trajectories. In: ICDE 2002: Proceedings of the 18th International Conference on Data Engineering, San Jose, CA, USA, pp. 673–684. IEEE Computer Society, Washington DC (2002)

18. Zhang, Z., Huang, K., Tan, T.: Comparison of similarity measures for trajectory clustering in outdoor surveillance scenes. In: ICPR 2006: Proceedings of the 18th International Conference on Pattern Recognition, pp. 1135–1138. IEEE Computer Society, Washington, DC, USA (2006)

19. Zhu, X., Elmagarmid, A., Xue, X., Wu, L., Catlin, A.: InsightVideo: toward hierarchical video content organization for efficient browsing, summarization and retrieval. IEEE Transactions on Multimedia 7(4), 648–666 (2005)

An Images-Based 3D Model Retrieval Approach

Yuehong Wang[1], Rujie Liu[1], Takayuki Baba[2], Yusuke Uehara[2],
Daiki Masumoto[2], and Shigemi Nagata[2]

[1] Fujitsu Research and Development Center LTD., Beijing, China
{wangyh,rjliu}@cn.fujitsu.com
[2] Fujitsu Laboratories LTD., Kawasaki, Japan
{baba-t,yuehara,masumoto.daiki,nagata.shigemi}@jp.fujitsu.com

Abstract. This paper presents an images based 3D model retrieval
method in which each model is described by six 2D images. The images are generated by three steps: 1) the model is normalized based on
the distribution of the surface normal directions; 2) then, the normalized
model is uniformly sampled to generate a number of random points; 3)
finally, the random points are projected along six directions to create
six images, each of which is described by Zernike moment feature. In the
comparison of two models, six images of each model are naturally divided
into three pairs, and the similarity between two models is calculated by
summing up the distances of all corresponding pairs. The effectiveness
of our method is verified by comparative experiments. Meanwhile, high
matching speed is achieved, e.g., it takes about 3e-5 seconds to compare
two models using a computer with *Pentium IV 3.00GHz CPU*.

Keywords: 3D retrieval, 2D images, pose normalization, sampling, projection, models comparison.

1   Introduction

With the ever-growing volume of 3D models generated and stored, 3D retrieval
techniques become fundamentally important to the management and reuse of the
existing models in various applications. Much effort has been spent on finding
the efficient 3D model retrieval approaches.

In the initial stage, 3D retrieval is based on key-words annotation. In this
approach, the 3D models are manually annotated by key words which provide
the semantic information, and then the models with the same or similar key
words as the query are retrieved. However, it becomes inapplicable when the size
of database becomes large because a great amount of manual labor is required
to annotate the whole database and inconsistency among different annotators
may exist in perceiving the same models.

To overcome these shortcomings, content based retrieval methods [1,2] are
proposed in which the model's own content, in particular shape characteristic
is taken into account. Nowadays, the research is focused on the content based
retrieval approaches which can be roughly divided into three categories: feature
vector based methods, topology based methods and images based methods.

S. Satoh, F. Nack, and M. Etoh (Eds.): MMM 2008, LNCS 4903, pp. 90–100, 2008.

In the feature vector based methods, the 3D model is characterized by a feature vector. One of the representative methods is shape distribution [3]. In this approach, the histogram of the distance between two random points on the surface is calculated to describe the global geometric characteristics, and the similarity between models is calculated through their histograms. This kind of approaches are simple, fast and robust, and they could be used as a pre-filter in a complete retrieval system.

In the topology based methods, 3D models are usually described by trees or graphs to express their topological structure, and 3D models are compared through some tree or graph matching algorithms. In [4], Multi-resolutional Reeb Graphs (MRGs) are automatically extracted from the 3D model to represent the skeletal and topological structure, and the distance of 3D models are calculated by matching their corresponding MRGs from coarse to fine level. This kind of descriptor is invariant to affine transformations, and robust against surface simplification and deformations caused by posture changes of an articulated model. In the experiment, it takes about 12 seconds to search through a database with 230 models, so it is not suitable for large database retrieval.

In the images based methods, the 3D model is represented by a series of 2D images, and the similarity between models is measured by comparing their 2D images. In these methods, the visual characteristics of 3D models can be well described, and thus these methods usually get good retrieval accuracy. Among these methods, light field descriptor (LFD) [5] is very famous and it also achieved the best performance among twelve different methods in the comparative study [6]. In LFD, the 3D model is described by 10 Light Field Descriptors, and 10 binary images are needed to create each descriptor, so totally 100 images need rendering from a model. Then the similarity between two models is measured by summing up the distances of all corresponding images. Compared to LFD, our images based method is more efficient in terms of feature extraction and model retrieval because much fewer images are used.

In our research, six 2D images are used to describe the 3D model, and 3D models are compared by an intuitive matching approach. Our method is composed of two main parts, and it is assumed that the surface of 3D models are comprised by triangle faces.

1) 3D model representation with six 2D images.

In this process, the 3D model is firstly normalized by a surface orientation based approach in which the distribution of all triangle faces' normal directions is utilized; After that, a number of random points are obtained by uniformly sampling the normalized model; Finally, the random points are projected along six directions to create six 2D images and each image is described by Zernike moment feature [7] for later retrieval. Therefore, each 3D model is described by six image features.

2) Model comparison.

Six 2D images of each model are naturally divided into three pairs, then the similarity between two models is calculated by the accumulative distance of corresponding pairs. Principal Component Analysis (PCA) is implemented to accelerate the retrieval process due to the demand of efficiency for large database retrieval.

The effectiveness of our method is verified by the comparative experiments and the high retrieval speed is also achieved. Therefore, our method is practical to retrieve desirable models from large database.

The rest of this paper is organized as follows: the next section describes the content about the six 2D images generation and 2D image description by Zernike moments; one intuitive model comparison algorithm and the accelerated retrieval approach are illustrated in section 3. Experimental results are presented in section 4, followed by the conclusion in section 5.

2   3D Model Representation with Six Images

This section introduces the 3D representation approach, where six 2D images are generated from each 3D model, and then described by Zernike moment feature. As a result, each 3D model is described by six image features.

2.1   Images Generation

Two dimensional images generation is one of the key issues in the images based 3D model retrieval techniques. In our method, six images of a 3D model are generated by three steps as in Fig.1. Firstly, the 3D model is normalized by an approach in order to deal with translation and rotation problem, in which the distribution information of all triangle faces' normal directions is exploited. Secondly, a number of evenly distributing random points are generated from the normalized 3D model through an effective sampling mechanism. Finally, the random points are projected along six different directions to create six 2D projection images. All the three steps will be illustrated in detail.

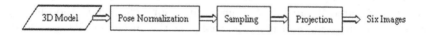

Fig. 1. The framework of images generation

2.1.1   Pose Normalization

Translation and rotation are two most common problems in 3D model retrieval. As to translation, it can be easily solved by moving the barycenter of the 3D model to the origin of the coordinate system. But it is not so easy to deal with the rotation problem.

Some methods attempted to generate a large number of images from many directions to reduce the rotation effect. For example, one hundred images and eighty images need rendering in light filed descriptor [5] and the characteristic views based method [8], respectively. However, rendering and describing such many images will cost a lot of time, and comparing the models is also time consuming.

Some other methods tried to normalize the orientation of 3D models prior to the images generation. Principal component analysis (PCA) is one of the best known methods due to its simplicity and efficiency. However, from many experiments, it is found that PCA may not detect the principal axes of some similar models stably. For example, different axes are obtained by PCA for three similar mugs [1].

In our study, a normalization approach is put forward, where the distribution of all triangles' normal directions is taken into account. With its help, three principal axes of the 3D model are detected firstly, then the 3D model is normalized so that rotation and translation problems are suppressed. This normalization approach will be called as *Normal Method* in the following parts and it is illustrated as follows.

1. The area a_i and normal direction $\mathbf{p}_i$ of each triangle t_i, $i = 1, 2, ..., fCnt$, are calculated, where $fCnt$ is the number of triangle faces in the 3D model.
2. The barycenter $\mathbf{c} = \frac{1}{S} \sum_{i=1}^{fCnt} g_i\, a_i$, where S is the total area of the surface and g_i is the center of the ith triangle.
3. Three principal axes are detected.

   – The weighted scatter matrix s of the normal directions is calculated as Eqn.1, where $\mathbf{p}_0$ is the average normal direction.

$$s = \sum_{i=1}^{fCnt} a_i(\mathbf{p}_i - \mathbf{p}_0)(\mathbf{p}_i - \mathbf{p}_0)^T \qquad (1)$$

   – Three eigenvectors are obtained by decomposing the matrix s, and then selected as principal axes $\mathbf{pa}_1, \mathbf{pa}_2, \mathbf{pa}_3$.

4. Each vertex of the model is normalized as the following formulas, where $\mathbf{v}_i$ and $\mathbf{v}_i' = \{v_{ix}', v_{iy}', v_{iz}'\}$, $(i = 1, 2, ..., vCnt)$, denote the original and normalized ith vertex, $\mathbf{c}$ is the barycenter of the original 3D model, and $\cdot$ denotes dot product.

$$v_{ix}' = (\mathbf{v}_i - \mathbf{c}) \cdot \mathbf{pa}_1$$

$$v_{iy}' = (\mathbf{v}_i - \mathbf{c}) \cdot \mathbf{pa}_2$$

$$v_{iz}' = (\mathbf{v}_i - \mathbf{c}) \cdot \mathbf{pa}_3$$

After normalization, the coordinate axes of the world system will be aligned with the three principal axes of the 3D model, and thus the rotation problem is suppressed. At the same time, the barycenter of the 3D model is translated to the origin of coordinate system, so the translation effect is reduced. From Fig.2, the principal axes are accurately detected by *Normal Method*.

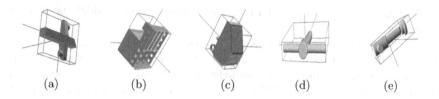

(a)   (b)   (c)   (d)   (e)

Fig. 2. Three principal axes detected by *Normal Method*

2.1.2   Uniform Sampling

The second step is to sample the surface of the normalized model uniformly to generate a number of random points. In our study, the suitable number of random points is chosen by the experiments to balance the accuracy and efficiency.

Unbiased random points should distribute uniformly over the model's surface, and an approach is proposed for this target. In the approach, for a triangle, the number of random points is set with respect to its area. Compared to the sampling approach in [3], the selection of one random triangle for sampling is removed, while all triangles comprising the surface are sampled orderly instead. Therefore, our sampling approach is more efficient and it is realized by the following steps.

1. The total area of the surface is calculated as $a_{total} = \sum_{i=1}^{fCnt} a_i$, where a_i is the area of ith triangle face and $fCnt$ is the number of triangle faces comprising the model surface.
2. For each triangle t_i $(i = 1, 2, ...fCnt)$, a number of points are sampled.
   - The number of points in t_i is calculated as $nCnt_i = \lfloor pCnt * a_i/a_{total} \rfloor$, where $pCnt$ is the expected total number of random points, and $\lfloor \cdot \rfloor$ denotes the integer part of a given real number.
   - $nCnt_i$ random points of the triangle t_i are generated in order. Every point $\mathbf{P}_j$ $(j = 1, 2, ..., nCnt_i)$ is obtained as Eqn.2, where $\mathbf{A}, \mathbf{B}, \mathbf{C}$ are the vertices of t_i, and $r_1, r_2 \in [0, 1]$ are the random numbers generated independently for each point.

$$\mathbf{P}_j = (1 - \sqrt{r_1})\, \mathbf{A} + \sqrt{r_1}\, (1 - r_2)\, \mathbf{B} + \sqrt{r_1}\, r_2\, \mathbf{C} \tag{2}$$

2.1.3   Parallel Projection

The last step of images generation is to project the random points along six directions to create six 2D images. Generally only one side of the model can be seen from a particular direction. Therefore in our study, about a half of random points are used for each image to accord with human perception. For example, the points with positive and negative z coordinate are used to create the top image and bottom image, respectively. In addition, the dimension of all images is identical and every image is square. In this way, both of the isotropic and anisotropic scaling can be effectively suppressed. Meanwhile, the resultant 2D images may be binary or gray images according to users' requirement. Taking top image for example, the process of image creation is illustrated as follows.

1. Suppose $P = \{p_1, p_2, ..., p_{cnt}\}$ be all the random points with positive z coordinate and the image dimension be $N * N$, the intensities of all pixels in the top image are initialized as zero.
2. Each point $\mathbf{p}_i = \{p_{ix}, p_{iy}, p_{iz}\}$, $i = 1, 2, ..., cnt$, is projected to its corresponding pixel (j, k). The intensity of the pixel (j, k) can be set as one to generate binary image, and it can also be set as the maximum or weighted z coordinates of the points locating in the position (j, k) to generate gray image.

The other five images are created in the similar way. Figure 3 shows the six binary images generated from the two similar models shown in Fig.2(d) and Fig.2(e), respectively. It is easy to see that these 2D images of two models are also similar to each other, which guarantees the accuracy of models comparison.

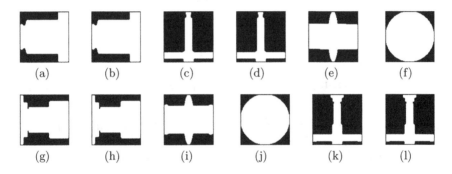

Fig. 3. Six binary images of the models in Fig.2(d-e). (a-f), (g-l) are top image, bottom image, right image, left image, front image and back image of two models, respectively

2.2 Image Feature Extraction

After the steps of images generation, six 2D images are created. In our method, Zernike moment feature, well known as efficient for shape representation, is adopted to describe the generated images and it has several merits such as robustness against noise, invariance to rotation and expression efficiency. Detailed information can be found in [7]. In our system, the descriptor of each 3D model consists of six image features, each of which is a 79-dimensional vector.

3   Model Retrieval

With the former steps, each model is described with six 79D image features. In this section, our intuitive comparison approach and its accelerated retrieval algorithm will be presented.

3.1 Similarity Between Two Models

The 3D models comparison by 2D images is another key point in the images based retrieval techniques. In our method, six images of each 3D model are naturally divided into three pairs as shown in Fig.4, and the similarity between two models is measured by the accumulative distance of corresponding pairs. Our method is based on a simple assumption: top image and bottom image, left image and right image, front image and back image always appear in pair, so each pair of images should be bound together to compare 3D models. Suppose (A_1, A_2, A_3) and (B_1, B_2, B_3) are three pairs of two models separately, the algorithm of models comparison is illustrated as follows.

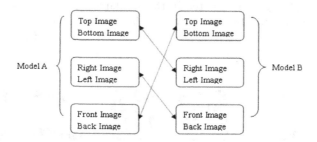

Fig. 4. The mechanism of comparing two models

1. The distance of every two pairs $d(A_i, B_j)$ is calculated as Eqn.3, $i, j = 1, 2, 3$, where (A_{i1}, A_{i2}) and (B_{j1}, B_{j2}) are two images in the pair A_i and B_j, respectively, and $l(\cdot, \cdot)$ is $L1$ distance of two image features.

$$d(A_i, B_j) = \min(l(A_{i1}, B_{j1}) + l(A_{i2}, B_{j2}),\ l(A_{i1}, B_{j2}) + l(A_{i2}, B_{j1}))\quad(3)$$

2. The distance of two models is calculated as Eqn.4, where $S = \{c = \{c_1, c_2, c_3\}\ |\ c_i \in \{1, 2, 3\}, and\ c_i \neq c_j\ if\ i \neq j.\}$ and A_k and B_j are assumed to be corresponding pairs when $c_k = j$. The size of S is six $(C_3^1 C2^1 C1^1 = 6)$.

$$dis = \min_{c \in S} \sum_{k=1}^{3} d(A_k, B_{c_k})\quad(4)$$

With the above comparison method, the resultant corresponding pairs of the two models (shown in Fig.2(d-e)) are $A_1 - B_1$, $A_2 - B_3$ and $A_3 - B_2$, where A_i and B_i are the ith image pair of the two models, respectively, and '$-$' links two corresponding pairs, and the result is consistent with human perception.

3.2 Accelerated Retrieval Algorithm

During the experiments, it is found that the algorithm illustrated in section 3.1 is not fast enough to search through the large database. Therefore, an accelerated matching approach is proposed and the basic idea of algorithm in section 3.1 is reserved. In the improved matching algorithm, there are two key points: 1) Lower dimensional features are used in the determination of the corresponding pairs in order to save time; 2) The original high dimensional features are used in the calculation of distance between two models to avoid much loss of retrieval accuracy. The accelerated approach is presented as follows.

1. Offline preparation: For each database model, two 79D features of each image pair are ranked according to their variance, and then catenated into one 158D feature. Then based on all 158D features of database models, PCA is applied to detect 10 principal directions, in which all 158D features are projected to get 10D ones. Therefore, three 158D and 10D features of each database model are available before online retrieval.

2. Preparation for the query: Six 79D features are converted into three 158 ones in the same manner as that for each database model. Then three 10D features are obtained by projecting three 158D ones along the 10 principal directions determined in the offline preparation.

3. Comparison of the query to all database models: The query is compared with each database model by two steps: determination of corresponding pairs, and similarity calculation of two models. In the first step, 10D features are used to calculate the distances of every two image pairs between two models, and then the optimal correspondence of image pairs is found by searching from all six possible cases. In the second step, 158D features are used to calculate the similarity between two models by summing up the distance of all corresponding pairs determined in the first step.

In the comparison of two models, it only needs nine times of calculating the absolute distance of 10D features to determine corresponding pairs, and three times of absolute distance computation of 158D features to calculate the distance of two models. Therefore, the retrieval process is greatly sped up. From the repetitive experiments, the average time cost to compare two modes is 3e-5 seconds using the computer with with *Pentium IV 3.00GHz CPU*.

4   Experiment Results

4.1   Test Data Sets

To evaluate the effectiveness of our method, two datasets are selected as the test sets. One is the training set of Princeton shape benchmark (PSB), and another is our own engineering models collection. All the models of two datasets are represented by triangle faces.

In the first data set, 907 models are contained and divided into 90 categories according to the semantic and shape information. The size of all categories ranges from 4 to 50. The dataset is publicly available from http://shape.cs.princeton. edu-/benchmark, and widely used as the ground-truth to compare different 3D shape descriptors. For example, it is adopted in SHREC-3D shape retrieval contest (http://www.aimatshape.net/event). For the detailed information, please refer to [6].

In the second data set, 1000 engineering models used in the real application are included and manually divided into 34 classes based on shape information. Besides some complex models (*e.g.* those shown in Fig.2), there are also some models with very simple structure. For example, Fig.5 shows five representative such simple models. In the dataset, rotation, translation, isotropic or anisotropic scaling may exist among some similar models.

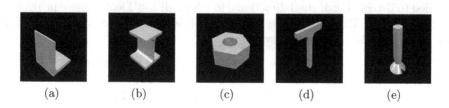

(a)   (b)   (c)   (d)   (e)

Fig. 5. Five model samples with simple structure in the second data set

4.2   Experimental Results

The experiments are conducted by leave one out manner, that is, each model of the database will be selected as the query at one time, and then the average retrieval result are obtained. The retrieval performance is measured by precision recall curve. In brief, *precision* denotes the proportion of retrieved models that are relevant, while *recall* is the proportion of relevant models that are accurately retrieved.

In the experiments, the parameters in our method are listed as follows:

- The number of random points: 100000;
- The image type: binary image;
- The dimension of 2D images: 100×100;
- The length of each image Zernike moment feature: 79.

Four other competing methods are selected to verify the effectiveness of our method, namely Light field descriptor (LFD)[5], Shape distribution (SD)[3], Thickness histogram (TH)[9] and Direction method (DF)[9]. As the former two methods are simply introduced in the introduction, the latter two methods are briefly introduced here. In the thickness histogram, the descriptor is created by uniformly estimating the thickness of a model in a statistical way, and then the similarity between two models are measured by the distance of their thickness histograms. The direction method is an improved form of thickness histogram, where the directional form of thickness histograms are calculated and then converted into harmonic representation as the descriptor of the model.

Figure.6(a) shows the precision recall curves of all five methods including our method on the first test dataset. From the result, our method and light field

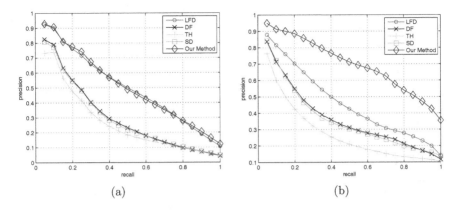

Fig. 6. Precision-recall curves on two test sets

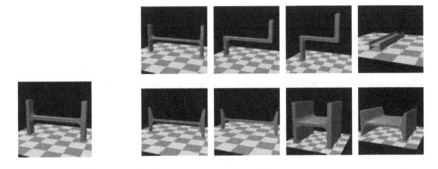

Fig. 7. One query sample   **Fig. 8.** First four retrieved models by LFD (above row) and our method (bottom row) for the query in Fig.7

descriptor achieve the best results. However, our method is more efficient than LFD in both the model representation and model comparison because much fewer images are applied.

Figure.6(b) shows the precision recall curves of the five methods on the second dataset. From the result on this engineering dataset, our method gets the best result and the performance is much better than that by LFD. We also found that our method is more effective than LFD to deal with anisotropic scale problem. For example, Fig.8 shows the first four retrieved models for the query (Fig.7) by our method and LFD, respectively, and it is found that the retrieval result by our method is more accurate than that by LFD.

5   Conclusion

In this paper, an efficient 3D model retrieval method is presented. The shape content of 3D model is well described by six images which are generated by pose normalization, uniform sampling and parallel projection, and these images are described by Zernike moment feature. Then 3D models are compared by an intuitive matching approach, where six images of each model are naturally divided into three pairs and the similarity between two models is calculated by summing up the distances of all corresponding image pairs. Comparative experiments verify the advantage of our method, and our method is practical for large database retrieval. Our method is also applicable for 3D retrieval by 2D image query.

References

1. Johan, W.H., Tangelder, Remco, C.V.: A Survey of Content Based 3D Shape Retrieval Methods. In: Proceedings of International conference on shape modeling, pp. 145–156 (2004)
2. Vranic, D.V.: 3D Model Retrieval. Ph.D.Dissertation (December 2003)
3. Osada, R., Funkhouser, R., Chazelle, T.: Shape Distributions. ACM Transactions on Graphics 21(5), 807–832 (2002)
4. Hilaga, M., Shinagawa, Y., Kohmura, T., Kunii, T.L.: Topology Matching for Fully Automatic Similarity Estimation of 3D Shapes. In: Proceedings SIGGRAPH, pp. 203–212 (2001)
5. Ding-Yun, C., Xiaopei, T., Yute, S., Ming, O.: On Visual Similarity Based 3D Model Retrieval. Proceedings of European association for Computer Graphics 22(3), 223–232 (2003)
6. Shilane, P., Min, P., Kazhdan, M., Funkhouser, T.: The Priceton Shape Benchmark. In: Proceedings of the international conference on Shape modeling, pp. 167–178 (2004)
7. Whoi-Yul, K., Yong-Sung, K.: A Region-based Shape Descriptor Using Zernike Moments. Signal Processing: Image Communication 16, 95–102 (2005)
8. Ansqry, T.F., Vandeborre, J., Daoudi, M.: A framework for 3D CAD Models Retrieval From 2D images. Annals of telecommunications technologies and tools for 3D imaging 60, 11–12 (2005)
9. Yi, L., Jiantao, P., Hongbin, Z.: Thickness Histogram and Statistical Harmonics Representation for 3D Model Retrieval. In: Proceedings of the international symposium on 3D data processing, visualization and transmission, pp. 896–903 (2004)

'Oh Web Image, Where Art Thou?'

Dirk Ahlers[1] and Susanne Boll[2]

[1] OFFIS Institute for Information Technology, Oldenburg, Germany
ahlers@offis.de
[2] University of Oldenburg, Germany
boll@informatik.uni-oldenburg.de

Abstract. Web image search today is mostly keyword-based and explores the content surrounding the image. Searching for images related to a certain location quickly shows that Web images typically do not reveal their explicit relation to an actual geographic position. The geographic semantics of Web images are either not available at all or hidden somewhere within the the Web pages' content. Our spatial search engine crawls and identifies Web pages with a spatial relationship. Analysing location-related Web pages, we identify photographs based on content-based image analysis as well as image context. Following the photograph classification, a location-relevance classification process evaluates image context and content against the previously identified address. The results of our experiments show that our approach is a viable method for Web image location assessment. Thus, a large number of potentially geographically-related Web images are unlocked for commercially relevant spatial Web image search.

1 Introduction

The relation of Web information to a physical place has gained much attention in recent years both in research and commercial applications. Web search started to become "local", meaning that users can search and access information that is mapped to an exact place or region of interest. However, currently a Web search for photos of a certain place remains at a keyword-level of known geographic names such as "New York" or "Singapore" but does not deliver a precise georeference for Web media content. To enable users to search for images at a specific geographical coordinate or its spatial vicinity, we need a Web image search with geo-spatial awareness.

The Web pages we find today seldomly provide explicit location-information. This also applies to the images contained in Web pages. Even though GPS has arrived at the end consumer, photos with an actual location stamp cover only a tiny fraction of all Web images. The challenge that remains for Web image retrieval is the derivation of reliable location information for Web images from unstructured Web pages. In our approach to spatially index Web images, we exploit address information that is hidden in Web pages. Employing our spatial Web search engine, we crawl and index Web pages for location information. If our geoparser identifies a reliable relaion between a Web pages' content and a

S. Satoh, F. Nack, and M. Etoh (Eds.): MMM 2008, LNCS 4903, pp. 101–112, 2008.

physical address, we can then determine whether the location of the Web page itself can also be assigned to the images embedded in it. Analysing the image content, we distinguish photographs from other images. Exploiting image and surrounding page content, a multi-criteria classification determines if the photograph can actually be related to the location identified for the Web page. We combine several heuristic approaches for analyzing and scoring relevant features to achieve an overall assessment of an image's connection to a location. Our test and evaluation show that only a small fraction of Web pages contain location-relevant photos but that these can be very well related to the spatial context. With a spatial Web image search engine thus established, we can answer the question "Oh Web image, where art thou?" Our spatial Web image index can then be applied for a variety of interesting applications such as searching for images along a route, extending personal photo collections, or illustrating and enhancing search results.

The paper is structured as follows. We present the related work in Section 2. Section 3 introduces the reader to our spatial search engine. In Section 4, we present our location-based image search approach. We evaluate and discuss our results in Section 5 and conclude the paper in Section 6 and give a perspective on ongoing work.

2   Related Work

One of the related fields is the *extraction of geographic meaning from unstructured Web pages* (Web-Geo-IR). An comprehensive overview of the state-of-the-art in this large field is presented in [8]. Central challenges in the field are the identification of geographical entities as described in [14] and [15] and the use of geographic features within a Web crawler as, e.g., discussed in [6]. The basis for our spatial Web image search is a spatial search engine we developed that employs geographically focused Web crawling and database-backed geoparsing to spatially index Web pages as presented in [2,1].

Related approaches for *Web image classification* can be grouped by their source of information, i.e., as HTML code and structure and Web image content. As an example for solely using the HTML code, [22] examines the attributes of the image tag, surrounding paragraph and title of the page. Aiming to understand and derive roles of Web images, [13] uses features taken from structural document data and image metadata but not from actual image content. Analysing HTML structure, [7] segments Web pages into semantic blocks whose semantics are inherited by embedded images. An early work [5] uses the HTML content and a few selected image content features for Web image search. Building upon this work, [3] developed a classifier for photographs against graphics using decision trees. The most recent work presents iFind [9], which considers context and content of images and examines their layout on a page for semantic annotation. A comprehensive discussion of existing technologies in Web image retrieval and how they address key issues in the field can be found in [11].

Considering the large field of *content-based image retrieval*, a good overview of the existing work, the state-of-the-art and challenges in the field can be found in [20] and [12]. Even though Web image analysis is not the explicit focus of many of these works, it became clear in the field of content-based retrieval that results in image understanding can only be advanced by looking at both the content and external sources of information.

Regarding the connection of location and Web images, some work has been done on deriving location by using only image content analysis for known locations. IDeixis [21] is an approach to compare pictures taken by a mobile device to previously taken photos to initiate a search. Work about inferring semantics by multimodal analysis of images and their spatial and temporal properties was done by, e.g., our group in [19]. On the way to location-aware images, Web 2.0 services that allow organizing and sharing personal photo collections provide for an assignment of location-related information by manual tagging and annotation. Often, user-chosen tags include names of locations or places. Some services such as Mappr (mappr.com), Flickr (flickr.com) or Placeopedia (placeopedia.com) even allow for assigning items a definite coordinate on a map and thus manually geocode the content. Content from existing directories such as yellow pages is mapped by services such as Yahoo! Maps (maps.yahoo.com) or MSN Live (maps.live.com), enabling map-based spatial search. Recently, Google Maps (maps.google.com) has allowed business owners to enhance entries with images of their business, clearly emphasizing the demand for accompanying images to location information.

Modern cameras with an integrated GPS-receiver can directly embed coordinated in a photo's EXIF metadata. However, such geo-located images are rare in the first place even in large photo collections and are even rarer in a general Web context, partly due to loss of information in editing processes. Regarding loss of metadata, [16] presents a system that captures metadata at media capture time and preserves it over the production process in a professional environment, but which ios not suitable for common use.

Unfortunately, tagged media collections or prepared geocoded images cover only a very small fraction of images on Web pages; many others still reside unrecognised in the World Wide Web. The remaining open issue is that explicit location information for Web pages and their images is given only for a small fraction of the Web which leaves a large number of potentially geographically-related images on Web pages as yet unrecognised for spatial search. We therefore need other methods of location assessment and additional sources of data for geo-referencing Web images.

3   Geospatial Search

Most current search engines are very efficient for keyword-based queries. Spatial search, i.e., querying for Web pages related to a certain location is starting to gain momentum. Services operating on prepared geo-referenced data receive widespread attention. This is consistent with the high relevance of location to the user. A study in 2004 [18] finds that as much as 20% of user's Web queries have a geographic relation while [10] estimates this at 5-15% for search on mobile devices. Web pages with location-related information represent an estimate of 10-20% of all Web pages. This makes their relation to a physical location a yet widely unused asset. A spatial Web search engine can discover and process this information for an interesting set of location-based applications.

For our own spatial Web search engine presented in [2], we use common Web crawler and indexing technology and extended it with our own location specific components. Our spatial crawler and indexer identify Web pages that promise a relation to a physical location, extract the desired information, and assign a geo-reference to the pages. They are designed to exploit the location information of a Web page that is not explicitly contained as metadata or structured annotation but is rather an implicit part of the textual content. Based on our research in mobile pedestrian applications [4], we tailor our search to a pedestrian user who needs precise geo-references at the level of individual buildings.

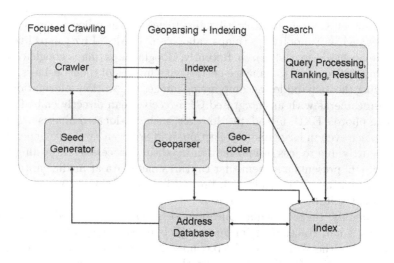

Fig. 1. Architecture of our spatial search engine

The architecture detailed in Figure 1 comprises the main components of our spatial Web search engine prototype, separated into function groups of crawling, indexing, and search. To enable an efficient geographically focused crawling, a seed generator feeds seed URLs that have a strong relationship to the desired physical location—such as, e.g., municipal sites—to enable the crawler to start with relevant pages. The crawler hands the pages found over to the indexer. Besides the common analysis of the textual Web content, a geoparser processes the page to extract geographic information. The extraction process is supported by an address database for enhanced accuracy. The key aspect of focused crawling is a feedback loop based on a page classifier to guide the crawler towards pages with the desired topic. Thus, the geoparser results are fed back to the crawler. Discovered location-related information is geo-coded, i.e., the hierarchical textual description is mapped to a coordinate. Along with the actual address and the URL it is inserted into a spatial index. The index of our search engine can then be used for a keyword-based search now extended by spatial search capability.

4   Web Image Location-Detection

While today an interesting set of semantics can be derived from image content, geographic location is usually not part of it. Apart from well-known geographic landmarks or existing annotations Web images cannot be processed by current techniques to assess and pinpoint an actual location.

The goal of our spatial Web image search is to be able to automatically illustrate locations with relevant images of their surroundings and for a given place to answer questions like "What does this place look like?" or "What is a representative image of this place?". We aim at a general approach to derive the location for those images that are contained in Web pages with an established spatial context. The mutual relation of a Web pages' text, its contained images, and accociated metadata is a main aspect of this method: The page's spatial semantics are extended to the embedded images which then will, to a certain degree and depending on detected features, inherit the location of the page.

Fig. 2. Images and location on a sample Web page

As one example of our approach, consider the Web page of a public library in Germany as shown in Figure 2. The page features various images – surrounded by dashed lines – with the one in the center prominently displaying the library building. Its address is present to the right of the image and its name and city in some of the metadata such as keyword and title. For a location-based image search, only this photograph should be retrieved since it is descriptive of the location.

4.1   Architecture of the Location Assessment

For the identification of a possible location-relation of images from Web pages, we propose a method and architecture for image location assessment. Using only the Web page data is not sufficient as only preliminary conclusions can be drawn about the image content. Thus, this has to be taken into account as well. The main logical components are two classifiers for photographs and for location relevance, respectively. These are arranged as weighted filter chains and utilize various criteria taken from the HTML content and metadata, the metadata of embedded images, image content, and the address previously found. The general process is outlined in Figure 3. Input is a Web page with a known location from, e.g., our spatial search. All images are extracted, downloaded and processed by a photograph classification, followed by a location assessment. Image and Web page are examined for hints towards a location reference, which are weighted and summarised. If a location can be reliably assigned, the process results in a geo-coded image. In the following we describe the two classifications.

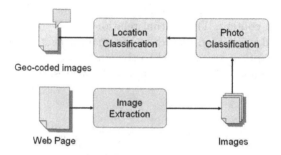

Fig. 3. Process of the location assessment

Photograph classification. Today, images on Web pages are used for different reasons. Distinguishing their different roles supports filtering certain images by their roles. A large group of images are those that serve an *illustrative* purpose: photographs, diagrams, graphics, sketches, titlebars, logos. Other images may serve as *formatting objects*, represent *advertisements* or are used for *user tracking*. Of these roles, we are interested in *photographs* being the main bearers of visual location information. Such photographs serve illustrative purposes; page authors use them with this in mind, and they clearly depict objects or scenery that is in most cases related to the text they accompany. This corresponds to the results of our initial surveys and probings. Therefore, we developed methods to identify images with a high probability to be a photograph of a place, drawing from low-level image features. While each of these features are inconclusive, in combination they yield satisfying results.

- *Image size and image ratio* is used to remove small formatting images as well as illustrative images that lack sufficient size or that have an unusual ratio such as banners etc.

- *Color count and histogram analysis* is used to distinguish photographs from illustrations, drawings or logos. Black & white images are detected to be treated with different thresholds.
- *Animation or transparency* in images usually indicates non-photographs.
- *EXIF-data* in JPG files is examined. Specific metadata such as camera type, focal length, flash usage etc. is considered strong evidence that an image was taken by a digital camera and is thus a photograph.
- *Vertical edges* in above-average quantity can indicate photographs of a place showing buildings, pieces of architecture or trees. For our purposes, a modified Sobel process operating on greyscaled images for edge detection worked best for urban buildings but is inconclusive for rural scenery.
- *Face detection* is used to distinguish mere snapshots of people at a location from images truly depicting the location itself since we found the number of such snapshots quite high.

Location-relevance classification. An image related to a location will exhibit certain characteristics which we exploit to create a set of measurements of how well the location of a Web page can be inherited by the images embedded in it. To establish a relation of a photograph and the location referenced on the Web page, we rely on content and structure of the page in question. From the photograph classification, we know all photographs on the page; from our spatial search engine, we know the geographic location of a Web page as a full address including street, number, zip code, city name and also geo-coordinate.

However, we assume this location reference may not necessarily stand for the entire page, it may rather determine a location for only a part of the page. We assume a decreasing relevance by increasing distance of the address and the image on the basis of a DOM-tree representation of the page. An image in the vicinity of an address has a higher probability for location relevance than one further away; if we can identify a page as generally dealing with the location, the probability also increases.

For the implementation of the location-relevance classification, we consider the distance of the image to each address on the page and the matching of image descriptors and key elements on the page to parts of the address. We use an in-page location keyword search. We interpret the given address as a small subsection of a geographic thesaurus. This allows for generalization of an address by traversing its hierarchy for keywords. We can broaden the search from full street address to only city or region. An address such as *"Escherweg 2, 26121 Oldenburg"* could be matched in decreasing levels of relevance as *"Escherweg, Oldenburg"* or *"Oldenburg"* alone. This truncation matching is already useful for searching the page, but absolutely necessary for searching features such as metatags, page title, or image attributes. They are very unlikely to contain full addresses, but will often contain at least the city name. Matches of this search are rated by the amount of matched keywords and—where applicable—the distance from the image based on the DOM-representation of the document. The process would repeat for each location associated to a Web page.

The examined image tag attributes are *alt*, *title*, and *name*. These descriptive fields for an image may contain descriptions of the image contents and are therefore highly relevant as well as the *src* attribute for meaningful image or path names. The page's metatag fields *description*, *keywords* and Dublin Core *DC.Subject*, *DC.Description* as well as page title can hint that the page as a whole is concerned with the location and therefore the parts on it get a higher rating. Other well-known tags such as dc.coverage, geo.location or icbm coordinates were not encountered during our crawls and were therefore not included at this time.

4.2   Combining Features for Location Assessment

The process in Figure 3 depicts two logical blocks for location assessment, photograph classification and location classification, each realised by an analysis chain. Inside each chain, several modules evaluate the aforementioned features and calculate a score for the assessed image.

The assessment chains are defined as follows: Let n be the number of evaluation modules in the chain. Each module $evaluation_i$ is assigned a weight w_i to express its relevance relative to other modules and allow for easy parameterization and tuning. The relevance score for an image img is calculated by summing up the evaluation scores for each feature:

$$relevance(img)_{chain} = \sum_{i=1}^{n} w_i \; evaluation_i(img) \qquad (1)$$

For each chain, the final relevance score of an image is compared to an empirically determined threshold $threshold_{chain}$ to decide whether it is in or out of scope.

$$pass(img)_{chain} = \begin{cases} 1 & threshold_{chain} \leq relevance(img)_{chain} \\ 0 & otherwise \end{cases} \qquad (2)$$

Having defined the general evaluation chains, we install two actual chains *photo* and *location* for photograph detection and location assessment respectively. An image is classified as location-relevant if it passes both chains; its overall location score is given as $relevance(img)_{location}$ and the relation between image and location is established.

5   Evaluation

To evaluate our approach, we performed a crawl of Rügen, Germany's largest island and a famous tourist area, and of the city of Oldenburg, Germany. The resulting testset comprises Web pages along with the addresses that were identified on them. In the following, we discuss the results of the crawl of Rügen only as the second crawl of the city of Oldenburg delivered quite similar results. We show the performance of photograph classification on a smaller testset and then present the location classification in a second step.

5.1   Evaluation of Photograph Classification

To create a small testset for the photograph classification we used a random sampling from our spatial index of 100 Web pages with an identified location relevance. Out of these, 78 pages could be used as 22 pages remained unreachable or had parsing problems. Within the remaining pages, we found 1580 images. Our photograph classification resulted in 86 images classified as photographs. Visual inspection of these images revealed that 69 were classified correctly. The remaining 17 images were misclassified graphics which still showed some of the relevant photographic features. 1538 images were classified as non-photographs and mainly comprised decorative items of Web pages. We also went through a visual inspection of these images and identified 1511 as classified correctly. The 27 falsely classified photographs contained only few colors or had untypical sizes or ratios such that their score fell beyond the threshold. The fact that we only found very few photographs is not surprising, as on the Web nowadays most images are used for decorative purposes. Within this small testset, the achieved values for $precision \approx 0,80$ and $recall \approx 0,72$ are promising.

5.2   Evaluation of Location Classification

To draw meaningful conclusions for the location assessment, we enlarged the testset to 1000 pages. Of these, 857 pages could be examined. A glance on the resulting photographs confirmed a similar performance as before, but was not manually assessed. A resulting 618 combinations of photos with locations were analysed. The ratings are depicted in Figure 4 as well as one sample image with a score of 13. An accumulation of images at the lower end of the scale around 4 can be observed. Since an address was present on the page, some evaluators such as city name matching generate a low initial score. But only with the combination of several well-matching criteria an image's score raises sufficiently to reach a high ranking above the determined threshold of 6 in our system. Manual inspection shows that indeed this group contains highly relevant images while low-rated images have mostly no discernible location associated.

Of the 74 images classified as having a location relevance we found 55 classified correctly and 19 with dubious or false results. Of the 544 images classified without location relevance, we have no exact values for the ratio of wrong classification. However, scanning these images seems to confirm that most of them are correctly classified; we estimate recall at above 0.7 and can calculate $precision \approx 0,74$. Examples of the images retrieved by our system are shown in Fig. 5. We find some well-related images *a-d*, some even from the interior of buildings, especially for holiday homes. However, we also return some false positives and mismatches. Images *e* and *g* depict a location, but the connection to the found location is uncertain. For *g* we can assume that it is just a general landscape of the island. Some uncertainties could only be solved by in-depth linguistic analysis of the pages, some are unsolvable even by a human user. Clearly mis-classified is the illustrative graphic *f*. The sketch of a chapel *h* shows good location relevance but is not a photo. It shows an interesting capability of our system: The major part of images falsely

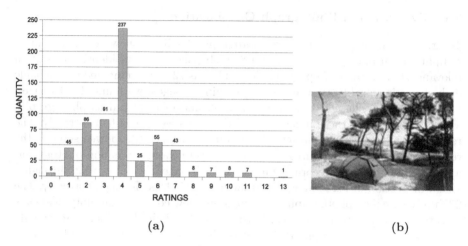

(a)   (b)

Fig. 4. (a) Distribution of location ratings (b) Example of the top-rated image

Fig. 5. Retrieved images, sample true positives (a–d) and false positives (e–h)

classified as photographs were rated lower for location relevance than true photographs. Apparently the location classification compensates for some errors in the photograph detection.

6   Conclusion

In this paper, we presented an approach to automatically geo-reference images embedded in Web pages on the address level. Based on our work on location-based Web search, we presented our method to reliably determine photographs on Web pages and the heuristics to determine if the location of the Web page can be reliably assigned to the photograph. We could show that a combined analysis of content and context is feasible for this task. Automatic location detection of images on unstructured Web pages now allows images to become part of the results of a spatial Web image search without previous manual tagging.

The initial results of our experiments are promising and show that we can achieve a precision for the location classification of about 0.74 with an estimated recall of 0.7. As the discussion of the evaluation revealed, it remains challenging to determine if a photo carries a location-relation. Still, the results and our chosen features show that context analysis for images alone is not sufficient but in combination with basic image content analysis we can reliably detect location-bearing photographs. In our ongoing work we will refine the parameters of the heuristics, analyse in more detail to what extent the filters each influence the results and how this can be exploited in more sophisticated classification by, e.g., decision trees and the use of more features for the classification. We will further increase the quality of our Web image location search.

Acknowledgements

We thank Jörg Baldzer and Norbert Rump for their work on the search engine project as well as our students Sebastian Stockfleth, Timo Scheffler, and Dorothea Eggers. Part of this research has been carried out as subproject of the Niccimon project [17] and was supported by the State of Lower Saxony, Germany.

References

1. Ahlers, D., Boll, S.: Geospatially Focused Web Crawling. Datenbankspektrum, Special Issue Focused Search (Fokussierte Suche) (2007)
2. Ahlers, D., Boll, S.: Location-based Web search. In: Scharl, A., Tochtermann, K. (eds.) The Geospatial Web, Springer, London (2007)
3. Athitsos, V., Swain, M.J., Frankel, C.: Distinguishing photographs and graphics on the World Wide Web. In: CAIVL 1997: Proceedings of the 1997 Workshop on Content-Based Access of Image and Video Libraries, p. 10. IEEE Computer Society, Los Alamitos (1997)
4. Baldzer, J., Boll, S., Klante, P., Krösche, J., Meyer, J., Rump, N., Scherp, A., Appelrath, H.-J.: Location-Aware Mobile Multimedia Applications on the Niccimon Platform. In: IMA 2004 (2004)
5. Frankel, C., Swain, M.J., Athitsos, V.: WebSeer: An Image Search Engine for the World Wide Web. Technical report, Chicago, IL, USA (1996)
6. Gao, W., Lee, H.C., Miao, Y.: Geographically focused collaborative crawling. In: WWW 2006: Proc. of the 15th Intl. Conf. on World Wide Web, pp. 287–296. ACM Press, New York (2006)
7. Gong, Z., U, L.H., Cheang, C.W.: Web image semantic clustering. In: Meersman, R., Tari, Z. (eds.) On the Move to Meaningful Internet Systems 2005: CoopIS, DOA, and ODBASE. LNCS, vol. 3761, pp. 1416–1431. Springer, Heidelberg (2005)
8. Gräf, J., Henrich, A., Lüdecke, V., Schlieder, C.: Geografisches Information Retrieval. Datenbank-Spektrum 6(18), 48–56 (2006)
9. He, X., Caia, D., Wen, J.-R., Ma, W.-Y., Zhang, H.-J.: Clustering and searching WWW images using link and page layout analysis. ACM Trans. on Multimedia Comput. Commun. Appl. 3 (2007)

10. Kamvar, M., Baluja, S.: A large scale study of wireless search behavior: Google mobile search. In: CHI '06: Proc. of the SIGCHI conf. on Human Factors in computing systems, pp. 701–709. ACM Press, New York (2006)

11. Kherfi, M.L., Ziou, D., Bernardi, A.: Image retrieval from the world wide web: Issues, techniques, and systems. ACM Comput. Surv. 36(1), 35–67 (2004)

12. Lew, M.S., Sebe, N., Djeraba, C., Jain, R.: Content-based multimedia information retrieval: State of the art and challenges. ACM Trans. Multimedia Comput. Commun. Appl. 2(1), 1–19 (2006)

13. Maekawa, T., Hara, T., Nishio, S.: Image classification for mobile web browsing. In: WWW 2006: Proc.of the 15th Intl. Conf. on World Wide Web, pp. 43–52. ACM Press, New York (2006)

14. Markowetz, A., Chen, Y.-Y., Suel, T., Long, X., Seeger, B.: Design and implementation of a geographic search engine. In: WebDB 2005, Baltimore (2005)

15. McCurley, K.S.: Geospatial mapping and navigation of the web. In: WWW 2001: Proc. of the 10th Intl. Conf. on World Wide Web, pp. 221–229. ACM Press, New York (2001)

16. Nack, F., Putz, W.: Designing annotation before it's needed. In: MULTIMEDIA 2001: Proceedings of the ninth ACM international conference on Multimedia, pp. 251–260. ACM Press, New York (2001)

17. Niccimon. Competence center of lower saxony for information system for mobile usage (2006), http://www.niccimon.de/.

18. Sanderson, M., Kohler, J.: Analyzing geographic queries. In: Workshop on Geographic Information Retrieval SIGIR (2004)

19. Sandhaus, P., Scherp, A., Thieme, S., Boll, S.: Metaxa – context- and content-driven metadata enhancement for personal photo albums. Multimedia Modeling 2007, Singapore (2007)

20. Smeulders, A.W.M., Worring, M., Santini, S., Gupta, A., Jain, R.: Content-based image retrieval at the end of the early years. IEEE Trans. Pattern Anal. Mach. Intell. 22(12), 1349–1380 (2000)

21. Tollmar, K., Yeh, T., Darrell, T.: Ideixis - image-based deixis for finding location-based information. In: MobileHCI (2004)

22. Tsymbalenko, Y., Munson, E.V.: Using HTML Metadata to Find Relevant Images on the World Wide Web. In: Proceedings of Internet Computing 2001, Las Vegas, vol. 2, pp. 842–848. CSREA Press (2001)

Complementary Variance Energy for Fingerprint Segmentation

Z. Hou[1], W.Y. Yau[1,2], N.L. Than[2], and W. Tang[2]

[1] Institute for Infocomm Research, Singapore 119613
[2] School of EEE, Nanyang Tech. Univ., Singapore 639798

Abstract. The paper presents a method for fingerprint segmentation, which executes in two phases. The enrolled image is partitioned into block by block and a preliminary segmentation is firstly carried out based on thresholding the blockwise variance. Afterwhich, the segmentation result is refined by energy information, where the blocks with the most "reliable" energy are selected to polish the preliminary result and yield the final segmentation map. Reliability of the method has been demonstrated using NIST and FVC data sets. Comparison with other methods is presented.

1 Introduction

Fingerprint segmentation in this paper refers to the segmentation of region where image contents are dominated by fingerprint structures. In literature, this term sometimes means the separation between ridges and valleys in the fingerprint region. However, it is more often to name the latter process as binarization.

In an automatic fingerprint identification system (AFIS), the stage of segmentation helps to reduce the perturbation of background on feature detection and facilitates the computation of subsequent processes. Many techniques have been presented [1-13] to address the issue.In general, to segment the fingerprint region from the background region, one needs to derive a feature which well characterizes the oriented pattern of the fingerprint structure. Frequently used features include mean, variance, contrast, eccentric moment, coherence, energy and x-signature statistics. It has been a trend to combine multiple feature values for fingerprint segmentation. After deriving the feature value/vector, the foreground can be segmented from the background using a classification method from the simple thresholding technique to more sophisticated ones.

Though many feature descriptors have been investigated, the strength and the weakness of a feature in characterizing the fingerprint structure as well as its relation to other features remains obscure. What is the more effective way to combine the individual features to yield a more efficient feature presentation? This is also a common problem for many other computer vision applications. Through our study, it was found that thresholding techniques like the Otsu method [14], or unsupervised clustering methods like k-means clustering [15], are not sufficient to produce a reliable solution under different circumstances.

S. Satoh, F. Nack, and M. Etoh (Eds.): MMM 2008, LNCS 4903, pp. 113–122, 2008.

More complicated classification methods may lead to more accurate results, but they often require a training stage, which limits their wide applications.

From the pratical point of view, it would be desirable for a method to be able to perform reliably for different sensors and for images with varying qualities. To that end, one can take into account the spatial relationship modeling in the process of fingerprint segmentation and apply more powerful segmentation methods such as random field modeling or active contour. However, real-time performance is critical for most AFISs. Also, the texture nature of the fingerprint structure imposes difficulty on spatial modeling.

In this paper, a novel technique is presented to reliably segment fingerprint images, which fuses information between variance and energy, takeing into consideration the spatial modeling without increasing much the computation load. The method is described in Section 2. Experiments and comparisons are presented in Section 3. Finally, the paper concludes in Section 4.

2   Method

The proposed method basically consists of two phases: preliminary segmentation and refined segmentation, where the former phase provides a preliminary foreground which is based on blockwise variance information and is often under-segmented. Then, starting from an over-segmented foreground based on the energy distribution, the latter phase refines the preliminary segmentation and derives the final segmentation map which would locate between these two ends. The detail is described in the following.

2.1   Preliminary Segmentation Based on Variance

Segmentation is usually application dependent. For AFIS, it often suffices to segment the fingerprint image in a coarse level. Thus, similar to most other techniques, the enrolled fingerprint image is partitioned into $w \times w$ blocks and the segmentation process is implemented in this coarse representation.

Firstly the image is segmented preliminarily using the variance information according to the following steps.

1. normalization The image is normalized to have mean value of 0 and standard deviation of 1. Let denote the intensity of image $\mathcal{F}$ at position x by $f(x)$, the mean and variance of image $\mathcal{F}$ by $\mu(\mathcal{F})$ and $D(\mathcal{F})$ respectively. Then the normalized image $\mathcal{G}$ is derived by

$$g(x) = \mu(\mathcal{F}) + \text{sgn}(f(x) - \mu(\mathcal{F}))\sqrt{\frac{(f(x) - \mu(\mathcal{F}))^2}{D(\mathcal{F})}}, \qquad (1)$$

where $g(x)$ denotes the intensity of the normalized image at x.
2. thresholding Global thresholding is applied to the variance of each block. A block will be labeled as background if its variance is lower than a prefixed threshold, T_{var}; otherwise, it will be a candidate block in foreground.

3. post-processing Morphological operations are employed to remove isolated small regions and result in continuous foreground. Connected component analysis is utilized to select the largest component as the preliminary segmentation map.

Fig. 1. Sample fingerprint images segmented by variance information alone: the result is reasonable for good quality image (upper) and under-segmented for poor quality one (bottom)

Due to the periodic occurrence of valley and ridge in the fingerprint region, it is reasonable to expect a large variance for a block with fingerprint structures present. However, it is also highly possible for a background block with high level of noise to be classified as foreground through this strategy since variance does not consider the spatial distribution of the intensity. Therefore, variance-based segmentation could deliver good results for images with reasonable quality, but tends to under-segment the foreground for images with quite noisy background. Fig. 1 illustrates the effects by two examples, where the first image (top left) is of good quality and the segmentation result (top right) is quite reasonable. But for the second image (bottom left), the quality is evidently degraded which may be due to the dirtyness of the sensor platen. The background region even contains fingerprint structure which might be impressed in the sensor platen in the previous scanning process. As a result, the image is clearly under-segmented (bottom right).

2.2 Segmentation Refined by Energy Information

To handle the under-segmentation problem, we resort to the energy information. In particular, blocks with most "reliable" energies are selected to refine the above preliminary solution. The processing steps are as follows.

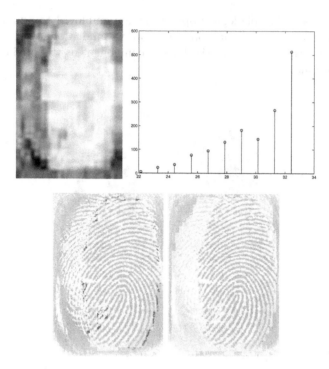

Fig. 2. Upper left is the energy image of the second sample image in Fig. 1 (Row 2 Left), and on the upper right shows the histogram of the energy image. In the bottom, the segmented image using threshold e_{th} is shown on the left, and the variance based result is shown on the right for reference.

1. **Energy computation.** The energy in a block is computed using the logarithm transform of the mean square of Fourier transform coefficients, where the log-transform is exploited to supress the large dynamic range of the Fourier spectra. To reduce the impact of noise, the image is smoothed using the directional filtering technique as frequently used in fingerprint image enhancement [3,12] where the filter consists of a separable low-pass filter in ridge direction and a band-pass filter in orthorgonal direction. Let e_i denote the energy at block i. Fig. 2 (upper left) shows the energy images of the noisy image in Fig. 1, where the histogram of the energy image is also presented on the upper right. From this figure, one can observe three points: (1) the energy response correlates closely with the fingerprint structures; (2) the energy response detects regular structures in the background as well; (3) the energy response is sensitive to the quality of the structure. Thus, how to mine the information from the energy response is a problem. In general, we do not favor an "optimal" solution from a conventional classifier, since in practice the class (particularly the background class) is highly possibly insufficiently sampled, or the class distribution is away from the theorectical

assumption, or the boundary between the foreground and the background in feature space could be not well defined, leading to bias from the theoretical solution. In the following, an alternative solution is presented, which is not optimal, but can be demonstrated to be stable and reliable.

2. **Energy selection.** The histogram of energy is computed and the *dominant component* located on the right side is identified, which corresponds to the most reliable structures from the energy response. Within the preliminary foreground as detected above, the foreground block whose energy falls in this component is preserved; otherwise, it will be relabeled as background. Suppose that the energy range is partitioned into L bins, and denote half of the bin width as Δ_e. Then the foreground component is identified as follows. In the energy histogram, the peak is firstly selected from energy $e_{(L/2)}$ to $e_{(L)}$, where $e_{(L)}$ corresponds to the energy of the Lth bin. For convenience, let denote the corresponding energy value as e^*. Then, the energy threshold is determined by

$$e_{th} = e^* - n_e \Delta_e, \tag{2}$$

where n_e is a parameter whose value depends on the background noise level. The foreground region will then be those blocks with energy value greater than e_{th}.

On the bottom left of Fig. 2 shows the segmented result using threhsold e_{th}. For reference, the variance based result is shown on the bottom right. It can be seen that the energy thresholded result is quite reasonable. The background structure is largely differentiated. Some falsely detected background or missing foreground can easily be resolved using the reference segmentation map as detected by variance.

3. **Post-processing.** Isolated blocks are removed and gaps between the foreground blocks are filled to yield the final continuous segmentation map.

Fig. 3. Segmentation results for the sample images in Fig. 1 after refining by energy information: the previously reasonable result for good quality image (left) is preserved, but the under-segmented result is much improved for the poor quality one (right)

Fig. 3 shows the results for the images in Fig. 1 after refining segmentation by energy information. It can be noted that for the good quality image the reasonable result in the preliminary segmentation map is well preserved, whereas the under-segmented noisy image is substantially improved.

3   Results and Discussion

To evaluate the performance of the proposed complementary variance energy (CVE) method, the following data sets have used for testing: fingerprint verification competition (FVC) data sets (2000, 2002 and 2004) (http://bias.csr.unibo.it), NIST special database 4 (http://www.nist.gov/srd/nistsd4.htm), which contains in total more than 10000 fingerprint images acquired using various sensors or synthetic methods with a wide variety of qualities. The parameters are set as follows: 8×8 windows, $T_{var} = 0.25$ for variance thresholding, $L = 10$ bins and $n_e = 3$ in energy thresholding.

The method has been compared with a Gabor filter (Gabor) method [16], which takes as the feature the standard deviation of a set of oriented Gabor filters. In order to see the effect of the information fusion between variance and energy in the presented method, another fusion method is also implemented for comparison, which takes the blockwise variance and energy as the input for k-means clustering (VE-k).

Fig. 4 shows two examples segmented by CVE (Column 2), Gabor (Column 3) and VE-k respectively. The first example presents high noise in the background, but the contrast with respect to the fingerprint region is pretty clear. Both the CVE and the VE-k result are satisfactory and the Gabor result is slightly over-segmented. As for the second example, the fingerprint structure is of poor quality, possibly due to wetness of the enrolled finger. The contrast between the ridge and the valley is not always visible. The Gabor method only detects a few isolated small blocks, some of which come from the background. The VE-k

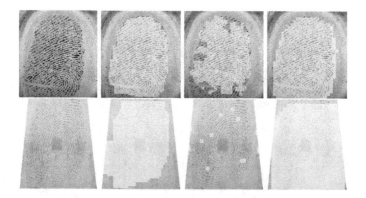

Fig. 4. A qualitative comparison among the three methods for some images, where from left to right are the original image, the CVE result, the Gabor result and the VE-k result

Table 1. Summary of the four manually segmented FVC data sets

	sensor	size / resolution
2000db2	low-cost capacitive sensor	256×364 / 500dpi
2000db3	optical sensor	448×478 / 500dpi
2004db2	optical sensor	328×364 / 500dpi
2004db3	thermal sweeping sensor	300×480 / 512dpi

result is obviously under-segmented. Comparatively, the CVE solution is slightly under-segmented, but quite reasonable.

To quantitatively compare the performance of different methods, we have manually segmented four data sets as summarized in Table 1. The following three error rates are computed to measure the accuracy:

– false negative segmentation error

$$\epsilon_{fn} = \frac{N_{fn}}{N_{FG}}, \tag{3}$$

where N_{fn} stands for the number of pixels that are foreground pixels but classified as background ones, and N_{FG} the number of foreground pixels in the manually segmented map.

– false positive segmentation error

$$\epsilon_{fp} = \frac{N_{fp}}{N_{BG}}, \tag{4}$$

where N_{fp} means the number of pixels that are background pixels but classified as foreground ones, and N_{BG} the number of background pixels in the manually segmented map.

– total segmentation error

$$\epsilon_{total} = \frac{N_{fn} + N_{fp}}{N_{BG} + N_{FG}}. \tag{5}$$

The results are given in Table 2. The proposed CVE method achieves minimal total segmentation error rate for all the data sets, illustrating the robustness and reliability of the proposed method. If the error rate is broken down into false negative (FN) error and false positive (FP) error, it can be noted that the VE-k method tends to have larger FP error, and the Gabor method results in larger FP for two data sets (FVC2000Db2 and FVC2004Db3). The FP error for these two data sets by the CVE method is smaller but still quite large (around 10%). In general, the requirement on error control is application dependent. For medical applications, the FN error could lead to the loss of a life. For fingerprint segmentation, although it would be ideal to have segmentation as accurate as possible, we argue that the FP error is more sever than the FN error because the former could introduce many false responses during feature detection near the boundaries. From this point, it would be desirable for future development to achieve small errors in the sense of both the total and the FP error.

As discussed in Section 2, the CVE solution would locate between a under-segmented map by the variance information and an over-segmented map by the energy information. Thus, in order to reduce the FP error, one can either increase the value of the parameter T_{var} to have a less under-segmented map, or decrease the value of the parameter n_e to have a more over-segmented map. As an example, Table 3 list the segmentation error rates for the CVE method to test on FVC2004Db3 when $n_e = 3, 2, 0$. One can see that the FP error decreases with respect to the decreasing of n_e, but the FN error increases at the same time.

Table 2. Segmentation error rates on FVC data sets by different methods

method	data set	ϵ_{fn}	ϵ_{fp}	ϵ_{total}
CVE	2000Db2	0.053	0.086	0.061
	Db3	0.046	0.056	0.046
	2004Db2	0.044	0.047	0.044
	Db3	0.012	0.119	0.053
Gabor	2000Db2	0.092	0.126	0.102
	Db3	0.116	0.052	0.086
	2004Db2	0.276	0.053	0.176
	Db3	0.013	0.176	0.074
VE-k	2000Db2	0.108	0.212	0.135
	Db3	0.024	0.134	0.070
	2004Db2	0.041	0.407	0.189
	Db3	0.022	0.238	0.112

Table 3. The segmentation error rates of the proposed method on the FVC2004Db3 under different n_e

n_e	ϵ_{fn}	ϵ_{fp}	ϵ_{total}
3	0.012	0.119	0.053
2	0.014	0.110	0.051
0	0.079	0.058	0.075

Before ending this section, we would like to point out the limitation of the proposed method. When the enrolled fingerprint image has very weak signal response in some fingerprint region, neither the variance information nor the energy information is sufficient for detection, resulting in the FN error. An example is shown in Fig. 5 (upper). Another issue is that fingerprint images often suffer from localized contamination, which are usually in-homogeneous in fingerprint region. As exemplified in Fig. 2, the energy information is sensitive to the quality of the image structure. Hence the energy information could miss some authentic fingerprint structure due to in-homogeneity, particularly when the structure is located near the boundary of the fingerprint region. Fig. 5 (bottom) gives an

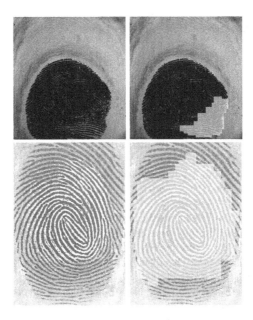

Fig. 5. This example shows the limitation of the proposed method, which tends to over-segment the fingerprint region when the signal response of the fingerprint structure is weak or markedly in-homogeneous

example, where the central portion of the fingerprint is evidently brighter than the periphery region and in the segmented image some useful structures are missing. This kind of error might be reduced through a mechanism that is adaptive to the local data quality.

4   Conclusion

In summary, this paper presents an approach to fingerprint segmentation, which executes in two phases. Firstly, a preliminarily segmented image is obtained using variance information. Then the result is refined based on "most" reliable energy information. The proposed method is advantageous in providing a mechanism to tradeoff the FP and the FN error and result in robust performance for images with different qualities acquired using various sensors. The method has been validated using more than 10000 fingerprint images and compared qualitatively and quantitatively with other methods. The experiments show that the proposed method is able to achieve more accurate results with more reliable performance. Implemented in Matlab and running in a PC with CPU of 3GHZ, the method takes about 1.5 seconds for an image of size 448×478.

It is noted that the error control design in the present study is quite straightforward and can be improved in two ways: (1) to select a feature or a feature vector which is more sensitive to the fingerprint structure to derive an "over-segmented" image; (2) to design more intelligent rules for the segmentation process to walk between the "under-segmented" and the "over-segmented" image.

References

1. Mehtre, B.M., Murthy, N.N., Kapoor, S., Chatterjee, B.: Segmentation of fingerprint images using the directional image. Pattern Recognition 20, 429–435 (1987)
2. Mehtre, B.M., Chatterjee, B.: Segmentation of fingerprint images: a composite method. Pattern Recognition 22, 381–385 (1989)
3. Hong, L., Wang, Y., Jain, A.K.: Fingerprint image enhancement: algorithm and performance evaluation. IEEE Trans. Patt. Analysis and Mach. Intell. 20, 777–789 (1998)
4. Bazen, A.M., Gerez, S.H.: Segmentation of Fingerprint Images. In: Proceedings of Workshop on Circuits Systems and Signal Processing, pp. 276–280 (2001)
5. Klein, S., Bazen, A.M., Veldhuis, R.N.J.: Fingerprint image segmentation based on hidden Markov models. In: The 13th Annual Workshop on Circuits, Systems and Signal Processing, pp. 310–318 (2002)
6. Bernard, S., Boujemaa, N., Vitale, D., Bricor, C.: Fingerprint segmentation using the phase of multiscale Gabor waveletes. In: The 5th Asian Conference on Computer Vision, Melbourne, Australia (2002)
7. Liu, Q., Yan, P.L., Zou, H., Xia, D.L.: Effective gradual segmentation algorithm for fingerprint image. Computer Applications 23, 81–83 (2002)
8. Sato, S., Umezaki, T.: A fingerprint segmentation method using a recurrent neural network. In: Proceedings of the 12th IEEE Workshop Neural Networks for Signal Processing, pp. 345–354 (2002)
9. Chen, X., Tian, J., Cheng, J., Yang, X.: Segmentation of fingerprint images using linear classifier. EURASIP Journal on Applied Signal Processing 4, 480–494 (2004)
10. Shi, Z., Wang, Y., Qi, J., Xu, K.: A new segmentation algorithm for low quality fingerprint image. In: The 3rd International Conference on Image and Graphics (2004)
11. Wang, S., Zhang, W., Wang, Y.: New features extraction and application in fingerprint segmentation. Acta Automatica Sinica 29, 622–626 (2004)
12. Chikkerur, S., Govindaraju, V., Cartwright, A.: Fingerprint image enhancement using STFT analysis. In: International Workshop on Pattern Recognition for Crime Prevention, Security and Surveillance, pp. 20–29 (2005)
13. Barreto Marques, A.C.P., Thome, A.C.G.: A neural network fingerprint segmentation method. In: The 5th International Conference on Hybrid Intelligent Systems (2005)
14. Otsu, N.: A threshold selection method from gray-level histograms. Man and Cybernetics 9, 62–66 (1979)
15. MacQueen, J.B.: Some Methods for classification and Analysis of Multivariate Observations. In: Proceedings of 5th Berkeley Symposium on Mathematical Statistics and Probability, Berkeley, vol. 1, pp. 281–297. University of California Press (1967)
16. Fernandez, F.A., Aguilar, J.F., Garcia, J.O.: An enhanced Gabor filter-based segmentation algorithm for fingerprint recognition systems. In: Proceedings of the 4th International Symposium on Image and Signal Processing and Analysis, pp. 239–244 (2005)

Similarity Search in Multimedia Time Series Data Using Amplitude-Level Features

Johannes Aßfalg, Hans-Peter Kriegel, Peer Kröger, Peter Kunath, Alexey Pryakhin, and Matthias Renz

Institute for Informatics, Ludwig-Maximilians-Universität München, Germany
{assfalg, kriegel, kroegerp, kunath, pryakhin, renz}@dbs.ifi.lmu.de

Abstract. Effective similarity search in multi-media time series such as video or audio sequences is important for content-based multi-media retrieval applications. We propose a framework that extracts a sequence of local features from large multi-media time series that reflect the characteristics of the complex structured time series more accurately than global features. In addition, we propose a set of suitable local features that can be derived by our framework. These features are scanned from a time series amplitude-levelwise and are called amplitude-level features. Our experimental evaluation shows that our method models the intuitive similarity of multi-media time series better than existing techniques.

1 Introduction

Time series data is a prevalent data type in multi-media applications such as video or audio content analysis. Videos are usually modeled as sequences of features extracted for each picture of the video stream. Analogously, audio content is also modeled as a series of features extracted continuously from the audio stream. Similarity search in such time series data is very important for multi-media applications such as query-by-humming, plagiarism detection, or content-based audio and video retrieval.

The challenge for similarity search in time series data is twofold. First, the adequate modeling of the intuitive similarity notion between time series is important for the accuracy of the search. For that purpose, several distance measures for time series have been defined recently, each of which works fine under specific assumptions and in different scenarios (e.g. the Euclidian distance or Dynamic Time Warping (DTW)). Most of them apply features comprising quantitative information of the time series. However, in particular for complex structured time series, features comprising quantitative information are often too susceptible to noise, outliers, and other interfering variables. Second, since time series are usually very large, containing several thousands of values per sequence, the comparison of two time series can be very expensive, particularly when using distance measures that require the access to the raw time series data (i.e. the entire sequence of time series values). For example, for a audio sequence we can derive 300 features per second. Thus, a 3 minute audio sequence is represented by a time series of length 54,000. Generally, shape-based similarity measures like the DTW are very expensive, and are usually not applicable for multi-media data.

In this paper, we propose a novel framework for shape-based similarity search on multi-media time series that addresses both mentioned problems. Our approach allows

S. Satoh, F. Nack, and M. Etoh (Eds.): MMM 2008, LNCS 4903, pp. 123–133, 2008.
© Springer-Verlag Berlin Heidelberg 2008

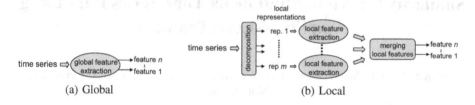

Fig. 1. Global vs. local feature extraction

to incorporate the relevant features that model qualitative characteristics of the time series and, thus, is able to represent the similarity of complex time series more accurately than recent approaches. In addition, the runtime complexity of our method is independent of the length of the time series which is important for very long multi-media time series. Figure 1 depicts our novel approach of local feature extraction (cf. Figure 1(b)) in comparison to the traditional global feature extraction strategies [1] (cf. Figure 1(a)). The traditional global approach extracts a set of n one-dimensional features representing the global characteristics of the time series. The resulting n features are used to build an n-dimensional feature vector and the Euclidean distance is used to measure the similarity between the derived features. In contrast, our approach is based on a decomposition of the complex structured time series into a reasonable set of more simple structured components which we call local representations. Then, we extract a set of local features of different types from these local representations. Subsequently, we merge the local features of each type into a feature vector. As a result, we obtain a set of n feature vectors. The main advantage of our strategy is that we dissect the complex feature extraction problem into a set of small subproblems which can be solved more easily. In order to reduce the complexity of the similarity measure based on the resulting features, we can subsequently compress the results using standard dimensionality reduction techniques. In this paper, we focus on one-dimensional time series. However, our approach can easily be adapted to the multi-dimensional case by extracting features for each dimension.

The rest of the paper is organized as follows. In Section 2, we survey related work. In Section 3, we present our feature extraction framework. A set of feature types reflecting the characteristics of time series in Section 4. Section 5 comprises the experimental results. The paper is concluded in Section 6.

2   Related Work

Modeling multimedia objects by time series. Recently, modeling multimedia data (e.g., audio streams, video sequences) as time series attracted more and more attention in the field of content-based multimedia object retrieval. In [2], a template matching method is presented. This approach measures similarity of videos by applying the time warping distance on sequences of low-level feature vectors. Another efficient scheme for video sequence matching was suggested in [3]. This method applies a time-series-based description of visual features from every video frame to capture the visual similarity w.r.t. the order of their appearance in the query video. The authors of [4] propose a clustering process and a weighted similarity measure between so-called key frames calculated for each shot in order to capture the dynamics of visual contents for matching. This keyframe based representation of a video can be viewed as a multi-dimensional time series in order to retain the temporal order of events.

In order to compare two multimedia objects represented by time series, a proper distance measure is required. The most prominent similarity measure for time series is the Euclidean distance. In the past years, the Dynamic Time Warping (DTW) [5] which is conceptually similar to sequence alignment has become as prominent as the Euclidean distance. Contrary to the Euclidean distance which is a measure for the similarity in time, DTW is a measure for the similarity in shape.

Feature extraction for time series. For long time series usually structure level similarity measures based on global features or model parameter extraction are used [6,7,8,9]. A similarity model for time series that considers the characteristics of the time series was recently proposed in [1]. A set of global features including periodicity, self-similarity, skewness, kurtosis among others are used to compute the similarity between the time series. Some of the features are generated from the raw time series data as well as from trend and seasonally adjusted time series. The authors focused on clustering as a special application of similarity search and showed that a small set of global features can be sufficient to achieve an adequate clustering quality. However, this approach is successful only as long as adequate features that reflect the time series characteristics can be identified. Unfortunately, long time series often feature very complex structures which cannot sufficiently be reflected by a single global feature, e.g. modeling the periodicity of a long time series with only one value may be too coarse in most cases.

In the multimedia community, publications about global features can be grouped in two main categories. Approaches belonging to the first category calculate features in the so-called frequency domain. The following feature transformations of this category are well known in the audio and signal processing area: Relative Spectral Predictive Linear Coding, Pitch [10], Spectral Flux, Mel Frequency Cepstral Coefficients, Bark Frequency Cepstral Coefficients [11], and coefficients calculated by basic time-frequency transformations (e.g., DCT, FFT, CWT, DWT). The second category consists of techniques that extract features in the so-called time domain. This category consists of the following features: Linear Predictive Coding coefficients[12], Zero Crossing Rate Periodicity Histogram [10], Sone and Short Time Energy [13], Length of High Amplitude Sequence, Length of Low Amplitude Sequence, or Area of High Amplitude [14].

In contrast to the existing features working in the time-based domain, the features proposed in this paper are calculated over the whole amplitude spectrum. This fact allows us capturing time-domain properties over the whole available amplitude range. Moreover, we suggest an automatical method for the combination of the derived features which results in a significant improvement of effectiveness.

3   Feature Sequence Extraction

As discussed above, traditional similarity measures like the Euclidean distance or DTW that work on the raw time series are not appropriate for multi-media applications. Rather, it is more suitable to extract features from qualitative representations of time

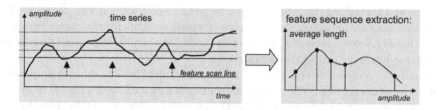

Fig. 2. Amplitude-level-wise feature extraction

series. Here, we propose a qualitative representation of time series that relies on sequences of intervals each representing all time slots at which the value of the original time series is above a given amplitude level.

3.1 Amplitude-Level-Wise Feature Extraction

Using only features according to one single amplitude level to describe a time series might be much too coarse to get satisfying results. Rather, we use several amplitude levels in order to capture the entire shape of the time series and extract features for each amplitude value. Instead of one feature value we get a sequence of feature values, called *feature sequence*, as illustrated in Figure 2. However, it is not very appropriate to consider all possible amplitude values for the feature extraction due to two reasons: First, the number of amplitude levels is infinite. Second, close amplitude values are likely to contain similar information, so that the feature sequence will contain a lot of redundant information.

We propose a framework that extracts time series features in two steps: In a first step, we generate sequences of feature values by scanning the amplitudes of the corresponding time series with a reasonable high resolution. In order to improve the similarity search quality we suggest to extract several features from the interval sequences. As depicted in Figure 2 we use the feature scan line (fsl) to vertically scan the time series from bottom to top and retrieve at each (relevant) amplitude level τ a set of features called *Amplitude-Level Features* (ALFs). Examples of simple ALFs include the fraction of time series values that exceed each amplitude level (denoted by ALF_{ATQ} in the following) and the number of intervals of consecutive time slots above each amplitude level (denoted by ALF_{TIC} in the following).

As a result, we obtain a sequence of ALFs $\langle (\tau_{min}, f_{\tau_{min}}), \dots (\tau_{max}, f_{\tau_{max}}) \rangle$, where τ_{min} denotes the global minimum of all amplitudes of all time series and τ_{max} denotes the corresponding global maximum of all amplitudes. The resolution r of the amplitude scan (i.e. the length of the ALF sequence) is a user-defined parameter that influences the length of the resulting feature sequence as well as the accuracy of the representation. If we choose a high value for the resolution r, we will obviously obtain a more accurate description of the time series and may achieve better results. On the other hand, a high value for the resolution r results in larger space required to store the ALF sequences and in a lower query performance. In order to reduce the size of the extracted features and to decrease redundant information, we subsequently apply appropriate dimensionality reduction methods to reduce the large feature sequences to a smaller set of coefficients.

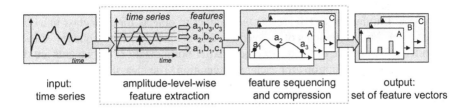

| input:
time series | amplitude-level-wise
feature extraction | feature sequencing
and compression | output:
set of feature vectors |

Fig. 3. Feature extraction framework

These coefficients correspond to the feature vectors that are finally used to represent the time series and are used for the similarity search methods.

3.2 Feature Sequence Compression

Depending on the resolution r of the feature extraction method, the ALF sequences may usually have a more or less smooth shape. Assuming a high resolution, the features extracted from adjacent amplitude thresholds do not vary very much. For this reason, common dimensionality reduction techniques for time series like DFT, PAA, or Chebyshev applied to the ALF sequences lead to shorter ALF sequences while accurately approximating the original ALF sequence. Finally, for each feature we generate a dimensionality reduced ALF sequence in the form of a vector which can be indexed by any spatial index structure. This strategy helps to solve the performance problems while keeping the quality of the similarity measure.

The principle of our framework is depicted in Figure 3. The framework takes a time series as input and produces a set of feature vectors as output. It consists of the two steps, the amplitude-level-wise feature extraction and the feature sequence compression. In particular, for a given time series and a given feature A we extract a sequence of local feature values a_1, a_2, and a_3. Subsequently, the generated ALF sequence is compressed by means of standard dimensionality reduction techniques resulting in a feature vector. This step is repeated for each feature extraction method so that finally a set of feature vectors is returned. This set is afterwards used to measure the similarity between the time series objects. Obviously, the final set of feature vectors and the dimension of each feature depends on the number and type of derived features, the resolution r, and the applied dimensionality reduction techniques. The length of the input time series however, has no influence on the dimensions of the resulting feature vectors. So the time complexity of a query is constant with respect to the length of the input time series. In the following section, we will present some high quality ALFs and discuss how to compute the similarity of the resulting set of feature vectors.

3.3 Feature Sequence Combination

As mentioned above, we generate a set of feature vectors for each time series. As the combination of different feature vectors usually improves the search quality we apply a combination approach similar to the techniques described in [15] and [16]. In order to compute weights for the different representations, we initially chose a small subset of training objects from the database. For each query object, we then perform a k-NN query on our training set and aggregate the number of objects for each class in a confidence vector. The coefficients of this confidence vector reflect the frequency of each class in the k-NN sphere of the query object. After normalization, the weights are derived by computing the entropy for each representation. The idea of this method is that feature spaces yielding a pure k-NN sphere are more suitable than representations containing objects from a lot of classes. After having determined the weights, a standard combination method like *sum*, *product*, *min*, or *max* can be used to combine the distances according to the different feature representations.

4   Amplitude-Level Features

The number and type of adequate features depend on the application and on the data. In the following, we propose a selection of features that mainly reflect shape characteristics of time series, and thus, might be suitable to common applications. Let us note that there may be other features that are sensible for special applications. However, we will show in our experiments that even the basic features described in the following already yield a rather accurate similarity model for shape-based similarity search in time series databases.

In the previous section, we already introduced two simple amplitude-level features, the Above Amplitude Level Quota (ATQ) that measures the fraction of time series values that exceed a given amplitude level τ and the Threshold Interval Count (TIC) that measures the relative number of amplitude level intervals. Both are easy to compute but reflect well the basic characteristic of time series. The resulting feature values obviously range from 0 to 1, where ALF_{ATQ} decreases monotonously for increasing values of τ. Noise has a stronger impact on ALF_{TIC} curve than on that of ALF_{ATQ} as a lot of noise can lead to a huge number of intervals. Similar to ALF_{ATQ} all chronological information is lost.

In the following, we present further adequate amplitude-level features. Here $ti_{\tau,X}$ denotes the qualitative representation of a time series X w.r.t. the amplitude level τ, i.e. the set of intervals where the value of X is above τ.

Threshold Interval Length (TIL). In contrast to the ALF_{TIC}, TIL tries to capture more complex characteristics of the intervals than just their existence. An obvious choice is the average and the maximal length of all intervals for a given amplitude level τ and a time series X, formally

$$ALF_{maxTIL}(X, \tau) = \max\{(u_j - l_j) : j \in ti_{\tau,X}\}$$

$$ALF_{\varnothing TIL}(X, \tau) = \frac{1}{|ti_{\tau,x}|} \sum_{j=0}^{M} (u_j - l_j)$$

ALF_{maxTIL} and $ALF_{\varnothing TIL}$ show similar behavior in most cases, whereas the former always yields monotonously decreasing feature values and naturally is more robust against noise (cf. Figure 4(a)). The contained information basically indicates at which amplitudes the time series contain high/low frequent sections. The same observation could be made for ALF_{ATQ}, however, for noisy data $ALF_{\varnothing TIL}$ is more effective than ALF_{ATQ} (cf. Figure 4(b)).

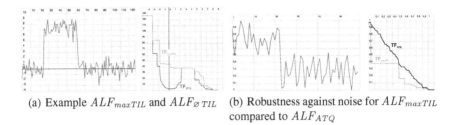

(a) Example ALF_{maxTIL} and $ALF_{\varnothing TIL}$ (b) Robustness against noise for ALF_{maxTIL}
compared to ALF_{ATQ}

Fig. 4. Examples of ALF sequences

Threshold Interval Distance (TID). A further reasonable feature is the distance between consecutive intervals. Generally, distances between intervals are ambiguous, so
we have some options for the feature generation. We can build distances between the
start points of the intervals only or between the end points only or we take both points
into account. Here, we use the distance between the start point l_j of an interval and the
start point l_{j+1} of the subsequent interval. We again consider both, the maximum and
the average distance value:

$$ALF_{maxTID}(X,\tau) = \max\{(l_{j+1} - l_j) : j \in 1..ti_{\tau,X} - 1\}$$

$$ALF_{\varnothing TID}(X,\tau) = \frac{1}{|ti_{\tau,X}| - 1} \sum_{j=1}^{|ti_{\tau,X}|-1} (l_{j+1} - l_j)$$

This feature differs from the others in being not invariant against mirroring of the time
series along the time axis. It is adequate to separate periodical signals having different
frequencies. Like ALF_{TIL}, ALF_{maxTID} is more robust against noise than $ALF_{\varnothing TID}$.

Threshold Crossing Angle (TXA). This feature differs slightly from the previous as it
does not take the interval sequences into account. Here, we consider the slopes of the
time series that occur at the start and end points of the time intervals.

First, we define the slope angle $\text{angle}(t_i)$ of a time series value $(x_i, t_i) \in X : i \in$
$2 \dots N$ as follows:

$$\text{angle}(t_i) := \arctan(x_i - x_{i-1}).$$

Based on this definition, we can define the features:

$$ALF_{absTXA}(X,\tau) = \frac{1}{N\pi} \sum_{j=1}^{|ti_{\tau,X}|} (|\text{angle}(l_j)| + |\text{angle}(u_j)|) * (u_j - l_j)$$

$$ALF_{diffTXA}(X,\tau) = 0{,}5 + \frac{1}{N\pi} \sum_{j=1}^{|ti_{\tau,X}|} (\text{angle}(l_j) + \text{angle}(u_j)) * (u_j - l_j)$$

We weight the slope angles according to the corresponding interval length. The factor
$\frac{1}{N\pi}$ as well as the constant value 0.5 are used to normalize the results to the range $(0, 1)$
and are necessary to compare time series of different lengths.

Obviously, this feature primarily aims at separating time series having different rate of changes. Unfortunately, the determination of such kind of patterns can be easily perturbed by noise. As a consequence, the quality of the similarity measures based on this feature mainly depends on the intensity of the noise in a dataset.

Threshold Balance (TB). The last feature incorporates the temporal behavior of the time series by considering the distribution of the amplitude values that are above the corresponding amplitude threshold. First, we need the auxiliary function

$$\mathrm{above}_\tau(x_i) := \begin{cases} 1 & \text{if } x_i > \tau \\ 0 & \text{else} \end{cases}.$$

By means of this function, we can define the Threshold-Balance feature ALF_{TB} that aggregates those values of the time series which are above the amplitude threshold, whereas values of different time slots are weighted differently. Formally

$$ALF_{TB}(X,\tau) = \frac{1}{N^2} \sum_{i=1}^{N} \left(i - \frac{N}{2} \right) \mathrm{above}_\tau(x_i).$$

Each of the presented features covers specific characteristics of a time series. Naturally, depending on the application, the full power of the features can be achieved if we use combinations of them.

5   Evaluation

We used four datasets from the UCR Time Series Data Mining Archive [17]. Dataset "DS1" contains 600 time series of length 60 divided into 6 classes. This dataset is the *SynthCtrl* dataset and contains artificially created time series. The *GunX* dataset will be denoted as "DS2". It contains tracking data of the movement of persons while either drawing or pointing a gun. This dataset contains 200 time series of length 150 grouped into 2 classes. The *Trace* dataset is a synthetic dataset which describes instrumentation failures in a power plant. It will be referred to as "DS3" and contains 200 time series in 4 different classes. The length of each time series is 275. The last dataset ("DS4") is the *Leaf* dataset. Images were used to create this dataset. It consists of 442 time series of length 150 grouped into 6 classes.

We compared our approach in terms of accuracy (average precision/recall of kNN classification experiments) with the following approaches: (1) Euclidean distance on the raw time series, (2) DTW on the raw time series, the global feature extraction approach from [1] with (3) unweighted and (4) weighted feature combination, and our approach using all proposed ALFs with (5) an unweighted feature combination as well as (6) the weighted feature combination. For both weighted competitors (approaches (4) and (6)), we applied the method proposed above using 20% of the particular datasets for learning the weights. Moreover, the k parameter of our weighting method was chosen to be 5 times the number of existing classes.

We ran a kNN classifier with several k values. The resulting average precisions for all competitors applied to our datasets are presented in Figure 5(a). As it can be observed,

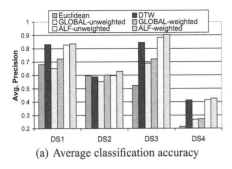

(a) Average classification accuracy

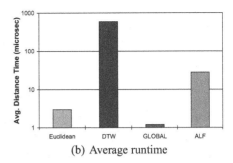

(b) Average runtime

Fig. 5. Comparison of different approaches

our ALF approaches outperform the competing techniques for all examined datasets (cf. Figure 5(a)). Let us note that we even achieved a higher classification accuracy than DTW which, in contrast to our approach, has a quadratic runtime w.r.t. the length of the time series. In addition, the experiments show that our novel weighted feature combination in average further boosts the classification quality. Even the global feature based classification can be improved with our proposed feature combination technique. Let us note, that the single precision results obtained for each tested k value look very similar. The average runtimes for one distance computation of the competitors are depicted in Figure 5(b). It can be observed that our approach clearly outperforms DTW by more than one order of magnitude. This is important because DTW is the only competitor that achieves roughly similar accuracy like our approach but for the cost of far higher runtimes.

We also evaluated the classification accuracy of each proposed ALF separately. Table 1 compares these accuracy values with the accuracy of the (weighted) combination of all ALFs. It can be observed, that on three out of four datasets choosing only one (the best) ALF is less accurate than combining all ALFs for similarity search.

In a further experiment, we evaluated the resolution r that specifies the number of amplitude-levels used for deriving the corresponding ALFs. Since r determines the length of the derived ALF sequences, this parameter seems to be important for the accuracy of the search. In fact, for a broad range of resolution values (r between 10 and 100), the average classification accuracy was very stable for all datasets. In Figure 6 we depicted the results for the two real-world datasets DS2 and DS4 for the unweighted and the weighted combination. The experiments showed that even for a very low value of r, i.e. rather short ALF sequences, we gain very accurate results.

Table 1. Classification accuracy of single ALFs (in percent)

ALF	ATQ	TIC	$\varnothing TIL$	$maxTIL$	$\varnothing TID$	$maxTID$	$absTXA$	$diffTXA$	TB	**combined**
DS1	77.2	**78.6**	64.8	73.5	56.4	64.0	78.5	44.9	62.8	**83.6**
DS2	59.2	54.8	56.2	59.9	52.4	52.5	**69.5**	55.9	53.8	**62.9**
DS3	63.8	43.8	65.4	74.5	74.8	**84.5**	65.3	81.3	54.7	**90.5**
DS4	**41.0**	37.6	32.4	30.9	30.7	33.3	26.0	27.1	18.8	**42.5**

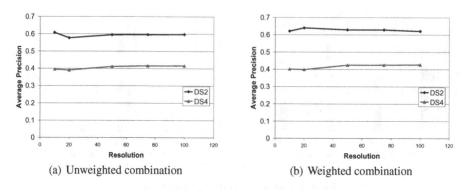

(a) Unweighted combination   (b) Weighted combination

Fig. 6. Average classification accuracy of ALF for different resolutions

6 Conclusions

In this paper we proposed a new general framework for generating high quality Amplitude-Level Features (ALF) from time series. An advantage when using ALFs for similarity search is that the runtime is independent of length of the time series. Thus, ALFs are adequate even for long sequences as occurring frequently in multimedia applications. We furthermore introduced several ALFs that are able to describe the characteristic properties of a time series. We also proposed a method to combine several feature representations. We showed in our experimental evaluation that our proposed technique outperforms traditional similarity search methods in terms of accuracy. In addition, our approach significantly outperforms the only competitor that achieves roughly similar accuracy in terms of runtime.

References

1. Wang, X., Smith, K., Hyndman, R.: Characteristic-based clustering for time series data. Data Min. Knowl. Discov. 13(3), 335–364 (2006)
2. Naphade, M., Wang, R., Huang, T.: Multimodal pattern matching for audio-visual query and retrieval. In: Proc. SPIE (2001)
3. Naphade, M., Yeung, M., Yeo, B.: A novel scheme for fast and efficient video sequence matching using compact signatures. In: Proc. SPIE (2000)
4. Yeung, M.M., Liu, B.: Efficient matching and clustering of video shots. In: Proc. ICIP (1995)
5. Berndt, D., Clifford, J.: Using dynamic time warping to find patterns in time series. In: Proc. AAAI 1994 W. on Knowledge Discovery and Databases, pp. 229–248 (1994)
6. Nanopoulos, A., Alcock, R., Manolopoulos, Y.: Feature-based classification of time-series data. Information processing and technology, 49–61 (2001) isbn 1-59033-116-8
7. Deng, K., Moore, A., Nechyba, M.: Learning to recognize time series: Combining arma models with memory-based learning. In: IEEE CIRA, pp. 246–250 (1997)
8. Ge, X., Smyth, P.: Deformable markov model templates for time-series pattern matching. In: Proc. ACM SIGKDD, pp. 81–90 (2000)
9. Keogh, E., Lonardi, S., Ratanamahatana, C.A.: Towards parameter-free data mining. In: Proc. ACM SIGKDD, pp. 206–215 (2004)

10. Sun, X.: Pitch determination and voice quality analysis using subharmonic-to-harmonic ratio. In: Proc. ICASSP (2002)
11. Liu, M., Wan, C.: Feature selection for automatic classification of musical instrument sounds. In: Proc. JCDL (2001)
12. Tremain, T.: The government standard linear predictive coding algorithm: Lpc-10 (1982)
13. Pampalk, E.: A matlab toolbox to compute music similarity from audio. In: Proc. ISMIR (2004)
14. Mitrovic, D., Zeppelzauer, M., Breiteneder, C.: Discrimination and retrieval of animal sounds. In: Proc. MMM (2006)
15. Bustos, B., Keim, D., Saupe, D., Schreck, T., Vranic, D.: Automatic selection and combination of descriptors for effective 3D similarity search. In: Proc. ICME (2004)
16. Kriegel, H.P., Pryakhin, A., Schubert, M.: Multi-represented knn-classification for large class sets. In: Zhou, L.-z., Ooi, B.-C., Meng, X. (eds.) DASFAA 2005. LNCS, vol. 3453, pp. 511–522. Springer, Heidelberg (2005)
17. Keogh, E.: The ucr time series data mining archive, University of California Riverside CA (2006), http://www.cs.ucr.edu/~eamonn/TSDMA/index.html

Sound Source Localization with Non-calibrated Microphones

Tomoyuki Kobayashi, Yoshinari Kameda, and Yuichi Ohta

Graduate School of Systems and Information Engineering, University of Tsukuba
1-1-1 Tennoudai, Tsukuba, Ibaraki, 305-8573, Japan
kobayashi@image.esys.tsukuba.ac.jp,
{kameda,ohta}@iit.tsukuba.ac.jp
http://www.image.iit.tsukuba.ac.jp

Abstract. We propose a new method for localizing a sound source in a known space with non-calibrated microphones. Our method does not need the accurate positions of the microphones that are required by traditional sound source localization. Our method can make use of wide variety of microphone layout in a large space because it does not need calibration step on installing microphones. After a number of sampling points have been stored in a database, our system can estimate the nearest sampling point of a sound by utilizing the set of time delays of microphone pairs. We conducted a simulation experiment to determine the best microphone layout in order to maximize the accuracy of the localization. We also conducted a preliminary experiment in real environment and obtained promising results.

Keywords: non-calibrated microphones, sound source localization, time-delay.

1 Introduction

Sound source localization can play an important role in surveillance and monitoring purposes, especially in intelligent support of safe and secured life in daily situation. Once the location of a sound source is estimated, it can be a very powerful clue for many applications such as event classification, intruder detection at night, classification of the behaviors, and so on.

Traditional sound source localization methods need precise geometry of the microphones of a microphone array. Microphones are linearly, squarely, or roundly set in popular array layout and their position intervals are given in advance. Or, their positions needs to be precisely measured beforehand when they are sparsely scattered in a room. Some of the advanced researches have reported that sound source localization worked very well with these calibrated microphones [1][2][3][4][5][6][7]. Their performance, however, mainly relies on the accuracy of the microphone positions, which are not always easy to obtain in some situations.

In the literature of intelligent life support[8] and sensing[9][10] of daily life, we can exploit pre-recorded sound samples as a clue to localize a newly observed

S. Satoh, F. Nack, and M. Etoh (Eds.): MMM 2008, LNCS 4903, pp. 134–143, 2008.

sound source because microphones are usually fixed for a long term in such a space and they can record a large number of samples during the term. In addition, for some monitoring purposes, they can be satisfied by finding the geometrically nearest sound sample for the newly observed sound in the space.

We propose a new method for localizing a sound source in a known space with non-calibrated microphones. It does not need to know the positions of the microphones.

We assume that the microphones are permanently fixed in the space. Our method can work with wide variety of microphone layout in a large space because it does not need calibration step on installing the microphones. After a number of sampling points have been stored in the database, our system can estimate the nearest sampling point for a new sound by utilizing the set of time delays of microphone pairs.

The rest of the paper is organized as follows. Section 2 briefly describes the overview of our sound localization system, and section 3 explains the similarity scale that estimates the "distance" between two sound locations. Then, we examine the layout of microphones so that localization error is minimized in section 4 and a preliminary experiment in real environment is shown in section 5. We conclude the paper in section 6.

2   Sound Localization System

As for monitoring purposes, we should consider various kinds of sound in a space. For example, people in a room may make many kinds of sounds such as voice, cough, sneezing, footsteps, opening and closing sound of door, etc. Therefore, we cannot exploit the features that are only effective for human voice. In this paper, we use a relatively simple sound feature in our sound localization system. We exploit time-delays of all the possible pairs of microphones in our system.

If there are N $(N \geq 3)$ microphones, the total number of microphone pairs becomes $_NC_2$. Therefore, a time-delay vector is expressed by $M = {}_NC_2$ elements. It holds rich information enough to estimate the spatial location of the sound source if the geometry of microphone layout is given to the system. Note that the time-delay vector only depends on the location of the sound source. It is uniquely given if a sound source is set in a certain place and all the microphones are fixed in the space. Therefore, if two time-delay vectors are same, it means the corresponding sound sources are placed in the same place.

We here assume that the temperature of the space is constant so that the sound speed is constant.

3   Query for Sound Sample

In our approach, a sound is localized by finding a sound sample that has the same time-delay vector. Sound samples had been recorded and their time-delay vectors were stored in a database in the system in advance.

As for applications, suppose the system has a calibrated camera and it found a new sound. The system will estimate the closest sound sample and point out the place of the sound source in the video image that has taken at the time when the sound was recorded.

The system needs a large number of sound samples in the database to cover the whole space. However, as the similarity estimation of our method is rather simple (explained in 3.2), the computation cost to find the closest sound sample in the database is within the practical range for various on-line applications.

3.1   Time-Delay Vector

By recording a sound with two microphones i and j, we can obtain a time-delay $\tau_{i,j}$ between i and j. With N microphones, we will have $M = {}_NC_2$ time-delay values for one sound. Time-delay vector T is denoted as $T = (\tau_{1,1}, \tau_{1,2}, \cdots, \tau_{N-1,N})$.

We basically estimate the time-delays of a microphone pair by simply searching the start time of sound wave at each microphone for an isolated single sound (such as closing sound of a door). We also plan to exploit Cross-Power Spectrum Phase (CSP)[11] and its improved approach to estimate more accurate time-delay τ because we need to handle various kinds of environmental noise such as noise of fans and motors of electric devices.

3.2   Similarity Scale for Time-Delay Vector

We define a similarity scale for evaluating the similarity between the time-delay vectors of two sound sources.

Obviously, the distance should be zero and the similarity should be high if the two time-delay vectors are same because it implies that the two relevant sound sources are at the same place.

Suppose there are two sound sources α and β, and the corresponding time-delay vectors T_α and T_β. We define the similarity scale $ss(T_\alpha, T_\beta)$ for two time-delay vectors based on the definition of the Euclidian distance.

$$ss(T_\alpha, T_\beta) = \left(\sum_{1 \le k \le M} (\tau_{\alpha_k} - \tau_{\beta_k})^2 \right)^{\frac{1}{2}} \qquad (1)$$

$\tau_{\alpha k}$ indicates the kth element of the time-delay vector T_α.

Since time-delay vector space is a none-linear projection of the real space where sound-α and sound-β exists, we need to examine the behavior of the similarity scale when the two sound sources are in different positions. For example, $ss(T_\alpha, T_\beta) = ss(T_\beta, T_\gamma)$ does not imply $ed(\alpha, \gamma) = 0$, where the function $ed(\ )$ shows the Euclidian distance betweem the two sound sources in the real space.

This behavior is affected by the layout of the microphones in a space and the location of sound source.

Therefore, if we find a good microphone layout in which the similarity scale has the strong correlation with the actual distance in the real space, we can use the scale to find the closest sound sample in the database for a newly observed sound.

As for a comparison of the proposed similarity scale, we also prepare the normalized inner product $ip()$ in this paper. It is often used as a similarity scale for two multidimensional vectors. Suppose there are two sound sources α and β, and the corresponding time-delay vectors T_α and T_β, the normalized inner product is defined as:

$$ip(T_\alpha, T_\beta) = \frac{(T_\alpha, T_\beta)}{\|T_\alpha\|\|T_\beta\|} \qquad (2)$$

4 Simulation Experiment

We have examined five kinds of popular microphone layout in a room in simulation experiment. We also compare the proposed similarity scale with a normalized inner product to evaluate the accuracy of the proposed method.

In the simulation, we set the size of experimental space as 6.201 by 7.288 by 3.094 (depth/width/height)[m], which is the size of our real experiment room. We prepare the pre-recorded sound samples at the interval of 0.3, 0.6, and 1.0 meter for depth, width, and height direction. The numbers of the pre-recorded sound samples are 223, 857, and 5,774 respectively. The corresponding time-delay vectors are calculated in advance. We assume ominidirectional and undamped sound sources and sound samples. And we do not consider reverberation during the simulation process.

The performance of sound source localization is evaluated as follows. A new sound sample is randomly placed in the space, and the corresponding time-delay vector is calculated. Then, the system finds the most similar time-delay vector

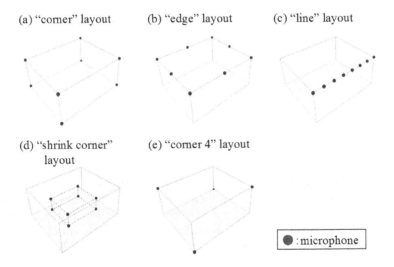

Fig. 1. Microphone layouts

Table 1. Simulation result

layout	method	interval	ref	success	neighbor	failure	average [m]	variance	deviation
corner	ss	1.0 [m]	a	4675	325	0	0.483	0.020	0.143
		0.6 [m]	b	4713	287	0	0.286	0.007	0.085
		0.3 [m]	c	4724	276	0	0.144	0.002	0.043
	ip	1.0 [m]	d	2009	1665	1326	0.904	0.308	0.555
		0.6 [m]	e	1846	1428	1726	0.647	0.233	0.483
		0.3 [m]	f	1728	1392	1880	0.380	0.123	0.351
edge	ss	1.0 [m]	g	1881	1586	1533	0.930	0.336	0.580
		0.6 [m]	h	1700	1423	1877	0.618	0.166	0.408
		0.3 [m]	i	1630	1346	2024	0.331	0.052	0.229
	ip	1.0 [m]	j	1831	1797	1372	0.920	0.319	0.565
		0.6 [m]	k	1869	1510	1621	0.609	0.200	0.448
		0.3 [m]	l	1787	1496	1717	0.337	0.086	0.294
linear	ss	1.0 [m]	m	714	1528	2758	1.425	0.639	0.799
		0.6 [m]	n	482	998	3520	1.256	0.659	0.811
		0.3 [m]	o	261	533	4206	1.134	0.612	0.782
	ip	1.0 [m]	p	427	1050	3523	1.939	1.374	1.172
		0.6 [m]	q	299	696	4005	1.532	0.865	0.930
		0.3 [m]	r	169	328	4503	1.280	0.676	0.822
shrink corner	ss	0.6 [m]	s	3240	1395	365	0.378	0.045	0.213
corner 4	ss	0.6 [m]	t	3454	1478	68	0.332	0.019	0.139

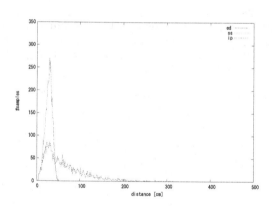

Fig. 2. Error distribution of "corner"

by applying the proposed similarity scale (and the normalized inner product for comparison). If the answer is also the closest sample to the new sound sample in the real space, it is marked as success. If the answer is not the closest one but is one of the 7 second-best pre-recorded samples (8 corners of a cube that involves the new sound source, excluding the closest corner itself), it is marked as neighbor. Otherwise, it is marked as failure. Each experiment is conducted with 5,000 randomly placed samples.

We have first examined the three kinds of microphone layouts to compare the proposed method ("ss") with the normalized inner product ("ip").

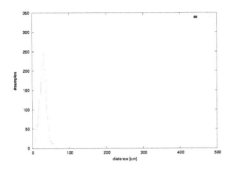

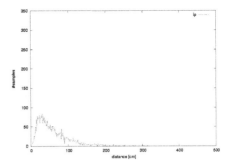

Fig. 3. Error distribution of "ss" on "corner" layout

Fig. 4. Error distribution of "ip" on "corner" layout

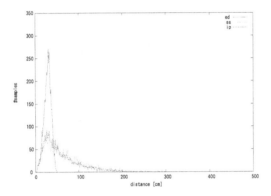

Fig. 5. Error distribution of "edge"

The first layout has 8 microphones at each corner of the space ("corner"). The second one has 4 microphones at the corners on the ceiling, and 4 microphones in the mid point of the 4 edges of the ceiling ("edge"). In the third layout, 8 microphones are linearly arranged and their intervals are equally set. This linear microphone array is set on one side of the wall at the ceiling height ("line"). Fig 1 (a) - (c) shows these three layouts.

The simulation results are shown in Table 1. The average indicates the average error distance between a random sample and the corresponding "closest" pre-recorded sample in the real space. The variance and the deviation show the distribution of the error.

The (a) - (c) rows in Table 1 clearly show that our proposed method achieved the best score with "corner" layout. The proposed method shows the better results than those of the comparison method "ip" in "corner" and "line" layouts at any resolution.

Fig 2 - 4 shows the distance distribution of the samples at 0.6 meter interval. The line "ed" in Fig 2 indicates the Euclidian distance between the random samples and their nearest pre-recorded samples. The line "ss" plots the Euclidian distance

140   T. Kobayashi, Y. Kameda, and Y. Ohta

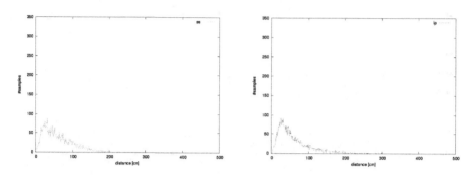

Fig. 6. Error distribution of "ss" on "edge" **Fig. 7.** Error distribution of "ip" on "edge"
layout   layout

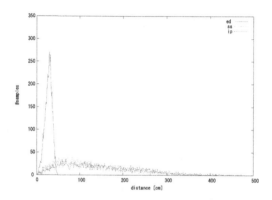

Fig. 8. Error distribution of "line"

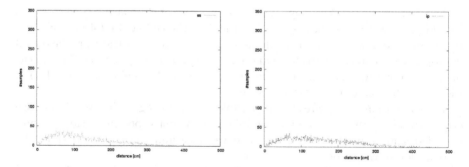

Fig. 9. Error distribution of "ss" on "line" **Fig. 10.** Error distribution of "ip" on "line"
layout   layout

between the random samples and their answers of the proposed method, and "ip"
plots the Euclidian distance between the samples and the answers given by the
normalized inner product method. Since "ss" is very similar to "ed", we can say

that "ss" can be treated as the real Euclidian distance in this case. In Fig 2, "ss" and "ed" have a very similar distribution and they are almost overlapped each other.

However, even with the "ss", the performance becomes worse if the microphone layout loses the cubic expansion of its baselines(see Table.1 (g-i)(m-o)). Fig 5 - 7 and Fig 8 - 10 also shows this fact because "ss" is different from "ed" in these cases. Therefore, we can say that the cubic layout is preferred to obtain good performance on sound source localization by our method.

We also conducted two additional experiments to examine the performance of the microphone layout that saves space and number. The row (s) in Table 1 is the result of the 8 microphones that are similar to "corner", but it is shrunk in half to the center of the space ("shrink corner"). This layout marked the better result than "edge" and "line". If we are allowed to place microphones at corners, we can get very good performance even if we use only 4 microphones (2 at the opposite corners on the floor and 2 at the other opposite corners on the ceiling) as shown in row (t), "corner 4".

5 Experiment in Real Environment

We also conducted a preliminary experiment in a real room. We placed 4 microphones so as to expand them three dimensionally. Fig 11 and Table 2 show the layout of microphones and the positions of sound sources. Fig 12 shows a snapshot of the room.

Table 2. Positions of microphones and sound sources

	mic1	mic2	mic3	mic4			place1	place2	place3	place4
X	5.090	5.643	2.210	3.059	X		2.182	4.814	4.771	2.723
Y	5.314	0.958	5.824	0.4130	Y		5.306	5.054	3.095	3.073
Z	0.159	1.229	0.812	2.599	Z		0.686	0.002	0.757	0.001

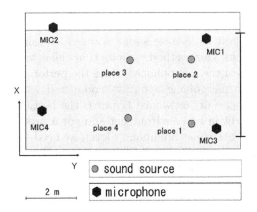

Fig. 11. Layout of microphones and positions of sound sources

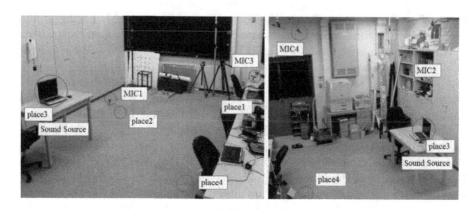

Fig. 12. Positions of microphones and sound sources

Table 3. The value of the similarity scale in real environment

		door			
		place 1	place 2	place 3	place 4
	place 1	47.0	868.9	789.7	460.0
voice	place 2	683.2	284.6	558.9	448.9
	place 3	848.1	894.5	75.1	433.5
	place 4	471.1	698.5	417.9	22.9

We prepared two kinds of recorded sounds. One is "voice" and the other is door closing sound of a locker ("door"). They were played on a speaker at 4 different places. Table 3 shows the values of the similarity scale between "voice" and "door". Note that the values are always low when the both sounds are observed at the same place.

6   Conclusion

We presented a method to localize sound sources by using a number of non-calibrated microphones. Our method exploits time-delay vectors and it does not need calibration step of the microphones. Since the performance of the proposed method is affected by microphone layout, we conducted a simulation experiment and concluded that spatially expanded layout is the best. We also conducted a preliminary experiment in real environment and got a promising result.

Since the experiments are at preliminary level, we need to apply the proposed method in various real situations to validate it. As for future works, we plan to improve the method to cope with multiple sound sources and reverberation that sometimes make influence on the performance of the sound source localization in real situations.

References

1. Brandstein, M., Ward, D. (eds.): Microphone Arrays: Signal Processing Techniques and Applications. Springer, Heidelberg (2001)
2. Brandstein, M., Adcock, J., Silverman, H.: A closed-form method for finding source locations from microphone-array time-delay estimates. In: ICASSP 1995, pp. 3019–3022 (1995)
3. Omologo, M., Svaizer, P.: Acoustic source location in noisy and reverberant environment using csp analysis. In: ICASSP 1996, pp. 921–924 (1996)
4. Peterson, J.M., Kyriakakis, C.: Hybrid algorithm for robust, real-time source localization in reverberant environments. In: ICASSP 2005, vol. 4, pp. 1053–1056 (2005)
5. Raykar, V.C., Yegnanarayana, B., Parasanna, S.R., Duraiswami, R.: Speaker localization using excitation source information in speech. IEEE Trans. Speech and Audio Processing 13(5), 751–761 (2005)
6. O' Donovan, A., Duraiswami, R., Neumann, J.: Microphone arrays as generalized cameras for integrated audio visual processing. In: CVPR 2007, pp. 1–8 (2007)
7. Scott, J., Dragovic, B.: Audio location: Accurate low-cost location Sencing. In: Gellersen, H.-W., Want, R., Schmidt, A. (eds.) PERVASIVE 2005. LNCS, vol. 3468, pp. 1–18. Springer, Heidelberg (2005)
8. Coen, M.H.: Design principles for intelligent environments. In: Proceedings of AAAI, pp. 547–554 (1998)
9. Mori, T., Noguchi, H., Takada, A., Sato, T.: Informational support in distributed sensor environment sensing room. RO-MAN 2004, pp. 353–358 (2004)
10. Nishiguchi, S., Kameda, Y., Kakusho, K., Minoh, M.: Automatic video recording of lecture's audience with activity analysis and equalization of scale for students observation. JACIII 8(2), 181–189 (2004)
11. Omologo, M., et al.: Acoustic event location using a crosspower-spectrum phase based. technique. In: ICASSP 1994, vol. 2, pp. 273–276 (1994)

PriSurv: Privacy Protected Video Surveillance System Using Adaptive Visual Abstraction

Kenta Chinomi, Naoko Nitta, Yoshimichi Ito, and Noboru Babaguchi

Graduate School of Engineering, Osaka University
2-1 Yamadaoka Suita, 565-0871 Japan
{chinomi,naoko,ito,babaguchi}@nanase.comm.eng.osaka-u.ac.jp

Abstract. Recently, video surveillance has received a lot of attention as a technology to realize a secure and safe community. Video surveillance is useful for crime deterrence and investigations, but may cause the invasion of privacy. In this paper, we propose a video surveillance system named PriSurv, which is characterized by *visual abstraction*. This system protects the privacy of objects in a video by referring to their privacy policies which are determined according to closeness between objects in the video and viewers monitoring it. A prototype of PriSurv is able to protect the privacy adaptively through *visual abstraction*.

1   Introduction

The concern about video surveillance has been growing in recent years in accordance with increasing demands for security. Video surveillance allows us to remotely monitor a live or recorded video feed which often includes objects such as people. It is recognized that video surveillance contributes to realizing a secure and safe community. When video surveillance systems are widely deployed, we are faced with a problem of privacy invasion. Objects' privacy may be exposed in the videos recorded by surveillance cameras set in public spaces. However, their privacy should be protected anytime even while surveillance is in operation. The challenge of video surveillance is to balance security and privacy appropriately.

Over the past few years, several studies have been made on privacy with video surveillance. Newton et al.[1], Cavallaro et al.[2] and Kitahara et al.[3] proposed the methods for protecting objects' privacy by image processing such as blur and mosaic. The methods presented by Wickramasuriya et al.[4] and Senior et al.[5] protect object's privacy based on the authority either of objects or viewers. Zhang et al.[6] proposed the method for embedding privacy information using digital watermarking technology. Embedded information is obtained only by authorized viewers. Considering more appropriate privacy protection, Sekiguchi et al.[7] proposed the system to protect object's privacy in accordance with the requests of viewers and objects. In this system, the viewer's request is prior to the object's request for practicality of the surveillance system.

These methods, however, are insufficient for privacy protection because the difference of each object's sense of privacy is not considered. For example, some objects may want their privacy to be protected from particular viewers, while

S. Satoh, F. Nack, and M. Etoh (Eds.): MMM 2008, LNCS 4903, pp. 144–154, 2008.

others may not care about their privacy at all. This implies that we must adaptively protect objects' privacy.

This work has been motivated by the need to protect objects' privacy considering the difference of each object's sense of privacy. The contribution of this work is as follows:

- To propose an approach to protecting privacy of people adaptively with video surveillance.
- To embody video/image processing for protecting visual privacy.
- To settle video surveillance as a secure social system.

In this paper, we propose Privacy Protected Video Surveillance System PriSurv. PriSurv aims to protect objects' privacy based on their privacy policies which are determined according to closeness between objects and viewers. A mechanism called *visual abstraction* is introduced to control disclosure of visual information according to objects' privacy policies. Objects' privacy policies give types of abstraction operators which are functions to control visual information of objects.

2   System Overview

We assume PriSurv should be used in a small community such as school areas. In the community, a certain number of members are registered and they would monitor each other. The members would sometimes be viewers and other times be objects.

It is noted that PriSurv is characterized by adaptive *visual abstraction*. PriSurv is capable of generating several kinds of images reflecting on the relationship between the objects and the viewers. The appearance of the objects should be open only to the viewers that objects feel close to, and be hidden to the viewers that objects feel distant from. In this way, PriSurv can control the objects' privacy for each individual viewer.

Fig. 1 is an example showing the feature of PriSurv. Let o, v and a denote an object, a viewer and an abstraction operator, respectively. An original image S including the object o is processed through the abstraction operator a, and the viewer v obtains a privacy protected image $S^a_{<o,v>}$. In Fig. 1, 'Taro' is the object and is monitored by four viewers: 'Stranger 1', 'Neighbor 1', 'Neighbor 2' and 'Family 1'. The appearance of 'Taro' should be changed to each viewer because the closeness levels between 'Taro' and four viewers are different. The original image S is processed through *visual abstraction* by the abstraction operators 'Dot', 'Silhouette', 'Mosaic' and 'As-Is', and the abstracted images $S^{Dot}_{<Taro,Stranger1>}$, $S^{Silhouette}_{<Taro,Neighbor1>}$, $S^{Mosaic}_{<Taro,Neighbor2>}$ and $S^{As-Is}_{<Taro,Family1>}$ are sent to 'Stranger 1', 'Neighbor 1', 'Neighbor 2' and 'Family 1', respectively.

Fig. 2 shows the system architecture of PriSurv. Viewers need to access the main server through an open network and be authenticated to monitor a surveillance video. The function of each module in Fig. 2 is as follows:

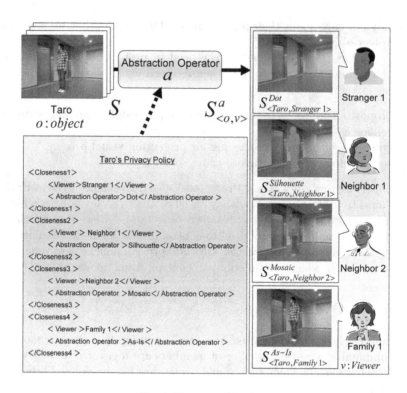

Fig. 1. Feature of PriSurv

- Analyzer

  Analyzer has a function of *object identification* which is a process to label IDs on each object in an image. On condition that each object has an RFID-tag, objects in images are identified with a combination of RFID-tags and video analysis.

- Profile Generator

  Profile Generator facilitates to set profiles of members. Profiles have members' privacy information, which are privacy policies and attributions such as name, age, gender and address. Registered members can set their privacy information simply on a graphical user interface, then Profile Generator converts the settings to XML based syntax. Profiles can be updated only by their owners and can not be accessed by other members.

- Profile Base

  Profile Base stores a set of profiles of the registered members securely in the server.

- Access Controller

  Access Controller reads XML based privacy policies of objects and look up viewers' IDs in objects' privacy policies to determine appropriate abstraction operators. Access Controller sends the types of operators to Abstractor.

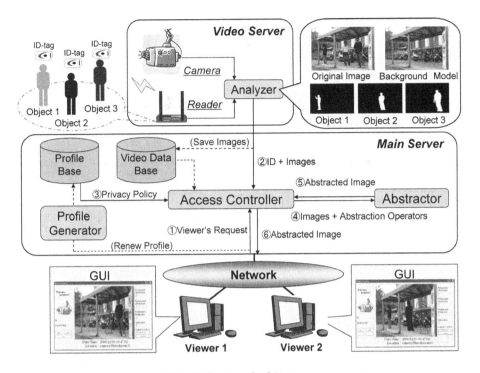

Fig. 2. System Architecture

– Abstractor
  Abstractor is an image processor for *visual abstraction* by the abstraction operators specified from Access Controller.
– Video Data Base
  Video Data Base stores past video data and supplies them to viewers through *visual abstraction* when necessary.

3   Object Identification

PriSurv needs to firstly identify objects in original images. Here, assuming that every member has his own RFID-tag, the surveillance space is divided into N × N areas and we estimate in which area each RFID-tag and object in images are present. IDs are then assigned to all objects in images by integrating these estimation results. Fig. 3 shows the process of object identification. The process consists of three steps:

1. Area estimation of RFID-tags carried by objects
2. Area estimation of objects in images
3. Integration of area estimation results

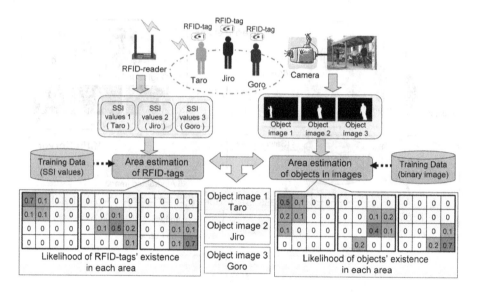

Fig. 3. Object Identification

These three steps are described below.

RFID-tags are useful for object identification since they provide the information about who and where their carriers are. Each tag emits a signal encoded with a unique ID number, which is received by an RFID-reader. As a result, the SSI (Signal Strength Indicator) values of the signals received by all RFID-readers set in the surveillance space are measured for each RFID-tag. We firstly prepare a training data by collecting a set of these SSI values when RFID-tags are at arbitrary locations in each area. When SSI values are measured from an unknown location, the likelihood of the RFID-tag's existence in each area is calculated by examining their k-nearest neighbors in the training data.

In order to identify objects in the original image, each object has to be extracted separately. Therefore, we firstly estimate a background model image by Gaussian mixture model and extract a foregound image per original image, where each detached region is considered as an object. Since the appearance of the object should be different depending on the spatial relationship between the object and the camera, we firstly prepare a training data by collecting binary images of each object, when the object is at arbitrary locations in each area. When a new original image is obtained, the likelihood of each object in the image to exist in each area is calculated by examining their k-nearest neighbors in the training data.

Finally, the calculated two likelihood values in each area are multiplied to calculate the likelihood of each RFID-tag and object to co-exist in the corresponding area. The ID of each RFID-tag is assigned to the object with the highest likelihood.

4 Privacy Policy

It is effective to set privacy policies based on closeness between objects and viewers [9]. Therefore, each registered member classifies other members into several closeness groups and sets an abstraction operator to each group. The members who are not classified in any group are grouped as a non-classified group.

Fig. 4 shows an example of Taro's privacy policy. This privacy policy is described in XACML which is a language for expressing access control policies. Note that the example policy is simplified for readability.

5 Visual Abstraction

Privacy protection is achieved by hiding object's visual information (e.g. expression, clothe, etc.). However, excess *visual abstraction* makes video surveillance meaningless. In PriSurv, both safety and privacy protection are needed. Therefore we implement several abstraction operators to control visual information gradually. We provide the following 12 operators as shown in Fig. 5.

- As-Is
  An object is not abstracted. All visual information is visible. The abstraction level is the lowest of all operators.
- See-through
  Pixel values of an object image and a background model image are blended. The background is visible through the object.
- Monotone
  Color information is hidden. An object is expressed in black and white.
- Blur
  An object is blurred. Details of the object are hidden.
- Mosaic
  An object is mosaicked. Details of the object are hidden.
- Edge
  An object is expressed by an extracted edge in one color.
- Border
  An object is expressed by an extracted border line in one color. The background is visible in the object's region.
- Silhouette
  An object is expressed by a silhouette painted out in one color. The background is not visible in the object's region.
- Box
  An object is expressed by a painted box. We can recognize the height and the width of the object.
- Bar
  An object is expressed by a painted bar. We can recognize the height of the object.
- Dot
  An object is expressed by a painted dot. We can recognize only the location of the object.

```
-<PolicySet Policy SetId="Taro's PolicySet">
  -<Policy PolicyId=" Closeness Level 1">
    -<Rule RuleId="WatchRule 1">
      -<Subject>Stranger1</Subject>
     </Rule>
    -<Obligation ObligationId=" Abstractor 1">
      -<Attribute Assignment>Dot< /AttributeAssignment >
     </Obligation>
   </Policy>
  -<Policy PolicyId=" Closeness Level 2">
    -<Rule RuleId="WatchRule 2">
      -<Subject>Neighbor 1</Subject>
     </Rule>
    -<Obligation ObligationId=" Abstractor 2">
      -<Attribute Assignment>Silhouette< /AttributeAssignment >
     </Obligation>
   </Policy>
  -<Policy PolicyId=" Closeness Level 3">
    -<Rule RuleId="WatchRule 3">
      -<Subject>Neighbor 2</Subject>
     </Rule>
    -<Obligation ObligationId=" Abstractor 3">
      -<Attribute Assignment>Mosaic< /AttributeAssignment >
     </Obligation>
   </Policy>
  -<Policy PolicyId=" Closeness Level 4">
    -<Rule RuleId="WatchRule 4">
      -<Subject>Family 1</Subject>
     </Rule>
    -<Obligation ObligationId=" Abstractor 4">
      -<Attribute Assignment>As-Is< /AttributeAssignment >
     </Obligation>
   </Policy>
 </PlicySet>
```

Fig. 4. Example of Privacy Policy

– Transparency
  All visual information of an object is hidden as if the object were not there.
  The abstraction level is the highest of all operators.

Visual information controlled by each operator is different as illustrated in
Table 1. In this figure, 'O', '△' and '×' mean disclosed, partially-hidden and

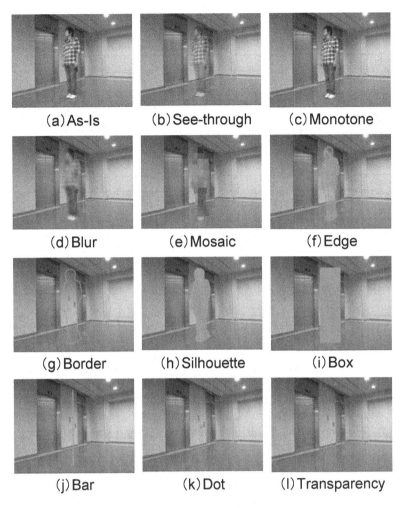

Fig. 5. Visual Abstraction

hidden, respectively. The operators are shown in increasing order of the abstraction level from top to bottom. In addition, the abstraction operators can be applied to a part of the object, i.e. his/her head or body.

6   Formulation

We formulate a process of generating privacy protected images.

An $M \times N$ original image can be represented as

$$S = \{s_{ij}\} \ (i = 1, 2, \cdots, M; j = 1, 2, \cdots, N) \tag{1}$$

where $s_{ij} = (s_{ij}^r, s_{ij}^g, s_{ij}^b)$ is a three-dimensional vector of RGB pixel values. In the original image S, let B denote the background region and F denote the

Table 1. Visual Information

	existence	location	height	width	silhouette	hairstyle	clothes	expression
As-Is	○	○	○	○	○	○	○	○
See-through	○	○	○	○	○	○	○	○
Monotone	○	○	○	○	○	○	△	○
Blur	○	○	○	○	○	△	△	×
Mosaic	○	○	○	○	○	△	△	×
Edge	○	○	○	○	○	△	△	×
Border	○	○	○	○	○	×	×	×
Silhouette	○	○	○	○	○	×	×	×
Box	○	○	○	○	×	×	×	×
Bar	○	○	○	×	×	×	×	×
Dot	○	○	×	×	×	×	×	×
Transparency	×	×	×	×	×	×	×	×

foreground region. Then a background image S_B and a foreground image S_F can be expressed as

$$S_B = \left\{ b_{ij} \left| \begin{array}{l} b_{ij} = 0 \quad (i,j) \in \bar{B} \\ b_{ij} = s_{ij} \ (i,j) \in B \end{array} \right. \right\} \tag{2}$$

$$S_F = \left\{ f_{ij} \left| \begin{array}{l} f_{ij} = 0 \quad (i,j) \in \bar{F} \\ f_{ij} = s_{ij} \ (i,j) \in F \end{array} \right. \right\} \tag{3}$$

where $\bar{B}$ is the complement region of B in S and $\bar{F}$ is the complement region of F in S. If there are N_o objects, F is divided into subregions F_n corresponding to objects $o_n (n = 1, 2, \cdots, N_0)$. Then, an object's image S_{F_n} is represented as follows:

$$S_{F_n} = \left\{ f_{ij}^n \left| \begin{array}{l} f_{ij}^n = 0 \quad (i,j) \in \bar{F}_n \\ f_{ij}^n = s_{ij} \ (i,j) \in F_n \end{array} \right. \right\} \tag{4}$$

b_{ij}, f_{ij} and f_{ij}^n are three-dimensional vectors of RGB pixel values. Using S_B and $S_{F_n} (n = 1, 2, \cdots, N_0)$, we represent the original image S in terms of stratified images as

$$S = S_B + S_{F_1} + S_{F_2} + \cdots + S_{F_{N_o}} \tag{5}$$

where the operator $+$ adds the pixel values of the same coordinate in S_B and each S_{F_n}.

We use the background model image $\tilde{S}_B$, estimated by Gaussian mixture model, as the background of the privacy protected image. Let a_0 denote the abstraction operator for the background model image $\tilde{S}_B$ and a_n denote the abstraction operator for the image S_{F_n} of the object o_n. We define two sets $a = (a_0, a_1, a_2, \cdots, a_{N_o})$ and $o = (o_1, o_2, \cdots, o_{N_o})$. Now we can say that access control based on objects' privacy policies is a process to determine a set of abstraction operators a to a given set of objects o.

Visual abstraction by a on objects' images S_{F_n} and the background model image $\tilde{S}_B$ generates abstracted images as follows:

$$S_{F_n}^{a_n} = \left\{ \boldsymbol{f}_{n,ij}^{a_n} \middle| \begin{array}{ll} \boldsymbol{f}_{n,ij}^{a_n} = \boldsymbol{0} & (i,j) \in \bar{F}_n^{a_n} \\ \boldsymbol{f}_{n,ij}^{a_n} = a_n(\boldsymbol{s}_{ij}) & (i,j) \in F_n^{a_n} \end{array} \right\}$$

$$\tilde{S}_B^{a_0} = \left\{ \tilde{\boldsymbol{b}}_{ij}^{a_0} \middle| \begin{array}{ll} \tilde{\boldsymbol{b}}_{ij}^{a_0} = \boldsymbol{0} & (i,j) \in \bar{\bar{B}}^{a_0} \\ \tilde{\boldsymbol{b}}_{ij}^{a_0} = a_0(\tilde{\boldsymbol{b}}_{ij}) & (i,j) \in \bar{B}^{a_0} \end{array} \right\}$$

where $F_n^{a_n}$ is the region of the foreground image in which *visual abstraction* is executed and $\bar{B}^{a_0}$ is the visible region of the background model image after *visual abstraction* for the foreground images. The privacy protected image $S_{<\boldsymbol{o},v>}^{\boldsymbol{a}}$, which is sent to the viewer v, is expressed as follows:

$$S_{<\boldsymbol{o},v>}^{\boldsymbol{a}} = \tilde{S}_B^{a_0} + S_{F_1}^{a_1} + S_{F_2}^{a_2} + \cdots + S_{F_{N_o}}^{a_{N_o}}$$

7   Implementation and Evaluation

Fig. 6 shows a graphical user interface of PriSurv prototype. The viewer is able to select the type of abstraction operators and the surveillance camera. Assume that a viewer 'yuta' is monitoring three objects: 'object 1', 'object 2' and 'object 3', from the left. In the shown image $S_{<\boldsymbol{o},v>}^{\boldsymbol{a}}$, v, $\boldsymbol{o}$ and $\boldsymbol{a}$ are as follows: $v = yuta$, $\boldsymbol{o} = (object1, object2, object3)$, $\boldsymbol{a} = (Box, Silhouette, Mosaic)$.

We experimented our object identification method with a 4.75m × 4.5m room as a surveillance space. The room is evenly divided into 16 square areas and has 4 RFID-readers, each of which obtains two SSI values. When two people consistently walk around in the room, the proposed method was able to identify both objects with the accuracy of 81%.

We also evaluated the performance of visual abstraction. The frame rate of the video should depend on the image size, the number of objects, and the type

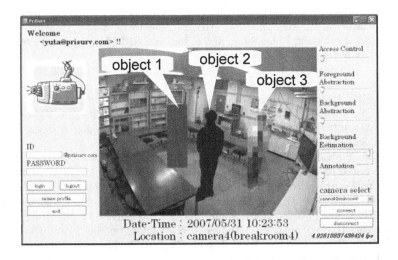

Fig. 6. Graphical User Interface

of the abstraction operator. When the size of images is 640×480, the average frame rate was 15.0 fps without any object. When there is one object whose region size is about 150×420, the average frame rate was the highest at 12.2 fps and the lowest at 8.8 fps when the abstraction operator was Transparency and See-through, respectively.

8   Conclusion

In this paper, we have proposed Privacy Protected Video Surveillance System PriSurv, focusing on *visual abstraction*. PriSurv refers objects' privacy policies, which are determined according to objects' closeness with viewers, and determines abstraction operators to hide visual information of objects. This method enables us to adaptively protect each object's privacy.

To make PriSurv more practical, we need to improve and integrate *object identification*. We also need to consider network security because there is a risk for the invasion of privacy by eavesdroppers.

Acknowledgments. This work was supported in part by a Grant-in-Aid for scientific research and by SCOPE.

References

1. Newton, E.M., Sweeny, L., Malin, B.: Preserving Privacy by De-Identifying Face Images. IEEE Trans. Knowledge and Data Engineering 17(2), 232–243 (2005)
2. Cavallaro, A., Steiger, O., Ebrahimi, T.: Semantic Video Analysis for Adaptive Content Delivery and Automatic Description. IEEE Trans. Circuits and Systems Video Technology 15(10), 1200–1209 (2005)
3. Kirahara, I., Kogure, K., Hagita, N.: Stealth Vision for Protecting Privacy. In: Proc. 17th International Conference on Pattern Recognition, vol. 4, pp. 404–407 (2004)
4. Wickramasuriya, J., Alhazzazi, M., Datt, M., Mehrotra, S., Venkatasubramanian, N.: Privacy-Protecting Video Surveillance. In: Proc. SPIE International Symposium on Electronic Imaging, vol. 5671, pp. 64–75 (2005)
5. Senior, A., Pankati, S., Hampapur, A., Brown, L., Tian, Y.-L., Ekin, A., Connell, J., Shu, C.F., Lu, M.: Enabling Video Privacy through Computer Vision. IEEE Security and Privacy Magazine 3(3), 50–57 (2005)
6. Zhang, W., Cheung, S.S., Chen, M.: Hiding Privacy Information in Video Surveillance System. In: ICIP2005. Proc. IEEE International Conference on Image Processing, pp. 868–871 (2005)
7. Sekiguchi, T., Kato, H.: Proposal and Evaluation of Video-based Privacy Assuring System Based on the Relationship between Observers and Subjects. IPSJ Trans. on Computer Security Proping up Ubiquitous Society 47(8), 2660–2668 (2006)
8. Stauffer, C., Grimson, W.E.L.: Learning Patterns of Activity using Real-Time Tracking. IEEE Trans. Pattern Analysis and Machine Intelligence 22, 747–757 (2000)
9. Koshimizu, T., Toriyama, T., Babaguchi, N.: Factors on the Sense of Privacy in Video Surveillance. In: Proc. Workshop on Capture, Archival and Retrieval of Personal Experiences, pp. 35–43 (2006)

Distribution-Based Similarity for Multi-represented Multimedia Objects

Hans-Peter Kriegel, Peter Kunath, Alexey Pryakhin, and Matthias Schubert

Institute for Informatics, Ludwig-Maximilians University, Munich, Germany
{kriegel,kunath,pryakhin,schubert}@dbs.ifi.lmu.de

Abstract. In modern multimedia databases, objects can be represented by a large variety of feature representations. In order to employ all available information in a best possible way, a joint statement about object similarity must be derived. In this paper, we present a novel technique for multi-represented similarity estimation which is based on probability distributions modeling the connection between the distance value and object similarity. To tune these distribution functions to model the similarity in each representation, we propose a bootstrapping approach maximizing the agreement between the distributions. Thus, we capture the general notion of similarity which is implicitly given by the distance relationships in the available feature representations. Thus, our approach does not need any training examples. In our experimental evaluation, we demonstrate that our new approach offers superior precision and recall compared to standard similarity measures on a real world audio data set.

1 Introduction

Similarity search and content-based object retrieval are important topics when handling multimedia data like sound files or music titles. In recent years, the research community introduced a large variety of feature transformations for all different types of sound data and music titles [1]. Systems like Muscle Fish [2] employ multiple representations like loudness, pitch, or harmonicity for the retrieval of audio data. Additionally, multiple representations are a common setting in various other areas of multimedia data, such as image or video data. Since most of the feature transformations focus on different aspects of the objects, it is beneficial to use more than one feature representation when processing similarity queries. Thus, the most suitable feature representations need to be selected or combined.

In this paper, we introduce a novel technique for combining distance values being observed in multiple representations. In our context, a representation is a method for calculating a distance value between two objects. Our approach assumes that there exist two probability distributions modeling the likelihood that a user would state that two objects displaying a certain distance value in some representation are similar or dissimilar. These distributions are influenced by the degree of similarity between the objects as well as the complete set of objects displaying the same given distance value. Furthermore, we assume that both distributions are connected by a third distribution modeling the ambiguity of the distance value, e.g. the likelihood that both distributions display the same distance value. Now, we can derive the likelihood that a given distance

S. Satoh, F. Nack, and M. Etoh (Eds.): MMM 2008, LNCS 4903, pp. 155–164, 2008.

value has a definite meaning, i.e. the likelihood for an ambiguous meaning is rather small. Since small distances correspond to similar objects, we can assume that distance values being smaller than all distances having an ambiguous meaning indicate object similarity. Based on the local likelihood for similarity in each representation, we can now calculate a joint probability score indicating object similarity.

An additional contribution of this paper is a method for explicitly describing the local similarity likelihoods as explicit functions. Furthermore, to fit the distributions to the given application, we propose an iterative algorithm which is based on maximizing the agreement between representations. To run this algorithm, it is not necessary to manually label pairs of similar objects. Instead our new approach is based on the fact that the feature representations are usually selected to be useful for the given application. Under the condition of meaningful feature transformations, very small distance values will imply similarity and very large distance values will imply dissimilarity. Exploiting this observation, our new algorithm finds a meaningful parametrization within a few iterations.

The rest of the paper is organized as follows. In Section 2, we survey related work in the area of multi-represented similarity search. Our new theory about mapping distances to similarity statements is introduced in Section 3. Section 4 presents solutions for calculating the similarity likelihood and unsupervised parameter tuning. Our experimental evaluation is presented in section 5. The paper concludes in Section 6 with a summary and some directions for future work.

2   Related Work

Considering objects with multiple representations has attracted more and more attention in the multimedia research community. The approaches proposed over the last years can be divided in two categories, namely supervised and unsupervised. The supervised techniques either revert to user feedback or assume that labeled data with known affiliation of objects to some classes are available. For both categories, a common framework is the use of a weighted linear combination.

Supervised by user feedback. Various approaches have been proposed to compute the weights with the help of user feedback. To give feedback, a user has to label if an object being retrieved by a similarity query is really similar to the given query object. In general, the weighted average of the distances observed in all representations was reported to provide good results in several publications (e.g., [3]). For instance, the approaches in [4,5] compute the weights based on the idea of relevance feedback. The authors of [6] suggest another relevance feedback based technique. This technique implements a weighted distance approach that uses standard deviations of the features. Another example is logistic regression w.r.t. user feedback [7]. From the user's point of view, it is rather inconvenient to provide feedback several times to get the result. In contrast, our method can operate without any training objects.

The interactive search fusion method [8] provides a set of fusion functions, e.g. min, max, sum and product function that can be used for combining different representations in order to improve the effectiveness of similarity search. This method supports a manual and an interactive search that is supervised by the user's assistance or by a user-defined query. In addition, Boolean operators on aggregation functions are supported, e.g. "AND" can be applied to the product aggregation function. This technique requires strong interaction with the user. This is not always desirable because in order to use this method the user has to understand its concepts first.

Supervised by labeled data. The authors of [9] introduce two methods for improving the effectiveness in a retrieval system that operates on multiple representations of 3D objects. The proposed techniques are based on the entropy impurity measure. The first method chooses the best representation w.r.t. a given query object. The second method performs a so-called dynamic weighting of the available representations that is computed at query time, and that depends on entropy impurity in the local neighborhood of a query object. This work also presents encouraging experimental results that demonstrate a significant improvement in effectiveness of the similarity search for both proposed techniques. The methods described in [9] need a set of labeled data in order to measure entropy impurity.

Unsupervised. An unsupervised way to determine the weights for a linear combination is counting the number of representations for which a similarity larger than zero is observed [3]. This method is strongly dependent on the occurrence of zero distances. An unsupervised technique for the weighted combination of multiple representations for similarity search in multimedia databases was proposed in [10]. This technique exploits the fact that it is often beneficial to summarize multimedia data, like e.g. videos, in order to achieve higher efficiency during query processing. Compared to our new method, this method has the general drawback that it is only applicable together with summarization. However, object summarization is not a necessary element of general multi-represented similarity search. In [11], a template matching method based on the time warping distance is presented. This approach can measure the temporal edit similarity in order to process audio-visual similarity queries. However, temporal order is not necessary in many applications.

3   A Distribution-Based Approach for Similarity Estimation

In this section, we will introduce our new method for estimating the similarity between two multimedia objects based on multiple feature representations. We can formalize a multi-represented object as follows:

Definition 1 (Multi-Represented Object). *Let $R = \{R_1, \ldots, R_n\}$ be a set of feature spaces. For each feature space R_i there exists a distance function $d_i : R_i \times R_i \to \mathbb{R}_0^+$. A multi-represented object o over the representations R is given by the n tuple $o = (r_1, \ldots, r_n) \in R_1 \times \ldots \times R_n$.*

To compare two multi-represented objects o_1 and o_2, we have to combine the distances that can be derived from each representation. In general, most systems combine the distances using the weighted average over all distances and all representation spaces [3,9,10]. Though this standard approach is adjustable by varying the weights, it considers that the dissimilarity is linearly decreasing in all representations. However, we argue that very small and very large distances indicate a more clear statement about object similarity and dissimilarity, respectively, than medium distance values and thus, have to be treated in a different way.

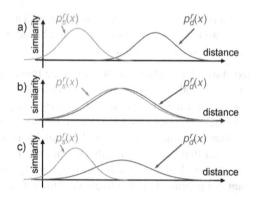

Fig. 1. Three examples for the distributions of similar and dissimilar distances

In our new model, we want to quantify similarity as the likelihood that a user would assign the label "similar" to the comparison of o_k and o_l given the distance value $d_i(o_k, o_l)$ in representation R_i. Let us note that in this model the complementary label to "similar" is not "dissimilar". Instead the user would assign a label "unknown" in the case if it is not clear whether the object should be considered as similar or not. Correspondingly, we can consider the likelihood that a user would assign the label "dissimilar" to both objects. For this distribution, not labeling two objects as similar would also indicate "unknown". As a conclusion, we can distinguish two types of distributions mapping a distance value to "similar", "dissimilar" or "unknown". The first distribution describes the likelihood that a user would consider two objects clearly as similar and the second distribution describes the likelihood that a user would consider two objects clearly as dissimilar. Thus, both distributions are not necessarily complementary because a user could be ambiguous about object similarity as well. However, both distributions are implicitly connected by a third distribution modeling the ambiguity of meaning of a given distance value.

In the following, we will refer to the probability density function over the distances in representation R_i implying similarity as $p_s^i(x)$ and the corresponding density function modeling the distribution of dissimilarity as $p_d^i(x)$. Figure 1 displays three examples of both distributions over the distance values in a data space. For this example, we assume Gaussian distributions. In Subfigure a), $p_s^i(x)$ and $p_d^i(x)$ are rather well separated. Therefore, a ranking query in this representation would most likely retrieve similar objects first and afterwards objects being dissimilar to the given query object. Subfigure b) displays the other extreme. Both distributions are rather identical. Thus, the distance in this representation is rather uncorrelated with object similarity. Therefore, similar as well as dissimilar objects are encountered for any given distance value. Finally, subfigure c) illustrates a more realistic distribution. $p_s^i(x)$ is much more dense for small distances and displays a small density for large distances. $p_d^i(x)$ displays medium densities for a large spectrum of small and large distance values. A corresponding ranking, would start with similar as well as with dissimilar objects. However, after a certain distance is reached, the ranking would contain mostly dissimilar objects.

Based on this observation, we can measure the suitability of a given representation R_i to distinguish similar from dissimilar objects. To measure how meaningful observing a certain distance δ between two objects o_k and o_l is, we can consider the likelihood that the distance δ is observed for similar as well as for dissimilar objects. If δ is common in both distributions $p_s^i(x)$ and $p_d^i(x)$ the meaning is rather ambiguous. However, if it is much likelier that δ is observed for similar objects, the meaning of δ is rather definite.

Formally, the complete likelihood that both distributions display the same distance in representation R_i can be expressed as follows:

$$p_{ambiguous}^i = \int_{-\infty}^{\infty} p_s^i(x) p_d^i(x) dx$$

The product of densities corresponds to the event that both distributions display the same distance and the integral sums up this joint density for all possible distance values. Since $p_{ambiguous}^i$ describes the complete amount of ambiguity in representation i, it can be considered as a measure of how far a given representation is suitable to model similarity. If $p_{ambiguous}^i$ is rather large, the implication of most distance values in R_i on similarity will be rather small. To calculate the probability that a given interval of distance values $[a, b]$ contains more ambiguous distances than the rest, we can determine the portion of the error relative to $p_{ambiguous}^i$:

$$P_{ambiguous}^i(a, b) = \frac{\int_a^b p_s^i(x) p_d^i(x) dx}{p_{ambiguous}^i}$$

To determine the probability that a distance $x < \delta$ has a definite meaning, we can now determine the probability of the ambiguity of distances which are larger than δ:

$$P_{definite}^i(x < \delta) = P_{ambiguous}^i(x \geq \delta) = \frac{\int_\delta^\infty p_s^i(x) \cdot p_d^i(x) dx}{p_{ambiguous}^i}$$

Since distances between similar objects are naturally smaller than distances between dissimilar objects, we can conclude that $p_{definite}^i(x < \delta)$ corresponds to the likelihood that two objects having a distance of δ or smaller are similar. Formally, we can define the local similarity likelihood in representation R_i as follows:

Definition 2 (Local Similarity Likelihood in R_i). *Let o_k and o_l be multi-represented objects over the representations $R = \{R_1, \ldots, R_n\}$. Then the similarity Likelihood for the comparison of o_k and o_l in representation R_i is defined as follows:*

$$L_S^i(o_k, o_l) = p_{definite}^i(x < d_i(o_k, o_l))$$

After having formalized the local similarity likelihood for representation R_i, we can now define the complete similarity likelihood over all representations:

Definition 3 (Similarity Likelihood). *Let o_k and o_l be multi-represented objects over the feature spaces or representations $R = \{R_1, \ldots, R_n\}$. For each representation R_i, we consider the similarity likelihood $L_S^i(x)$. The similarity likelihood P_{SIM} between o_k and o_l is defined as follows:*

$$P_{SIM}(o_k, o_l) = \prod_{R_i \in R} L_S^i(o_k, o_l),$$

Let us note that the similarity likelihood assumes independence between the representations. This is a valid assumption because the benefit of combining multiple representations strongly depends on the use of independent object representations. Thus, when using a set of representations which always have the same implication on object similarity, any combination rule will follow this implication anyway.

4   Efficient Calculation and Parameter Fitting

After describing the general model, we will now turn to calculating the similarity likelihood. Therefore, we need to explicitly describe our distribution functions and fit the parameters of the distributions to the data objects in the given application.

In order to select a suitable distribution function, we have to examine co-occurrence between distance values and object similarity. Let us note that our technique can work with an arbitrary probability distribution function. In our application, we observed that Gaussian distribution functions seem to be a suitable description of the density of object pairs being labeled as similar or dissimilar. Furthermore, when modeling $p_s^i(x)$ and $p_d^i(x)$ as Gaussian distribution, it can be shown that $p_{ambiguous}^i(x)$ again follows a Gaussian distribution.

A Gaussian distribution function is characterized by the mean value and the standard deviation which can be calculated in a straight-forward way.

In order to calculate $L_S^i(o_k, o_l)$, we would need to integrate over a Gaussian distribution function modeling $p_{ambiguous}^i(x)$. Unfortunately, there is no known antiderivative for the Gaussian density function and thus, we need to employ an approximation in order to calculate our similarity likelihoods. To solve this problem, we employ the sigmoid function which is quite often used to approximate the integral from $-\infty$ to a or from a to ∞ over a Gaussian distribution. The sigmoid function is defined as follows:

$$sig_{\alpha,\beta}(x) = \frac{1}{1 + \exp(\alpha \cdot x + \beta)}$$

The local similarity likelihood is modeled by a sigmoid function having a negative α-value. To determine the sigmoid function approximating the cumulative density for a given Gaussian, there are various methods. In our system, we employed the following: We derived a set of sample points by cumulating the values of the Gaussian. Afterwards we employed the method of Levenberg and Marquadt [12] for fitting a sigmoid function to the sample points.

Finally, to employ the similarity likelihood, we have to find suitable function parameters for each representation. Our method is based on distinguishing the distributions of distance values implying similarity and dissimilarity. Thus, we need to find a way for approximating the likelihood that two objects are similar or dissimilar. Our solution to this problem is based on the following observation. If the distances observed in all representations for a given pair of objects are rather small, it is very likely that the objects are considered as similar. Correspondingly, if the distances between two objects are rather large in all representations, we can assume that the objects are dissimilar. To apply this observation for determining a good parametrization, we have to find a way

```
FUNCTION unsupervisedParameterTuning()
    D = generateDistanceVectors()
    FOR EACH representation R_i ∈ R DO
        initSimilarityLikelihoods(R_i,D)
    END FOR
    DO
        L_S^AVG = calculateAVGSIM(D)
        FOR EACH representation R_i ∈ R DO
            calcDistributions(D, L_S^AVG)
            p_ambiguous^i = calcAmbiguity(D, L_S^AVG)
            approximateSimilarityLikelihoods(D, L_S^AVG,p_ambiguous^i)
        END FOR
    WHILE(old parameters ≠ new parameters)
```

Fig. 2. The algorithm for unsupervised parameter tuning

to maximize the agreement between the similarity likelihoods. In other words, the density functions modeling the ambiguity of a distance in each representation should be synchronized in a way that $d_i(o_k, o_l)$ has a comparable probability density in representation R_i as $d_j(o_k, o_l)$ in representation R_j. In order to avoid a costly computation of the distances between all database objects, we sample a small example data set S. We observed in our experiments that using about 100 - 200 objects is sufficient to compute a good approximation. Formally, we can capture the agreement between the similarity likelihoods in all representations by the average variance of estimate values on a sample data set S:

Definition 4. *Let $R = \{R_1, \ldots, R_n\}$ be a set of representations and let $L_S^i(o_k, o_l)$ be the similarity for R_i with $1 \leq i \leq n$. Then the average similarity $L_S^{AVG}(o_k, o_l)$ for the comparison of two multi-represented objects o_k, o_l is defined as :*

$$L_S^{AVG}(o_k, o_l) = \frac{\sum_{R_i \in R} L_S^i(o_k, o_l)}{|R|}$$

Consequently, the average variance of a given example set S consisting of multi-represented objects is given as:

$$Var(S) = \sum_{o_n, o_m \in S} \sum_{R_i \in R} (L_S^i(o_n, o_m) - L_S^{AVG}(o_n, o_m))^2$$

After providing a measure of the agreement between the distributions in each representation on a given example set S, we now introduce an iterative method to find estimate parameters minimizing $Var(S)$. Our method iteratively minimizes a target function, i.e. $Var(S)$, and updates the parameters in each representation to better resemble the similarity value induced by $L_S^{AVG}(o_k, o_l)$.

In the following, we describe the method in more detail. Figure 2 depicts the algorithm in pseudo code. In the initialization step, we calculate all distances in all representations between two example objects. As a result, each object comparison is described by a distance vector $\overrightarrow{d_{m,n}}$ of dimensionality $|R|$ containing the distance in each representation. It makes sense to store the distance vectors for all pairs of objects to avoid recalculating the distances in each iteration. To derive an initial parametrization for the distribution function in representation R_i, all distance vectors are sorted w.r.t. the i-th component. The initial similarity likelihoods are now computed under the assumption that the s smallest observed distance values correspond to similarity. Based on this initial notion of similarity, the parameters of the underlying Gaussian distribution are derived. To get an initialization of dissimilarity, we assume that the d largest distances correspond to dissimilarity. After approximating both distributions, we can derive $p^i_{ambiguous}$ and fit a sigmoid to model $L^i_S(o_k, o_l)$. Now the algorithm can enter the iteration loop. In a first step, we calculate $L^{AVG}_S(o_k, o_l)$ for each distance vector and thus, receive a joint notion of similarity for each object comparison.

After building the current notion of similarity, we first of all can update the Gaussian distributions describing similar and dissimilar distances in each representation. Each distance is weighted with the current likelihood that the corresponding distance vector induces similarity or dissimilarity. After updating the distributions, we continue by calculating $p^i_{ambiguous}$ and transform both Gaussian distributions into our probability distribution describing ambiguity. Now the sigmoid functions describing $L^i_S(o_k, o_l)$ can be updated to fit the joint notion of similarity in a better way. After having updated the similarity in each representation, we can check if any parameter value was indeed optimized. If this was the case, we proceed with an additional iteration. If the parameters did not change, the algorithm converges and we have found a suitable set of parameters maximizing the agreement between distributions. In our experiments, we observed that the algorithm usually terminates after 5 to 10 iterations.

5   Evaluation

All methods were implemented in Java 1.5, the experiments were performed on a workstation having 2GB main memory and an Intel Pentium IV (2.6 GHz) processor. We conducted our experiments on a music collection consisting of almost 500 songs which were taken from 15 different musical genres as the basis for the audio data set. We generated 6 different feature representations per song and depending on the representation, we extracted 30 to 300 features per second. Timbre features are derived from the frequency domain and were mainly developed for the purpose of speech recognition. The extraction of the timbral texture is performed by computing the short time fourier transform. We use the Mel-frequency cepstral coefficients (MFCCs), spectral flux, spectral deviation and spectral rolloff as timbral representations [1]. Rhythmic content features are useful for describing the beat frequency and beat strength of a piece of music. Features derived from beat histograms [1] are used for the description of the rhythmic content. Pitch extraction tries to model the human perception by simulating the behavior of the cochlea. Similar to the rhythmic content features, we derive pitch features from pitch

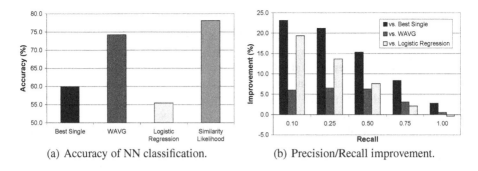

(a) Accuracy of NN classification.   (b) Precision/Recall improvement.

Fig. 3. Quality results on audio data set

histograms which were generated by a multipitch analysis model [13]. For each representation, we applied a vantage point based instance reduction [14] and transformed the corresponding feature vector set into one feature vector of about 500 dimensions.

We compared our approach with three competitors, namely logistic regression [7], the weighted distances approach "WAVG", and the best single representation "Best Single", which provides the best single model for similarity and dissimilarity. The weights for each representation for WAVG are selected in the following way which is known as mean normalization. We normalize the distance with regard to the mean value μ_i^{orig} of the original distance $dist_i^{orig}$ in representation R_i, i.e. $dist_i^{norm}(o, q) = dist_i^{orig}(o, q)/\mu_i^{orig}$. The mean value can be approximated by sampling a small set of objects from the current representation R_i.

Nearest Neighbor Classification. In this type of experiment, we employed nearest neighbor classification in combination with 10-fold cross validation to avoid overfitting. We employed our unsupervised method for parameter fitting and compared the classification accuracy of a nearest neighbor classifier. The results are depicted in Figure 3(a). The classification accuracy when using the similarity likelihood was higher than the accuracy of the classification employing logistic regression, WAVG, or any of the underlying representations. Thus, the similarity likelihood provided a even better notion of similarity than the supervised approach employing logistic regression.

Precision-Recall Results. A final type of experiment tries to capture precision and recall of the proposed method by constructing so-called precision-recall graphs. For this type of experiment a ranking query is posed for each object in the test set. For each query, we now measure the precision for 5 different levels of recall. Afterwards, the average precision for each recall level over all queries is computed. Thus, the 0.25 bin of the precision/recall graph corresponds to average precision observed in the result sets containing 25 % of the objects belonging the same class as the query object. We examined the performance of each representation separately and additionally, examined the performance of WAVG and logistic regression (cf. Figure 3(b)). For all measured recall values, the similarity likelihood achieves a significantly higher precision than both WAVG and the best single representation. Only logistic regression was able to slightly outperform our method for very high recall values.

6   Conclusions

In this paper, we proposed a novel method for multi-represented similarity search. Unlike previous methods which only focus on achieving comparability between the distances derived in each representation space, our new method additionally distinguishes the meaning of distance relationships in each representation. To capture this meaning, we define a so-called similarity likelihood which approximates the probability that two compared objects are truly similar. We propose an unsupervised method which finds parameters that resemble the current notion of similarity in a best possible way. This method employs the idea that the selection of representation spaces itself yields an implicit statement about the notion of similarity of the given application. Thus, our approach maximizes the agreement between the similarity likelihoods in the given representations in order to find a meaningful parameter setting. In our experimental evaluation, we demonstrate on a real world audio data set that our new likelihood based technique outperforms standard combination methods w.r.t precision and recall. For future work, we plan to investigate the use of other distribution functions to model distances between similar and dissimilar objects.

References

1. Tzanetakis, G., Cook, P.: Musical genre classification of audio signals. IEEE TSAP 10(5), 293–302 (2002)
2. Wold, E., Blum, T., Keislar, D., Wheaton, J.: Content-based classification, search, and retrieval of audio. IEEE Multimedia 3(3), 27–36 (1996)
3. Lee, J.H.: Analyses of multiple evidence combination. In: ACM SIGIR Conf. on Research and Development in Information Retrieval, Philadelphia, US, pp. 267–276 (1997)
4. Chua, T.S., Low, W.C., Chu, C.X.: Relevance feedback techniques for color-based image retrieval. In: Proc. MMM, p. 24 (1998)
5. Rui, Y., Huang, T.S., Mehrotra, S.: Content-based image retrieval with relevance feedback in mars. In: Proc. ICIP, pp. 815–818 (1997)
6. Aksoy, S., Haralick, R.M., Cheikh, F.A., Gabbouj, M.: A weighted distance approach to relevance feedback. In: Proc. ICPR, p. 4812 (2000)
7. Gey, F.: Inferring probability of relevance using the method of logistic regression. In: ACM SIGIR Conf. on Research and Development in Information Retrieval, Dublin, Ireland, pp. 222–231 (1994)
8. Smith, J.R., Jaimes, A., Lin, C.Y., Naphade, M., Natsev, A.P., Tseng, B.: Interactive search fusion methods for video database retrieval. In: Proc. ICIP, pp. 741–744 (2003)
9. Bustos, B., Keim, D.A., Saupe, D., Schreck, T., Vranic, D.V.: Using entropy impurity for improved 3d object similarity search. In: Proc. ICME, pp. 1303–1306 (2004)
10. Kriegel, H.P., Kröger, P., Kunath, P., Pryakhin, A.: Effective similarity search in multimedia databases using multiple representations. In: Proc. MMM, pp. 389–393 (2006)
11. Naphade, M., Wang, R., Huang, T.: Multimodal pattern matching for audio-visual query and retrieval. In: Proc. SPIE, pp. 188–195 (2001)
12. Gill, P.E., Murray, W.: Algorithms for the solution of the nonlinear least-squares problem. SIAM J. Num. Anal. 15(5), 977–992 (1978)
13. Tolonen, T., Karjalainen, M.: A computationally efficient multipitch analysis model. IEEE TSAP 8(6), 708–716 (2000)
14. Brecheisen, S., Kriegel, H.P., Kunath, P., Pryakhin, A.: Hierarchical genre classification for large music collections. In: ICME, pp. 1385–1388 (2006)

A Multimodal Input Device for Music Authoring for Children

Yasushi Akiyama[1] and Sageev Oore[2]

[1] Dalhousie University, Halifax Canada
`yasushi[at]cs.dal.ca`
[2] Saint Mary's University, Halifax Canada
`sageev[at]cs.smu.ca`

Abstract. We present a novel interface of a digital music authoring tool that is designed for children. Our system consists of a unique multimodal input device and corresponding platform to support children's music authoring. By departing from the conventional design approaches of existing tools, our system provides a simple and intuitive environment for young children to use. The proposed interface is tested with children in a focus group study, and the results of the study are encouraging in that the children were able to perform some of complicated multitrack recording tasks within a single session that lasted for 15 to 20 minutes.

Keywords: HCI, multimodal interaction, multimedia authoring, interface design for children, digital music creation.

1   Introduction

Providing tools to assist children in exploring their creative ideas is important for the development of their creativity. Children are capable of using their voices to express a variety of musical ideas without formal training, however, unlike scrap paper and crayons with which children can try out their drawing ideas, they do not seem to have tools that allow themselves to further develop their musical ideas. The design of music creation tools is traditionally based on the look and functionality of hardware counterparts, and they are designed to accommodate the demand by experienced adult users. The reproduction of tiny knobs and other controls on computer screens makes these tools look very complicated and presents physical difficulties for manipulation as depicted in Figure 1. Although there exist many dedicated hardware devices, such as HUI controllers [1] or MIDI keyboards to control software programs, the complicated appearance of the software still remains the same, and it is very unlikely to greatly reduce the complexity so that the new users with no experience in manipulating audio equipment can start using these tools without long struggling hours of learning. Needless to say, younger children are virtually completely excluded as intended users because of the complexity of the software.

This paper presents our novel interface design that allows young children to intuitively learn to manipulate digital music data, by employing multimodal

S. Satoh, F. Nack, and M. Etoh (Eds.): MMM 2008, LNCS 4903, pp. 165–174, 2008.

Fig. 1. Screenshot of a popular program, Cakewalk's *Sonar* [2]. The screen is cluttered with small controls. One can easily imagine how awkward it is to manipulate these tiny controls with a mouse. Although there exist some hardware devices to control the software tools, the complexity will remain the same.

interaction techniques and a unique spatial allocation approach of musical objects for easy authoring.

1.1 Motivation

Although most children can use their voices to express a variety of musical ideas without formal vocal lessons, it is unlikely for them to skilfully manipulate musical instruments and/or recording equipment. For recording of a vocal or instrumental performance, they tend to lack the ability or knowledge of the complex tasks of sound engineering. Furthermore, as noted above, designers of existing authoring tools have made an effort to create *replicas* of hardware devices on computer screens, and this replication may have benefited some users when switching from hardware to software programs. However, the resulting software tools appear quite unfriendly to new users, and sometimes clumsy even for professionals to use. For instance, a very large recording control board with knobs, buttons, and faders was shrunk to fit in a computer screen. A monitor screen is cluttered with those miniature *virtual* controls that have to be manipulated with a mouse (Figure 1). Although using specially designed hardware devices, such as HUI controllers [1] or MIDI keyboards for manipulation of software tools, may ease the physical difficulty, the cluttered view still remains the same, and novice users understandably would find the software quite difficult to use. This is a typical example of the interface design that presents a *gulf of execution* [3].

Another recurring issue in the related literature is the linearity of existing authoring tools. [4, 5] The majority of these programs provide an interface that looks like a spread sheet [5], on which users place musical motifs one after another to create a sequence for each instrument (or a vocal track). This method works well if the user already has an idea of the overall structure of the musical piece. However, the music creation process involves many non-linear steps–not many composers start writing from the introduction of a piece and gradually proceed towards the ending, but rather, they tend to come up with a few themes/motifs that are rearranged and manipulated through different compositional techniques and combined through their own creativity. Providing an interface that can accommodate multiple creation processes may be desired.

1.2   Inherent Issues in Music Authoring Tools

Our own discussions with adult users and observations of children using existing tools led us to identify two types of issues that may affect the usability of music creation tools.

1. Issues due to user's overall ability.
   - Lack of prior knowledge of sound engineering.
   - Varied levels of musical/instrumental and computer skills.
2. Design issues of interfaces of these programs.
   - Cluttered view as a result of recording software devices with many virtual controls crammed into a screen.
   - Physical difficulties of manipulation of tiny controls.
   - Linear/sequential approach of music creation that may not be suitable for all compositional habits.

1.3   Related Work

There are a very few music creation tools that are intended for use by young children. Two products that are commercially available are Sony's Super Duper Music Looper [6] and FlexiMusic's Kids Composer [7]. These products use the interface and concept of the standard multitrack sequencers and linear sequencing approach. Informal observations of children trying to use these tools showed that multitrack sequencing programs require prior knowledge of concept of tracks and basic compositional skills (e.g., careful planning of the music structure), and thus these programs are more appropriate for older children. (e.g., Super Duper Music Looper is designed for children ages 6 to 9). By incorporating multimodal interaction techniques and presenting music clips in a different manner, we are able to include children of younger ages.

As part of MIT Media Laboratory's Toy Symphony project, Farbood et al. introduced HyperScope [8], a sketch-based composition tool for novice users. The user draws a curve to create a musical motif, and then using those created motifs, she will specify the structure of a music piece, again by drawing lines (simple repetition of original motifs) or curves (with moderate pitch alterations).

There are also other related systems for children. Tomitsch et al. [9] presented the evaluation of the prototype of their tangible music toy *MusicPets*, which allows children to record and playback audio. MusicPets encouraged children to exchange messages, collaboratively compose tunes, and play DJ with multiple MusicPets. Breinbjerg et al. [10] have created a system for novice users to record, manipulate, and mix sounds of everyday life. *Acousmatic Composition Environment* consists of three stands with a soundproof box, tangible interface for sound manipulation, and a two-touch screen for mixing recorded audio. The system is intended to encourage children's auditory curiosity in the context of Musique Concréte. These results are encouraging in that appropriately designed tools can help children to explore their musical creativity, which might have been otherwise unexplored. Although not specifically designed for children, various other systems incorporated motion sensors for music/sound manipulation and for other forms of arts including [11, 12, 13, 14].

Duignan et al. [4] have identified metaphors used in existing music sequencing programs and proposed the taxonomy of their interfaces design characteristics. Seago et al. [15] have performed a heuristic review on interface designs of both hardware and software synthesisers. The issues which they have identified are in fact of our own interest, as both synthesisers and authoring tools share design issues such as crude emulation of hardware devices and control of music data which are typically high-dimensional and elusive.

We describe our proposed multimodal input device and software platform, along with some implementation details in Section 2. We then discuss our focus group studies with children in Section 3, and conclusions are presented in Section 4.

2   Implementation

2.1   System Overview

We address the issues discussed in Section 1.2 by designing a unique input device that allows users to interact multimodally (Figure 2) and by introducing an interface that enables casual yet intuitive placement of music clips (Figure 3),

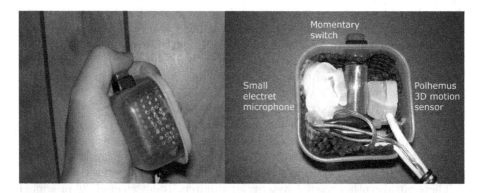

Fig. 2. The input device for the system consists of an electret microphone, a momentary switch, and a Polhemus 3D motion sensor. User holds the switch to drag the musical objects on the screen. The location of the pointer is determined by the 2D coordinate values on a plane that is parallel to the monitor screen. It is also used as the sound input device, thus it frees users from constant switching between the standard mouse and a microphone.

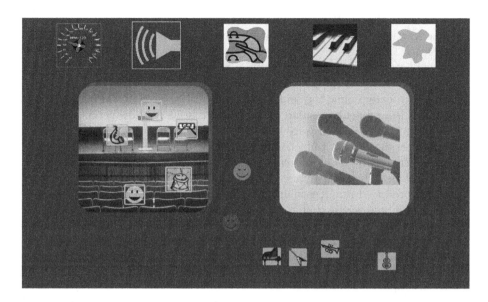

Fig. 3. Screenshot of the system. A user places a musical object on one of the 3 distinct areas, stage, recording, or neutral, for intuitive activation and arming of music clips. A unique integrated input device is used as a pointing device as well as sound input device, eliminating cumbersome switching between the devices.

as opposed to the constrained linear organisation employed in typical authoring tools. A user moves a tangible input device to manipulate musical objects. This input device is also equipped with a microphone, thus it allows the user to record a vocal performance without switching to a separate sound input device. It also supports vocal-based instrument-sound synthesis and sound effects, by real-time transcription and sound analysis of the incoming vocal signal, respectively.

The implementation was written in Java and JOGL [16] for the graphical interface and visual feedback, and in Max/MSP [17] for sound processing. The device construction is described in Section 2.3.

2.2   Multimodal Platform

- Integrated input device consisting of an electret microphone, a momentary switch, and a Polhemus 3D motion sensor, supporting pointing, clicking and sound input, without the necessity to switch to another device.
- Vocal-based instrument playback by realtime transcription. Children can sing musical phrases into the microphone, and the system plays back the same phrase by synthesising a chosen instrument sound. This is done by a simple algorithm using the Fast Fourier transform to detect the dominant frequency and the frequency-to-MIDI conversion equation:

$$n = 12 \times \frac{\log \frac{f}{220}}{\log 2} + 57 \; . \tag{1}$$

where n is the MIDI pitch value and f is the detected dominant frequency. The fraction of n is represented as the additional *detune* parameter in MIDI message.

- Vocal-based sound effects by realtime sound analysis. Most children do not have knowledge of specific sound effect parameters, but they are oftentimes able to vocally mimic the sound of the effect. Our system allows children to control the predefined sound effects such as *wah-wah*, distortion, or pitch-shifting with their own voice mimicking the sound.

  Wah-wah effect is implemented as the band-pass filter with the centre of the frequency band shifted based on the frequency band width of the controlling sound that mimics the effect. Using the incoming sound's band width produced a perceptually more stable result than using the weighted or unweighted average of the incoming sound's frequencies. Distortion is implemented as the amplitude distortion whose strength is proportional to the incoming voice sound's amplitude. The louder the controlling sound, the more distorted the target sound is. Pitch-shifting is a frequency-domain pitch shifter, whose shifting amount is proportional to the incoming controlling voice's pitch shifting.

- A location based playback/recording mode selection. It provides a clear distinction of the clip status, compared to the standard button-based approach, as described in Section 2.4.

2.3   Input Device Design

We created a prototype of a unique tangible device that consists of an electret microphone, a momentary switch, and a Polhemus 3D motion sensor (Figure 2). Polhemus Isotrak [18] is used for the 3D motion tracking. The user holds the switch to drag the musical objects on the screen. The location of the pointer is determined by the 2D coordinate values on a plane that is parallel to the monitor screen. To reduce the influence of the jittering movements of the cursor due to some environmental noise, we have applied a dynamic low-pass filter [19] and incorporated the Bubble cursor [20], which is known to enhance the interaction time and accuracy in the case of the standard mouse.

In addition to being a pointing device, it is also a sound input device. The user can directly sing into this device. This gives younger children a more toy-like impression than the standard mouse.

2.4   Object Representation and Graphical Interface Design

The graphical interface of our system provides three distinct areas, *neutral, stage*, and *recording* areas, on to which children drag and drop sound objects. Objects are either instruments (prerecorded music clips) or happy faces (clips that they can freely record/playback their own sounds). When these objects are placed on the stage area, they are activated for playback, and when on the recording area, they are armed (activated for recording). This simple change from the conventional multitrack representation of music clips to the location-based method by allowing the objects to move around freely not only helps children to understand the object's status more intuitively, but it may also allow users quick auditioning of their ideas, which may not have been possible with the spreadsheet style sequencing.

3   User Studies

3.1   Study Setting

We conducted a set of focus group studies with 11 children aged from 3 to 6 (1 three-year old, 7 four-year olds, 2 five-year olds, and 1 six-year old children) in order to introduce our musical authoring tool, and then observe their behaviours and reactions. They had varied experience in general computer usage, music, and video games (4 had a frequent use of computer and 3 had some experience with computer. 4 had a piano/toy piano at home and had played it before. 1 child had frequent experience playing video games, and 3 had some experience with video games).

Figure 4 shows the system in use by children. Each session lasted 15 to 20 minutes, depending on their interests and the quickness to get used to the system, and we had 2 or 3 children in a group for each session. We began each session by demonstrating how to drag the musical objects holding the integrated input device, and explained the basic concepts of musical object activation/arming (i.e., stage and recording areas). We also showed them how to choose songs and voice-based instruments/effects. After a few minutes of familiarising themselves with the input device and the concept, we had asked them to perform easy tasks in a very casual manner with questions like "Do you want to record your singing?" or "Do you want to move a saxophone to hear how it sounds?" in order to observe the levels of their understanding of the system. We asked the subjects to switch between the standard mouse and our integrated device, and then observed their behaviours.

3.2   Observation

Although a few of the younger children took a longer time to get used to the physical manipulation of the input device, all of them were able to move the musical objects to specific targets by the end of the sessions. Compared with the standard mouse, children who had frequently used computers seemed to have taken a longer time to get used to our integrated input device, while we did not see any obvious difference between the two types of input devices in performance of others with little or no previous computer experience. Most children seemed encouraged to play with our tangible device, which they can move in mid-air to manipulate virtual objects on screen. We also noticed that while using a mouse, a couple of children mistakenly picked it up and started to sing into the mouse. This behaviour suggests that our device helps children to intuitively perform the relevant tasks such as moving objects with it and then singing into it as a

Fig. 4. The system in use by children. Although the time each child took to get used to the system varied, by the end of the session, all of them were able to place musical objects in target areas for playback and recording.

natural sequence of actions, which may be less fluid in case of a mouse and a separate microphone.

They were very quick to realise the concept of activation, presumably due to the location based approach and the visual feedback. Only the currently played clips change the icon sizes based on the amplitude of each clip, while the rest of the icon sizes remain unchanged. Once the children understood the activation of the clips (i.e., placing them on the stage), it seemed relatively easy for them to grasp the concept of arming. Most children did not seem to know the different types of instruments, however, they were nonetheless able to make connections between the instrument names and the icons towards the end of the sessions. When asked, they were able to move a specific instrument object. As we had expected, most children had no experience in recording their own voice, and thus listening to themselves singing, talking, or sometimes yelling was apparently a fun activity for them. One 4 year old who had no musical experience went on to record multiple clips of her singing, and played them back simultaneously, accomplishing her first attempt at multitrack recording.

We also noticed some aspects that need to be improved. The children tended to constantly change their locations during a single session. Because the base station of the 3D tracker was fixed at one spot and the sensor's location was an absolute location relative to this station, the cursor was sometimes out of the viewing area and we had to move the children back to the original location where the device was calibrated. One solution to this is to use the relative positioning used with the regular pointing devices. When the cursor reaches one of the edges of the viewing area, it cannot move further in that direction. It resumes its movement when the pointing device moves in a different direction.

Another issue that we noticed at the early sessions with the youngest group was that the initial number of happy faces (blank objects) was set to nine and this number seemed a little too big for them. Because most children use only one or two blank objects, we changed so that they had only 3 happy faces and they could add more if needed. This created a more spacious and cleaner view. Our system currently provides 7 prerecorded songs for 7 instruments. Commercial products like [6, 7] come with a large list of prerecorded clips, and this may be helpful when the users are older. However, it is probably impossible for children who are unable to read to select a song from the long list of song names, and we believe that keeping the list shorter may be a more age-appropriate approach.

Overall, the system attracted most children and they successfully enjoyed this new way of creating music. Our studies took place at a daycare facility where there were many other children who were not participating in the study but were still able to see their peers playing with our system, and they actually started forming a line eager to have their own turns.

4   Conclusions and Future Work

We have described a new multimodal input device and corresponding platform for digital music authoring for children. Our approach is different from complex existing tools in that it fluidly integrates multimodal interaction techniques such as a motion sensor, voice-based playback of instruments and sound effects in such a way as to allow younger users, who do not have high-level computer or musical skills, to explore their musical creativity. Our integrated input device consists of a small microphone, an on/off switch, and a Polhemus motion sensor and thus serves as a pointing device as well as a sound input device. This is supported by a location-based object manipulation interface in lieu of the standard button/light based mode selection.

The focus group sessions that we have conducted show some promising results of our system. Unlike existing tools that use the conventional multitracking concepts, our system provides an intuitive and easy approach to digital music creation.

We are planning to conduct a series of user evaluation studies with children in the near future. These studies will include further investigation and comparison of aspects of the system such as the standard multitracking versus casual placement of music clips, and the conventional lighted/coloured button-based versus spatial allocation of music clips.

We believe that allowing this younger age group of children to freely explore their creativity is very important and making supporting tools available to them is an essential step.

Acknowledgements. This research is funded by NSERC. Yasushi Akiyama is a recipient of NSERC PGS. We would like to thank Dirk Arnold for giving us very helpful feedback, and Sharon Woodill for assisting to conduct the user studies with children.

References

1. MACKIE: http://www.mackie.com/index.html
2. Cakewalk: Sonar, http://www.cakewalk.com/products/sonar/default.asp
3. Norman, D.A.: The design of everyday things. Basic Books, New York (2002)
4. Duignan, M., Noble, J., Barr, P., Biddle, R.: Metaphors for electronic music production in *Reason* and *Live*. In: Masoodian, M., Jones, S., Rogers, B. (eds.) APCHI 2004. LNCS, vol. 3101, pp. 111–120. Springer, Heidelberg (2004)
5. Project-Bar-B-Q: http://www.projectbarbq.com/
6. Sony: http://www.sonycreativesoftware.com
7. FlexiMusic: Kids composer,
   http://www.fleximusic.com/kidscomposer/preview.htm
8. Farbood, M.M., Pasztor, E., Jennings, K.: Hyperscore: A graphical sketchpad for novice composers. IEEE Emerging Technologies, 50–54 (2004)
9. Tomitsch, M., Grechenig, T., Kappel, K., Koltringer, T.: Experiences from designing a tangible musical toy for children. In: IDC. International Conference for Interaction Design and Children 2006, Tampere, Finland (2006)
10. Breinbjerg, M., Caprani, O., Lunding, R., Kramhoft, L.: An acousmatic composition environment. In: NIME 2006. The 2006 International Conference on New Interfaces for Musical Expression, Paris, France (2006)
11. Mulder, A.G.E., Fels, S.S.: Sound sculpting: Manipulating sound through virtual sculpting. In: WCGS 1998, Whistler, BC, Canada, pp. 15–23 (1998)
12. Ip, H.H.S., Law, K.C.K., Kwong, B.: Cyber composer: Hand gesture-driven intelligent music composition and generation. In: MMM, pp. 46–52 (2005)
13. Lim, M.Y., Aylett, R.: Interactive virtual graffiti system. In: IEEE Virtual Reality International Conference 2004, p. 131 (2004)
14. Godoy, R.I., Haga, E., Jensenius, A.R.: Playing "air instruments": Mimicry of sound-producing gestures by novices and experts. In: Gibet, S., Courty, N., Kamp, J.-F. (eds.) GW 2005. LNCS (LNAI), vol. 3881, pp. 256–267. Springer, Heidelberg (2006)
15. Seago, A., Holland, S., Mulholland, P.: Synthesizer user interface design–lessons learned from a heuristic review. Technical Report 2004/20, Depatment of Computing, Faculty of Mathematics and Computing, The Open University, Milton Keynes, UK (2004)
16. java.net: Jogl api project, https://jogl.dev.java.net/
17. Cycling'74: Max/msp, http://www.cycling74.com/products/maxmsp
18. Polhemus: http://www.polhemus.com
19. Vogel, D., Balakrishnan, R.: Distant freehand pointing and clicking on very large, high resolution displays. In: User Interface Software and Technology 2005 (UIST 2005), Seattle, Washington, USA (2005)
20. Grossman, T., Balakrishnan, R.: The bubble cursor: enhancing target acquisition by dynamic resizing of the cursor's activation area. In: CHI 2005. Proceedings of the SIGCHI conference on Human factors in computing systems, pp. 281–290. ACM Press, New York (2005)

Free-Shaped Video Collage*

Bo Yang[1], Tao Mei[2], Li-Feng Sun[1], Shi-Qiang Yang[1], and Xian-Sheng Hua[2]

[1] Department of Computer Science and Technology, Tsinghua University, P.R. China
[2] Microsoft Research Asia, P.R. China
bo.yang02@gmail.com, {tmei,xshua}@microsoft.com,
{sunlf,yangshq}@mail.tsinghua.edu.cn

Abstract. With the explosive growth of multimedia data, video presentation has become an important technology for fast browsing of video
content. In this paper, we present a novel video presentation technique
called "Free-Shaped Video Collage" (FS-Collage), which is motivated
from and built upon our previous work on Video Collage [3]. Video Collage is a kind of static summary which selects the most representative
regions-of-interest (ROI) from video and seamlessly arranges them on
a synthesized image. Unlike Video Collage in which both the shapes of
ROI and final collage are fixed as rectangle, we support arbitrary shapes
of ROI and a set of collage templates in FS-Collage. Furthermore, we
design three ROI arrangement schemes (i.e., *book*, *diagonal*, and *spiral*)
for satisfying different video genres. We formulate the generation of FS-
Collage as an energy minimization problem and solve the problem by
designing a random sampling process. The experiment results show that
our FS-Collage achieves satisfying performance.

Keywords: video collage, region of interest.

1 Introduction

Driven by the rapid development of digital devices, the quantity of video data
is significantly increasing in recent years. One way for efficient browsing such
large amounts of data is video presentation, which aims at producing visually
pleasing and compact summary of video content while preserving the storyline.

There exists rich research on video or photo set representation. From the
viewpoint of presentation style, the existing methods can be classified into two
categories, i.e., dynamic skimming and static summary. Dynamic skimming is
a new generated video sequence composed of a series of sub-clips from one or
multiple video sequences or a collection of photos [6][7][8][11][12], while static
summary is usually one or multiple images extracted or generated from video
key-frames or selected from a set of photos [1][9][10] so that it is more convenient for transmission and storage. On the other hand, from the perspective of
presented content, video or photo presentation can be classified into two para-
digms, i.e., frame-based and Regions-of-Interest (ROI)-based. The first paradigm

---

* This work was performed when Bo Yang visited Microsoft Research Asia as an intern.

S. Satoh, F. Nack, and M. Etoh (Eds.): MMM 2008, LNCS 4903, pp. 175–185, 2008.

(a) rectangle collage   (b) heart shaped collage

Fig. 1. Sample "Free-Shaped Video Collage" of two videos. Arbitrary shaped ROI are extracted from the representative key-frames, and then resized and seamlessly arranged in collage according to user-selected shape template.

extracts a set of representative key-frames and then arranges these key-frames into a synthesized image according to temporal structure [1][10]. However, such approaches are not compact enough due to many non-informative areas in key-frames. Thus, more research work on video presentation has focused on the arrangement of ROI rather than the whole key-frames. The second paradigm first extracts saliency regions in the key-frames and then arranges in a static or dynamic manner [7][9]. However, these approaches do not make the ROI as a visually pleasing integration, either because of non-compactness or sharp transitions between ROI.

Recently, Rother *et al.* proposed a compact and smooth presentation for photo collections, called "AutoCollage," which automatically and seamlessly arranges the ROI within a photo collage [2]. Wang *et al.* further extended this idea to video and proposed "Video Collage" [3], which extracts ROI from representative key-frames in video sequence and arranges them according to temporal structure, as well as blends the seams between ROI. However, Video Collage also has several unsolved issues. First, the ROI are fixed to rectangles and thus cannot well preserve the saliency regions within key-frames. Second, the final collage is also fixed to a rectangle, which lacks diversity of visual styles. Furthermore, ROI can be only arranged by a predefined temporal order, and thus there are no choices for users to produce other kinds of collages. We believe that a great diversity of collage templates with arbitrary shaped ROI and different ROI arranging styles will significantly improve user experience of browsing video content.

Considering the above issues in Video Collage that affect user experience, we propose in this paper a kind of enhanced video collage, called "Free-Shaped Video Collage" (FS-Collage), which is generated by arranging arbitrary shaped ROI smoothly on a user-specified collage template, as well as providing users more choices to produce their preferred collage. Figure 1 shows two examples of the proposed FS-Collage of two home videos, whose template is indicated by user. In FS-Collage, we first extract key-frames by image attention analysis [5] and get the ROI using color and motion based method [4]; then according to collage template and ROI arrangement style, we put as more ROI as possible into the collage with several constraints satisfied; finally, the seams between different images are blended to produce visually smooth collage by probabilistic alpha matting.

Compared with "AutoCollage" [2] and "Video Collage" [3], the proposed "Free-Shaped Video Collage" has the following distinctive characteristics:

- The ROI and the final collage are free in shape rather than fixed as rectangles. Moreover, users can assign any shaped collage template.
- Unlike Video Collage which arranges ROI in the order of "left-to-right" and "top-to-down," the ROI in FS-Collage can be arranged in temporal order or in salience order.
- The arbitrary shaped seams are better blended by a probabilistic alpha matting approach.

The remaining of this paper is organized as follows. In Section 2, we formulate the process of generating the collage as an energy minimization problem; then the energy minimization approach is presented in Section 3; we detail seamless blending in Section 4; Section 5 gives experiment results, followed by conclusions in Section 6.

2   Energy Definition

A collage is a tool which facilitate users' browsing video content; therefore, any collage should have some basic properties. We summarize them as follows:

- **Representative.** Since the target of collage is to efficiently browsing video data, The collage should present the main story of the video. In other words, users could have a quick glance at video content from the collage.
- **Compact.** For efficiently browsing video content, a collage needs to show as much informative information as possible. As mentioned in Section 1, for each key-frame, only some parts attract users' attention and provide useful information. Therefore, the collage should have ROI as more as possible while including background as less as possible.
- **Visually smooth.** In order to provide users better experience, a collage needs to be a visually smooth integration instead of a set of independent regions. Therefore, seams between different images should be smooth enough.

These properties can be formulized as a series of energies, and generating a collage can be viewed as a labeling problem with minimized energy. Given a video sequence V containing M frames $\{F_1, F_2, \ldots, F_m\}$, the goal of free-shaped video collage is to find the best labeling L, which minimizes an energy function $E(L)$. For each pixel p in a collage template C its label has the form $L(p) = \{n, r, s\}$, in which n denotes the number of frame, so that $F_n \in \{F_1, F_2, \ldots, F_m\}$, r denotes the resize factor of frame F_n to make more saliency regions larger, and

s denotes the 2D shift of the resized image with respect to the collage so that $C(p) = I(F'_n(r), p - s)$, where $F'_n(r)$ is the resized image from an original image F_n with factor r, and $I(x, p)$ denotes pixel p in image x. We derive the energy of a labeling L from [3], but make a few changes as:

$$E(L) = \omega_1 E_{rep}(L) + \omega_2 E_{comp}(L) + \omega_3 E_{trans}(L) \tag{1}$$

where $E_{rep}(L)$, $E_{comp}(L)$, and $E_{trans}(L)$ denotes representative cost, compact cost, and visually smooth cost, respectively, and ω_1, ω_2, and ω_3 are their corresponding weights, which are set empirically.

Representative Cost. Similar to [3], we define representative cost as a combination of image saliency, quality, and distribution. Intuitively, if a collage includes more salient regions and covers more key stories, it is more representative. Moreover, low quality frames provide little visual information, and thus should be excluded. Accordingly, the representative cost is defined as

$$E_{rep}(L) = -(\alpha A(L) + \beta Q(L) + \gamma D(L)) \tag{2}$$

where $A, Q, and D$ measures the saliency, quality, and frame distribution, respectively. $\alpha, \beta, and \gamma$ are corresponding weights. However, we modify definition of the saliency and distribution in order to extract better representative keyframes. Let all images used in L are $\{F_{l1}, F_{l2}, \ldots, F_{lN}\}$, and their corresponding ROI are $\{R_{l1}, R_{l2}, \ldots, R_{lN}\}$. Then, we define $A(L)$ on ROI instead of on the whole image in [3] as $A(L) = \sum_i A(R_{li}) \cdot \epsilon A(R_{li})/A_{max}$, where $A(R_{li})$ measures the saliency of R_{li} [4], and ϵ is a parameter controlling the resize factor. In the ROI extraction process, faces are especially preserved, since they often attract human's attention. $Q(L) = \sum_i (C(F_{li}) - B(F_{li}))$, where $C(F_{li})$ denotes the color contrast and $B(F_{li})$ measures blurring degree [5]. Similar to [3], we use information entropy to measure $D(L)$ as

$$D(L) = -\frac{1}{\log N} \sum_{i=1}^{N-1} p(F_{li}) \cdot \log p(F_{li}) \tag{3}$$

Unlike [3], we consider the intrinsic video temporal structures, i.e., shot and sub-shot, and use sub-shot distribution here instead of direct frame distribution as in [3] to avoid selecting two frames in one long sub-shot. Thus, $p(F_{li}) =$(sub-shot interval between F_{li} and $F_{l,i+1}$)/(the number of sub-shots).

Compact Cost. To measure the compactness of collage, we introduce the compact cost. Owing to the space limitation of a collage, we should endeavor to make the collage present as much important information as possible. Thus, the compact cost is defined as

$$E_{comp}(L) = \sum_i Area(R_{li})/Area(C) \tag{4}$$

where $Area(R_{li})$ denotes the area of R_{li}, and $Area(C)$ the area of collage template C.

Transition Cost. A visually smooth collage should avoid sharp transitions between different pictures. Here, we derive the cost definition from that in [3].When two 4-connected pixels p, q have different labels, i.e. $L(p) \neq L(q)$, a seam is detected. Thus, the transition cost is defined as

$$E_{trans}(L) = \sum_{p,q \in C} (\| F'_{L(p)}(p) - F'_{L(q)}(p) \| + \| F'_{L(p)}(q) - F'_{L(q)}(q) \|) \quad (5)$$

where $F'_{L(p)}(q)$ denotes the color of pixel q in the resized image $F'_{L(p)}$. Similar to [2], the minimization of $E(L)$ is done under two constraints: uniform shift and connectivity. The former assures the images appearing in the collage only have one unique shift each. For example, for two pixels $p, q \in C$, $L(p) = \{n, r, s\}$ and $L(q) = \{n', r', s'\}$, if $n = n'$, then $s = s'$. The latter constraint indicates that for each set $S_n = \{p \in C : L(p) = \{n, r, s\}\}$, it should form a 4-connected region.

3 Implementation of Energy Minimization

In order to find the best labeling L, we need to decide the parameters in each pixel's labeling: $L(p) = \{n, r, s\}$. As Eq. (2), r is fixed for each frame, we only need to find an optimized n and s. However, due to large search space of n (often larger than $10k$ frames) and s (often larger than $10k$ pixels), it is quite difficult for traversing the whole search space. We design a random sampling process to first find N frames from all M frames in the video sequence, and then decide each pixel's label $L(p)$. By such an approach, we optimized E by minimizing E_{rep}, E_{comp}, and E_{trans} respectively. Unlike [3] where heuristic searching algorithm of sub-shot selection does not consider the distribution constraint of sub-shot, the proposed process achieves better performance by iterative random sampling.

Figure 2 gives our energy minimization algorithm. Unlike [3] in which the number of image is given by the user, the proposed algorithm automatically adjusts it to adapt according to collage template in Step 1 and 4. We iteratively use random sampling approaches in step 2 and 3 to choose key-frames and to make ROI arrangement with random disturbance, to minimize $E_{rep}(L)$ and $E_{comp}(L)$. Once the ROI and their positions have been decided, we make a minor ROI position adjustment to cover as more collage area as possible in Step 6. Finally, graph cut is adopted to minimize the overall energy E. We will then detail the approaches to ROI arrangement in Step 3 and ROI adjustment in Step 6.

3.1 ROI Arrangement

As shown in Fig. 2, ROI arrangement (Step 3) is a crucial step for minimizing $E_{comp}(L)$. Given a set of ROI, our target is to find the best arrangement which minimizes $E_{comp}(L)$ according to user's specific collage style, i.e., making ROI cover as much space of the collage as possible and assuring no ROI occlusions. To provide users more collage styles, we design three kinds of ROI arrangement schemes for users to choose: book, diagonal, spiral, as shown in

> **Input:** Sub-shots **Output:** L
>
> 1. Initialize $N = Area(C)/$Average ROI $Area(R_i)$
> 2. Uniformly select N sub-shots with each disturbed by a random variable, select a key-frame from each sub-shot with $\max\{A(L) + Q(L)\}$ to minimize $E_{rep}(L)$.
> 3. ROI in these key-frames are arranged with random disturbance for several times, and choose the one with least $E_{comp}(L)$
> 4. If all the selected n key-frames have been put into the collage, $N++$; else, $N--$;
> 5. Repeat step 2 to step 4 for several times to select the arrangement with $\min \omega_1 E_{rep}(L) + \omega_2 E_{comp}(L)$
> 6. Adjust ROI positions to make corresponding images cover as more area of the collage as possible
> 7. If the covering percentage is less than a threshold t, repeat step 2 to step 6; otherwise, adopt graph cut to minimize the overall energy E, $\omega_1 E_{rep}(L) + \omega_2 E_{comp}(L) + \omega_3 E_{trans}(L)$

Fig. 2. Algorithm for energy minimization

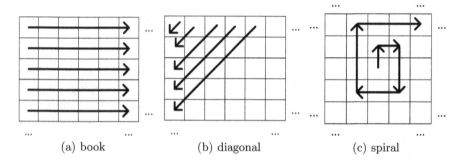

(a) book   (b) diagonal   (c) spiral

Fig. 3. Three collage styles for users to choose: *book, diagonal,* and *spiral*. ROI are ordered by temporal sequence in (a) (b) and by salience in (c).

Figure 3. Book and diagonal are designed for generating collage preserving temporal orders, while spiral is designed for putting important items, i.e., regions with more saliency, in the center in case of temporal information being not so important(e.g., home videos.)

Unlike rectangle ROI used in Auto Collage [2], each of which can be represented by four parameters, the proposed free-shaped ROI can be hardly represented by a fixed number of parameters, and it is difficult to traverse the whole searching space. Thus, we also introduce a random sampling approach to find a good ROI arrangement as follows. According to collage styles, i.e., book, or diagonal, or spiral, we can order pixels in the collage in sequence, as well as order the ROI according to temporal information or their saliencies. Thus, for each ROI, according to collage pixel sequence, we find the first position the ROI could be put without occlusion, and then make a random shift. We make the arrangement of ROI in sequence, until all ROI are successfully put into the collage, or no more ROI could be put.

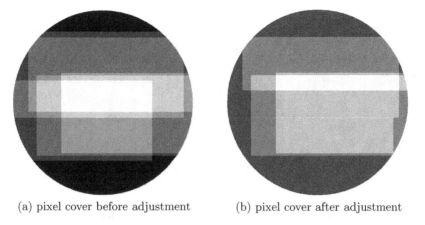

(a) pixel cover before adjustment   (b) pixel cover after adjustment

Fig. 4. Pixel cover before and after ROI adjustment. Higher intensities indicate pixels covered by more images. Black area is not covered by any image. The non-covered black parts in the top and bottom of (a) are covered in (b) after the adjustment.

3.2   ROI Adjustment

Except for ROI arrangement, another key issue of generating the collage is ROI adjustment Step 6 in Figure 2. After assigning each ROI to a position, there may still exist pixels which are not covered by any images, as shown in Figure 4(a). Such problem is easy to deal with when using rectangle images to cover the rectangle collage in Video Collage [3]. However, in FS-Collage, users can assign any shaped template to generate a collage, and it is not quite easy to cover each pixel. Therefore, we propose the following ROI adjustment strategy to cover more pixels.

For each image, we attempt four directions for position adjustment: up, down, left, right. In the adjustment process, ROI should not be occluded with each other, and the adjustment only occurs when more pixels are covered. To avoid the adjustment process stopping at a local minimum, we adjust all images in turn, in which the order is generated randomly, and then iterate such process for several times to produce better covering results.

4   Seamless Blending

Although in the energy minimization process, graph cut is adopted to find the smooth cut between different images, the clear seams will affect the visual appearance of the collage and make not smooth as shown in Figure 5(a). Thus, seamless blending is required to create smooth transitions between different images.

In "video collage" [3], images are put in rows, and seams are only vertical or horizontal. Thus, simple Gaussian blending work well in "video collage." However, in the proposed FS-Collage, seams are arbitrary. In "auto collage" [2],α-Poisson is adopted to make edge-sensitive blending. It works well for high quality images, but may produce poor results when working on videos, since edge gradient often contains much noise.

(a) collage before blending   (b) Poisson blending[2]   (c) Proposed blending

Fig. 5. Effects of different seamless blending approaches. Border lines between images are still quite clear in (b), while clear edges are well smoothed in (c).

Therefore, we introduce a probabilistic alpha matting approach to better blending seams between images. For each pixel p in the collage, we attach it to a list of labels $\{L_{p1}, L_{p2}, \ldots, L_{pN}\}$ and their corresponding probabilities $\{Prob_{p1}, Prob_{p2}, \ldots, Prob_{pN}\}$. Initially, according to graph cut results, only one $Prob_{pi}$ is assigned to 1, while others are assigned to 0. Then, each pixel's probabilities are distributed equally to its 4-connected neighboring pixels, so that neighboring pixels tend to have similar probability after enough iterations. Then, the probabilities are used as alpha values for alpha matting among different images. Fig. 5 shows the edges before blending and after blending using Poisson blending in [2] and the proposed probabilistic alpha matting. From the enlarged parts, we can see that there still exist clear borderlines after Poisson blending as shown in Fig. 5(b), while such clear edges are smoothed using the proposed blending approach in Fig. 5(c).

5   Experiments

We test our free-shaped video collage on four home videos and four movie clips with more than 10 hours, 500 shots and $5k$ sub-shots. We produced 10 different kinds of collages for each video using the following six schemes: (1) "AutoCollage" [2]; (2) "Video Collage" [3]; (3) "FS-Collage" of rectangle template using *book* order; (4) "FS-Collage" of rectangle template using *diagonal* order; (5) "FS-Collage" of rectangle template using *spiral* order; (6) "FS-Collage" of five templates shown in Fig. 6 using *spiral* order.

Since our target is to produce user specified collage, we first collect users' preferred non-rectangle templates from evaluators. As a result, we get the above five most popular templates. Since these templates are obviously difficult to preserve temporal order, we only generate collages in spiral style when using them as templates.

We invited 12 evaluators majored in computer science, including nine graduate and three undergraduate students. Each evaluator is first required to provide

Fig. 6. Five non-rectangle templates used for user study: circle, ellipse, heart, mickey, and fan, which are provided by evaluators

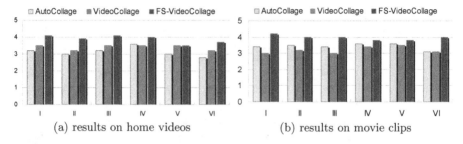

(a) results on home videos   (b) results on movie clips

Fig. 7. Average rating scores of the above six questions on home videos and movie clips. The x-axis is question ids, and the y-axis is average rating scores.

his/her preference of the collage template within the five non-rectangle templates shown in Fig. 6 and the rectangle one. If the rectangle collage is selected, then the evaluator needs to choose one of the three collage order styles, i.e., book, diagonal, spiral. After viewing a video, each evaluator is given three collages, which are generated by video collage, auto collage, and our free-shaped video collage according to his/her preference. Then the evaluator is asked to answer the following questions with 1 (definitely no) to 5 (definitely yes):

   I Are you satisfied with the collage in general?
  II Do you believe the collage is representative of the video?
 III Do you consider the collage is visually pleasing?
  IV Do you believe the representation is compact?
   V Can you get to know the story line from collage?
  VI Would you like to use the collage as a poster of the video?

The averaged results on home videos and movies are shown in Figure 7. We can see the overall satisfaction of proposed free-shaped video collage is much higher than both auto collage and video collage, which indicates that our free-shaped video collage is an effective collage tool. From the representative score, we can see that our random sampling approach is able to select well representative key-frames. However, Auto Collage does not leverage the temporal structure of video, and thus could not well select key-frames; video collage's heuristic searching of sub-shots focuses too much on saliency and quality, but weakens the importance of frame distribution, and thus fails to select most representative key-frames. Furthermore, visually pleasing scores show superior performance of our approach to others. This verifies the effectiveness of our ROI arrangement algorithm and

(a) "AutoCollage"   (b) "Video Collage"

(c) "FS-Collage" in circle template   (d) "FS-Collage" in heart template

Fig. 8. Results comparison of "AutoCollage," "Video Collage," and our "FS-Collage"

our seamless blending approach, both of which have great impact on visual effect of the collage. In addition, by using free shaped ROI instead of rectangle ones, more ROI could be put in one collage so that making the collage more compact, which is verified by the scores of the fourth question.

It is a little surprise that evaluators do not give video collage a high score in the fifth question, and even get the lowest score compared with the proposed FS-collage and auto collage. The results are surprising that auto collage has even higher scores than video collage on movies clips. Such results indicate that users often fail to well recognize the temporal order of a collage even in movie clips, which have obvious story line.

Figure 8 gives the generated collages by AutoCollage [2], Video Collage [3], and our Free-Shaped Video Collage. We can see that AutoCollage does not well smooth borders between different images, while Video Collage often produces abrupt color changes between different images due to its ignoring of the transition cost when strictly putting ROI in rows. The FS-Collage produces more compact collages, and the edges are better smoothed.

6   Conclusion

In this paper, we have proposed a novel video representative technique called "Free-Shaped Video Collage" (FS-Collage), which is an automatically synthesized image presenting video content, as well as being compact and visually pleasing. We formulate the above properties of FS-Collage as a series of energies, and transform the generation of FS-Collage as an energy minimization problem. We introduce a random sampling process to solve this problem. The experiments have indicated that our free-shaped video collage is an effective video representation for video browsing. The proposed FS-Collage produces an image abstract on their own videos, and also can be used for efficient browsing of large amount of web videos.

Acknowledgments. This work is supported by the National Natural Science Foundation of China under Grant No. 60573167 and the National High-Tech Research and Development Plan of China (863) under Grant No. 2006AA01Z118. We would like to express the appreciation to Xueliang Liu and Xinyuan Fu for implementing comparative algorithms for our experiments.

References

1. Ma, Y.-F., Zhang, H.-J.: Video snapshot: A bird view of video sequence. In: Proceedings of MMM (January 2005)
2. Rother, C., Bordeaux, L., Hamadi, Y., Blake, A.: Autocollage. In: SIGGRAGPH (2006)
3. Wang, T., Mei, T., Hua, X.-S., Liu, X., Zhou, H.-Q.: Video Collage: A Novel Presentation of Video Sequence. In: Proceedings of ICME (July 2007)
4. Ma, Y.-F., Zhang, H.-J.: Contrast-based image attention analysis by using fuzzy growing. In: Proceedings of ACM Multimedia, pp. 374–381 (2003)
5. Mei, T., Hua, X.-S., Zhu, C.-Z., Zhou, H.-Q., Li, S.: Home Video Visual Quality Assessment with Spatiotemporal Factors. IEEE Transactions on Circuits and Systems for Video Technology 17(6), 699–706 (2007)
6. Smith, M.A., Kanade, T.: Video Skimming and Characterization through the Combination of Image and Language Understanding Techniques. In: Proceedings of CVPR, pp. 785–781 (1997)
7. Kang, H.-W., Matsushita, Y., Tang, X., Chen, X.-Q.: Space-Time Video Montage. In: Proceedings of CVPR, pp. 1331–1338 (2006)
8. Kawai, Y., Sumiyoshi, H., Yagi, N.: Automated Production of TV Program Trailer using Electronic Program Guide. In: Proceedings of CIVR, pp. 49–56 (2007)
9. Girgensohn, A., Chiu, P.: Stained Glass Photo Collages. In: Proceedings of UIST, pp. 13–14 (October 2004)
10. Diakopoulos, N., Essa, I.: Mediating Photo Collage Authoring. In: Proceedings of UIST, pp. 183–186 (October 2005)
11. Graham, J., Erol, B., Hull, J.J., Lee, D.-S.: The Video Paper Multimedia Playback System. In: Proceedings of ACM Multimedia (November 2003)
12. Chen, J.-C., Chu, W.-T., Kuo, J.-H., Weng, C.-Y., Wu, J.-L.: Tiling Slideshow. In: Proceedings of ACM Multimedia, pp. 25–34 (October 2006)

Aesthetics-Based Automatic Home Video Skimming System

Wei-Ting Peng[1], Yueh-Hsuan Chiang[2], Wei-Ta Chu[2], Wei-Jia Huang[2],
Wei-Lun Chang[2], Po-Chung Huang[2], and Yi-Ping Hung[1,2]

[1] Graduate Institute of Networking and Multimedia,
National Taiwan University, Taipei, Taiwan
[2] Department of Computer Science & Information Engineering,
National Taiwan University, Taipei, Taiwan

Abstract. In this paper, we propose an automatic home video skimming system based on media aesthetics. Unlike other similar works, the
proposed system considers video editing theory and realizes the idea
of computational media aesthetics. Given a home video and a inciden-
tal background music, this system generates a music video (MV) style
skimming video automatically, with consideration of video quality, music tempo, and the editing theory. The background music is analyzed so
that visual rhythm caused by shot changes in the skimming video are
synchronous with the music tempo. Our work focuses on the rhythm over
aesthetic features, which is more recognizable and more suitable to describe the relationship between video and audio. Experiments show that
the generated skimming video is effective in representing the original input video, and the audio-video conformity is satisfactory.

Keywords: Video skimming, content analysis, media aesthetics.

1 Introduction

With growing availability and portability of digital video cameras, making home
videos has become much more popular. But editing home videos remains difficult
for most people because most home videos are captured without auxiliary tools,
such as tripods, so that there is usually severe shaking and vibration. Insufficient
photography knowhow of lighting techniques also results in bad visual quality.
Moreover, editing is a skill as well as an art. Without solid editing knowledge and
media aesthetics, it is not easy to generate an effective and lively summary video.

Therefore, we propose an automatic home video skimming system which con-
forms to the editing theory and enables amateurs to make an MV style video
without difficulties. An MV style video means a music video accompanied by a
piece of background music. Figure 1 illustrates the proposed system framework,
which will be described in the following sections.

Video summarization systems have been developed for years, yet many problems still remain to be solved. Ma et al. [1] proposed a framework of user attention

S. Satoh, F. Nack, and M. Etoh (Eds.): MMM 2008, LNCS 4903, pp. 186–197, 2008.

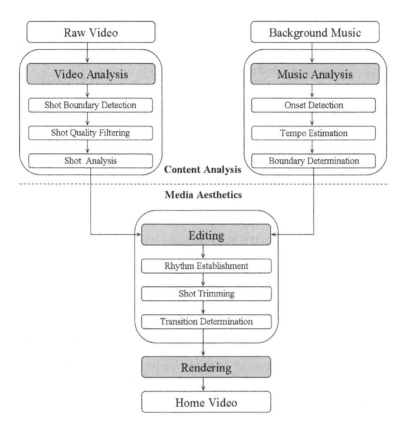

Fig. 1. Structure of the proposed system

models to extract essential video content automatically. Hanjalic [2] modeled the influence of three low level features on user excitement.

There also have been researches about automatic editing systems. Foote et al. [3] presented methods for automatic and semi-automatic creation of music videos. But they merely considered camera motion and image brightness and left out motion blur and ambiguity between underexposure images and night scenes. In [4], their work failed to elaborate on the application of transition effects, which are crucial for video composition and music tempo synchronization. Lee et al. [5] proposed a video pre-processing and authoring technique facilitating music video creation. However, the visual rhythm extraction is not accurate, and the editing theory is not considered in clip selection.

Computational media aesthetics [6] has aroused discussions in recent years. Mulhem et al. [7] used a pivot vector space method to match video shots with music segments based on aesthetic cinematographic heuristics. But their results failed to draw a link between video and audio for viewers. Therefore, our work focuses on the rhythm over aesthetic features, which is more recognizable and is more appropriate to describe the relationship between video and audio.

The remainder of this paper is organized as follows. Section 2 describes the editing theory. Section 3 shows content analysis processes in our system. The aesthetics-based editing method is proposed in Section 4. Section 5 shows experimental results, while conclusions are made in Section 6.

2   Editing Theory

In this section, we will briefly introduce the editing theory, and describe some crucial concepts for automatic editing. They are the foundations of our system. Details can be found in related literature [8,9,10,11,12].

2.1   Motion

The first essential editing concept is motion. Based on Zettl's theory [11], motion can be categorized into three classes: primary motion, secondary motion, and tertiary motion. Primary motion is event motion in front of the camera, including the movements of objects such as people and vehicles. Because extracting primary motion robustly is still an open issue in video analysis, we don't consider primary motion in this paper.

Secondary motion is camera motion. Camera motion analysis in our work will be described in the next section. More specifically, we will introduce pan, tilt, and zoom to clarify the priority rules of editing. Pan and tilt can be considered at the same time because they are similar and only differ in directions. The importance of pan is illustrated in [10]: *"It should be borne in mind that it is better to pan from a weak to a stronger dramatic situation than the reverse—in other words, to build toward strength."* In the case of zoom, zoom in stresses the last subject appearing in a shot, while zoom out emphasizes the scope. Therefore, in terms of automatic video editing, we should prioritize the tail over the rest of a video shot when there is pan, tilt or zoom camera motion.

Tertiary motion is editing motion. It is the visual rhythm caused by transition effects of shot changes. Tertiary motion is crucial for editing aesthetics. But most people just randomly apply transition effects without considering the editing theory. Three kinds of transition effects, i.e. cut, dissolve, and fade, are elaborately selected and incorporated into our system according to the characteristics of consecutive music tempo. These transition effects were depicted in the literature as follows: *"A cut usually generates a staccato rhythm; dissolves generate a legato rhythm"* [11]. *"Longer dissolves will slow the pace of the video, shorter ones will keep it moving quickly"* [12]. *"The function of the fade is to signal a definite beginning (fade-in) or end (fade-out) of a scene or sequence"* [11].

2.2   Rhythm

The length and playback rate of a video shot can be adjusted so that visual rhythm is in conformity to music tempo. We will introduce three methods to change video rhythm in the following.

Rhythmic Control. Lengths of successive shots constitute the rhythm of the output video. Different combinations of shots result in different rhythms. According to the temporal variations of music tempo, we can accordingly vary the visual rhythm by changing the lengths of successive shots.

Cut tight or Cut loose. Concatenating short shots would draw tight visual rhythm. On the contrary, consecutive long shots would moderate the visual presentation. In editing theory, they are respectively called as 'cut tight' and 'cut loose'. For example, in a movie trailer, the editor often applies cut tight editing to increase the visual rhythm and to attract viewers.

Slow and Accelerated Motion. Another method to change the visual rhythm is to adjust the playback rate. In reality, we seldom increase the playback rate, because it is visually unfavorable, and details could be neglected. However, slow motion is a common technique and is included in our system.

3   Content Analysis

Given the input video $\mathcal{V}$ and the background music $\mathcal{M}$, this section describes video and music analysis in our system. The results of these processes are the material for our automatic aesthetics-based editing method.

3.1   Video Analysis

In order to extract most favorable parts of the input video $\mathcal{V}$, we apply the following video analysis, including frame quality estimation, shot change detection, motion analysis, and face detection.

Quality Estimation. Ill-quality frames of the input video are detected and dropped at first. Blur, overexposure, and underexposure are detected in this work. When blur occurs, due to out-of-focus or object/camera motions, edges in the video frame will become indistinguishable [13]. In our system, we use a Laplacian filter to obtain edge intensities, and utilize them to achieve blur detection.

To detect overexposed/underexposed frames, we calculate the mean brightness M_{all}, M_L, and M_D of all pixel, top 10% lightest pixels, and top 10% darkest pixels, respectively. In overexposed frames, most pixels are over lit and have high brightness. So we consider a frame overexposed if both M_{all} and M_D exceed some predefined thresholds. On the contrary, most pixels are dark in underexposed frames, and M_{all} should be low in this case. However, night scene images share this characteristic with underexposed ones. But there are probably some bright pixels such as bulbs or street lamps in night scene images. So we further consider the difference between M_L and M_D to distinguish night scene images from underexposed ones:

$$
\begin{aligned}
&\text{If } M_{all} \text{ is low and } (M_L - M_D) \text{ is high} \Rightarrow \text{night scene image.} \\
&\text{If both } M_{all} \text{ and } (M_L - M_D) \text{ are low} \Rightarrow \text{underexposed image.}
\end{aligned}
\tag{1}
$$

Video Segmentation. To segment the home video $\mathcal{V}$ into clips, we just use the most well-known histogram-based shot change detection [14], since shot changes mostly occur with sudden cuts, instead of man-made transitions such as dissolve or fade. After dropping ill-quality frames and detecting shot change, we segment the input video $\mathcal{V}$ into N_{shot} filtered shots:

$$\mathcal{V}_{good} = \{\text{shot}_i : i = 1, \ldots, N_{shot}\}. \tag{2}$$

Motion Analysis. We also perform motion analysis to determine the camera motion types (pan, tilt, zoom, or still) with an optical flow based approach [15]. In addition to camera motion types, directions and magnitudes, we advocate considering camera motion acceleration. If motion acceleration varies frequently and significantly, the video segment is usually annoying and is less likely to be selected in the automatic editing phase.

Face Detection. Face information is an important clue to select attractive video segments at the automatic editing stage. So, we apply Viola-Jonse face detection algorithm [16] in our system.

3.2 Audio Analysis

To coordinate visual and aural presentation, shot changes need to be in conformity to the music tempo. So we estimate music tempo of the background music $\mathcal{M}$ at this stage.

We first detect onsets based on energy dynamics. Onsets generally occur when there is significant energy change. We apply the Fourier transform with a Hamming window $w(m)$ to $\mathcal{M}$. The kth frequency bin of the nth frame, $F(n,k)$, of the background music $\mathcal{M}$ can be described as:

$$F(n,k) = \sum_{m=\frac{-N}{2}}^{\frac{N}{2}-1} \mathcal{M}(hn+m)w(m)e^{\frac{2j\pi nk}{N}}, \tag{3}$$

where N is the windows size, and h is the hop size. If the sampling rate of the background music $\mathcal{M}$ is 44100Hz, N and h are set as 2048 and 441 in our system. Spectral flux [17] is one of the onset functions that can measure the changes of magnitudes between frequency bins:

$$\text{Flux}(n) = \sum_{k=\frac{-N}{2}}^{\frac{N}{2}-1} H(|F(n,k)| - |F(n-1,k)|), \tag{4}$$

where $H(x) = (x+|x|)/2$ is the half-wave rectifier function. Then a peak at the nth frame is selected as an onset if it fulfils the peak-peaking algorithm in [18]. Let peak(n) represent this onset detection function. If the nth frame conveys a peak, the output of peak(n) is one. Otherwise, the output is zero. Finally, we formulate the tempo of the nth frame of the background music $\mathcal{M}$ as the sum of tempo(n) over a local window with size w:

$$\text{tempo}(n) = \sum_{k=n-\frac{w}{2}}^{n+\frac{w}{2}} \text{peak}(k). \tag{5}$$

4   Media Aesthetics-Based Editing

With the shots of the filtered video $\mathcal{V}_{good}$ and the tempo information of the background music $\mathcal{M}$, we are now ready to turn to our aesthetics-based editing method, which consists of three steps: rhythm establishment, shot trimming, and transition determination.

4.1   Rhythm Establishment

Since the lengths of the input video and background music are not necessary the same, the durations of video shots must be adjusted to match the length of the background music, and the visual rhythm caused by shot changes is desired to be synchronous with the music tempo. As we mentioned in Section 2.2, the easiest way to achieve this is exploiting 'cut tight' and 'cut loose'. Figure 2 illustrates how we use a transfer function for this purpose, and details are described as follows.

We first linearly map the shot durations to the length of the background music. The begin time of shot$_i$ in $\mathcal{V}_{good}$ after this pre-mapping process can be written as:

$$t_i^{\text{pre}} = \frac{\sum_{k=1}^{i-1} \text{length}(\text{shot}_k)}{\text{length}(\mathcal{V}_{good})} \text{length}(\mathcal{M}). \tag{6}$$

To synchronize the visual rhythm with the music tempo, we try to alter the duration of each shot after pre-mapping. Motivated by the idea of histogram equalization, we try to design a transfer function, which is monotonically increasing and transforms the starting time of each shot according to the music tempo. The transfer function $TF(n)$ is defined as:

$$TF(n) = \sum_{k=1}^{n} (\text{tempo}_{max} - \text{tempo}(k)), \tag{7}$$

where tempo$_{max}$ denotes the maximum value of all tempo(n). Then, the begin time of shot$_i$ is further mapped according to this transfer function $TF(n)$ in this post-mapping process:

$$t_i^{\text{post}} = \frac{TF(t_i^{\text{pre}})}{TF(\text{length}(\mathcal{M}))} \text{length}(\mathcal{M}). \tag{8}$$

After post-mapping, the visual rhythm caused by shot changes is better synchronized with the music tempo of the background music $\mathcal{M}$.

In order to make shot changes occurred exactly at music onsets in the output music video, we further adjust t_i^{post} to align with its nearest onset peak t_i^{onset}, as shown in Fig. 2.

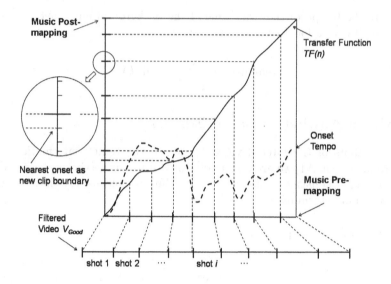

Fig. 2. Illustration of rhythm establishment

4.2   Shot Trimming

After the beginning time, so that the length of each shot in the output music video have been determined, there are still two choices to be decided: how many subshots should be extracted from each shot, and where the most favorable subshots are. We solve these two problems as follows.

We normally do not segment a shot into too many subshots. Because superfluous subshots result in information redundancy and decrease visual aesthetics. Generally, we choose only one subshot for static shots. For motion shots, the higher the music tempo is, the more subshots we extract. And the maximum number of subshots is decided as three in this work.

After the number of subshots for $shot_i$ has been determined, we then select the most suitable subshots based on visual importance. Each subshot within the same shot has the same duration. We denote f_{ij} the jth frame of the $shot_i$, then we estimate its importance based on face region $\text{Face}(f_{ij})$, camera motion $\text{Motion}(f_{ij})$, and frame temporal position $\text{Pos}(f_{ij})$:

$$\text{Face}(f_{ij}) = \frac{\text{Region}(f_{ij})}{\max_j \text{Region}(f_{ij})}, \tag{9}$$

$$\text{Motion}(f_{ij}) = 1 - \frac{\text{Acc}(f_{ij})}{\max_j \text{Acc}(f_{ij})}, \tag{10}$$

$$\text{Pos}(f_{ij}) = \frac{j}{\text{length}(shot_i)}, \tag{11}$$

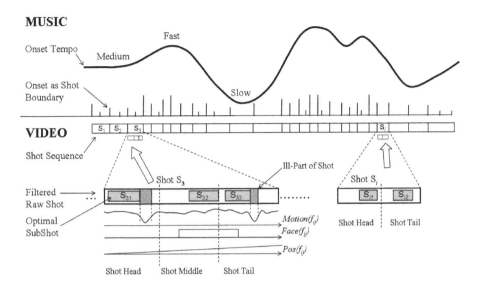

Fig. 3. Illustration of shot trimming

where $\text{Region}(f_{ij})$ and $\text{Acc}(f_{ij})$ denote the face region in frame f_{ij} and the magnitude of camera motion acceleration of f_{ij}. By these three elements, we then formulate the frame importance as:

$$\text{Imp}(f_{ij}) = w_f \text{Face}(f_{ij}) + w_m \text{Motion}(f_{ij}) + (1 - w_f - w_m)\text{Pos}(f_{ij}), \qquad (12)$$

where w_f and w_m are weighting coefficients controlling the importances of face, motion, and temporal position. Then, the optimal subshots with highest frame importance are extracted from different segments of each shot, as shown in Fig. 3.

4.3   Transition Determination

Now we consider transition effects, which occurs in three different situations: at the beginning and the end of the output video, between adjacent shots, and between adjacent subshots. According to the editing theory in Section 2.1, fade-in and fade-out are applied to the beginning and the end of the output video.

For transition effects between adjacent shots, we consider the average music tempo of shot$_i$:

$$\text{ShotTempo}(i) = \frac{\sum_{n=t_i^{\text{onset}}}^{t_{i+1}^{\text{onset}} - 1} \text{tempo}(n)}{t_{i+1}^{\text{onset}} - t_i^{\text{onset}}}. \qquad (13)$$

Each shot is classified as fast, medium, or slow according to its average tempo. Then the transition applied to two adjacent shots is determined according to their shot tempos as Table 1.

When transitions between adjacent subshots are considered, unlike the case of shots, the tempo classes of subshots are derived from their containing shots

Table 1. Transition effects between adjacent shots

shot$_i$	shot$_{i+1}$	Transition
Fast	Fast	Cut
	Medium	Short Dissolve
	Slow	Long Dissolve
Medium	Fast	Short Dissolve
	Medium	Short Dissolve
	Slow	Long Dissolve
Slow	Fast	Short Dissolve
	Medium	Long Dissolve
	Slow	Long Dissolve

Table 2. Transition effects between adjacent subshots

shot$_i$	Transition
Fast	Cut
Medium	Short Dissolve
Slow	Long Dissolve

Table 3. Experiment 1 specification

	MV1	MV2
Video	16m02s	25m15s
Video description	Travel in Europe	Travel in Taiwan
Music	3m40s (popular)	3m08s (piano)

directly, instead of being further classified. Transition effects applied to adjacent subshots in fast, medium, and slow shots are cut, short dissolve, and long dissolve, respectively, as shown in Table 2.

5   Experiments

5.1   Experiment 1 and User Study

In the first experiment, we apply our method to two different kinds of input videos and background musics. The specification is shown in Table 3. We invited seventeen users (eleven males and six females) to compare the results of our system with that of two commercial software, PowerDirector [19] and MuVee [20].

In order to obtain convincing comparison, the evaluators do not know in advance which video was generated by which system. After watching the output music videos, the users are required to answer the following four questions and give scores ranging from one to ten for each question, where ten is the best:

Q1: In visual expression, please rate according to your perceptual satisfaction .
Q2: Do you think the transition effects are comparable with that of a designers touch?
Q3: Do you think the visual rhythm matches the music tempo?
Q4: In general, which result do you prefer?

Figure 4 shows the average scores of the three systems. The results indicate that both our system and MuVee excel PowerDirector in average. In terms of visual expression, our system and MuVee do not differ much, which is probably because MuVee provides fancy atmosphere for travel style and diverts evaluators' attention (**Q1**). Since PowerDirector fails to rule out shaky shots, its output

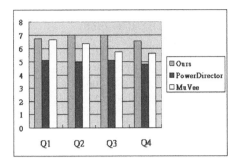

Fig. 4. Average scores of three systems in Experiment 1

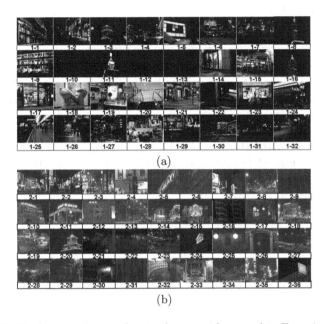

Fig. 5. Keyframes of every shot in the two videos used in Experiment 2

videos induce visual discomfort. Our system outperforms the others with better conformity between visual rhythm and music tempo (**Q3**), which is one of the main objectives of this work.

5.2 Experiment 2 and Results

In Experiment 2, to compare these systems in terms of quality estimation, we use two videos that contain 68 shots totally, in which 53 shots are captured in night scenes. The night scene shots are likely to be underexposed (eight shots), and blur (five shots) in all clips. The keyframe of each shot is shown in Fig. 5.

Table 4. Detection results of underexposed and blur shots. (S1: Our System, S2: PowerDirector, S3: MuVee, F: fail, D: totally drop)

	Underexposure								Hit (%)	Blur					Hit (%)
	1-10	1-12	1-13	2-6	2-9	2-16	2-21	2-31		2-25	1-11	1-16	2-12	2-24	
S1	D	D	D	D	D	D	D	D	100	D	F	D	D	D	80
S2	D	D	F	F	F	F	F	F	25	D	D	F	F	F	40
S3	D	D	D	D	D	D	D	D	100	D	D	D	D	D	100

Table 5. False alarm for ordinary night scenes

	Shots that caused false alarm	False Alarm (%)
S1	2-13, 2-22, 2-36	5.7 (=3/53)
S2	1-26, 1-27, 1-32, 2-22	7.5 (=4/53)
S3	1-3, 1-4, 1-7, 1-31, 1-32, 2-13, 2-17, 2-22, 2-23, 2-26, 2-27, 2-28, 2-29, 2-30, 2-34	28.3 (=15/53)

Tables 4 and 5 show the results of the Experiment 2. Both PowerDirector and MuVee can detect and remove most underexposed and blur shots. However, MuVee mis-detects fifteen ordinary night scene shots as underexposed ones, their false alarm rate is about 28.3%, while ours is 5.7%. PowerDirector can better preserve ordinary night shots, at the cost of selecting six underexposed shots. The hit rate of PowerDirector is about 25%, while ours is 100%. Overall, our system outperforms these two commercial software in bad shot removal and night scenes preservation.

6   Conclusions

We proposed an automatic home video skimming system based on media aesthetics. Editing theory is considered in algorithm design and is incorporated into our system. Experimental results demonstrated that our system is superior to two existing commercial software. Low quality shots can be detected and removed automatically and the conformity between video rhythm and music tempo can be achieved at the same time. More video processing techniques can be integrated into our system in the future, such as stabilizing or de-blurring, so that better video clip slection and more lively audiovisual presentation are possible. Moreover, it is also desired to improve possible inconsistent video rhythm when the music tempo changes significantly in a short period of time.

Acknowledgements

This work was partially supported by grants from NSC 96-2752-E-002-007-PAE.

References

1. Ma, Y.F., Hua, X.S., Lu, L., Zhang, H.J.: A generic framework of user attention model and its application in video summarization. IEEE Transactions on Multimedia 7(5), 907–919 (2005)
2. Hanjalic, A.: Multimodal approach to measuring excitement in video. In: ICME (2003)
3. Foote, J., Cooper, M., Girgensohn, A.: Creating music videos using automatic media analysis. In: ACM international conference on Multimedia (2002)
4. Hua, X.S., Lu, L., Zhang, H.J.: Optimization-based automated home video editing system. IEEE Transactions on CSVT 14(5), 572–583 (2004)
5. Lee, S.H., Yeh, C.H., Kuo, C.C.: Home video content analysis for MV-style video generation. In: International Symposium on Electronic Imaging (2005)
6. Nack, F., Dorai, C., Venkatesh, S.: Computational media aesthetics: finding meaning beautiful. Multimedia, IEEE 8(4), 10–12 (2001)
7. Mulhem, P., Kankanhalli, M., Yi, J., Hassan, H.: Pivot vector space approach for audio-video mixing. Multimedia, IEEE 10(2), 28–40 (2003)
8. Goodman, R., McGrath, P.: Editing Digital Video. McGraw-Hill/TAB Electronics (2002)
9. Chandler, G.: Cut by cut: editing your film or video. Michael Wiese (2004)
10. Communication Production Technology: The Pan Shot, http://www.saskschools.ca/curr_content/cpt/projects/musicvideo/panshots.html
11. Zettl, H.: Sight, sound, motion: applied media aesthetics. Wadsworth (2004)
12. Loehr, M.: Aesthetics of editing, http://www.videomaker.com/article/2645/
13. Tong, H., Li, M., Zhang, H., Zhang, C.: Blur detection for digital images using wavelet transform. In: ICME (2004)
14. Hanjalic, A.: Shot-boundary detection: unraveled and resolved? IEEE Transactions on CSVT 12(2), 90–105 (2002)
15. Dibos, F., Jonchery, C., Koeper, G.: Camera motion estimation through quadratic optical flow approximation. Technical report, Universite de PARIS V DAUPHINE (2005)
16. Viola, P., Jones, M.J.: Robust real-time face detection. IJCV 57(2), 137–154 (2004)
17. Masri, P.: Computer modeling of sound for transformation and synthesis of musical signal. PhD thesis, University of Bristol (1996)
18. Dixon, S.: Onset detection revisited. In: International Conference on Digital Audio Effects (2006)
19. CyberLink: PowerDirector, http://www.cyberlink.com
20. muvee Technologies: muvee autoProducer, http://www.muvee.com

Using Fuzzy Lists for Playlist Management

François Deliège and Torben Bach Pedersen

Department of Computer Science, Aalborg University, Denmark
{fdeliege,tbp}@cs.aau.dk

Abstract. The increasing popularity of music recommendation systems and the recent growth of online music communities further emphasizes the need for effective playlist management tools able to create, share, and personalize playlists. This paper proposes the development of generic playlists and presents a concrete scenario to illustrate their possibilities. Additionally, to enable the development of playlist management tools, a formal foundation is provided. Therefore, the concept of fuzzy lists is defined and a corresponding algebra is developed. Fuzzy lists offer a solution perfectly suited to meet the demands of playlist management.

1 Introduction

The proliferation of broadband Internet connections and the development of new digital music formats have led to the explosion of online music communities and music recommendation systems. The increasing popularity of these systems has created a strong demand for the development of *playlist manipulation engines*. Hence, playlist models are highly needed. However, playlists are by nature *imprecise*. One song could probably be replaced by another while preserving the essence of the playlist. Similarly, two songs can sometimes be permuted. The way playlists are built explains this phenomenon. For individual music lovers, the manual construction of a playlist results in some kind of consensus between the various aspects defining the songs [1,2]. In large automated music recommendation systems, user collaborative filtering and co-occurrence analysis approaches are commonly used to construct playlists [3]. While imprecise, each playlist can exactly characterize a trend, a dynamic, a mood. Additionally, playlists also have a *subjective* nature, i.e., they are highly dependent on their audience. Listeners might have strong musical preferences or may not have access to all the music. Therefore, playlist management tools have to include *personalization mechanisms*.

The contributions of this paper are twofold. (i) A new scheme for constructing and sharing playlists is described via a concrete scenario. The scenario illustrates how the imprecise and subjective characteristics of playlists can be handled in order to improve playlist management engines. (ii) *Fuzzy lists*, a generalization of lists and fuzzy sets, are defined and their corresponding algebra is developed. The proposed algebra is inspired by relational algebra in order to facilitate future implementation in an RDBMS. Fuzzy lists offer the formal foundation for the development of playlist management tools as the provided examples illustrate.

The remainder of this paper is organized as follows. The creation of fuzzy lists for playlist management is motivated by a scenario presented in Section 2. Section 3 discusses the related work. Section 4 provides a formal definition of fuzzy lists, their operators and functions. Concrete playlist manipulation examples are shown to underline

S. Satoh, F. Nack, and M. Etoh (Eds.): MMM 2008, LNCS 4903, pp. 198–209, 2008.

their utility. Finally, after evoking some implementation considerations in Section 5, conclusion and future work are presented in Section 6.

2 Motivation

In this section, a playlist management engine that respects both the imprecise and subjective nature of playlists is envisioned. The users of the system want to create and share playlists. The playlists are built by user communities in a collaborative fashion rather than by individual users. Automated classification systems could possibly be incorporated as well as classical users participating in the playlist building process. Additionally, the generated playlists are adaptable to the users' profiles to respect their musical taste. The setup is as follows.

The objective is to create a playlist composed of a given number of songs and a theme. For example, 100 users are asked to build a playlist composed of ten songs, the first 3 songs should be rock, the next 3 should sound jazzy, the following 3 romantic, and the last one should be a blues song. Furthermore, the users are asked to provide smooth transitions between the songs, e.g., the third rock song should sound a bit jazzy. Agreement between the different users is achieved thanks to a voting mechanism. Finally, independently from the playlist building process, registered users have lists of songs they like and dislike.

The playlists created by the voters are merged into a single playlist, referred to as a *generic playlist*. The generic playlist stores the "election score," referred to as the *membership degree*, obtained for each song and each position. The generic playlist can then be shared among all the registered users of the system. However, the generic playlist cannot be used directly by the users as for each position in the playlist many songs will probably coexist. Furthermore, if some songs have been previously tagged as the user's favorites then they should preferably be played, or if the user has no access to a song, an accessible song should be alternatively chosen. The personalization mechanism selects songs from the generic playlist with respect to the user preferences and constraints. For each possible song, a preference grade is given; songs with a high grade should preferably be played while songs with a low grade should be played less often. A selection score is calculated using the user's preference list and the generic playlist.

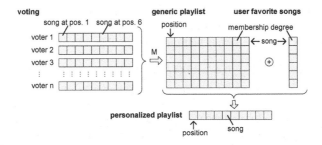

Fig. 1. Generic Playlists Usage Scenario

Table 1. Users votes count

song	#1	#2	#3	#4	#5	#6	#7	#8	#9	#10
s1	50	20	20	10	0	0	0	0	0	0
s2	20	50	30	0	0	0	0	0	0	0
s3	20	20	40	0	0	0	0	0	0	0
s4	10	10	10	10	0	0	0	0	0	0
s5	0	0	0	20	20	0	0	0	0	0
s6	0	0	0	60	40	0	0	0	0	0
s7	0	0	0	0	40	20	30	30	0	0
s8	0	0	0	0	0	80	20	0	0	0
s9	0	0	0	0	0	0	40	60	10	0
s10	0	0	0	0	0	0	10	10	10	70
s11	0	0	0	0	0	0	0	0	80	30
s12	0	0	0	0	0	0	0	0	0	0

Table 2. Generic Playlist

song	A_1	A_2	A_3	A_4	A_5	A_6	A_7	A_8	A_9	A_{10}
s1	0.5	0.2	0.2	0.1	0	0	0	0	0	0
s2	0.2	0.5	0.3	0	0	0	0	0	0	0
s3	0.2	0.2	0.4	0	0	0	0	0	0	0
s4	0.1	0.1	0.1	0.1	0	0	0	0	0	0
s5	0	0	0	0.2	0.2	0	0	0	0	0
s6	0	0	0	0.6	0.4	0	0	0	0	0
s7	0	0	0	0	0.4	0.2	0.3	0.3	0	0
s8	0	0	0	0	0	0.8	0.2	0	0	0
s9	0	0	0	0	0	0	0.4	0.6	0.1	0
s10	0	0	0	0	0	0	0.1	0.1	0.1	0.7
s11	0	0	0	0	0	0	0	0	0.8	0.3
s12	0	0	0	0	0	0	0	0	0	0

Table 3. Modified generic playlist

song	A_1	A_2	A_3	A_4	A_5	A_6	A_7	A_8	A_9	A_{10}
s1	0.50	0.35	0.35	0.30	0.25	0.25	0.25	0.25	0.25	0.25
s2	0.30	0.45	0.35	0.20	0.20	0.20	0.20	0.20	0.20	0.20
s3	0.30	0.30	0.40	0.20	0.20	0.20	0.20	0.20	0.20	0.20
s4	0.05	0.05	0.05	0.05	0.00	0.00	0.00	0.00	0.00	0.00
s5	0.20	0.20	0.20	0.30	0.30	0.20	0.20	0.20	0.20	0.20
s6	0.35	0.35	0.35	0.65	0.55	0.35	0.35	0.35	0.35	0.35
s7	0.30	0.30	0.30	0.30	0.50	0.40	0.45	0.45	0.30	0.30
s8	0.25	0.25	0.25	0.25	0.25	0.65	0.35	0.25	0.25	0.25
s9	0.25	0.25	0.25	0.25	0.25	0.25	0.45	0.55	0.30	0.25
s10	0.25	0.25	0.25	0.25	0.25	0.25	0.30	0.30	0.30	0.60
s11	0.25	0.25	0.25	0.25	0.25	0.25	0.25	0.25	0.65	0.40
s12	0.35	0.35	0.35	0.35	0.35	0.35	0.35	0.35	0.35	0.35

The songs with the highest score win. Figure 1 illustrates the overall construction of a generic playlist and how it is derived into a personalized playlist a latter stage.

The merging and personalization mechanisms will now be described and illustrated by a concrete example. The functions presented were chosen for their simplicity as the aim here is to motivate the use of generic playlists.

Table 1 represents the vote counts for the creation of a playlist with a length of 10 songs where the base song set is composed of 12 songs. The merging function, denoted M, grants a low membership degree to songs that have receive only a few votes, and a high membership degree to songs that have received many votes, at a given position. Let the generic playlist A, shown in Table 2, be generated by applying M to Table 1.

Assume a user u has rated his music preferences using a fuzzy song set as follows. The user's preference list, denoted F_u, assigns to each song in the system a preference score reflecting if the user likes, is neutral to, or dislikes, the song.

$$F_u = \{0.5/s1, 0.4/s2, 0.4/s3, 0.0/s4, 0.4/s5, 0.7/s6,$$
$$0.6/s7, 0.5/s8, 0.5/s9, 0.5/s10, 0.5/s11, 0.7/s12\}$$

The generalized playlist and the user's preferences are used to construct the modified generic playlist, presented in Table 3. For each song at a given position in the generic playlist, the average between the membership degree of the generic playlist and the user's preference score is calculated.

Finally, the personalized playlist, denoted P, is generated by selecting, for each position, the song with the highest membership degree.

$$P = [s1, s2, s3, s6, s6, s8, s7, s9, s11, s10]$$

The personalized playlist generated is sensible: $s12$ that has not received any votes is not present; $s4$ that has a preference score of zero, e.g., the user does not own the song, is not present; $s6$ and $s8$ that have the highest preference score are present; and the rest of the songs are at placed in accordance with the votes. The consecutive repetition of song $s6$ could be avoided by using a slightly more sophisticated personalization method, e.g., by lowering the preference score of songs previously selected at a nearby position.

The merging and personalization functions used in the previous example were solely chosen for their simplicity. Experiments on a real system should be conducted to obtain reasonable weight estimates for both the creation of generic playlists from multiple sources and their personalization. However, the correct weights to be used, if they can be estimated, are domain specific and are considered as external parameters.

Proportional positioning of the song elements, where positions are specified with respect to the whole playlist, e.g., a song is located at 20% of the playlist length, is commonly found in playlist management systems. Proportional positioning offers relative comparisons that a simple index of the songs positions does not capture, e.g., blues songs are generally located in the second third of the playlists of given group of users. Fuzzy lists can simply be adapted to support proportional positioning by transforming the generic playlist to generic playlists having a common length, e.g., by dividing the position of each element by the total length m and multiplying it by a reference length, say, 100. The algebra proposed in Section 4 supports transformations that accomodate both playlists shorter and longer than the reference length. More generally, relative positioning of elements, where elements are positioned relatively to each other, can be captured by functions such as, for example, sliding windows that take into account membership degrees of songs in a given position neighborhood in a generic playlist.

If generic playlists were modeled with *ordinary lists*, then the membership degrees would either be 0 or 1, and all songs that have received votes would have an identical probability of being part of the playlist. Instead, if *fuzzy sets* were used to model generic playlists, then the position dimension of the playlist would be lost and all songs would have the same probability of being part of the playlist regardless of the position. Thus, *fuzzy lists* are the best choice to model playlists as they capture the interdependency between song, position, and membership degree.

3   Related Work

Recently, work on fuzzy sets was reported for modeling music similarities and user preferences [4]. Three different storage schemes are discussed. This paper reuses the idea of user favorite song sets to provide playlist personalization features. Fuzzy lists, a generalization of lists and fuzzy sets, were studied previously [5]. However, the approach described is not appropriate to represent playlists for two reasons. First, some positions may be undefined, i.e., they have no corresponding elements or membership degrees. Second, multiple membership degrees may be defined for a single element at a given position. By contrast, the present paper allows an element to have the same membership degree at different positions, e.g., songs having a zero membership degree regardless of their position in the generic playlist.

Previous work on playlist generation dealt with algorithms to efficiently find a playlist which fulfills given constraints [6,7,8]. Work on dynamic playlist generation where songs are retrieved one at a time and listeners can intervene in the playlist creation is presented by Pampalk et al. [9]. A data and query model for dynamic playlist generation was proposed by Jensen et al. [10]. The authors are able to retrieve songs similar to a given seed while avoiding songs with respect to the user preferences. However, no solution is proposed to the issues of sharing and personalizing existing playlists. Additionally, the playlists are created in a song by song fashion and aggregating playlists to capture mood or genre similarities is not possible. However, some applications require functionalities, e.g., searching missing songs in a playlist, that require capturing the essence of the playlist [11].

A traditional approach to store musical information in a database is to use classical relational models such as the one proposed by Rubenstein [12]. The model extends the entity-relationship data model to implement the notion of hierarchical ordering, commonly found in musical data. Wang et al. have presented a music data model and its algebra and query language [13]. The data model is able to structure both the musical content and the metadata. However, all these models are limited to individual music performances and do not cover playlists.

Finally, the most related work is probably the foundation for query optimization on ordered sets proposed by Slivinskas et al. where a list-based relational algebra is presented [14]. However, the framework does not cover neither multiple elements coexisting at a given position of the list, nor membership degrees. Furthermore, the framework does not address playlist management issues.

4   The Fuzzy List Algebra

This section provides a formal foundation for generic playlists. A definition of fuzzy lists is first provided, followed by a description of fuzzy list operators. The operators are divided in three categories. Operators similar to the list operators are first presented, followed by unary operators, and finally by binary operators.

4.1   Definition

A finite fuzzy list, A, of length m_A over a domain X is defined as follows.

$$A = \{\mu_A(x,n)/n/x \mid x \in X, n \in \{1, \ldots, m_A\}, \mu_A : X \times \mathbb{N} \mapsto [0;1]\}$$

Here x is an element of X, n is a non-negative integer, and $\mu_A(x,n)$, referred to as the sequential membership degree of x at position n, is a real number belonging to $[0;1]$. $\mu_A(x,n) = 0$ when case x does not belong to A at position n, and $\mu_A(x,n) = 1$ when x completely belongs to A at position n. The length of A, length(A), is defined as m_A.

4.2   List-Like Operators

In the following, let A, A_1, and A_2 be three fuzzy lists defined over a domain X.

Equality

A_1 and A_2 are equal iff A_1 and A_2 have the same length and have the same membership degree between identical pairs of element and position:

$$A_1 = A_2 \Leftrightarrow \text{length}(A_1) = \text{length}(A_2), \text{ and}$$
$$\forall x \in X, n \in \{1, ..., \text{length}(A_1)\} : \mu_{A_1}(x, n) = \mu_{A_2}(x, n)$$

Sublist

A_1 is a fuzzy sublist of A_2 iff a sequence exists in A_2 where all the membership degrees of A_1 are less than or equal to the membership degrees of A_2:

$$A_1 \subseteq A_2 \Leftrightarrow \exists i \in \mathbb{N} \mid \forall x \in X, \forall n \in \{1, ..., \text{length}(A_1)\} :$$
$$\mu_{A_1}(x, n + i) \leq \mu_{A_2}(x, n)$$

Note that the empty fuzzy list of length 1, denoted ϕ_1, is a fuzzy sublist of all fuzzy lists. Note also that $A_1 = A_2 \Leftrightarrow A_1 \subseteq A_2$ and $A_2 \subseteq A_1$. In the playlist context, a sublist is a sequence of a playlist where the probability of a song being played at a given position is lowered. Songs not present in a generic playlist will remain excluded in all its sublists.

Concatenation

The concatenation of A_1 and A_2 is the fuzzy list of length(A_1) + length(A_2) where the fuzzy list A_2 succeeds A_1 as follows.

$$A_1 \| A_2 = \{\mu_{\|}(x, n)/n/x \mid \forall x \in X, \forall n \in \{1, ..., \text{length}(A_1) + \text{length}(A_2))\} :$$
$$\mu_{\|}(x, n) = \begin{cases} \mu_{A_1}(x, n) & \text{for } n \leq \text{length}(A_1), \\ \mu_{A_2}(x, n - \text{length}(A_1)) & \text{for } n > \text{length}(A_1) \end{cases} \}$$

Note that $A_1 \subseteq (A_1 \| A_2)$ and $A_2 \subseteq (A_1 \| A_2)$. The concatenation operator is inspired by the UNION ALL operator in SQL. In the playlist context, the concatenation operator allows short playlists to be used as the building blocks of longer playlists, e.g., to propose playlists constructed based on the succession of different generic playlists.

4.3   Unary Operators

The operators presented below modify the position, e.g., to reorder a generic playlist, and the nature, e.g., to capture the likelihood of an artist to be played rather than a song, of the elements.

Unary Reordering, Selection, and Aggregation

The unary aggregation is a generalization of the unary selection that is, in turn, a generalization of the unary reordering. For ease of understanding, the three operators are progressively introduced. They transform the fuzzy list based on the elements' positions. Each of the operators is defined by a different mapping function as illustrated in Figure 2.

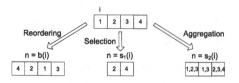

Fig. 2. Examples of position mapping for unary reordering, selection and aggregation operators

Unary Reordering:
Given a bijection $b : \{1, \ldots, \text{length}(A)\} \leftrightarrow \{1, \ldots, \text{length}(A)\}$, the bijection of A with respect to b is defined as follows.

$$A_b = \{\mu_{A_b}(x, n)/n/x \mid \forall x \in X, \forall n \in \{1, \ldots, \text{length}(A)\} :$$
$$\mu_{A_b}(x, n) = \mu_A(x, b^{-1}(n))\}$$

A unary reordering of a fuzzy list is defined by a permutation, and allows the creation of, e.g., a shuffling function that randomly reorders the playlist. The *invert* operator defined as follows, is another example of unary ordering.

$$\text{Invert}(A) = \{\mu_{\text{Invert}}(x, n)/x/n \mid \forall x \in X, \forall n \in \{1, \ldots, \text{length}(A)\} :$$
$$\mu_{\text{Invert}}(x, n) = \mu_A(x, \text{length}(A) - n)\}$$

Unary Selection:
Given a set $A' \subseteq \{1, \ldots, \text{length}(A)\}$, and a bijection $s_1 : A' \leftrightarrow \{1, \ldots, \text{size}(A')\}$, a selection of A over s_1 is defined as follows.

$$A_{s_1} = \{\mu_{A_{s_1}}(x, n)/n/x \mid \forall x \in X, \forall n \in \{1, \ldots, \text{size}(A')\} :$$
$$\mu_{A_{s_1}}(x, n) = \mu_A(x, s_1^{-1}(n))\}$$

A reordering is a particular case of a selection where $A' = \{1, \ldots, \text{length}(A)\}$. The selection operator removes the elements at a given position of the fuzzy list. Therefore, if s_1 is chosen to verify a given predicate, only the elements that fulfill the predicate will be kept. Thus in a playlist, the positions in the generic playlist where the songs made by U2 have a high membership degree could be removed or kept.

Unary Aggregation:
Given a set $A' \subseteq \{1, \ldots, \text{length}(A)\}$, and a surjective mapping $s_2 : A' \mapsto \{1, \ldots, \text{max}(s_2)\}$, let S_n be the set of all fuzzy list elements $\{\mu(x, i)/i/x\}$ of A with $n = s_2(i)$, and let $a : 2^{S_n} \mapsto [0; 1]$ be a surjective mapping. The aggregation of A with a over s_2 is defined as follows.

$$A_{s_2}^a = \{\mu_{A_{s_2}^a}(x, n)/n/x \mid \forall x \in X, \forall n \in \{1, \ldots, \text{max}(s_2)\} :$$
$$\mu_{A_{s_2}^a}(x, n) = a(S_n)\}$$

A selection is a particular case of an aggregation where $A' = \{1, \ldots, \text{length}(A_1)\}$ and $a(S_n) = \mu(x, s_2^{-1}(n))$. Aggregations can be used to reinforce the membership degree of certain songs at a given position in a generic playlist if similar songs also have a high membership degree in nearby positions. Aggregations can also be used to generate an overview over different positions in a generic playlist, e.g., an average over a sliding window. The unary aggregation operator is similar to aggregations in SQL.

Projection
Let Y be a set of elements, and let y be one of its elements. Let $p : X \mapsto Y$ be a surjection, let S_y be the set of all fuzzy list elements $\{\mu(x, n)/n/x\}$ of A with $x = p^{-1}(y)$, and let $a : 2^{S_y} \mapsto [0; 1]$ be a function. The projection of A with respect to p and a is defined as follows.

$$\Pi_p^a(A) = \{\mu_\Pi(y, n)/n/y \mid \forall n \in \{1, \ldots, \text{length}(A)\}, \forall y \in Y :$$
$$\mu_\Pi(y, n) = a(S_y)\}$$

Since p is a surjection, $\mu_\Pi(y, n)$ is defined $\forall y \in Y$. The projection operator allows grouping elements of the fuzzy lists, e.g., it is possible to obtain an overview of the generic playlist in terms of artists or genre categories by mapping each song to at least one or more artists or genres. The mapping is specified by p and the new membership degree is determined by a.

4.4   Binary Operators

The following operators are defined over two fuzzy lists. They allow generic playlists to be merged, aggregated, or compared.

Binary Reordering, Selection and Aggregation
Binary operators allow merging two fuzzy lists, e.g., two playlists, into one by specifying an ordering, i.e., the position of the songs, and optionally how the membership degrees should be changed, i.e., the likelihood for a song to be selected in the playlist. To define binary operators, three position mapping functions b, s_1, and s_2 are used as illustrated in Figure 3. As presented earlier in the case of unary operators, the binary reordering, selection and aggregation will be successfully introduced for clarity reasons. Binary aggregations are a generalization of binary selections that are, in turn, a generalization of binary reorderings.

Binary Reordering:
Let $b : \{1, \ldots, \text{length}(A_1)\} \times \{1, \ldots, \text{length}(A_2)\} \leftrightarrow \{1, \ldots, \max(b)\}$ be a bijection as, e.g., illustrated by Figure 3. Let $\star : [0; 1] \times [0; 1] \mapsto [0; 1]$ be a binary operator. The binary reordering between A_1 and A_2 with b and $\star$ is defined as follows.

$$A_1 \underset{b}{\star} A_2 = \{\mu_\star(x, n)/n/x \mid \forall x \in X_1, \forall n \in \{1, \ldots, \max(b)\},$$
$$\forall (i, j) = b^{-1}(n) : \mu_\star(x, n) = \mu_{A_1}(x, i) \star \mu_{A_2}(x, j)\}$$

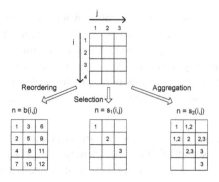

Fig. 3. Examples of position mapping for unary reordering, selection and aggregation operators

Common operators are for example the product, the minimum, the maximum, and the average. The average, e.g., of two generic playlists built by different user groups that were given the same constraints, can be performed as follows.

$$A_1 \underset{b}{\text{AVG}} A_2 = \{\mu_{\text{AVG}}(x, n)/n/x \mid \forall x \in X_1, \forall n \in \{1, \dots, \max(b)\},$$

$$\forall(i, j) = b^{-1}(n) : \mu_{\text{AVG}}(x, n) = \frac{\mu_{A_1}(x, i) + \mu_{A_2}(x, j)}{2}\}$$

Binary Selection:
Let $A'_1 \subseteq \{1, \dots, \text{length}(A_1)\}$ and $A'_2 \subseteq \{1, \dots, \text{length}(A_2)\}$ be two sets. Let $s_1 : \{1, \dots, \text{size}(A'_1)\} \times \{1, \dots, \text{length}(A'_2)\} \mapsto \{1, \dots, \max(s_1)\}$ be a bijection as, e.g., illustrated in Figure 3, and let $\star : [0; 1] \times [0; 1] \mapsto [0; 1]$ be a binary operator. The binary selection of A_1 and A_2 with s_1 and $\star$ is defined as follows.

$$A_1 \underset{s_1}{\star} A_2 = \{\mu_\star(x, n)/n/x \mid \forall x \in X, \forall n \in \{1, \dots, \max(s_1)\},$$

$$\forall(i, j) = s_1^{-1}(n) : \mu_\star(x, n) = \mu_{A_1}(x, i) \star \mu_{A_2}(x, j)\}$$

Binary selections over fuzzy lists are very common operations. Intersection and union operators are particular cases where the $\star$ operators are respectively the minimum and the maximum with some corresponding changes to the position mapping function s_1.

The *intersection* of A_1 and A_2 is defined as a fuzzy list where the membership degree for any element at a particular position is its minimum value in A_1 and A_2.

$$A_1 \cap A_2 = \{\mu_\cap(x, n)/n/x \mid \forall x \in X, \forall n \in \{1, \dots, \min(\text{length}(A_1), \text{length}(A_2))\}\} :$$
$$\mu_\cap(x, n) = \min(\mu_{A_1}(x, n), \mu_{A_2}(x, n))\}$$

Note the following properties: $(A_1 \cap A_2) \subseteq A_1$, $(A_1 \cap A_2) = (A_2 \cap A_1)$, $A_1 \cap \phi_1 = \phi_1$, and $A_1 \cap A_1 = A_1$.

The *union* of A_1 and A_2 is defined as a fuzzy list where the membership degree for any element at a particular position is set to its maximum value in A_1 and A_2.

$$A_1 \cup A_2 = \{\mu_\cup(x,n)/n/x \mid \forall x \in X, \forall n \in \{1, \ldots, \max(\text{length}(A_1), \text{length}(A_2))\} :$$

$$\mu_\cup(x,n) = \begin{cases} \mu_{A_1}(x,n) & \text{for } n > \text{length}(A_2) \\ \mu_{A_2}(x,n) & \text{for } n > \text{length}(A_1) \\ \max(\mu_{A_1}(x,n), \mu_{A_2}(x,n)) & \text{otherwise} \end{cases} \quad \}$$

Note the following properties: $A_1 \subseteq (A_1 \cup A_2)$, $(A_1 \cup A_2) = (A_2 \cup A_1)$, $A_1 \cup \phi_1 = A_1$, and $A_1 \cup A_1 = A_1$.

Intuitively, the intersection operator returns a generic playlist where only the songs strongly present in both of the two provided generic playlists will be very present in the resulting one. The intersection and the union operators are commonly used to build new generic playlists from existing ones.

Binary Aggregation:
Let $A_1' \subseteq \{1, \ldots, \text{length}(A_1)\}$ and $A_2' \subseteq \{1, \ldots, \text{length}(A_2)\}$ be two sets, let $s_2 : \{1, \ldots, \text{length}(A_1')\} \times \{1, \ldots, \text{length}(A_2')\} \mapsto \{1, \ldots, \max(s_2)\}$ be a surjective mapping as, e.g., illustrated in Figure 3, and let $\star : [0;1] \times [0;1] \mapsto [0;1]$ be a binary operator. Let S_n be the set of all the pairs of fuzzy lists elements $(\mu_{A_1}(x_{A_1}, i); i; x_{A_1})$ and $(\mu_{A_2}(x_{A_2}, j); j; x_{A_2})$ so that $s_2(i,j) = n$. Let $a(S_n) : 2^{S_n} \mapsto [0;1]$ be a function. The aggregation of A_1 and A_2 with a and s_2 is defined as follows.

$$A_1 \underset{s_2}{\overset{a}{\,}} A_2 = \{\mu_{\frac{a}{s_2}}(x,n)/n/x \mid \forall x \in X, \forall n \in \{1, \ldots, \max(s_2)\} :$$

$$\mu_{\frac{a}{s_2}}(x,n) = a(S_n)\}$$

For example, the average of two generic playlists can be perform over two sliding windows as illustrated by $s2$ in Figure 3. Such an average, less sensitive to small position differences between the two generic playlists, can be defined as follows.

$$s_2(i,j) = n \mid i = j, \{(i-1,j), (i,j-1), (i,j), (i,j+1), (i+1,j)\} \mapsto n$$

$$a(S_n) = \frac{\sum_{(i,j)=s_2^{-1}(n)} \mu_{A_1}(x,i) + \mu_{A_2}(x,j)}{\sum_{(i,j)=s_2^{-1}(n)} 1}$$

The binary aggregation operator is an adaptation to fuzzy lists of the join and aggregation operators found in SQL.

Cartesian Product
Let A_1 and A_2 be two fuzzy lists defined over the two domains X_1 and X_2. Let $s : \{1, \ldots, \text{length}(A_1)\} \times \{1, \ldots, \text{length}(A_2)\} \mapsto \{1, \ldots, \max(s)\}$ be a surjective mapping and let $S_n : \{((\mu_{A_1}; i; x_{A_1}); (\mu_{A_2}; j; x_{A_2}))\}$ be the set of all the pairs of fuzzy lists elements so that $s(i,j) = n$. The Cartesian product of A_1 and A_2 with respect to a and s is defined as follows.

$$A_1 \underset{s}{\overset{a}{\times}} A_2 = \{\mu_\times(x_{A_1 \times A_2}, n)/n/x_{A_1 \times A_2} \mid \forall x_{A_1 \times A_2} \in X_1 \times X_2,$$

$$\forall n \in \{1, \ldots, \max(s)\} : \mu_{\times_s^a}(x_{A_1 \times A_2}, n) = a(S_n)\}$$

Typical selection and aggregation functions for the Cartesian product are for example $s(i,j) = i = j$ and $a(S_n) = \mu_{A_1}(x_{A_1}, i) \cdot \mu_{A_2}(x_{A_2}, j)$, that computes the probability of two songs to be played at identical positions in two independent generic playlists.

The Cartesian product operator for fuzzy lists is related to the Cartesian product in SQL. As joins in SQL, binary aggregations are derived operators that can expressed using projections, selections, and Cartesian products. The concatenation of two fuzzy lists is also a derived operation. Other derived operators inspired from SQL such as Top_k could be useful, e.g., for capturing in a generic playlist the songs that have received the most votes. The fundamental operators of fuzzy lists are: the unary aggregation, the projection, and the Cartesian product.

5 Prototyping Considerations

The fuzzy lists and the operators defined above raise many interesting implementation issues. A first implementation option is to develop the fuzzy lists algebra with its own storage, query planner, query executor and to create a database management system, (DBMS), working on fuzzy lists rather than on multi-sets. While this would certainly be a neat solution and provide the most efficiency, it would also require to rewrite most parts of the DBMS, from the storage representation, to the query optimizer.

Another approach is to build an abstraction layer that reuses the relation operators defined for multi-sets. Fuzzy lists could be represented as tables including a position and a membership degree for each tuple. The queries should then be mapped to classical Relational DBMS operators. The main advantage of such an approach is that existing DBMS abstraction and features, e.g., physical storage, query planner and optimizer, can be reused, thus considerably reducing the implementation work. However, efficient storage representations and specific query optimizations will not be available, therefore reducing the scalability of the system. Object Relational DMBSs offer the possibility to specify both storage representations and query optimizations by allowing the definition of Abstract Data Types. However, their underlying algebra still remains confined in a relational model based on multi-sets.

As fuzzy lists are a generalization of lists that are commonly used to represent playlists, the integration of generic playlists into existing workflows of playlist management systems for playlist representation requires only minor adaptations such as having only 0 or 1 as possible membership degrees. For such usage, using an abstraction layer over a classical Object Relational DBMS is certainly the best approach. Previous work on storage representation for fuzzy song sets [4] using compressed bitmaps is a very interesting starting point to address storage representation issues of generic playlists and fuzzy lists.

6 Conclusion and Future Work

Generic playlists offer a pragmatic answer to the need for playlist management tools that has recently arisen in online music communities. Generic playlists respect both the consensual and the subjective nature of playlists by defining for each position in the sequence a likelihood degree for the presence of a given song. As illustrated by a concrete scenario, generic playlists are a flexible and concrete solution for constructing, sharing and personalizing playlists. This paper provides a solid foundation for the development of generic playlists by formally defining fuzzy lists and their algebra. Examples of generic playlists motivate the use of the presented fuzzy lists operators. Three basic operators are proposed. Their similarity with relational algebra operators facilitates their implementation in database systems. Future work encompasses research on efficient implementations of the basic operators, exploration of new operators, and experiments on a large scale playlist management engine.

Acknowledgments

This work was supported by the Danish Research Council for Technology and Production, through the framework project "*Intelligent Sound*", http://www.intelligentsound.org (STVF No. 26-04-0092).

References

1. Deliège, F., Pedersen, T.B.: Music warehouses: Challenges for the next generation of music search engines. In: LSAS. Proc. 1st Workshop on Learning the Semantics of Audio Signals, pp. 95–105 (2006)
2. Pachet, F.: Musical metadata and knowledge management. In: Encyclopedia of Knowledge Management, pp. 672–677. Idea Group (2005)
3. Cohen, W.W., Fan, W.: Web-collaborative filtering: recommending music by crawling the Web. Computer Networks 33, 685–698 (2000)
4. Deliège, F., Pedersen, T.B.: Using fuzzy song sets in music warehouses. In: ISMIR. Proc. 8th International Conference on Music Information Retrieval, pp. 21–26 (2007)
5. Tripathy, B., Pattanaik, G.: On some properties of lists and fuzzy lists. Information Sciences 168, 9–23 (2004)
6. Aucouturier, J.-J., Pachet, F.: Scaling up music playlist generation. In: Proc. IEEE International Conference on Multimedia and Expo, pp. 105–108 (2002)
7. Alghoniemy, M., Tewfik, A.: A network flow model for playlist generation. In: Proc. IEEE International Conference on Multimedia and Expo, pp. 445–448 (2001)
8. Pohle, T., Pampalk, E., Widmer, G.: Generating similarity-based playlists using traveling salesman algorithms. In: DAFx. Proc. 8th International Conference on Digital Audio Effects, pp. 220–225 (2005)
9. Pampalk, E., Pohle, T., Widmer, G.: Dynamic playlist generation based on skipping behavior. In: ISMIR. Proc. 4th International Conference on Music Information Retrieval, pp. 634–637 (2005)
10. Jensen, C.A., Mungure, E.M., Pedersen, T.B., Sørensen, K.: A data and query model for dynamic playlist generation. In: IEEE-MDDM. CDROM Proc. 2nd IEEE International Workshop on Multimedia Databases and Data Management (2007)
11. Hicken, W.T.: US Patent #20060265349A1: Sharing music essence in a recommendation system (2006)
12. Rubenstein, W.B.: A database design for musical information. In: Proc. ACM SIGMOD, pp. 479–490 (1987)
13. Wang, C., Li, J., Shi, S.: A music data model and its application. In: MMM. Proc. 10th International Multimedia Modelling Conference, pp. 79–85 (2004)
14. Slivinskas, G., Jensen, C.S., Snodgrass, R.T.: Bringing order to query optimization. SIGMOD Rec. 31, 5–14 (2002)

Tagging Video Contents with Positive/Negative Interest Based on User's Facial Expression

Masanori Miyahara[1], Masaki Aoki[1], Tetsuya Takiguchi[2], and Yasuo Ariki[2]

[1] Graduate School of Engineering, Kobe University
{miyahara,masamax777}@me.cs.scitec.kobe-u.ac.jp
[2] Organization of Advanced Science and Technology, Kobe University
1-1 Rokkodai, Nada, Kobe, Hyogo, 657-8501 Japan
{takigu,ariki}@kobe-u.ac.jp

Abstract. Recently, there are so many videos available for people to choose to watch. To solve this problem, we propose a tagging system for video content based on facial expression that can be used for recommendations based on video content. Viewer's face captured by a camera is extracted by Elastic Bunch Graph Matching, and the facial expression is recognized by Support Vector Machines. The facial expression is classified into Neutral, Positive, Negative and Rejective. Recognition results are recorded as "facial expression tags" in synchronization with video content. Experimental results achieved an averaged recall rate of 87.61%, and averaged precision rate of 88.03%.

Keywords: Tagging video contents, Elastic Bunch Graph Matching, Facial expression recognition, Support Vector Machines.

1 Introduction

Recently, multichannel digital broadcasting has started on TV. In addition, video-sharing sites on the Internet, such as "YouTube," are becoming very popular. These facts indicate that there are too many videos with such a diversity of content for viewers to select. To solve this problem, two main approaches have been employed. One analyzes the video content itself, and the other analyzes the viewer's behavior when watching the video.

For video content analysis, many studies have been carried out[1], such as shot boundary determination, high-level feature extraction, and object recognition. However, generic object recognition remains a difficult task.

On the other hand, for a viewer's behavior analysis, most often remote control operation histories, registration of favorite key words or actors, etc. are used. K. Masumitsu[2] focused on the remote control operation (such as scenes, etc. that the viewer chose to skip), and calculated the importance value of scenes. T. Taka[3] proposed a system which recommended TV programs if viewers gave some key words. But these methods acquire only personal preferences, which a viewer himself already knows. Furthermore, registering various key words or actors is cumbersome for a viewer.

S. Satoh, F. Nack, and M. Etoh (Eds.): MMM 2008, LNCS 4903, pp. 210–219, 2007.

Moreover, there are some studies that focused on a viewer's facial direction and facial expression. M. Yamamoto[4] proposed a system for automatically estimating the time intervals during which TV viewers have a positive interest in what they are watching based on temporal patterns in facial changes using the Hidden Markov Model. But it is probable that TV viewers have both positive interest and negative interest.

Based on the above discussion, we propose in this paper a system for tagging video content with the interest labels of Neutral, Positive, Negative and Rejective. To classify facial expressions correctly, facial feature points must be extracted precisely. From this viewpoint, Elastic Bunch Graph Matching (EBGM)[5][6] is employed in the system. EBGM was proposed by Laurenz Wiskott and proved to be useful in facial feature point extraction and face recognition.

The rest of this paper is organized as follows. In section 2, the overview of our system is described. In sections 3 and 4, the methods used in our system are described. Experiments and evaluations are described in section 5. Future study themes will be discussed in section 6.

2   Overview of Proposed System

Fig. 1 shows our experimental environment where a viewer watches video content on a display. The viewer's face is recorded into video by a webcam. A PC plays back the video and also analyzes the viewer's face.

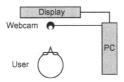

Fig. 1. Top View of Experimental Environment

Fig. 2 shows the system flow for analyzing the viewer's facial video. At first, exact face regions are extracted by AdaBoost[7] based on Haar-like features to reduce computation time in the next process, and the face size is normalized. Secondly, within the extracted face region, facial feature points are extracted by Elastic Bunch Graph Matching based on Gabor feature. Thirdly, the viewer is recognized based on the extracted facial feature points. Then, the personal model of his facial expression is retrieved. In the personal model, the facial feature points that were extracted from the viewer's neutral (expressionless) image and the facial expression classifier are already registered. Finally, the viewer's facial expression is recognized by the retrieved classifier, Support Vector Machines[8], based on the feature vector computed as the facial feature point location difference between the viewer's image at each frame and the registered neutral image.

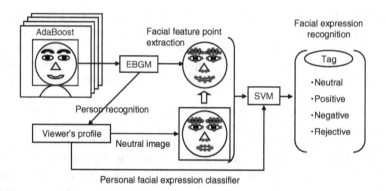

Fig. 2. System flow

Recognition results are recorded as "facial expression tags"(Neutral, Positive, Negative, Rejective) in synchronization with video content.

3 Facial Feature Point Extraction and Person Recognition Using EBGM

3.1 Gabor Wavelets

Since Gabor wavelets are fundamental to EBGM, it is described here. Gabor wavelets can extract global and local features by changing spatial frequency, and can extract features related to a wavelet's orientation.

Eq. (1) shows a Gabor Kernel used in Gabor wavelets. This function contains a Gaussian function for smoothing as well as a wave vector $\vec{k}_j$ that indicates simple wave frequencies and orientations.

$$\psi_j(\vec{x}) = \frac{\vec{k}_j^2}{\sigma^2} exp\left(-\frac{\vec{k}_j^2 \vec{x}^2}{2\sigma^2}\right)\left[exp\left(i\vec{k}_j\vec{x}\right) - exp\left(-\frac{\sigma^2}{2}\right)\right] \quad (1)$$

$$\vec{k}_j = \begin{pmatrix} k_{jx} \\ k_{jy} \end{pmatrix} = \begin{pmatrix} k_\nu \cos\varphi_\mu \\ k_\nu \sin\varphi_\mu \end{pmatrix} \quad (2)$$

Here, $k_\nu = 2^{-\frac{\nu+2}{2}}\pi C\varphi_\mu = \mu\frac{\pi}{8}$. We employ a discrete set of 5 different frequencies, index $\nu = 0, ..., 4$, and 8 orientations, index $\mu = 0, ..., 7$.

3.2 Jet

A jet is a set of convolution coefficients obtained by applying Gabor kernels with different frequencies and orientations to a point in an image. Fig.3 shows an example of a jet. To estimate the positions of facial feature points in an input image, jets in an input image are compared with jets in a facial model.

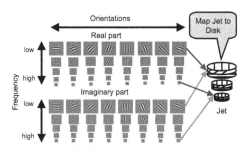

Fig. 3. Jet example

A jet $\mathcal{J}$ is composed of 40 complex coefficients (5 frequencies $\times$ 8 orientations) and expressed as follows:

$$\mathcal{J}_j = a_j exp(i\phi_j) \qquad (j = 0, ..., 39) \tag{3}$$

where $\overrightarrow{x} = (x, y)$, $a_j(\overrightarrow{x})$ and $\phi_j(\overrightarrow{x})$ are the facial feature point coordinate, magnitude of complex coefficient, and phase of complex coefficient, which rotates the wavelet at its center, respectively.

3.3 Jet Similarity

For the comparison of facial feature points between the facial model and the input image, the similarity is computed between jet set $\{\mathcal{J}\}$ and $\{\mathcal{J}'\}$. Locations of two jets are represented as $\overrightarrow{x}$ and $\overrightarrow{x}'$. The difference between vector $\overrightarrow{x}$ and vector $\overrightarrow{x}'$ is given in Eq. (4).

$$\overrightarrow{d} = \overrightarrow{x} - \overrightarrow{x}' = \begin{pmatrix} dx \\ dy \end{pmatrix} \tag{4}$$

Here, let's consider the similarity of two jets in terms of the magnitude and phase of the jets as follows:

$$S_D(\mathcal{J}, \mathcal{J}') = \frac{\sum_{j=0}^{N-1} a_j a_j' \cos(\phi_j - \phi_j')}{\sqrt{\sum_{j=0}^{N-1} a_j^2 \sum_{j=0}^{N-1} a_j'^2}} \tag{5}$$

where the phase difference $(\phi_j - \phi_j')$ is qualitatively expressed as follows:

$$\phi_j - \phi_j' = \overrightarrow{k}_j \overrightarrow{x} - \overrightarrow{k}_j \overrightarrow{x}' = \overrightarrow{k}_j \left(\overrightarrow{x} - \overrightarrow{x}' \right) = \overrightarrow{k}_j \overrightarrow{d} \tag{6}$$

To find the best similarity between $\{\mathcal{J}\}$ and $\{\mathcal{J}'\}$ using Eq. (5) and Eq. (6), phase difference is modified as $\phi_j - (\phi_j' + \overrightarrow{k}_j \overrightarrow{d})$ and Eq. (5) is rewritten as

$$S_D(\mathcal{J}, \mathcal{J}') = \frac{\sum_{j=0}^{N-1} a_j a_j' \cos(\phi_j - (\phi_j' + \overrightarrow{k}_j \overrightarrow{d}))}{\sqrt{\sum_{j=0}^{N-1} a_j^2 \sum_{j=0}^{N-1} a_j'^2}} \tag{7}$$

In order to find the optimal jet J' that is most similar to jet J, the best $\vec{d}$ is estimated that will maximize similarity based not only upon phase but magnitude as well.

3.4   Displacement Estimation

In Eq. (7), the best $\vec{d}$ is estimated in this way. First, the similarity at zero displacement ($dx = dy = 0$) is estimated. Then the similarity of its North, East, South, and West neighbors is estimated. The neighboring location with the highest similarity is chosen as the new center of the search. This process is iterated until none of the neighbors offers an improvement over the current location. The iteration is limited to 50 times at one facial feature point.

3.5   Facial Feature Points and Face Graph

In this paper, facial feature points are defined as the 34 points shown in Fig. 2 and Fig. 4. A set of jets extracted at all facial feature points is called a face graph. Fig. 4 shows an example of a face graph.

Fig. 4. Jet extracted from facial feature points

3.6   Bunch Graph

A set of jets extracted from many people at one facial feature point is called a bunch. A graph constructed using bunches at all the facial feature points is called a bunch graph. In searching out the location of facial feature points, the similarity described in Eq. (7) is computed between the jets in the bunch graph and a jet at a point in an input image. The jet with the highest similarity, achieved by moving $\vec{d}$ as described in Section 3.4, is chosen as the target facial feature point in the input image. In this way, using a bunch graph, the locations of the facial feature points can be searched allowing various variations. For example, a chin bunch may include jets from non-bearded chins as well as bearded chins, to cover the local changes. Therefore, it is necessary to train data using the facial data of various people in order to construct the bunch graph. The training data required for construction of bunch graph was manually collected.

3.7   Elastic Bunch Graph Matching

Fig. 5 shows an elastic bunch graph matching flow. First, after a facial image is input into the system, a bunch graph is pasted to the image, and then a local search for the input face commences using the method described in Section 3.4.

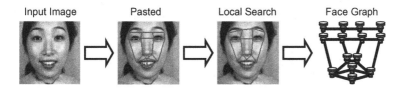

Input Image   Pasted   Local Search   Face Graph

Fig. 5. Elastic Bunch Graph Matching procedure

Finally, the face graph is extracted after all the locations of the feature points are matched.

3.8 Person (Face) Recognition

The extracted face graph is used for face recognition. For the comparison between the extracted face graph G and the stored graph G', the similarity is computed between face graphs G and G'. Here, let's consider the similarity of two face graphs as follows:

$$S_{jet}(G, G') = \frac{1}{M} \sum_{j=0}^{M-1} S_D(\mathcal{J}_j, \mathcal{J}'_j) \tag{8}$$

where M is the number of the facial feature points for recognition. $\mathcal{J}, \mathcal{J}'$ are sets of Jets for graphs G and G' respectively. A person with the maximum S_{jet} score is recognized as the input person.

4 Facial Expression Recognition Using SVM

4.1 Definition of Facial Expression Classes

To classify the viewer's facial expression, the classes were conventionally defined as "interest" or "disinterest." But it is probable that the viewer's interest is positive, negative or neutral. For example, if the viewer watches a video that is extremely unpleasant, he may be interested in watching it once, but never again. From this viewpoint, in this study, three facial expression classes are defined; Neutral, Positive and Negative. In addition, if the viewer does not watch the display in a frontal direction or tilts his face, the system classifies it as Rejective because their correct classification is difficult. Table 1 shows the class types and the meanings.

4.2 SVM Algorithms

Support Vector Machines were pioneered by Vapnik[8]. SVM separate the training data in feature space by a hyperplane defined by the type of kernel function employed. In this study, Radial Basis Function (RBF) is employed as a kernel function. SVM finds the hyperplane with the maximum margin, defined as the distances between the hyperplane and the nearest data point in each class. To recognize multi-class data, SVM is extended by one-against-the-rest method.

Table 1. Facial expression classes

Classes	Meanings
Neutral (Neu)	Expressionless
Positive (Pos)	Happiness, Laughter, Pleasure, etc.
Negative (Neg)	Anger, Disgust, Displeasure, etc.
Rejective(Rej)	Not watching the display in the front direction, Occluding part of face, Tilting the face, etc.

4.3 Feature Vector

The viewers of our system register their neutral images as well as the personal facial expression classifier in advance. After EBGM recognizes a viewer in front of the display, the system retrieves his neutral image and the personal facial expression SVM classifier. Then, the differences between the viewer's facial feature points extracted by EBGM and the viewer's neutral facial feature points are computed as a feature vector for SVM.

5 Experiments

5.1 Experimental Conditions

In the experimental environment shown in Fig. 1, two subjects, A and B, watched four videos. They were instructed not to exaggerate or suppress their facial expressions. The length of the videos was about 17 minutes in average. The categories were "variety shows" because these shows often make viewers change their facial expressions, compared to other categories such as "drama" or "news." While they watched the videos, the system recorded their facial video in synchronization with the video content at 15 frames per second. Then subjects A and B tagged the video with four labels, Positive, Negative, Neutral and Rejective according to Table 1. To tag the video, an interface was used as shown in Fig. 6. In the left window, the video content and the viewer's facial video were displayed. The subjects were asked to press the buttons in the right window to classify the video frames into three classes while they watched both the video content and their facial video in the left window. If no button was pressed, the frame was classified as Neutral. Tagged results for all frames in the experimental videos are shown in Table 2. We used those experimental videos and the tagging data as training and test data in the subsequent section.

Table 2. Tagged results (frames)

	Neu	Pos	Neg	Rej	Total
Subject A	49865	7665	3719	1466	62715
Subject B	56531	2347	3105	775	62758

Fig. 6. Tagging interface

5.2   Facial Region Extraction Using AdaBoost

Facial regions were extracted using AdaBoost based on Haar-like features[7] in all frames of the experimental videos except Reject frames. Extracted frames were checked manually to confirm whether they were false regions or not. The experimental results are shown in Table 3.

Table 3. Experimental results of facial region extraction

a. Subject A

	Neu	Pos	Neg
False extraction	20	3	1
Total frames	49865	7665	3719
Rate (%)	0.040	0.039	0.027

b. Subject B

	Neu	Pos	Neg
False extraction	132	106	9
Total frames	56531	2347	3105
Rate (%)	0.234	4.516	0.290

In the experiments, extraction rates of the facial regions for both subject A and B were 100%. On the other hand, averaged Neu, Pos and Neg false extraction rates were 0.0354% for subject A and 1.68% for subject B. The reason for the worse false extraction rate for subject B is attributed to his habit of raising his head when he is excited.

5.3   Person Recognition Using EBGM

All faces correctly extracted by AdaBoost were recognized by Elastic Bunch Graph Matching. Experimental results are shown in Table 4.

Table 4. Person recognition experiment

a. Subject A

	Neu	Pos	Neg
False recognition	2	0	0
Total frames	49845	7662	3718
Rate (%)	0.004	0.000	0.000

b. Subject B

	Neu	Pos	Neg
False recognition	2	20	0
Total frames	56399	2241	3096
Rate (%)	0.004	0.893	0.000

As the data in the table shows, the false recognition rate was so low, in fact, that we can say that our proposed system is able to select almost without error a personal facial expression classifier from the viewer's profile.

Table 5. Experimental results of facial expression recognition

a. Confusion matrix for subject A

	Neu	Pos	Neg	Rej	Sum	Recall (%)
Neu	48275	443	525	622	49865	96.81
Pos	743	6907	1	14	7665	90.11
Neg	356	107	3250	6	3719	87.39
Rej	135	0	5	1326	1466	90.45
Sum	49509	7457	3781	1968	62715	
Precision (%)	97.51	92.62	85.96	67.38		

b. Confusion matrix for subject B

	Neu	Pos	Neg	Rej	Sum	Recall (%)
Neu	56068	138	264	61	56531	99.18
Pos	231	2076	8	32	2347	88.45
Neg	641	24	2402	38	3105	77.36
Rej	203	0	21	551	775	71.10
Sum	57143	2238	2695	682	62758	
Precision (%)	98.12	92.76	89.13	80.79		

5.4   Facial Expression Recognition Using SVM

For every frame in the experimental videos, facial expression was recognized by Support Vector Machines. Three of four experimental videos were used for training data, and the rest for testing data. The cross-validation method was used to create the confusion matrices shown in Table 5.

The averaged recall rate was 87.61% and the averaged precision rate was 88.03%. When the subjects modestly expressed their emotion, even though the subjects tagged their feeling as Positive or Negative, the system often mistook the facial expression for Neutral. Moreover, when the subjects had an intermediate facial expression, the system often made a mistake because one expression class was only assumed in a frame.

6   Conclusion

In this paper, we proposed the system that tagged video contents with Positive, Negative, and Neutral interest labels based on viewer's facial expression. In addition, a "Rejective" frame was automatically tagged by learned SVM classifiers. As an experimental result of the facial expression recognition for two subjects, the averaged recall rate and precision rate were about 88%. This makes our proposed system able to find those intervals of a video in which the viewer interested, and it also enables the system to recommend video content to the viewer. Evaluation of the video contents of various categories and evaluation of various subjects will be the theme of future work. Moreover, we plan to construct a system that can automatically recommend video content for viewers based on a combination of facial expression, speech and other multimodal information.

References

1. Smeaton, A.F., Over, P., Kraaij, W.: Evaluation campaigns and TRECVid. In: MIR 2006. Proceedings of the 8th ACM International Workshop on Multimedia Information Retrieval, Santa Barbara, California, USA, October 26 - 27, 2006, pp. 321–330. ACM Press, New York (2006)
2. Masumitsu, K., Echigo, T.: Personalized Video Summarization Using Importance Score. J.of IEICE J84-D-II(8), 1848–1855 (2001)
3. Taka, T., Watanabe, T., Taruguchi, H.: A TV Program Selection Support Agent with History Database. IPSJ Journal 42(12), 3130–3143 (2001)
4. Yamamoto, M., Nitta, N., Babaguchi, N.: Estimating Intervals of Interest During TV Viewing for Automatic Personal Preference Acquisition. In: PCM2006. Proceedings of The 7th IEEE Pacific-Rim Conference on Multimedia, pp. 615–623 (November 2006)
5. Wiskott, L., Fellous, J.-M., Kruger, N., von der Malsburg, C.: Face Recognition by Elastic Bunch Graph Matching. IEEE Transactions on Pattern Analysis and Machine Intelligence 19(7), 775–779 (1997)
6. Bolme, D.S.: Elastic Bunch Graph Matchin. In: partial fulfillment of the requirements for the Degree of Master of Science Colorado State University Fort Collins, Colorado (Summer 2003)
7. Viola, P., Jones, M.: Rapid Object Detection using a Boosted Cascade of Simple Features. In: Proc. IEEE Conf. on Computer Vision and Pattern Recognition Kauai, USA, pp. 1–9 (2001)
8. Vapnik, V.N.: The Nature of Statistical Learning Theory. Springer, Heidelberg (1995)
9. Lyons, M.J., Akamatsu, S., Kamachi, M., Gyoba, J.: Coding Facial Expressions with Gabor Wavelets. In: Proceedings, Third IEEE International Conference on Automatic Face and Gesture Recognition, April 14-16, 1998, pp. 200–205. IEEE Computer Society, Nara Japan (1998)

Snap2Play: A Mixed-Reality Game Based on Scene Identification

Tat-Jun Chin[1], Yilun You[1], Celine Coutrix[2], Joo-Hwee Lim[1],
Jean-Pierre Chevallet[1], and Laurence Nigay[2]

[1] Image Perception, Access and Language Lab
Institute for Infocomm Research, Singapore
{tjchin,ylyou,joohwee,viscjp}@i2r.a-star.edu.sg
[2] Laboratoire d'Informatique de Grenoble
Université Joseph Fourier, B.P. 53, 38041 Grenoble cedex 9 France
{celine.coutrix,laurence.nigay}@imag.fr

Abstract. The ubiquity of camera phones provides a convenient platform to develop immersive mixed-reality games. In this paper we introduce such a game which is loosely based on the popular card game "Memory", where players are asked to match a pair of identical cards among a set of overturned cards by revealing only two cards at a time. In our game, the players are asked to match a "physical card", which is an image of a scene in the real world, to a "digital card", which corresponds to a scene in a virtual world. The objective is to convey a mixed-reality sensation. Cards are matched with a scene identification engine which consists of multiple classifiers trained on previously collected images. We present our comprehensive overall game design, as well as implementation details and results. Additionally, we also describe how we constructed our scene identification engine and its performance.

1 Introduction

The increase in functionality and processing power of mobile phones in conjunction with the massive bandwidth afforded by advanced telecommunication networks allow a plethora of innovative and interesting game applications to be developed for mobile phone users, e.g. [1,2]. In addition, the existence of high-resolution cameras on many mobile phones opens up another interesting direction for games based on image or video processing techniques.

In this paper we describe an innovative game application which exploits cameras on mobile phones. Our game consists of using the phone camera as an input interaction modality (a way for the user to interact with the game). The aim of our game, apart from the obvious role of providing entertainment, is to convey a feeling of "mixed reality" (i.e. a seamless interchange between a virtual world and the real world) to the user. Indeed our design approach is based on providing similar input modalities for interacting with the virtual world and with the real world. The game is inspired by the popular card game "Memory", where players are asked to match a pair of identical cards among a set of overturned cards by

S. Satoh, F. Nack, and M. Etoh (Eds.): MMM 2008, LNCS 4903, pp. 220–229, 2008.

revealing only two cards at a time. In our game, the players are asked to match a "physical card", which represents the real world, to a "digital card", which is a token of the virtual world.

The game begins with the process of collecting a digital card: The player goes to a pre-determined location, and, with the aid of a custom software on the phone which exploits orientation sensing hardware, points the phone camera at a pre-determined direction and orientation (i.e. at a "virtual scene"). This is to simulate a photo taking experience in the virtual world, and it is emphasized that the corresponding real-world scene at which the player is inadvertently guided to aim is inconsequential for the game. Upon "snapping" the virtual scene at the right vantage point, the player receives the digital card which is actually an image of a real-world scene in a separate location.

Drawing from his familiarity of the local geography or guidance from the system, the player proceeds towards the location inferred from the digital card. Upon reaching the correct area, the player attempts to capture the scene with an image (the physical card) which resembles the digital card contents as closely as possible. The physical card is then transmitted to a service provider which employs a scene identification engine to verify the card. If verification is obtained, the player has successfully matched a pair of cards, and he can continue to collect the remaining card pairs (by first receiving directions to the next digital card). In a competitive setting, the player who collects all cards first is the winner.

We call this game "Snap2Play", and the overall success of the game is indicated when the player, apart from being entertained, is immersed during the interchange between the physical and virtual world i.e. he is only mildly aware of the differences between capturing the digital card and the physical card.

The rest of the paper is organized as follows: §2 describes in detail the rules and flow of the game. §3 describes a very important aspect of the game which is how we simulate a photo taking experience on a mobile phone for collecting the digital card. §4 explains the other major aspect of our game which is how our scene identification engine is constructed. §5 reports the progress we have obtained thus far, while a conclusion is drawn in §6.

2   How the Game Works

Snap2Play can be implemented as a single- or multiplayer (co-operative or competitive) game. The player interacts with the game through a mobile phone installed with the Snap2Play application. The overall flow of the game is coordinated through the mobile phone network (i.e. GPRS) by a game server (henceforth, the "game system"). Upon starting, the player is first introduced to the rules and objectives of the game, and is prompted to select his preferred game trail[1] based on the descriptions provided by the application. The player then proceeds to hunt for the first digital card by receiving, from the game system

---

[1] The design of the game trail allows the incorporation of various vested interests, e.g. introduction to tourist spots or shopping precincts, promotion of physical fitness.

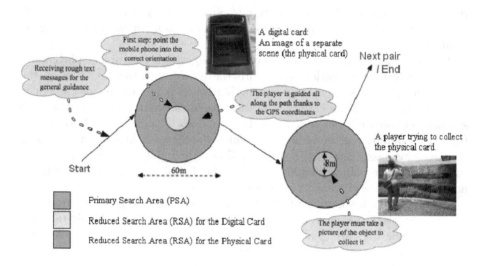

Fig. 1. The Snap2Play game scenario

through the phone network, a message with the rough location of the card. The aim is for him to enter the "Primary Search Area (PSA)" of the card; See Fig. 1.

The system will automatically detect when the player enters the PSA, after which a 2D digital compass which points to the direction of the digital card is activated on the phone. Based on the guidance by the compass, the player moves towards the digital card until he eventually reaches a "Reduced Search Area (RSA)". This is the pre-determined physical location, with a certain level of tolerance, where the digital card is embedded at a pre-defined orientation in space. The above steps are achieved through using GPS navigation.

Once the player enters the RSA, a text notification is given to activate the phone camera and to use it to locate and snap the digital card. The player is guided with a software that exploits attached orientation sensors on the phone to aim the camera at a pre-determined vantage point of the digital card. When the correct view-point is established, the player is notified through a superimposed image on the video feed or through tactile feedback, and the player can trigger the camera to collect the digital card. The elaborate manner in which the digital card is obtained is aimed at simulating the experience of capturing an image in a virtual world. §3 describes in detail how this is achieved.

The digital card is actually an image of a scene in a separate location. The player will need to find the location inferred from the digital card based on either his familiarity of the local geography or guidance from the system. When the player reaches the PSA of the physical card, the compass will be invoked to guide the player towards the corresponding RSA; See Fig. 1. The player proceeds by trying to snap an image of the scene (the physical card) to match the contents of the digital card. The physical card is sent (e.g. via MMS) to the system to be verified by a scene identification engine. §4 describes how the scene identification engine is constructed. If the cards are deemed matching, the player can continue to collect the remaining cards (by receiving a message with the rough location of the next digital card) if the game has not finished.

3   Collecting a Digital Card

The goal of this subsystem is to simulate a photo-taking experience in a virtual world. In essence the intention is to guide the player to take aim and acquire the image of a physically non-existent "virtual scene" (the digital card) while simultaneously imparting, as much as possible, the feeling of taking a photo of a real scene. A successful execution renders the player only mildly aware of the differences. The following describes how we propose to achieve this.

3.1   Embedding and Locating a Virtual Scene

Three parameters are required to embed a virtual scene in the physical world: A 2D coordinate (i.e. a GPS location), the direction (relative to the north) to face the scene, and the orientation (relative to the ground) to view the scene. The three different sensing instrument to achieve this, respectively a GPS receiver, a compass and a tri-axis accelerometer, are described in §3.2. When designing the game trail, the three parameters of all digital cards are recorded. Locating a digital card during play is a matter of re-producing its embedding parameters.

Acquiring the first parameter involves the straightforward process of reading from a GPS receiver and digital compass attached to the phone by the Snap2Play application. When locating a digital card during play, the system iteratively monitors the GPS location and heading of the player through the GPRS network and notifies the player when he is sufficiently close to a PSA or RSA (c.f. §2 and Fig. 1). Once the correct GPS coordinate is obtained, the system notifies the Snap2Play application to activate the video feed and begins to monitor the compass and accelerometer reading in order to provide guidance to the pre-determined "vantage point" (orientation) from which to view a virtual scene. Feedback to the player is given visually through the video feed, whereby a variable sized image of the digital card (to signify divergence from the correct orientation) is superimposed. Feedback via video is crucial to compel the player to acquire a digital card as though he is acquiring a physical card. Once the right orientation is obtained, the player triggers the phone to collect the digital card.

3.2   The Hardware

In our implementation, two standalone devices are required apart from the mobile phone. First is the Holux GPSlim 236 Bluetooth GPS receiver which contains a SiRF-Star-III chipset, allowing it to have an accuracy within 3m; See Fig. 2(a). This is digitally connected to the mobile phone via the Bluetooth protocol. Its small size allows the player to carry it conveniently in a pocket. Despite the impressive accuracy, the existence of high-rise buildings and frequently overcast sky in our game trails make GPS reading unrepeatable, hence the inclusion of

(a) Holux GPSlim 236   (b) SHAKE SK6   (c) Nokia N80

Fig. 2. Some of the hardware in our implementation

the PSA and RSA (see §2) to allow some degree of tolerance of positioning error in the game. Note that more advanced phone models with on-board GPS receivers will render such an extra device unnecessary.

In addition, a compass and a tri-axis accelerometer are also needed for the game. While the compass gives heading relative to the magnetic north, the tri-axis accelerometer provides orientation-sensitive readings. These functions can be conveniently provided by an instrument called the "Sensing Hardware Accessory for Kinaesthetic Expression (SHAKE)" device. The "SK6" model is used in our game. The accelerometer needs to be attached to the phone, and fortunately the small form factor of the SK6 allows this to be easily achieved; see Fig. 2(b). It is also digitally interfaced to the phone via the Bluetooth protocol. Finally, the mobile phone used in our system is the Nokia N80 model which has a 3 Megapixel camera. Fig. 2(c) shows the actual phone used in our system.

4   Collecting a Physical Card

The collection of a physical card requires the determination of, preferably without soliciting manual attention, whether a physical card (an image) corresponds to the scene at which a player should be seeking to match the current digital card he is holding. Many previous work on object and scene category recognition (e.g. [3,4,5,6]) provide excellent potential solutions. We take a *discriminative* machine learning approach for this task. Our scene identification engine consists of classifiers trained on previously collected sample images of the scenes. A discriminative approach is favoured here due to its simplicity, in that less parameter selection effort is required, and effectiveness, as is evident in [5,6].

4.1   Multiple Classifiers for Scene Identification

Our scene identification engine consists of N classifiers H_n, where N is the number of physical cards to be collected in a particular route, and $1 \leq n \leq N$. Given a physical card $\mathbf{I}$, the following result is obtained:

$$n^* = \arg\max_n H_n(\mathbf{I}) \ , \tag{1}$$

where $H_n(\mathbf{I})$ evaluates the possibility of $\mathbf{I}$ belonging to the n-th scene. Provided that $H_{n^*}(\mathbf{I})$ is larger than a pre-determined threshold, $\mathbf{I}$ is assigned the label n^*.

Fig. 3. Sample images of 5 physical cards in the Campus trail. Observe the variations that exist for a particular scene. Points in these images are detected SIFT keypoints.

Otherwise, the system is programmed to decline classification. If n^* matches the digital card that is currently pending, then $\mathbf{I}$ is successfully paired.

Before training H_n, a set of sample images of the N scenes have to be collected. Ideally, the samples should be captured in a manner that includes, as much as possible, the variations expected from images taken by the players as Fig. 3 illustrates. Secondly, the type of feature to be extracted from input images $\mathbf{I}$ on which H_n operates has to be determined. Experimental results from object and scene category classification [3,4,5] suggest that local features which are invariant to affine transformations are very suited for the task. In particular, the SIFT framework [7] has proven to be effective and robust against distortions caused by rotation, scaling, affine transformations and minor lighting changes. It involves two stages, namely keypoint detection and local descriptor extraction. Each descriptor is typically a 128-dimension feature vector which allows the the keypoint to be compared. Fig. 3 shows the SIFT keypoints of the sample images.

4.2   Training Classifiers Via Boosting

Many possibilities exist to construct H_n given a set of local features of $\mathbf{I}$. We apply the technique of *boosting* to train H_n. A popular boosting algorithm, the AdaBoost procedure, was adapted in [5] for object-class recognition with impressive results, and we apply their method here. Basically boosting constructs the desired classifier H_n by linearly combining T *weak* classifiers:

$$H_n(\mathbf{I}) = \frac{1}{\sum_{t=1}^{T} \alpha_n^t} \sum_{t=1}^{T} \alpha_n^t h_n^t(\mathbf{I}) \ , \tag{2}$$

where h_n^t is the t-th weak classifier of H_n and α_n^t is its corresponding weight ($\alpha_n^t \geq 0$). A weak classifier h_n^t determines whether $\mathbf{I}$ belongs to scene n. Each h_n^t must be able to classify correctly at least only half of the time (hence "weak classifiers"), but when their decisions are aggregated a competent overall classifier H_n can be obtained. For our task, a weak classifier is defined as

$$h_n^t(\mathbf{I}) = \begin{cases} 1 & \text{if } \min d(\mathbf{v}_n^t, \mathbf{v}^m) \leq \theta_n^t \text{ for all } 1 \leq m \leq M \\ 0 & \text{otherwise} \end{cases}, \tag{3}$$

where $\mathbf{v}_n^t$ is the defining feature of h_n^t, and $\mathbf{v}^m$ is one of the M SIFT descriptors of $\mathbf{I}$. Function $d(\cdot, \cdot)$ is a pre-determined distance metric (e.g. Euclidean) in the descriptor space, while constant θ_n^t is a closeness criterion for h_n^t. More intuitively, h_n^t is activated (returns '1') if there exists at least one descriptor in $\mathbf{I}$ that is sufficiently similar to $\mathbf{v}_n^t$. In addition, it can be seen that $0 \leq H_n \leq 1$.

For a particular scene, any feature extracted from its sample images can be used to define a weak classifier. The goal of AdaBoost is to select a subset of all available weak classifiers for which the defining features, as far as possible, simultaneously exist in the images of that scene while at the same time do not appear in images of other scenes. The algorithm iteratively chooses weak classifiers depending on how well they perform on sample images with different weightings, which are in turn computed based on how well previously selected weak classifiers perform on these samples. See Table 1. The closeness criterion for a weak classifier is provided by the weak hypothesis finder. See Table 2.

5   Results

5.1   Our System

We implemented Snap2Play as a single-tier Java Platform Micro-Edition (J2ME) client application. The application is designed using the "Interaction Complementarity Assignment, Redundancy and Equivalence (ICARE)" methodology [8], a

Table 1. The AdaBoost algorithm for scene classification

Input: Training images $(\mathbf{I}_1, l_1), \ldots, (\mathbf{I}_K, l_K)$, where $l_k = +1$ if $\mathbf{I}_k$ belongs to class n, and $l_k = -1$ otherwise.
Initialization: Set weights $w_1 = \ldots = w_K = 1$.
1. **for** $t = 1, \ldots, T$ **do**
2.   If $(\sum_k^K w_k < th_{Ada})$ set $T = t$ and terminate.
3.   Find best weak hypothesis h_n^t with respect to $w_1, \ldots, w_K$ using the weak hypothesis finder (Table 2).
4.   Compute $\mathcal{E}_n^t = (\sum_{k=1, h_n^t(\mathbf{I}_k) \neq l_k}^K w_k)/(\sum_{k=1}^K w_k)$.
5.   Compute $\beta_n^t = \sqrt{(1 - \mathcal{E}_n^t)/\mathcal{E}_n^t}$ and $\alpha_n^t = \ln \beta_n^t$.
6.   Update $w_k \leftarrow w_k \cdot (\beta_n^t)^{-l_k \cdot h_n^t(\mathbf{I}_k)}$.
7. **end for**
Output: T weak classifiers h_n^t with corresponding weights α_n^t.

Table 2. The weak hypothesis finder

Input: Labeled local features $(\mathbf{v}_k^f, l_k)$ and weights w_k, where $1 \leq k \leq K$ and $1 \leq f \leq F_k$. F_k is the total number of local features extracted from the k-th image.

1. Define distance metric $d(\cdot, \cdot)$ for local features.

2. For all local features $\mathbf{v}_k^f$ and all images $\mathbf{I}_j$, find the minimal distance between $\mathbf{v}_k^f$ and local features in $\mathbf{I}_j$:

$$d_{k,f,j} = \arg\min_{1 \leq g \leq F_j} d(\mathbf{v}_k^f, \mathbf{v}_j^g).$$

3. Sort the minimal distances as such: For all (k, f), find a permutation $\pi_{k,f}(1), \ldots, \pi_{k,f}(K)$ such that

$$d_{k,f,\pi_{k,f}(1)} \leq \cdots \leq d_{k,f,\pi_{k,f}(K)}.$$

4. Select the best weak hypothesis as such: For all v_k^f, compute the following value

$$\arg\max_s \sum_{j=1}^{s} w_{\pi_{k,f}(j)} l_{\pi_{k,f}(j)}$$

and select $\mathbf{v}_k^f$ for which the above value is the largest.

5. Compute threshold for best weak hypothesis as

$$\theta = \tfrac{1}{2}(d_{k,f,\pi_{k,f}(s^*)} + d_{k,f,\pi_{k,f}(s^*+1)})$$

where s^* is the value of s at the maximum in Step 4.

Output: Best weak classifier defined by the selected $\mathbf{v}_k^f$ and its corresponding θ.

---

component-based approach which enables the rapid development of multiple active or passive input modalities such as tactile messages, GPS and orientation sensory readings. Snap2Play requires an interface to capture and perform scene identification on the physical card. We built an interface with a client-server architecture which allows transmission of the image to the game server via GPRS or WiFi. The communication layer of the our interface is developed using Java Platform Standard-Edition (J2SE) and the scene identification engine is built in C++ for performance. Fig. 4 illustrates the actual user interface on the mobile phone of our system.

5.2   Scene Identification

We have implemented our game on a trail which is situated in our campus (henceforth, the "Campus" trail). This trail contains 10 pairs of digital and physical cards. Fig. 3 illustrates 5 of the 10 physical cards, while Fig. 5 depicts the configuration of the trail. We present scene identification results for the physical cards (scenes) in this trail. A total of 183 images were used for training the scene identification engine, while 300 images captured on a different day were used for testing. As shown in Fig. 3, the images were captured in a manner that aims to include the variations expected during game play. Several scene identification methods are compared. First, given the apparent visual similarity of the images from the same class despite the view-point changes imposed during collection, one is tempted to apply a straightforward Euclidean distance with a nearest neighbour search to classify the testing images. Secondly, we also tried a naive feature matching approach i.e. store all SIFT features from training images and test a query image by matching its features to the feature database. We have also implemented the "discriminative patch selection" method of [6] since it

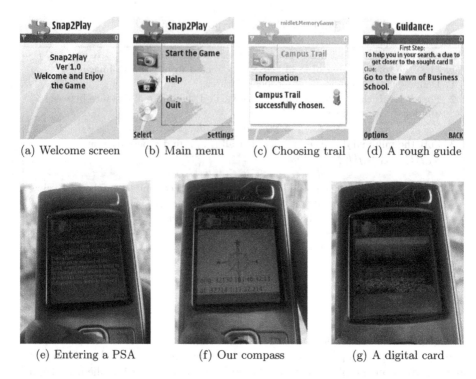

(a) Welcome screen   (b) Main menu   (c) Choosing trail   (d) A rough guide

(e) Entering a PSA   (f) Our compass   (g) A digital card

Fig. 4. Sample screen shots of the user interface on the Nokia N80 of our system

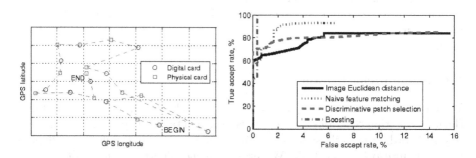

Fig. 5. Left: The Campus trail. Each grid is approximately 300m x 300m. Right: Scene identification results (in the form of ROC curves) of 4 methods on the Campus trail.

provides an alternative sampling-based approach to boosting [5]. Fig. 5 illustrates the scene identification results in the form of Receiver Operating Characteristic (ROC) curves. It can be seen that despite the vast similarity between the images, trivial approaches like Euclidean distance and naive feature matching do not perform well. Boosting returned the best results, justifying our selection of this method for our game. On the query set it is capable of achieving a true accept rate of 99.33% with a corresponding false accept rate of only 0.67%.

6   Conclusion

In this paper we propose a novel mixed-reality game which is implemented on mobile camera phones. The game requires the player to match a physical card in the real world to a digital card in a virtual world. This was achieved by exploiting orientation sensing hardware and a scene identification engine. Experimental results show that boosting SIFT features is an effective technique for constructing the scene identification engine. The next step is to deploy Snap2Play to evaluate the usability of the interaction modalities as well as the experience of the players (in Singapore in September 2007 and in Grenoble-France during autumn).

Acknowledgements

We reserve enormous gratitude to Emelie Annweiler, Wee-Siang Tan, Kelvin Kang-Wei Goh and Clement Yuan-Loong Tung for their tireless effort in implementing the various aspects of our game. This work is partly funded by the ICT-Asia MoSAIC project and by the OpenInterface European FP6 STREP focusing on an open source platform for multimodality (FP6-035182).

References

1. Strachan, S., Williamson, J., Murray-Smith, R.: Show me the way to monte carlo: density-based trajectory navigation. In: Proceedings of ACM SIG CHI (2007)
2. Ballagas, R.A., Kratz, S.G., Borchers, J., Yu, E., Walz, S.P., Fuhr, C.O., Hovestadt, L., Tann, M.: REXplorer: a mobile, pervasive spell-casting game for tourists. In: CHI 2007. Extended Abstracts on Human Factors in Computing Systems (2007)
3. Fergus, R., Perona, P., Zisserman, A.: Object class recognition by unsupervised scale-invariant learning. In: Computer Vision and Pattern Recognition (2003)
4. Li, F.F., Perona, P.: A Bayesian hierarchical model for learning natural scene categories. In: Computer Vision and Pattern Recognition (2005)
5. Opelt, A., Pinz, A., Fussenegger, M., Auer, P.: Generic object recognition with boosting. Pattern Analysis and Machine Intelligence 28(3), 416–431 (2006)
6. Lim, J.H., Chevallet, J.P., Gao, S.: Scene identification using discriminative patterns. In: International Conference on Pattern Recognition (2006)
7. Lowe, D.G.: Distinctive image features from scale-invariant keypoints. International Journal of Computer Vision 60(2), 91–110 (2004)
8. Bouchet, J., Nigay, L.: ICARE: A component-based approach for the design and development of multimodal interfaces. In: Extended Abstracts of CHI 2004 (2004)

Real-Time Multi-view Object Tracking in Mediated Environments

Huan Jin[1,3], Gang Qian[2,3], and David Birchfield[3]

[1] Dept. of Computer Science and Engineering and
[2] Dept. of Electrical Engineering and
[3] Arts, Media and Engineering Program,
Arizona State University, Tempe, AZ 85287, USA
{Huan.Jin,Gang.Qian,dbirchfield}@asu.edu

Abstract. In this paper, we present a robust approach to real-time tracking of multiple objects in mediated environments using a set of calibrated color and IR cameras. Challenges addressed in this paper include robust object tracking in the presence of color projections on the ground plane and partial/complete occlusions. To improve tracking in such complex environment, false candidates introduced by ground plane projection or mismatching of objects between views are removed by using the epipolar constraint and the planar homography. A mixture of Gaussian is learned using the expectation-maximization algorithm for each target to further refine the 3D location estimates. Experimental results demonstrate that the proposed approach is capable of robust and accurate 3D object tracking in a complex environment with a great amount of visual projections and partial/complete occlusions.

1 Introduction

Movement-driven mediated environments attract increasing interests in interactive learning, performing arts, and rehabilitation and many other applications. The well-known immersive virtual reality system CAVE [2] can be seen as a good example of such movement-driven interactive environment. A mediated environment has both a movement sensing/analysis module and a feedback module. Users interact with the environment through their body movements (e.g. 2D/3D locations, facing direction, gestures), and/or by manipulating objects being tracked. Based on the movement analysis results, the feedback module produces real-time video and audio feedback which correlates with the users' movement.

Although a large amount of effort has been made to develop video-based human movement analysis algorithms, (see for example [9,12] for recent literature survey), reliable tracking and understanding of human movement in a mediated environment remains a significant challenge to computer vision. In this paper we focus our discussion on robust 3D object tracking in complex environment. Objects can be tracked using different sensing modalities. In spite of many commercially available object tracking systems (e.g. InterSense IS-900 Precision

S. Satoh, F. Nack, and M. Etoh (Eds.): MMM 2008, LNCS 4903, pp. 230–241, 2008.

Motion Tracker [3] built on hybrid ultrasound-inertial tracking technology, and Flock of Birds electromagnetic tracking from [1]), video-based systems pose as an attractive solution to object tracking mainly due to the fact that it's a low cost setup. However, reliable and precise tracking of multiple objects from video in mediated environments is a nontrivial problem for computer vision. Visual projections as part of the real-time feedback present a fast-changing dynamic background. Multiple users interacting with each other in the environment often make the objects being tracked partially or fully occluded in some of the camera views. In addition, to increase the visibility of the visual projection, the lighting condition of the environment is often dimmed and sub-optimal for video tracking. Reliable object tracking in 3D space with dynamic background presents a challenging research problem. Many existing object tracking algorithms focus on robust 2D tracking in cluttered/dynamic scenes [7,10,13]. Some 3D object tracking algorithms utilize background subtraction and temporal filtering techniques to track objects in 3D space with the assumption of simple or stationary background [5,8].

In this paper, we address the aforementioned specific challenges and present a working system we have developed for real-time 3D tracking of objects in a mediated environment where visual feedback is projected onto the ground plane covered by white mats using an over-head projector through a reflecting mirror. To deal with the dimmed lighting conditions, we use custom-made battery-powered glowing balls with built-in color LEDs as the objects to be tracked by the system. Different balls emit different color light. To alleviate the ambiguity caused by visual projections, we adopt a multimodal sensing framework using both color and infrared (IR) cameras. IR cameras are immune to visual projections while color cameras are necessary to maintain the target identities. IR-reflective patches were put on the balls to make them distinct from the background in the IR cameras. Homography mappings for all camera pairs with respect to the ground plane are recovered and used to remove false candidates caused by the projections on the ground plane. To better handle occlusions and minimize the effects on the objects' 3D locations caused by partial occlusion, a mixture of Gaussian is obtained for each object from the possible 3D location candidates using the expectation-maximization algorithm, under the assumption that most of the 3D location candidates are from non-occluded camera views. The presented tracking system has been extensively tested in real-life scenarios and satisfactory results have been obtained.

1.1 Background

The driving application for our research in vision-based tracking is the development of a new student-centered learning environment for K-12 mediated education [4]. This learning environment engages the naturally expressive movement paths and gestures of participants. It facilitates collaboration, active learning, and structured play in service of education. This framework allows our work to address the needs of students with diverse learning styles and to prepare students for the dynamic digital world they are entering. We are partnered with

K-12 teachers to design modular curricula that address concepts in physics, dance, art, and language arts. The physical constraints of the interactive space, and the design of specific learning scenarios provide important constraints on our approach to object tracking. For example, in the Spring Sling learning scenario, as students move a tracked physical object in the environment, the movement of the object will interact with a virtual spring model that is projected onto the floor. Students explore the physical attributes of a spring by moving in the space and changing the parameters of the model. The nature of the interaction leads students to stand in a relatively stationary position while repeatedly extending and contracting one arm that is holding the tracked physical object. Typically, one or two students will be actively interacting with the virtual spring model at a given time while up to 10 students will stand along the perimeter of space, observing the activity.

2   Tracking Objects and Appearance Representation

To ensure the visibility of the visual feedback, the ambient illumination needs to be on a dim level. As a result, a color object is very hard to be seen by color cameras. Therefore, we use custom-designed glowing balls built with sufficient color LEDs as tracking objects. Sufficient small IR-reflective patches are attached on them evenly so that they can be detected as bright blobs in IR cameras lightened by IR illuminators.

2.1   Color Modeling

Color histogram provides an effective feature for object tracking as it is computationally efficient, robust to partial occlusion, and invariant to rotation and scale. We adopt hue, saturation, value (HSV) color space because it separates out hue (color) from saturation and brightness channels and hue channel is relatively reliable to identify different objects. A color histogram H_j for target object j is computed in the tracking initialization stage using a function $b(\mathbf{q}_i) \in \{1, ..., N_b\}$ that assigns the hue value $\mathbf{q}_i$ to its corresponding bin.

$$H_j = \{h^u(R_j)\}_{u=1...N_b} = \lambda \sum_{i=1}^{N_{R_j}} \delta[b(\mathbf{q}_i) - u] \tag{1}$$

where δ is the Kronecker delta function, λ is the normalizing constant and N_{R_j} is the number of pixels in the initial object region R_j. In our practice, we divide the hue channel into $N_b = 16$ bins in order to make the tracker less sensitive to color changes due to visual projections on the objects.

2.2   Grayscale Thresholding

We use grayscale thresholding to detect the reflective objects that have bright blobs in IR camera views. Since all objects being tracked share the same reflective material, they have the same grayscale lower and upper-bound thresholding

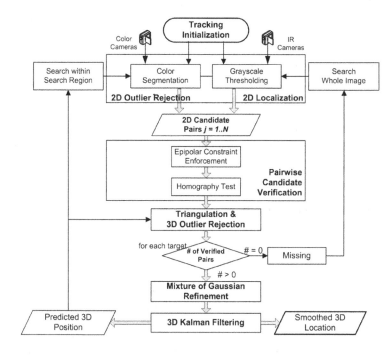

Fig. 1. Diagram of Object Tracking in Mediated Environments

parameters $T = \{T_{min}, T_{max}\}$. The grayscale thresholding parameters need to be adjusted only when the infrared spectrum of the ambient illumination is substantially changed.

3   Multi-view Tracking

3.1   System Calibration and Tracking Initialization

A diagram of the proposed multi-view tracking system is given by Figure. 1. System calibration consists of camera calibration, scene calibration and object template retrieval. The cameras are calibrated using the multi-camera self-calibration toolkit developed by Svoboda *et al.*[11]. We use a small krypton flashlight bulb as the calibration object that is visible in both color and IR cameras. Given N camera projection matrices $\{P_i\}_{i=1}^{N}$, the fundamental matrices, $\{F_{ij}\}_{i,j=1;i\neq j}^{N}$, which are useful to enforce the epipolar constraint, can be computed easily [6].

The purpose of the scene calibration is to obtain the equation of the 3D plane (or planes if there are more than one projection surfaces in the space) on which visual feedback is projected. In our case, it's the ground plane. The plane equation is used to get the planar homography which removes visual projections on the plane. The reason that we do not use 2D feature correspondences to compute homography is that the color points projected on the plane are invisible in IR cameras. Thus, we fit a plane based on the 3D point locations computed by triangulation using the 2D feature correspondences in color cameras. Once we have the 3D plane equation and camera projection matrices, planar homography $\{\mathbf{H}_{ij}\}_{i,j=1;i\neq j}^N$ can be computed between any different cameras.

An object template includes objects' color histograms, grayscale thresholds and 2D size range in each camera view. Currently, the object templates are obtained manually as part of the system calibration process. The color histogram is computed for each color camera by choosing the area of an object in that camera view, while the grayscale thresholds are learned by waving a reflective ball evenly in 3D mediated space and then extracting blobs' minimum and maximum brightness value in IR cameras. An object's 2D size is useful to reject 2D false candidates. 2D size range for each object is retrieved by counting the number of pixels in the object's area. Given system calibration and object templates, tracking can be initialized automatically.

3.2   2D Segmentation and Outlier Rejection

In our mediated environment, the background subtraction is not helpful to detect desired objects because of the projected visual feedback and human interaction in the space. Therefore, we directly segment out the object candidates based on its color histogram and grayscale thresholds for the color and IR cameras, respectively. Given a color image, we identify all the pixels with hue values belonging to the object's color histogram. Given a grayscale image from an IR camera, we segment out all the pixels whose brightness values are within T_{min} and T_{max}. Then, we employ connected component analysis to get all pixel-connected blobs in both color or grayscale image. A blob is valid only if its size is within the corresponding object's size range. Finally, we take the blob's center to represent its 2D coordinates. Size control is useful to combat the background projection, especially when a ball is submerged by a large projection with similar color in some color camera views. After size control, the projection will be removed from the list of valid 2D candidates. Essentially, the ball is considered to be "occluded" by the projection in such cases.

For color images, we further verify each valid blob k by comparing its histogram H_k, with the object template histogram H using the Bhattacharyya coefficient metric , which represents a similarity metric with respect to the template histogram. The metric is given by $\rho(H_k, H) = \sum_{b=1}^{N_b} \sqrt{h_k^{(b)} h^{(b)}}$, where N_b is the number of bins and $h_k^{(b)}$ is the normalized value for bin b in the k-th blob's histogram H_k. $\rho(H_k, H)$ ranges from 0 to 1, with 1 indicating a perfect match. A blob is a valid object candidate only if its Bhattacharyya coefficient is greater than a certain similarity threshold T_s. A small threshold $T_s = 0.8$ was taken because of high occurrence of uniformly colored targets in our applications.

To remove 2D outliers introduced by cluttered and varying scenes, we specify a search region. It is given by a circular region centered at the predicted 2D location which is reprojected from 3D Kalman predicted location (3.6). The radius of the search region depends upon the 2D object's moving speed. A 2D blob for the target is identified as an outlier if it is out of the target's search region. After 2D outlier rejection, a list containing the blobs' 2D locations, $\{X_{k,i}^{(u)}\}$, is formed for object k in camera view i, where u is the index of the blob.

3.3 2D Pair Verification

A valid pair of 2D candidates from two different views is a prerequisite to compute accurate 3D location using triangulation. Let $\mathbf{X}^c = \{X_i^{(u)}, X_j^{(v)}\}_{i<j}$ denote the set of initial candidate pairs, where $X_i^{(u)}$ is the 2D homogeneous coordinates of the blob u in camera i, including false candidate pairs not corresponding to any ball, such as pairs related to floor projections, or pairs not related to any 3D points.

To remove such false pairs, we first verify each pair by the epipolar constraint, i.e., $X_2^T \mathbf{F_{21}} X_1 = 0$. The pair with epipolar distance $ED(X_2, X_1) < \mathrm{T}_{ED}$ will be classified into the valid pair set $\mathbf{X}^e$, where T_{ED} is the epipolar distance threshold.

Due to the visual feedback projected on the ground plane, some projections sharing a similar color histogram with the target may be observed in two color camera views. Such projections satisfy the epipolar constraint. To remove projections, we apply the planar homography test against the pairs in $\mathbf{X}^e$. The pair who passes the homography test, i.e., $\|X_2 - \mathbf{H}_{21} X_1\| > \mathrm{T}_H$, is not corresponding to projections and will be put into the final set $\mathbf{X}^f$, where T_H is the homography test threshold.

The ball, however, may actually be laid on the floor. To prevent valid pairs from being removed by the homography test in this case, we first search through all the color-IR pairs to see if there is any color-IR pair $\{X_2^e, X_1^e\} \in \mathbf{X}^e$ satisfying $\|X_2 - \mathbf{H}_{21} X_1\| < \mathrm{T}_H$. If there are such color-IR pairs, it is a good chance that the ball is on the floor. All the indices of related color blobs in those color-IR pairs are recorded in a valid blob list B. If a color-color candidate pair fails the homography test (i.e. they satisfy the homography constraint w.r.t. the ground plane), but one of the blobs is in B, meaning the ball is on the plane and it is expected for the related color blobs to fail the homography test, this color-color pair is still regarded as a valid pair and put into $\mathbf{X}^f$. In our experiment, we set both T_{ED} and T_H to a small threshold (2 pixels).

3.4 3D Localization and Outlier Rejection

Given a pair of 2D locations from two different camera views, the triangulation is able to compute 3D location efficiently [6]. For each pair $X_k^f \in \{\mathbf{X}_k^f\}_{k=1}^{N_p}$ where N_p is the number of the verified pairs, we compute the 3D location Z_k using the triangulation $Z_k = T(X_k^f) \in \{\mathbf{Z}_k\}_{k=1}^{N_p}$. The triangulation algorithm can be fed a tuple of more than two feature points. But, given three feature points, there are three pair combinations which may have different distributions. To minimize the risk, we use multi-sensor fusion in Sec. 3.5 to refine 3D location.

However, a 2D false candidate can be paired to be a valid candidate pair if it is located along the epipolar line. And it is also possible that some visual feedbacks are projected on human body and form an area visible in two color camera

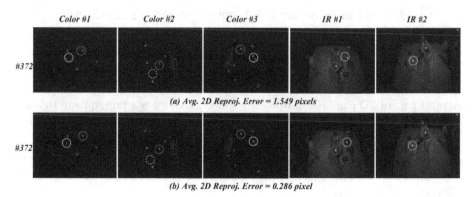

(a) Avg. 2D Reproj. Error = 1.549 pixels

(b) Avg. 2D Reproj. Error = 0.286 pixel

Fig. 2. Comparison of two fusion methods. (a) 3D location is computed by taking the mean of all 3D points; (b) 3D location is obtained from MoG using EM. Green object is missing in the second view.

views. Likewise, some reflective or bright spots, such as watches and glasses, may exist in two IR camera views. Those pairs are still alive through the pairwise candidate verification. To eliminate the outliers caused by the foresaid scenarios, we perform outlier rejection based on the Kalman predication introduced in Sec. 3.6. Let $Z_{k,t}$ be the k-th 3D location for one target at time t and Z_{t-1}^t be the 3D Kalman prediction for time t at time $t-1$, $Z_{k,t}$ is identified as an outlier if $\|Z_{k,t} - Z_{t-1}^t\| > \mathrm{T}_{3D}$, where T_{3D} indicates the tolerance of outliers.

3.5   Multi-view Fusion and Partial Occlusion Handling

Given a list of candidate 3D locations for one ball after 3D outlier rejection, we need to determine an 3D location estimate of the ball. Due to partial occlusion, some of the candidate locations are biased from the true 3D location of the ball. In addition, when two balls are close, the 3D location of one ball obtained from an IR-IR pair might be within the proximity of the predicted location of the other ball. Hence, 3D locations from different balls might be mixed together in the candidate 3D location list of one object.

When there are more color cameras than IR cameras, and ball is non-occluded in most of the cameras views, true 3D candidates will outnumber the false candidates. Hence we cluster the 3D points into two groups and choose the the center of the group with more candidate points as the final 3D target location. We use a dual component mixture of Gaussian (MoG) to model the clustering problem (2).

$$p(Z_k) = \sum_{i=1}^{2} \pi_i p(Z_k | C_i) \tag{2}$$

where π_i is the mixture C_i's weight and $p(Z_k | C_i) \sim \mathrm{N}(\mu_i, \Sigma_i)$.

The Expectation-Maximization (EM) algorithm is used to obtain the MoG model from the 3D location list. To make the EM training more robust without bias to two mixture components, initial weights of two components are equal. The initial center of the first component is the mean of all 3D points while the initial guess for the second component is the 3D point farthest from the mean of the first component. After the EM training, we extract the mean of the component with the larger weight to represent the 3D location of the target. In Figure. 3.5, we compare results from the MoG method with results by simple average. It can be seen that the results from the MoG method are closer to the true location of the ball in all the camera views. Partial occlusions occur frequently during the tracking and the center of 2D partially occluded object is difficult to obtain correctly. However, the effects of partial occlusions have been alleviated through the MoG refinement. Inaccurate 3D points are mostly clustered into the "inaccurate" component.

3.6   3D Kalman Filtering and Complete Occlusion Handling

Each target is assigned with a Kalman filter to perform smoothing and prediction. The first-order motion model is adopted. The Kalman filter takes the result from the mixture of Gaussian refinement as input. The smoothed 3D location is output as the target's final 3D location. Kalman filtering also predict the 3D location for the next time instant. The predicted target location is projected onto all camera views to form 2D search region that can substantially reduce the number of 2D false candidate blobs.

Complete occlusions that occur in some camera views are automatically compensated by other non-occluded camera views. If the target is only detected in one camera view, the tracking system reports the missing event for that target as no pair exists. Whether or not the tracking can resume depends on the existence of a valid color-IR pair, since color-color pairs may be interfered with visual projections and IR-IR pairs do not have identity information.

4   Experimental Results

Our tracking system consists of three color CCD cameras, two IR CCD cameras (Dragonfly2, Point Grey Research) and a PC (Intel Xeon 3.6GHz, 1GB RAM). Image resolution is 320×240. The cameras are synchronized and calibrated in advance. The dimension of the space is aligned as $1 unit = 15 feet$. To better cover the activity space, we set large FOV for each camera. So, lens distortion [6] is also recovered for every frame. The fitted plane's homogeneous coefficients are $[-0.0047, -0.0017, 0.9998, 0.0142]$. The tracking system with five cameras can run at 60 fps in real-time. Figure. 4 illustrates the real system setup in top-down view.

To evaluate the tracking performance of the tracking system, we project a large amount of visual projections with similar colors to the tracked objects. Sequence 1 is used to demonstrate the capability of tracking under visual projections on the floor. Sequence 2 is to demonstrate the capability of tracking with 5 people interacting with the mediated environment. Partial and complete occlusions frequently occur.

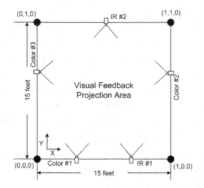

Fig. 3. Illustration of the real system setup in top-down view

In the first experiment (Figure. 4), two glowing balls (green and red, 6 inch in diameter) patched with reflective material are tracked with interference of visual projections in the same colors as the balls. In (a), sample frames from five cameras (*Frame 84, 149, 316, 598, 848 and 871*) are shown with 2D reprojection locations (small bold circles) and search regions (large slim circles) superimposed for both targets. The bold green and red circles indicate the green and red objects' 2D locations reprojected from the final 3D locations, respectively. The large slim yellow circle is the predicted search region to remove 2D false candidates. In these frames, 2D false candidates did appear in the entire image but they were effectively removed through the predicted search region. The floor projections are successfully eliminated by the homography test. Some bright spots, *e.g.* , the spots on the upper body of the subjects in *Frame 84 and 316* or incandescent lights shed on the control panel side in *IR Camera 2*, have no effects on the tracking due to the proper outlier rejection procedure presented early. Target identity is successfully maintained when two objects are close in *Frame 149 and 316*. In *Frame 848 and 871*, we show that the balls can be continually tracked when they were put on the floor without being confused with floor projections. Figure. 4 (b) and (c) show the 3D tracking trajectories. It can be seen that the trajectories are smooth. Since there is no ground-truth for comparison, we projected 3D location onto all camera views and found the corresponding 2D blob candidate and computed the error distance. In this experiment, the average reprojection errors over all frames and all cameras are 0.483 pixels for the green ball and 0.598 pixels for the red ball.

In Figure. 4, we show two ball tracking with five people interacting with the mediated environment, which caused a lot of occlusions of the balls during the tracking. In *frame 570*, the green ball is completely occluded in *Color Camera 1 and IR Camera 1* and the red ball is partially occluded in *Color Camera 1 and Color Camera 2*. But our approach can still provide consistent and accurate tracking. In *frame 605*, two balls are merged together in *IR Camera 1*. The red ball is accidently covered by a red visual projection and simultaneously occluded in other

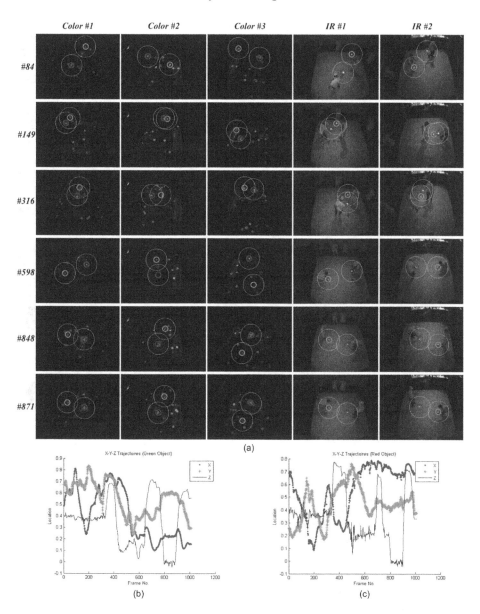

Fig. 4. (a) Sequence 1: two object tracking under visual feedback projected on the floor [*1174 frames*] (Bold green and red circles indicate the green and red balls' 2D locations reprojected from final 3D locations, respectively. The large slim yellow circle is the predicted search region to remove 2D false candidates.); (b) 3D trajectories of the green ball with an average 2D reprojection error of 0.483 pixels; (c) 3D trajectories of the red object with an average 2D reprojection error of 0.598 pixels.

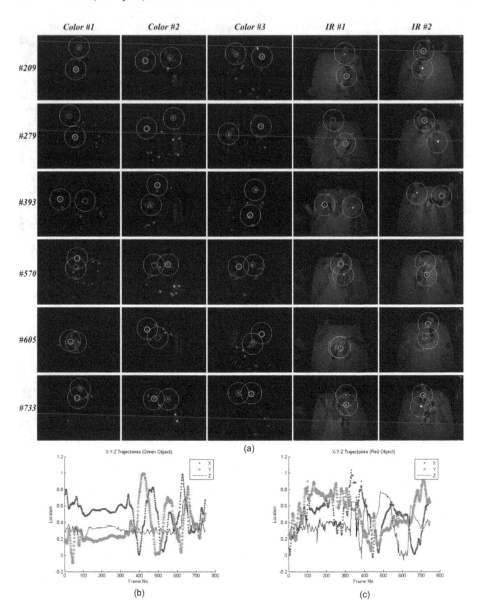

Fig. 5. (a) Sequence 2: two object tracking with five people interacting with the mediated environment [747 frames]; (b) 3D trajectories of the green ball with an average 2D reprojection error of 0.761 pixels; (c) 3D trajectories of the red object with an average 2D reprojection error of 0.860 pixels.

views. However, the proposed system can successfully maintain the tracking in this extreme case and 3D locations are computed accurately. The average 2D reprojection errors for the green and red ball are 0.761 and 0.860 pixels, respectively.

5   Conclusions

In this paper, we present an approach to real-time multi-view object tracking in mediated environments. The experiment results show that our approach can robustly and accurately provide consistent 3D object tracking in the presence of dynamic visual projection on the ground plane sometimes with partial or full occlusions. As part of the future work, we will merge the MoG modeling of the distributions of multiple balls from related 3D candidate list to improve the dependence and consistency of the tracking of multiple objects. In addition, we are currently working on an improved version of the system which allows multiple visual projection planes.

References

1. Ascension, `http://www.ascension-tech.com/`
2. Cave, `http://en.wikipedia.org/wiki/Cave_Automatic_Virtual_Environment`
3. Intersense, `http://www.isense.com/`
4. Birchfield, D., Ciufo, T., Minyard, G., Qian, G., Savenye, W., Sundaram, H., Thornburg, H., Todd, C.: Smallab: a mediated platform for education. In: Proceedings of ACM SIGGRAPH, Boston, MA (2006)
5. Black, J., Ellis, T., Rosin, P.: Multi view image surveillance and tracking. In: IEEE Workshop on Motion and Video Computing (2002)
6. Hartley, R.I., Zisserman, A.: Multiple View Geometry in Computer Vision, 2nd edn. Cambridge University Press, Cambridge (2004)
7. Huang, Y., Essa, I.: Tracking multiple objects through occlusions. In: IEEE Conf. on Computer Vision and Pattern Recognition, II, pp. 1051–1058 (2005)
8. Jurie, F., Dhome, M.: Real time tracking of 3D objects with occultations. In: Int'l Conf. on Image Processing, I, pp. 413–416 (2001)
9. Moeslund, T.B., Hilton, A., Kruger, V.: A survey of advances in vision-based human motion capture and analysis. Computer Vision and Image Understanding 104(2), 90–126 (2006)
10. Pan, J., Hu, B.: Robust occlusion handling in object tracking. In: IEEE Workshop on Object Tracking and Classification Beyond the Visible Spectrum, pp. 1–8 (2007)
11. Svoboda, T., Martinec, D., Pajdla, T.: A convenient multi-camera self-calibration for virtual environments. PRESENCE: Teleoperators and Virtual Environments 14(4), 407–422 (2005)
12. Wang, L., Hu, W., Tan, T.: Recent development in human motion analysis. Pattern Recognition 36, 585–601 (2003)
13. Yang, T., Li, S.Z., Pan, Q., Li, J.: Real-time multiple objects tracking with occlusion handling in dynamic scenes. In: IEEE Conf. on Computer Vision and Pattern Recognition, I, pp. 970–975 (2005)

Reconstruct 3D Human Motion from Monocular Video Using Motion Library

Wenzhong Wang[1,2,3], Xianjie Qiu[1], Zhaoqi Wang[1], Rongrong Wang[1,2], and Jintao Li[1]

[1] Institute of Computing Technology, Chinese Academy of Sciences
[2] Key Laboratory of Intelligent Information Processing, Chinese Academy of Sciences
[3] Graduate School of Chinese Academy of Sciences
{wangwenzhong,qxj,zqwang,wr,jtli}@ict.ac.cn

Abstract. In this paper, we present a new approach to reconstruct 3D human motion from video clips with the assistance of a precaputred motion library. Given a monocular video clip recording of one person performing some kind of locomotion and a motion library consisting of similar motions, we can infer the 3D motion from the video clip. We segment the video clip into segments with fixed length, and by using a shape matching method we can find out from the motion library several candidate motion sequences for every video segment, then from these sequences a coarse motion clip is generated by performing a continuity test on the boundaries of these candidate sequences. We propose a pose deformation algorithm to refine the coarse motion. To guarantee the naturalness of the recovered motion, we apply a motion splicing algorithm to the motion clip. We tested the approach using synthetic and real sports videos. The experimental results show the effectiveness of this approach.

1 Introduction

Creating realistic human motion has been a great challenge in the domains of computer graphics and computer vision in recent years; it turns out to be a time-consuming and expensive process which requires the talents of a professional animator using specialized software or exotic motion capture hardware.

There are several kinds of technologies for this task, the most popular one is maker-based optical motion capture and has been used commercially for a number of years in variant applications. Though this technique succeeds in many applications, it requires expensive hardware and special apparel which hinders its popularization and limits its flexibility; and the use of markers is intrusive in some extent, restricts the range of applications.

Due to the deficiency of the above techniques, researchers seek for means to accomplish markerless motion capture. A lot of work has been done in this area. This is really challenging and little practical achievements have been obtained so far. There are many reasons for this situation: the state-of-the-arts motion tracking techniques cannot meet high accuracy requirements in motion capture; inter-part occlusions make problems for the tracking task; and limbs are difficult to distinguish automatically.

S. Satoh, F. Nack, and M. Etoh (Eds.): MMM 2008, LNCS 4903, pp. 242–252, 2008.
© Springer-Verlag Berlin Heidelberg 2008

In this paper, we offer a new approach to marker-free motion capture based just on ordinary monocular videos recording of one actor whose motions are to be captured. The approach is illustrated in Figure 1. The key idea in our work is to establish a sound map between the 2D motions in the video and the 3D motions in the motion library. We regard this as a 2D shape matching problem. We construct a model contour set from the motion library by projecting a human model performing the motions onto a 2D plane. Then we extract the human body contour from the input video. For each video contour, we retrieve a candidate list of similar contours from the model contour set by shape matching. By doing so, we can assign for each video segment a list of candidate motions. To make the result motion more similar to the motion in the video, we deform the approximate postures so that their 2D projections are more similar to the video contours, and then we stitch the candidate motions to obtain a smoothed motion sequence.

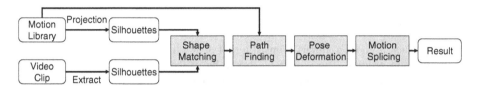

Fig. 1. Processing Flowchart

In section 2, we briefly review previous work related to ours. Section 3 describes our approach in detail. In section 4, we show our experiments and results. Conclusions and future work is presented in section 5.

2 Previous Work

Many researchers have tackled the challenge of human motion capture from single view image sequences in a marker free manner.

C.J Taylor [5][6] recovers the 3D configuration of joints can be inferred using a scaled orthographic projection model given the aspect ratio of the image. Sminchisescu and Triggs [9][13] proposed algorithms based upon propagating a mixture of Gaussians PDF, representing the probable 3D configurations of a body over time. In [15], a body model is rendered at different poses and compared with the silhouette using core-weighted XOR and image features as the metric. Ankur Agarwal et.al [16] regresses a function using shape context descriptor of example's contours and their corresponding 3D poses. Wachter and Nagel[3] use articulated kinematics and a shape model built from of truncated cones, and estimate motion in a monocular sequence, using edge and intensity (optical flow) information. Sidenbladh et al. perform tracking in monocular cluttered image sequences using an articulated 3D model with shape represented in terms of cylinders and intensity-based image cues [4]. Their later work [8] integrates flow, edge and ridge cues using Laplacian-like error distributions learned from training data for tracking, and their more recent work [11] extends snippets example-based motion models, learned using PCA from small pieces of motion. Chih-Yi Chiu et.al [17] proposed a model-based approach to reconstruct 3D human posture from a single image. They utilized a posture library and a set of constraints to guide the reconstruction. In their approach, a 3D pivotal posture is retrieved for a given 2D human figure from the posture library, and then physical and environmental constraints are automatically applied to reconstruct the 3D posture.

In our work, we attempts to automatically recover 3D motions in uncalibrated monocular videos. We leave aside the tough problem of referring 3D body configurations directly from single-view images and try to incorporate knowledge from precaptured motion data into the reconstruction process. Unlike the previous works using auxiliary captured motion data, our method features a simple treatment for 2D to 3D mapping and an intuitive way for concatenation of motion pieces.

3 Our Approach

3.1 Preprocessing

We construct a motion library consisting of many motion clips to facilitate the reconstruction process. These motions should be of the same kind of the ones to be captured. The motion data in the library are captured using VICON8. We assume that the actor performs in almost the same speed as the captured motions and sample the motion data so that all the clips have the same frame rate as the input videos. If this assumption is not held, our approach may be failed. This is not a serious problem since a little amendment can be made to the approach to handle the situation. This is nonessential to our overall goal; so we do not take it into consideration currently.

The body silhouettes in each frame of the video are extracted by background subtraction. These silhouettes are called video silhouettes. We then orthographically project all poses in the motion library to a 2D plane to obtain pose silhouettes of the motion library. These silhouettes are called model silhouettes. Each of the model silhouettes corresponds to a 3D pose in the motion library. Given clean silhouette images, we can effectively extract the contours of these silhouettes. These contours constitute the model contour set. The contours of the video silhouettes and model silhouettes are called video contours and model contours, respectively.

In order to obtain better match between video contours and model contours, the 3D postures should be projected onto a 2D plane in almost the same view angle as that of the video. In our experiments, this is done by manually adjust the viewpoint of the 3D model. Nuances are admitted in this process since the shape matching algorithm we employed can overcome these nuances.

3.2 Shape Matching

In this stage, we represent a shape by a discrete set of n sample points $P = \{p_1, p_2, \cdots p_n\}$, $p_i \in R^2$ $(i = 1, 2 \cdots n)$. We employ the shape context local descriptor of [10] for shape feature description. We use a fast contour matching method with approximate EMD embedding [12] and nearest neighbor searching. In this paper, we employ the embedding algorithm of [14] for shape matching, and we adopt Locality-Sensitive Hashing (LSH) to improve the performance of shape matching. See [2] for detail. For a given video silhouette, we retrieve a list of K closest matches using approximate NN search from model silhouettes, each silhouette in this candidate list corresponds to a 3D pose from which it is projected, and this 3D posture is an approximation of the pose in the video. Our experiences state that K should be of a small proportion to the size of the motion library; in our tests, it is set to 20.

3.3 Path Finding

Now that we have K candidate 3D poses for each pose in the video, we can immediately pick one from each of these candidate lists and connecting them directly into a motion clip. However, this usually results in very unnatural motions.

The resulting motion is apparently more pleasing if it is composed of consecutive fragments of the original motion data rather than a messy corpus of discrete postures. Consequently, we segment the video clip into a series of fragments of a fixed length s ($s = 30$ frames in our experiments) and search for motion chunks of the same length that best match the 2D motion in each video fragment. What is more, we only make use of the first silhouette in each video fragment to retrieve approximate 3D poses by shape matching, and we treat every motion segment with length of s which starts at these 3D poses as a candidate motion for the video fragment; this policy reduces the cost for shape matching significantly while sacrifices a spot of overall performance. By this means, we obtain a list of possible motion clips for each video segment.

Then we must choose a path through these candidates to create a single coherent motion and make the resulted motion satisfactory. Our approach towards this problem is based on the observation that in a motion, the velocity, position and orientation of the body change continuously with respect to time. We define a test function to evaluate the continuity of two sequential motion clips. It is based on the continuity function of two poses p_1 and p_2 :

$$T(p_1, p_2) = w_v V(p_1, p_2) + w_o O(p_1, p_2) + w_p P(p_1, p_2) \tag{1}$$

$V(p_1, p_2), P(p_1, p_2)$ are Euclidean distances of velocities and positions between p_1 and p_2, and $O(p_1, p_2)$ is the orientation distance defined as

$$O(p_1, p_2) = \arccos(q(p_1) * q(p_2)) \tag{2}$$

where $q(p_1), q(p_2) \in S^3$, and w_v, w_o, w_p are weights of V, O, and P, respectively. In our implementation, these weights are set to 0.1, 0.4, and 0.5.

The continuity test function of two consecutive clips c_1, c_2 with length n is defined as

$$F(c_1, c_2) = \sum_{i=1}^{k} w_i T(p_1(n-i), p_2(i)) \tag{3}$$

($p_1(i)$ and $p_2(i)$ are the ith poses in c_1 and c_2, respectively. $k = 3$ in our implementation. For simplification, we equalize w_i 's.)

Since we have no other information in the selection of motion clips for the first video fragment, it is not arbitrary to choose the first entry in the candidate motion list as the best approximate of the first video fragment. This treatment relies the overall results on the shape matching effect of the first silhouette greatly. Thanks to the efficient shape matching algorithm, this tip works well in our experiments. Another choice may be to select a right motion clip by users.

For each of the remaining video fragments, we choose from its candidate list a motion clip which minimizes $F(c, c_i)$ (c is the best approximate motion of the previous video clip, c_i is a candidate motion of current video clip) as its best approximation.

3.4 Pose Deformation

The approximate poses obtained above may not exactly accord with the poses in the video. We employ a pose deformation technique for this problem. The idea is that if the dissimilarity between the video silhouette and its corresponding candidate model silhouette exceeds a given threshold, the retrieved 3D posture should be adjusted so that its 2D projection in the same viewpoint as the video will be more close to the video silhouette. The dissimilarity is defined as the average distance between the sample points in the video silhouette and their matched points in the model silhouette. In our experiments, we use 10 (in pixels) as the threshold.

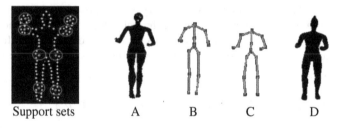

Support sets   A   B   C   D

Fig. 2. Left: Support sets; Right: Pose Transformation. A and D are two similar contours, C is the 3D pose of D, and B is the result of pose transformation from C. Notice that the limbs in B are more closer to that in A.

We assume that there is a transformation between the candidate model silhouette and the video silhouette, and this transformation is determined by the correspondences between the sample points of the two silhouettes. To address locality of the transformation, we define for each joint of the body a support set (Figure 2) consisting of a set of sample points around the joint, and the correspondences between the points in the support sets of two corresponding joint define a local transformation T of that joint.(See Figure 2).

We choose affine transformation for T. We use the algorithm of [1] for linear assignment problem (LAP) to calculate a perfect match between two sets of sample points using their shape contexts. This match gives the correspondences of every two support sets of the corresponding joints, and with these correspondences, we can determine the least squares solution of T for each joint.

All the joints in the candidate model silhouette are now transformed to new position. By using an unprojection operation on these new 2D positions together with the 3D configuration with which the 2D projections are obtained, we can evaluate the position information of the joints and thus generate new 3D poses from the original 3D poses. These novel 3D poses are rough reconstruction of the poses in the video.

3.5 Motion Splicing

Pose selection does not guarantee the smoothness at the boundaries of the clips, and pose transformation may introduce oscillation in the results. In order to make the synthesized motion more natural looking, we employ the algorithm of [7] to stitch the approximate motion clips. Readers are refered to [18] and [7] for details.

After splicing, we obtain a convincing result which attains the realism of the motion captured data and is similar to the motion in the input video.

4 Experimental Results

We built two motion libraries respectively using gymnastics and trampoline motions captured by VICON8. The gym library contains 7 clips of different motion each lasts about 26 seconds and total postures count up to 5424. The trampoline library contains 13 motion clips with 6245 postures. We ran two experiments on each motion library.

In the first test, we aimed to evaluate the accuracy of our method, so we simulated video contours by projecting 3D poses of a virtual human model performing some motions in the databases onto a 2D plane, and then we add nonuniform noises to these contours. Each model contour set is generated by projecting 3D poses of another virtual human model sequentially performing all motions in the database in almost the same viewpoint in which the video contour set is generated. Each contour is sampled to 200 points from which the shape context is computed. We compare the recovered motions with the ground truth motions, and state the average errors of root positions and joint angles in Table 1. The statistics tells that the root translations and the average joint angle errors are very trivial respect to the motions. This proves the accuracy of our method. Figure 7 and Figure 8 show the resulted motions. In the first row are synthetic video contours, and the last two rows are their corresponding 3D poses in two different view directions. It is obvious that the inferred poses look very similar to the test silhouettes.

In the second test, we captured two video clips (Figure 3): a gymnastics video clip consisting of a piece of gym motion which lasts about 5 seconds and a trampoline video clip lasting 3.5 seconds. In the preprocessing stage, we manually adjust the

Table 1. Reconstuctioin Errors

Test	Root Position (cm)			Joint Angle		
	x	y	z	x	y	z
Gymnastics	0.53	0.01	0.03	1.73	0.78	0.57
Trampoline	0.66	6.19	2.72	11.0	0.40	3.09

Fig. 3. Example frames of two video clips: Gymnastics(1st row) and Trampoline(2nd row)

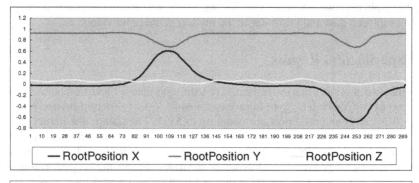

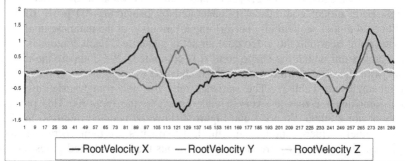

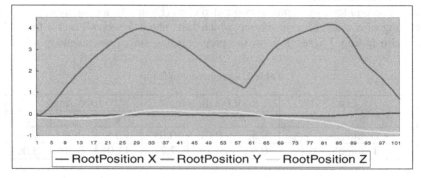

Fig. 4. Motion curves of recontstucted Gymnastics motion

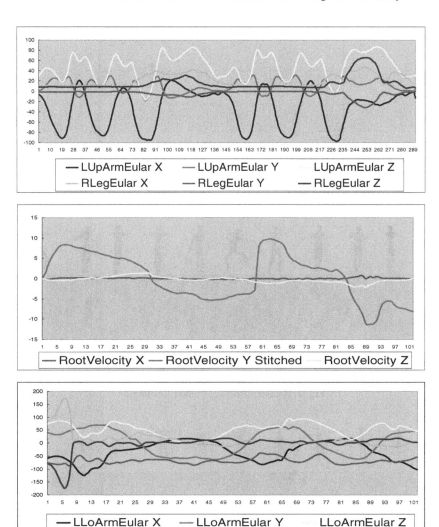

Fig. 5. Motion curves of recontstucted Trampoline motion

projection view point according to that in the video. Figure 4 and 5 show the continuity of root positions and joint angles of result motions. These curves indicate the overall effect of our approach. It is clear that the motions generated by the proposed method attain smoothness. Figure 9 and Figure 10 illustrate the inferred motions of gym video and trampoline video.

Though motion splicing improved the results greatly, our tests on trampoline motions reveal the deficiency of motion splicing technique. It introduces artifacts in the resulted motions as shown in figure 6: the sports girl jumps up without hitting the ground. This is because the root position is amended in the splicing process without any consideration for constraints of real motions.

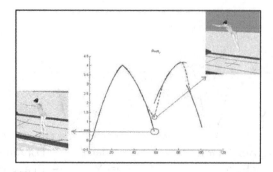

Fig. 6. Deficiency of motion splicing

Fig. 7. Reconstruction of gymnastics motion

Fig. 8. Reconstruction of trampoline motion

Fig. 9. Reconstruction of gymastics video

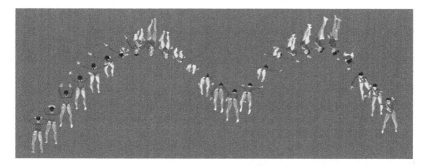

Fig. 10. Reconstruction of trampoline video

5 Conclusions and Future Work

In this paper, we present a video based approach for 3D motion recovering using a motion library. We employ shape matching technique to facilitate the reconstruction. We propose a method to select most appropriate poses from the retrieved posture lists based on the continuity of the motion. Besides, we perform pose deformation on the approximate poses and use a multiresolution stitching algorithm to splice the motion clips. Our experiments produced promising results and proved the effectiveness of the approach.

The current implementation of this work arbitrarily cut the video clip into segments with fixed length; this is unjustly in a sense. A more improving strategy should be segmentation according to the nature of the motion.

The current means for path finding doesn't take into consideration the shape matching results of video silhouettes except for the first one in each fragment and will no doubt miss a lot of useful information for better path finding. This motivates our further investigation on more effective method for path finding.

Another improvement should be a more robust motion splicing techniques incorporating physical constraints to overcome the distortion introduced by current stitching method.

Acknowledgements

This work is supported by NSF of China (60473002), Beijing Nature Science Foundation (4051004) and National Special Item for Olympics (Z0004024040231).

References

1. Goldberg, A., Kennedy, R.: An Efficient Cost Scaling Algorithm for the Assignment Problem. Math. Prog. 71, 153–178 (1995)
2. Indyk, P., Motwani, R.: Approximate Nearest Neighbor - Towards Removing the Curse of Dimensionality. In: Proceedings of the 30th Symposium on Theory of Computing, pp. 604–613 (1998)
3. Wachter, S., Nagel, H.: Tracking Persons in Monocular Image Sequences. Computer Vision and Image Understanding 74(3), 174–192 (1999)

4. Sidenbladh, H., Black, M., Fleet, D.: Stochastic Tracking of 3D Human Figures Using 2D Image Motion. In: European Conference on Computer Vision (2000)

5. Taylor, C.J.: econstruction of Articulated Objects from Point Correspondences in a Single Uncalibrated Image. In: IEEE International Conference on Computer Vision and Pattern Recognition, pp. 677–684 (2000)

6. Taylor, C.J.: Reconstruction of articulated objects from point correspondences in a single image. Computer Vision and Image Understanding 80(3), 349–363 (2000)

7. Lee, J., Shin, S.Y.: A Coordinate-invariant Approach to Multiresolution Motion Analysis. Graphics Model 63(2), 87–105 (2001)

8. Sidenbladh, H., Black, M.: Learning Image Statistics for Bayesian Tracking. In: IEEE International Conference on Computer Vision (2001)

9. Sminchisescu, C., Triggs, B.: Covariance scaled sampling for monocular 3d body tracking. In: Proc. Conf. Computer Vision and Pattern Recognition (2001)

10. Belogie, S., Malik, J., Puzicha, J.: Shape Matching and Object Recognition Using Shape Context. IEEE Transactions On Pattern Analysis and Machine Intelligence 24(24) (2002)

11. Sidenbladh, H., Black, M., Sigal, L.: Implicit Probabilistic Models of Human Motion for Synthesis and Tracking. In: Heyden, A., Sparr, G., Nielsen, M., Johansen, P. (eds.) ECCV 2002. LNCS, vol. 2352, pp. 784–800. Springer, Heidelberg (2002)

12. Indyk, P., Thaper, N.: Fast Image Retrieval via Embeddings. In: 3rd International Workshop on Statistical and Computational Theories of Vision (2003)

13. Sminchisescu, C., Triggs, B.: Kinematic jump processes for monocular 3d human tracking. In: Proc. Conf. Computer Vision and Pattern Recognition (2003)

14. Grauman, K., Darrell, T.: Fast Contour Matching Using Approximate Earth Mover's Distance. In: Proceedings of the IEEE Conference on Computer Vision and Pattern Recognition (2004)

15. Chen, Y., Lee, J., Parent, R., Machiraju, R.: Markerless Monocular Motion Capture Using Image Features and Physical Constraints. In: Computer Graphics International 2005, Stony Brook, USA (June 2005)

16. Agarwal, A., Triggs, B.: Recovering 3D Human Pose from Monocular Images. IEEE Trans. On Pattern Analysis and Machine Intelligence(PAMI) 28(1), 44–58 (2006)

17. Chiu, C.Y., Wu, C.C., Wu, Y.C., Wu, M.Y., Chao, S.P., Yang, S.N.: Retrieval and Constraint-Based Human Posture Reconstruction from a Single Image. Journal of Visual Communication and Image Representation 17(4), 892–915 (2006)

18. Wang, R., Qiu, X., Wang, Z., Xia, S.: A Video-Driven Approach to Continuous Human Motion Synthesis. In: Nishita, T., Peng, Q., Seidel, H.-P. (eds.) CGI 2006. LNCS, vol. 4035, pp. 614–621. Springer, Heidelberg (2006)

Appropriate Segment Extraction from Shots Based on Temporal Patterns of Example Videos

Yousuke Kurihara, Naoko Nitta, and Noboru Babaguchi

Graduate School of Engineering, Osaka University
2-1 Yamadaoka Suita, 565-0871 Japan
{kurihara,naoko,babaguchi}@nanase.comm.eng.osaka-u.ac.jp

Abstract. Videos are composed of shots, each of which is recorded continuously by a camera, and video editing can be considered as a process of re-sequencing shots selected from original videos. Shots usually include redundant segments, which are often edited out by professional editors. This paper proposes a method for automatically extracting appropriate segments to be included in edited videos from shots based on temporal patterns of audio and visual features in appropriate segments and redundant segments in example videos learned with Hidden Markov Models. The effectiveness of the proposed method is verified with experiments using original shots extracted from movies and appropriate segments extracted from movie trailers as example videos.

Keywords: video editing segment extraction Cshot, example videos.

1 Introduction

In recent years, with the advance of information technology of the Internet and digital TV, a large amount of video content with great variation has become available. In addition, high performance digital devices, such as video cameras and computers, can be obtained at low prices. Therefore, it has become easy for average users to edit videos. Today, there are many video editing tools that can be used easily, for example, Windows Movie Maker [1] or Adobe Premiere [2].

Video editing is to create a new video content by combining segments selected from original videos. There are two purposes of video editing, 1)efficiently conveying information to viewers and 2)stimulating viewers' interests. As a way to achieve the former purpose, many video summarization methods which extract only semantically important video segments have been proposed [3] [4]. For example, Takahashi et al. have proposed a method of summarizing sports videos by selecting important shots based on the semantic information of each shot obtained from the metadata of the videos. Although they have verified that the videos created by their method include the same content as professionally created broadcast digest videos, they are inferior in quality to professionally edited videos in terms of stimulating viewers' interests. This is attributed to the fact that most existing methods consider shots, each of which is recorded continuously by a camera, as the minimum units of video segments. However, a

S. Satoh, F. Nack, and M. Etoh (Eds.): MMM 2008, LNCS 4903, pp. 253–264, 2008.

shot often includes redundant segments. For example, a shot where people are having a conversation consists of voice and non-voice segments. In such cases, professional editors tend to consider only the voice segments as appropriate to be included in edited videos and discard the redundant non-voice segments. Therefore, extracting an appropriate segment from a shot is necessary to create videos which more effectively stimulate viewer's interests. In what follows, the segment selected by professional editors from a shot is referred to as an *appropriate segment* and the other parts of the shot as *redundant segments.*

There are some work related to extracting appropriate segments from shots. Aoyanagi et al. have proposed a method of extracting appropriate segments from shots based on rules about how frame-based audio and visual features change in appropriate segments[5]. Takemoto et al. have proposed a method for extracting appropriate segments based on rules about how shots of certain length are aligned to create a specific impression[6]. However, since the rules to evaluate the appropriateness of segments are determined manually, questions still remain in their legitimacy.

We therefore propose a method for extracting appropriate segments from shots based on temporal audio-visual patterns automatically obtained from example videos. First, given sets of appropriate segments and redundant segments as examples, the proposed method learns the temporal patterns of how frame-level audio and visual features change in each type of segment with Hidden Markov Models(HMMs). Then, when an original shot is given, the method extracts an appropriate segment from the shot based on its likelihood value to be observed in the learned HMMs. In this paper, we obtain examples from movies and their trailers, that is, when given a shot from movie trailers as appropriate segments, other parts of the corresponding original shot in movies are obtained as redundant segments.

2   Appropriate Segment Extraction

2.1   Outline of the Proposed Method

Fig. 1 shows the outline of the proposed method. The proposed method consists of two phases: Learning Phase and Segment Extraction Phase. We assume that audio and visual features change in a characteristic way in appropriate segments selected by professional editors. Therefore, in Learning Phase, given sets of appropriate segments and redundant segments as examples, the temporal patterns of how frame-level audio and visual features change in each type of segment are learned with HMMs. After extracting audio and visual features from frames of the given segments, each feature is discretized to represent frames with similar audio and visual features with a symbol. Then, symbol sequence patterns in appropriate segments and redundant segments are learned with HMMs, generating a HMM for appropriate segments and a HMM for redundant segments respectively. Finally, in Segment Extraction Phase, when an original shot and the length of the segment to be extracted are given, a symbol sequence for the original shot is obtained and the likelihoods for all segments of the specified

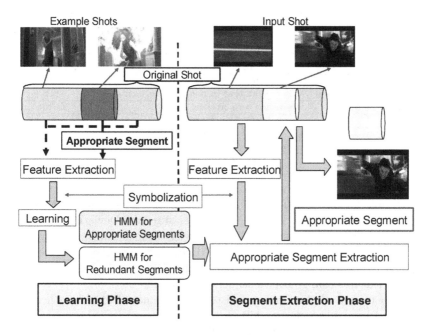

Fig. 1. Outline of the method

length to be observed in each HMM are calculated. The segment with the maximum ratio between the likelihood values for the HMM for appropriate segments and for the HMM for redundant segments is extracted as the most appropriate segment. The proposed method requires the following four procedures.

1. Feature Extraction
2. Symbolization
3. Symbol Sequence Pattern Learning with HMMs
4. Segment Extraction

2.2 Feature Extraction

Shots can be classified into some categories and which audio or visual features change characteristically in appropriate segments should depend on the shot categories. Therefore, the audio and visual features which suit for each shot category need to be extracted. In this paper, focusing on *conversation* and *action* shots, we extract features suitable for each shot category. For example, in conversation shots, as shown in Fig. 2, the appropriate segments include clearly audible voices, which cause the zero crossing ratio to vary widely [7], and the frequency spectrum largely differs from that in the redundant segments. On the other hand, appropriate segments in action shots include the intervals which have large luminance changes, loud sound effects and large zero crossing ratio change as shown in Fig. 3.

Table 1. Relations between characteristics of appropriate segments and audio and visual features

Shot Category	Characteristics of appropriate segments	audio and visual features
Conversation	clearly audible voice	STE, ESTD, LSTER
	frequency spectrum which largely differs from that in non-voice segments	ERSB
	widely varied zero crossing ratio	ZCR
Action	large luminance change	Luminance
	widely varied zero crossing ratio	ZCR
	sharp loud sound effects	STE

Considering the above observations, we summarize the audio and visual features suitable for conversation and action shots in Table 1. In this table, STE stands for Short-Time Energy, ESTD for STE Standard Deviation, LSTER for Low Short-Time Energy Ratio, ERSB for Energy Ratio of SubBand at frequency band, and ZCR for Zero Crossing Ratio [7]D According to the table, we extract relevant features for each category from each frame as follows in order to see how these features change over a sequence of frames.

Here, let us note that a frame consists of a sequence of fixed length windows of L audio samples, which are shifted by F_s samples. $STE(n)$ denotes STE of the nth window. When $x(l)$ denotes audio signal of the lth sample, $STE(n)$ is calculated by

$$STE(n) = \sqrt{\frac{1}{L}\sum_{l=-\infty}^{\infty}[x(l)i(n)]^2} \tag{1}$$

where $i(n)$ is defined as

$$i(n) = \begin{cases} 1 \text{ for } nL \leq l < (n+1)L \\ 0 \text{ otherwise} \end{cases} \tag{2}$$

(a) $\overline{STE}(p)$

$\overline{STE}(p)$ denotes the average $STE(n)$ in the pth frame, calculated by

$$\overline{STE}(p) = \frac{1}{N}\sum_{n=(p-1)N}^{pN-1} STE(n) \tag{3}$$

where N denotes the number of windows in a frame.

(b) $LSTER(p)$

$LSTER(p)$ denotes the ratio of $STE(n)$ which exceeds $\overline{STE}(p)$ in the pth frame, calculated as follows.

$$LSTER(p) = \frac{1}{N}\sum_{n=(p-1)N}^{pN-1} sgn[\overline{STE}(p) - STE(n)] \tag{4}$$

where

$$sgn[y] = \begin{cases} 1 \text{ if } y \geq 0 \\ 0 \text{ otherwise} \end{cases} \tag{5}$$

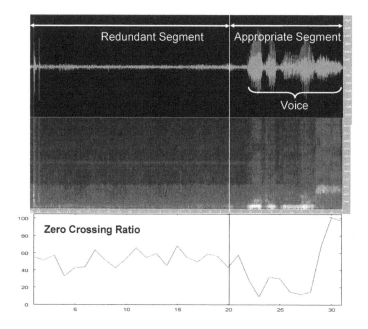

Fig. 2. Volume and Spectrum of a Conversation Shot

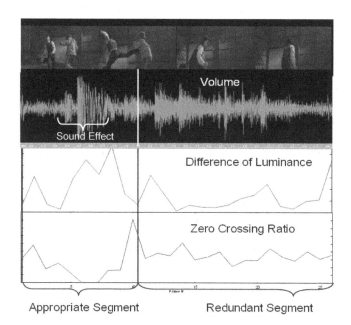

Fig. 3. Luminance Change in an Action Shot

(c) $ESTD(p)$

$ESTD(p)$ denotes the standard deviation of $STE(n)$ in the pth frame.

$$ESTD(p) = \sqrt{\sum_{n=(p-1)N}^{pN-1} (STE(n) - \overline{STE}(p))^2} \qquad (6)$$

(d) $ZCR'(p)$

$ZCR(n)$ denotes the Zero-Crossing Ratio in the nth window, defined as follows.

$$ZCR(n) = \sum_{l=-\infty}^{\infty} \frac{1}{2}|\text{sgn}[x(l)] - \text{sgn}[x(l-1)]|i(n-l) \qquad (7)$$

Then, J denotes the number of frames in a shot, and $ZCR'(p)$ is calculated as follows.

$$ZCR'(p) = \frac{\overline{ZCR}(p)}{\frac{1}{J}\sum_{p=1}^{J} \overline{ZCR}(p)} \qquad (8)$$

where

$$\overline{ZCR}(p) = \frac{1}{N} \sum_{n=(p-1)N}^{pN-1} ZCR(n) \qquad (9)$$

(e) $\overline{ERSB[0/1/2/3]}(p)$

$ERSB_n$ is extracted by transforming audio signals in the nth window from time domain into frequency domain with FFT(Fast Fourier Transform). There are four $ERSB(n)$s, $ERSB[0](n)$ – $ERSB[3](n)$. $ERSB[0](n)$ is the total energy of all frequencies, $ERSB[1](n)$ is that between 0 and 630Hz, $ERSB[2](n)$ is that between 630 and 1720Hz, and $ERSB[3](n)$ is that between 1720 and 4400Hz. We calculate the average of $ERSB[0/1/2/3](n)$ in the pth frame, $\overline{ERSB[0/1/2/3]}(p)$.

(f) Change of Luminance$I_{diff}(p)$

The average image luminance of the pth frame, $\overline{I}$, is calculated from the average RGB, $\overline{R}(p), \overline{G}(p)$, and $\overline{B}(p)$ as below.

$$\overline{I}(p) = 0.2989 \times \overline{R}(p) + 0.5866 \times \overline{G}(p) + 0.1445 \times \overline{B}(p) \qquad (10)$$

$\overline{I}$ is then normalized to handle the luminance difference between videos caused by their recording situations, and we obtain $\hat{I}(p)$. With $\hat{I}(p)$ and $\hat{I}(p+1)$, $I_{diff}(p)$ is calculated by

$$I_{diff}(p) = \begin{cases} 0 & \text{if } p = J \\ |\hat{I}(p+1) - \hat{I}(p)| & \text{otherwise} \end{cases} \qquad (11)$$

2.3   Symbolization

We use Principal Component Analysis(PCA) to reduce the noise contained in features, and as a result, to reduce the dimension of features. In this paper, we adopt z principal components for each shot category, where the cumulative contribution is more than 90%. In addition, since different features are measured in different units, all features are standardized before PCA.

Since the principal component scores are continuous values, we transform them into discrete values in order to capture the rough characteristics of each frame. Each mth principal component score ranging from $t_{m,min}$ to $t_{m,max}$ is equally divided into d_m intervals. After discretization each component, all features in each discretized feature vector space is represented with a symbol. Consequently, a sequence of frames is transformed into a sequence of symbols.

2.4   Symbol Sequence Pattern Learning with HMMs

Hidden Markov Models(HMMs) are used to learn the temporal patterns of the symbol sequence of appropriate segments and redundant segments. HMM is one of the popular techniques to construct an efficient model which describes the temporal patterns of data sequence [8]. The main advantages over other methods, such as Support Vector Machines and Neural Networks, are their ability to model variable-length patterns. Since the length of the symbol sequences to learn is varied for each shot, we need to use a recognition model which can learn variable-length patterns.

A HMM consists of a finite set of states, and the transitions between states are described by a set of probabilities $A = a_{ij}$, where a_{ij} indicates the transition from the state i to j. At each state, there are observation probabilities $B = b_i(O)$, where $b_i(O)$ indicates the occurrence of symbol O at the state i. The initial state is determined by the initial state distribution $\pi = \pi_i$.

The symbol sequences of appropriate segments and redundant segments for each shot category are fed into two separate HMMs. In this paper, we use 3-state left-to-right HMM. The parameters of HMM are learned with Baum-Welch algorithm[8].

2.5   Segment Extraction

Finally, when given an original shot and the time length of the segment to be extracted, the proposed method extracts an appropriate segment of the specified length based on the learned HMMs. Fig. 4 shows the flow of segment extraction. k denotes the number of frames of the appropriate segment specified by the user. First, a symbol sequence is extracted from the given original shot. $h_k(f)$, the log likelihood for a sequence of k symbols centered at the fth symbol to be observed in the HMM for appropriate segments, and $g_k(f)$, the log likelihood for the same sequence to be observed in the HMM for redundant segments, are

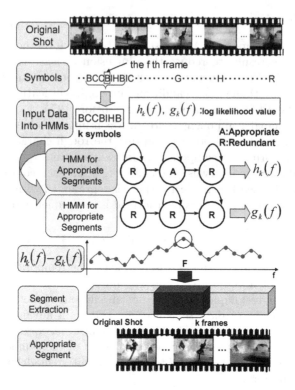

Fig. 4. Appropriate Segment Extraction

calculated with Forward algorithm. Then, a segment with the maximum ratio between $h_k(f)$ and $g_k(f)$, centered at the Fth frame, is extracted as follows.

$$F = \arg\max_f (h_k(f) - g_k(f)) \qquad (12)$$

3 Experiments

We evaluated our proposed method using movies and their trailers. Movie trailers are one of the representative professionally edited videos, mainly designed to attract viewers' interests. Another benefit of using these videos are that both of the original videos and edited videos are easily available. Here, we extracted shots from movie trailers as the appropriate segments, and the corresponding shots as the original shot. Then, the segments excluding the appropriate segments are extracted from the original shot as the redundant segments. Table 2 shows the titles and the number of sample and test original shots. Here, appropriate and redundant segments obtained from sample original shots are used as examples and an appropriate segment is extracted from the test original shot by the proposed method. We used the original shots, which are different from the sample shots, as the test shots. k is set to the number of frames of the segments

Table 2. Sample and Test Shots

Movie Title	Action		Conversation	
	Sample Shot	Test Shot	Sample Shot	Test Shot
New Police Story	1	0	1	1
MI:2	0	0	1	0
MI:3	2	4	0	0
Mr. and Mrs. Smith	3	2	4	2
Day After Tomorrow	1	3	2	1
Minority Report	0	0	3	1
Butterfly Effect	0	0	1	2
I, ROBOT	3	6	0	0
Dead Man's Chest	0	7	0	3
Star Wars I	0	1	0	3
Star Wars II	0	13	0	2
Star Wars III	0	4	0	2
BIOHAZARD2	0	1	0	0
Harry Potter I	0	0	0	1
Harry Potter II	0	5	0	2
Harry Potter III	0	1	0	2
Total	10	47	12	22

used in movie trailers. On average, the original shot length was 41.2 frames, and $k = 13.3$, which corresponds to 32.3% of the original shot length.

The parameters used in the experiments are as follows. The frame rate is 10fps, $z = 5$, $d_1 = 3$, $d_2 = 3$, $d_3 = 2$, $d_4 = 2$, and $d_5 = 2$ for conversation shots, and $z = 3$, $d_1 = 4$, $d_2 = 3$, and $d_3 = 2$ for action shots. We set the initial parameters of left-to-right HMMs as $\pi_1 = 1$, $\pi_2 = 0$, $\pi_3 = 0$, and

$$A = \begin{pmatrix} 1/2 & 1/2 & 0 \\ 0 & 1/2 & 1/2 \\ 0 & 0 & 1/2 \end{pmatrix}.$$

The initial output probability at each state is set equally to all symbols,

$$B = \begin{pmatrix} 1/c & 1/c & \cdots & 1/c \\ 1/c & 1/c & \cdots & 1/c \\ 1/c & 1/c & \cdots & 1/c \end{pmatrix},$$

where $c = 72$ for conversation shots and $c = 24$ for action shots.

3.1 Objective Evaluation

As an objective evaluation, we compared the appropriate segments extracted by the proposed method with the segments used in movie trailers, and evaluated the results with the accuracy defined as follows.

$$\text{Accuracy} = \frac{\text{the number of correctly extracted appropriate segments}}{\text{the number of all original shots}} \quad (13)$$

Table 3. Results of Objective Evaluation

	Accuracy	
	Action	Conversation
t=2	53%(25/47)	60%(11/22)
t=3	60%(28/47)	64%(14/22)
t=5	72%(34/47)	73%(16/22)

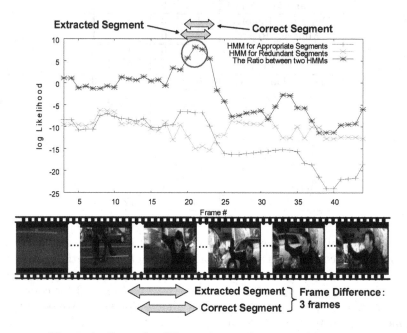

Fig. 5. An Example of Extracting an Appropriate Segment

In what follows, we will call segments extracted by the proposed method *extracted segments*, and segments used in movie trailers *correct segments*. In evaluation, we allowed the frame difference between the extracted segment and the correct segment up to t frames.

Table 3 shows the results of objective evaluation. When $t = 5$, the appropriate segments were correctly extracted from 72.5% of the original shots. Fig. 5 shows an example of extracting an appropriate segment. The original shot includes a crash scene in which a truck nearly hits a character, which corresponds to the correct segment, and the proposed method was able to extract the same segment within 3-frame difference by the proposed method.

3.2 Subjective Evaluation

As a subjective evaluation, we also conducted a questionnaire to evaluate if users feel the extracted segments are appropriate to be used in edited videos.

This questionnaire was administered to 14 people. First, we presented them the original shot and then three segments as the appropriate segment, 1)correct segment, 2)extracted segment, and 3)random segment, and asked them to rank the three segments in terms of their adequacy. In this questionnaire, we allowed them to rank more than two segments in the same rank. Assuming that extracting the first k frames, the middle k frames, or the last k frames of the original shot is the most simple way to select segments, we adopted one of these three segments as random segment. Fig. 6 shows the results of the subjective evaluation. The graph shows that 80.0% of the extracted segments received higher evaluation ratings than that of random segments. Although the correct segments received the highest evaluation rating, 53.9% of the extracted segments received equivalently high evaluation rating as the correct segments. These results have verified that the proposed method was able to extract subjectively appropriate segments.

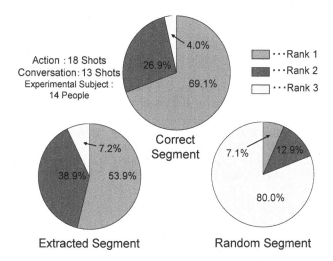

Fig. 6. Result of Subjective Evaluation

4   Conclusion

In this paper, we proposed a method for extracting an appropriate segment from an original shot based on the temporal patterns of how the audio and visual features change both in the appropriate and redundant segments, which are automatically learned from examples. We experimented the proposed method using examples obtained from movies and their trailers. According to the objective evaluation, the appropriate segments were correctly extracted from 72.5% of the original shots within the error of the 5-frame difference. In addition, according to the subjective evaluation, 80% of the extracted segments received higher evaluation ratings than the random segments, and in particular, 53.9% of them received equivalently high evaluation ratings as the correct segments. These results have verified the effectiveness of the proposed method in extracting appropriate segments.

There is room for argument on selecting audio and visual features. In this paper, we used only difference of average luminance between frames as the visual features; therefore, we should use a feature which describes movements of objects in videos. We also need to consider other shot categories and how to determine suitable audio and visual features for each category. An algorithm to automatically discriminate the shot category should also be contrived.

References

1. Windows Movie Maker, http://www.windowsmoviemakers.net/
2. Adobe Premiere, http://www.adobe.co.jp/products/premiere/main.html
3. Takahashi, Y., Nitta, N., Babaguchi, N.: Video Summarization for Large Sports Video Archives. In: Proceedings of IEEE ICME (July 2005)
4. Tanimoto, M., Mukunoki, M., Ikeda, K.: Sports Video Indexing by Detecting the Events that Consist Scene -Indexing of golf program- Technical Report of IEICE PRMU, pp. 67–74 (October 2001)
5. Aoyanagi, S., Kourai, K., Sato, K., Takada, T., Sgawara, T.: Evaluation of New Video Skimming Method Using Audio and Video Information. In: Proceedings of DEWS 2003 2-A-01 (March 2003)
6. Tkakemoto, R., Yoshitaka, A., Hirashima, T.: Video Editing based on Movie Effects by Shot Length Transition, Technical Report of IEICE PRMU pp.19–24 (January 2006)
7. Wang, Y., Liu, Z., Huang, J.C.: Multimedia Content Analysis Using Both Audio and Visual Clues. IEEE Signal Processing Magagine, 12–36 (2000)
8. Rabiner, L.R.: A Tutorial on Hidden Markov Models and Selected Applications in Speech Recognition. Proceedings of IEEE 77, 257–285 (1989)

Fast Segmentation of H.264/AVC Bitstreams for On-Demand Video Summarization

Klaus Schöffmann and Laszlo Böszörmenyi

Department of Information Technology (ITEC), University of Klagenfurt
Universitätsstr. 65-67, 9020 Klagenfurt, Austria
{ks,laszlo}@itec.uni-klu.ac.at

Abstract. Video summarization methods need fast segmentation of a video into smaller units as a first step, especially if used in an on-demand fashion. We propose an efficient segmentation algorithm for H.264/AVC bitstreams that is able to segment a video in appr. 10% of the time required to decode the video. This is possible because our approach uses features available after entropy-decoding (which is the very first stage of the decoding process) only. More precisely, we use a combination of two features, especially appropriate to H.264/AVC, with different characteristics in order to decide if a new segment starts or not: (1) L1-Distance based partition histograms and (2) ratio of intra-coded macroblocks on a per-frame basis. Our results show that this approach performs well and works for several different encoders used in practice today.

Keywords: video segmentation, video analysis, shot detection, shot boundary detection, cut detection, H.264, AVC, compressed domain.

1 Introduction

Due to many improvements in several areas of computing, the amount of digital videos has been dramatically increased in recent years. It is often not easy for users to decide whether they are interested in one particular video or not. To solve this problem researchers have started to work on video summarization methods. The goal of video summarization is to create abstracts of digital videos. Many articles have been published on this topic in recent years. While the proposed solutions differ in the methods used to create the abstracts, most of them are based on an elementary video segmentation, where a whole video sequence is divided into small units, called *shots*. Although there has been intensive research on shot-detection methods in the last two decades and this topic is considered to be a solved problem, it seems to reobtain importance with video summarization. Since practically every video is stored in compressed form and video coding standards have reached a very high level of compression efficiency, decoding a video can be a time-consuming process. With applications where on-demand video abstracts should be created, a user might not accept a long delay since he/she wants to see the abstract as soon as possible. In such cases it is obviously a better solution for video summarization methods to rely on

S. Satoh, F. Nack, and M. Etoh (Eds.): MMM 2008, LNCS 4903, pp. 265–276, 2008.

shot-detection methods which can operate directly in the compressed domain in order to enable fast processing, although they might not be as precise as algorithms working in the decompressed domain. Even though there have been many proposed algorithms for performing video shot segmentation in the compressed domain, only a few of them are suited for the most recent state-of-the-art video coding standard H.264/AVC [3], frequently used in practice due to its high compression efficiency.

With this article, we propose a novel shot detection algorithm for H.264/ AVC bitstreams that completely operates in the entropy-decoding stage, which is the very first one in the entire decoding process. As shown in Fig. 1, our shot-detection approach is composed of two main processes and uses some further refinement steps. The details of these post-processing steps are not described in this article, but can be found in [10]. Our algorithm allows segmentation of a video in about 10% of the time required to decode the video. This makes it perfectly suited for the usage in the video summarization area. Our approach has been evaluated with the baseline profile of H.264/AVC since we used our own decoder for evaluation which currently supports baseline profile only, but we expect similar results for higher profiles. In the further sections we show that our algorithm works for three very popular encoders with quite equal results and uses simple threshold parameters whose settings can be easily understood by a non-expert end-user as well.

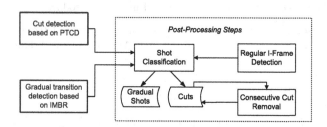

Fig. 1. Overview of our shot-detection approach

2 Shot Detection in H.264/AVC

2.1 Macroblock Types and Partitions

The H.264/AVC standard [3] allows encoding different *types of macroblocks* within a particular type of frame. For instance, a predicted (P) frame may consist of intra-coded macroblocks (I-MBs), predicted macroblocks (P-MBs), bidirectional predicted macroblocks (B-MBs), and skipped macroblocks (S-MBs). Macroblocks are further partitioned into smaller blocks whereby the size of a partition can be: 16x16 Pixel, 16x8 Pixel, 8x16 Pixel, 8x8 Pixel, 8x4 Pixel, 4x8 Pixel, or 4x4 Pixel. Which *macroblock type* and which *partitioning* is applied to a specific block, is decided by the encoder. Which type of macroblock an encoder chooses mainly depends on the residual. The encoder tries to find the corresponding block(s) in a previous or future frame which will give the smallest residual. If even the smallest residual is too high, the encoder will use intra-coding. Which partitioning is chosen for a macroblock mainly depends on the strategy of the encoder. However, an encoder will typically apply partitioning depending on the "*noise/energy*" of a block, the shapes and contours in the block, the location of "*homogeneous*" areas in the block. The chosen type of a macroblock does also constraint the partitioning[1]. An encoder will use such a partitioning that will result in the lowest residual for the entire block. More details about H.264/AVC can be found in [3], [9], and [11].

2.2   Related Work

In difference to algorithms operating on decompressed data, video shot detection algorithms working in the compressed domain have the advantage that no full decoding (which costs time and memory space) is necessary. Several shot detection algorithms operating on compressed videos have been proposed in the last decade. However, only a few of them use features newly introduced by the H.264/AVC coding standard.

Usually, the performance of a shot detection algorithm is measured in *Recall* and *Precision*. Recall denotes the proportion of the number of detected shots to the number of existing shots. Precision quantifies how many of the detected shots are correct shots. In many cases we are also interested in the correct detection of the starting and the ending location of a shot, nevertheless in this article we use recall and precision as the only metric of evaluation. The reason for this is that this is the most comparable metric since many other published shot-detection algorithms use it as well. We wished to compare the performance of our algorithm to the already proposed algorithms, but the test-videos are, unfortunately, not available for public use[2].

In [5] the authors proposed a shot detection approach for H.264/AVC which is based on the prediction modes of macroblocks. Their approach works in two stages. First, the *dissimilarity distance* of inter-prediction histograms in two adjacent I frames is calculated. If this distance is above a predefined threshold, the GOP starting with the corresponding I frame is further analyzed. This first stage is used to limit the number of GOPs for the second stage. In the second stage, they use *Hidden Markov Models* (HMM) to detect shots based on seven types of inter-prediction of 4x4 partitions. If used with both stages, their approach is able to detect up to 94.7% of the shots with a precision of 98.16%. If only the second stage is used, the precision decreased down to 88.7%. However, their approach takes some assumptions which may not hold in practice. First, many H.264/AVC encoders with default settings do only sparsely insert I frames into the bitstream. Instead of an I frame rather, a P or B frame with many I macroblocks is inserted. This means, that the first stage of the described

---

[1] I-MBs may only be composed of one 16x16/four 8x8/sixteen 4x4 partitions; S-MBs may only be composed of one 16x16 partition.

[2] We use this opportunity to raise a plea for unrestricted publication of material needed for reconstruct any published experiments. This is a basic req. for scientific work.

approach would miss many shots if they do not start with an I frame, and the whole sequence must be analyzed with the technique of the second stage. Next, the inter-prediction type of a macroblock is strongly dependent on the settings of the encoder. For instance, a video encoded with baseline profile does only use backward prediction. The authors of [1] proposed a shot detection approach which is based on SAD values (SAD = Sum of Absolute Differences). The SAD value is calculated by the encoder at encoding time and sums up the Pixel-differences between the current block and the referenced block. With dynamic thresholding their approach achieved a recall of 97% with precision of 97% for a sports video. However, while this is a good result, the proposed approach is only applicable for video bitstreams that include SAD values calculated by the encoder at encoding time. Another shot-detection algorithm for H.264/AVC bit-streams has been presented in [12]. However, their approach separately considers I, P, and B frame coded videos, rather than one single video consisting of several frame types. A detailed summary of related work can be found in [10].

3   IBR Approach

If the residual of a P- or B-MB tends to be too high, an encoder will typically use intra-coding instead of predictive coding for that macroblock. Such situations occur frequently at shot boundaries especially if backward prediction is used. The reason is, that the first frame of a shot is usually very different to earlier frames in the video. Our shot detection algorithm exploits this behavior as it uses the *I-MB Ratio* (IBR) to create a set of candidate-cuts. A candidate frame i is added to the candidate set CS by the following rule, where TH_I is the threshold [0-1] for the required ratio of I-MBs in a frame:

$$CS = CS \cup Frame_i, IBR_i \geq TH_I \tag{1}$$

A frame will be added to the candidate set if and only if it contains more I-MBs than the specified threshold (as a percentage value). Although this algorithm successfully detects shot boundaries (e.g. cuts), it needs some further refinement. Those post-processing steps are described in Section 5.

4   PHD Approach

The shot detection process solely based on IBR achieves good performance, as our results show. However, typically the algorithm lacks of accuracy which results in many false positives and, thus, a low precision value. Therefore, we have developed another shot detection algorithm that exploits the partitioning-decisions taken by the encoder.

In Section 2.1 the partitioning of macroblocks has been briefly discussed. Intuitively, an encoder will use uniform partitioning for macroblocks of a slow-changing scene, and differ from that partitioning scheme if a shot-change occurs and the homogenous areas, shapes, contours, noise etc. significantly change. As our results show, this assumption is true for several encoders, thus, the change of the *partitioning scheme* is another well-suited feature for shot detection of H.264/AVC encoded bitstreams. We specify a weighted value, called *Partition Histogram Difference* (PHD), which expresses how much the partitioning scheme changes between two consecutive frames. Therefore, we use a partition histogram consisting of 15 bins according to the macroblock-related partition sizes defined in the H.264/AVC standard (with except to partitions of I-MBs)[3]:

$$H = \{P^{16\times16}, P^{16\times8}, P^{8\times16}, P^{8\times8}, P^{8\times4}, P^{4\times8}, P^{4\times4},$$
$$B^{16\times16}, B^{16\times8}, B^{8\times16}, B^{8\times8}, B^{8\times4}, B^{4\times8}, B^{4\times4}, S^{16\times16}\}$$

The reason we do not use partition-types of intra-coded macroblocks is that we do not want to detect candidate-cuts in consecutive frames with changing I-MBs. This relies on the observation that such I-MBs could have been inserted by the encoder due to fast motion. Furthermore, if from one frame to another many I-MBs have been inserted by the encoder, this fact will influence the number of other partition-types (i.e. S/P/B partitions). Thus, if a frame consists primarily of many I-MBs it cannot consist of many P-,S-, or B-macroblocks. Hence, the number of such partitions will go dramatically down and increase at the next P/B frame, if this frame will contain only a few I-MBs.

The PHD is calculated as the sum of differences of the histogram bins between the current frame i and the preceding frame $i - 1$:

$$PHD = \sum_{b=1}^{15} \left(H_i^b - H_{i-1}^b \right) \tag{2}$$

The histogram difference defined in Equation 2 was originally specified as an L_1 *Difference* (i.e. sum of absolute differences). However, as our measurements have shown, absolute differences lead to much more false detections (i.e. lower precision). This correlation is shown in Figure 2. The reason for this behavior is, that there are situations where macroblocks at the same spatial position change their partitioning not due to real content change, but due to compression efficiency decisions of the encoder. Such a situation might occur if an encoder starts to use *Skipped* macroblocks instead of *Predicted* macroblocks. In this case, a sum of absolute differences will produce a high and double-evaluated PHD value, possibly causing false detections. On the other hand, using just differences instead of absolute differences has the problem, that the (e.g. negative) difference of one bin may compensate the (e.g. positive) difference of another bin. However, as we have performed many measurements with many different video files encoded with different encoders and the sum of differences always produced better results than the sum of absolute differences, we can conclude that such situations do rarely happen.

To enable uniform rating of different partition types, a scaling vector for the histogram bins should be used. We use scaling to 4×4 blocks, thus, our scaling vector looks like this: $S = \{16, 8, 8, 4, 2, 2, 1, 16, 8, 8, 4, 2, 2, 1, 16\}$.

---

[3] In our measurements, we have not used partition types of B-MBs, thus, we use in fact only eight partition-types due to the baseline profile limitation of our decoder.

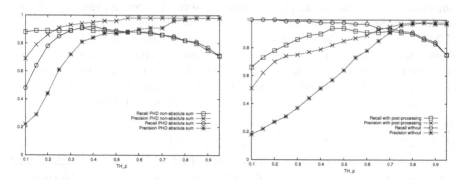

Fig. 2. PHD results when using L1-Distance or sum of differences for video I enc. with x264

Fig. 3. Influence of post-processing in video I enc. with x264

Furthermore, we perform a weighting of the sum of scaled differences in order to enable an easier threshold setting. The refinement of Equation 2 including scaling of histogram bins and weighting of the result is shown here:

$$PHD = \frac{1}{W} \sum_{b=1}^{15} \left(H_i^b - H_{i-1}^b \right) S^b \tag{3}$$

The dynamic weight W is specified as the maximum number of 4×4 partitions (i.e. blocks) for frame i and frame $i - 1$, whereas intra-coded partitions are not considered, as shown in Equation 4. This will produce PHD values in the range $[0 - 1]$[4]:

$$W = \frac{2}{16} Framesize - (P_i^{I16 \times 16} + P_{i-1}^{I16 \times 16}) S^{I16 \times 16} - (P_i^{I4} + P_{i-1}^{I4}) S^{I4 \times 4} \tag{4}$$

A candidate frame i is added to the candidate set CS if and only if the absolute PHD value of frame i is greater than or equal to a predefined threshold TH_P.

$$CS = CS \cup Frame_i \ , \ |PHD_i| >= TH_P \tag{5}$$

5   Post-processing Steps

In the previous two sections we described two simple shot-detection algorithms which rely on different features extracted from compressed data of H.264/AVC bitstreams. The algorithms described so far are quite simple and their general goal is to detect candidate cuts. However, since shot-boundaries are sometimes represented as *gradual transitions* rather than cuts, we need to detect them

---

[4] *Framesize* specifies the size of a frame in pixel dimension. It is assumed that this value is constant for the entire duration of a video.

as one single shot remaining over several frames. Such consecutive candidate cuts are grouped together to one single shot (a *gradual transition*) by the *Shot Classification* Process which is described in [10]. The IBR algorithm described in Section 3 has another problem which needs to be solved: every I frame will be detected as a candidate cut due to its IBR of 100%, even if it has been inserted by the encoder due to Group-of-Picture (GOP) limitations[5]. To avoid this problem our approach removes such frames from the candidate set which seem to be inserted due to the regular end of a GOP. There are several possibilities to detect this correlation, the details are described in [10]. Another post-processing step, called *Consecutive Cut Removal* (CCR), is used to remove such "consecutive" candidate cuts which have not been grouped together by the process of *Shot Classification*.

Figure 3 shows the influence of the post-processing steps on the recall and precision values. For low thresholds the shot classification process will group together a lot of adjacent candidate cuts (which reduces the number of false detections when applying such evaluation rules as described in Section 7) and the consecutive cut removal will further remove many consecutive candidate cuts. This causes both, an increase of precision and a decrease of recall, especially for low threshold settings, as shown in the figure. More details about the post-processing steps can be found in [10].

6   Combining PHD and IBR

Figure 4 shows how the PHD and IBR approach performs if used solely. As shown in the figure, the PHD approach produces much better precision values, especially for low threshold settings, while the IBR approach produces better recall values. As our measurements have shown, the PHD approach works fine for detecting cuts in the video but lacks of the detection of gradual-transition. In contrast, the IBR approach works better for gradual-transition detection but produces many false positives in some specific situations (see [10]). As those observations hold for all of our test videos, we propose a combination of both approaches, whereas the IBR approach is used to detect gradual transitions which have not yet been detected by PHD (cuts detected by IBR are discarded). For the example presented in Figure 5, the cuts at frames 2646 and 2678 will be detected by the PHD algorithm while both gradual transitions from 2650-2657 and 2665-2674 will be detected by the IBR algorithm. In this example a threshold of 0.4 has been chosen for both, TH_I and TH_P. The light-gray vertical bars in the figure denote the positions of shot-changes.

Figures 6 and 7 show the results of solely used IBR and PHD in direct comparison with the IBR/PHD combined approach. The figures show that for most of the threshold values the combination of IBR/PHD produces both, better recall and better precision results. In Figure 8, the Recall/Precision graph of all

---

[5] Some videos are encoded with a constant GOP size which means that the distance between two adjacent I frames will be usually the same for the entire video. In addition to constant GOP sizes encoders do also manage a maximum GOP size.

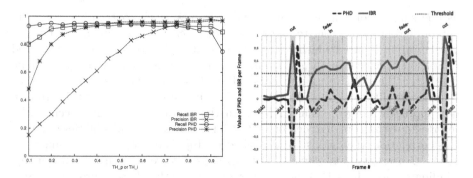

Fig. 4. Comparison of PHD and IBR for video II enc. with QT

Fig. 5. PHD and IBR applied to frames 2640-2680 of video-I (enc. with x264)

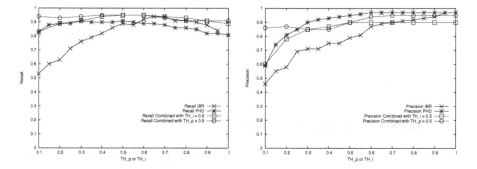

Fig. 6. Recall-Comparison of IBR, PHD, and IBR/PHD combined, video I enc. with Nero

Fig. 7. Precision-Comparison of IBR, PHD, and IBR/PHD combined, video I enc. with Nero

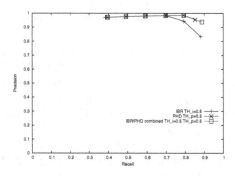

Fig. 8. Recall/Precision Graph for video I enc. with QT

three methods (IBR, PHD, and IBR/PHD) is presented. Please note, that in this graph lower recall values are not shown, since our results are of weak order where several entries may have the same rank. It should be further noted, that very high recall values in this graph are avoided by our post-processing steps (as they avoid false-positives).

7   Performance Measurements

Our measurements have been performed with several test-videos. In this article we present the results for three videos (more results can be found in [10]):

I. *James Bond - Casino Royale*, Movie Trailer[7]; 320x176 Pixel; 1024 kb/s
3650 Frames; 136 Cuts; 33 Gradual Transitions

II. *Sex-and-the-City*, Season-1, Episode-1; 352x288 Pixel; 1024 kb/s
29836 Frames (only the first 20 minutes including intro); 114 Cuts; 117 Gradual Transitions

III. *TRECVID-BOR03*[8]; 320x240 Pixel; 512 kb/s
48451 Frames; 231 Cuts; 11 Gradual Transitions

At least two of the three videos above are publicly available, the first one has been downloaded from the website [7]. The second video is a popular sitcom recorded from TV. The last video has been taken from the public *TREC-2001 Video Track*[8]. For this video the shot-annotation specified by TRECVID has been used. For the other videos the types and locations of shots have been identified by ourselves in a time-consuming manual annotation process. All analyzed videos have been encoded and evaluated with the H.264/AVC *Baseline Profile* by using three popular encoders: (1) Apple QuickTime 7 Pro [2], (2) x264 [4], and (3) Nero Recode 7 [6]. For our implementations and measurements we used our self-implemented H.264/AVC decoder which currently supports baseline profile only. We defined the following rules in order to decide if a shot-change has been correctly detected or not:

- A cut happening at frame i has been correctly detected if our algorithm has detected a shot-change at frame $i \pm 1$.
- A gradual transition happening from frame i to frame $i+n$ has been correctly detected if a shot-change from frame k to frame j has been detected, where either $i \le k \le i + n$ or $i \le j \le i + n$. In other words, a detected gradual transition must either start or stop within frame i and $i + n$.

Table 1 summarizes the best measurement results of the IBR/PHD combined approach applied to all videos. The combined approach produces better results than any of the single ones (IBR or PHD). For instance, with $TH_P = 0.6$ and

Table 1. Best results of the *IBR/PHD combined* approach

video	TH_P / TH_I	detected cuts/grads	false	R	P	average shot detection time in relation to the decoding time
I (Nero)	0.60 / 0.60	135/25	6	94%	96%	9.54%
II (QT)	0.50 / 0.60	112/108	14	95%	94%	8.41%
III(QT)	0.50 / 0.50	228/3	22	95%	91%	9.17%

$TH_I = 0.6$ the combined approach achieves 94% recall with 96% precision for video-I. With the same threshold value, the IBR-alone approach achieves 92% recall with 87% precision and the PHD-alone approach achieves 89% recall with 97% precision. From our results, we can conclude, that the IBR/PHD combined approach produces well results when both thresholds TH_P and TH_I are within 0.4 and 0.9, whereas 0.5 will be a good start value. This correlation is also shown in Figures 9, 10, 11 and 12, where the performance of the IBR/PHD combined approach with different threshold settings for video I (encoded with Nero Recode and QuickTime) have been summarized.

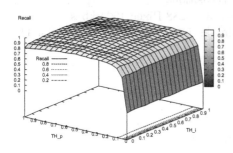

Fig. 9. Recall of the IBR/PHD comb. approach for video I (Nero)

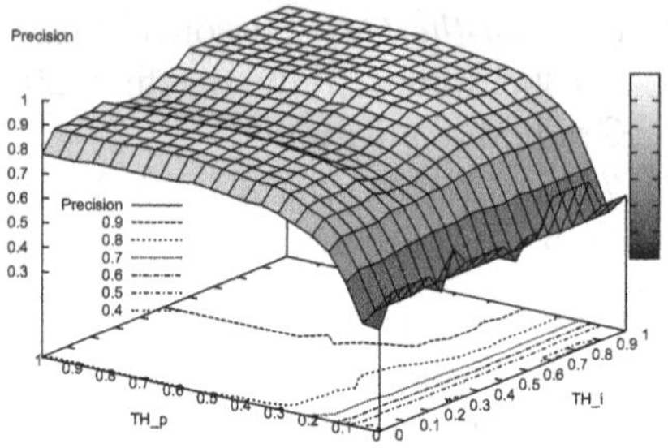

Fig. 10. Precision of the IBR/PHD comb. approach for video I (Nero)

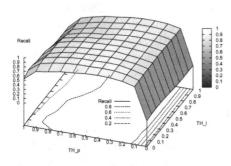

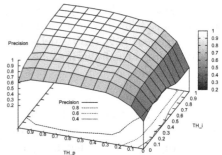

Fig. 11. Recall of the IBR/PHD comb. approach for video I enc. with QT

Fig. 12. Precision of the IBR/PHD comb. approach for video I enc. with QT

In the last column of Table 1 the results of our measurements regarding runtime performance are given. We used our self-written decoder (implemented in C#) for all the measurements, which has currently suboptimal decoding-performance. Since the aim of our program was rather portability and extendibility, it does not use any platform specific optimization. As we can see, our approach requires an average runtime of 9.04% of the overall decoding time for a video. Furthermore, we have directly compared the influence of the chosen encoder for video-I. The results of the combined approach are very similar: while with x264 a recall of 95% with a precision of 95% has been achieved, with

QuickTime-7 the algorithm achieved 91% recall with 95% precision and with Nero Recode 7 94% recall with 96% precision. Moreover, we have evaluated the influence of the chosen encoding bitrate. Although not illustrated here due to space limitations (please see [10]), our measurements have shown that IBR is highly dependent on the encoding bitrate and produces the more false alarms the higher is the encoding bitrate i.e. the quality of the video. PHD seems to be more independent from the encoding bitrate. In contrast, the recall of both methods is quite independent from the encoding bitrate although PHD is more resistant against higher bitrates than IBR.

8   Conclusion and Further Work

We have developed a simple and efficient shot detection method for H.264/AVC bitstreams. The algorithm uses information from the entropy decoding process and calculates the difference of partition histograms in combination with the ratio of intra-coded macroblocks. Our method uses a very simple and transparent threshold setting which can be understood by a non-expert user as well. Our approach does not depend on any specific video encoder and has only little dependence on the encoding-bitrate. Finally, our proposed method works fast, i.e. takes only about 10% of the entire decoding time for a video. This is especially advantageous in cases, where no successive decoding is needed. Our proposed algorithm can be used for applications which require very fast segmentation of a video into shots, as for instance video summarization, video indexing, or shot-based adaptation. The next step is to evaluate our method with higher profiles of H.264/AVC too and to directly compare it with other shot detection methods which work in the compressed domain of H.264/AVC as well.

References

1. Dimou, A., Nemethova, O., Rupp, M.: Scene Change Detection for H.264 using Dynamic Threshold Techniques. In: Proceedings of 5th EURASIP Conference on Speech and Image Processing, Multimedia Communications and Service (July 2005)
2. Inc., A.: Quicktime 7 pro, Online (last accessed on: 04/01/07) (2007), http://www.apple.com/quicktime/pro/
3. ISO/IEC JTC 1/SC 29/WG 11. ISO/IEC FDIS 14496-10: Information Technology - Coding of audio-visual objects - Part 10: Advanced Video Coding (March 2003)
4. Aimar, L., Merritt, L., Petit, E., Chen, M., Clay, J., Rullgard, M., Czyz, R., Heine, C., Izvorski, A., Wright, A.: x264 - a free h264/avc encoder. Online (last accessed on: 04/01/07), http://www.videolan.org/developers/x264.html
5. Liu, Y., Wang, W., Gao, W., Zeng, W.: A Novel Compressed Domain Shot Segmentation Algorithm on H.264/AVC. In: ICIP 2004. 2004 International Conference on Image Processing, vol. 4, pp. 2235–2238 (October 2004)
6. Nero Inc., G.: Nero recode 7, Online (last accessed on: 04/01/07) (2007), http://www.nero.com/eng/index.html
7. Neuveglise, J.: PocketMovies.net

8. N.N.I. of Standards and Technology. Trec video retrieval evaluation. Online (last accessed on: 04/01/07) http://www-nlpir.nist.gov/projects/trecvid/

9. Richardson, I.: H.264 and MPEG-4 Video Compression: Video Coding for Next Generation Multimedia. John Wiley & Sons Ltd. The Atrium. Southern Gate, Chichester, West Sussex PO19 8SQ, England (2003)

10. Early Stage Shot Detection for H.264/AVC Bitstreams. Technical Report TR/ITEC/07/2.04, Department of Information Technology, University of Klagenfurt, Austria, Jul, Online (2007),
http://www-itec.uni-klu.ac.at/~klschoef/papers/shotdetection.pdf

11. Wiegand, T., Sullvian, G.J., Bjontegaard, G., Luthra, A.: Overview of the H.264/AVC Video Coding Standard. In: IEEE Transactions on Circuits and Systems for Video Technology (July 2003)

12. Zeng, W., Gao, W.: Shot change detection on H.264/AVC compressed video. In: ISCAS 2005. IEEE International Symposium on Circuits and Systems, vol. 4, pp. 3459–3462 (May 2005)

Blurred Image Detection and Classification

Ping Hsu and Bing-Yu Chen

National Taiwan University
vivace@cmlab.csie.ntu.edu.tw, robin@ntu.edu.tw

Abstract. Digital photos are massively produced while digital cameras are becoming popular, however, not every photo has good quality. Blur is one of the conventional image quality degradation which is caused by various factors. In this paper, we propose a scheme to detect blurred images and classify them into several different categories. The blur detector uses support vector machines to estimate the blur extent of an image. The blurred images are further classified into either locally or globally blurred images. For globally blurred images, we estimate their point spread functions and classify them into camera shake or out of focus images. For locally blurred images, we find the blurred regions using a segmentation method, and the point spread function estimation on the blurred region can sort out the images with depth of field or moving object. The blur detection and classification processes are fully automatic and can help users to filter out blurred images before importing the photos into their digital photo albums.

1 Introduction

Image degradation comes into existence in different environments: unstable camera, night scene, moving object, etc. Many users take photos excursively and it turns out that there exist a lot of low quality photos. It is not convenient that the users have to take much time to find these defective photos out after a tour. The goal of blur classification in this paper is to help the users to automatically detect the blurred photos and classify them into some categories to let the users make further decisions.

Since the image gradient model is highly related to image blurring [1], our blur detector uses *support vector machine* (SVM) to verify the gradient model and estimate the magnitude of blur in an image, and then the blurred image is also determined to globally or locally blurred. Either camera shake or out of focus may cause globally blurred image, yet we can verify them by the *point spread function* (PSF). The PSF describes the response of an image to a point source or point object. After calculating the PSF of an image, the globally blurred image can be classified into camera shake or out of focus. Simultaneously the locally blurred image can be classified into two types: depth of field and moving object. We find the blurred regions by segmentation method, and the PSF estimation on the blurred region can sort out the image with depth of field or moving object.

S. Satoh, F. Nack, and M. Etoh (Eds.): MMM 2008, LNCS 4903, pp. 277–286, 2008.
© Springer-Verlag Berlin Heidelberg 2008

Therefore, every image, by our blur detector, can be classified into one of the following five types: non-blurred, camera shake, out of focus, moving object, and depth of field. Fig. 1 shows the procedure of the blur detection.

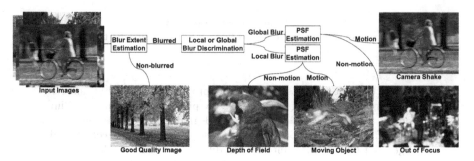

Fig. 1. The procedure of the blur detection

2   Related Work

Tong *et al.* [2] proposed a scheme that makes the use of the ability of Harr wavelet transform in both discriminating different types of edges and recovering sharpness from the blurred version, and then determines whether an image is blurred or not and to what extent an image is blurred. Elder *et al.* [3] proposed an algorithm to detect local scale control and localize the edges over a broad range of the blur scale. This method for edge detection leads to a method for estimating the local blur of image contours.

Ben-Ezra *et al.* [4] proposed a hybrid image system that uses a secondary detector to estimate the motion in the image. Combining the blurred image and the acquired motion information, a PSF is estimated that represents the path of the camera during the integration. Rooms *et al.* [5] assumed the PSF can be modeled with a single parameter, and they used a Gaussian function to estimate the single-parameter PSF from a single observation of a degraded image. Fergus *et al.* [1] adopted a variational Bayesian approach to estimate the PSF of an image. Given the grayscale blurred image B, the blur kernel K and the latent image L are going to be estimated by finding the values with the highest probability from the statistics of L. These statistics are based on the image gradients rather than the intensities, so the optimization is working on gradient domain. The variational algorithm minimizes a cost function that can represent the distance between the approximation and the true posterior. The updates are repeated until the change converges. The mean of the distribution is then taken as the final value of K.

Pedro *et al.* [6] proposed an algorithm using a graph-based representation of the image and applied it to image segmentation. Let $G = (V, E)$ be an undirected graph with vertices $v_i \in V$ to be segmented and edges $(v_i, v_j) \in E$ corresponding to pairs of neighboring vertices. A segmentation S is a partition of V such that each component $C \in S$ is a connected component in graph $G' = (V, E')$ where

$E' \subseteq E$. Let S^0 be the initial segmentation, where each vertex v_i is in its own component, and the algorithm merges the vertices repeatedly. After m steps, S^m is the output that segments V into r components $S = (C_1, \ldots, C_r)$.

3 Blur Extent Estimation

3.1 Image Gradient Model

Gradient can be considered as a gradation from low to high values. The gradient of an image is a function that at each pixel the gradient vector points in the direction of largest possible intensity increase with the components given by the derivatives in the horizontal and vertical directions. The gradient of a two variables function $F(x, y)$ is defined as

$$\nabla F = \frac{\partial F}{\partial x}\hat{i} + \frac{\partial F}{\partial y}\hat{j}. \tag{1}$$

If we define F as the source image, $G_x = \frac{\partial F}{\partial x}\hat{i}$ and $G_y = \frac{\partial F}{\partial y}\hat{j}$ are two images which at each pixel contain the horizontal and vertical derivative values. At each pixel in the image, the resulting gradient values can be combined to give the gradient magnitude, using $G = \sqrt{G_x^2 + G_y^2}$. We can also calculate the gradient's direction as $\theta = \arctan(G_y/G_x)$.

Fig. 2 shows that the gradient histogram distribution of a clear image is massive on small values but there also exist some small noises on large values. Besides the magnitude histogram, we can find that every direction has almost the same probability in the direction histogram. On the contrary, the gradient magnitude distribution of a blurred image is almost empty on the large values and there only exists small values, and the gradient direction histogram also shows there are some values higher than others. According to the difference of the gradient distribution between a normal image and a blurred image, we can discriminate them by examining an image's gradient histogram.

3.2 Support Vector Machines

SVM, which has been proposed as a very effective method for pattern recognition [7,8], is a set of related supervised learning methods used for classification. A special property of SVM is that it minimizes the classification error and maximizes the geometric margin. SVM maps input vectors to a higher dimensional space and constructs a hyperplane to separate the data into two groups. Two parallel hyperplanes are built up on each side of the hyperplane that maximize the distance between the two groups.

Given a training set of pre-labeled data points (x_i, y_i), $i = 1, \ldots, l$ where $x_i \in R^n$ belongs to either of two classes and $y_i \in \{1, -1\}$ denotes the label, the support vector machines, to establish a hyperplane that can divide all

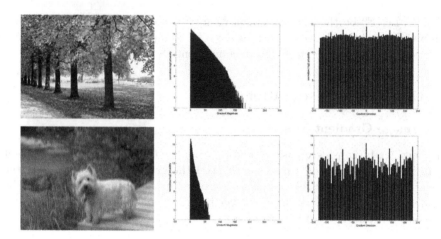

Fig. 2. Left: original images. Middle: gradient magnitude histogram. Right: gradient direction histogram.

x with maximizing the distance between the two classes, solves the following optimization problem:

Minimize
$$\frac{1}{2}\mathbf{w} \cdot \mathbf{w} + C \sum_{i=1}^{N} \xi_i$$

Subject to
$$y_i(\mathbf{w} \cdot \phi(x_i) + b) \geq 1 - \xi_i, \quad \xi_i > 0$$

The nonnegative variable $\xi = \{\xi_1, \xi_2, \dots \xi_N\}$ allows a small number of misclassified points for better generalization, and $C > 0$ is the penalty parameter of the error term. Furthermore, $K(x_i, x_j) = \Phi(x_i) \cdot \Phi(x_j)$ is called the kernel function and we use the radial basis function (RBF) as the kernel function where $K(x_i, x_j) = e^{-|x_i - x_j|^2 / 2\sigma^2}$.

Instead of predicting the label, sometimes we are looking for a probability prediction $Pr(y = 1|x)$, Platt [9] proposed a method to approximate the posterior by a sigmoid function:

$$Pr(y = 1|x) \approx P_{A,B}(x) \equiv \frac{1}{1 + exp(Af(x) + B)}, \quad (2)$$

where the parameters (A, B) are estimated by solving a maximum likelihood problem.

3.3 Blur Extent Estimation Using SVM

There are two types of training data: clear images and blurred images. Every labeled image I_i, $i = 1 \dots l$ is converted to grayscale, so the gradient magnitude and direction maps can be built up first. By adding up the counts of the gradient values, the gradient magnitude histogram can be made as well as the gradient direction histogram. The magnitude histogram is segmented to a n_1 dimensional vector while the direction histogram is segmented to a n_2 dimensional vector. Therefore, every patch becomes a $n_1 + n_2$ dimensional vector. The training set consists of pre-labeled data points (x_i, y_i), where $x_i \in R^{n_1+n_2}$ and $y_i \in \{+1, -1\}$ denotes it is a blurred image or a clear one.

The unknown image I_u, the same as the training data, is converted to one vector x_u by the gradient magnitude histogram and the gradient direction histogram. The vector $x_u \in R^{n_1+n_2}$ will be classified by SVM and the output is one probability value $0 \leq p_u \leq 1$. If p_u is higher, relatively, the chance I_u belongs to a blurred image is higher.

4   Blur Discrimination for Local and Global Blur

In order to distinguish the locally blurred images with the globally blurred images, we segment the image into many grids and apply the blur estimation on each grid. A decision map is made to show where the blurred region is. The estimation does not need to be very precise since we just want to find locally or globally blurred image. Sometimes the monochrome scene with low gradients such as sky or wall might be treated as a blur region by the method described in the previous section. Thus, the monochrome identification is needed to eliminate the fake blur. Both monochrome region and blurred region have small gradient value, however, the difference between them is the color variance. By checking the variance with a threshold, we can verify if the region is blur or monochrome. After counting the number of blurred grids and non-blurred grids, the globally blurred image and locally blurred image can be discriminated.

5   Classification of Globally Blurred Images

5.1   Point Spread Function

Given a globally blurred image, it is possibly caused by either camera shake or out of focus. For a given blurred image B, the blurring effect can be modeled as $B = K \otimes L + N$, where $\otimes$ denotes the discrete image convolution and L is the latent image convoluted by a blur kernel K with sensor noise N. The blur kernel K is a PSF, which is the key to distinguish the camera shake and out of focus, since they have significant difference. The PSF of a camera shake image has line structures and the blurred direction matches the PSF direction, but the PSF of an out of focus image is flat and dispersed, which means every pixel is polluted by nearby pixels. A common problem is that the blur kernel $K(x, y)$ is often unknown, or only partially known. In this case, the unknown K has to be estimated from the blurred image B.

5.2   PSF Estimation

Many PSF estimation algorithms have been proposed, and in this paper we follow the work of Fergus et al. [1]. The advantage of their algorithm is that only one image required. The approximation of the posterior distribution can be expressed by Bayes' Rule, and the variational algorithm minimizes a cost function that can represent the distance between the approximation and the true posterior. The parameters of the distributions are updated alternately by coordinate descent. The updates are repeated until the change converges. The mean of the distribution is then taken as the final value of the PSF.

5.3 PSF Classification

The PSF classification is rather similar to the blur estimation. The training images consist of half camera shake blurred images and half out of focus blurred ones. Every image is estimated to find the $n \times n$ blur kernel K, and the kernel is the feature of SVM classification. The kernel of every image is then transmuted, row by row, to a n^2 dimensional vector, and the model is built from these vectors. The predicting data, the same as training data, is converted to a vector from the estimated blur kernel, and then predicted to camera shake or out of focus by SVM.

6 Classification of Locally Blurred Images

If an image has some blurred regions and some clear regions at the same time, it is considered as a locally blurred image. There are two possible occasions that locally blurred region occurs: moving object and depth of field. To discriminate the two kinds of locally blurred images, we have to segment the foreground object from the background first. Image segmentation is a historical problem and there are many algorithms in this area. Pedro *et al.* [6] proposed an algorithm using a graph-based representation of the image and applied it to image segmentation. Their method is fast in practice and can preserve the details in low-variability regions while ignoring the details in high-variability regions.

Our goal is to find where the blurred region exactly is. For this reason, we apply the blur estimation on each region after the image segmentation to find the blur extent of each region. The fake blur problem arises here that the following two reasons may cause misclassification: 1. if the region is too mall; 2. if the region is monochrome. The fake blur can be judged by the neighboring pixels. If there is a region in the image with fake blur and its blur extent is unknown, we examine all pixels around the region to find the most frequent value and assign the value to the region.

In order to distinguish the moving object and depth of field, we apply the PSF estimation as described in the previous section. The estimated patch, however, is not decided only by the gradient. Since there are still some clear regions in the image, the PSF estimation should not be performed on the clear regions. We find the patch P that can maximize the blur probability. The PSF classification on the patch can decide if the blurred patch is caused by motion or camera focus. If the blur is from motion, we can conclude that the image has moving object. If the blur is from camera focus, relatively, we can conclude that the image has depth of field.

7   Results

7.1   Blur Extent Estimation

From 200 blurred images and 200 clear images, half of the images are randomly chosen as the training data, and the remaining images are the predicting data. The gradient magnitude histogram is segmented to a 360 dimensional vector as well as the direction histogram. It turns out that the accuracy is 99.5% since only one image is wrong for 100 blurred images and 100 clear images. Fig. 3 shows some images and their blur extent values.

(a) Blur extent value = 0.889063

(b) Blur extent value = 0.879511

(c) Blur extent value = 0.007651

(d) Blur extent value = 0.043577

Fig. 3. Different images and their blur extent values

7.2   Blur Discrimination for Local and Global Blur

For those images with blur extent larger than 0.5, we segment the image into many grids to check if the blur is globally or locally. The width and the height of the grid may affect the prediction result: if the grids are too large, the prediction will not be accurate; if the grids are too small, there will be a multitude of fake blurred regions. The width and height of the grid is set to 10% of the image. If the prediction value of the grid is larger than 0.5, it is a blurred region. The non-blurred region, vice versa, are the grids with value less than 0.5. The variance of monochrome identification is heuristically set to 30. It turns out a decision map that can tell where the blurred region is. Every image is segmented to k regions including k_1 blurred regions, k_2 non-blurred regions, and k_3 fake blurred regions in the decision map. If $k_1/(k_1 + k_2) \geq 0.7$, then the image is a globally blurred image, otherwise it is a locally blurred image. Fig. 4 shows the grid structure and

Fig. 4. Blur region detection

the visualization of the prediction result. The image is considered as a locally blurred image because there exist both blurred regions and non-blurred regions.

7.3   Classification of Globally Blurred Images

From 80 camera shake blurred images and 80 out of focus image, half of the images are randomly chosen as the training data. We rescale all images to no more than 800x600 because the blur kernel size is related to the image size. Assuming the camera shake is not huge, we set the kernel size to 49x49. Every image is then given a probability value p, $0 \leq p \leq 1$ denotes the chance to be an out of focus image or a camera shake image. If p is higher, relatively, the chance of the image to belongs to an out of focus image is higher. The prediction on the 40 camera shake images and 40 out of focus image results 4 wrong prediction which means the accuracy is 95%. Fig. 5 shows the prediction on different globally blurred images and the estimated PSFs.

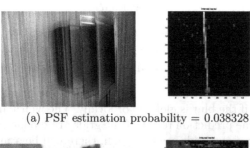

(a) PSF estimation probability = 0.038328

(b) PSF estimation probability = 0.842785

Fig. 5. The classification of globally blurred images

7.4   Classification of Locally Blurred Images

The accuracy of the classification of the locally blurred images is about 70% when predicting 40 depth of field and 40 moving object images. Fig. 6 shows the visualized result after segmentation, the blur estimation on each region with fake blur, and the final probability map.

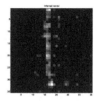

(a) Original image   (b) Blur extent estimation result   (c) Estimated PSF on the blurred region

Fig. 6. Locally blur detection

8   Conclusions and Future Work

In this paper, we propose a framework to estimate the blur extent of an image and classify different types of blurred images. Blur extent estimation is performed on every input image, and those blurry image are chosen. The grid search is then applied to distinguish between locally blurred images and globally blurred ones. For the globally blurred image, we estimate its PSF and it can be classified into camera shake or out of focus. For the locally blurred image, we find the blurred regions using a segmentation method, and the PSF estimation on its blurred region can sort out the image with depth of field or moving object. The advantage of our framework is that the processes are automatic, so that the users can easily find the images they want by these hints.

The method proposed in [2] requires several rules and steps to calculate the blur extent of an image. Relatively, our method for blur extent estimation is highly accurate and not heuristic because the classification error is minimized automatically via SVM. Furthermore, our method can verify the images from different types of blur which is not proposed in other previous methods. The idea is new and has the potential for further researches.

Acknowledgments

This paper was partially supported by the National Science Council of Taiwan under NSC95-2622-E-002-018 and also by the Excellent Research Projects of the National Taiwan University under NTU95R0062-AE00-02.

References

1. Fergus, R., Singh, B., Hertzmann, A., Roweis, S.T., Freeman, W.T.: Removing camera shake from a single photograph. ACM Transactions on Graphics 25, 787–794 (2006) (SIGGRAPH 2006 Conference Proceedings)
2. Tong, H., Li, M., Zhang, H., Zhang, C.: Blur detection for digital images using wavelet transform. In: Proceedings of IEEE 2004 International Conference on Multimedia and Expo, pp. 17–20 (2004)
3. Elder, J.H., Zucker, S.W.: Local scale control for edge detection and blur estimation. In: Buxton, B.F., Cipolla, R. (eds.) ECCV 1996. LNCS, vol. 1065, pp. 57–69. Springer, Heidelberg (1996)
4. Ben-Ezra, M., Nayar, S.K.: Motion-based motion deblurring. IEEE Transactions on Pattern Analysis and Machine Intelligence 26(6), 689–698 (2004)
5. Rooms, F., Philips, W., Portilla, J.: Parametric PSF estimation via sparseness maximization in the wavelet domain. In: Proceedings of SPIE Wavelet Applications in Industrial Processing II, pp. 26–33 (2004)
6. Felzenszwalb, P.F., Huttenlocher, D.P.: Efficient graph-based image segmentation. International Journal on Computer Vision 59(2), 167–181 (2004)
7. Boser, B.E., Guyon, I.M., Vapnik, V.N.: A training algorithm for optimal margin classifiers. In: Proceedings of 1992 Workshop on Computational Learning Theory, pp. 144–152 (1992)
8. Cortes, C., Vapnik, V.: Support-vector networks. Machine Learning 20(3), 273–297 (1995)
9. Platt, J.: Probabilistic outputs for support vector machines and comparison to regularize likelihood methods. In: Smola, A., Bartlett, P., Schoelkopf, B., Schuurmans, D. (eds.) Advances in Large Margin Classifiers, pp. 61–74 (2000)
10. Chang, C.C., Lin, C.J.: LIBSVM: a library for support vector machines (2001)
11. Raskar, R., Agrawal, A., Tumblin, J.: Coded exposure photography: motion deblurring using fluttered shutter. ACM Transactions on Graphics 25, 795–804 (2006) (SIGGRAPH 2006 Conference Proceedings)
12. Miskin, J., MacKay, D.J.: Ensemble learning for blind image separation and deconvolution. In: Advances in Independent Component Analysis (2000)
13. Reeves, S.J., Mersereau, R.M.: Blur identification by the method of generalized cross-validation. IEEE Transactions on Image Processing 1(3), 301–311 (1992)

Cross-Lingual Retrieval of Identical News Events by Near-Duplicate Video Segment Detection

Akira Ogawa[1], Tomokazu Takahashi[1], Ichiro Ide[1,2], and Hiroshi Murase[1]

[1] Graduate School of Information Science, Nagoya University,
Furo-cho, Chikusa-ku, Nagoya, 464–8601, Japan
{aogawa,ttakahashi,ide,murase}@murase.m.is.nagoya-u.ac.jp
http://www.murase.m.is.nagoya-u.ac.jp/
[2] National Institute of Informatics,
2–1–2, Hitotsubashi, Chiyoda–ku, Tokyo, 101–8430, Japan
ide@nii.ac.jp

Abstract. Recently, for reusing large quantities of accumulated news video, technology for news topic searching and tracking has become necessary. Moreover, since we need to understand a certain topic from various viewpoints, we focus on identical event detection in various news programs from different countries. Currently, text information is generally used to retrieve news video. However, cross-lingual retrieval is complicated by machine translation performance and different viewpoints and cultures. In this paper, we propose a cross-lingual retrieval method for detecting identical news events that exploits image information together with text information. In an experiment, we verified the effectiveness of making use of the existence of near-duplicate video segments and the possibility of improving retrieval performance.

1 Introduction

1.1 Background

Recently, the importance of archiving news videos has increased, and its utility value as a social property has also been focused on. Therefore, for reusing large quantities of accumulated news video, technology for news topic searching and tracking is necessary. When news programs from all over the world become available, understanding a certain topic from various viewpoints increases. So, we focus on identical news event detection in various news programs from different countries.

Currently, the retrieval of news videos is generally performed using only the text information in a similar way to the retrieval of newspaper stories [1,2]. The retrieval of news video in the same language can be achieved rather easily and with high performance. However, news video broadcasts not only exist domestically but also in other countries as information resources. Utilizing such video resources effectively is our aim. When existing methods, which exploit text information, retrieve video resources in other languages, performance falls due

S. Satoh, F. Nack, and M. Etoh (Eds.): MMM 2008, LNCS 4903, pp. 287–296, 2008.
© Springer-Verlag Berlin Heidelberg 2008

to low machine translation performance and the necessity for advanced natural language understanding for handling different viewpoints and cultures. Besides, since transcript text called *closed-caption* (CC) does not always accompany every news video, outputs from automatic speech recognition may have to be used, which further complicates the task. In this paper, we circumvent such difficulty in cross-lingual retrieval for detecting identical news events by image information in news video together with text information.

When reporting a certain news event over a long period of time, news programs tend to repeat the same footage. Moreover, video sources of events in other countries are frequently provided by local broadcasters to distribute and broadcast throughout the world. From these properties, when identical video footage is contained in different news videos, a certain relation should exist between them; perhaps they are identical events.

From the above assumption, we detect identical news events by detecting near-duplicate video segments from news video broadcasts in two or more countries in different languages.

1.2 Definition of Terminology

Before describing the details of the process, we must define the terminology of news videos. News video is composed of images and audio, and sometimes closed-caption text. It is structured as follows:

- **Frame:** A still image, which is the minimal unit of a video stream.
- **Shot:** A sequence of frames that are continuous when seen as an image.
- **Cut:** A boundary between shots.
- **Story:** A semantic unit, which contains one event in a news video.
- **Event:** A real-world phenomenon, which occurred at a certain place and time.

2   Related Works

Many works relevant to the retrieval and tracking of news video using text information have been reported, including bidirectional retrieval by matching TV news videos and newspaper articles [1], topic segmentation, and tracking and thread extraction [3]. However, most use text information from the same language. When extending these methods to consider cross-lingual retrieval between news texts of two or more languages, performance generally falls due to low machine translation and speech recognition performances as well as different viewpoints or cultures. The problem of declining retrieval performance cannot be solved easily.

In our work, we retrieve news video using the existence of near-duplicate video segments together with text information. In this case, the detection of identical video segments in different video sources is important. Regarding this technology, some methods exist, including time-series active search [4], which finds identical video segments from a long video stream. In addition, some methods detect

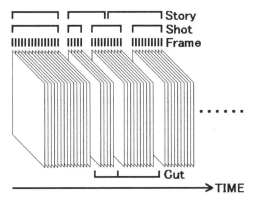

Fig. 1. Composition of broadcast news video

arbitrary pairs of identical video segments using the features of short video fragments, such as a method for the fast retrieval of identical video segments by feature dimension compression using *Principal Component Analysis* (PCA) [5].

3   Retrieval of Identical News Events by Near-Duplicate Video Segment Detection

An overview of the retrieval process of identical news events by near-duplicate video segment detection is shown in Fig. 2. In this experiment, since the input videos are two news programs in different languages, each channel is expressed as C1 and C2, and each language is expressed as L1 and L2, respectively.

3.1   Preparation

As preparation for the detection of identical news events, each news video is segmented into stories. Identical events are detected in each story. As story segmentation in news video, various methods have been proposed, such as those that utilize the appearance of anchor-person shots and others that apply NLP methods to CC text [3,10]. Because we can exploit such segmentation methods, in this paper we assume that stories have already been extracted. In case CC text is not available, output of automatic speech recognition or existing story segmentation methods that refers to the existence of anchor-shots may be used.

3.2   Extraction of Matching Region

As the first part of the main processing, the matching region, the region in each frame used when matching between videos, is extracted. Here telops and logos are often inserted by each news program. Therefore, they may be judged as different video segments despite using the same source video. Setting the threshold to a low degree of similarity is one method for avoiding this. But such a strategy

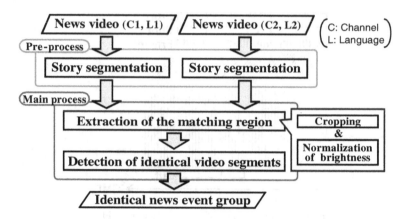

Fig. 2. Retrieval flow of identical news events using image information

increases the number of false detections. So in our work, since telops and logos are usually not inserted in the center of each frame, the central region of each frame is clipped as the matching region.

However, the problem of matching news video is not limited to such video editing. There is also a problem regarding the color differences of video between broadcast stations. In our work, since RGB pixel values are used as features, we cope with this critical problem by normalizing the brightness by histogram equalization [6] in the whole frame. In the following experiment, normalization is performed by changing the RGB value into a YUV value and then performing histogram equalization on Y, which is the brightness value, and returning it to an RGB value. In the following process, the RGB color features are those after the normalization.

3.3   Detection of Identical Video Segments

The brute force frame-by-frame comparison method can be considered the simplest method of detecting arbitrary pairs of identical video segments between videos. However, with this method the computation time increases drastically in proportion to the length of videos. So, we use the fast identical segment detection method proposed in [5] that compresses feature dimensions using PCA. Its basic idea is to detect identical video segments as quickly and accurately as possible by 1) comparing the features of short video fragments instead of a frame, and by 2) compressing the dimension of feature vectors. The first approach makes the comparison efficient and at the same time robust to noise. Meanwhile, the second approach reduces computation time together with i/o time and storage space, which is a significant problem when processing a long video stream. As the feature vector, all the RGB values of pixels from a group of consecutive frames are extracted from a video stream and compressed spatiotemporally by PCA. Secondly, the candidates of identical video segments are detected by comparisons using compressed spatiotemporal feature vectors for every video segment.

Fig. 3. Extraction of matching region (Top: original frame images, Bottom: extracted region for matching)

Identical video segments are correctly detected from video segments obtained as candidates by comparison in the original (high-dimension) feature space.

4   Experiment

Following the process introduced in Section 3, we conducted an experiment that compared the detection results using only text information with the results using image information together with text information and verified the effectiveness of making use of the existence of near-duplicate video segments and the possibility of improving the retrieval performance.

4.1   Data Set

The experiment used news videos broadcast in Japan (NHK: News7) and in the U.S. (CNN: NewsNight Aaron Brown) in November 2004. The U.S. news video was provided by TrecVid2005 [7], and the corresponding CC texts were obtained from CNN's web page[1]. One Japanese news video (News7: half-hour) and two English news videos (NewsNight: one hour each) within a ±24-hour time range were treated as one group, where matching processing is performed

---

[1] http://transcripts.cnn.com/TRANSCRIPTS/asb.html

within the group to cover the time differences between the two countries and the time of the news transfer. In verification of this experiment, the accuracy of the identical news event pair detected by near-duplicate video segment detection is judged manually from the contents of actual video and text data. In the following experiment, the result of four such groups is shown.

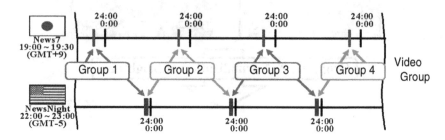

Fig. 4. Relation of broadcast time between a Japanese and U.S. news program

Table 1. Broadcast time of video data in each video group (All data are from November 2004)

	NHK News7	CNN NewsNight (previous)	CNN NewsNight (after)
Group 1	9th 19 : 00 - 19 : 30	8th 22 : 00 - 23 : 00	9th 22 : 00 - 23 : 00
Group 2	10th 19 : 00 - 19 : 30	9th 22 : 00 - 23 : 00	10th 22 : 00 - 23 : 00
Group 3	11th 19 : 00 - 19 : 30	10th 22 : 00 - 23 : 00	11th 22 : 00 - 23 : 00
Group 4	12th 19 : 00 - 19 : 30	11th 22 : 00 - 23 : 00	12th 22 : 00 - 23 : 00

4.2   Experimental Procedure

In the experiment, the detection of identical news events only using image information was performed based on the procedure shown in Fig. 2 to evaluate the detection performance by near-duplicate video segment detection. For story segmentation of the Japanese news video, since CC texts exist, the method proposed by Ide et al. [3] was used, which is based on the similarity of keyword vectors between CC sentences. On the other hand, for story segmentation of the English news, participant shared data of TRECVid2005 were used. For identical video segment detection, parameters were set to detect segments longer than four seconds. Furthermore, to reduce false detection, we precisely matched the candidates from low-dimension matching using color correlograms [9]. As a result, event pairs in which identical video segments exist are detected as identical events. However, because short segments in headlines cause false detections, they were ignored in the evaluation.

Second, we detected identical news events using only text information. This experiment compared detection results using image and text information and using only text information. CC texts of each video were used as text information. Identical news events were detected from them based on the following process. In addition, English text was translated automatically by commercial MT software[2].

Step 1. Story segmentation was performed as in the experiment using image information (See Sect. 3.1).

Step 2. The character strings that serve as keywords were extracted from the CC text of each event by morphological analysis (JUMAN 5.1 [8] was used).
- The following two kinds of character strings were extracted as keywords.
  - Nouns: "personal pronoun" and "formal noun" were ignored, "prefix" and "postfix" in front and behind of words were combined, and the combined noun sequence was regarded as a keyword.
  - Undefined words

Step 3. After extracting *keywords*, the inner product of the frequency-of-appearance vectors was computed among all stories.
- Only a keyword that appears twice or more is matched.
- Only when an inner product is larger than a threshold, the story pair is detected as stories discussing an identical news event.

4.3   Results

The following are the experiment results. The number of identical news events detected with only image information, only text information, and image information together with text information is shown in Table 2, where "Total" denotes the number of detected news events, "Correct" denotes the number of detected identical news events, "Groundtruth" denotes the manually provided answers by us, "Recall" denotes the ratio of "Correct" to "Groundtruth," and "Precision" denotes the ratio of "Correct" to "Total." Similarity by image information in addition to text information is defined as

$$R_{fusion}(S_i, S_j) = \alpha R_{text}(S_i, S_j) + (1 - \alpha) R_{image}(S_i, S_j), \tag{1}$$

where $R_{text}(S_i, S_j)$ and $R_{image}(S_i, S_j)$ are the similarities between stories S_i and S_j by text and image information respectively and α is a constant to balance the importance of their similarities. In this paper, $R_{text}(S_i, S_j)$ is defined as the inner product of keyword frequency vectors between stories S_i and S_j, and $R_{image}(S_i, S_j)$ is defined as

$$R_{image}(S_i, S_j) = \frac{1}{2} \left(\frac{M_{ij}}{L(S_i)} + \frac{M_{ji}}{L(S_j)} \right), \tag{2}$$

where $L(S_i)$ and $L(S_j)$ are the time length of stories S_i and S_j, respectively, M_{ij} is the total time length of identical video segments in S_i that also appear in S_j, and M_{ji} is the total time length of identical video segments in S_j that also appear in S_i. Moreover, the simplest way to select constant α is to let $\alpha = 0.5$. From this result, we can see that four identical news events that couldnft be detected by text information were detected by near-duplicate video segment detection, and recall became 94% using both types of information. So we conclude that

---

[2] The Translation Professional V10 [TOSHIBA].

Table 2. Detection results of identical news events

	Total	Correct	Groundtruth	Recall	Precision
Image only	11	9	18	50%	82%
Text only	35	14	18	78%	40%
Image and text	20	17	18	94%	85%

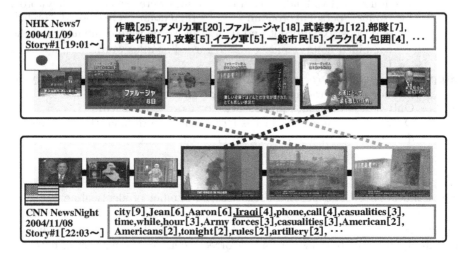

Fig. 5. Example of detected identical news events

the proposed method makes it possible to obtain better retrieval performance by using image information together with text information.

4.4 Discussion

First, we consider the detection accuracy of identical news events by image information. The precision of detection by near-duplicate video segment detection was 82% and the recall was 50%. Considering recall, since identical video segments are not always included in identical news events, this result is also sufficient. On the other hand, although precision is 82%, the following two kinds of false detection exist:

- Trailers for upcoming news before commercials
- False detection of identical video segments

Although eliminating the former case is difficult, it is possible to eliminate the latter case by introducing other image features.

We also considered whether the method can be applied to news videos from countries other than Japan and the U.S. After applying the method to other data from TRECVid, some identical news events were detected from Chinese and Lebanese programs base on the existence of near-duplicate video segments.

5   Conclusion

In this paper, we proposed a cross-lingual retrieval method of identical news events that uses image information in addition to text information and verified the effectiveness of making use of the existence of near-duplicate video segments and the possibility of improving retrieval performance. In addition, although text information is used for the story segmentation of the proposed method, it can also be implemented by a method that uses image information. That is, even when text information cannot be used, detecting identical news events is possible only using image information. Moreover, there are near-duplicate detection methods which use the SIFT features to detect near-duplicate video segments taken from slightly different angles or in different sizes [11]. However, since those methods compare still images, there are problems that huge computation time required to compare all the frame pictures in video segments, thus motion features of objects may not be taken into consideration.

Future study includes a more effective way to use image and text information together by investigating the effect of weighting and the combination of image and text information. Moreover, the implementation of an application that can actually be used for retrieval of identical news events should also be considered.

Acknowledgments

Parts of this work were supported by the Grants-In-Aid for Scientific Research from the Ministry of Education, Culture, Sports, Science and Technology. The video data used in the experiment were provided by the US National Institute of Standards and Technology, and the National Institute of Informatics through a joint research project. This work is developed based on the MIST library (*http://mist.suenaga.m.is.nagoya-u.ac.jp/*).

References

1. Watanabe, Y., Okada, Y., Kaneji, K., Sakamoto, Y.: Multimedia database system for TV newscasts and newspapers, Advanced Multimedia Content Processing. In: Nishio, S., Kishino, F. (eds.) AMCP 1998. LNCS, vol. 1554, pp. 208–220. Springer, Heidelberg (1999)
2. Araya, K., Tsunoda, T., Ooishi, T., Nagao, M.: A retrieval method of relevant newspaper articles using word's cooccurrence frequency and location. Trans. of Information Processing Society of Japan 38(4), 855–862 (1997) (in Japanese)
3. Ide, I., Mo, H., Katayama, N., Satoh, S.: Threading news video topics. In: Proc. Fifth ACM SIGMM Intl. Workshop on Multimedia Information Retrieval, pp. 239–246 (November 2003)
4. Kashino, K., Kurozumi, T., Murase, H.: A quick search method for audio and video signals based on histogram pruning. IEEE Trans. Multimedia 5(3), 348–357 (2003)
5. Ide, I., Noda, K., Takahashi, T., Murase, H.: Genre-adaptive near-duplicate video segment detection. In: Proc. 2007 IEEE Int. Conf. on Multimedia and Expo, pp. 484–487 (July 2007)

6. Finlayson, G., Hordley, S., Schaefer, G., Tian, G.Y.: Illuminant and device invariant colour using histogram equalisation. Pattern Recognition 38(2), 179–190 (2005)
7. TREC Video 2005 Evaluation (2005), http://www-nlpir.nist.gov/projects/tv2005/tv2005.html
8. Japanese morphological analysis system JUMAN version 5.1 (September 2005), http://www.kc.t.u-tokyo.ac.jp/nl-resource/juman.html
9. Huang, J., Kumar, S.R., Mitra, M., Zhu, W.-J., Zabih, R.: Image indexing using color correlograms. In: Proc. IEEE Conf. on Computer Vision and Pattern Recognition 1997, pp. 762–768 (1997)
10. Zhai, Y., Yilmaz, A., Shah, M.: Story segmentation in news videos using visual and text cues. In: Leow, W.-K., Lew, M.S., Chua, T.-S., Ma, W.-Y., Chaisorn, L., Bakker, E.M. (eds.) CIVR 2005. LNCS, vol. 3568, pp. 92–102. Springer, Heidelberg (2005)
11. Ngo, C.-W., Zhao, W.-L., Jiang, Y.-G.: Fast tracking of near-duplicate keyframes in broadcast domain with transitivity propagation. In: Proc. ACM 14th Int. Conf. on Multimedia, pp. 845–854 (October 2006)

Web Image Gathering
with a Part-Based Object Recognition Method

Keiji Yanai

Department of Computer Science,
The University of Electro-Communications
1–5–1 Chofugaoka, Chofu-shi, Tokyo, 182–8585 Japan
`yanai@cs.uec.ac.jp`

Abstract. We propose a new Web image gathering system which employs a part-based object recognition method. The novelty of our work is introducing the bag-of-keypoints representation into an Web image gathering task instead of color histogram or segmented regions our previous system used. The bag-of-keypoints representation has been proven that it has the excellent ability to represent image concepts in the context of visual object categorization / recognition in spite of its simplicity. Most of object recognition work assumed that complete training data is available. On the other hand, in the Web image gathering task, since images associated with the given keywords are gathered from the Web fully-automatically, complete training images cannot be available.

In this paper, we combine the HTML-based automatic positive training image selection and the bag-of-keypoints-based image selection with an SVM which is a supervised machine learning method. This combination enables the system to gather many images related to given concepts with high precision fully automatically needing no human intervention. Our main objective is to examine if the bag-of-keypoints model is also effective for the Web image gathering task where training images always include some noise. By the experiments, we show the new system outperforms our previous systems, other systems and Google Image Search greatly.

1 Introduction

The recent explosive growth of the World Wide Web has enabled easy acquisition of a huge number of various kinds of images. Our goal is to build a large scale data set consisting of many highly relevant images for each of thousands of concepts by gathering images from the Web. To realize that, we have proposed several Web image gathering systems so far [8,9,10]. In our previous work [10], we proposed the method with region segmentation and a probabilistic model based on a Gaussian mixture model. The proposed method worked very well for "scene" images such as sunset and mountain, but not for "object" images such as lion and apple. This is because region-based image representation is effective for "scene" images, but not for "object" images. Sometimes region segmentation algorithms fail to separate "object" regions from background regions.

Then, in this paper we present a new system employing a state-of-the-art image representation for visual object categorization / recognition, which is

S. Satoh, F. Nack, and M. Etoh (Eds.): MMM 2008, LNCS 4903, pp. 297–306, 2008.
© Springer-Verlag Berlin Heidelberg 2008

bag-of-keypoints representation [1]. The bag-of-keypoints representation got popular recently in the research community of object recognition. It is proven that it has excellent ability to represent image concepts in the context of visual object categorization/recognition in spite of its simplicity.

The basic idea of the bag-of-keypoints representation is that a set of local image points is sampled by an interest point detector or randomly, and a vector of visual descriptors is evaluated by the Scale Invariant Feature Transform (SIFT) descriptor [5] on each point. The resulting distribution of description vectors is then quantified by vector quantization against a pre-specified codebook, and the quantified distribution vector is used as a characterization of the image. The codebook is generated by the k-means clustering method based on the distribution of SIFT vectors extracted from all the target images in advance. As a classifier to classify images associated with quantified vectors as relevant or irrelevant, we use a Support Vector Machine (SVM) classifier. An SVM is a supervised learning methods, so that we have to prepare training samples. To prepare training images automatically without human intervention, we propose using the HTML-based automatic positive image selection based on simple heuristics on HTML tags.

Most of object recognition work assumes that complete training images are available. On the other hand, since our system selects training images automatically based on HTML analysis, complete training images cannot be available and training data always include some noise.

In this paper, we describe an Web image-gathering system with the HTML-based automatic selection of training samples and the bag-of-keypoints-based image selection employing an SVM as a classifier. Our main objective is to examine if the bag-of-keypoints model is also effective for the Web image gathering task where training images always contains some noise. By the experiments we show the new system outperforms our previous systems and other systems greatly.

Note that the objective of our image gathering is absolutely different from ones of the other Web image search systems including commercial Web image search engines. While their objective is searching for highly relevant but relatively a small number of images, ours is to gather a large number of relevant images to build image concept database. So that we call our system not Web image search system but "Web image gathering system".

The rest of this paper is organized as follows: In Section 2 we overview our system which consists of a collection stage and a selection stage. In Section 3 we describe about the collection stage which employs HTML-based image selection and in Section 4 we explain the detail of the selection stage which performs image-based image selection. In Section 5 we presents the experimental results and evaluations, and in Section 6 we conclude this paper.

2   Overview

The system we propose in this paper gathers images associated with the keywords given by a user fully automatically. Therefore, an input of the system is just keywords, and the output is several hundreds or thousands images associated with the keywords.

Our proposed system consists of two stages, which are a collection stage and a selection stage.

In the collection stage, we carry out an HTML-text-based image selection which is based on the method we proposed before [8,9]. The basic idea on this stage is gathering as many images related to the given keywords as possible from the Web with their surrounding HTML texts, and selecting candidate images which are likely to be associated with the given keywords by surrounding HTML text analysis based on simple heuristics. In addition, initial positive images are selected from all the candidate images for the supervised learning employed in the next stage.

In the selection stage, we perform an image-feature-based image selection using the bag-of-keypoints model [1] as an image representation and an SVM classifier as a classification method. In general, to use supervised machine learning methods like an SVM, we need to prepare training samples. Then, we use initial positive images selected in the previous stage automatically as positive training samples.

3   Collection Stage

In the collection stage, the system obtains URLs using several commercial Web search engines, and by using those URLs, it gathers images from the Web. The algorithm is as follows:

1. A user provides the system with two kinds of query keywords. One is a main keyword that best represents an image, and the other is an optional subsidiary keyword. For a polysemous word, subsidiary keywords can restrict the meaning of the main keyword. For example, when we like to obtain images of "bank" of a river, we should use "river" as a subsidiary keyword in addition to the main keyword "bank".
   B
2. The system sends the main and subsidiary keywords as queries to the commercial Web search engines and obtains the URLs of the HTML documents related to the keywords. To examine as many HTML documents as possible, we use several Web search engines.
3. It fetches the HTML documents indicated by the obtained URLs, no matter whether images are embedded in the HTML documents or not.
4. It analyzes the HTML documents, and extracts the URLs of images embedded in the HTML documents with image-embedding tags ("IMG SRC" and "A HREF"). Documents having no images are ignored. For each of those images, the system calculates a score that represents the relevancy of the relation between the image and the given keywords based on the following simple heuristics:

   Condition 1: Every time one of the following conditions is satisfied, 3 points are added to the score.

- If the image is embedded by the "SRC IMG" tag, the "ALT" field of the "SRC IMG" includes the keywords.
- If the image is linked by the "A HREF" tag directly, the link words between the "A HREF" and the "/A" include the keywords.
- The name of the image file includes the keywords.

Condition 2: Every time one of the following conditions is satisfied, 1 point is added.

- The "TITLE" tag includes the keywords.
- The "H1, ..,H6" tags include the keywords, assuming these tags are located just before the image-embedding one.
- The "TD" tag including the image-embedding tag includes the keywords.
- Ten words just before the image-embedding tag or ten words after it include the keywords.

If the score of an image is higher than 1, the image is classified into a candidate image set. In addition, an image the score of which is higher than 3 is also marked as initial positive images. This evaluation is carried out before fetching image files from the Web actually. For an HTML document having several images, the above evaluation is repeated for each image.

5. The system fetches only image files belonging to a candidate image set.

The condition 1 is strongly restrictive. However, by examining a great many images, this condition can find out highly relevant images which can be used as positive training images. In the experiments, we examined several thousands of image URLs extracted from about 5000 HTML documents for each concept. Since this heuristic is very simple, we can apply this methods for any words including proper nouns such as person's names and place names.

4   Selection Stage

In this section, we describe the detail of the selection stage, especially how to generate feature vectors based on the bag-of-keypoints model [1]. The main idea of the bag-of-keypoints model is representing images as collections of independent local patches, and vector-quantizing them as histogram vectors.

The main steps of the method are as follows:

1. Sample many patches from an image.
2. Generate feature vectors for the sampled patches by the SIFT descriptor [5].
3. Construct a codebook with k-means clustering over extracted feature vectors. A codebook is constructed for each concept independently.
4. Assign all feature vectors to the nearest codeword of the codebook, and convert a set of feature vectors for each image into one k-bin histogram vector regarding assigned codewords. In addition, background images which are prepared as negative training samples in advance are also converted into k-bin histograms based on the same codebook.
5. Train an SVM classifier with all the histogram vectors of initial positive images and background images.

6. Classify all the histogram vectors of candidate images as relevant or irrelevant with applying the trained SVM. Note that a candidate image set includes initial positive images.

4.1   Sampling Image Patches

We use two kinds of strategies to sample patches from images. One is Difference of Gaussian (DoG) which is a multi-scale keypoint detector included in the SIFT method [5]. The other is random sampling [6]. Intuitively, using a keypoint detector seems to be better than random sampling. However, according to [6], random sampling is equivalent to or outperforms using a keypoint detector. The advantage of random sampling is that we can decide the number of sampling patches as we like, while the algorithm of a keypoint detector decides the number of keypoints. In the experiment, about 500-1000 points depending on images are sampled by the DoG keypoint detector, and we sample 3000 points by random sampling.

4.2   SIFT Descriptors

Scale Invariant Feature Transform (SIFT) proposed by D. Lowe [5] provides a multi-scale representation of an image neighborhood in addition to DoG-based keypoint detection. They are Gaussian derivatives computed at 8 orientation planes over a 4 × 4 grid of spatial location, giving 128-dimension vector. The biggest advantage of SIFT descriptor is invariant to Affine transformation including rotation and scale-change. Many researches [1,6] show the SIFT descriptor is the best as representation of image patches for object recognition.

4.3   Generating Codebook and Quantization

We obtain a collection of 128-dimension vectors for each images after the previous two steps. The amount of data to represent a image is still too much. Then, we apply vector quantization for them.

Firstly, we compute a codebook by applying k-means clustering for all or part of extracted SIFT vectors over all the positive training samples and negative training samples. Regarding negative samples we describe about it in the next sub-section. In the experiment, we tried $k = 500$ and $k = 1000$ for 1,000,000 SIFT vectors at most. Secondly, we assign all the SIFT vectors to the nearest codewords. This is the same as nearest neighbor search. To speed up, we used SR-tree indexing [4] in the experiment. Finally, we convert a set of the SIFT vectors for each image into one k-bin histogram of assigned codewords. Each histogram is represented by a k-dimension vector, so we have converted one image into one k-dimension feature vector based on the bag-of-keypoints representation.

4.4   Classifying with an SVM

To classify candidate images as relevant and irrelevant, we use a one-to-one SVM classifier. This classifier needs negative training samples as well as positive training samples. We use all the initial positive images selected in the collection stage as positive training samples. In addition we need to prepare negative images in advance. In the experiment, we collected 1200 images randomly from the Web by supplying random keywords to the Google Image Search and used them as negative training sample. In the same way as positive images, we convert each of them into a k-dimension feature vector based on the bag-of-keypoints representation.

We train an SVM classifier with positive and negative samples. Next, we classify all the vectors of candidate images with the trained SVM. Finally, we can get only images classified as relevant to the given keywords as a result.

In the experiment, we used the SVM-light package created by T. Joachims as SVM implementation. As a kernel, we used radial basis function (RBF).

5   Experimental Results

We made experiments for the following ten concepts independently: sunset, mountain, waterfall, beach, flower, lion, apple, baby, notebook-PC, and Chinese noodle. The first four concepts are "scene" concepts, and the rest are "object" concepts. For only "lion" and "apple", actually we added subsidiary keywords "animal" and "fruit" to restrict its meaning to "lion of animal" and "apple of fruit" in the collection stage, respectively.

In the collection stage, we obtained around 5000 URLs for each concept from several Web search engines including Google Search and Yahoo Web Search. The exact numbers vary depending on concepts, since we excluded duplicate URLs from the URL list for each concept.

Table 1 shows the results of the collection stage including the number of initial positive images and the number of candidate images, and we added to it the subjective evaluation of the top 500 images of Google Image Search and the two previous systems which employ the CBIR-based image selection method [8] and GMM-based probabilistic method [10] for comparison. Both CBIR-based and GMM-based methods selected relevant images from the same candidate images as ones constructed for the experiments of the new method proposed in this paper. In the CBIR-based method, one image are represented as one color histogram simply, and image selection is done by image search for initial positive images. On the other hand, the GMM-based method employs region segmentation, one image are represented as a collection of region features regarding color, texture and shape of regions, and region features are probabilistically modeled by the Gaussian Mixture Model (GMM).

In the table, numerical values in the parentheses represent the precision and the recall. To evaluate the precision and the recall, we randomly selected 500 images from each result and evaluated their relevancy by the human's subjective evaluation by hand. Note that for the results of the collection stage we cannot estimate the recall, since the denominator to compute it corresponds to the number of images associated to the given concept on whole the Web and we do not know it. Regarding the results of Google Image Search, we show the precision of output images ranked between 1 and 500 in the table. The average precision

Table 1. Results of the collection stage and the selection stage by the CBIR-based method [8] and the GMM-based probabilistic method [10]. From the right column, this table describes the precision of the top 500 output images of Google Image Search evaluated by hand for comparison, the number of initial positive images and candidate images selected in the collection stage, the number of output images by the two previous methods. Numerical values in () represent the precision and the recall.

concepts	Goo. prec.	after the collection stage		CBIR-based	GMM-based
		positive	candidates		
sunset	79.8	790 (67)	1500 (55.3)	828 (62.2, 62.1)	**636 (91.0, 70.2)**
mountain	48.8	1950 (88)	5837 (79.2)	3423 (82.6, 61.2)	**3510 (89.0, 65.0)**
waterfall	72.4	2065 (71)	4649 (70.3)	3281 (71.4, 71.7)	**3504 (76.8, 74.6)**
beach	63.2	768 (69)	1923 (65.5)	1128 (67.3, 60.3)	**983 (73.3, 62.5)**
flower	65.6	576 (72)	1994 (69.6)	952 (79.3, 54.4)	**758 (71.9, 41.0)**
lion	44.0	511 (87)	2059 (66.0)	967 (71.0, 50.5)	**711 (69.4, 53.6)**
apple	47.6	1141 (78)	3278 (64.3)	1495 (68.8, 48.8)	**1252 (67.2, 37.7)**
baby	39.4	1833 (56)	3571 (54.5)	1831 (55.1, 51.8)	**1338 (63.9, 45.9)**
notebook PC	60.2	781 (57)	2537 (43.6)	1290 (46.9, 54.6)	**867 (56.0, 47.6)**
Chinese noodle	65.2	901 (78)	2596 (66.6)	1492 (71.0, 61.3)	**1266 (77.0, 53.2)**
TOTAL/AVG.	58.6	11316 (72)	29944 (62.2)	16687 (66.0, 57.7)	**14825 (73.5, 55.1)**

Table 2. Results of the selection stage by the bag-of-keypoints with SVM. This table describes the number of output images in case that point detection is performed by DoG keypoint detector and random sampling, and the codebook size (cb) is 500 and 1000, respectively. Numerical values in () represent the precision and the recall.

	DoG, cb=1000	DoG, cb=500	random, cb=1000	random, cb=500
sunset	**563 (93.3, 62.5)**	546 (92.9, 60.3)	**652 (91.5, 70.9)**	642 (90.9, 69.4)
mountain	**2762 (93.7, 68.7)**	2656 (94.2, 66.5)	**2778 (93.7, 69.1)**	2343 (93.6, 58.3)
waterfall	**3261 (82.3, 82.0)**	3285 (81.9, 82.2)	**3211 (81.4, 79.8)**	3127 (82.6, 78.9)
beach	**701 (86.5, 48.7)**	699 (87.0, 48.9)	**737 (91.0, 53.9)**	733 (91.2, 53.7)
flower	**707 (86.7, 45.0)**	695 (86.1, 43.8)	**711 (87.4, 45.6)**	716 (87.7, 46.1)
lion	**790 (85.5, 56.1)**	754 (85.5, 53.6)	**719 (86.7, 51.8)**	724 (85.3, 51.4)
apple	**970 (85.3, 38.5)**	961 (82.7, 36.9)	**1089 (86.0, 43.6)**	1180 (82.3, 45.1)
baby	**2042 (55.7, 58.4)**	1961 (53.9, 54.3)	**2114 (59.1, 64.2)**	2073 (57.3, 61.0)
notebook PC	**1213 (55.0, 66.3)**	1183 (54.3, 63.8)	**1090 (52.9, 57.3)**	1111 (51.5, 56.9)
Chinese noodle	**1020 (86.9, 54.2)**	996 (84.1, 51.2)	**809 (92.0, 45.5)**	780 (93.2, 44.5)
TOTAL/AVG.	**13297 (81.1, 58.0)**	13000 (80.3, 56.2)	**13153 (82.2, 58.2)**	12872 (81.6, 56.5)

of candidate images, 62.2%, was slightly superior to the average precision of top 500 results of Google images, 58.6%, while we collected about 3000 images a concept. This shows that the simple heuristic method employed in the collection stage can improve the output of Web image search engines.

Table 2 corresponds to the results of the selection stage by the proposed method with the bag-of-keypoints representation and an SVM, which shows the number, the precision and the recall of the outputs. We carried out four combinations of experiments, changing sampling methods of image patches and the size of codebooks: (1) DoG with 1000 codewords, (2) DoG with 500 codewords, (3) random with 1000 codewords and (4) random with 500 codewords. In the experiments, we used the parameter setting so that the recall rates are close to the recall rate by two old methods shown in Table 1 for easy comparison. Note that in the Web image gathering task, the recall rate is less important than the precision rate, since the more Web sites we crawl, the more images we can get easily. So we mainly evaluate the system performance by the precision below.

In case of (1), we obtained the 81.1% precision on the average, which outperformed the 66.0% precision by the CBIR method and the 73.5% precision by the GMM-based probabilistic method. Except "baby" and "notebook PC" (Figure 2), the precision of each concept were also improved. Especially, in case of "flower", "lion" (Figure 3) and "apple", the precision were improved prominently. This shows that the bag-of-keypoints representation and SVM is very effective to classify "object" images, since the bag-of-keypoints representation does not need region segmentation algorithms which sometimes fail to separate "object" regions from background regions for complicated images and cause to fail the GMM-based method.

On the other hand, the precisions of "baby" and "notebook PC" were not good, which were less than the precision by the probabilistic methods. This is because the precision of the initial positive images of these two concepts were relatively low, 56% and 57%, respectively. In short, training data for two concepts contained too many irrelevant samples. That is why the precisions were not improved. To overcome that, we need to prepare better initial positive images or to develop a mechanism to remove irrelevant training samples.

When the size of codebooks is 500 in the case of (2), the precision on the average was slightly degraded, but almost the same, although the dimension of image vectors is half compared to the case of (1).

Surprisingly, random sampling outperformed DoG keypoint detector in terms of the precision on the average in case of both 500 codebooks and 1000 codebooks. The result of (3) was the best among the four experiments. This result is consistent with the fact described in [6] that random sampling is equivalent to or outperforms a keypoint detector as a method to sample image patches.

To compare the results shown in Table 1 and 2, we show a graph in Figure 1. In this graph, "RAW", "CBIR", "GMM", "BOK (DoG)" and "BOK (rand)" means results just after the collection stage, results by the CBIR-based method, results by the GMM-based method, results by the bag-of-keypoints with DoG keypoint detection, and results by the bag-of-keypoints with random sampling, respectively. For both "BOK", the size of the codebook is 1000.

As comparison to other work, the result of (3) also outperforms by far the 54% F-measure by H. Feng et al.[2] for 15 keywords, the 65.9% precision and the 15% recall by P. Fergus et al.[3] for 10 keywords, and the about 50% precision by Y. Sun et al.[7] for 5 keywords, although some keywords used in the experiments are different.

Unfortunately we can show only small parts of the result images due to space limitation. Instead we have prepared the Web site to show the experimental results we provided in this paper. The URL is as follows:
http://mm.cs.uec.ac.jp/yanai/mmm08/

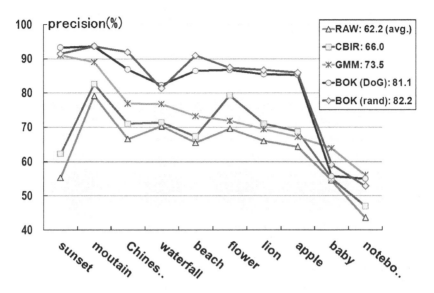

Fig. 1. Comparison of the precision by five methods

Fig. 2. "Notebook PC" images

Fig. 3. "Lion" images

6   Conclusions

In this paper, we described a new system employing the bag-of-keypoints representation [1] which was paid much attention to as a new excellent image representation for visual object categorization / recognition. The HTML-based positive sample selection methods enabled us to use an SVM which is a supervised classifier. In the experiments for ten concept keywords, we obtained the 82.2% precision on the average in case of 1000 codebooks with random sampling, which outperformed the 66.0% precision by the CBIR method and the

73.5% precision by the GMM-based probabilistic method. The experimental results shows that the bag-of-keypoints representation is very effective to classify "object" images as well as "scene" images, although initial training is not perfect and contains much noise. However, in case that the precision of the training data is very low (less than 60%), the proposed method still cannot improve the precision.

As future work, we plan to prepare better initial training images by improving HTML analysis methods and combining query keywords for Web search engines with effective subsidiary keywords, and plan to investigate how to remove irrelevant data in training data or how to learn from imperfect training data.

References

1. Csurka, G., Bray, C., Dance, C., Fan, L.: Visual categorization with bags of keypoints. In: Proc. of ECCV Workshop on Statistical Learning in Computer Vision, pp. 1–22 (2004)
2. Feng, H., Shi, R., Chua, T.: A bootstrapping framework for annotating and retrieving WWW images. In: Proc. of ACM International Conference Multimedia, pp. 960–967 (2004)
3. Fergus, R., Perona, P., Zisserman, A.: A visual category filter for google images. In: Proc. of European Conference on Computer Vision, pp. 242–255 (2004)
4. Katayama, N., Satoh, S.: The SR-tree: An index structure for high-dimensional nearest neighbor queries. In: Proc. of ACM SIGMOD International Conference on Management of Data, pp. 369–380 (1997)
5. Lowe, D.G.: Distinctive image features from scale-invariant keypoints. International Journal of Computer Vision 60(2), 91–110 (2004)
6. Nowak, E., Jurie, F., Triggs, W., Vision, M.: Sampling strategies for bag-of-features image classification. In: Leonardis, A., Bischof, H., Pinz, A. (eds.) ECCV 2006. LNCS, vol. 3954, pp. 490–503. Springer, Heidelberg (2006)
7. Sun, Y., Shimada, S., Morimoto, M.: Visual pattern discovery using Web images. In: Proc. of ACM SIGMM International Workshop on Multimedia Information Retrieval, pp. 127–136 (2006)
8. Yanai, K.: Image collector: An image-gathering system from the World-Wide Web employing keyword-based search engines. In: Proc. of IEEE International Conference on Multimedia and Expo, pp. 704–707 (2001)
9. Yanai, K.: Generic image classification using visual knowledge on the web. In: Proc. of ACM International Conference Multimedia, pp. 67–76 (2003)
10. Yanai, K., Barnard, K.: Probabilistic Web image gathering. In: Proc. of ACM SIGMM International Workshop on Multimedia Information Retrieval, pp. 57–64 (2005)

A Query Language Combining Object Features and Semantic Events for Surveillance Video Retrieval

Thi-Lan Le[1,2], Monique Thonnat[1], Alain Boucher[3], and François Brémond[1]

[1] ORION, INRIA, 2004 route des Lucioles, B.P. 93, 06902 Sophia Antipolis, France
{Lan.Le_Thi,Monique.Thonnat,Francois.Bremond}@sophia.inria.fr
[2] International Research Center MICA Hanoi University of Technology, Viet Nam
[3] Equipe MSI, Institut de la Francophonie pour l'Informatique, Hanoi, Viet Nam
Alain.Boucher@auf.org

Abstract. In this paper, we propose a novel query language for video indexing and retrieval that (1) enables to make queries both at the image level and at the semantic level (2) enables the users to define their own scenarios based on semantic events and (3) retrieves videos with both exact matching and similarity matching. For a query language, four main issues must be addressed: data modeling, query formulation, query parsing and query matching. In this paper we focus and give contributions on data modeling, query formulation and query matching. We are currently using color histograms and SIFT features at the image level and 10 types of events at the semantic level. We have tested the proposed query language for the retrieval of surveillance videos of a metro station. In our experiments the database contains more than 200 indexed physical objects and 48 semantic events. The results using different types of queries are promising.

1 Introduction

Video surveillance is producing huge video databases. While there are many works dedicated to object detection, object tracking and event recognition [7], few works have been done for accessing these databases. For surveillance video indexing and retrieval, apart from object tracking, object classification and event recognition, we have 4 main issues: **data modeling**, **query formulation**, **query parsing** and **query matching**. The **data modeling** determines which features are extracted and how they are organized and stored in the database. The **query formulation** specifies the way in which the user expresses his/her query while the **query parsing** [5] specifies the way in which the system analyzes (parses) this query into an internal representation. The aim of **query matching** is to compare elements stored in the database with the query.

The first works dedicated for the surveillance video indexing and video concentrate on data modeling. In [7], IBM smart surveillance engine successfully detects moving objects, tracks multiple objects, classifies objects and events. However, for retrieving in the database, the queries are done based on only recognized

S. Satoh, F. Nack, and M. Etoh (Eds.): MMM 2008, LNCS 4903, pp. 307–317, 2008.
© Springer-Verlag Berlin Heidelberg 2008

events and metadata. In [6], a data model is built for online video surveillance. Various query types are also presented. In [3], Saykol et al. presented a framework and a visual surveillance querying language (VSQL) for surveillance video retrieval. These previous works have three main drawbacks. Firstly, they work with an assumption that in the indexing phase objects are perfectly tracked and events are perfectly recognized. It is the reason why video retrieving is based on the exact matching of semantic events and metadata. However, object detection and event recognition are not always successful. The video retrieving must work well under imperfect indexing. In this case, the similarity matching on object features is necessary. Secondly, these approaches limit the search space. Because the videos are only indexed by a set of recognized events, the users' queries are restricted to a limited set of predefined events. Thirdly, it is not flexible and does not take into account various users' interests and users' degrees of knowledge. The users could need more or less information according to their interest and could define differently an 'event' in the form of a query in function of their knowledge in this domain.

Our main contributions are designing a video data model and proposing a novel query language. Our data model is different from the model proposed in [6] because it contains object visual features. Our query language overcomes the previous works [7], [6], [3] because it (1) enables users to make queries both at the image level and at the semantic level (2) allows the users to define their own scenarios based on semantic events and (3) retrieves videos with both exact matching and similarity matching.

The rest of this paper is organized as follows: Section 2 describes the proposed approach including data model, query language and query matching. In section 3, we describe some experimental results and their performance evaluation. We conclude this paper in section 4.

2   Proposed Approach

Figure 1 shows the general architecture of the proposed approach. This approach is based on an external **Video Analysis module** and on two internal phases: an **indexing phase** and a **retrieval phase**. The external Video Analysis module performs tasks such as mobile object detection, mobile object tracking and event recognition. The results of this module are some Recognized Video Content. These Recognized Video Content can be physical objects, trajectories, events, scenarios, etc. So far, we are only using physical objects and events but the approach can be extended to other types of Recognized Video Content. The indexing phase takes results from the Video Analysis module as input data. The indexing phase has two main tasks: **feature extraction** and **data indexing**. It performs feature extraction to complete the input data by computing missing features and data indexing using a data model. The retrieval phase is divided into five main tasks: **query formulation**, **query parsing**, **query matching**, **result ranking** and **result browsing**. In the query formulation task, in order to make the users feel familiar with the query language, we propose a SVSQL

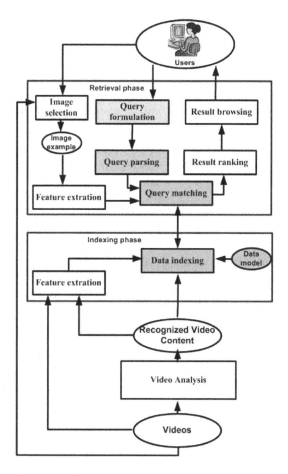

Fig. 1. Global architecture of our approach. This approach is based on an external **Video Analysis module** and on two internal phases: an **indexing phase** and a **retrieval phase**. The indexing phase takes results from the Video Analysis module as input data and performs **feature extraction** and **data indexing** using a **data model**. The retrieval phase takes queries from users (by the **query formulation** task), analyzes and evaluates them (by **query parsing** and **query matching** tasks) using indexed data in the indexing phase. The retrieval results are ranked and returned to the users (by the **result ranking** and the **result browsing** tasks). The focus of this paper concerns the parts in blue.

(Surveillance Video Structured Query Language) language. The vocabulary and the syntax are described in the next section. In the query, the users can select an image example global or a region in an image from the database (by the image selection task). In this case, the feature extraction task computes some features in the image example which are used by the query matching task. In the query parsing task, queries built with the proposed language are transmitted to a parser. This parser checks the vocabulary, analyzes the syntax and separates the query into several parts. The query matching task searches in the database the elements that satisfy the query. The obtained results are ranked and returned to the users.

2.1 Data Model

Our data model contains two main components of interest form the user's point of view: *physical objects* and *events*.

Physical objects: they are the detected objects in the video database. A physical object can be a static object (e.g. contextual object) or a moving object (e.g. a person, a vehicle). Let P be a physical object, P is defined as follows: $P = (Id,$ *[Type], [Name], 2D_positions, 3D_positions, MBRs (Minimum Bounding Box), Features, Time_interval)* where *Id* is the label of the object, the *Type* and *Name* attributes are optional. The *2D_positions, 3D_positions, MBRs* are the sets of 2D positions, 3D positions, MBRs of this object during its lifetime indicated by *Time_interval*. The *Features* currently available in the system are the color histogram and a set of detected keypoints by using SIFT (Scale Invariant Feature Transform) descriptors. These features are computed by the Feature extraction task. We use the SIFT descriptors because the SIFT descriptors are invariant to image scale and rotation and they are shown to provide robust matching across a substantial range of affine distortion change in 3D view point, addition of noise, and change in illumination. Therefore, they help to match efficiently images. However, SIFT descriptors do not focus on color information like the color histogram. The methods for extracting these features can be found in [4] for the color histogram and in [1] for the SIFT descriptors.

Events: They are the recognized events in the video database. Let E be an event, E is defined as follows: $E = (Id, Name, Confidence\_value,$ *Involved_Physical_objects, [Sub_events], Time_interval)*. Where *Id* is the label of the event and *Name* is the name of the event. The *Confidence_value* specifies the confidence degree of recognized event. The work presented in Section 2 does not take into account this information. In our work, the *Confidence_value* is used to compute the final distance between video frames and the query. The *Involved_Physical_objects* specifies which physical objects are involved in this event, while the *Sub_events* are optional, and the *Time_interval* indicates the frames in which the event is recognized.

The advantage of our data model is that it is independent of any application and of any feature extraction, learning and event recognition algorithms. Therefore, we can combine results of different algorithms for feature extraction, learning and event recognition (both descriptive and stochastic approaches) and use it for different application domains.

2.2 Proposed Language and Query Syntax

The syntax of a query expressed by our language is the following:

SELECT < Output > FROM < Database > WHERE < Condition >

Where: **SELECT, FROM, WHERE** are keywords for a query and they are mandatory. A graphic interface can be developed to generate this syntax but it is out of the scope of this paper.

- **Output** specifies the format of the retrieved results. It can have two values: one is *video_frames* indicating that the retrieved results are video frames in which the <Condition> is satisfied and the other is *number_of_events* indicating that the retrieved result is the number of events in the database satisfying the <Condition>.
- **Database** specifies which parts of the video database are used to check the <Condition>. It can be either * for the whole video database or a list of named subparts. This is interesting for surveillance because the video database can be divided into several parts according to time or location. It allows to accelerate the retrieval phase in the case that the users know already which parts of the video database they are interested in.
- **Condition** specifies the conditions that the retrieved results must satisfy. The users express their requirements by defining this component. The condition may have more than one expression connected together by logic operators (AND, OR, NOT), each expression is started by "(" and ended by ")". This component is the most important component in the language.

There are two types of expression in the condition component: a declaration expression (α_d) which is mandatory and a constraint expression (α_r) which provides additional conditions. The declaration expression indicates the types of variable while the constraint expression specifies constraints the variable must satisfy.

The syntax for a declaration expression is: ($v : type$) where v is a variable. It is the place where the user specifies if the retrieval is at the image level, the semantic level or both levels. The authorized types are : *Physical_object* and its subtypes (*Person, Group, Luggage*) and *Event*. In image and video retrieval applications, users usually want to retrieve indexed data that is similar to an example they have. Therefore, besides Physical objects and Events, we add another type SubImage. SubImage has Features attribute like the Physical objects. In query, (v : SubImage) means that v will be set by users image example.

The syntax for a constraint expression is very rich. The constraint expression can be expressed by using a set of projections, functions, predicates, algebra operators and constants. Currently, the authorized projections are { *'s Id, 's Type, 's Name, 's 2D_positions, 's 3D_positions, 's MBRs, 's Features, 's Time_interval*} for physical object and { *'s Id, 's Name, 's Confidence_value, 's Involved_Physical_objects, 's Sub_events, 's Time_interval*} for event; there are two authorized functions which are *histogram_distance* that returns the distance between color histograms and *number_matched_keypoint* that returns the number of matched keypoints between an example image and an indexed object; there are four authorized predicates which are *color_similarity* and *keypoints_matching* that return true if an image example and an indexed object are similar in term of color histogram or keypoints, *involved_in* which verifies whether one indexed object belongs to an event and *before* which verifies whether an event occurs before another event; the authorized algebra operators are =, <, >, >=, =<, ! =}; the constants can be either numbers or strings.

This language is rich enough to express numerous possible queries. Based on the technique proposed in [5], we implement a parser to check automatically the syntax of each query. This parser automatically analyzes the syntax of the query. The results of this parsing allow to locate which databases will be used to match query, which variables must be set and which results must be returned.

An example expressed by this language at the semantic level is: Find Close_to_Gates events occurring in videos of all databases.

*SELECT video_frames FROM * WHERE ((e: Events) AND (e's Name = "Close_to_Gates"))*

where e is a variable of Events, $e's\ Name$ gets Name of e.

Another example expressed by this language at the image level is: Find indexed persons in the database named Video_Database that are similar to a given image.

SELECT video_frames FROM Video_Database WHERE ((p: Person) AND (i: SubImage) AND (i color_similarity p))

where p is a variable of Person, i is a variable that will be set by an image example, *color_similarity* is predicate that decide whether two images are similar (in color).

2.3   Query Matching

For each expression α in the condition field, the evaluation of the expression α is performed by matching the indexed database D and the expression α. The results of this process are a set of physical objects and events extracted from D that satisfy α. Let $\eta_i = \{\varsigma_i, \mu_i, I_i\}$ be the ith result instance of the expression α and η be the set of the result instances of α where ς_i are the physical objects or the events, μ_i is the similarity degree that determines how much ς_i satisfy α in a time interval I_i. Currently, we have defined the similarity degree for the predicates based on the feature similarity (e.g. nearest neighbors for SIFT descriptors and histogram intersection for color histograms). With the other types the default value of the similarity degree is set to 1.

If the query has more than one expression in the condition, the similarity degrees are computed according to the operator linking these expressions as follows: $\mu = min(\mu_j, \mu_k)$, $\mu = max(\mu_j, \mu_k)$, $\mu = (1 - \mu_k)$ for AND, OR, NOT operators where μ_j, μ_k are the similarity degrees of the expressions α_j, α_k respectively.

3   Implementation and Experimental Results

3.1   Video Event Database

In order to validate our approach, we have used two videos of 10 minutes and 2 hours acquired by two fixed cameras at different positions that record human activities in a metro station. An example of two scenes in two videos is shown in

Fig.2. The scene contains a platform and several gates. The Video Analysis such as automatic object tracking, object classification and event recognition proposed in [5] have been automatically applied to these videos. As results, we have 221 indexed physical objects (101 for the first video and 120 for the second one) with their labels, 3D positions, 2D positions, MBRs and time intervals. The 120 physical objects in the second video are classified as 29 persons, 27 groups, 16 crowds, 25 luggages et 23 unknowns. One physical object is perfectly tracked and recognized if in all frames in which this object appears, this object is detected and has one sole label. In addition, 10 event types have been defined and recognized for each frame (inside Platform, close to Gates i (i from 1 to 9)) for the second video. These events are defined in the language proposed in [5] as follows:

*Event(**close_to**,*
PhysicalObjects((p : Person), (eq : Equipment))
Constraints((p distance eq $\leq$ Close_Distance))
    where eq is Gate i (i from 1 to 9), Close_Distance is a threshold.
*Event(**inside_zone**,*
PhysicalObjects((p : Person), (z : Zone))
Constraints((p in z))

where z is a Platform, *in* is a predicate that checks whether p's center belongs to the polygon z.

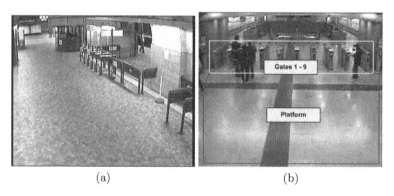

(a)   (b)

Fig. 2. Two scenes describe human activities in some metro stations(a) in the first video. (b) in the second video.

3.2 Experimental Results and Performance Evaluation

In order to evaluate the retrieval performance, we use the average normalized rank proposed in [2]. We do not use the measures of true positives, true negatives, false positives and false negatives like in classification problem because for the retrieval problem, the retrieval algorithm is good if it return relevant results first.

$$\widetilde{Rank} = \frac{1}{NN_{rel}} \left(\sum_{i=1}^{N_{rel}} (R_i) - \frac{N_{rel}(N_{rel} + 1)}{2} \right) \tag{1}$$

where N_{rel} is the number of relevant result for a particular query, N is the size of the tested set, and R_i is the rank of the ith relevant result. $\widetilde{Rank}$ is zero if all N_{rel} are returned first. The $\widetilde{Rank}$ measure lies in the range 0 (good retrieval) to 1 (bad retrieval), with 0.5 corresponding to a random retrieval.

Experiment 1: The goal of this experiment is to check whether our proposed language enables users to retrieve effectively persons in the database even though they are not successfully detected and tracked. For this experiment, the query is: Find in the second video the video frames having persons that are similar (in term of keypoint matching) to the person in this example image. This query is expressed as follows:

SELECT video_frames FROM Video2 WHERE ((i: SubImage) AND (o: Person) AND (i keypoints_matching o))

where keypoints_matching is a predefined predicate of our language, i is an example image.

Figure 3.a shows the average normalized rank for this experiment. There are 120 indexed persons in the second video. The retrieval performance is measured over all 120 images using each in turn as a query. Each image query has from 3 to 5 relevant images. The small obtained average normalized ranks (the maximum value being 0.3183) show that the proposed approach retrieve successfully the indexed objects even when they are imperfectly indexed.

Experiment 2: This experiment aims at pointing out the advantage of our language. It allows to retrieve interesting events with a detailed description. For instance, the event *close_to_Gate1*(p) indicates that person p is close to the Gate 1. In the case of many *close_to_Gate1* recognized instances, the user may be interested in only *close_to_Gate1* frames containing a person that is similar to a given example. The user can ask a query as follows:

SELECT video_frames FROM Video2 WHERE ((i: SubImage) AND (o: Person) AND (e: Event) AND (e's Name = close_to_Gate1) AND (o involved_in e) AND (i keypoints_matching o))

where i is an image example, 's Name is a predefined projection of event's name, *involved_in* is a predefined predicate that determines whether one person is involved in an event and *keypoints_matching* is a predefined predicate described in section 2.

To answer this query, the persons involved in all *close_to_Gate1* events are used for *keypoints_matching* with the given example. The returned results for each query is a list of *close_to_Gate1* events ranked by the number of matched keypoints between the involved persons and the given example. Among 19 *close_to_Gate1* events of the second video, there are several events concerning one sole person. We have 15 distinct persons concerned to these 19 events. For each person, we have chosen one image example. Totally, we have 15 example images. Each image turns as input for the query. Figure 3.b gives the obtained average normalized rank over 15 image examples and 19 events of *close_to_Gate1* in the second video. The ground truth is made by hand for these 15 queries. A returned result is considered relevant if it is a *close_to_Gate1* event whose the involved persons show the same person as in the given image example.

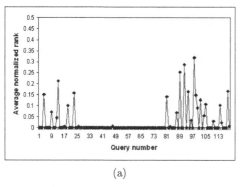
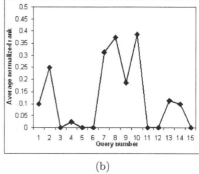

(a)   (b)

Fig. 3. (a) The average normalized rank for experiment 1 over 120 queries. (b) The average normalized rank for experiment 2 over 15 queries. The value 0 of average normalized ranks corresponds to good retrieval, value 1 corresponds to bad retrieval and 0.5 corresponds to random retrieval.

Experiment 3: The objective of this experiment is to measure the capacity of this language to define and retrieve new events from the recognized ones. From two recognized events in the database: inside_zone_Platform and close_to_Gate1, the user may write a query such as: Find the frames in which one person is going from the Platform to Gate1.

This query is expressed as follows:

SELECT video_frames FROM Video2 WHERE ((o_1: Person) AND (e_1: Event) AND (e_2: Event) AND (o_1 involved_in e_1) AND (o_1 involved_in e_2) AND (e_1's Name = inside_zone_Platform) AND (e_2's Name = close_to_Gate1) AND (e_1 before e_2))

This query is automatically analyzed by the parser presented in the section 2.

Because of imperfect indexing, one person in the real world may be indexed as different persons within the database. Thanks to similarity matching returned results must consider all *inside_zone_Platform* and *close_to_Gate1* events containing indexed persons that are similar (an exact matching that matches the indexed persons by their labels would have returned for this query incomplete results and sometimes empty ones as shown in Figure 4.a). With our technique to answer this query, the system first matches the involved persons in both *inside_zone_Platform* and *close_to_Gate1* by keypoint matching. For each person involved in *close_to_Gate1* event, it computes the number of matched keypoints between this person and the persons involved in the *inside_zone_Platform* event. A set of persons ordered by their matched keypoints are returned. The *inside_zone_Platform* events containing these persons become candidate for retrieval results. Then, these events are used to check whether they satisfy the *before* constraint with the *close_to_Gate1* events. The *before* constraint performs based on the starting frames and the ending frames of *inside_zone_Platform* and *close_to_Gate1* events.

For each *close_to_Gate1* event, the retrieval result is a list of *inside_zone_Platform* events that satisfy the *before* constraint with *close_to_Gate1* event and that are ranked by the number of matched keypoint between their involved persons and the person involved in *close_to_Gate1* event. The returned result is considered relevant if it contains an *inside_zone_Platform* event that satisfies the *before* constraint and if their involved persons show the same person in the real world.

The average normalized rank for this experiment is given in Fig.4.b over 19 events of close_to_Gate1.

This experiment shows the capacity of this language to define new event from the recognized ones with satisfying results (average normalized ranks of all 19 events are smaller than 0.3).

As shown in Fig.3 and Fig.4, most of the average normalized ranks of the three experiments are small but there are some cases where these measures are quite high (maximum value is respectively 0.3183, 0.3875, 0.262 for the experiment 1, the experiment 2 and the experiment 3) because of the error in object tracking. Therefore, in addition of keypoints and color histogram we intend to use more features or to use a combination of features to solve these problems.

The experiments 1, 2 and 3 show that the proposed approach overcomes the first and the second drawback presented in the introduction. We present another example of query to explain how the proposed approach can do to overcome the third drawback. In the first video, we do not have the results of event recognition. Users may define a new Close to Gates event by stating query as follows:

SELECT video_frames FROM Video1 WHERE ((o: Person) AND (z: Gates) AND (o distance z < threshold))

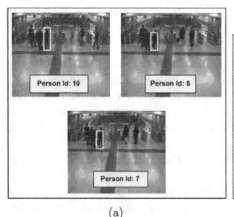 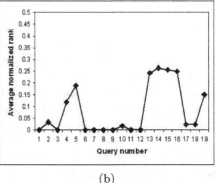

(a)   (b)

Fig. 4. (a) Three indexed persons with labels 10, 8, 7 describe the same person in the real world. These indexed persons belong to close_to_Gate1 and inside_zone_Platform events that satisfy *before* constraint. The exact matching based on persons' label gives only one result of person label 10 while our similarity matching gives three persons label 10, 8, 7 with respectively 1, 2, 5 of rank (b) The average normalized rank for experiment 3 over 19 close_to_Gate1 events. The value 0 of average normalized ranks corresponds to good retrieval, value 1 corresponds to bad retrieval and 0.5 corresponds to random retrieval.

One person is close to gates if the distance between this person and the gates is smaller than a given threshold. The distance is computed based on the 3D position of the persons and the gates. This query takes into account users interest by using a threshold. User can set the value of a threshold as he/she wants. By setting two different values for the threshold, 100 and 150, we have two different results. The first result returns 10 indexed persons with 320 recognized instance of the Close to Gates event. The second one returns 20 indexed persons with 727 recognized instances.

4 Conclusions

In this paper, we have proposed an approach for video indexing and retrieval for surveillance based on a query language. This new language enables both image and semantic queries and similarity matching. The obtained results for three experiments show that: combining the image level and the semantic level (in experiment 2 and 3) and similarity matching (in experiment 1, 2 and 3) manage imperfect object tracking and imperfect event recognition. New events defined by the user from the recognized ones have been successfully retrieved (in the experiment 3).

Currently, similarity matching has been limited to the color histogram and the keypoints. We plan to study and use more features to enrich the proposed language. In addition, the users may want to make a complex query containing several subqueries. How to combine the results from these subqueries is an issue that we plan to study in the future.

References

1. Lowe, D.G.: Distinctive image features from scale-invariant keypoints. International Journal of Computer Vision 60(2), 91–110 (2004)
2. Müller, H., Marchand-Maillet, S., Pun, T.: The truth about corel - evaluation in image retrieval. In: Lew, M.S., Sebe, N., Eakins, J.P. (eds.) CIVR 2002. LNCS, vol. 2383, pp. 28–49. Springer, Heidelberg (2002)
3. Saykol, E., Güdükbay, U., Ulusoy, O.: A database model for querying visual surveillance by integrating semantic and low-level features. In: Candan, K.S., Celentano, A. (eds.) MIS 2005. LNCS, vol. 3665, pp. 163–176. Springer, Heidelberg (2005)
4. Swain, M.J., Ballard, D.H.: Color indexing. International Journal of Computer Vision 7(1), 11–32 (1991)
5. Vu, V.T., Brémond, F., Thonnat, M.: Automatic video interpretation: A novel algorithm for temporal scenario recognition. In: International Joint Conference on Artificial Intelligence (IJCAI 2003), Acapulco, Mexico, August 9-15, 2003, pp. 1295–1302 (2003)
6. Durak, N., Yazici, A., George, R.: Online Surveillance Video Archive System. In: Proc. of International Multimedia Modeling Conference, Singapore, pp. 376–385 (January 2007)
7. Hampapur, A., Brown, L., Connell, J., Ekin, A., Haas, N., Lu, M., Merki, H., Pankanti, S., Senior, A., Shu, C., Tian, Y.L.: Smart Video Surveillance: Exploring the concept of multiscale spatiotemporal tracking. IEEE Signal Processing Magazine 22(2), 38–51 (2005)

Semantic Quantization of 3D Human Motion Capture Data Through Spatial-Temporal Feature Extraction

Yohan Jin and B. Prabhakaran

Department of Computer Science
University of Texas at Dallas
Richardson, Texas 75083-0688, USA
{yohan,praba}@utdallas.edu

Abstract. 3D motion capture is a form of multimedia data that is widely used in animation and medical fields (such as physical medicine and rehabilitation where body joint analysis is needed). These applications typically create large repositories of motion capture data and need efficient and accurate content-based retrieval techniques. 3D motion capture data is in the form of multi-dimensional time series data. To reduce the dimensions of human motion data while maintaining semantically important features, we quantize human motion data by extracting Spatial-Temporal Features through SVD and translate them onto a 1-dimensional sequential representation through our proposed sGMMEM (semantic Gaussian Mixture Modeling with EM). Thus, we achieve good classification accuracies for primitive human motion categories (walking 92.85%,run 91.42%,jump 94.11%) and even for subtle categories (dance 89.47%,laugh 83.33%,basketball signal 85.71%,golf putting 80.00%).

1 Introduction

In terms of human perception, human can understand the "semantic" meaning of an image with small number of colors after color-quantization (that is, similar color shades are expressed with one representative color). Thus, the level of human understanding does not change after decreasing enormous amount of information for storage, which is quite useful for compression and recognition of multimedia data [7]. This is also true for human motion capture data. 3D human motion capture is widely used in various applications such as animation authoring and medical fields (such as physical medicine and rehabilitation). Here, sophisticated motion capture facilities aid in mapping the complex human motion in the three dimensional (3D) space. Each row of data matrix corresponds to a single frame that consists of information for 29 segments (corresponding to different parts of human body) depending on degree of freedom. The degree of freedom for each segment is the ability of the segment to rotate or translate along three axes, according to the hierarchical structure of the human segment. Altogether, these segments form a 62-dimensional data along time axis. Human motion is characterized by spatial relationships between each of these body

S. Satoh, F. Nack, and M. Etoh (Eds.): MMM 2008, LNCS 4903, pp. 318–328, 2008.

segments/joints over a period of time. Hence, we need to extract these spatial and temporal relationships from the multi-dimensional 3D motion capture data matrix and map them onto a lower-dimension (1-dimensional, in our approach) representation by the following steps;

- **Spatial Feature Extraction:** Human motions are primarily identified by movements of arms, legs, and the associated body or "torso". Hence, the human motion matrix is divided into three main body parts (or sub-matrices): 'torso','arms' and 'legs'. For extracting spatial relationships among body parts, we use Singular Value Decomposition (SVD)[12].
- **Semantic Quantization Through Temporal Feature Extraction:** We semantically quantize spatial 3-dimensional singular values by identify temporal distributions among body parts in a human by measuring the responsibility of each body component [torso, arms, and legs] and the associated combinations (8 combinations among the 3 components) to the observed frame values. For this, we map 3 dimensional singular values of frames into Gaussian Mixture Semantic Space. Then, we apply Expectation Maximization (EM)[11] to find the most probable semantic quantization value of each frame. We consider continuous singular spatial values as the "observation" values and discrete ("quantized") body components as the "latent (hidden)" values. Hence, multi-dimension 3D motion data frames can be reduced to 1-dimensional quantization value that can be used for classification and retrieval.

In this paper, we show that time series, multi-dimensional 3D human motion capture data can be semantically quantized through statistical modeling (Gaussian Mixture) based on temporal distribution of spatial features of human motion data. We proposed a novel approach which can extract human motion's semantic characteristics successfully during reducing dimensions so much and demonstrated its usefulness by matching the most closest motion with real subtle 3D human motion queries.

2 Related Work

To index 3D human motion data, there are approaches which use principle components of human motions. Li et al.[2] extracted geometric structure as exposed by SVD of matrices of human motion data and indexed using interval-tree based index structure and classified human motions with SVM on geometric extracted motion vectors [1]. Guodong et el.[6] selected small set of leading eigenvectors as principle features and tried to represent motion frames as simplified "cluster transition signature", which is conceptually similar to 1-dimensional quantization representation in this paper. Other approaches utilized hierarchical trees for indexing 3D human motions. Gaurav et al.[4] used hierarchical structure of the human body segments. Each level of index tree is associated with the weighted feature vectors of a body segment. Feng et al.[8] proposed content-based motion retrieval (CBMR) by building motion-index tree on hierarchial motion description, which serves as a classifier to determine a sub-library that contains promising similar motions to the query example. For dealing with temporal invariance between similar motions, used "elastic match"[8], a combination of DTW (Dynamic Time Warping) and dynamic programming. To overcome the limit of DTW technique ('local scaling') for time-series data comparison, Keogh et al.[9] proposed a uniform scaling , which can scaling globally and showed that it can speed up indexing using bounding envelopes. Most recently, Muller et al.[5] contributed content-based human motion retrieval through "qualitative" geometric description for bridging the numerical and perceptual human motion similarity gap. However, a user has to select suitable features in order to obtain high-quality retrieval results. In this paper, we use SVD for extracting spatial characteristics of human motion frames while reducing dimensions similar to [2], and our approach don't need to specify the retrieval condition description. Furthermore, we also try to find temporal continuity with similar frames and represent each frames as semantic quantization values by applying statistical distribution modeling (Semantic Gaussian Mixture Space Modeling). Thus, this is the novel approach which exploit 'statistical distribution' in 3D human motion database and 'quantize' it for content-based 3D Human Motion Retrieval.

3   Spatial Feature Extraction

We consider one human motion is characterized by different combination of three main body parts: torso, arms and legs. Each body parts include several segments. For example, we divide 29 segments of human body into three sets, namely "torso," "arms," and "legs." The torso consists of 7 segments (with degree of freedom in parenthesis),namely root (6), lower back(3), upper back(3), thorax(3), lower neck(3), upper neck(3), and head(3) segments. The arms consists of 7 pairs of segments including left and right side, namely clavicle(2), humerus(3), radius(1), wrist(1), hand(2), fingers(1), and thumb(2). And, finally, legs consists of 4 pairs of segments including left and right side, namely femur(3), tibia(1), foot(2), and toes(1). For extracting spatial relationships and reducing dimensions (from 62 to 3 dimensions) among the 3 different body components, we separate a motion data matrix ($M_{f \times m}$) into three sub matrices ($M^{\alpha} = M_{f \times k}, M^{\beta} = M_{f \times j}, M^{\gamma} = M_{f \times r}$, where $m = k + j + r$) belonging to torso,arms and legs part respectively. From three sub matrices, SVD decomposes "singular" values (see Figure 1).

$$M^i = U \Sigma V^T, M^i v_1 = \sigma^i v_1, i \in \{\alpha, \beta, \gamma\} \tag{1}$$

Now, three "singular" values ($\sigma^{\alpha}, \sigma^{\beta}, \sigma^{\gamma}$) which represent torso,arms and legs parts are the coefficient of each frame as the spatial feature, then we have a reduced matrix $M_{f \times 3}$ for a single human motion clip. Singular values represent the periodic and continuous characteristics of human's motion. Increasing singular value of one body part indicates that part is used more intensively than other part for a particular motion (see Figure 2).

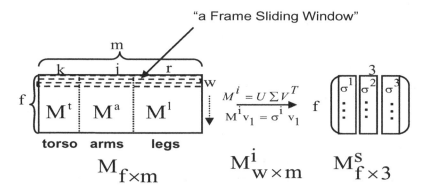

Fig. 1. SVD Spatial Feature Extraction using Frame Sliding Window

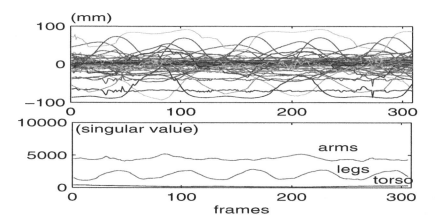

Fig. 2. SVD Spatial Feature Dimension Reduction ('walking' motion)

4 Semantic Gaussian-Mixture Quantization Through Temporal Feature Extraction

4.1 Gaussian Mixture Semantic Space

We map spatially extracted 3-dimensional singular values of each motion file into Gaussian Mixture Semantic Space [10] (see Figure 3), this space is to find "latent" semantic quantization components(A(rms), T(orso), and L(egs)) which is corresponding to the given observation (i^{th} frame of one motion file). It computes $\Re_{ki}$ of 3 body component, which is probability of "latent" component k's responsibility for observing i^{th} frame (O_i).

$$\Re_{ki} = P(k|O_i) = \frac{P(O_i|k)P(k)}{P(O_i)} = \frac{g(O_i; \mu_k)\Phi_k}{\sum_{k=1}^{K} P(O_i, k)} \qquad (2)$$

Let $P(O_i|k)$ be the Gaussian function $g(O_i; \mu_k)$ of latent component k, and P(k) be the mixing parameter Φ_k of latent component k. $P(O_i)$ is the "prior" probability that we can get from marginalization of joint probability.

Human can express one action using more than one body component at the same time, so we need to extend Gaussian Mixture Semantic Space from three main body parts (Triangle) to a combination of the three main parts (Cube). We add three combined "latent" components corresponding to each edge of Triangle, which is 'TL', 'AT' and 'AL' respectively. Thus, overall number of "latent" component in Cube space is 8 including null (Φ) and all (TAL) components. Each quantizing component has its semantic meaning: for example, if one frame window has a mixture value close to 'L', it means that this frame window belongs to "legs intensive" actions. And if one frame window's mixture value is close to 'TAL', then it means that this frame has action using "legs" ,"arms" and "torso" actively.

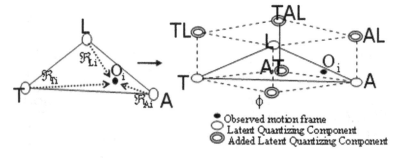

Fig. 3. Gaussian Mixture Semantic Space for finding "latent" component's responsibilities

4.2 Extension of GMM with EM for Semantic Quantization of Human Motion Data

We can extend GMM with EM (Expectation Maximization) for finding local maximal values based on the initial GMM values of human motions. After iteratively running with GMM and EM model, we get the locally maximized mixture value. Then, we assign each maximized value to the closest quantization value in order to get the quantized representation of each frame window from spatially extracted feature vectors through following steps.

1. **Initialization Phase:** After running the k-means cluster algorithm with all singular value coefficients matrices and 8 central points, we get the initial values (mixing Φ_k and initial memberships π_i) of GMM

$$\Phi_k = \frac{\sum_i (\pi_i; i = k)}{\sum_i \pi_i} \tag{3}$$

Every membership variable has the value of 0 or 1. We need to do this iteratively (from phase 2 to phase 5) until the values converge.

2. **Evaluation Phase:** Let $\lambda(i,k)$ is the k quantizing component's Gaussian function value of the current motion observation (i^{th} frame window) with the recently updated Gaussian parameters from "Update Phase". At the first iteration, evaluate with initial parameters.

$$\lambda(i,k) = g(O_i; \mu_k) = \frac{1}{(2\pi\varepsilon)^{1/2}} exp(-\frac{\| O_i - \mu_k \|^2}{2\varepsilon}) \tag{4}$$

$$\Re_{ki} = \frac{\Phi_k \lambda(i,k)}{\sum_k \Phi_k \lambda(i,k)}, k \in \{\Phi, T, A, L, ..., TAL\} \tag{5}$$

3. **Update Phase:** Follows to the re-evaluated "responsible" parameters ($\Re_{ki}$) from previous phase, it updates Gaussian parameters ($\widetilde{\mu_k}$) and "mixing" parameters ($\widetilde{\Phi_k}$),

$$\widetilde{\mu_k} = \frac{1}{S_k} \sum_{i=1}^{I} \Re_{ki} O_i \tag{6}$$

$$\widetilde{\Phi_k} = \frac{S_k}{I}, S_k = \sum_{i=1}^{I} \Re_{ki} \tag{7}$$

4. **Convergence Phase:** In each iteration, we compute the maximum likelihood (ML) function with the updated Gaussian parameter $P(O|\mu)$ and mixing parameter $P(\Phi)$ from previous phase;

$$ML(O; \Phi, \mu) = \ln P(O|\Phi, \mu) = \ln P(O|\mu) P(\Phi) \tag{8}$$

Next, we compute the convergence of this maximum-likelihood (*ConvML*) function as;

$$ConvML = \ln \prod_{i=1}^{I} \sum_{k=1}^{K} (\widetilde{\Phi_k} - \Phi_k)(\lambda(i,k) - \lambda(i,\widetilde{k})) \tag{9}$$

where I is the number of observations and K is the number of quantizing components (K=8). $\widetilde{\Phi_k}$ and $\lambda(i,\widetilde{k})$ are updated mixing parameter and Gaussian function values with re-evaluated parameters. If the difference between current and previous iteration's is smaller than some convergence threshold (*ConvML* $< \varpi$), then the iterative process is complete and we proceed to the 'Quantization Phase'. Else, we go back to the 'Evaluation Phase' for the subsequent iteration.

5. **Quantization Phase:** After convergence of the maximum-likelihood function is reached, we generate the locally-maximized P matrix of one motion clip:

$$lmP(i,k) = \frac{P(i,k)\Phi_k^{conv}}{\sum_{k=1}^{K} P(i,k)\Phi_k^{conv}} \tag{10}$$

$lmP(i,k)$ is the maximized probability that component k is representative of the ith motion frame. For each motion frame window, we can compute

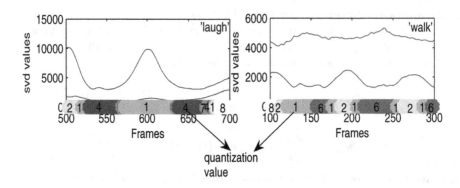

Fig. 4. Temporal Segmentation Effect From GMMEM Quantization Modeling ('laugh' & 'walk' examples)

the jth quantizing component that has the maximum probability among all k components, and then assign the quantization value of this j^{th} component to that motion frame (QuantP(i)).

$$QuantP(i) = \arg \max_{k}(lmP(i,k)) \tag{11}$$

In Figure 4, we observe that quantization value representation from semantic GMMEM has been segmented with temporally similar frames [5][8]. Thus, finally extracted quantization value has spatial and temporal characteristics of a specific motion.

5   Query Resolution

We can notice that similar motions have quite similar patterns of quantization values lie in time series since quantization values we chose is the implication

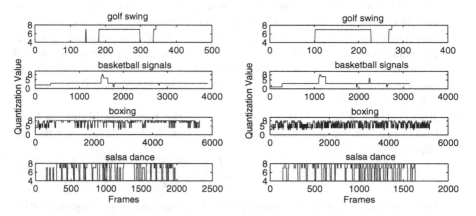

Fig. 5. Quantization Value Representation of Similar Motions

of body segment usages, quantization values are corresponding to semantic description of specific motion. For example, 'boxing' motion has repeated intensive action primitive and 'golf swing' has one big cycle of swing primitive action (see Figure 5). For similarity comparison, we transform quantization values of each motion into histogram values (see Figure 6). We randomly selected a query motion ('laugh','salsa dance' and so on) in the motion database [3] and search the database for the most closest match (using k=1) using kNN (K-Nearest Neighbor) classifier since we're interested in the best single matching motion as in [9].

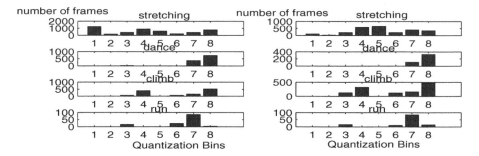

Fig. 6. Histogram Comparison of Quantized Similar Motions

6   Implementation and Performance Analysis

For experiments, we used the Pentium (R) D CPU 3.0 GHz and MATLAB 7.3.0 (R2006b) and the publicly used motion capture data files (CMU Motion Capture Database)[3] and chose 209 human motion clips (370,294 frames) in our experiment. There are 14 different semantic motion categories, which are 'dance','laugh', 'salsa dance','pantomime','siton & standsup','jump','golf swing', 'run','boxing','basketball signal','golf putting','walk','stretching','climb'. Classify and retrieve these subtle actions are quite challengeable problem because of following reasons;

- First, some action categories are semantically very similar to each other. For example, 'dance' vs. 'salsa dance', 'golf swing' vs. 'golf putting', and some other actions are syntactically similar, in that, their actions need to use similar body parts, but they have different meanings. For instance, 'laugh' vs. 'pantomime', 'pantomime' vs 'basketball signal'.
- Second, the lengths of each motion are quite different. For example, a motion may consists of only hundreds frames (it is only 1 second duration since frame rate of AMC motion capture data is 120 frames/sec.) and other one may have ten thousands frames (this motion has more than 125 seconds duration). Frame ranges in our experiment are from 124 frames to 15021 frames.

– Third, variety of frame sizes and human actors (subjects) in the same action category. For example, 'pantomime' category includes 4 different subjects and sizes are from 3508 to 15021, 'climb' has 4 subjects and their size is from 1198 to 6956 frames and so on.

In Figure 7, for showing how much dimensional reduction from spatial feature reduction (62 to 3 dimensions) affects the 3D motion recognition. We compare kNN classification accuracies with original (62) data dimension and reduced (3) dimension that have been quantized using K-means technique. It demonstrates that dimensional reduction by extracting spatial features doesn't deteriorate motion recognition rate, but it increase the accuracies for some motion categories.

We compare with LVQ (Learning Vector Quantization) technique[13] and our proposed sGMMEM(semantic GMMEM) quantization method (in Figure 8), LVQ and sGMMEM quantized spatially extracted data, which got from the first stage of our approach. We can observe sGMMEM can improve kNN classification accuracies so much than LVQ does with 3 dimensional human motion data (see Figure 8). Finally, in Table 1,we can see overall precision and recall values for 14 different motion categories. sGMMEM quantization shows quite good performance in most of motion categories. Especially, for such subtle motion categories as dance (89.47%),laugh (83.33%),basketball signal (85.71%),golf putting(80.00%), golf swing(81.81%) show good recall values. In other hands, LVQ demonstrates much lower accuracies about those subtle motion categories (dance(31.57%),laugh(33.33 %),golf swing(36.36%) and so on). About primitive motion categories, sGMMEM achieves more than 90% precision accuracies (walk (92.85%), run (%91.42),jump (94.11%)) -see Table 1.

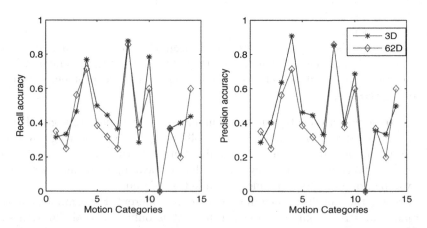

Fig. 7. Comparison Accuracies with 3-dimensional and 62-dimensional Motion Representations

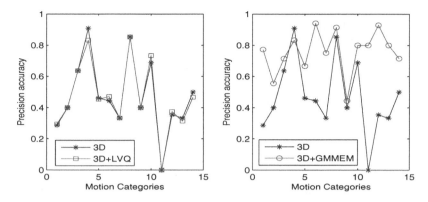

Fig. 8. Comparison Accuracy Improvements between LVQ and Semantic GMMEM Quantization with 3-dimensional Motion Representations

Table 1. Accuracy Comparison for all Motion Categories

Categories	LVQ		Semantic GMMEM	
	precision	recall	precision	recall
1.dance	0.2857	0.3157	0.7727	0.8947
2.laugh	0.4000	0.3333	0.5555	0.8333
3.salsa	0.6363	0.4666	0.7142	0.6666
4.pantomime	0.9090	0.7692	0.8333	0.7692
5.siton standup	0.4615	0.5000	0.6666	0.6666
6.jump	0.4444	0.4444	0.9411	0.8888
7.golf swing	0.3333	0.3636	0.7500	0.8181
8.run	0.8529	0.8787	0.9142	0.9696
9.boxing	0.4000	0.2857	0.4444	0.5714
10.baskeball signal	0.6875	0.7857	0.8000	0.8571
11.golf putting	0.0000	0.0000	0.8000	0.8000
12.walk	0.3548	0.3666	0.9285	0.8666
13.stretching	0.3333	0.4000	0.8000	0.4000
14.climb	0.5000	0.4375	0.7142	0.6250
average	0.4713	0.4533	0.7596	0.7591

7   Conclusions and Future Work

In this paper, we extract spatial (using SVD) and temporal features (using statistical distribution of spatial feature values) of 3D motion clips and map into Gaussian Mixture Semantic Space. The mapped values are then quantized into one of the 8 motion components (corresponding to body movements involving Arms, Torso, and Legs) using Expectation Maximization (EM). In performance analysis, although multi-dimensional(62) human motion capture data are reduced to one-dimensional expression, we demonstrated our approach can keep the semantic characteristics of each human motion clip. As the sequentially quantized compact representation imply human motion's semantics (body components relationship in the statistical distribution), the quantized representation could bridge the gap between 3D human motion matrix data and human understandable languages with possible extensions with information retrieval research area such as motion vocabulary and motion classification with LSI (Latent Semantic Indexing) through translating 1-dimensional quantization values into repeated rules.

References

1. Li, C., Kulkarni, P.R., Prabhakaran, B.: Motion Stream Segmentation and Recognition by Classification. International Journal of Multimedia Tools and Applications (MTAP) by Springer-Verlag 35(1) (2007)
2. Li, C., Pradhan, G., Zheng, S.Q., Prabhakaran, B.: Indexing of Variable Length Multi-attribute Motion data. In: Proc. of the Second ACM International Workshop on Multimedia, Washington D.C., USA, pp. 75–84 (November 2004)
3. CMU Motion Capture Library, http://mocap.cs.cmu.edu/
4. Pradhan, G.N., Li, C., Prabhakaran, B.: Hierarchical Indexing Structure for 3D Human Motion. In: Int'l Proceedings of ACM Multimedia Modeling Conference (MMM) 2007, Singapore, January 9-12 (2007)
5. Muller, M., Roder, T., Clausen, M.: Efficient content based retrieval of motion capture data. ACM Transactions on Graphics (TOG) 24, 677–685 (2005)
6. Liu, G., Zhang, J., Wang, W., McMillan, L.: A system for analyzing and indexing human-motion databases. In: Proc. 2005 ACM SIGMOD International conference on Management of data (2005)
7. Ketterer, J., Puzicha, J., Held, M.: On Spatial Quantization of Color Images. IEEE Transactions on Image Processing 9, 666–682 (2000)
8. Liu, F., Zhuang, Y., Wu, F., Pan, Y.: 3D motion retrieval with motion index tree. Computer Vision and Image Understanding 92, 265–284 (2003)
9. Keogh, E., Palpanas, T., Zordan, V.B., Gunopulos, D., Cardle, M.: Indexing large human-motion databases. In: Proc. 30th VLDB Conference, Toronto, Canada, pp. 780–791 (2004)
10. Bishop, C.M.: Pattern Recognition and Machine Learning. Springer, New York (2006)
11. Dempster, A.P., Laird, N.M., Rubin, D.B.: Maximum likelihood from incomplete data via the EM algorithm. Journal of Royal Statistical Society B39, 1–38
12. Golub, G.H., Loan, C.F.: Matrix Computations. The Johns Hopkins University Press, Baltimore, Maryland (1996)
13. Kohonen, T., Kangas, J., Laaksonen, J., Torkkola, K.: A program package for the correct application of Learning Vector Quantization algorithms. In: Proceedings of the International Joint Conference on Neural Networks, Baltimore, pp. 725–730 (June 1992)

Fast Intermode Decision Via Statistical Learning for H.264 Video Coding

Wei-Hau Pan, Chen-Kuo Chiang, and Shang-Hong Lai

Department of Computer Science, National Tsing Hua University, Hsinchu, Taiwan
{whpan,ckchiang,lai}@cs.nthu.edu.tw

Abstract. Although the variable-block-size motion compensation scheme significantly reduces the compensation error, the computational complexity of motion estimation (ME) is tremendously increased at the same time. To reduce the complexity of the variable-block-size ME algorithm, we propose a statistical learning approach to simplify the computation involved in the sub-MB mode selection. Some representative features are extracted during ME with fixed sizes. Then, an off-line pre-classification approach is used to predict the most probable sub-MB modes according to the run-time features. It turns out that only possible sub-MB modes need to perform ME. Experimental results show that the computation complexity is significantly reduced while the video quality degradation and bitrate increment is negligible.

Keywords: Variable block-size, H.264, motion estimation, statistical learning.

1 Introduction

H.264/AVC, the latest video coding standard of Joint Video Team (JVT), outperforms previous standards such as MPEG-4 and H.263 in terms of coding efficiency and video quality. This is due to the fact that many new techniques are adopted in this standard. Variable-block-size ME is one of the most important features in H.264. There are seven kinds of block sizes, 16×16, 16×8, 8×16, 8×8, 8×4, 4×8 and 4×4. An MB (16×16) can be partitioned to 16×8, 8×16 and 8×8. A sub-MB (8×8) can be further partitioned to 8×4, 4×8 and 4×4. Different types of partitions are shown in Fig. 1.

In [1], the degrees of homogeneous and stationary regions are determined as the criteria for block partition. This is based on the assumption that the higher the degree of homogeneous and stationary blocks, the larger the block partition is used. However, the thresholds to determine the degree of homogeneity are empirically selected, and the resulting criteria can not provide very accurate block partitioning. Another approach [2] analyzes the likelihood and the correlation of motion fields for a suitable block mode selection.

In this paper, we propose an algorithm by using statistical learning to analyze representative features for variable-block-size ME and determined the most probable modes. More accurate mode decision can be obtained by statistical learning results rather than heuristic thresholding on simple features. On the other hand, it eliminates all unnecessary computation involved in variable-block-size ME. The rest of the

S. Satoh, F. Nack, and M. Etoh (Eds.): MMM 2008, LNCS 4903, pp. 329–337, 2008.

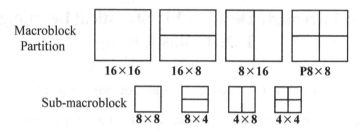

Fig. 1. MB partitions and sub-MB partitions in H.264

paper is organized as follows. Section 2 introduces the selection of representative features based on experimental results. Section 3 presents how a sub-MB mode decision problem can be modeled to a classification problem and training steps and an alternative testing method for SVM. The proposed algorithm is presented in Section 4. Experimental results are shown in Section 5. Finally, Section 6 concludes this paper.

2 Feature Selection

In this section, we will introduce some representative features for variable-block-size mode selection. These features can be used to predict the most probable partition type of the current MB. All of them are well chosen and examined carefully in our experiments. The results show that they are helpful to the variable-size mode selection.

2.1 Inter Best SAD

For an Inter prediction MB, the ME procedure determines the best matching reference MB. The distortion measure used in this ME procedure in H.264 is the sum of absolute difference (SAD). The Inter Best SAD is the lowest SAD value of the ME results to the current MB. This value may indicate not only the accuracy of ME procedure but also the possibility of being a background MB. The lower this value is, the higher probability the current MB contains still background. Thus, small Inter Best SAD value means it is very unlikely that this MB will be split up into sub-MBs. This is due to the fact that a background MB is stationary and can be matched well by a large MB. On the other hand, we need to consider the bitrate overhead caused by more motion vectors if we split up a MB into sub-MBs. Fig. 2(A) shows that lower SAD value indicates higher probability of being a 16×16 or an 8×8 partition mode.

2.2 Motion Vector Difference and Motion Vector Magnitude

Motion Vector Difference (MVD) is the sum of absolute value of the difference between the predicted MV and the motion vector after ME in horizontal and vertical directions. In the H.264 standard, the predicted MV is defined as the median MVs of the adjacent blocks in both x and y directions. MVD may represent the motion smoothness between current MB and adjacent MBs. Fig. 2(B) indicates that if MVD

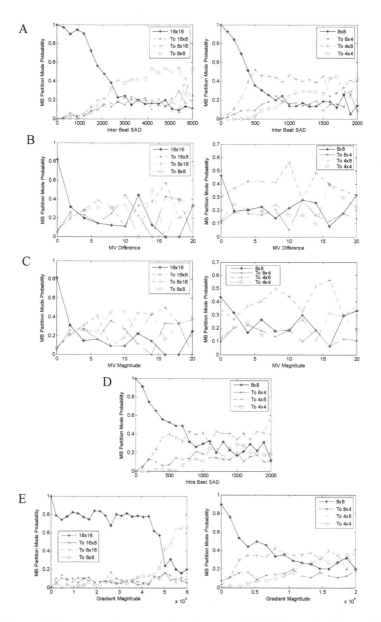

Fig. 2. The probability of partition mode for 16×16 and 8×8 MBs under different (A) Inter Best SAD, (B) MVD, (C) MVM, (D) Intra Best SAD and (E) Gradient Magnitude in News sequence

is small, the current MB has more chance to be a background block. In this case, it is not necessary to partition this MB into sub-MBs.

Motion Vector Magnitude (MVM) is the sums of absolute value of the motion vector itself regardless of the MV prediction. It indicates that whether this MB is stationary or not. Stationary MBs are still temporally. That is, little change between the current block and the collocated block in the previous frame can be detected. If the MB is stationary, it can be matched well by large MBs. Another reason to consider MVM is that it may show more precise MB activity than MVD when the camera is fixed. Fig. 2(C) shows that MVM is helpful to decide the mode when the MB is stationary.

2.3 Intra Best SAD

Intra Best SAD is the minimum SAD value after Intra prediction of the current MB. An MB with a large SAD value after Intra prediction usually contains complicated texture or object boundaries. Therefore, such kind of MBs tend to be partitioned into smaller sub-MBs. It is obvious especially for 8×8 MBs, so we take this feature for 8×8 MBs. In Fig.2(D), the 8×8 MBs with high Intra SAD value have larger probability to be partitioned into smaller sub-MBs.

2.4 Gradient Magnitude

The gradient magnitude of the current $M \times N$ MB is defined as the summation of the gradient magnitudes of all pixels inside the MB obtained by applying the Sobel operator.

The gradient magnitude is low in homogeneous regions. An MB with low gradient magnitude tends to be a background block, which is unlikely to be partitioned into sub-MBs. It is obvious in Fig.2(E) that the gradient magnitude provides useful information for our purpose.

3 Problem Formulation and Solution

We will formulate a sub-MB mode decision problem into a classification problem and provide a solution in this section. Firstly, ME is performed on 16×16 MBs. Then, the most possible sub-MB mode is predicted based on the selected features.

3.1 Problem Formulation for a 16×16 MB and an 8×8 MB

There are four possible partition modes for a 16×16 MB, including 16×16, 16×8, 8×16 and P8×8. Since we have performed ME for 16×16 MBs, we need to decide which mode to perform ME in the next step. Our experiments indicate that 1616, 16×8, and 8×16 modes usually have similar features. Thus, partition mode 16×16, 16×8 and 8×16 are grouped to class one (C_1) and P8×8 is set as class two (C_2). Four features, mentioned in the Section 2 are used for the classification, including Inter Best SAD (SAD_P), Motion Vector Difference (MV_D), Motion Vector Magnitude (MV_{mag}), and Gradient Magnitude (G). Thus, the binary classification results can be decided from the class conditional probabilities given the features, i.e.

$$\text{Decide } C_1 \text{ if}$$
$$P(C_1 \mid SAD_P, MV_D, MV_{mag}, G) > P(C_2 \mid SAD_P, MV_D, MV_{mag}, G);$$
$$\text{otherwise decide } C_2.$$

(1)

For an 8×8 MB, there are also four possible partition modes including 8×8, 8×4, 4×8 and 4×4. Similar to the case for a 16×16 MB, we set partition mode 8×8 as class three (C_3) and the mode 8×4, 4×8 and 4×4 are grouped to class four (C_4). In addition to the four features used for 16×16 MB, the Intra Best SAD (SAD_I) is included in the binary classification for an 8×8 MB. The decision is still based on the class conditional probability given as follows

Decide C_3 if

$$P(C_3 \mid SAD_P, MV_D, MV_{mag}, G, SAD_I) > P(C_4 \mid SAD_P, MV_D, MV_{mag}, G, SAD_I) ; \qquad (2)$$

otherwise decide C_4.

3.2 Training and Off-Line Pre-classification

In the above, two decision rules are defined for our classification problem. However, it is difficult to model the joint probability of those features well from limited training samples. The Support Vector Machine (SVM) is used here to solve the classification problem.

The training data is obtained by applying the H.264 reference code JM 11.0 to four video sequences; namely, News, Akiyo, Foreman and Coastguard. For the 16×16 MBs, the required features and the MB partition mode results (C_1 or C_2) are collected, similarly for the case of the 8×8 MBs (C_3 or C_4). The collected data is regarded as the input training samples for SVM. Experimental results show that the accuracy of cross validation is very high by using SVM on these two classification problems.

For the consideration of real-time encoding, it takes too much time for run-time classification for SVM. Thus, an off-line pre-classification approach is proposed to minimize the computation time involved in the classification procedure. The idea is to generate all possible combinations of the feature vectors and pre-classify them with SVM. However, the total number of possible combinations is too large for real applications. A useful method is to quantize each feature based on the feature distribution. Instead of using the uniform quantizer, Llyod-Max quantizer [3] which has adaptive step size is applied on the training samples since it can approximate a distribution much better than the uniform quantizer. Each feature is quantized into 20 bins in our implementation.

From the trained SVM classifiers, we can decide the class for each possible input sample. The classification results for all possible input samples are stored. During the encoding, we only need to collect the necessary features, quantize them and search the look-up table for classification. Hence, the computation time in the classification can be significantly reduced by using this off-line pre-classification approach.

4 Proposed Intermode Decision Algorithm

The procedure of the proposed Intermode decision algorithm is given as follows:

Step 1) Perform 16×16 ME.

Step 2) Collect four features: SAD_P, MV_D, MV_{mag}, and G_{mag} for 16×16 MB.

Step 3) Quantize these features from the Lloyd-Max quantizer.

Step 4) Obtain the classification result from the table look-up. If the results is

$C1$, perform 16×8, 8×16 ME and go to Step 12.

Step 5) Perform 8×8 ME.

Step 6) Collect five features: SAD_P, MV_D, MV_{mag}, G_{mag} and SAD_I for 8×8 MB.

Step 7) Quantize these features from the Lloyd-Max quantizer.

Step 8) Classify via table look-up procedures. If $C3$ is preferable, go to Step 11.

Step 9) Perform 8×4, 4×8, and 4×4 ME.

Step 10) Determine the best P8×8 MB partition mode.

Step 11) Repeat from Step 5 to Step 10 until all the 8×8 MBs are performed.

Step 12) Select the best MB partition mode as the Intermode. Go to Step 1 and proceed to the next MB.

Notice that the feature quantization and the classification step are simply via table look-up. Thus, they have insignificant computation overhead for the encoding. The 8×8 Intra prediction is performed before Step 6 since the four features, SAD_P, MV_D, MV_{mag} and SAD_I, are required for encoding. The main overhead of the proposed algorithm is on the calculation of $Gmag$ for each MB. Fig.3 illustrates the flow chart of the proposed algorithm.

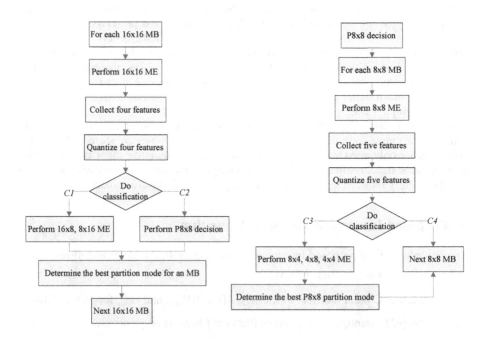

Fig. 3. Flow chart of the proposed algorithm

5 Experimental Results

The proposed algorithm and the algorithm by Wu *et al.* [1] are implemented in JM11.0 using the fast ME, EPZS [4]. The motion search range is set to 32 and the number of reference frame is set to 1. The RD optimization is disabled and the CABAC entropy encoding is enabled in our experiments. All test sequences are in QCIF format and tested on an Intel Pentium M processor of 1.73GHz. All frames except the fist frame are encoded as P-frames. The training data for our algorithm is collected from News, Akiyo, Foreman, Coastguard sequences. The QP is set to 28.

We applied Full Search (FS), EPZS, our proposed algorithm and the method by Wu *et al.* [1] to six test sequences. The PSNR increase and bitrate increase compared with Full Search are listed in Table 1 when QP is set to 24, 28 and 32, respectively. The speedup ratios are calculated for three methods compared with FS in terms of execution time and number of search points per MB when QP is set to 24, 28 and 32. Note that SP stands for the number of search points per MB, which is the number of search points per mode multiplied by a weight proportional to the size of the partition

Table 1. PSNR and Bitrate decrease compared with the Full Search for the three algorithms when QP is set to 24, 28 and 32

Sequence	PSNR increase (dB)			Bitrate increase (%)		
(QP 24)	EZPS	Proposed	Wu's	EZPS	Proposed	Wu's
Mobile	0.01	0.01	0.04	-0.64	-0.25	-0.65
HallMonitor	0.02	0.01	0.02	0.07	1.35	0.02
Container	0.05	0.02	0.04	-0.55	-0.64	-0.59
Akiyo	0.01	0.00	0.01	-0.62	0.21	-0.62
News	0.02	0.01	0.02	-1.37	0.09	-1.25
Foreman	0.01	-0.00	0.01	-0.12	1.12	-0.05
(QP 28)	EZPS	Proposed	Wu's	EZPS	Proposed	Wu's
Mobile	0.03	0.02	0.03	-0.97	-0.56	-1.01
HallMonitor	0.02	0.04	0.07	0.79	1.41	1.07
Container	0.08	0.08	0.08	-0.75	-0.46	-0.40
Akiyo	0.04	0.05	0.04	-1.23	-0.51	-1.23
News	0.04	0.04	0.03	-0.94	0.30	-0.88
Foreman	0.02	0.01	0.00	-0.96	1.32	-0.83
(QP 32)	EZPS	Proposed	Wu's	EZPS	Proposed	Wu's
Mobile	0.07	0.06	0.07	-2.34	-1.74	-2.32
HallMonitor	0.00	0.02	0.03	-0.17	1.35	-0.55
Container	0.21	0.21	0.21	-0.11	-0.10	-0.11
Akiyo	0.10	0.14	0.10	-3.38	-2.46	-3.38
News	0.22	0.16	0.17	-2.01	-0.53	-1.30
Foreman	0.03	0.04	0.03	-2.39	-1.18	-2.85

Table 2. Average speedup ratios of ME time and SP/MB compared to the Full Search for the three algorithms

Sequence	Avg. speedup ratio of ME time			Avg. speedup ratio of SP/MB		
	EZPS	Proposed	Wu's	EZPS	Proposed	Wu's
Mobile	33.94	98.65	32.34	112.41	213.21	112.76
HallMonitor	24.28	81.13	23.36	148.72	274.40	150.15
Container	27.69	87.60	28.10	149.32	283.93	151.25
Akiyo	23.13	79.93	23.34	126.46	244.09	127.37
News	24.28	75.70	24.91	74.13	231.89	127.62
Foreman	21.29	65.88	25.42	109.32	219.34	121.72

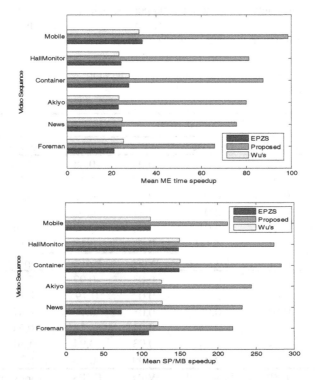

Fig. 4. Average speedup ratios of ME time and SP/MB compared with the Full Search for the three algorithms, including EPZS, Wu's and the proposed method

mode. Table 2 and Fig. 4 show the average speedup ratios of the results when QP is set to 24, 28 and 32 for different sequences. The speedup ratio is the execution time of ME compared to Full Search of each algorithm. It indicates that the number of search points in the proposed algorithm is about half of those of the other two methods in JM while the execution time is about three times faster than the other methods.

From these results, it is obvious that our algorithm has similar performance compared with FS. Both the average PSNR and bitrate variations are negligible, but the average ME time speedup (81.48) and average SP/MB speedup (244.47) factors of our proposed algorithm are significantly greater than those of the other two algorithms.

6   Conclusions

In this paper, we presented a variable-block-size mode decision algorithm based on statistical learning. In this work, several representative features are investigated to help decide the best Intermode from variable block sizes. Experimental results show that they can provide good discriminating features for the Intermode classification problem. To our knowledge, this is the first work that introduces the statistical learning technique into the variable-block-size Intermode decision problem. Experimental results show that the number of search points required in the proposed algorithm is about half of the previous methods, including the EPZS method used in JM. The execution speed of our algorithm is about three times faster than these existing methods while achieving nearly the same compression quality in terms of PSNR and bitrate.

Acknowledgements

This work was supported by MOEA research project under grant 96-EC-17-A-01-S1-034 and National Science Council, under grant 96-2220-E-007-028.

References

1. Wu, D., Pan, F., Lim, K.P., Wu, S., Li, Z.G., Lin, X., Rahardja, S., Ko, C.C.: Fast Intermode Decision in H.264/AVC Video Coding. IEEE Trans. Circuits & Systems For Video Technology 15(6), 953–958 (2005)
2. Kuo, T.-Y., Chan, C.-H.: Fast Variable Block Size Motion Estimation for H.264 Using Likelihood and Correlation of Motion Field. IEEE Trans. Circuits & Systems for Video Technology 16(10), 1185–1195 (2006)
3. Jain, A.K.: Fundamentals of digital image processing, ch. 4. Prentice-Hall, Englewood Cliffs (1989)
4. Tourapis, A.M.: Enhanced Predictive Zonal Search for Single and Multiple Frame Motion Estimation. In: SPIE Proceedings of the Visual Comm. Image Proc. (2002)

A Novel Motion Estimation Method Based on Normalized Cross Correlation for Video Compression

Shou-Der Wei, Wei-Hau Pan, and Shang-Hong Lai

Department of Computer Science, National Tsing Hua University, Hsinchu, Taiwan
{greco,whpan,lai}@cs.nthu.edu.tw

Abstract. In this paper we propose to use the normalized cross correlation (NCC) as the similarity measure for block-based motion estimation (ME) to replace the sum of absolute difference (SAD) measure. NCC is a more suitable similarity measure than SAD for reducing the temporal redundancy in video comparison since we can obtain flatter residual after motion compensation by using the NCC as the similarity measure in the motion estimation. The flat residual results in large DC term and smaller AC term, which means less information is lost after quantization. Thus, we can obtain better quality in the compressed video. Experimental results show the proposed NCC-based motion estimation algorithm can provide similar PSNR but better SSIM than the traditional full search ME with the SAD measure.

Keywords: Motion estimation, normalized cross correlation, SSIM.

1 Introduction

Motion estimation (ME) is widely used in many applications related to computer vision and image processing, such as object tracking, object detection, pattern recognition and video compression, etc. Especially, block-based motion estimation is very essential for motion-compensated video compression, since in principle it finds the temporal correlation to reduce the data redundancy between frames and achieve high compression ratio. Many block-based ME algorithms have been proposed in the past. All of these block-based motion estimation algorithms are developed for finding the block with the smallest matching error, which can mostly reduce the temporal redundancy in the current target block. In terms of block distortion measure, the sum of absolute difference (SAD) is commonly used in video compression. It is defined in equation (1), where the block size is $N \times N$, (u,v) is the motion vector, and I_t and I_{t-1} denote the current image and reference image, respectively.

Most of the previous motion estimation methods can be roughly categorized into two categories; namely the approximate block matching methods [1][2][3] and the optimal block matching methods [4][5][6], which have the same solution as that of full search but with less operations by using the early termination in the computation of SAD, given by

S. Satoh, F. Nack, and M. Etoh (Eds.): MMM 2008, LNCS 4903, pp. 338–347, 2008.
© Springer-Verlag Berlin Heidelberg 2008

$$SAD_{x,y}(u,v) = \sum_{j=0}^{N-1}\sum_{i=0}^{N-1}\left|I_t(x+i,y+j) - I_{t-1}(x+u+i,y+v+j)\right| \qquad (1)$$

Beside the SAD and SSD, the NCC is also a popular similarity measure. The NCC measure is more robust than SAD and SSD under linear illumination changes, so the NCC measure has been widely used in object recognition and industrial inspection. The definition of NCC is given as follows:

$$NCC(x,y) = \frac{\displaystyle\sum_{i=1}^{M}\sum_{j=1}^{N}I(x+i,y+j)\cdot T(i,j)}{\sqrt{\displaystyle\sum_{i=1}^{M}\sum_{j=1}^{N}I(x+i,y+j)^2} \cdot \sqrt{\displaystyle\sum_{i=1}^{M}\sum_{j=1}^{N}T(i,j)^2}} \qquad (2)$$

In this paper, we propose a block-based motion estimation method by using the NCC as similarity measure. The experimental results show that the proposed algorithm has similar PSNR and bit rate but it provides better SSIM value compared to full search SAD. The rest of this paper is organized as follow: we first briefly review the integral image scheme for speeding up the NCC computation. Then, we describe the reason of applying the NCC as the similarity measure for ME in section 3. The experimental results are shown in section 4. Finally, we conclude this paper in the last section.

2 Normalized Cross Correlation by Integral Image

The traditional NCC needs to compute the numerator and denominator, which is very time-consuming. Later, the integral image scheme [7][8][9] has been proposed to reduce the computation in the denominator. Below we describe the integral image scheme briefly.

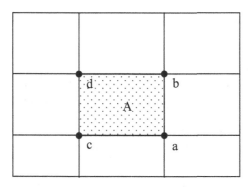

Fig. 1. An example of integral image

Equation 3 is the definition of integral image. Note that I is the original image, and S is the integral image of I. We can calculate the square sum of any subimage very efficiently by the integral image. As shown in Figure 1, the square sum of subimage A can be calculated by $S(a)+S(d)-S(b)-S(c)$. This approach can be used to calculate the denominator of NCC computation.

$$S(x, y) = \sum_{i=1}^{x} \sum_{j=1}^{y} I(i, j)^2 \qquad (3)$$

3 Motion Estimation by Normalized Cross Correlation

The NCC is a more robust similarity measure than the SAD, especially under linear illumination change. If we apply the NCC as the similarity measure in motion estimation, we can obtain flatter residual between the current MB and the best MB. Here is an example of applying the NCC and SAD measures for ME on the MB (the black square 8×8) to the frame shown in Figure 2 and the corresponding residuals are depicted in Figure 3. Because the SAD is to find the best one who has the lowest error and the NCC is to find the best MB whose overall intensity variations is most similar to the current MB, the error of SAD (539) is less than that of NCC (623). Although the error of NCC is larger than SAD, the residual obtained by using NCC for ME is flatter than that of SAD as shown in Figure 3. Thus, we can get larger DC term and smaller AC terms after DCT. The smaller AC terms mean we lose less information after the quantization. Thus, we can obtain better quality of the reconstructed frame.

The peak signal-to-noise ratio (PSNR) is a traditional and well-known image quality measurement, which measures the difference between two input signals by mean-square error. It is defined as follows:

$$PSNR = 10 \times \log(\frac{MAX_I^2}{MSE}), \qquad (4)$$

where MAX_I is the maximum intensity value of the signal, MSE is the mean-square error of the two given signals. However, research in [10] indicates that the magnitude of PSNR may not well represent the perceptual quality evaluated by human eyes since PSNR only consider the mean-square error of two given signals.

Recently, lots of video quality assessment methods based on human vision system (HVS) are proposed, as we know that PSNR may not represent the perceptual quality very well. Wang et al. [11] proposed a measure of image structural distortion called SSIM, which is widely used as a new quality measure for HVS. In [11], the luminance, contrast and structure measures are defined as:

$$l(x, y) = \frac{2\mu_x\mu_y + C_1}{\mu_x^2 + \mu_y^2 + C_1}, \; c(x, y) = \frac{2\sigma_x\sigma_y + C_2}{\sigma_x^2 + \sigma_y^2 + C_2}, \; s(x, y) = \frac{\sigma_{xy} + C_3}{\sigma_x\sigma_y + C_3}, \qquad (5)$$

Fig. 2. The example of frame 58 of Forman sequence, the black square indicate a current MB

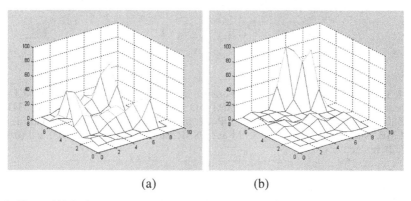

(a)   (b)

Fig. 3. The residual of current MB and best MB in Figure 2. The best MBs are determined by different similarity. (a) NCC. (b) SAD. The total error value of (a) is 623 and (b) is 539.

where x and y are two input signals, μ_x, μ_y are the sample mean of x and y, respectively, σ_x, σ_y are the variances of x and y, respectively, σ_{xy} is the covariance between x and y, and C_1, C_2 and C_3 are the parameters. The SSIM is defined by:

$$SSIM(x, y) = l(x, y) \cdot c(x, y) \cdot s(x, y) \tag{6}$$

With this measure, we can evaluate the quality of reconstructed frames in a much more meaningful way for HVS instead of PSNR.

4 Experimental Results

We implemented NCC-based ME in JM 11.0. The experiments are carried out with five sequences in QCIF format and the number of encoded frame is set to 150 for

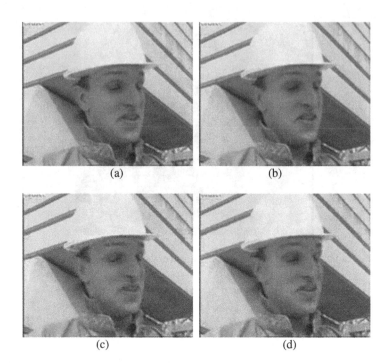

Fig. 4. The 74th reconstructed frame of Foreman by using (a) SAD-based and (b) NCC-based ME with QP=28. The corresponding SSIM and PSNR values are (0.94103, 35.5341) and (0.94680, 35.5926), respectively. When QP=32, the results of (c) SAD-based and (d) NCC-based ME, with the corresponding SSIM and PSNR values (0.91972, 33.0963) and (0.92606, 33.1782), respectively.

each sequence. The search range is set to 16, and only the 8×8 DCT is enabled. Since we focused on the performance between NCC and SAD, only the 8×8 block type is active to perform ME in order to adapt to the 8×8 DCT. We compared these two different ME algorithm by PSNR and SSIM, parameters of SSIM are set to the default value in [11].

To prove that NCC-based ME works better for perceptual quality, the 74-th and 51-th reconstructed frames of Foreman and Suzie sequence with QP=28,32 are listed in Figure 4 and Figure 5. From the reconstructed frames we can observe that the artificial noise made by quantization/dequantization error in high frequency DCT coefficients is significantly reduced by using NCC-based ME. Moreover, there is also a great increment of SSIM in the listed figures. It is obvious that SSIM is a more appropriate measurement with objective video quality. The SSIM value comparison between SAD-based and NCC-based ME of Foreman and Suzie sequences are listed in Figure 6. It is clear that the NCC-based ME performs better in terms of SSIM evaluation than the SAD-based ME.

The detail experimental results of SSIM, PSNR, and bit rate are listed in Table 1, 2 and 3 with different QP values. Table 4 shows the average performance increments to

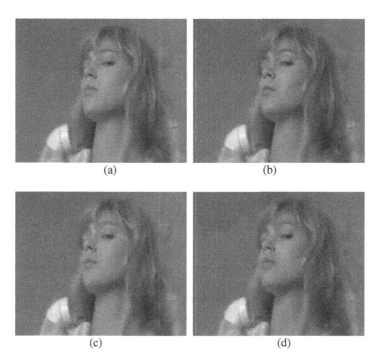

Fig. 5. The 51st reconstructed frame of Suzie by using (a) SAD-based and (b) NCC-based ME with QP=28. The corresponding SSIM and PSNR values are (0.94508, 37.8209) and (0.95388, 38.0996), respectively. When QP=32, the results of (c) SAD-based and (d) NCC-based ME, with the corresponding SSIM and PSNR values (0.92012, 35.5657) and (0.93517, 35.6596), respectively.

Table 1. Performance comparison for SAD-based ME and NCC-based ME for different video sequences with QP=24

Sequence	SAD-based ME			NCC-based ME		
	SSIM	PSNR (dB)	Bit Rate (kbits/s)	SSIM	PSNR (dB)	Bit Rate (kbits/s)
Foreman	0.9607	39.042	431.83	0.9630	39.136	436.04
Suzie	0.9579	40.195	305.82	0.9598	40.259	320.02
Silent	0.9607	38.571	195.64	0.9619	38.622	197.55
Coastguard	0.9550	38.064	647.16	0.9554	38.075	646.21
News	0.9737	39.571	220.01	0.9748	39.562	230.68

compare the NCC-based ME with the SAD-based ME. With the increment of QP value, the SSIM increment is also larger since the quantization/dequantization error in high frequency DCT coefficients is greatly increased for the SAD-based ME.

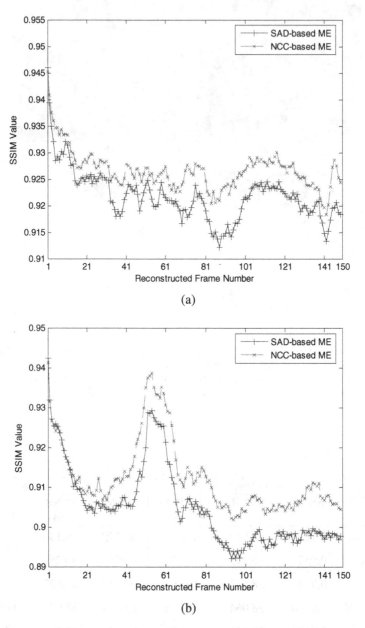

(a)

(b)

Fig. 6. Comparison of SSIM values between the SAD-based ME and NCC-based ME for different reconstructed frames of (a) Foreman and (b) Suzie sequences under QP=32

Table 2. Performance comparison for SAD-based ME and NCC-based ME for different video sequences with QP=28

Sequence	SAD-based ME			NCC-based ME		
	SSIM	PSNR (dB)	Bit Rate (kbits/s)	SSIM	PSNR (dB)	Bit Rate (kbits/s)
Foreman	0.9437	36.564	276.47	0.9472	36.658	285.96
Suzie	0.9347	37.839	186.95	0.9391	37.889	207.22
Silent	0.9372	36.235	125.72	0.9396	36.325	131.21
Coastguard	0.9165	35.087	383.29	0.9182	35.126	384.54
News	0.9629	37.118	155.76	0.9629	37.041	172.51

Table 3. Performance comparison for SAD-based ME and NCC-based ME for different video sequences with QP=32

Sequence	SAD-based ME			NCC-based ME		
	SSIM	PSNR (dB)	Bit Rate (kbits/s)	SSIM	PSNR (dB)	Bit Rate (kbits/s)
Foreman	0.9218	34.293	189.43	0.9269	34.341	204.41
Suzie	0.9053	35.755	129.24	0.9128	35.672	139.48
Silent	0.9121	34.545	84.97	0.9159	34.624	92.86
Coastguard	0.8563	32.284	214.51	0.8628	32.346	223.37
News	0.9460	34.899	115.36	0.9474	34.909	130.30

Table 4. Comparison of average performance increments (difference) between NCC-based ME and SAD-based ME with different QP values

QP	Average performance increment		
	Δ SSIM*10^3	Δ PSNR(dB)	Δ Bit Rate(%)
24	1.37	0.042	2.259
28	2.36	0.039	5.944
32	4.78	0.023	8.440

Table 5. Average execution time per frame for NCC-based ME and SAD-based ME

ME algorithm	SAD-based ME	NCC-based ME
Average execution time per frame (ms)	390	360

We implemented the NCC by applying the integral image approach to efficiently calculate the denominator. Table 5 shows the executing time of applying NCC as the similarity measure in motion estimation in comparison with the traditional full search SAD. We perform our experiments with the AMD64 X2 processor in 2.01 GHz. The execution time of NCC is less than that of the SAD-based full search ME. For practical applications, there are some efficient NCC methods that can be used to reduce the computational cost of the numerator in NCC for implementation under the PC platform. For the DSP platform, there are more and more DSPs have the inner product instruction and the calculation of numerator only needs one operation. Furthermore, we can even use the predefined search pattern to find an approximate solution, like the fast ME methods [1][2][3].

5   Conclusion

In this paper, we apply the normalized cross correlation as the similarity measure for motion estimation to find the best MB for the current MB. The residual between the current MB and the best MB by using the NCC-based ME is normally much flatter than that obtained by the SAD-based ME. The flatter residual results in larger DC value and smaller AC values, thus leading to better quality in the reconstructed frame. The experimental results show the NCC-based ME can provide higher quality and better SSIM in the reconstructed frame than the SAD-based ME. In the future we can further adopt more efficient NCC methods to reduce the computational cost in the NCC-based ME. For practical applications, we can use a predefined pattern to find an approximate solution, like DS and TSS for SAD-based ME. Furthermore we plan to apply NCC and SAD in a hybrid way for motion estimation with an appropriate criterion to obtain better quality in the decompressed video.

Acknowledgements

This work was supported by MOEA research project under grant 96-EC-17-A-01-S1-034 and National Science Council, under grant 96-2220-E-007-028.

References

1. Zhu, S., Ma, K.K.: A new diamond search algorithm for fast block-matching motion estimation. IEEE Trans. Image Processing 9(2), 287–290 (2000)
2. Li, R., Zeng, B., Liou, M.L.: A new three-step search algorithm for block motion estimation. IEEE Trans. Circuits Systems Video Technology 4(4), 438–442 (1994)
3. Po, L.M., Ma, W.C.: A novel four-step search algorithm for fast block motion estimation. IEEE Trans. Circuits Systems Video Technology 6(3), 313–317 (1996)
4. Li, W., Salari, E.: Successive elimination algorithm for motion estimation. IEEE Trans. Image Processing 4(1), 105–107 (1995)
5. Gao, X.Q., Duanmu, C.J., Zou, C.R.: A multilevel successive elimination algorithm for block matching motion estimation. IEEE Trans. Image Processing 9(3), 501–504 (2000)

6. Lee, C.-H., Chen, L.-H.: A fast motion estimation algorithm based on the block sum pyramid. IEEE Trans. Image Processing 6(11), 1587–1591 (1997)
7. Lewis, J.P.: Fast template matching. Vision Interface, 120–123 (1995)
8. Mc Donnel, M.: Box-filtering techniques. Computer Graphics and Image Processing 17, 65–70 (1981)
9. Viola, P., Jones, M.: Robust real-time object detection. In: Proceeding of International Conf. on Computer Vision Workshop Statistical and Computation Theories of Vision (2001)
10. Wang, Z., Bovik, A.C., Lu, L.: Why is image quality assessment so difficult. In: IEEE International Conference on Acoustics, Speech, and Signal Processing, Orlando (May 2002)
11. Wang, Z., Bovik, A.C., Sheikh, H.R., Simoncelli, E.P.: Image quality assessment: From error visibility to structural similarity. IEEE Transactions on Image Processing 13(4) (April 2004)

Curved Ray-Casting for Displacement Mapping in the GPU

Kyung-Gun Na and Moon-Ryul Jung

Department of Media Technology
School of Media, Sogang Univ., Korea
{gun,moon}@sogang.ac.kr

Abstract. To achieve interactive speed, displacement mapping in the GPU is typically implemented in two steps: vertex shading/rasterization of the base surface and pixel shading. Pixel shading applies the height map relative to the image plane of the base surface, casts view rays to the height field through each pixel, finds the intersection point with the height field, and computes the color of that point. Here, the ray-casting process involves significant errors; The spatial relationship between the ray and the base surface is not preserved between the ray and the image plane of the base surface. The errors result in incorrect silhouettes. To address this problem, we curve the ray so that the spatial relationship between the (linear) ray and the base surface is preserved between the curved ray and the image plane of the base surface. This method reduces intersection errors, producing more satisfactory silhouettes, self-occlusions and shadows.

Three-Dimensional Graphics and Realism: shading, texture, displacement mapping, GPU.

1 Introduction

Texture mapping is widely used to make rendering more realistic, but cannot represent the fine geometry of a surface. Bump mapping [1] produces impressive shading effects, but this technique is also incapable of modeling self occlusions, shadows, or silhouettes. However, displacement mapping is able to achieve these effects.

Displacement mapping was introduced by Cook [2]. It applies the height map to the base surface and obtains the detailed surface. To apply the height map, it uses the normal map, the texture of the normal vectors to the base surface. This method requires heavy computation.

Recent displacement mapping approaches take advantage of the programmable pixel pipeline of the GPU. We can apply vertex shading to the surface obtained by applying the height map to the base surface, and rasterize the resulting surface using the attributes of vertices. Because the resolution of height maps is typically very high, this method can take much time. So, to achieve interactive speed, displacement mapping in the GPU is typically implemented in two steps: vertex shading/rasterizing and pixel shading. Vertex shading/rasterizing

S. Satoh, F. Nack, and M. Etoh (Eds.): MMM 2008, LNCS 4903, pp. 348–357, 2008.

compute the attributes of the vertices and rasterize the base surface. Pixel shading applies the height map relative to the image plane of the base surface, casts view rays to the height field through each pixel, finds the intersection point with the height field, and computes the color of that point.

Many methods implement the ray-casting process approximately, causing significant intersection errors. The early method is parallax method [4], which is similar to bump mapping. The difference is that parallax mapping shifts the texture coordinates by considering the view point and the height field. Parallax mapping is not capable of detecting self-occlusions and silhouettes at steep view angles. More satisfactory silhouettes can be generated by using view-dependent displacement data as in [9,10,11]. These methods store pre-computed displacements for each texel relative to many sampled viewing directions. They can produce nice results at a high frame rate. However, they require large size data. Due to pre-computed displacement and resolution, the method is not suitable for close-up rendering and surface deformation. "Relief mapping"[8] casts view rays to the height field applied to the image plane and finds intersections between the rays and the height field (Figure 1.(b)). This method assumes that the base surface is the flat near the currently processed pixel. This method has been improved by reducing the time spent for intersection [3,5,6]. A significant disadvantage of these approaches is the inability to produce satisfactory object silhouettes due to the intersection errors.

Relief mapping has been improved to get better silhouettes by Oliveira et al. [7]. The idea is to represent the base surface "faithfully" near the currently processed pixel. To represent the local base surface around a given pixel point, this method constructs a quadric surface using the curvature information of the base surface, and displaces the height field by the heights of the quadratic surface from the image plane of the base surface. This method tries to overcome the assumption that the base surface is flat near the currently processed pixel. This extended relief mapping method [7] generates reasonably good silhouettes in general. However, as the ray moves far from the given pixel point and thus intersects the height field away from the pixel, a significant difference occurs between the approximate local quadric surface and the original base surface. See Figure 1.(c). Thus, there is still the lack of satisfactory object silhouettes at steep view angles.

We propose a new GPU-based ray-casting method to produce visual effects including accurate silhouettes. As illustrated in Figure 1, the fundamental problem for typical GPU-based ray-casting methods is that the relative relationship between the ray and the height field relative to the image plane of the base surface does not approximate that between the ray and the height field relative to the base surface well enough. To solve this problem, we "curve" the ray that has passed through the surface point corresponding to the current pixel, so that the spatial relationship between the (linear) ray and the base surface is approximately preserved between the curved ray and the image plane of the base surface and, as shown in Figure 2. Here, the ray should be also curved horizontally because there is typically deformation between the texture space and the 3D space.

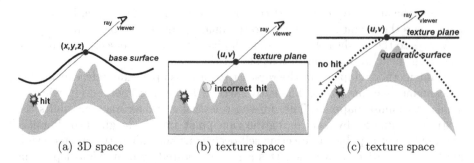

(a) 3D space   (b) texture space   (c) texture space

Fig. 1. The shaded areas are obtained by adding the height field to (a) the base polygonal surface, (b) the texture plane and (c) the local quadric surface. (a) The ray is cast through the surface point corresponding to the current pixel and intersects the height field. (b) The height field is interpreted relative to the texture plane. If linear ray casting is used, the intersection may occur at a wrong position. (c) The height field is interpreted relative to the quadric surface at the current pixel. In case the ray travels far from the given pixel to find an intersection, a considerable difference occurs between the quadric surface and the original base surface. So, there may be no intersection with the height field, causing incorrect silhouettes.

We call this method as "the curved ray casting", whereas we call the typical method as the "linear ray casting". The curved ray reduces incorrect intersections. Our approach has several advantages as follows:

- Silhouettes can be generated with less distortions at steep viewing angles compared with the extended relief mapping method [7].
- Curved ray casting method doesn't require any extra data storage in contrast to the methods using view dependent displacement data [9,10,11].

2   Height Mapping

We assume that the base surface is a triangular mesh, and the height mapping is defined by the correspondence between the 2D points on the texture plane and the vertices on the base surface. This correspondence is typically defined by the modeler. In this paper, we represent the height mapping as a piecewise linear mapping between the texture space and the tangent spaces in 3D space.

We now define the piecewise linear height mapping. Let the i-th triangle of the base surface be defined by the vertices p_{i1}, p_{i2}, p_{i3}. Let the corresponding texture coordinates for height be (u_{i1}, v_{i1}, h_{i1}), (u_{i2}, v_{i2}, h_{i2}), (u_{i3}, v_{i3}, h_{i3}), respectively. The piecewise linear mapping between the texture space and the tangent space is defined by determining the basis vectors T_i, B_i, N_i for the tangent space as shown in Figure 3. The tangent space is used to define the height map, and is simply the tangent plane plus the normal vector. The tangent space consists of basis vectors T_i, B_i, N_i. Here, T_i corresponds to the basis vector of the texture space where the first texture coordinate u increases. B_i corresponds to the basis of the

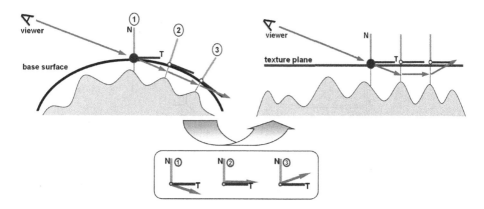

Fig. 2. Left (in 3D space): The ray, which passes through the surface point corresponding to the current pixel, does not intersect the height field defined on the original base surface. **Right** (in texture space): To simulate the non-intersection in the top figure, the ray passing through the current pixel changes its direction piecewise by using the inverse of the piecewise linear height mapping from the texture space to the tangent space of the base surface.

texture space where the second texture coordinate v increases. N_i is chosen to be perpendicular to T_i and B_i. Note that T_i and B_i are not necessarily orthogonal to each other, because there is typically deformation between the texture space and the 3D space. Also, the basis vectors do not necessarily have the unit length, because there is typically scaling transformation between the texture space and the 3D space.

The basis vectors T_i, B_i, and N_i are determined to satisfy equation(1).

$$p_{i2} - p_{i1} = (u_{i2} - u_{i1})T_i + (v_{i2} - v_{i1})B_i$$
$$p_{i3} - p_{i1} = (u_{i3} - u_{i1})T_i + (v_{i3} - v_{i1})B_i$$
$$N_i = T_i \times B_i \tag{1}$$

The piecewise linear height mapping between displacement $(\triangle u_i, \triangle v_i, \triangle h_i)$ in the texture space and displacement $\triangle p_i = (\triangle p_{ix}, \triangle p_{iy}, \triangle p_{iz})$ in tangent space is given by equation(2):

$$\triangle p_i = \triangle u_i T_i + \triangle v_i B_i + \triangle h_i N_i$$
$$= \begin{bmatrix} B_i \ T_i \ N_i \end{bmatrix} \begin{bmatrix} \triangle u_i \ \triangle v_i \ \triangle h_i \end{bmatrix}^T$$
$$= M_i \begin{bmatrix} \triangle u_i \ \triangle v_i \ \triangle h_i \end{bmatrix}^T \tag{2}$$

The transformation M for each vertex is computed by averaging M_i's of the triangles adjacent to the vertex. The average of M_i's is obtained by computing the averaged T and B out of basis vectors T_i and B_i, and getting N as the cross product of T and B. This method of averaging does not create any mathematical difficulty because in M, T and B need not be orthogonal to each other, and vectors T, B, N need not have the unit length. For arbitrary (u, v), $M(u, v)$ is

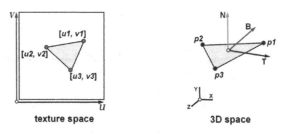

Fig. 3. Tangent space

obtained by linearly interpolating the values of M at the vertices of the triangle containing point (u, v).

Given a 3D displacement d, the inverse height mapping M_i^{-1} can be computed by equation(3), using only the fact that the normal vector N_i is orthogonal to T_i and B_i. Note that (u, v) depends on only the horizontal components of d, and h on the vertical component of d.

$$u = \frac{(T_i \cdot d)B_i^2 - (B_i \cdot d)(B_i \cdot T_i)}{B_i^2 T_i^2 - (B_i \cdot T_i)^2}$$

$$v = \frac{(B_i \cdot d)T_i^2 - (T_i \cdot d)(B_i \cdot T_i)}{B_i^2 T_i^2 - (B_i \cdot T_i)^2}$$

$$h = \frac{N_i \cdot d}{N_i^2} \tag{3}$$

To preserve the relative spatial relationship between the base surface and a ray passing through it, the ray should be curved as much as as the base surface is curved to be flat. To obtain the curved ray in the texture space, we apply the inverse transformation $M(u_i, v_i)^{-1}$ to the linear ray. This is the core idea of our method.

The inverse transformation $M(u, v)^{-1}$ maps the height field $(\triangle u, \triangle v, \triangle h)$. It can be also applied to the ray vectors. The ray vector can be decomposed into the horizontal component on the tangent plane and the normal component. We can apply $M(u, v)^{-1}$ to the horizontal component of the ray vector to obtain the horizontal component of the corresponding ray vector in the texture space. The normal component of the ray vector in the texture space is defined accordingly. Confer equation(3). The detail will be discussed more in section 3.

3   Curved (Piecewise Linear) Ray Casting

Our method curves the ray so that the spatial relationship between the (linear) ray and the base surface is preserved between the curved ray and the image plane of the base surface. The problem is how to deform the ray passing through the base surface as the base surface is deformed to the image plane. The information about the base surface is not available within the pixel shader where the ray-height field intersection is processed. The inverse of the piecewise linear height mapping describes how the height field on the base surface is deformed to the height field with respect to the texture space. So, we curve the ray by using the inverse of the height mapping $M(u, v)$ as in **Algorithm 1.**

Algorithm 1.   Repeat the steps 2 - 6 for every pixel (x_i, y_i):
1. Given the ray direction $r(u_0, v_0)$ for a given pixel (x_i, y_i), where $(u_0, v_0) = texel(x_i, y_i)$, get $M(u_0, v_0)$. Let $cr(u_0, v_0, t)$ refer to the curved ray passing through the point (u_0, v_0) in the texture space. $cr(u_0, v_0, 0) = (u_0, v_0, 0)$.
2. $k := 0$.
3. Loop: Get the ray segment $\triangle t_k[r(u_0, v_0)]$, and transform it to the texture space ray vector $r'(u_k, v_k)$, by $r'(u_k, v_k) := M(u_k, v_k)^{-1} \triangle t_0[r(u_0, v_0)]$
4. $cr(u_0, v_0, \sum_{n=0}^{k+1} \triangle t_n) := cr(u_0, v_0, \sum_{n=0}^{k} \triangle t_n) + r'(u_k, v_k)$.
5. $k := k + 1; (\triangle u_k, \triangle v_k) := (r'(u_k, v_k)[0], r'(u_k, v_k)[1]);$
   $(u_k, v_k) := (u_{k-1}, v_{k-1}) + (\triangle u_k, \triangle v_k)$.
6. If the height of the curved ray, i.e. $cr(u_0, v_0, \sum_{n=0}^{k} \triangle t_n)[2]$, is greater than the height of the height map at (u_k, v_k), break the loop with (u_k, v_k) as the texel corresponding to the intersection point. Otherwise goto Loop.

The step size $\triangle t_i$ is controlled by the user, and is fixed as constant in our implementation. Given the ray direction $r(u_0, v_0)$ step (3) initially transforms the ray segment $\triangle t_0[r(u_0, v_0)]$ by $M(u_0, v_0)^{-1}$. Then the algorithm obtains the current ray segment $\triangle t_1[r(u_0, v_0)]$ and tries to transform it. To do so, we need to get an appropriate transformation for the vector $\triangle t_1[r(u_0, v_0)]$. As indicated in section 2, we use the inverse of the height mapping, $M(u, v)^{-1}$, for some (u, v) for this purpose. Here we provide how. We demand that the current ray segment $\triangle t_1[r(u_0, v_0)]$ be deformed according as the base surface is deformed to be flat. The information for doing it exactly is no longer available in the GPU. This demand can be satisfied approximately if the current ray segment $\triangle t_1[r(u_0, v_0)]$ is deformed by $M(u, v)^{-1}$ where (u, v) is the horizontal component of the starting point of the ray segment $\triangle t_1[r(u_0, v_0)]$. The starting point of the current ray segment $\triangle t_1[r(u_0, v_0)]$ is the end point of the previous ray segment $\triangle t_0[r(u_0, v_0)]$. The $\triangle t_0[r(u_0, v_0)]$ lies in the tangent space defined by $M(u_0, v_0)$, and its coordinates in the texture space are given by $(\triangle u_0, \triangle v_0, \triangle h_0) := M(u_0, v_0)^{-1} \triangle t_0[r(u_0, v_0)]$. So, the end point of the horizontal component of the previous ray segment $\triangle t_0[r(u_0, v_0)]$is given $(u_1, v_1) := (u_0, v_0) + (\triangle u_0, \triangle v_0)$. This process is iterated for (u_k, v_k). If many ray segments are used to curve the ray, the errors in curving each segment will be accumulated.

4   Curved Ray Casting Using the Ray Direction Texture

In Algorithm 1, we transform the ray segment $\triangle t_k[r(u_0, v_0)]$ for a given pixel with respect to the reference frame $M(u_0, v_0)$ to the ray segment $(\triangle u_k, \triangle v_k, \triangle h_k)$ by transformation $M(u_k, v_k)^{-1}$ for each k. The iterative transformations of ray directions require a considerable computation time, since this procedure has to be repeated several times for each pixel. A simpler approximate solution can be obtained if we can use the precomputed ray directions $r'(u, v)$ in the texture space for each pixel (u, v). If we assume that the ray direction $r(u_0, v_0)$ is the same for every pixel (x_i, y_i), such approximation is possible. That assumption is reasonable if the camera is sufficiently far away from the surface points. Under this assumption, the Z-axis of the camera is taken to be the ray direction. Let $r(u, v)$ be the ray direction relative to the tangent space defined by $M(u, v)$. Then, the algorithm I works even if we replace $M(u_k, v_k)^{-1} \triangle t_k [r(u_0, v_0)]$ by $M(u_k, v_k)^{-1} \triangle t_k [r(u_k, v_k)]$ in step 3. In this case, the texture space ray directions $r'(u_k, v_k)$ for all (u_k, v_k) relative to the texture space can be pre-computed and stored as a texture called the "ray direction" texture. Thus, our algorithm using the ray direction texture is implemented by 2-pass rendering procedure. The first pass generates the texture image of ray directions in the texture space. The ray direction texture $r'(u, v)$ is computed every time the camera position is changed. We only need to compute the texture space ray directions for vertices of the base surface in the first pass rendering. The ray directions for arbitrary (u_k, v_k) can be interpolated from the ray directions of the vertices during rasterization.

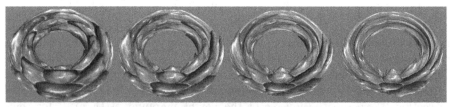

(a) extended relief mapping method

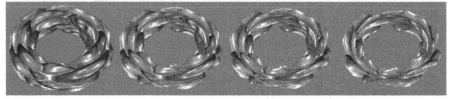

(b) curved ray casting method with ray direction map

Fig. 4. (a) and (b) show tori rendered with the height field; The height field becomes higher as we go to the right. Our method produces less distortions of silhouettes compared with the extended relief mapping method.

5   Results

We have implemented the techniques described in this paper using the OpenGL Shading Language(GLSL). We used 512×512 RGBα textures except for the ray direction texture, to create the illustrations shown in this paper. All the shown results are obtained by the ray direction texture method. In order to generate a texture for ray directions $r'(u, v)$ in the first rendering pass we used a high performance method that avoids an actual data copy by using *EXT-framebuffer-objects* extension in OpenGL 2.1. Using high-resolution ray direction texture in

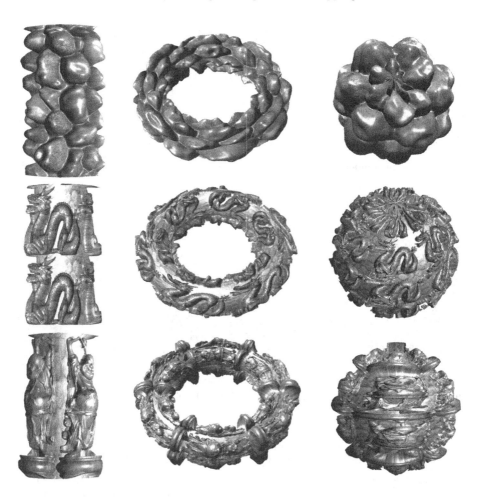

Fig. 5. The cylinders, tori and spheres rendered with ray direction map

the first pass may lower the whole rendering performance. When the surface has a simple geometry (Figure 5), we set the resolution of the ray direction texture to 32×32. This gross texture will be interpolated up to the resolution of the final image, when it is used in the rendering pass 2. In case of a more general surface as shown in Figure 7, we used a ray direction texture of a 64×64 resolution. We demonstrate there is little difference between results rendered with different resolutions of the ray direction texture (Figure 6).

We compared our method with the extended relief mapping method [7]. The higher the height field becomes, the further the ray travels, and there is a more significant difference occurs between the approximate quadric surface and the original base surface. Figure 4 demonstrates that our method produces less distortions of silhouettes compared with the extended relief mapping method. The scenes in the video are rendered at the resolution of 700×700 pixels at 60.3

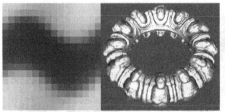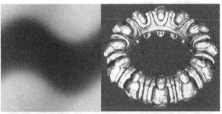

rendered torus with 16x16 ray direction map   **rendered torus with 256x256 ray direction map**

Fig. 6. The tori rendered with different resolutions of the ray direction map show little difference

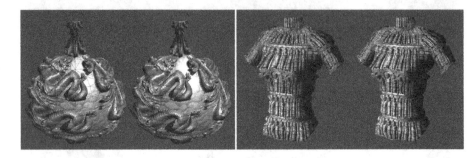

Fig. 7. The images show the arbitrary polygon surface rendered by the proposed technique. We used a ray direction texture of 64×64 resolution because of their complex geometry.

frames per second. These measurements were made on a 3.2 GHz PC using a NVIDIA Quadro FX 3400/4400. We used a linear and binary search proposed in [8] to find intersection points between curved rays and the height field. In general, the root-finding procedure is slower at steep view angles, but faster at the front view angle. Thus, we adjusted size of searching step depending on a angle between the surface normal and the view direction during ray casting [6].

6   Conclusion

We have presented a new GPU-based ray casting for displacement mapping technique to render silhouettes of highly detailed surfaces. The basic idea is to curve the view ray passing through each pixel of the rasterized base surface so that it would not intersect the height field applied to the image plane of the base surface if it would not have intersected the height field defined on the original base surface. We curve the ray so that the spatial relationship between the ray and the base surface is preserved between the curved ray and the image plane of the base surface. The method generates satisfactory silhouettes. Our technique takes advantage of the programmable GPU pipeline resulting in highly interactive frame rates with no extra data storage.

Acknowledgements

This work has been supported by the Korea Culture and Content Agency (KOCCA) for three years.

References

1. Blinn, J.F.: Simulation of Wrinkled Surfaces. In: Proceedings of the 5th annual conference on Computer graphics and interactive techniques, pp. 286–292. ACM Press, New York (1980)
2. Cook, R.L.: Shade Trees. In: Proceedings of the 11th annual conference on Computer graphics and interactive techniques, pp. 223–231 (1984)
3. Donnelly, W.: Per-Pixel Displacement Mapping With Distance Functions. In: GPU Gems 2, pp. 123–136. Addison Wesley, Reading (2005)
4. Kaneko, T., Takahei, T., Inami, M., Kawakami, N., Yanagida, Y., Maeda, T., Tachi, S.: Detailed Shape Representation with Parallax Mapping. In: Proceedings of ICAT 2001, pp. 281–286 (2001)
5. Kolb, A., Rezk-Salama, C.: Efficient empty space skipping for per-pixel displacement mapping. In: Proc. Vision, Modeling and Visualization (2005)
6. Natalya, T.: Dynamic parallax occlusion mapping with approximate soft shadows. In: I3D 2006, pp. 63–69 (2006)
7. Oliveira, M.M., Policarpo, F.: An Efficient Representation for Surface Details. UFRGS Technical Report (2005)
8. Policarpo, F., Oliveira, M.M., Comba, J.: Real-Time Relief Mapping on Arbitrary Polygonal Surfaces. In: I3D 2005, pp. 359–368 (2005)
9. Wang, L., Wang, X., Tong, X., Lin, S., Hu, S., Guo, B., Shum, H.-Y.: View-dependent displacement mapping. ACM Trans. Graph., 334–339 (2003)
10. Wang, X., Tong, X., Lin, S., Hu, S., Guo, B., Shum, H.-Y.: Generalized displacement maps. In: Eurographics Symposium on Rendering 2004, pp. 227–233 (2004)
11. Wu, H., Wei, L., Wang, X., Guo, B.: Silhouette Texture. In: Eurographics Symposium on Rendering 2006, pp. 285–296 (2006)

Emotion-Based Music Visualization Using Photos

Chin-Han Chen[1], Ming-Fang Weng[2], Shyh-Kang Jeng[1], and Yung-Yu Chuang[2]

[1] Department of Electrical Engineering,
[2] Department of Computer Science and Information Engineering,
National Taiwan University,
No. 1, Sec. 4, Roosevelt Road, Taipei, 10617, Taiwan
b90030@csie.ntu.edu.tw, mfueng@cmlab.csie.ntu.edu.tw,
skjeng@ew.ee.ntu.edu.tw, cyy@csie.ntu.edu.tw

Abstract. Music players for personal computers are often featured with music visualization by generating animated patterns according to the music's low-level features such as loudness and spectrum. This paper proposes an emotion-based music player which synchronizes visualization (photos) with music based on the emotions evoked by auditory stimulus of music and visual content of visualization. For emotion detection from photos, we collected 398 photos with their emotions annotated by 496 users through the web. With these annotations, a Bayesian classification method is proposed for automatic photo emotion detection. For emotion detection from music, we adopt an existing method. Finally, for composition of music and photos, in addition to matching high-level emotions, we also consider low-level feature harmony and temporal visual coherence. It is formulated as an optimization problem and solved by a greedy algorithm. Subjective evaluation shows emotion-based music visualization enriches users' listening experiences.

Keywords: Emotion detection, Music visualization.

1 Introduction

Media such as music and photos bring us different *emotions*, from *sadness* to *joy*, depending on the content of media. The integration of different forms of media could evoke even more feelings and give a more touching presentation as long as they are synchronized in emotions. Most music players for personal computers, such as *Winamp* and the *Microsoft Media Player*, are featured with *music visualization* by generating animated imagery when playing music. Some simply display patterns irrelevant to the music content while elaborate ones present visual effects with coordination to the music's low-level features such as loudness and frequency spectrum. There exists other more sophisticated forms of music visualization, for example, man-made music videos. However, their production involves experts and requires a lot of manual efforts. On the other hand, photo slideshow is also often accompanied with music and photos are switched at beat time to enhance viewer's watching experience. For better composition of

S. Satoh, F. Nack, and M. Etoh (Eds.): MMM 2008, LNCS 4903, pp. 358–368, 2008.

music and photos, this paper proposes a system to create emotion-based music visualization using photos. By coordinating emotions in both auditory and visual contents, emotional expression is enhanced and user's listening experience is enriched. Same technique could also be used to create more touching photo slideshows.

Recently, a lot of work has been done for emotion detection from music based on acoustical feature analysis. Lu *et al.*adopted a hierarchical framework to detect musical moods [1]. Though good performance was achieved, taxonomy of emotion classification is quite restricted in that paper, only four categories. Wu and Jeng expanded the taxonomy of music emotion to eight categories [2]. On the contrary, there are very few papers on automatic photo emotion detection if any. In this paper, we used the same emotion taxonomy proposed by Wu and Jeng [2] for both music and photos. The identical taxonomy facilitates the emotion-based integration of music and photos. With such an emotion taxonomy, we collected a set of images and annotated their emotion categories. For automatic photo emotion detection, we propose a set of visual features that influence human visual emotion perception. A Bayesian classification framework using these visual features is proposed and leads to satisfied classification results for our application.

There are various aesthetical strategies for combining visual and auditory media empirically and many methods to measure the similarity of two media according to their content. Perceptually, tempo and timbre of music are often related to camera motions and colors in images. In Tiling Slideshow [3], photos are displayed in a tiled fashion with background music and photos are switched in synchronization with tempo of the music. In Hua *et al.*'s work [4], the tempos of music and video are extracted and matched to create music videos. hilippe Mulhem *et al.* [5] tried to give additional impacts by combining video and audio from the view of aesthetics. There is however not much connection between high-level notions of both media. In this paper, we propose a system to combine two media based on their emotions. User evaluation shows that emotion-based presentation of music and photos is more impressive and affecting. Specifically, this paper has the following contributions: (1) a collection of images with emotion annotations, (2) an automatic photo emotion detection algorithm and (3) a scheme for composition of music and photos.

The rest of this paper is organized as following. Section 2 gives an overview of our system. Section 3 introduces the method for automatic photo emotion detection. The algorithm for composition of photos and music is described in Section 4. Finally, Section 5 presents evaluation for results and Section 6 concludes the paper.

2 Overview

Figure 1 gives an overview of the proposed system. The inputs to our system is a song and a set of photos. As the first step, emotion categories are automatically extracted from the input music and photos. Based on Hevner's work [6], our

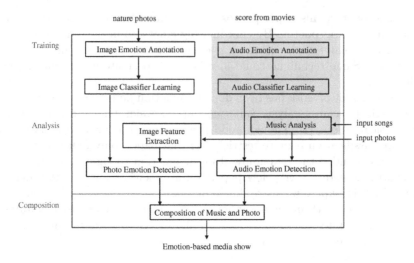

Fig. 1. System framework for emotion-based media show

emotion taxonomy consists of eight emotion classes: *sublime, sad, touching, easy, light, happy, exciting* and *grand*. For more details on the taxonomy, please refer to Wu and Jeng's paper [2]. For automatic music emotion detection, we directly apply Wu and Jeng's method [2]. In their method, the music features are selected by F-scores and a multi-class classifier is built by SVM. The average precision and recall are around 70%.

For automatic photo emotion detection, at the training stage, we collected and annotated a set of natural photos. From these images and their annotations, the distribution of emotion class is computed and classification models are learned. At the analysis stage, input photos are analyzed to predict their emotion classes by using the classifiers and models learned at the training stage. At the composition stage, based on beat analysis and music emotion detection, music is first divided into several segments, each of which contains a homogeneous emotional expression. We then attempt to assign a photo to each segment so that both have the same emotion expression. In addition to high-level emotional labels, two more criteria are considered to increase the harmony between music and photos. The first criterion is the harmonization between timbre of the music and color of the images. The second criterion is the temporal visual coherence of the photo sequence. Based on these criteria, photo sequence selection is formulated as an optimization problem and solved by a greedy algorithm.

3   Photo Emotion Detection

For automatic photo emotion detection, we collected and annotated a set of natural photos (Section 3.1). From them, Bayesian classifiers are learned. For a photo to be categorized, three types of visual features are extracted (Section 3.2) and fed into classifiers to determine its emotion category (Section 3.3).

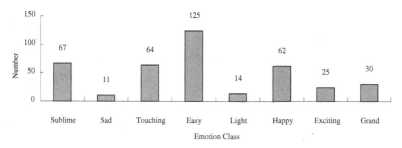

Fig. 2. The emotion class statistics of the image database

3.1   Training Data Collection

There are few image datasets with emotion annotations. In psychology, Lang conducted a series of experiments [7] using a database of photographs, the International Affective Picture System (IAPS), as the emotional stimulus. Unfortunately, IAPS has a different emotion taxonomy. In addition, most photos in IAPS are not what we will experience in our daily life. Thus, we collected 398 photos from internet and had them subjectively labeled by 496 participants through an on-line tagging system. To make the presentation joyful to watch and avoid dealing with high-level semantics, we selected photos according to two criteria: (1) we prefer images related to our daily life and without specific semantic meaning; and (2) we avoid photos containing human faces because facial expressions likely dominate the moods of photos. As a result, most photos are scenic photographs containing forrest, mountains, beaches, buildings and so on. There are also some photos on activities such as surfing and parties.

To be consistent with music emotion detection, we used the same tagging interface of emotion annotation as Wu and Jeng's work [8] for labeling photos. Because each photo is labeled by many users and they could perceive different emotions to it, instead of a single label, we represent the aggregated annotation of an image as a distribution vector over the eight emotion classes. To show some statistics about the dataset, Fig. 2 gives the numbers of images for all eight emotion classes by assigning each image to the dominant class in its distribution. Fig. 3 shows representative photos from each emotion class.

3.2   Visual Features

To construct a good computational model for photo emotion detection, we need to select a set of visual features which effectively reflect emotions. Except for high-level semantics which is still difficult to annotate accurately, among low-level visual features related to emotion, color is probably the most important one. Generally speaking, warm colors bring viewers warmth, excitement of emotions or even anger, while images dominated by cool colors tend to create cool, clamming, and gloomy moods. In some situations, a great deal of detail gives a sense of reality to a scene, and less detail implies more smoothing moods. As a result, textureness of an image also affects the viewer's emotion. Moreover, the

easy happy grand sad

sublime touching light exciting

Fig. 3. Sample images with different emotion tags from collection

directions of lines can express different feelings. Strong vertical elements usually indicate high tensional states while horizontal ones are much more peaceful. In this paper, we characterize three visual features for photo emotion detection: color, textureness, and line.

Color. The HSV color space is more suitable for human perception. We apply the method of Zhang *et al.* [9] to quantize the color space into 36 non-uniform bins. H channel is considered differently from S and V channels in a more similar way to the human vision model.

Textureness. Texture is an important cue for image feelings. In this paper, as a measure for local textureness, an entropy value is calculated for each pixel from the CIE Lab color histogram of its 32×32 neighborhood. Then, the image is divided 4×4 blocks and an average entropy value is calculated for each block.

Line. To model the line properties in images, edge features are obtained by a Canny edge detector, and then a wavelet transform is applied. The energy of spatial graininess, vertical stripes and horizontal elements are evaluated from moments of wavelet coefficients at various frequency bands.

3.3 Photo Emotion Detection

Because the annotated images are too few to cover the visual feature space, we can't obtain good classification performance by directly applying supervised learning approaches such as SVM. Instead, we propose a Bayesian approach to use unlabeled data to boost classification performance. We randomly selected 2,000 unlabeled images from another database, IAPR [10], of natural images. Visual features are extracted from these 2,000 images. Affinity propagation algorithm [11], a recently introduced powerful unsupervised clustering method, is used to group similar features into the same cluster. Assume that m clusters are formed and X_i is the representative vector of the ith cluster. From the clustering results, we adopt the package of support vector machine (SVM), LIBSVM [12], to construct a model M_i by feeding all features in the ith cluster and fivefold number of features in other clusters. The SVM model is used to predict the probability $p(X_i|I, M_i)$ that a new image I belongs to the ith cluster given its visual feature. We applied a standard sigmoid function to convert the output margin of SVM to a probability.

As explained earlier, emotion annotation for an image is expressed as a distribution over the eight defined emotions. For these 398 annotated photos, we use affinity propagation again to cluster the annotations into several discriminating clusters according to their emotional distributions. The clustering results represent major emotional distribution types. In our implementation, 19 clusters are generated, implying there are 19 major emotional distribution types. E_j denotes the representative distribution of the jth major emotional distribution type.

At the analysis stage, given a novel image I_t, we use the following formula to classify I_t into one of the 19 major emotional distributions.

$$E_t = \arg\max_{E_j} p(E_j|I_t) = \arg\max_{E_j} \sum_{i}^{m} p(E_j|X_i)p(X_i|I_t, M_i), \qquad (1)$$

where $p(X_i|I_t, M_i)$ is the probability that I_t belongs to the feature cluster X_i, estimated by the model M_i, and $p(E_j|X_i)$ is prior indicating the probability of belonging to the major emotional distribution E_j given that an image belongs to the feature cluster X_i. To evaluate $p(E_j|X_i)$, we adopt Bayes' rule

$$p(E_j|X_i) \propto p(X_i|E_j)p(E_j),$$

where $p(E_j)$ is the prior probability for the major emotional distribution E_j (Fig. 2), and $p(X_i|E_j)$ indicates the probability that an image's visual feature belongs to cluster X_i given that the image belongs to the major emotional distribution E_j. Assuming that P_{E_j} denotes the set of photos belonging to the major emotional distribution E_j in the training set, $p(X_i|E_j)$ is then approximated as

$$p(X_i|E_j) = \frac{1}{|P_{E_j}|} \sum_{I \in P_{E_j}} p(X_i|I, M_i).$$

Finally, we assign the test image I_t to the emotion category having the maximal probability in the emotional distribution E_t. By using this Bayesian framework, we can use help from unlabeled data and work around the problem of not having sufficient photos with emotion labels. From preliminary experiments, the accuracy of Bayesian framework is 43%. Although the number does not look impressive, mis-classified photos are often classified as nearby emotions. Therefore, it is unlikely to assign an opposite emotion to a photo. Thus, even if not extremely accurate, for our emotion-based music visualization, the detection results are good enough because music and photos are similar in emotion even if they could be labeled differently.

4   Composition of Music and Photos

In this section, we describe the method for music visualization composition. The music is first divided into several segments of homogenous emotional expressions. Next, for each music segment, we have to select a photo with the same emotion. In order to express various emotions in music, the number of photos is preferred to be large enough to cover a variety of emotions. As discussed in the previous section, the input photos are first grouped into different emotion classes. For each music segment, we must select a photo whose emotion label is the same as the music segment. Since we have many photos in an emotion category, we have the luxury to select a better one from multiple photos with the same emotion. Thus, in addition to matching high-level emotion category, we consider two additional criteria to further improve coordination between music and photos: (1) the consistence between low-level features of music and photos, and (2) visual coherence between successive photos.

4.1   Music Segmentation

A song often consists of more than one emotion. Thus, to detect emotion, we have to divide the song into several independent sections, each of which contains a homogeneous emotion. However, it is difficult to define where emotions switch. In fact, different emotion transition boundary decision strategies may result in different emotion detection results. Here, we present a three-stage analysis method to divide music into segments.

First, beat tracking is used to detect the rhythmic pulse of a piece of music. It is the salient part of music we often notice. As a result, the beat time is the good time to switch photos because synchronization of photo switching to music beats often improves enjoyment of watching the visualization. We use the beat tracking algorithm by Dixon [13] to divide music into many clips. Because the durations between beats are often too short for music emotion detection, we group adjacent clips into five-second segments according to the beat information. The boundary of each segment is picked to be as close to the beat time as possible. In our system, segments are the basic units from which the emotions are extracted and each segment will be associated with a photo in the visualization. Thus, the music emotion detection method is used to extract an emotion label for each segment.

After we obtain the emotion label of each segment, a regrouping process is invoked to find better emotion transition boundaries. Successive segments with the same emotion are grouped together as a longer section (Fig. 4). The emotion transition boundaries between sections are then further refined with the method proposed by Lu *et al.* [1].

4.2   Photo Sequence Selection

For music visualization composition, after finding segments of the music, we have to assign a photo to each segment. The input photos are first classified into different emotion categories. For a section S with an emotion label e, assume that S

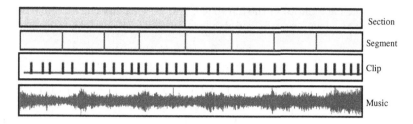

Fig. 4. The music segmentation process

has n segments and is denoted as $S = \langle s_1, s_2, \ldots, s_n \rangle$ where s_i is the ith segment of S. For the emotion class e, we have a set of m photos, $P_e = \{p_1, p_2, \ldots, p_m\}$, which has the same emotion label e. The photo sequence selection problem is to find a photo sequence $o = \langle \hat{p}_1, \hat{p}_2, \ldots, \hat{p}_n \rangle$ for section S, where $\hat{p}_i \in P_e$ and photo $\hat{p}_i$ is displayed when music segment s_i is played. The photo sequence selection is performed for each section independently. To select a proper sequence, in addition to matching high-level emotion notions, we further include the following two criteria to enhance the harmony between music and photo sequence.

Criterion 1: The coordination between low-level features of the music and photos. To be more consistent in visual and auditory perception, some low-level attributes of music and photos are selected to coordinate each other. As we listen to music, its timbre greatly affects our feelings to it. Qualities of timbre are often described as an analogy to color, since timbre is perceived and understood as a gestalt impression reflective of the entire sound. Ox pointed out that timbre is an essential feature to music in a similar way that color is to a painting [14]. Indeed, timbre literally means the color of sound. Hence, timbre is selected as the music attribute to be matched with the color of photos. Among the timbrel features, spectral centroid and spectral flux are important perceptual properties in the characterization of musical timbre [15]. According to these clues, we define a fitness function D_{feature} for measuring the coordination between the timbre of a music segment s_i and the color of a photo p as

$$D_{\text{feature}}(s_i, p) = \omega_{\text{centroid}} \cdot d_{\text{centroid}}(s_i, p) + \omega_{\text{flux}} \cdot d_{\text{flux}}(s_i, p) \ .$$

The function d_{centroid} measures the distance between spectral centroid of a music segment and brightness of a photo. If the centroid of music is large, we prefer a brighter photo. And the function d_{flux} expresses the distance between spectral flux of music and color contrast of a photo. If the flux variation in one segment is large, it means that the variation of the music timbre is large. Thus, a photo with higher color contrast is more suitable to be displayed with the segment.

Criterion 2: The temporal visual coherence of the photo sequence. We prefer a sequence whose visual appearance changes gradually along time. To measure temporal coherence of a photo sequence, the Lab color space is used. A histogram is computed for each photo in the a,b space, and we measure the distance between a pair of photos as the chi-squared distance between their ab-histograms.

$$D_{\text{coherence}}(p_i, p_j) = \begin{cases} d_{\chi^2}(H_{ab}(p_i), H_{ab}(p_j)) & \text{if } p_i \neq p_j \\ \infty & \text{otherwise} \end{cases}$$

where $H_{ab}(\cdot)$ is the histogram constructed in a,b space and $d_{\chi^2}(\cdot)$ is the chi-squared distance. An infinity distance is assigned if p_i and p_j are the same photo. This is to prevent the case that the same photo appears in succession.

The problem of photo sequence selection can then be modeled as selecting an optimal sequence $o = \langle \hat{p}_1, \hat{p}_2, \ldots, \hat{p}_n \rangle$ that minimizes the following function,

$$D(o) = \alpha \sum_{i=1}^{n} D_{\text{feature}}(s_i, \hat{p}_i) + \beta \sum_{i=1}^{n-1} D_{\text{coherence}}(\hat{p}_i, \hat{p}_{i+1}), \qquad (2)$$

where α and β are weighting parameters, D_{feature} and $D_{\text{coherence}}$ are defined above to measure the harmony between music and photos and the temporal visual coherence of a photo sequence.

It is time-consuming to solve the optimization by exhaustive search. Instead, a greedy algorithm is used to find a local optimum solution. Let the mapping $\Phi(i) = j$ denote that the optimal sequence selects photo p_j for segment s_i. The greedy algorithm sequentially finds the optimal mapping from the first segment to the last segment. Assuming that we already have solved up to the ith segment. That is, the values of $\Phi(1), \cdots, \Phi(i)$ are solved. Then, we evaluate $\Phi(i+1)$ as

$$\Phi(i+1) = \arg\min_j \alpha D_{\text{feature}}(s_{i+1}, p_j) + \beta D_{\text{coherence}}(p_{\Phi(i)}, p_j).$$

Locally best photos are sequentially found from the first segment to the last segment by repeatedly evaluating the above equation. Finally, the sequence $o = \langle p_{\Phi(1)}, p_{\Phi(2)}, \ldots, p_{\Phi(n)} \rangle$ is returned as the photo sequence to be played with the music section. All sections are processed in the same way independently to generate the whole visualization for the input music.

5   Evaluation Results

Since emotional perception of acoustic and visual media is subjective, objective evaluation of our system is difficult. Thus, we evaluate our system through a subjective user evaluation. Three types of music visualization are compared. In addition to the one generated by our system, we generate another visualization by randomly selecting photos without considering emotions. The third one is the visualization from Microsoft media player. Twenty-one evaluators aged from 20 to 50 were invited to evaluate the presentations. Particularly, we focus on evaluating how well our system bridges and enhances perception of music and photos through coordinating their emotional expressions. The following questions were asked.

Question 1 coordination: How do you think of the connection between music and photos?

Question 2 interestingness: How do you think of the presentation style?

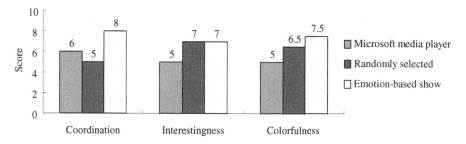

Fig. 5. Results of user evaluation

Question 3 colorfulness: How well do you think the visual contents enrich the audio?

Evaluators were asked to give scores from 1 to 10 (higher scores for more contentment) to show their satisfaction with these presentations. Fig. 5 summarizes the evaluation results. The presentation[1] generated by our method consistently has the highest scores for all questions. From the evaluation, we find that music visualization using photos is more interesting to watch than the animated patterns in traditional music visualization. Even the presentation with randomly selected photos is more fun to watch than media player. Our emotion-based music visualization coordinates the presence of music and photos much better than media player as our visualization captures higher-level notions of media in addition to low-level features. Thus, the music listening experience is enriched by synchronized emotional expressions of photos.

6   Conclusion and Future Work

In this paper, we have proposed a framework for creating emotion-based music visualization. To achieve this goal, we have collected and annotated 398 photos and proposed an automatic photo emotion detection method based on a Bayesian framework. For composition of music and photos, in addition to high-level emotion notions, we also consider temporal coherence of photo sequence and coordinate the presence of music and photos by their low-lever features of timbre and color. User evaluations indicates that emotion-based music visualization effectively enriches music listening experience.

There are several research avenues that we would like to explore in the future. For example, there is certainly room for improvement on the accuracy of emotion detection algorithms. Some transition effects could be added to harmonize with emotions. With little modification, our method could be used to create emotion-based photo slideshows. In addition to matching emotion categories, the composition method described in Section 4 could also be applied to other problem domains, such as situation types. Furthermore, the proposed method could be embedded into digital photo displays, making them more fun to watch.

---

[1] It can be found at http://www.csie.ntu.edu.tw/~b90030/emotionbased.wmv

Acknowledgment

This paper is primarily based on the work supported by the National Science Council (NSC) of Taiwan, R.O.C., under contracts NSC95-2752-E-002-006-PAE and NSC95-2622-E-002-018.

References

1. Lu, L., Liu, D., Zhang, H.J.: Automatic mood detection and tracking of music audio signals. IEEE Transactions on Audio, Speech & Language Processing 14(1), 5–18 (2006)
2. Wu, T.L., Jeng, S.K.: Probabilistic estimation of a novel music emotion model. In: The 14th International Multimedia Modeling Conference, Kyoto, Japan (2008)
3. Chen, J.C., Chu, W.T., Kuo, J.H., Weng, C.Y., Wu, J.L.: Tiling slideshow. In: ACM Multimedia, Santa Barbara, CA, USA (2006)
4. Hua, X.S., Lu, L., Zhang, H.J.: Automatic music video generation based on temporal pattern analysis. In: ACM Multimedia, New York, NY, USA (2004)
5. Mulhem, P., Kankanhalli, M.S., Yi, J., Hassan, H.: Pivot vector space approach for audio-video mixing. IEEE MultiMedia 10(2), 28–40 (2003)
6. Hevner, K.: Expression in music: a discussion of experimental studies and theories. Psychol. Rev. 42, 186–204 (1935)
7. Lang, P.J., Bradley, M.M., Cuthbert, B.N.: International affective picture system (iaps): technical manual and affective ratings. NIMH Center for the Study of Emotion and Attention (1997)
8. Wu, T.L., Jeng, S.K.: Regrouping expressive terms for musical qualia. In: WOCMAT on Computer Music and Audio Technology, Taiwan (2007)
9. Zhang, L., Lin, F., Zhang, B.: A cbir method based on color-spatial feature. In: IEEE Region 10 Annual International Conference (1999)
10. Grubinger, M., Clough, P., Muller, H., Deselears, T.: The iapr tc-12 benchmark – a new evaluation resource for visual information systems. In: International Workshop OntoImage'2006 Language Resources for Content-Based Image Retrieval (2006)
11. Frey, B.J.J., Dueck, D.: Clustering by passing messages between data points. Science (2007)
12. Chang, C.C., Lin, C.J.: LIBSVM: a library for support vector machines. (2001) Software, available at http://www.csie.ntu.edu.tw/~cjlin/libsvm
13. Dixon, S.: Mirex 2006 audio beat tracking evaluation: Beatroot. MIREX (2006)
14. Ox, J.: Two performances in the 21st century virtual color organ: GridJam and Im Januar am Nil. In: Proceedings of the Seventh International Conference on Virtual Systems and Multimedia, p. 580 (2001)
15. Grey, J.: An exploration of musical timbre. Ph.D. Dissertation, Stanford University (1975)

LightCollabo: Distant Collaboration Support System for Manufacturers

Tetsuo Iyoda, Tsutomu Abe, Kiwame Tokai, Shoji Sakamoto, Jun Shingu,
Hiroko Onuki, Meng Shi, and Shingo Uchihashi

Fuji Xerox, Co., Ltd.
430 Sakai, Nakai-machi, Ashigarakami-gun, Kanagawa, Japan

Abstract. This paper introduces our LightCollabo system which is a
distant collaboration tool designed for manufacturers. For distant collaboration between factory workers and members of a product design
team, it is important to support interactive discussion over actual objects. LightCollabo enables remotely located people to share a view of
actual objects and to annotate on the objects by using a camera and a
projector whose optic axes and view angles are precisely aligned. Light-
Collabo has been experimentally deployed in several locations in China
and Japan and proven to be effective. Initial results of our use case study
are also described.

1 Introduction

We have been designing a distant collaboration system for manufacturers. Glob-
alization is an inevitable trend in industry and demands for efficient telecommunication are increasing. Production engineers have special needs. Most video
conference systems in the market are designed to support face-to-face communication, however, watching views from remote sites is not sufficient for distant collaboration. We consider the capability to interact with remotely located objects
to be crucial. For example, when a problem is found with a product component
at a factory, remotely located engineers of the design team would want to not
only see the componet but also indicate where to investigate. Initial interviews
with engineers revealed that sending digital images via email is a popular solution to report problems and to send feedback for the reported problems. This
scheme obviously lacks interactivity and often cannot meet with time requirements. Without a proper solution, manufacturing companies are reconciled to
either sending people to the factory or shipping the defective product by express
to the design branch. Both methods are costly and the expense may ruin other
advantages of running factories globally.

Our LightCollabo system enables distant collaboration by making any physical object surface into a virtually shared workspace. Remote users can see the
object and activities of local users through video. They can also draw annotations on the video image and the annotations are projected back onto the original
object so that the local users can see. To handle 3D objects, we added several
implementation efforts upon preceding systems including iLight [3].

S. Satoh, F. Nack, and M. Etoh (Eds.): MMM 2008, LNCS 4903, pp. 369–379, 2008.
© Springer-Verlag Berlin Heidelberg 2008

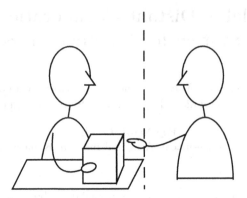

Fig. 1. A scene of collaboration over a physical object

This paper describes the design process of our LightCollabo system. We adapted a request-based approach to incrementally improve the system. Several LightCollabo systems have been already installed in our factories and product design centers located in China and Japan. Demands and feedbacks from the installed sites are collected and analyzed to update the system. This paper summarizes our activities in the last two years.

2   Problem with Distant Collaboration

2.1   Outline of Problem

Figure 1 illustrates a typical collaboration scene that we are considering. The person on the left has an object and the person on the right is pointing at a region of the object to call attention to it. Even a simple situation like this becomes a challenging task when the two people are not at the same location. The distance between them makes the dashed line in the middle of Figure 1 very difficult to get across. We need to provide a way for the person on the right to point at the remote object and for the person on the left to see the *hand* of the partner.

2.2   Current Solutions

We investigated how engineers communicate over distance especially in cases of problem solving by interviewing seven production engineers in Japan. Each interview session was organized in a semi-structured manner and lasted approximately 30 to 40 minutes. From the investigation we learned that telephone and email are the main tools of communication. Digital photos of problem scenes are often attached with email messages.

What happens frequently is that the photos and associated reports do not carry enough information for remotely located engineers to figure out the cause of the problem so that they have to request photos taken from different angles and additional descriptions of the scene. Typically, they have to iterate the process several times to establish a common understanding of the problem scene. Obviously, current solutions are not satisfactory for supporting the above communication: sending photos by email takes too long and phones alone cannot carry visual information. Video conferencing systems are not suitable either because they send blurred images tuned for face-to-face communication. Needless to say, people cannot point at an object to show "here" from a remote site using a video conferencing system.

3   LightCollabo System: Basic Design

3.1   Remote Workspace Sharing with Procam

LightCollabo uses a **pro**jector and a **cam**era (procam) to mix the local scene with gestures from the remote site. The camera captures a targeted object as well as hand movements of local participants and annotations they make around the object. The captured images are delivered through the network to remote participants for viewing. The remote participants can draw annotations on the images and the annotations are projected back onto the object. The basic design concept of LightCollabo is to let remotely located people virtually share the same workspace. As the first step, we let them share the same view and be jointly aware of it. We consider this design to facilitate joint visual attention, which is a notion known to development psychologists as the first step to establish communication [2][5].

Wellner proposed an interface using a camera and a projector to interact with both physical and virtual worlds [11]. Underkoffler *et al* investigated various arrangements of a camera and a projector for displaying virtual information onto the physical world [10]. Among others, we have chosen the 'zero-parallax' configuration where a camera and a projector are optically aligned (See Figure 2). It is the only arrangement with which annotations made by remote participants are projected as intended on any 3D object surface (See Figure 3).

Providing support for distant collaboration using a camera and a projector is an actively researched topic [3,6,9]. Most previously reported work adapts simpler arrangements so that their workspaces are restricted to near the desktop surface. To avoid the parallax issue, Bauer *et al* used a head-mounted display instead of a projector [1].

Remote collaboration using a tabletop configuration is an emerging research area [8]. We consider the tabletop as a workspace and interacting with both physical and digital objects in the workspace from local and remote sites is important.

3.2   Implementation Efforts

To make the LightCollabo procam unit practical, we had to overcome three major issues. The first issue is stray light. As Underkoffler pointed out, the 'zero-parallax' scheme is an ideal method, however it inherently suffers from stray

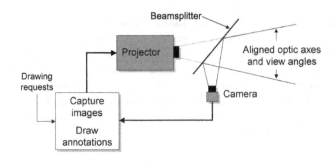

Fig. 2. Diagram of LightCollabo server

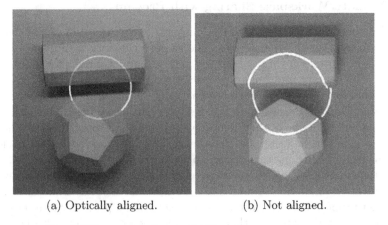

(a) Optically aligned.   (b) Not aligned.

Fig. 3. View comparisons of differently arranged cameras

light [10]. Light from the projector partially travels through the beamsplitter and becomes stray light that is eventually captured by the camera causing contrast degradation in the captured image. We collect and absorb such light using a light trap as shown in Figure 4.

The second and the third issues are both related to the projector lens. Projectors in the market have shifted lens with which images are projected upward from a horizontally set up device. This disagrees with our assumption illustrated in Figure 2 and Figure 4 where images are projected straight in front. Also, a regular projector lens has a focal depth that is just wide enough for projecting an image onto a flat surface and is too narrow for projecting annotations onto an object with modest depth. To solve the shifted-projection and the off-focus issues, we installed a specially tailored zero-shift lens with large focal depth in our system (See Figure 5).

3.3   Remote Participation

Remote participants interact with the collaborative workspace using view application software. A sequence of JPEG images from the LightCollabo procam

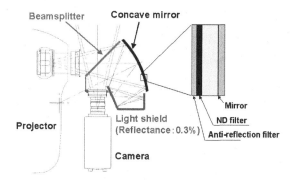

Fig. 4. Light trap structure

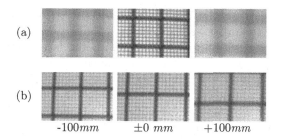

Fig. 5. Captured images around 1,000mm from the projector taken by (a)regular lens, and (b)zero-shift lens

unit is delivered through the network and shown in the application window. The remote participants can draw annotations on the images and the annotations are projected back onto the physical object through the procam unit. Figure 6 shows the interface of the viewer. Buttons are provided for selecting annotation types including text and various shapes such as eclipse, rectangle, line, and arrow. Annotations can be put in several different colors.

We chose to deliver images as a sequence instead of video stream because of the limited bandwidth to remote factories. Most of factories are located in distant places from major cities. Even today, network connection to such places is still costly and unreliable. In addition, international connectivity tends to be narrower than domestic network. Given these considerations, we concluded that sending high-resolution images at lower rate is more suitable for our purpose than streaming low-resolution video.

3.4 Sharing Physical Workspace

Local and remote participants can virtually share the same physical object in the sense that they all can see the object and locate any region on the object surface. We consider there are two ways to set up the LightCollabo procam unit. The

Fig. 6. GUI of client viewer application   **Fig. 7.** LightCollabo system

first way is to place it in front of a target object just like a projector is placed in front of a screen. The other way is to place it above a table looking down using a mirror. A larger workspace is available with the latter configuration; local participants can put related objects and documents on the table and even write on the table with markers, and remote participants can also put their annotations on the tabletop in addition to the object surface. To enable switching between the two setups, we designed a table combined with a lift (See Figure 7). Note that LightCollabo in Figure 7 is equipped with devices that were not included in the initial prototype. The additional devices are described in Section 4.

4 Preliminary Deployment

4.1 Experimental Launch

We demonstrated an early prototype of the LightCollabo system to our engineers in production sections and it was well-accepted. To further understand how they collaborate over distance and what support can be added to LightCollabo, we installed our system in several locations and observed the system usage in practical environments. Feedback from users was collected through informal interviews. We spent several months for the observation. Training sessions were held each time a system was installed at a new location for promotion.

4.2 Feedback Analysis

Considerable feedback on a wide range of topics was obtained through our deployment efforts. Below we list summaries of what we learned from the feedback and observations focusing on functionality for effective remote collaboration. Although feedback such as requests for user interface improvements is not discussed in this section, it was taken care of separately.

First, we observed that the tabletop configuration described in Section 3.4 was used most of the time. We consider it is partially because the size of physical objects that our trial users typically handle were more appropriate for placing on the table. Another explanation is that people simply wanted a larger space to work with. It was observed that people sometimes used the tabletop for chatting; local participants wrote their messages on the table with markers and messages from remote participants responded were projected on the table. The chatting worked effectively especially in multi-lingual situations. People also wrote notes on the table. The LightCollabo in the table configuration certainly provided a remotely shared physical and contextual workspace.

Secondly, we found that demands for 'zoom-up' views are high. Since the camera in the LightCollabo procam unit covers the entire tabletop, it is only good for table-top-size objects. The scale of the workspace varies depending on objects. Multiresolution structure of the workspace has to be considered to capture finer objects or even more subtle details.

Third, people occasionally see documents with objects during a distant collaboration session. Document sharing has been a popular collaboration tool. It will be ideal to incorporate document sharing capability into our system.

5   LightCollabo Updates

In response to the feedbacks from users described in Section 4, we updated our LightCollabo system. The modifications focused on handling objects in different scales and documents.

5.1   Optional Cameras

We provided two optional cameras to capture objects in different scales. The first solution uses a Pan-Tilt-Zoom (PTZ) camera. Coordinates of the procam unit's camera and parameters to drive a PTZ camera are registered in advance so that remote participants can simply specify a desired region on a viewer screen to let the system steer and zoom in the PTZ camera to obtain a detailed view of the specified region [7]. The obtained image is converted to a JPEG image and delivered by the image server. The viewer software receives the image and shows it in a pop-up window. Figure 8 shows the pop-up window. It is also equipped with control buttons of the PTZ camera. For on-site participants, the captured region is highlighted by a projected rectangle so that they can see where remote participants are looking at.

The second solution is a free arm camera which is an endoscope with a grip (See Figure 9). This camera is provided for viewing details in sub-millimeters. LED lights are placed around the lens for illuminating a target area. NTSC signals from a free arm camera are digitized as a JPEG image sequence and delivered to clients. Figure 10 illustrates a pop-up window showing a view from a free arm camera.

Note that shared workspaces using the above described cameras will be too small for projecting remote annotations and also for direct observation. Hence the workspaces are shared only on computer screens.

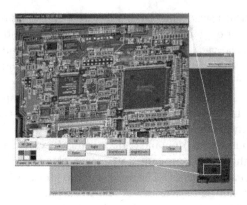

Fig. 8. Sub-window for PTZ camera

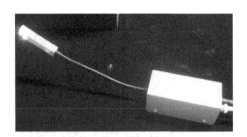

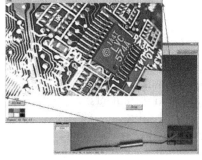

Fig. 9. A free-arm camera   **Fig. 10.** Sub-window for free arm camera

5.2 Document Sharing

We implementeded a primitive document sharing feature to the viewer application. In addition to regular annotations such as line and circle, remote participants can place any image file for sharing. The contents of the image file is projected onto the physical object or the tabletop as specified. Naturally, the system should evolve such that a remote participant can retrieve a document from a regular document sharing system and the document is projected as an image.

6   Field Test

6.1   Expectation

With the above updates, we continued installing LightCollabo in our factories and product design centers located in China and Japan. In total, 15 systems have been deployed. By observing how the systems are used, we expect we can spot the cases where LightCollabo works most effectively, and evaluate strengths and shortcomings of the current system. Especially, we expected LightCollabo can contribute in the following three areas.

- Pointing at a problem region
- Sharing circumstances where a problem occured
- Understanding what caused the problem

6.2 Settings

At each site, a LightCollabo system was installed in a conference room equipped with a phone audio teleconferencing. The conference room was located next to production lines so that engineers have immediate access to the system when a problem occurs in the lines.

We conducted intensive investigations of the system usage at 4 domestic sites and 4 oversea sites. Each investigation took one week during the period between November of 2005 and March of 2007. We observed 12 use cases of LightCollabo: 4 cases for solving emergency problems, 4 cases in regular meetings, 2 cases for changing designs, 1 case for training, and 1 case during brainstorming. Except for 1 case used for solving an emergency problem, LightCollabo was used as a part of a scheduled teleconference. Approximately 30 people from 15 different departments used the system among more than 100 participants of the teleconferences.

6.3 Case Study

This section lists scenes from our observations where LightCollabo successfully contributed in problem solving. Combinations of various features of LightCollabo were used to share the workspace. In all cases, we noticed people intensively used reference terms during discussions, for example "Put this part in this hole" or "What is the length of here?". Also they sent many gestures using LightCollabo both conciously by making annotations and unconciously by moving cursors. We consider these natural behaviors in remote communication are evidences that prove local and remote participants successfully share the same workspace using LightCollabo.

Pointing at a problem region. In order to train a product design engineer located at a remote site, local participants indicated improper points in a design plan drawn by the engineer using LightCollabo. Prior to the session, the local participants built a product component for trial based on the plan and found errors. The component was placed on the table of LightCollabo and the local participants explained where the errors are by pointing at the region and drawing on the table using markers. The remote engineer sent his feedback that was projected onto the component with which both sides confirmed that mutual understanding was achieved.

Sharing circumstances where problem occured. In a regular meeting, an engineer reported problem analysis results to a remote site using LightCollabo. The free arm camera was used to show cases where actual parts were assmbled correctly and incorrectly. The engineer drew arrows on the client view image to emphasize the difference.

Understanding what caused the problem. LightCollabo successfully led to solve a problem that a conventional method could not. A screw was conflicing with other parts of the component. First, the problem was reported by email and attached digital photos. Because none of the photos were not taken from a desired angle, engineers at the remote location decided to use LightCollabo. A local engineer was instructed to hold the component at a certain angle, while the remote engineers watched it using the PTZ camera.

6.4   Discussion

Both the PTZ camera and the free arm camera were frequently used in most of sessions. Interestingly, the free arm camera was used rather like a pointing device. On-site participants held the camera focusing at a spot where they wanted remote participants to see. In other words, the free arm camera was used to "push" the view to be shared from the local site to the remote sites.

Each of the three cameras of LightCollabo has a different role. The main camera of the procam unit is used to provide an overview image or context. Remote participants use the PTZ camera when they want to see an area in details.

Document sharing was also popularly used. People requested more views to be shared such as whiteboard for accelerating remote discussions. Often participants had to confirm whether people on the other end were watching the LightCollabo screen. A support for people on one side to know what people on the other side are watching is neccessary for fully realizing the joint visual attention concept.

7   Conclusions and Future Work

We introduced our LightCollabo system. A procam unit for LightCollabo was built by optically aligning a camera and a projector. Using the unit, LightCollabo allows remote and on-site participants to share the same workspace where all participants can see physical objects, point any region, and annotate on the objects. In response to feedbacks from our deployment efforts, two optional cameras were added to handle objects in different scales as well as a capability to share digital images along with physical objects. Observations from our deployment indicated that our system facilitates distant collaboration.

As a next step, we are planning to conduct formal user study to evaluate advantages of LightCollabo quantitatively. The task for the evaluation will be determined based on our observation. Analysis on usage logs and feedbacks from our test users in the field should reveal where users need more support and how we should further improve the LightCollabo system. To make the system more durable in practical environment, new features such as session contents archiving, network traffic control and managing secured connections, must be investigated from both system and computer-human interaction aspects.

Further, there is a challenge of expanding the shared workspace beyond the tabletop. People want to share not only viewing physical objects, but also documents, computer screens, whiteboard, and other activities in the rooms for smoother discussion over distance.

Acknowledgement

Our partners experimentally produced various components of LightCollabo. Among others, we thank Fujinon Corporation, Saitama, Japan, for their efforts in making the zero-shift projector lens.

References

1. Bauer, M., Kortuem, G., Segall, Z.: "Where Are You Pointing At?" A Study of Remote Collaboration in a Wearable Videoconference System. In: Proc. International Symposium on Wearable Computers, pp. 151–158 (1999)
2. Bruner, J.S.: Child's Talk - Learning to Use Language. Oxford University Press, Oxford (1983)
3. Foote, J., Kimber, D., Hirata, K.: Remote Interactive Graffiti. In: Proc. ACM Multimedia 2004, pp. 762–763 (2004)
4. Fussell, S.R., Setlock, L.D., Yang, J., Ou, J., Mauer, E.M., Kramer, A.: Gestures over Video Streams to Support Remote Collaboration on Physical Tasks. Human-Computer Interaction 19(3), 273–309 (2004)
5. Gergle, D., Kraut, R.E., Fussell, S.R.: Language Efficiency and Visual Technology: Minimizing Collaborative Effort with Visual Information. Journal of Language and Social Psychology 23(4), 491–517 (2004)
6. Kirk, D., Fraser, D.S.: Comparing Remote Gesture Technologies for Supporting Collaborative Physical Tasks. In: Proc. ACM CHI, pp. 1191–1200 (2006)
7. Liu, Q., Kimber, D., Foote, J., Wilcox, L., Boreczky, J.: FLYSPEC: A Multi-User Video Camera System with Hybrid Human and Automatic Control. In: Proc. ACM Multimedia 2002, pp. 484–492 (2002)
8. Perron, R., Laborie, F.: Augmented Tabletops, an Incentive for Distributed Collaboration. In: TABLETOP 2006. Proc. IEEE International Workshop on Horizontal Interactive Human-Computer Systems (2006)
9. Takao, N., Baker, S., Shi, J.: Telegraffiti: A Camera-projector based Remote Sketching System with Hand-based User Interface and Automatic Session Summarization. International Journal of Computer Vision 53(2), 115–133 (2003)
10. Underkoffler, J., Ullmer, B., Ishii, H.: Emancipated Pixels: Real-World Graphics in the Luminous Room. In: Proc. SIGGRAPH 1999, pp. 385–392 (1999)
11. Wellner, P.: Interacting with Paper on the DigitalDesk. Communications of the ACM 36(7), 87–96 (1993)

Accurate Identifying Method of JPEG2000 Images for Digital Cinema

Takahiro Fukuhara[1], Kazuhisa Hosaka[1], and Hitoshi Kiya[2]

[1] Sony Corporation B2B Solution Department,
4-14-1, Asahi-chou, Atsugi-city, Kanagawa, 243-0014
[2] Faculty of System Design, Tokyo Metropolitan University,
6-6, Asahigaoka, Hino-city, Tokyo, 191-0065

Abstract. JPEG2000 has been selected as the image compression and decompression technology for digital cinema by DCI(Digital Cinema Initiatives). In a few years, large amount of JPEG2000 compressed files will be widely used and delivered. Identifying a target compressed file out of image sequences or database is highly demanded. In this paper, very unique identifying method is presented. It takes advantage of the feature of JPEG2000 codestream structure. The proposed method has advantages of low computation and high accuracy over conventional methods.

Keywords: JPEG2000, Digital Cinema, Image Compression, Image Identification, Image Search.

1 Introduction

JPEG2000[1][2] is standardized by ISO in December, 2000. JPEG2000 has lots of functions such as high compression efficiency, lossless/lossy compression, scalability and adaptation for motion pictures. The lossy compression efficiency of JPEG2000 is about two times of that of JPEG. In 2005, JPEG2000 Part-1 was officially selected as the standard compression/decompression technology for digital cinema by DCI(Digital Cinema Initiatives)[3]. It is expected that more and more JPEG2000 files of movies will be widely used. At the same time, in the committee of ISO/IEC/JTC1/SC29/WG1, a new standardization related to JPEG2000 search[4][5] has just begun. The goal of the standardization is to define a new framework to search effectively JPEG2000 compressed files spread on the Internet and database.

One of the conventional methods to identify JPEG2000 images is to use sign(+/-) information of DWT(Discrete Wavelet Transform) coefficients[6]. This method consists of the following procedures; (1)extract sign information of DWT coefficients of both JPEG2000 compressed images(in database) and a query image, (2)calculate the similarity of the sign information in each subband region. However, this method inevitably requires entropy decoding(EBCOT:Embedded Block-based Coding with Optimized Truncation) that is the most heavy-duty part of JPEG2000 elements. It leads to lots of calculation time to identify a target JPEG2000 image. It is a bottleneck for fast identification. New study on identifying JPEG images has also been underway[7][8][9].

S. Satoh, F. Nack, and M. Etoh (Eds.): MMM 2008, LNCS 4903, pp. 380–390, 2008.

This paper presents a new method to identify the same image as the original image(uncompressed) out of JPEG2000 sequence of images more quickly and more robustly(without loss) than the conventional methods.

2 Feature of JPEG2000 Technology

In this section, the fundamental technology of JPEG2000 is described, because the proposed method effectively takes advantage of the feature of JPEG2000.

2.1 Basic Technology

JPEG2000 was standardized by ISO/IEC/JTC1/SC29/WG11 in December, 2000. JPEG2000 has been expected to take over JPEG as the next generation still-picture coding technology. In 2002, new part of JPEG2000("Motion JPEG2000") for motion pictures was standardized successfully. JPEG2000 is an unique format supporting not only sitll pictures but also motion pictures with completely the same algorithm. JPEG2000 has the following many functions; [1]high compression efficiency(30- 50 percents better than JPEG) [2]abundant scalability(resolution, quality, component) [3]supporting still pictures and motion pictures [4]error robustness(partial image decoding is possible when some part of codestream is lost) [5]high bit precision(up to 38bits/pel).

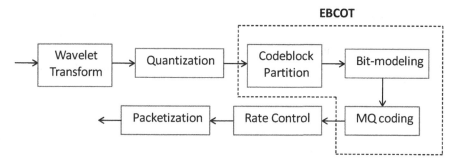

Fig. 1. JPEG2000 encoder block diagram

Fig.1 is a block diagram of JPEG2000 encoder. Wavelet transform analyzes input image and generates subband domains which are groups of wavelet coefficients. Wavelet coefficients in subband domains are quantized to generate quantized coefficients. Quantized coefficients are grouped in codeblocks. Value of the coefficients is represented as the bitplane of sign and absolute value(Fig.2). EBCOT is an unique entropy coder of JPEG2000 and generates compressed codestream by the combination of bit-modeling and MQ coding(arithmetic coding). In rate control, some coding-passes are truncated so as to adjust the amount of the codestream within the target size. In the last part of encoder, an incremental packet header is added to the codestream to generate JPEG2000 compliant codestream.

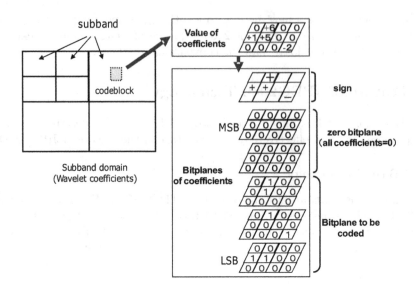

Fig. 2. Codeblock and bitplane

2.2   Bitplane

JPEG2000 adopts the technology of bitplane which is completely different from the other compression technologies such as JPEG and MPEG. Quantized coefficients are represented in three dimensions; horizontal, vertical and bit-depth. There are the same number of bitplanes as the number of the bit-depth from MSB(Most Significant Bit) to LSB(Least Significant Bit). Each bitplane contains the number of samples in a codeblock. All of the samples in bitplane are either 0 or 1.

Fig.2 is an example of codeblock with 12 samples(4 rows x 3 lines). However, the codeblock size is usually either 32x32 or 64x64 in JPEG2000.

Zero bitplane is a special bitplane which samples are all zeros. Zero bitplane is located from MSB to lower significant direction. Bitplanes except zero bitplanes are the object of encoding and decoding.

Four examples of zero bitplane are shown in Fig.3. The number of zero bitplanes in the first codeblock(left-hand side) equals to one, because the only MSB bitplane is zero bitplane. In the same manner, the number of zero bitplanes in the second one and the fourth one(right-hand side) are two and four respectively. But the third codeblock should be taken care, because all of the bitplanes are zero bitplanes. In JPEG2000 standard, this codeblock is defined as "not included", because the codeblock does not include any data to be encoded. Rate control in JPEG2000 usually employs the trick of truncating bitplanes from LSB to MSB. It leads to that the proposed method using zero bitplanes has an advantage of being hard to be influenced by compression rate, because zero bitplanes are located from MSB to the most recent non-zero bitplane. In this paper, zero bitplane plays a very important role for identifying JPEG2000 images.

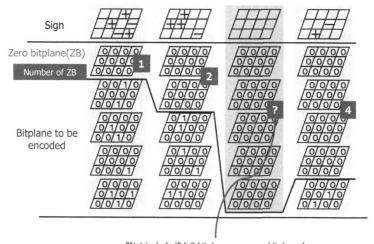

"Not included" (all bitplanes are zero bitplanes)

Fig. 3. Zero bitplane and encoding bitplanes

3 Identification of JPEG2000 Images

3.1 Background and Goal

JPEG2000 has been selected as the standard compression/decompression technology for digital cinema by DCI(Digital Cinema Initialtives)[3]. Movie films will be digitized and compressed as JPEG2000 files. They will be widely used in digital movie theaters and post-production houses.

The most recent requirement is building editing system such as re-encoding and replacement of definite pictures. For example, if some picture needs to be re-compressed with better quality, the target picture requires to be extracted, re-compressed and replaced with the old one. These editing work will be usually operated in post production house or movie studios, where original master pictures are saved and utilized. Since there are tremendous amount of pictures in movie sequence, very fast and accurate identifying method is very important. Our study is very usefull for building the editing systems.

3.2 Requirements of Proposed Method

The proposed identification method respects the following items.

Req-A. Identifying the same image before compression.

Req-B. Target image never fails to be identified(No identification lost).

Req-C. Identifying the image in the codestream level(smaller computation)

Req-D. Identification result is hard to be influenced by the change of compression ratio(robustness to bit-rate).

3.3   Identification by Each Level

The evaluation system in this study is shown in Fig.4. JPEG2000 compressed images are stored in database. Query image is the original image before compression. The query image is supposed to be compared with ones in database. Fig.5 shows the processing elements of JPEG2000 encoder/decoder and identification level. Advantage and disadvantage in the identification of each level are described in Table.1.

Considering the above analysis, Level-B is chosen as the base method for identification.

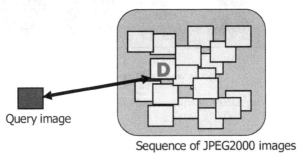

D ∈ Sequence of JPEG2000 images
Check if "D" is the image of compressing query image with JPEG2000

Fig. 4. Query image and JPEG2000 images

3.4   Proposed Method

Proposed method identifies between query image(image-A) and database images (image-B) with the following decision criteria. In order to increase the success rate of identification when either image-A or image-B is "not included", the number of zero bitplane is used. The third codeblock in Fig.6 is defined as "5+", instead of "not included" in Fig.3. It is because 5 zero bitplanes actually exist in the codeblock. But if there were non-zero bitplanes before truncation in the LSB direction, the number of zero bitplanes would be 5 or more.

[1]Rule-1: Identification of picture is successful if all codeblocks of image-A and image-B are perfectly the same.

[2]Rule-2: Identification is successful if the number of all zero bitplanes in the same position of codeblocks of image-A and image-B are perfectly the same.

[3]Rule-3: If a codeblock of image-B is "not included", identification is skipped.

[4]Rule-4: If a codeblock of image-A is "not included", the number of zero bitplanes is counted. If the number is "K", it is defined as "K+". If the number of zero bitplane of image-B is equal to or more than "K", they are identified as the same codeblock. According to the above rule, "4+" of image-A is identified as the same as "5" of image-B. Fig.7 shows the examples of the identification process.

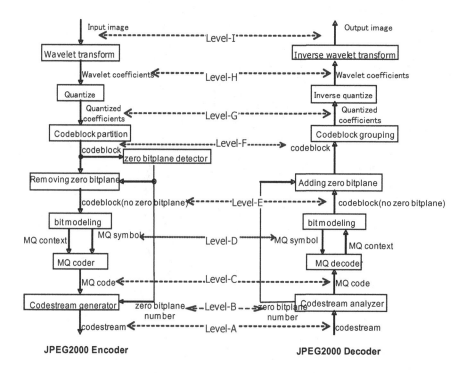

Fig. 5. Identification level in JPEG2000 encoder and decoder

Table 1. Each identification level

Level	Advantage	Disadvantage
Level-I	Only comparing baseband images is required(Encoder is not required).	Decoding codestream is required.
Level-EtoLevel-H	Only comparing coefficients is required.	All coefficients must coincide.
Level-C **Level-D**	Inverse quantization and inverse wavelet transform are not required in decoding.	EBCOT is required.
Level-B	EBCOT is not needed. Only parsing packet header is required.	Prevention of error identification is required.
Level-A	Only comparing files in binary level is required.	All of the coding conditions such as quantization step, rate control and compression ratio shall be the same.

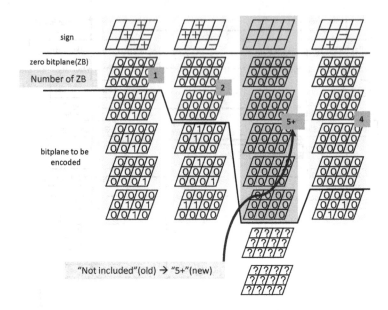

Fig. 6. Identification using the number of zero bitplanes

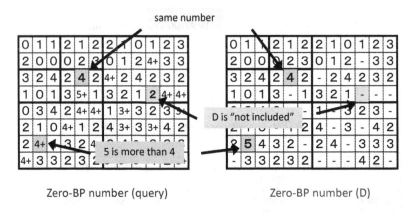

Zero-BP number (query)   Zero-BP number (D)

Fig. 7. Example of succeeded identifiation between query and D

4   Experiments and Results

Firstly, sequence of JPEG2000 compressed images are stored in database. A query image is searched and identified out of the JPEG2000 images in database.

The computational complexity of processing image-B in decoder is very small, because level-B as shown in Fig.5 requires only analyzing codestream and detecting zero bitplanes. On the other hand, processing image-A needs wavelet transform, quantization and codeblock partitioning in encoder. But it does not require EBCOT encoding which is the most heavy-duty part of JPEG2000. In addition, since the JPEG2000 DCI compliant encoding parameters is definite, query image does not need to be encoded every time in actual case(just one time encoding is needed).

4.1   Experimental Condition

In the experiment, "StEM"(DCI standard test sequence)(Fig.8) is used. The number of test frames is 14,981(there are more original frames in StEM, but those images with full black-color are rejected from the test sequence). The resolution is 4,096x1,714, which is about four times as large as full-HDTV. Encoding codition is shown in Table 2.

Table 2. Test sequence and encoding condition

Test sequence	StEM (DCI standard), 14,981 frames
Resolution	4,096(H) x 1,740(V)
Format	RGB(4:4:4) 12 bits
Bitrate	250Mbps (Peak rate) 159.17Mbps (Average)
Rate control	VBR (Variable Bit Rate)
Codestream	DCI Compliant (JPEG2000 Part-1) Wavelet decomposition level=5 Codeblock size=32x32 Precinct size=256x256 (LL=128x128) 1 Picture=1 Tile

4.2   Experimental Results

In movie sequences, there are lots of images with sub-title or mono-toned color. Since these images are easy to compress, the data size of compressed files will be small. On the other hand, those images with high-density texture and computer graphics are hard to compress. All of the test images were compressed with VBR(variable bit rate) control which is mandatory for DCI standard. It is to maintain the picture quality and decrease the difference of quality among the test images.

- 1. Identification Speed:
  Eleven query images(query-1 to query-11) were picked up from the original StEM images with the same interval. Each query image was compared with JPEG2000 images in database. Table 3 shows the total processing time in identifying the target images from 14,981 images. Average time of the proposed method and the DWT sign method[6] are 1.2253[msec/frame] and

Fig. 8. DCI test sequence (StEM)

Table 3. Identification speed of 11 query images

	Proposed method [sec]	DWT sign method [6] [sec]
query-1	15.6712	1527.8395
query-2	19.8713	30.3451
query-3	25.5569	92.3585
query-4	16.6355	29.7709
query-5	19.4924	64.7342
query-6	20.7858	39.0409
query-7	20.7057	43.4866
query-8	16.2215	61.9498
query-9	16.7342	37.6436
query-10	15.2219	370.8234
query-11	15.0202	897.7490
Average	18.3561	290.5220

19.3927[msec/frame] respectively. The proposed method is about 16 times faster than the DWT sign method. Another important point is that the proposed method is not influenced by the content of image and the processing time is very stable in all query images, but DWT sign method spends much time in some query images.

- 2. Identification accuracy:
  There was no lost of identification in both methods. Wrong identification rate of DWT sign method was 4.183 percents, although there was not any wrong identification in the proposed method. Wrong identification occurred in such images as fade-in and fade-out.

- 3. Identification of different images:
  In order to identify the target image from vast amount of images quickly, not only the small amount of calculation but also the function to skip different images in as eary stage as possible are very important. Table 4 shows in what number of codeblock, query image was identified as different from images in database and its frequency of occurrence. The proposed method succeeded in skipping different images in 0 to 16 codeblocks almost perfectly(98.96 percents). But DWT sign method did not succeed in skipping some images until very late stage. It causes lots of processing time.

Table 4. Identification of different images

Codeblock number	Frequency of occurence (Proposed)	Frequency of occurence [DWT sign]
0	0	59,361 (36.02%)
1~16	163,084 (98.96%)	96,059 (58.29%)
17~256	1,674 (1.02%)	1,550 (0.94%)
257~1,024	0 (0%)	10 (0.01%)
1,025~4,096	10 (0.01%)	11 (0.01%)
4,097~16,384	12 (0.01%)	895 (0.54%)
16,385~20,976	11 (0.01%)	6,905 (4.19%)

5 Footnote

Identification method of JPEG2000 images is proposed. It takes advantage of the characteristic of JPEG2000 codestream. The experimental results show the proposed method satisfies the requirements of high speed and high accuracy identification. Since the method does not fail identifying the target JPEG2000 image theoretically, it will be very useful for searching and identifying important images.

References

1. ISO/IEC 15444-1: JPEG2000 Part-1 Second Edition (July 2002)
2. Taubman, D., Marcellin, M.: JPEG2000: Image Compression Fundamentals, Standards and Practice, KAP (2001)
3. Digital Cinema Initiatives, LLC Member Representatives Committee: Digital Cinema System Specification V1.0, Final Approval (July 20, 2005)
4. JPSearch Part1 Technical Report(Type3): ISO/IEC PDTR 24800-1: Framework and System Components, JPSearch AHG (November 2006)
5. JPSearch WG: An Introduction to the JPSearch effort, JPSearch AHG (2006)
6. Watanabe, O., Kawana, A., Kiya, H.: An Identification Method for JPEG2000 Images Using the Signs of DWT Coefficients, Technical Report of IEICE, Vol.106(449) No.IE2006-217, pp.177-181 (January 2007)
7. Arnia, F., Iizuka, I., Fujiyoshi, M., Kiya, H.: An Identification Method for JPEG2000 Images Using the Signs of DWT Coefficients, Technical Report of IEICE, Vol. 106, No. 449, No. IE2006-217, pp. 177–181 (January 2007)
8. Arnia, F., Iizuka, I., Fujiyoshi, M., Kiya, H.: Fast and Robust Indentification Methods for JPEG Images with Various Compression Ratios. In: Proc.IEEE International Conference on Acoustics, Speech and Signal Processing, vol. IMDSP-P4.6 (May 2006)
9. Iizuka, I., Arnia, F., Fujiyoshi, M., Kiya, H.: Consideration on DCT Sign Only Correlation for Image Indentification. In: Proc. International Technical Conference on Circuits/Systems, Computers and Communications, vol. II(WPM2-6-3), pp. 481–484 (July 2006)

Optimization of Spatial Error Concealment for H.264 Featuring Low Complexity

Shih-Chia Huang and Sy-Yen Kuo

Fellow IEEE
Department of Electrical Engineering, National Taiwan University, Taipei, Taiwan
{d94921019,sykuo}@ntu.edu.tw

Abstract. Transmission of highly compressed video bitstreams can result in packet erasures when channel status is unfavorable. Spatial error concealment (SEC) techniques are very useful in the recovery of impaired video sequences, especially in the presence of scene changes, irregular motion, and appearance or disappearance of objects. As errors occur in the first frame, the corrupted MBs must be recovered by utilizing SEC schemes in order to prevent the propagation of errors to the succeeding inter-coded frames. We propose two SEC methods; one conceals the variances of the different kinds of damaged Macroblocks (MBs) targeted at any condition, and the other is speed-up which utilizes a H.264 coding tool, directional spatial intra prediction, in order to conceal the entire spectrum of damaged MBs targeted at intra-coded block(s). The experimental results show that when compared to other state of the art methods, our proposed SEC techniques significantly improve video quality up to 3.62 – 4.22 dB while reducing computational complexity.

Keywords: Spatial Error Concealment, H.264.

1 Introduction

The Spatial Error Concealment (SEC) approach basically exploits the spatial redundancy in a frame to conceal the missing pixels without reference to other frames. One SEC method referred to in [1] recovers the lost pixels through weighted pixel value averaging, the weights being inversely proportional to the distance of source and destination pixels. This technique is usually most applicable in intra mode when replacement is attempted without relying on additional information beyond the source-end. The reference software Joint Model (JM) decoder implements error concealment for impaired MacroBlocks (MBs) [2]; its SEC methods bear substantial similarity to those mentioned in [1]. Meisinger and Kaup present an approach that is distinct from most general SEC methods in that the estimated missing spatial information is in the frequency domain [3]. The approach of Wang et al. [4][5] suggests hybrid methods that operate in the frequence domain by minimizing the spatial variation between nearby samples within the damaged blocks and between adjacent blocks using the principle of "maximally smooth recovery" and thus

S. Satoh, F. Nack, and M. Etoh (Eds.): MMM 2008, LNCS 4903, pp. 391–401, 2008.

restoring an optimally smooth transition across the block boundary [6]. Park et al. [7] and Hemani et al. [8] also make use of a method similar to Wang's [4] in which they utilize the smooth connection property of image to estimate low frequency coefficients and recover the lost blocks in frequency concealment. Other efficient hybrid methods [9] are also reported in the findings of Alkachouh and Bellanger, in which they state under the assumption that if the set of pixels consisting of the missing block and its border pixels is transformed by the DCT, then the high frequency coefficients obtained can be set to zero. In this interpolation scheme, only eight border pixels are used in the computation of any missing pixel.

In related strains of spatial domain research, many other important approaches have been conducted including sequential recovery framework [10], spatial split-match EC method [11], [12], fuzzy logic reasoning [13], projection onto convex sets (POCS) [14], [15], maximum a posteriori (MAP) estimation procedure [17], best neighbor matching (BNM) [26], bilinear interpolation (BI) [1], [2], [16] and directional interpolation (DI) [14],[18]-[24]. Rongfu et al. [25] combine three methods: bilinear interpolation (BI), directional interpolation (DI), and best neighbor matching (BNM). Agrafiotis et al. [27] provide a novel SEC model that involves the switching of bilinear (BI) and directional (DI) interpolation based on the entropy of the edge direction data in the neighborhood of each missing MB. This model employs directional entropy to characterize the features of the different video sequences, and exploits the advantages of both BI and DI approaches. The performance quality of concealing visual errors using the two approaches interchangeably creates a result that is superior to the singular use of BI and DI methods.

2 Previous Works

Considerable research has been conducted in the field of error concealment (EC) in the hopes of ascertaining new spatial recovery methods. This section will focus on the introduction and discussion of traditional SEC methods.

2.1 Bilinear Interpolation

The Bilinear Interpolation (BI) spatial error concealment algorithm uses the principle that each corrupted pixel can be replaced by linear interpolation using a weighted average of the nearest pixels existing along the one-pixel-wide boundary of the four adjacent MacroBlocks (MBs) in both horizontal and vertical directions. The weights of the nearest four pixels on the boundary of the four adjacent MBs are inversely proportional to the distance of source and destination pixels.

2.2 Directional Interpolation

Directional Interpolation (DI) consists of two main parts: edge direction detection and 1-D interpolation. The initial step consists of using the edge direction filter to estimate the direction of each pixel contained within MBs surrounding the lost MB.

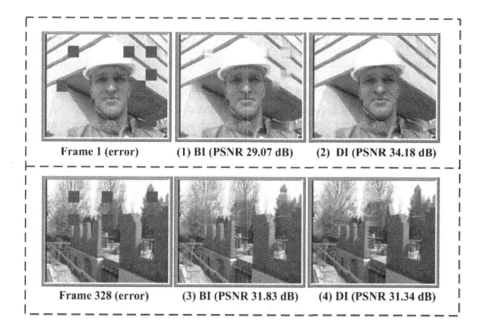

| Frame 1 (error) | (1) BI (PSNR 29.07 dB) | (2) DI (PSNR 34.18 dB) |
| Frame 328 (error) | (3) BI (PSNR 31.83 dB) | (4) DI (PSNR 31.34 dB) |

Fig. 1. The damaged MBs concealed by BI and DI

The edge direction is classified into 8 directions from 0 to 157.5 using a step of 22.5. The missing pixels are recovered by weighted 1-D interpolation along the strongest direction decided on the edge strength using border pixels of surrounding MBs.

2.3 Best Neighborhood Matching

Different from the above interpolation methods, Wang et al. propose the best neighborhood matching (BNM) method which discerns block-wise similarity within the vicinity of the search range of the single frame in effort to recover the entire missing MB.

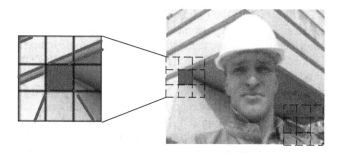

Fig. 2. Damaged MB with multiple edge directions

2.4 Discussion

So far, this paper has discussed three basic SEC methods. Now we will summarize and analyze the main facets of and differences between BI, DI and BNM. Human visual perception is highly sensitive to distortion of edges including impairments on existing edges (blurring) and the creation of false edges (blockiness) [32]. Additionally, according to psychovisual studies, an individual edge does not influence our perception but rather interacts with other neighboring edges to create a composite effect which we are then able to recognize [33]. Thus, since edges play such an important role in the human visual system, it is equally important that they are protected from deterioration, and that false edges are safeguarded against. DI exhibits many advantages in the area of edge protection. It can facilitate the preservation of the existing strong edges, as well as avoiding strong edge blur when the strong edges of the damaged MBs have only single directions, as illustrated in Fig. 1(2). Unfortunately, because DI is interpolated along a single direction it can result in the creation of false edges or the emphasis of relatively weak ones if there is more than one edge in the neighborhood, as illustrated in Fig. 1(4). On the other hand, the use of BI can help avoid the creation of false strong edges, as illustrated in Fig. 1(3). However, BI can blur original strong edges if only one edge exists in the neighborhood, as illustrated in Fig. 1(1). The damaged block replaced by interpolation will smoothly connect with its adjacent neighborhoods. But in areas of higher complexity, the spatial interpolation methods cannot completely describe missing or damaged blocks because the necessary reference blocks may simply not exist. BNM can recover damaged information in high detail, but may create edge discontinuity. It will also cause higher computation complexity than BI and DI when searching for a match and will thus be less time-efficient.

3 Proposed SEC Methods

3.1 Normal SEC Mode

In recent years research conducted in the area of SEC has been oriented towards a combination method using several SEC techniques whose respective uses are determined according to image content and complexity. The most current findings, as of the publication of this paper, were conducted by Agrafiotis et al. [27] and discuss a combination method by which the switching of Bilinear and Directional Interpolation proved extremely useful in the replacement of missing MBs. Although this method is very successful in many situations, there are instances when the image is too complex to be repaired entirely by this technique. This paper will now analyze the situations in which the method of Agrafiotis et al. [27] is least effective and suggest a novel way in which its problems may be solved. For more complicated situations in which the surrounding MBs exhibit many different directions, vertical-horizontal interpolation (BI) or one directional interpolation (DI) are alone not sufficient to recover the real image. For example, Fig. 2 below illustrates a multidirectional nature. Increasing recovered video quality is essential in the consideration of important factors in the above situation. With these issues in mind, we will employ a novel and enhanced DI method in order to accomplish multi-directional interpolation. Initially in normal SEC mode, we make use of the 3*3 Sobel edge direction filter to calculate gradient and magnitude of surrounding pixels which exist in the four-pixel-wide external boundary around the missing MB and thus correspond to one of eight different edge directions. Based on the calculated edge strength value, the strong edges are reserved as candidate edges which are then used in the calculation of the directional entropy (H_d). Entropy describes the state of disorder in a system [34]. Large H_d indicates the existence of no specific edge direction, since edges of different directions interact with each other, whereas small H_d indicates the existence of only one dominant edge direction in the area. The surrounding pixels within the four-pixel-wide external boundary are disjoined into 4×4-pixel blocks, as shown in Fig. 3. For each 4×4-pixel block a threshold β between 0 and 0.85 indicates that the 4×4-pixel block possesses a clear dominant edge and can be marked as a candidate block. The formula for threshold β is given by

$$\beta = \frac{-\sum p(d_x)\log_2 p(d_x)}{Max(H_d)}, \quad where \quad H_d = -\sum p(d_x)\log_2 p(d_x) \tag{1}$$

where $p(d_x)$ is the directional probability density function associated with the candidate edge direction data (d_x). A threshold β equal to 1 corresponds to all directions being equally probable. When using the surrounding 4×4-pixel blocks to estimate the missing MB, the deficient content can be classified into one of the following four categories: no-directional background area, single-directional edge area, textural multi-directional edge area, and complex multi-directional edge area.

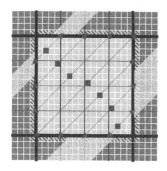
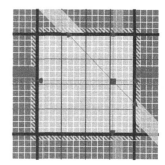

(a) Example of DI   (b) Example of Multi-DI

Fig. 3.

1) No-directional Background:
The 4×4-pixel surrounding blocks completely lack strong edge directions. It allows reasonably good approximation of damaged MBs that exist as the background or panning region of an image. Each pixel of damaged MBs can be replaced by Bilinear Interpolation.

2) Single-directional Edge Area:
Each 4×4-pixel surrounding candidate block exhibits the same singular strong edge direction. Directional Interpolation is the most useful method for this scenario, as it is

most beneficial in the protection of strong edges and avoidance of the creation of false strong edges, as shown in Fig. 3(a).

3) Textural Multi-directional Edge Area:
Each 4×4-pixel surrounding candidate block exhibits more than two strong edge directions. The direction of each missing pixel is approximated by the corresponding directional strong edge within the surrounding candidate blocks. Three-directional weighted interpolation (multi-DI) of the one-pixel-wide border along the corresponding horizontal, vertical, and one and forty-five degree directions, is the most useful method in the identification of the directions of the missing pixel, and is illustrated in Fig. 3(b). If the missing pixels do not have a corresponding strong edge direction, the lost pixels can be interpolated along the same direction corresponding to that of the nearest missing pixel.

4) Complex Multi-directional Edge Area
Each 4×4-pixel surrounding candidate block has more than two strong edge directions, with the direction of each missing pixel either corresponding to different strong edge directions within the candidate blocks or maintains a threshold β of more than 0.85 for most surrounding blocks. If the damaged MB exhibits complex content, then BNM may be adopted in order to reconstruct the damaged block. The effectiveness of the BNM method in terms of recovery image quality is very useful for complex areas [25], [26], but the time requirement for the computation load is relatively high. Conversely, the BI method for complex areas [27] offers a diminished time constraint, however the quality of the result will usually be lower than that of BNM.

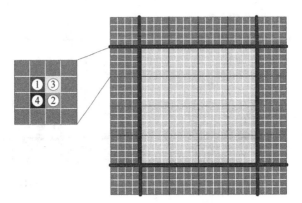

Fig. 4. The order of calculation of Sobel Filter

3.2 Intra High-Speed SEC Mode

In terms of time expenditures, the detection of edge direction of DI, of the switching method of DI and BI [27], and of normal SEC methods, takes 42% - 86% of computation on average and is obviously the processing bottleneck of these SEC methods. To reduce the complexity of edge direction detection, we shift the emphasis away from the role of damaged content classification to the role of edge direction detection. The initial event of note is that there is a correlation between intra-prediction modes and edge direction. With the exception of DC prediction mode, the coding modes of the eight directional 4×4 prediction modes and the three directional 16×16 prediction modes provide a strong estimation for the edge direction of the real images in H.264/AVC intra coding [35]. The intra prediction modes provide useful clues about edge direction that serve to reduce the initially large number of Sobel edge filter calculations. Then, it can reduce the complexity of the process of edge direction detection by 74% - 96% on average. The mode information of intra 16×16 prediction mode tends to be chosen for background or flat regions and intra 4×4 prediction mode tends to be used for foreground or highly textured regions [35]. By utilizing the intra prediction mode information of the surrounding area, the initial step of the Intra High-Speed SEC method classifies each damaged MB into two categories: flat region and compound region

1) Flat region

For the six neighborhoods of each damaged MB (Top, Top-Right, Left, Right, Bottom, and Bottom-Left), there are at least five adjacent MBs chosen via 16×16 prediction mode. It does not need to use any Sobel filters in the detection of edge direction for the panning region of an image. Each pixel of damaged MBs can be interpolated along a single direction (vertical, horizontal or diagonal) or bi-direction (vertical-horizontal) decided by majority decision based on the intra 16×16 prediction mode, mode 0 (vertical), mode 1 (horizontal), mode 3 (plane), and mode 2 (DC), of corresponding surrounding MBs.

2) Compound region

For the mixed 16×16 and 4×4 prediction modes of surrounding MBs, the four-pixel-wide boundary is disjoined into 4×4-pixel blocks, as shown towards the right in Fig. 4. In order to ascertain the existence of the dominant edge of each 4×4-pixel block and mark it as a candidate, we use the intra mode information and a small amount of the edge direction filter. The order of calculation of the Sobel filter to estimate the direction and magnitude of the inner pixels, p1, p2, p3, and p4, is depicted on the left in Fig. 4. The calculation is stopped if the candidate block is decided upon. For each 4×4-pixel block, edge detection begins at the p1 and p2, at least one of them exhibiting an existing strong edge in the same direction as obtained by intra mode prediction and marked as a candidate block. If neither p1 nor p2 exhibit an existing strong edge, then two additional points, p3 and p4, will be calculated. Intra DC prediction mode is regarded directly as no singular prominent edge exists in the 4×4-pixel block without the need of any Sobel filters. The final part is similar to the normal SEC method; both classify the deficient content into four categories: no-directional background area using BI method, single-directional edge area using DI method, textural multi-directional edge area using multi-DI method, and complex multi-directional edge area using BMN or BI method.

4 Experiment

The experimental environment is based around the H.264 reference software of Joint Model (JM) [36] supplied by the JVT [37] committee (Joint Video Team of ISO/IEC MPEG and ITU-T VCEG). The error concealment algorithms were tested on several

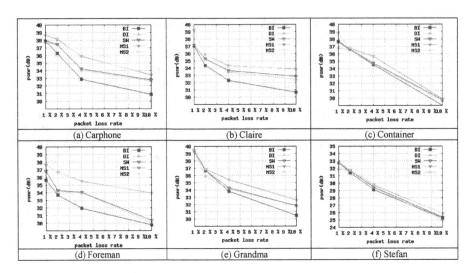

Fig. 5. PSNR results at different packet error rates are shown for sequences. (a) "Carphone", (b) "Claire", (c) "Container", (d) "Foreman", (e) "Grandma", and (f) "Stefan".

standard video sequences in both CIF (352×288) and QCIF (176×144) in order to evaluate the video quality in the experiment. The resolution video sequences were coded at 1 I-frame for every 12 P-frames with a slice size of 536 bytes, using interleaving technique of flexible macroblock ordering (FMO), with random packet lost errors at different specified loss ratios (different rates), which are assumed to be caused by transmission errors. Ten different random packet lost errors were used simultaneously at each different specified loss ratio. The average peak signal-to-noise ratio (PSNR) of a video sequence is employed to give a quantitative evaluation of the quality of the reconstructed image. The proposed Normal (SM1) and Intra High-Speed (SM2) SEC methods (Note: we adopt BI method on complex multi-directional edge area by the principle of equity) are compared to the DI SEC method which resembles [24], BI SEC method from [2], and the SEC switching method of DI and BI [27], with each pixel in the damaged MB concealed by linear interpolation along a one-pixel wide boundary. In order to show the performance of each SEC method, the rates at which random packets are lost, in regard to their effect on intra-frames, are approximately 1%, 2%, 4%, and 10%. The simulation average PSNR results of different rates of packet erasure are presented only for the specific spatially concealed intra-frames. As shown in Fig. 5, our proposed SM1 and SM2 SEC methods result in the best performance in regard to the "Foreman" sequence, one that is significantly better than the BI approach adopted in the JM decoder up to 4.16 dB and 4.22 dB at the 10% error rate, the DI approach adopted in the JM decoder up to 3.84 dB and 3.9 dB at the 10% error rate, and the SEC switching method of DI and BI (SW) up to 3.56 dB and 3.62 dB at the 10% error rate. Next, we discuss the computational complexity between SM1, SM2, and switching of DI and BI (SW) [27] SEC methods, because the SW [27] SEC methods make an assured calculation of the total amount of Sobel filter for the pixels of each available MB surrounding that which is damaged. Table 1 shows the speed-up factors of Normal (SM1) and Intra High-Speed (SM2) SEC methods in comparison to the SW [27] SEC method based on the execution time of total SEC processes at the error rate of 1% and 4%. The results show that the SM1 and SM2 SEC methods significantly speed up when compared to the SW [27] SEC method, because the complexity of the process of edge direction detection is reduced.

Table 1. Execution time speed-up of SW method

Speed-up	Error rate 1%		Error rate 4%	
	SM1	SM2	SM1	SM2
Container	3.57	6.23	2.98	4.92
Foreman	3.52	4.85	3.02	4.24
Football	3.58	5.25	2.96	4.78

5 Conclusion

In this work, we propose the following two SEC methods. The first, Normal SEC, is a novel hybrid method which uses DI, BI, multi-DI, or BMN targeted at any condition. The second, Intra High-speed SEC, is a proposed hybrid method which uses DI, BI, multi-DI, or BMN can be invaluable when targeted at intra coded block which utilizes the H.264/AVC coding tool of directional spatial domain intra prediction for intra coding in order to reduce the number of calculations needed to ascertain the quantity of direction edge filter, and in so doing reduces enormously the overall computational complexity. The proposed SEC schemes offer significant performance gains in comparison to other state of the art methods.

Acknowledgements

This research was supported by ASUS Corporation, Taiwan under Grant 96-S-B09 and by the National Science Council, Taiwan under Grant NSC 95-2221-E-002-068.

References

1. Salama, P., Shroff, N.B., Delp, E.J.: Error concealment in encoded video streams. In: Katsaggelos, A.K., Galatsanos, N.P. (eds.) Signal Recovery Techniques for Image and Video Compression and Transmission. ch. 7, Kluwer, Norwell, MA (1998)
2. Wang, Y.K., Hannuksela, M.M., Varsa, V., Hourunranta, A., Gabbouj, M.: The error concealment feature in the H.26L test model. In: ICIP, 2nd edn. Proc. Int. Conf. Image Processing, Rochester, New York, USA, pp. 729–732 (September 2002)
3. Meisinger, K., Kaup, A.: Spatial error concealment of corrupted image data using frequency selective extrapolation. In: ICASSP. Proc. Int. Conf. Acoust., Speech, Signal Process, pp. 209–212 (2004)
4. Wang, Y., Zhu, Q.F., Shaw, L.: Maximally smooth image recovery in transform coding. IEEE Trans. Commun. 41, 1544–1551 (1993)
5. Zhu, Q.F., Wang, Y., Shaw, L.: Coding and cell loss recovery for DCT-based packet video. IEEE Trans. Circuits Syst. Video Technol. 3, 248–258 (1993)

6. Zhu, W., Wang, Y.: A comparison of smoothness measures for error concealment in transform coding. In: Proc. SPIE Conf. Visual Communication and Image Processing, Taipei, Taiwan, vol. II, pp. 1205–1214 (1995)
7. Park, J.W., Kim, J.W., Lee, S.U.: DCT coefficients recovery-based error concealment technique and its application to MPEG-2 Bit stream error. IEEE Trans. Circuits and Systems for Video Technology 7, 845–854 (1997)
8. Hemami, S., Meng, T.: Transform coded image reconstruction exploiting interblock correlation. IEEE Trans. Image Processing 4, 1023–1027 (1995)
9. Alkachouh, Z., Bellangerh, M.G.: Fast DCT based spatial domain interpolation of blocks in images. IEEE Trans. Image Process. 9(4), 729–732 (2000)
10. Li, X., Orchard, M.T.: Novel sequential error concealment techniques using orientation adaptive interpolation. IEEE Trans. Circuits Syst. Video Technol. 12(10), 857–864 (2002)
11. Tsekeridou, S., Pitas, I.: MPEG-2 error concealment based on block matching principles. IEEE Trans. Circuits Syst. Video Technology 10(4), 646–658 (2000)
12. Tsekeridou, S., Pitas, I., Le Buhan, C.: An error concealment scheme for MPEG-2 coded video sequences. In: Proc. 1997 Int. Symp. Circuits and Systems, vol. 2, pp. 1289–1292 (1997)
13. Lee, X., Zhang, Y., Leon-Garcia, A.: Information loss recovery for block-based image coding techniques—A fuzzy logic approach. IEEE Trans. Image Processing 4, 259–273 (1995)
14. Sun, H., Kwok, W.: Concealment of damaged block transform coded images using projection onto convex set. IEEE Trans. Image Processing 4, 470–477 (1995)
15. Jung, K., Chang, J., Lee, C.: Error concealment technique using projection data for block-based image coding. In: Proc. SPIE Conf. Visual Communication and Image Processing, vol. 2308, pp. 1466–1476 (1994)
16. Aign, S., Fazel, K.: Temporal and spatial error concealment techniques for hierarchical MPEG-2 video codec. In: Proc. ICC, vol. 3, pp. 1778–1783 (June 1995)
17. Bajic, I.V.: Adaptive MAP Error Concealment for Dispersively Packetized Wavelet-Coded Images. IEEE Trans. Image Process 15(5), 1226–1235 (2006)
18. Suh, J.W., Ho, Y.S.: Error concealment based on directional interpolation. IEEE Trans. Consumer Electron 43, 295–302 (1997)
19. Kwok, W., Sun, H.: Multi-directional interpolation for spatial error concealment. IEEE Trans. Consumer Electron 39(3), 455–460 (1993)
20. Zeng, W., Liu, B.: Geometric-Structure-Based Error Concealment with Novel Applications in Block-Based Low-Bit-Rate Coding. IEEE Trans. on Circuits and Systems for Video Tech. 9(4), 648–665 (1999)
21. Kung, W.Y., Kim, C.S., Kuo, C.: A spatial-domain error concealment method with edge recovery and selective directional interpolation. In: Proc. of IEEE International Conference on Acoustics, Speech, and Signal Processing, vol. 5, pp. 6–10 (2003)
22. Chen, J., Liu, J., Wang, X., Chen, G.: Modified Edge-oriented Spatial Interpolation for Consecutive Blocks Error Concealment. In: ICIP. Proc. of IEEE International Conference, Image Processing, pp. 11–14 (September 2005)
23. Zhao, Y., Tian, D., Hannukasela, M.M., Gabbouj, M.: Spatial error concealment based on directional decision and intra prediction. In: Proc. ISCAS, pp. 2899–2902 (2005)
24. Xu, Y., Zhou, Y.: H.264 video communication based refined error concealment schemes. IEEE Trans. Consum. Electron. 50(4), 1135–1141 (2004)
25. Rongfu, Z., Yuanhua, Z., Xiaodong, H.: Content-adaptive spatial error concealment for video communication. IEEE Trans. Consum. Electron. 50(1), 335–341 (2004)

26. Wang, Z., Yu, Y., Zhang, D.: Best neighborhood matching: An information loss restoration technique for block-based image coding systems. IEEE Trans. Image Process. 7(7), 1056–1061 (1998)

27. Agrafiotis, D., Bull, D.R., Canagarajah, C.N.: Enhanced Error Concealment With Mode Selection. IEEE Trans. Circuits Syst. Video Technology 16(8), 960–973 (2006)

28. Chen, W.L., Leou, J.J.: A New Hybrid Error Concealment Scheme for H.264 Video Transmission. In: Proc. Int. Conf on Communications and mobile computing, Vancouver, Canada (July 2006)

29. Varsa, V., Hannuksela, M.M., Wang, Y.K.: Nonnormative error concealment algorithms. ITU-T SG16 Doc, VCEGN62, Santa Barbara, CA, USA (September 2001)

30. Davies, E.R.: Machine Vision. Academic Press Inc., San Diego (1990)

31. Kang, L.W., Leou, J.J.: A hybrid error concealment scheme for MPEG-2 video transmission based on best neighborhood matching algorithm. J. Vis. Commun. Image Represent 16(3), 288–310 (2005)

32. Ong, E., Lin, W., Lu, Z., Yao, S., Etoh, M.: Visual distortion assessment with emphasis on spatially transitional regions. IEEE Trans. Circuits Syst. Video Technol. 14(4), 559–566 (2004)

33. Ran, X., Farvardin, N.: A perceptually motivated three component image model—Part I: description of the model. IEEE Trans. Image Process., 401–415 (April 1995)

34. Shannon, C.E.: A Mathematical Theory of Communication. Bell Sys. Tech. J. 27, 379–423, 623–656 (1948)

35. Huang, Y.-W., Hsieh, B.-Y., Chen, T.-C., Chen, L.-G.: Analysis, fast algorithm, and VLSI architecture design for H.264/AVC intra frame coder. IEEE Trans. Circuits Syst. Video Technol. 15, 378–401 (2005)

36. H.264/AVC Reference Software JM, Available: http://bs.hhi.de/~suehring/tml/

37. Joint Video Team (JVT) of ISO/IEC MPEG & ITU-T VCEG, Working draft number 2, revision 2 (WD-2), Joint Video Team (JVT) (2002)

Temporal Error Concealment for H.264 Using Optimum Regression Plane

Shih-Chia Huang and Sy-Yen Kuo

Fellow IEEE

Department of Electrical Engineering, National Taiwan University, Taipei, Taiwan
{d94921019,sykuo}@ntu.edu.tw

Abstract. Highly compressed video bitstreams transmitted over error-prone communications networks can suffer from packet erasures. In order to avoid error-catalyzed artifacts from producing visible corruption of affected video frames, the use of error concealment at the video decoder becomes essential, especially in regard to wireless video transmission which can suffer packet loss more easily due to fluctuating channel conditions. Temporal error concealment techniques are usually successful when there is continuous high correlation between the frames of the coded sequence. The proposed temporal error concealment techniques consist of a novel and unique mathematical model, the optimum regression plane, developed for the repair of damaged motion vectors, and the creation of a framework to perform the variable block size motion compensation based on predictive motion vectors in Laplacian distribution model space for H.264 decoder. Experiments performed using the proposed temporal error concealment method resulted in excellent gains of up to 3.89 dB compared to those of the Joint Model (JM) method for a wide range of benchmark sequences.

Keywords: Temporal Error Concealment, H.264.

1 Introduction

The Temporal Error Concealment (TEC) approach exploits temporal redundancy in a sequence to recover the impaired MacroBlocks (MBs) by utilizing reference frames. The most common motion-compensated temporal prediction concealment approach combines both temporal replacement and motion compensation by exploiting the generally strong correlation between correlative motion vectors in the current decoded frame and the previous one. Unfortunately, the motion vector of the damaged MB may also be lost because of the variable length coding employed.

A number of varying simple approaches used in the estimation of the missing motion vector follow:

1) Using a zero motion vector involving the corrupted MB which is then replaced with one at the same spatial location within the previous frame.

2) Using the neighboring motion vectors (MVs) of the damaged MB.

S. Satoh, F. Nack, and M. Etoh (Eds.): MMM 2008, LNCS 4903, pp. 402–412, 2008.
© Springer-Verlag Berlin Heidelberg 2008

3)   Using the available MV of the spatially corresponding MB in the previous or forward frame [2].
4)   Using the median (or average) of the spatially adjacent MVs [3].
5)   Using conjunctively any of the set of the above candidate MVs [1], [4]-[8], [20].

Recently, a surge of research ([9]-[15]) has been conducted in the area of MV estimation by motion field interpolation methods. To improve the performance, the best motion vector is determined from the above MV candidates by the boundary matching algorithm (BMA) [5], [16], which calculates the minimum sum of absolute differences (SAD) along the one-pixel-wide boundary between the damaged MB and its candidate replacements in the H.264 JM decoder [17]-[18]. Other improved modified versions of boundary matching measure have been designed such as weighted SAD, external boundary matching, and so on [5]-[8], [19], [21], [23]. In addition to BMA-based methods, Tsekeridou and Pitas developed a block-matching (BM) algorithm [25], called the forward–backward block-matching EC (F-B BM EC) method, to match the upper and/or lower adjacent MBs between current and reference frames in effort to conceal the damaged MBs of an MPEG-2 coded video sequence.In order to find the best match in the reference frame, the use of fast search algorithms is suggested [6]-[8], [20], [21], [25]-[29]. More extensive research includes multi frame TEC approaches being reported in [30] and [31] at the detriment of increased complexity and time demand, as well as the concealment of whole missing frames as reported in [32] and [33].

2 Proposed TEC Method

In this section, we propose a mathematically optimized TEC approach for H.264/ AVC decoders. Using spatial redundancy, the optimum regression plane utilizes the spatial neighborhood MVs of the lost MB in order to estimate the sixteen MVs within each 4×4 block of the damaged MB. One of the spatial and temporal candidate MVs of each 4×4 block in the damaged MB that minimizes the boundary matching error is selected. The most suitable MB partition (including the sizes 16×16, 16×8, 8×16, and 8×8) is decided upon, according to the motion field distributions and correlations between the sixteen MVs of each 4×4 block within the damaged MB. At the end of this process, the winning MVs are subjected to variable block size motion refinement and motion-compensated temporal concealment, resulting in new MVs derived from a motion search carried out in the decoder.

2.1 Optimum Regression Plane

We make use of the significantly strong correlation between spatial MVs to estimate the missing motion vectors based on the optimum regression (OR) plane. For the approach proposed in H.264/AVC, we have assumed that the location of corrupted MBs has been accurately detected, and all the related surrounding MBs are correctly received and decoded due to the interleaving technique of flexible macroblock ordering (FMO) [22], [24],[34], [35] that is used to avoid successive lost MBs. In the two-dimensional (2-D) real space current frame with each pixel size equaling one

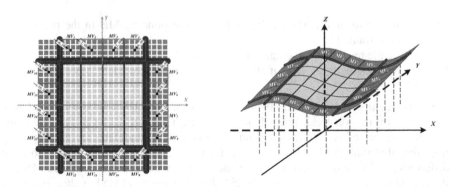

Fig. 1. (a) Left: Coordinates of neighboring 4×4 block centers, (b) Right: The Optimum Regression plane estimated by the surrounding motion vectors

unit, we first set up the coordinates of the damaged MB with center at (0, 0), and the corresponding coordinates of the surrounding 4×4 block centers at the following: Block 1 : (x_1, y_1) = (-6, 10), Block 2 : (x_2, y_2) = (-2, 10), Block 3 : (x_3, y_3) = (2, 10), Block 4 : (x_4, y_4) = (6, 10), Block 5 : (x_5, y_5) = (10, 6), Block 6 : (x_6, y_6) = (10, 2),Block 7 : (x_7, y_7) = (10, -2), Block 8 : (x_8, y_8) = (10, -6), Block 9 :(x_9, y_9) = (6, -10), Block 10 : (x_{10}, y_{10}) = (2, -10), Block 11 : (x_{11}, y_{11}) = (-2, -10), Block 12 : (x_{12}, y_{12}) = (-6, -10), Block 13 : (x_{13}, y_{13}) = (-10, -6) , Block 14 : (x_{14}, y_{14}) = (-10, -2), Block 15 : (x_{15}, y_{15}) = (-10, 2), Block 16 : (x_{16}, y_{16}) = (-10, 6), respectively. An illustration of the coordinates of neighboring 4×4 block centers and their corresponding motion vectors, MV_1, MV_2 , MV_3, MV_4 , MV_5, MV_6, MV_7, MV_8, MV_9, MV_{10} , MV_{11}, MV_{12} , MV_{13}, MV_{14}, MV_{15}, MV_{16}, are shown in Fig. 1(a). We have developed the multiple polynomial regression model to reconstruct the corrupted motion vectors based on the corresponding positions of the surrounding 4×4 blocks while utilizing the spatially correlated MVs. The OR plane is as follows.

$$Z(x, y) = c + a_1 x + a_2 x^2 + b_1 y + b_2 y^2 \qquad (1)$$

The value of the set of coefficients (a_1, a_2, b_1, b_2, c) are estimated by the minimum of the sum of squares of residuals (method of least squares). The estimated motion vectors will then be located on the OR plane, as illustrated in Fig. 1(b). The sixteen MVs for each 4×4 block within the damaged MB will be estimated by using the corresponding coordinates of each 4×4 missing block center, and are (-6, 6), (-6, 2), (-2, 6), (-2, 2), (6, 6), (6, 2), (2, 6), (2, 2), (6, -6), (6 , -2), (2, -6), (2, -2), (-6, -6), (-6,-2), (-2, -6), (-2, -2), as follow.

$$Z(x, y) = \left[\frac{1}{106496} \sum_{i=1}^{16} MV_i \cdot (27x_i^2 + 25y_i^2 - 3120) \right] x^2 + \left[\frac{1}{960} \sum_{i=1}^{16} MV_i \cdot x_i \right] x +$$

$$\left[\frac{1}{106496} \sum_{i=1}^{16} MV_i \cdot (25x_i^2 + 27y_i^2 - 3120) \right] y^2 + \left[\frac{1}{960} \sum_{i=1}^{16} MV_i \cdot y_i \right] y -$$

$$\frac{1}{512} \sum_{i=1}^{16} MV_i \cdot (15x_i^2 + 15y_i^2 - 1832) \qquad (2)$$

2.2 Realized Candidate MVs

For accurately estimating the MV from a comparison between the available candidates, we primarily exploit high spatial correlation and the similar Boundary Matching Algorithm (BMA) [46], [32] to evaluate the spatial and temporal candidate MVs of each 4×4 block in the damaged MB; the spatial motion vector is estimated based on the OR plane, whereas the other is the temporally correlated MV of the same spatial position. First, the external 4-pixel-wide boundary of the lost MB is divided into 12 different areas, after which the spatial and temporal MV candidates of the 4×4 block are evaluated in terms of the external boundary matching error (EBME) of the adjacent external boundary pixels of the lost 4×4 block and the same external boundary pixels of the candidate 4×4 block in the previous frame. An illustration of the adjacent external boundary pixels is shown in Fig. 2.

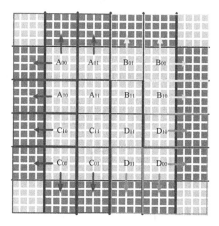

Fig. 2. Spatial and temporal MVs of each missing 4×4 blocks are evaluated by comparing the corresponding adjacent external boundary pixels

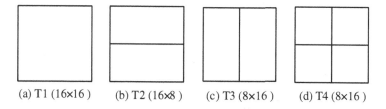

(a) T1 (16×16)   (b) T2 (16×8)   (c) T3 (8×16)   (d) T4 (8×16)

Fig. 3. Four modes of different block sizes

The A_{00} 4×4 block and its adjacent external boundary pixels are directly above and towards the left, the A_{01} 4×4 block and its adjacent external boundary pixels are directly above, the A_{10} 4×4 block and its adjacent external boundary pixels are directly left, and so on. The estimated MV is that which effectively minimizes the adjacent external boundary matching error (AEBME). However, the inner corrupted 4×4 blocks (A_{11}, B_{11}, C_{11}, and D_{11}) are all bordered by the outer corrupted blocks and have no adjacent boundary pixels. A_{11}, for instance, has a limited choice for the adoption of either spatial or temporal MV, which it therefore evaluates by majority decision based on A_{00}, A_{01}, and A_{10}s' preference for estimated MV. This same procedure is used also for B_{11}, C_{11}, and D_{11}, respectively.

2.3 Variable Block Size

After estimating one motion vector for each of the 16 4×4 blocks within the damaged MB by AEBME, the damaged MB will hasten the partition into four block modes (Fig. 3) of 16×16 (T_1), 16×8(T_2), 8×16 (T_3), and 8×8(T_4) based on the Laplacian distribution of the motion field. The maximum probability of the arrangement of the four partition modes (T_1, T_2, T_3, T_4) within the macroblock given the character of the motion field is defined by the following formulae. We begin with the definition of condition probability, using Bayes's theorem.

$$\hat{T} = max\left\{P(T_j|mv)\right\}, j \in \{1,2,3,4\} = max\left\{\frac{P(T_j \cap mv)}{P(mv)}\right\} = max\left\{\frac{P(mv|T_j)P(T_j)}{P(mv)}\right\} \qquad (3)$$

If we undertake an analysis of the entire video sequence, the value $P(T_j)$ of each mode could be differentiated, but in order to prohibit two-pass analysis, the probability of all initial modes $P(T_j)$ are equalized. The probability of the maximum likelihood of the four partition modes is expressed as

$$\hat{T}' = max\left\{P(mv|T_j)\right\} = max\left\{\prod_{k=1}^{N_j} P(mv_k|B_{k,j})\right\}$$

$$= max\left\{\prod_{k=1}^{N_j}\left[\prod_{mv_k \in B_{k,j}} P(mv_k^x|B_{k,j}) \cdot P(mv_k^y|B_{k,j})\right]\right\} \qquad (4)$$

where $B_{k,j}$ represents the kth partition in T_j; mv_k represents the motion vectors of the partition B_k; mv_k^x represents the horizontal character of the motion vector (mv_k); mv_k^y represents the vertical character of the motion vector (mv_k); N_j represents the number of partitions in the damaged macroblock ($T_1 = 1$, $T_2 = 2$, $T_3 = 2$, $T_4 = 4$).

The probability of maximum likelihood is evaluated by using the Laplacian-modeled motion field.

$$\hat{T}' = max\left\{\prod_{k=1}^{N_j}\left[\prod_{mv_k \in B_{k,j}} P(mv_k^x|B_{k,j}) \cdot P(mv_k^y|B_{k,j})\right]\right\}$$

$$= max\left\{\prod_{k=1}^{N_j}\left[\prod_{mv_k \in B_{k,j}} \frac{1}{2\sigma_k^x}exp(\frac{-\left|mv_k^x - \mu_k^x\right|}{\sigma_k^x}) \cdot \frac{1}{2\sigma_k^y}exp(\frac{-\left|mv_k^y - \mu_k^y\right|}{\sigma_k^y})\right]\right\} \qquad (5)$$

where μ_k^x represents the median of the horizontal character of the motion vector within the kth partition in T_j; μ_k^y represents the median of the vertical character of the motion vector within the kth partition in T_j; σ_k^x and σ_k^y are expressed in terms of the absolute difference of the median μ_k^x and μ_k^y, as follows:

$$\sigma_k^x = \frac{1}{\sqrt{2a}} \sum_{mv_k \in B_{k,j}} \left| mv_k^x - \mu_k^x \right|; \mu_k^x = median\left\{ mv_k^x \right\}$$

$$\sigma_k^y = \frac{1}{\sqrt{2a}} \sum_{mv_k \in B_{k,j}} \left| mv_k^y - \mu_k^y \right|; \mu_k^y = median\left\{ mv_k^y \right\}$$

(6)

where a denotes the number of motion vectors in $B_{k,j}$.

We then take the nature log of (10)

$$\hat{T'} \approx \max_j \left\{ \sum_{k=1}^{N_j} \left(-aln\sigma_k^x - aln\sigma_k^y \right) \right\}$$

(7)

When the different major clusters are too close to separate and classification results in high probability of error in terms of partitioning, the Bhattacharyya bound is used as the measurement of the separability of two clusters [38], [39].

For Laplacian probability distribution functions, minimum error of a Bayesian classifier for two different clusters is bounded by

$$P(error) \leq P^\beta(D_1) \times P^{1-\beta}(D_2) \times e^{-k(s)}$$

(8)

Where

$$k(s) = \frac{s(1-s)}{2}(u_2 - u_1)^t \left[s\Sigma_1 + (1-s)\Sigma_2 \right]^{-1}(u_2 - u_1) + \frac{1}{2}ln\frac{|s\Sigma_1 + (1-s)\Sigma_2|}{|\Sigma_1|^s|\Sigma_2|^{1-s}}$$

(9)

We use Bhattacharyya bound ($s = 1/2$), the upper limit of error, and D_k to denote the cluster in the motion field; u is the 2-component mean vector and Σ is 2-by-2 covariance matrix, with $|\Sigma|$ and Σ^{-1} as its determinant and inverse, respectively. In our case, the probabilities of two clusters are initially equal. When $k(s)$ between two clusters is large enough ($k(s) > 2$), it means the error probability of classification is very small, and then we define two clusters as separable.

After the partition mode is decided upon, it can be used to more accurately represent the motion character of the macroblock. If the damaged macroblock is thought to exhibit low or regular motion (i.e. Container sequence), the larger block size is more suitable for motion refinement; however, if the damaged macroblock is thought to exhibit higher and irregular motion (i.e. Stefan sequence), smaller block size is more suitable for motion refinement.

2.4 Motion Refinement

In order to make a refined estimate of the replacement MB, we apply motion refinement for each sub-macroblock partition (size of 16×16 or 16×8 or 8×16 or 8×8) of the damaged MB. For each sub-macroblock partition, motion refinement implies that the corresponding motion vector (u, v), the median of the estimated motion vector of the corresponding 4×4 blocks within the sub-macroblock, is used as the starting point for a motion search process to find a more accurate motion vector replacement, for which AEBME (and in this case the external 8-pixel-wide boundary) is employed as the matching measure. To minimize the computational complexity of the motion search process, we propose a novel method: the outward spiral scanning path, with adaptive search range and early stop augmenting and improving the search process. The adaptive search range (ASR) is based on the first adjacent external boundary matching error at the starting point of the spiral scanning path, along with the motion vector values of all surrounding 4×4 blocks. The ASR for motion search is determined by

$$ASR = \frac{|AEBME(u,v) - \mu|}{\mu} \times max(D_x, D_y) \times \frac{W}{\lambda} + \varepsilon, \quad \begin{array}{l} D_x = max \, | \, X(MVs) - u \, | \\ D_y = max \, | \, Y(MVs) - v \, | \end{array} \quad (10)$$

$AEBME(u, v)$ denotes the first adjacent external boundary matching error at the starting point, (u, v) is the corresponding motion vector for the sub-macroblock partition, μ denotes the original residual values of the *SADs* (sum of absolute difference) in the corresponding surrounding boundary blocks, W is the maximum search size, λ and ε are constant factors ($\lambda = 32$, $\varepsilon = 0$), $X(MVs)$ that denotes the x component of the set of motion vectors of corresponding surrounding blocks, and $Y(MVs)$ denotes the y component of the set of the motion vectors of the corresponding surrounding blocks. The early stop of our search process technique is dependent on the proximity of the adjacent external boundary matching error value to the original residual values of the SADs, μ, in the corresponding boundary blocks. The dynamic threshold (DT_a) is expressed as

$$DT_a = \mu + N \times \alpha \qquad (11)$$

where N is the total number of pixels in the corresponding boundary blocks, and α is the constant factor for each pixel. Occasionally μ is not available, in which case we need to increase α in order to calculate the dynamic threshold (DT_a). If the *AEBME* of the corresponding surrounding blocks is less or equal than the dynamic threshold (DT_a), we immediately stop the search for the damaged sub-macroblock. An important point to emphasize is that the use of overlapped block motion compensation (OBMC) [20] - the division of the damaged MB into four 8×8 blocks with motion refinement employed for each 8×8 block - results in better video quality when compared to those lacking the use of OBMC, however it causes higher computational complexity for a motion search process. Compared with OBMC, the use of variable block size motion compensation (VBSMC) not only represents the motion characteristic more accurately but also reduces the number of motion search processes from 4 times to 1~4 times for each damaged MB.

3 Experiment

The experimental environment is based around the H.264 reference software of Joint Model [36] supplied by the JVT [37] committee (Joint Video Team of ISO/IEC MPEG and ITU-T VCEG). The error concealment algorithms were tested on several standard video sequences in both CIF (352×288) and QCIF (176×144) in order to

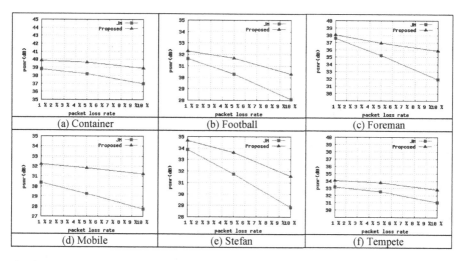

Fig. 4. PSNR results at different packet error rates are shown for various sequences. (a) "Container", (b) "Football", (c) "Foreman", (d) "Mobile", (e) "Stefan", and (f) "Tempete".

evaluate the video quality in the experiment. The resolution video sequences were coded at 1 I-frame for every 12 P-frames with a slice size of 536 bytes, using interleaving technique of flexible macroblock ordering (FMO), with random packet lost errors at different specified loss ratios (different rates), which are assumed to be caused by transmission errors. Ten different random packet lost errors were used simultaneously at each different specified loss ratio. The average peak signal-to-noise ratio (PSNR) of a video sequence is employed to give a quantitative evaluation of the quality of the reconstructed image. In the TEC scenario, we assume that packet erasure has not occurred on the initial decoded frame. The performance of the proposed TEC method is compared to the JM method by using several standard video sequences (with the exception of the first frame of each sequence) at the 1%, 5% and 10% erasure rates. Fig. 4 illustrates that the proposed TEC method outperforms the JM method. The "Foreman" video sequence is 3.89 dB, the "Mobile" video sequence is 3.5dB, the "Stefan" video sequence is 2.75 dB, the "Football" video sequence is 2.21 dB, the "Container" video sequence is 1.94 dB, and the "Tempete" video sequence is 1.76 dB, with all sequences at the 10% erasure rate. Now we will compare video quality and computational complexity of the variable block size motion compensation (VBSMC) with those of the overlapped block motion compensation (OBMC) [20], in effort to discern the more beneficial of the two. In order to compare computational complexity and performance, the proposed Temporal Error Concealment (TEC) method featuring the part of VBSMC is substituted with OBMC, and the remainder is fixed in accordance with the total TEC scheme. The average speed-up of VBSMC was found to be 1.12 times faster then that of OBMC for TEC process time, with VBSMC PSNR improvements of up to 0.09 dB more than OBMC.

4 Conclusion

In this paper we propose an optimized temporal error concealment algorithm with several novel techniques: the spatial damaged motion vectors are estimated based on the optimum regression plane, suitable MB partition is based on predictive motion vectors of the Laplacian distribution model, a significant speed-up on motion refinement with variable block size motion compensation, and early stop by dynamic threshold. The proposed temporal error concealment shows significant gains in improvement when compared with the JM method.

Acknowledgements

This research was supported by ASUS Corporation, Taiwan under Grant 96-S-B09 and by the National Science Council, Taiwan under Grant NSC 95-2221-E-002-068.

References

1. Wang, Y., Zhu, Q.F.: Error control and concealment for video communication: A review. Proc. IEEE 86(5), 974–997 (1998)
2. Peng, Q., Yang, T., Zhu, C.: Block-based temporal error concealment for video packet using motion vector extrapolation. In: IEEE 2002 International Conference on Communications, Circuits and Systems and West Sino Expositions, vol. 1, pp. 10–14 (June 29 -July 1, 2002)
3. Haskell, P., Messerschmitt, D.: Resynchronization of motion compensated video affected by ATM cell loss. In: Proc. ICASSP, vol. 3, pp. 545–548 (March 1992)
4. Agrafiotis, D., Chiew, T.K., Ferr, P., Bull, D.R., Nix, A.R., Doufexi, A., Chung-How, J., Nicholson, D.: Seamless wireless networking for video surveillance applications. In: Proc. SPIE Image Video Commun. Process. (January 2005)
5. Valente, S., Dufour, C., Groliere, F., Snook, D.: An efficienct error concealment implementation for MPEG-4 video streams. IEEE Transactions on Consumer Electronics 47(3), 568–578 (2001)
6. Yan, B., Ng, K.W.: A novel selective motion vector matching algorithm for error concealment in MPEG-4 video transmission over error-prone channels. IEEE Transactions on Consumer Electronics 49(4), 1416–1423 (2003)
7. Zhang, J., Arnold, J.F., Frater, M.R.: A cell-loss concealment technique for MPEG-2 coded video. IEEE Trans. Circuits Syst. Video Technol. 10(4), 659–665 (2000)
8. Pyun, J.-Y., Lee, J.-S., Jeong, J.-W., Jeong, J.-H., Ko, S.-J.: Robust error concealment for visual communications in burst-packet-loss networks. IEEE Trans. Consum. Electron. 49(4), 1013–1019 (2003)
9. Tsekeridou, S., Cheikh, F.A., Gabbouj, M., Pitas, I.: Vector rational interpolation schemes for erroneous motion field estimation applied to MPEG-2 error concealment. IEEE Trans. Multimedia 6(6), 876–885 (2004)
10. Al-Mualla, M.E., Canagarajah, N., Bull, D.R.: Temporal error concealment using motion field interpolation. Electron. Lett. 35, 215–217 (1999)
11. Al-Mualla, M.E., Canagarajah, C.N., Bull, D.R.: Error concealment using motion field interpolation. In: Int. Conf. Image Processing, vol. 28, pp. 512–516 (October 1998)

12. Chen, C., Chen, M., Huang, C., Sun, S.: Motion vector based error concealment algorithms. In: Chen, Y.-C., Chang, L.-W., Hsu, C.-T. (eds.) PCM 2002. LNCS, vol. 2532, pp. 425–433. Springer, Heidelberg (2002)

13. Zheng, J., Chau, L.-P.: Error-concealment algorithm for H.26L using first-order plane estimation. IEEE Trans. Multimedia 6(6), 801–805 (2004)

14. Zheng, J., Chau, L.-P.: Efficient motion vector recovery algorithm for H.264 based on a polynomial model. IEEE Trans. Multimedia 7(3), 507–513 (2005)

15. Zheng, J., Chau, L.P.: A motion vector recovery algorithm for digital video using Lagrange interpolation. IEEE Trans. Broadcast. 49(4), 383–389 (2003)

16. Lam, W.-M., Reibman, A.R.: Recovery of lost or erroneously received motion vectors. In: ICASSP. Proc. Int. Conf. Acoust., Speech Signal Process, p. V-417-V-420 (1993)

17. Wang, Y.-K., Hannuksela, M.M., Varsa, V., Hourunranta, A., Gabbouj, M.: The error concealment feature in the H.26L test model. In: ICIP. Proc. Int. Conf. Image Processing, pp. 729–732 (2002)

18. Sullivan, G., Wiegand, T., Lim, K.-P.: Joint model reference encoding methods and decoding concealment methods Doc. JVT-I049 (September 2003)

19. Xu, Y., Zhou, Y.: H.264 video communication based refined error concealment schemes. IEEE Trans. Consum. Electron. 50(4), 1135–1141 (2004)

20. Agrafiotis, D., Bull, D.R., Canagarajah, C.N.: Enhanced Error Concealment With Mode Selection. IEEE Trans. Circuits Syst. Video Technology 16(8), 960–973 (2006)

21. Chen, T.: Refined boundary matching algorithm for temporal error concealment. In: Proc. Packet Video, pp. 875–887 (2002)

22. Zhu, Q.F., Wang, Y., Shaw, L.: Coding and cell-loss recovery in DCT-based packet video. IEEE Trans. Circuits Syst. Video Technol. 3, 248–258 (1993)

23. Kuo, Y., Tsao, S.-C.: Error concealment based on overlapping. In: Proc. SPIE, vol. 4671, pp. 146–153 (January 002)

24. Suh, J.W., Ho, Y.S.: Directional interpolation for spatial error concealment. In: Int. Conf. Consumer Electronics, pp. 26–27 (June 1997)

25. Tsekeridou, S., Pitas, I.: MPEG-2 error concealment based on block-matching principles. IEEE Trans. Circuits Syst. Video Technol. 10(4), 646–658 (2000)

26. Suh, J.W., Ho, Y.S.: Error concealment techniques for digital TV. IEEE Trans. Broadcast. 48(4), 299–306 (2002)

27. Hsu, C.T., Chen, M.J., Liao, W.-W., Lo, S.-Y.: High-performance spatial and temporal error-concealment algorithms for block-based video coding techniques. ETRI J. 27(1), 53–63 (2005)

28. Hong, M.C., Scwab, H., Kondi, L., Katsaggelos, A.K.: Error concealment algorithms for compressed video. Signal Process, Image Commun. 14, 473–492 (1999)

29. Kang, L.W., Leou, J.J.: A hybrid error concealment scheme for MPEG-2 video transmission based on best neighborhood matching algorithm. J. Vis. Commun. Image Represent. 16(3), 288–310 (2005)

30. Lee, Y.-C., Altunbasak, Y., Mersereau, R.: Multiframe error concealment for MPEG-coded video delivery over error-prone networks. IEEE Trans. Image Process. 11(11), 1314–1331 (2002)

31. Park, Y.O., Kim, C.-S., Lee, S.-U.: Multi-hypothesis error concealment algorithm for H.26L video. In: ICIP. Proc. Int. Conf. Image Processing, pp. 465–468 (2003)

32. Belfiore, S., Grangetto, M., Magli, E., Olmo, G.: Concealment of whole-frame losses for wireless low bit-rate video based on multiframe optical flow estimation. IEEE Trans. Multimedia 7(2), 316–329 (2005)

33. Baccichet, P., Bagni, D., Chimienti, A., Pezzoni, L., Rovati, F.: Frame concealment for H.264/AVC decoders. IEEE Transactions on Consumer Electronics 51(1), 227–233 (2005)
34. Wenger, S., Horowitz, M.: Scattered Slices: A New Error Resilience Tool for H.264 (2002), [Online]. Available: ftp://ftp.imtcfiles.org/jvt-experts/0202_Gen/JVT-B027.doc
35. Wenger, S.: H.264/AVC over IP. IEEE Trans. Circuit Syst. Video Technol. 13(7), 645–656 (2003)
36. H.264/AVC Reference Software JM [Online], Available: http://bs.hhi.de/ suehring/tml/
37. Joint Video Team (JVT) of ISO/IEC MPEG & ITU-T VCEG, "Working draft number 2, revision 2 (WD-2)," Joint Video Team (JVT) (2002)
38. Kuo, T.Y., Chan, C.H.: Fast Variable Block Size Motion Estimation for H.264 Using Likelihood and Correlation of Motion Field. IEEE Trans. Circuits Syst. Video Technology 16(10), 1185–1195 (2006)
39. Richard, O.D., Peter, E.H., David, G.K.: Pattern Classification, pp. 46–48. Wiley-Interscience, New York (2000)

Transform Domain Wyner-Ziv Codec Based on Turbo Trellis Codes Modulation*

J.L. Martínez[1], W.A.R.J. Weerakkody[2], P. Cuenca[1], F. Quiles[1], and W.A.C. Fernando[2]

[1] Albacete Research Institute of Informatics
Universidad de Castilla-La Mancha
02071 Albacete, Spain
{joseluismm,pcuenca,paco}@dsi.uclm.es
[2] Center for Communications Research
University of Surrey
Guildford GU2 7XH, United Kingdom
{W.Fernando,r.weerakkody}@surrey.ac.uk

Abstract. In recent years, with emerging applications such as wireless video surveillance, multimedia sensor networks, disposable video cameras, medical applications and mobile camera phones, the traditional video coding architecture is being challenged. For these emerging applications, *Distributed Video Coding* (DVC) seems to be able to offer efficient and low-complexity encoding video compression. In this paper, we present a novel transform domain distributed video coding algorithm based on *Turbo Trellis Coded Modulation* (TTCM). As in the conventional turbo based Wyner-Ziv encoder, transform quantized coefficients are applied to the TTCM encoder and parity bits are generated from both constituent encoders. However, TTCM symbols are not generated at the encoder since they are not sent to the decoder. Parity bits produced by the TTCM encoder are stored in a buffer and transmitted to the decoder upon request. TTCM symbols are generated at the decoder and these symbols are passed to the TTCM decoder for demodulation. Experimental results show that significant rate-distortion (RD) gains compared to the state-of-the-art results available in the literature can be obtained.

Keywords: Distributed Video Coding, Transform Domain, Turbo Trellis Coded Modulation.

1 Introduction

Distributed Video Coding is one of the fastest growing coding techniques among the researchers in video coding due to its attractive and promising features. It has been motivated by the emerging and progressively more popular new applications

---

* This work has been jointly supported by the Spanish MEC and European Commission FEDER funds under grants ``Consolider Ingenio-2010 CSD2006-00046" and ``TIN2006-15516-C04-02", and by JCCM funds under grant "PAI06-0106".

S. Satoh, F. Nack, and M. Etoh (Eds.): MMM 2008, LNCS 4903, pp. 413–424, 2008.
© Springer-Verlag Berlin Heidelberg 2008

involving more encoders than decoders, such as multimedia wireless sensor networks, wireless video surveillance, disposable video cameras, medical applications or mobile camera phones. For these emerging applications, DVC seems to be able to offer efficient and low-complex encoding in video compression. DVC proposes a dramatic structural change to video coding by shifting the majority of complexity conventionally residing in the encoder towards the decoder. The major task of exploiting the source redundancies to achieve the video compression is accordingly placed in the decoder. The DVC encoder thus performs a computationally very inexpensive operation enabling a drastically low cost implementation of the signal processor in DVC based video cameras. Matching the rate-distortion (RD) performance of the standardized MPEG and H.26x based systems is a challenge ahead of the researchers promoting DVC.

The Slepian-Wolf theorem [1] and Wyner-Ziv model [2] were the basis for the DVC. Current practical schemes developed for DVC are based in general on the following principles: the video frames are organized into two types; Key frames and Wyner-Ziv frames, while the key frames are encoded with a conventional intraframe codec, the frames between them are Wyner-Ziv encoded. At the decoder, the side information is obtained using previously decoded key frames and a motion interpolation scheme, responsible to obtain the most accurate representation of the original frame.

The rate-distortion performance of the DVC codec has a large bearing on the quality of the side information stream since the parity input to the turbo coding based DVC decoder suffers a significant loss in information content due to the puncturing process carried out as a mechanism for achieving video compression. The quality of the side information stream is typically determined by its closeness to the corresponding original Wyner-Ziv frame used at the DVC encoder.

Based on this theoretical framework, several DVC codecs have been proposed recently [3,4,5] in the pixel domain using traditional turbo coding. In [3,4] the authors have proposed a Wyner-Ziv codec for motion video using a simple frame interpolation. In [5] the authors proposed a more sophisticated motion interpolation and extrapolation techniques to predict the side information.

The distributed video coding paradigm may be also applied in the transform domain. The RD performance of the DVC pixel domain codecs can be further improved by using a transform coding tool with the same purpose as in traditional video coding, i.e. to exploit spatial correlations between neighboring sample values and to compact the block energy into as few transform coefficients as possible. Several proposals have been reported in the literature aiming to implement different transform coding tools, using the well-known Discrete Cosine Transform (DCT) [6,7] and Discrete Wavelet Transform (DWT) [8,9], among others. However, it still exist a significant gap between the RD performance of this proposals and the standardized MPEG and H.26x based systems.

In this work, we present an improved transform domain Wyner-Ziv video codec based on *Turbo Trellis Coded Modulation* (TTCM) with significant rate-distortion (RD) gains compared to the state-of-the-art results available in the literature. As in the conventional turbo based Wyner-Ziv encoder, transform quantized coefficients are applied to the TTCM encoder and parity bits are generated from both constituent encoders. However, TTCM symbols are not generated at the encoder since they are not sent to the decoder. Parity bits produced by the TTCM encoder are stored in a buffer and transmitted to the decoder upon request. TTCM symbols are generated at the decoder and these symbols are passed to the TTCM decoder for demodulation.

This paper is organized as follows. Section 2 presents a review of the state-of-the-art of the transform domain DVC codecs proposed in the literature. The section 3 introduces the proposed Transform Domain Wyner-Ziv video codec based on TTCM. In Section 4, some experimental results are presented to evaluate the performance of our proposal with regard to the best solutions presented in the literature. Finally, conclusions are presented in Section 5.

2 Related Work

Many on-going research efforts are focused on improving the RD performance of Distributed Video Coding. Many studies have revealed that the RD performance of the DVC pixel domain codecs can be further improved by using transform coding. Several proposals have been reported in the literature aiming to implement different transform coding tools. In the following paragraphs, some of the most prominent ones which use DCT and DWT are introduced.

Aaron et al [6] proposed a transform domain Wyner-Ziv coding scheme for motion video based on turbo codes that uses intraframe encoding, but interframe decoding. In this system, the DCT transform coefficients of a Wyner-Ziv frame are encoded independently using a scalar quantizer and a turbo coder. The decoder uses previously reconstructed frames to generate side information to conditionally decode the Wyner-Ziv frames. Simulation results show significant gains above DCT-based intraframe coding and improvements over the pixel-domain Wyner-Ziv video coder [3].

Based on *Aaron et al* scheme, *Brites et al* [7] proposed an improved transform domain Wyner-Ziv video codec including: 1) the integer block-based transform defined in the H.264/MPEG-4 AVC standard, 2) a quantizer with a symmetrical interval around zero for AC coefficients, and a quantization step size adjusted to the transform coefficient bands dynamic range, and 3) advanced frame interpolation for side information generation. The combination of these tools provided significant rate-distortion gains compared to the codec proposed by *Aaron et al* [6].

Aaron's and Brites's schemes are built on DCT domain. It has been proved that DWT can overcome the 'block-effect' brought by block-wise DCT and achieve better coding performance in image coding. Based on this observation, recently, several wavelet-domain DVC schemes have been proposed in the literature. In [8] *Wang et al* proposed a DVC paradigm based on lattice vector quantization in wavelet domain. In this scheme, the authors use a fine and a coarse lattice vector quantizer to wavelet coefficients and the difference of two lattice quantizers is coded by turbo encoder, which is different to [6] based on scalar quantization. At the decoder, side information is gradually updated by motion-compensated refinement. The results obtained outperform the Aaron's scheme. However the refinement is not so useful in low-motion sequences and experiment results were not very impressive. Also, there are some drawbacks, for example, the rate is determined by feedback and the scalable nature of wavelet transform is not included.

Finally, *Bernardini et al* [9] have proposed a wavelet domain distributed coder for video which allows scalability and does not require a feedback channel. Efficient distributed coding is obtained by processing the wavelet transform with a suitable folding function and compressing the folded coefficients with a wavelet coder. At the receiver side, the authors use the statistical properties between similar frames to recover the compressed frame. Experimental results show that the proposed scheme has good performance when compared with similar asymmetric video compression schemes.

3 Transform Domain Wyner-Ziv Codec Based on TTCM

The majority of the well-know research works on DVC have been carried out using a Turbo Wyner-Ziv codec. However, our recent experimental results in [10] show that the Turbo Trellis Coded Modulation based pixel domain DVC codecs can improve the PSNR up to 6dB at the same bit rate with less memory compared to the pixel domain Turbo Coded DVC codecs. Within the research context of this paper we intend to continue this effort to a further paradigm, i.e. transform domain TTCM based DVC codec.

As described in [10], it is seen that the TTCM based codec performs significantly better irrespective of the motion level whereas turbo coding based implementation has a dependency on the motion level as evident when comparing the results for the test video sequence used. In this work [10] also analyzed the effects of the probability distribution of the noise in the side information and it resembled both Gaussian and Laplacian distributions with corresponding variance parameters depending on the high or low motion level in each frame. As a result, when using the video codecs with side information, some dependency on the noise distribution related parameters employed in the maximum a posteriori (MAP) based decoders, on the performance is naturally expected. However, the TTCM based decoder used in our implementation shows a significant immunity to the variations in the noise distribution related parameters.

3.1 Overall Architecture

Figure 1 shows the block diagram of the proposed video codec implementation in transform domain. There are some differences between our solution and the previous solutions proposed in the literature (see section 2), particularly in channel codes employed, the behavior of Slepian – Wolf codec, DCT and quantizer modules.

The even frames {X2, X4, ...} are the Wyner-Ziv frames which go through the interframe encoder to generate the parity sequence to be transferred to the decoder. The odd frames are directly passed to the decoder as Key-Frames and are considered to be available lossless at the decoder as in the equivalent codecs under study from the literature [6-9].

3.2 Transform Coding

In this architecture, the first stage towards encoding a Wyner-Ziv frame, X_{2i}, is transform coding (represented by the DCT module). The transform employed by us relies on the integer 4x4 block based discrete cosine transform, as define by the

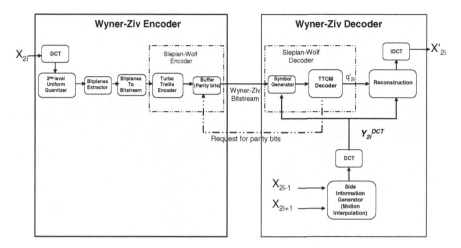

Fig. 1. Transform Domain DVC codec Architecture

H.264/MPEG-4 AVC standard [11]; the transform is applied to all 4x4 non-overlapping blocks of the X_{2i} frame, from left to right and top to bottom. The transform tool converts pixel values (which are always positives) into integer values (both positives and negatives); this concept is meaningful for quantization module. It is an integer transform; all operations can be carried out with integer arithmetic, with loss of accuracy. The core part of the transform only requires additions and shifts, keeping the philosophy of low-complexity encoder devices. As define the H.264/MPEG-4 AVC standard [11], a scaling multiplication (part of the complete transform) is integrated into the quantizer. Our architecture relies on this concept and also employs the quantizer like a part of the transform tool but fitting the QP factor to 0 due to the quantization operation is done using different quantizer matrix depicted in Figure 2.

3.3 Quantization

Once DCT module is applied, the coefficients are passed to quantization tools. The amplitude of the AC coefficients, within a 4x4 DCT coefficients block, tends to be higher for the coefficients close to DC coefficient and decrease as the coefficients approach the higher spatial frequencies. In fact, within a 4x4 coefficients block, the lower spatial frequencies enclose more relevant information about the block than the higher frequencies, which often correspond to noise or less important details for the human visual system (HVS) [12]. Since the HVS is more sensitive to lower spatial frequencies, the DCT coefficients representing lower spatial frequencies are quantized using low quantization step sizes, i.e. with a higher number of quantization intervals (levels).

By letting the decoder know, for each X_{2i} frame, the dynamic range of each DCT coefficients band (i.e. in what range the DCT coefficients vary) instead of using a fixed value, it is possible to have a quantization interval width adjusted to the dynamic range of each band similar to [7]. Besides we also need the number of quantization levels associated to that band. For this propose we use one of nine quantization matrices depicted in figure 2. The DCT coefficients are passed through one of them based on the expected quality of output and the available channel bandwidth. In our transform domain DVC codec nine 4x4 quantization matrixes are employed (see Figure 2) and different performances can be achieved; in the codec evaluation nine rate – distortion points were considered corresponding to the various quantization matrixes depicted in Figure2. The first seven matrices (1-7) in Figure 2 are equal to the ones used in [6], the matrix 8 in Figure 2 is proposed by *Brites et al* in [7] and, the final matrix (9) in Figure 2 is proposed by the authors of this paper in order to allow comparing the performance of our transform domain DVC codec for higher bitrates. That is due to the fact that our solution based on TTCM codes generates less bitrate for the same quality than the rest of literature which are based on turbo codes. In our simulations we have used the first eighth quantization matrix in order to comparing our proposal and the solution proposed in [6,7]. Within a 4x4 quantization matrix, the value at position k in Figure 2 indicates the number of quantization levels associated to the DCT coefficients band b_k; the value zero means that no Wyner-Ziv bits are transmitted for the corresponding band; in this case, the decoder will replace the DCT bands to which no Wyner-Ziv bits are sent by the corresponding DCT coefficients bands in the side information determined at the decoder. In our solution, we use the sign bit of the DC coefficient band to enhance the precision since all DC coefficients are always positives.

3.4 Bitplanes Extractor

After quantizing the DCT coefficients bands, the quantized symbols (represented by integer values) are converted into a binary stream. The bits of same significance in the quantized symbols (e. g. the most significant bit) are grouped together forming the corresponding bitplane array. In [6,7] these arrays are independently turbo encoded, i.e. the turbo encoder works on different bands independently (for example, for QCIF sequences, the turbo encoder uses 176x144/(4x4) = 1584 bits; that is input-length of Slepian – Wolf encoder). In our solution, the input-length of turbo encoder was studied and we observed better performance, based on several test, for a input size of 7 bits instead of 1584 that is used in other literature [6,7]. Moreover, in most solutions discussed in the literature based on turbo codes and DCT [6,7] the turbo decoder operates by each band and all bitplanes for the considered band. In our solution, we generate a bitstream that contain all bitplanes of all coefficients according to a linear reading of a frame, i. e. from left to right and top to bottom. These bits of each biplane are read according to their significance (we start with the most significant bit of each coefficient).

3.5 The Slepian – Wolf Codec

The Slepian-Wolf based encoder incorporates the bit plane extractor and then the turbo trellis encoder. Each rate ½ component encoder of our implementation has a constraint length K= M+1 =4 and a generator polynomial of [11 02] in octal form. A Pseudo-random interleaver is used in front of the second constituent encoder. Only the parity bit sequence thus generated is retained in the parity buffers and the systematic bits are discarded. The side information is generated at the decoder using

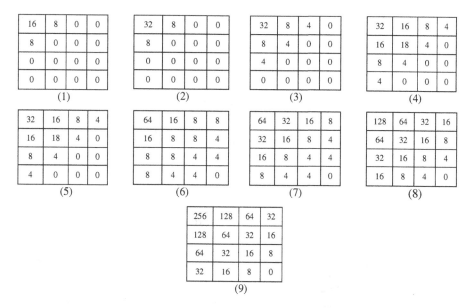

Fig. 2. Quantization matrices associated to our transform domain DVC codec

interpolation techniques between adjacent key frames; the proposed transform domain DVC codec uses the block – based frame interpolation framework proposed in [5] in order to compare the proposed results with the results presented in the literature. In a nutshell, the side information for an even frame at time index t is generated by performing motion-compensated interpolation using the decoded key frames at time $t+1$ and $t-1$ (in this scenario we suppose lossless coding). In addition to forward and bidirectional motion estimation, a spatial motion smoothing algorithm to eliminate motion outliers is employed.

This side information together with the parity bits passed from the encoder, upon request, form the PSK symbols to be processed in the TTCM decoder. A multi level set partitioning is done with the constellation mapping of the TCM symbols in order to maintain the maximum Euclidian distance between the information bits. Where ever parity bits are not available due to puncturing being effective, the symbol automatically reduces to a lower modulation level. In the implementation under discussion, a combination of 4 PSK and Binary-PSK is used based on the availability of the parity bits for the constellation mapping. As commonly understood, Trellis Coded Modulation is conceptually a channel coding technique used to optimize the bandwidth requirements of a channel while protecting the information bits by increasing the size of the symbol constellation. Our effort is to exploit the high coding gain and the noise immunity inherent in this technique.

A block diagram of the Turbo-TCM decoder implementation is shown in Figure 3. A symbol based MAP algorithm is used in the turbo trellis decoder which is run for 6 iterations as a complexity performance trade-off. A modification was done to the branch metric calculation to take care of the independent distributions of side

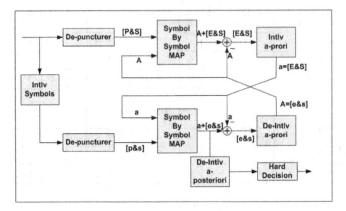

Fig. 3. Block Diagram of TTCM Decoder

information and parity bits. The parity bits are supplied to the decoder through an "on-demand" approach using a reverse channel for passing the request to the parity buffer maintained in the encoder. The de-puncturer function in the decoder basically watches the parity availability and manipulates the symbols fed to the SISO based MAP decoder accordingly. A reconstruction function similar to the one proposed in [3] is used to smoothen some adverse effects in the output sequence including some contribution by the quantization noise.

The side information generated of two key frames is assumed to be a form of the original Wyner-Ziv frame subjected to noise. The probability distribution of this noise was a part of the detailed study. It was noticed that both the Gaussian noise distribution and the Laplacian noise distribution resembled the interpolation noise with distinct variance parameters. However, most interestingly, it was noted that our implementation of the codec was not susceptible to error by sub-optimal approximations of the distribution for the purpose of taking the results; an additive White Gaussian noise (AWGN) with variance 0.125 was assumed.

4 Performance Evaluation

In this section, a comparative performance evaluation in terms of the RD performance results of the proposed Transform Domain Distributed Video Codec is carried out with other transform domain architectures proposed in the literature by *Aaron*, *Brites*, *Wang* and *Bernardini*, described in section 2.

The puncturing pattern is varied dynamically inside the codec in order to generate an optimum decoded output with respected to the quantized input fed to the encoder. The methods of estimating the accuracy of the decoded bit stream are beyond the scope of this paper. The PSNR of the decoded frames is then calculated and plotted against the transmitted bit rate, averaged over the sequence. The bit rate and PSNR are calculated for the luminance of the Wyner-Ziv frames, or the odd frames of the sequence, only with a frame size of 176x144 (QCIF) with a Wyner-Ziv frame rate of 15fps.

Further, it is noted that our implementation of the encoder uses a memory length of 3 whereas the codec proposed in [6,7] uses length 4. Shorter memory length means reduced computational complexity.

For a better comparative performance analysis of rate-distortion function, we also show the average PSNR difference (ΔPSNR) and the average bit-rate difference (ΔBitrate). The PSNR and bit-rate differences are calculated according to the numerical averages between the RD-curves derived from the proposed transform domain DVC codec and the *Aaron, Brites, Wang* and *Bernardini* codecs, respectively. The detailed procedures in calculating these differences can be found in the JVT document authored by *Bjontegaard* [13]. Note that PSNR and bit-rate differences should be regarded as equivalent, i.e., there is either the decrease in PSNR or the increase in bit-rate, but not both at the same time.

Figure 4 shows the RD analysis results for the Wyner-Ziv frames for all transform domain schemes under study for the first 101 frames of *Foreman* QCIF sequence. The performance is compared against H.264 intraframe coding (worst case) and H.264 interframe coding with an I-B-I-B structure (best case). In the last case, only the rate and PSNR of the B frames is shown. From the results illustrated in Figure 4, it is also possible to conclude that the RD performance obtained with our transform domain DVC codec outperforms the other transform domain DVC codecs presented in the literature. Coding improvements up to 0.58 dB compared to the best compatible solutions available in the literature can be obtained.

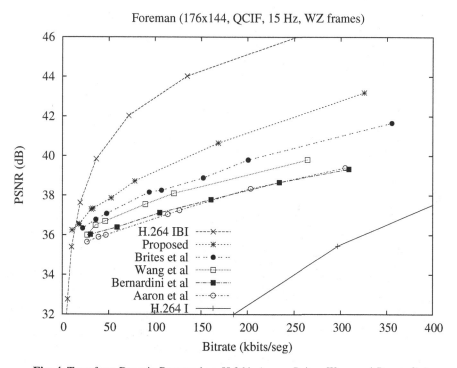

Fig. 4. Transform Domain Proposed vs. H.264, *Aaron, Brites, Wang* and *Bernardini*

The results for the first 101 frames of *Mother and Daughter* QCIF sequence are shown in Figure 5. For the plots, we only include the rate and distortion of the luminance of the even frames. The even frame rate is 15 frames per second. We compare our results to *Brites et al* and *Aaron et al*. We also plot the compression results of H.264 intraframe and interframe in a similar way to Figure 4. From the results illustrated in Figure 5, it is also possible to conclude that the RD performance obtained with our transform domain DVC codec also outperforms the other transform domain DVC codecs when another sequence is employed. In Figure 5 also shows better performance for our DVC architecture against Traditional Video Coding for lower bitrates.

Table 1. Quantitative Comparative Performance (Transform Domain Proposed vs. H.264, *Aaron, Brites, Wang* and *Bernardini* Architectures. *Foreman* Sequence)

Method	ΔPSNR (dB)	ΔBitrate (%)
H.264 IBI	-1.572	23.29
Brites et al	0.579	-118.9
Wang et al	0.77	-48.08
Bernardini et al	1.052	-133.67
Aaron et al	1.095	-97.21
H.264 I	3.891	-217.24

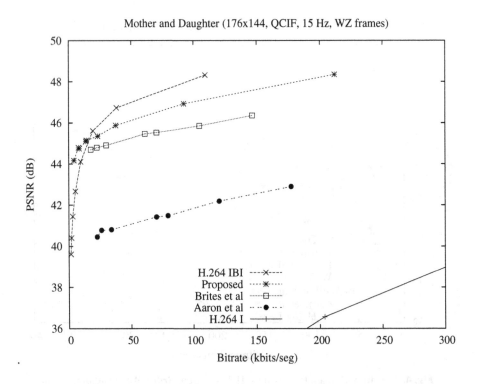

Mother and Daughter (176x144, QCIF, 15 Hz, WZ frames)

Table 1 shows quantitative results for a better comparative performance of rate-distortion function, in terms of the average PSNR difference (ΔPSNR) and the average bit-rate difference (ΔBitrate). As seen in the Table 1, the usage of the our transform domain DVC codec outperforms the other codecs by 0.58 dB 0.77 dB, 1.05 dB, and 1.09 dB on average, with respect *Brites*, *Wang*, *Bernardini* and *Aaron* proposals respectively, using significant less bit-rate.

Table 2 shows similar results of Figure 1 according to *Mother & Daughter* sequence, as we can see our transform domain DVC codec outperforms by 0.52 dB and 3.23 on average with respect to *Brites* and *Aaron* proposals, using significant less bit-rate.

Table 2. Quantitative Comparative Performance (Transform Domain Proposed vs. H.264, *Aaron, Brites,* Architectures. *Mother and Daughter Sequence*)

Method	ΔPSNR (dB)	ΔBitrate (%)
H.264 IBI	-0.555	41.02
Brites et al	0.522	-117.81
Aaron et al	3.237	---

5 Conclusions

In this work, an improved transform domain DVC codec was presented with significant RD performance gains compared to the state-of-the-art results available in the literature. This codec is based on TTCM codes, a novel channel coding approach for DVC unlike the most employed techniques in the literature such as turbo codes.

We have shown that the proposed codec outperforms the turbo coding based coded in transform domain with a very high PSNR at a lower data rate, enabling to be used over low bandwidth transmission media with a higher viewing quality. Moreover, this architecture is compatible with the DVC concepts with a very simple low cost encoder employing a DCT composes only by additions and shifts operations, the memory length of TTCM encoder is shorter and the fact that the TTCM symbols are not generated at the encoder side. Furthermore, the proposed codec performs equally well irrespective of the motion level in the video sequence and is immune to the variations of the probability distribution of the interpolation noise introduced at the side information generation.

References

1. Slepian, D., Wolf, J.K.: Noiseless Coding of Correlated Information Sources. IEEE Transaction on Information Theory 19, 471–480 (1973)
2. Wyner, D., Ziv, J.: The Rate-Distortion Function for Source Coding with Side Information at the Decoder. IEEE Transaction on Information Theory 22, 1–10 (1976)
3. Aaron, A., Zhang, R., Girod, B.: Wyner-Ziv Coding of Motion Video. In: Proceeding of Asilomar Conference on Signals and Systems, Pacific Grove, USA (2002)
4. Girod, B., Aaron, A., Rane, S., Monedero, D.R.: Distributed Video Coding. IEEE Special Issue on Advances in Video Coding and Delivery 93, 1–12 (2005)

5. Ascenso, J., Brites, C., Pereira, F.: Improving Frame Interpolation with Spatial Motion Smoothing for Pixel Domain Distributed Video Coding. In: 5th EURASIP Conference on Speech and Image Processing, Multimedia Communications and Services (2005)
6. Aaron, A., Rane, S., Setton, E., Griod, B.: Transform-domain Wyner-Ziv Codec for Video. In: VCIP 2007. Visual Communications and Image Processing, San Jose, USA (2004)
7. Brites, C., Ascenso, J., Pereira, F.: Improving Transform Domain Wyner-Ziv Video Coding Performance. In: ICASSP 2006. IEEE International Conference on Acoustics, Speech and Signal Processing, Toulouse, France (2006)
8. Wang, A., Zhao, Y., Wei, L.: Wavelet-Domain Distributed Video Coding with Motion-Compensated Refinement. In: ICIP 2006. Proceedings of IEEE International Conference on Image Processing, Atlanta, USA (2006)
9. Bernardini, R., Rinaldo, R., Zontone, P., Alfonso, D., Vitali, A.: Wavelet Domain Distributed Coding for Video. In: ICIP 2006. Proceedings of IEEE International Conference on Image Processing, Atlanta, USA (2006)
10. Weerakkody, W.A.R.J., Fernando, W.A.C., Adikari, A.B.B., Rajatheva, R.M.A.P.: Distributed video coding of Wyner-Ziv frames using Turbo Trellis Coded Modulation. In: ICIP 2006. Proceedings of International Conference on Image Processing, Atlanta, USA (2006)
11. ISO/IEC International Standard, 6-10:2003, Information Technology – Coding of Audio - Visual Objects – Part 10: Advanced Video Coding (1449)
12. Clarke, R.: Transform Coding of Images. Academic Press, San Diego (1990)
13. Bjontegaard, G.: Calculation of Average PSNR Differences between RD-Curves. In: 13th VCEG-M33 Meeting, Austin, USA (2001)

Selective Sampling Based on Dynamic Certainty Propagation for Image Retrieval

Xiaoyu Zhang, Jian Cheng, Hanqing Lu, and Songde Ma

National Laboratory of Pattern Recognition,
Institute of Automation, Chinese Academy of Sciences, Beijing 100080, China
{xyzhang,jcheng,luhq}@nlpr.ia.ac.cn, songde.ma@mail.ia.ac.cn

Abstract. In relevance feedback of image retrieval, selective sampling is often used to alleviate the burden of labeling by selecting only the most informative data to label. Traditional data selection scheme often selects a batch of data at a time and label them all together, which neglects the data's correlation and thus jeopardizes the effectiveness. In this paper, we propose a novel Dynamic Certainty Propagation (DCP) scheme for informative data selection. For each unlabeled data, we define the notion of *certainty* to quantify our confidence in its predicted label. Every time, we only label one single data point with the lowest degree of certainty. Then we update the rest unlabeled data's certainty dynamically according to their correlation. This *one-by-one labeling* offers us extra guidance from the last labeled data for the next labeling. Experiments show that the DCP scheme outperforms the traditional method evidently.

Keywords: Image retrieval, Relevance feedback, Active learning, Selective sampling, Semi-supervised learning.

1 Introduction

In Content-Based Image Retrieval (CBIR) [1, 2], relevance feedback [3] is a powerful and wildly-used approach to bridge the gap between high-level semantic concepts and low-level image features by human-computer interaction. In each round of relevance feedback, some images are returned for the user to label, and then the labeled images will be used to refine the output of the CBIR system. It is common that in an image retrieval system the image database is very huge, while the images labeled by the user are quite limited. Therefore, how to explore the abundant unlabeled images as well as the small number of labeled images effectively has become one of the key problems in relevance feedback. From the viewpoint of machine learning, the process of image retrieval can be regarded as a binary classification problem which classifies the images in the database as relevant or irrelevant to the query. So advanced machine learning algorithms can be introduced into relevance feedback to improve the classification performance.

Active learning (or more precisely, *selective sampling*) [4] is a useful machine learning algorithm dealing with classification problems in which labeled data are scare while unlabeled data are abundant and easy to get. Its main idea is selecting the

S. Satoh, F. Nack, and M. Etoh (Eds.): MMM 2008, LNCS 4903, pp. 425–435, 2008.

most informative data so that knowing their labels can greatly boost the performance of the classifier. The selected data will then be labeled and added to the training set to retrain the classifier. This procedure can be iterated, and the goal is to label as little data as possible to achieve a certain performance. Examples of selective sampling being used in image retrieval include SVM$_{Active}$ proposed by Tong and Chang [5], SSAIR by Zhou et al. [6], Co-SVM by Cheng and Wang [7], etc. In each round of relevance feedback, they label a batch of images either with minimum confidence to the classifier or with maximum disagreement among multiple classifiers. However, as will be indicated later, the traditional *batch labeling* schemes are not effective enough since they neglect the correlation between the data.

In this paper, we present the Dynamic Certainty Propagation (DCP) scheme for informative data selection in selective sampling. In our method, the unlabeled data are selected *one by one* in terms of their *certainty*. Once a data point is labeled, its certainty will change and then *propagate dynamically* to the nearby unlabeled data points. By utilizing the data's correlation as an aid, we make the data selected by the DCP scheme more informative.

2 Related Work

As mentioned above, the key point with selective sampling is to find out a way to choose the most informative data for labeling.

SVM$_{Active}$ is a representative algorithm introducing selective sampling to relevance feedback. It considers the images closest to the current SVM boundary to be the most informative data. In recent years, a trend in image retrieval is to combine selective sampling with *multi-view semi-supervised learning* [8], such as *co-training* [9], *co-testing* [10], etc. It is a natural choice since multi-view learning is another powerful algorithm dealing with the same issue as selective sampling, i.e. labeled data are scare while unlabeled data are abundant. SSAIR and Co-SVM are algorithms of this kind. They train different classifiers on different views separately, and regard the images on which the classifiers most disagree as the most informative data.

As we can see, both the "sole" selective sampling and the selective sampling combined with multi-view learning use the similar *batch labeling* model: They first attach a measurement to each unlabeled data to quantify the confidence in its predicted label. Then they return the top N_l data points with the lowest confidence at a time and label them all together, where N_l is the number of images to be labeled in a round of relevance feedback.

Zhang and Oles [11] theoretically analyzed the value of unlabeled data for classification problems, and presented two principles for the selection of informative unlabeled data in selective sampling:

- Choose the unlabeled data with low confidence;
- Choose the unlabeled data that are not redundant with the data already chosen.

The former is quite intuitive based on pervious studies, while the latter is not so apparent at first glance. We can explain it in a specific two-dimensional classification problem for simplicity. As illustrated in Fig. 1, the batch labeling schemes discussed above with $N_l = 2$ will undoubtedly label data A and B, since they are the top 2 closest

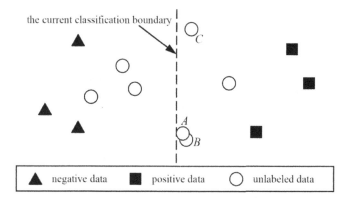

Fig. 1. After point *A* has been labeled, it seems that *B* becomes less informative than *C*, although *B* is relatively closer to the current trained classification boundary

to the classification boundary, and thus have the top 2 lowest confidence. However, after the most uncertain data *A* has been labeled, *C* is perhaps more informative, because *B* is so similar to *A* that its confidence has sharply increased after its neighbor *A* is known. The traditional batch labeling schemes fail to consider the correlation between the data to be labeled because they select the batch of data all together. As a result, they are inclined to violate the *non-redundancy* principle, which is largely responsible for their ineffectiveness.

Perhaps the optimal way for informative data selection is to label only one most informative data point, and retrain the classifier immediately. Then the updated classifier will decide the next most informative one to be labeled. We call this *one-by-one training*, since after each labeling there is a training of classifier. It can be seen as an extreme of batch labeling where $N_l = 1$. With the same number of data to label, the one-by-one training model will perform better than batch labeling. However, since the process of training is the most complex part in the process of relevance feedback, the time consumption of one-by-one training, which needs frequent training, will be unbearable. So in image retrieval, batch labeling is often adopted instead of one-by-one training as a trade-off between efficiency and performance [12].

3   Dynamic Certainty Propagation Scheme

3.1   Algorithm

In this paper, we propose a novel data selection scheme, the Dynamic Certainty Propagation (DCP) scheme, for selective sampling. We take both the *low-confidence* and *non-redundancy* principle into account, and present our *one-by-one labeling* model: we select and label the data one by one, using the last labeled data point to guide the selection of next; after a batch of data has been labeled and added to the training set, we perform training once to get a better performing classifier. In a word, in our DCP scheme, we use one-by-one labeling but still batch training, which can be seen as a compromise of batch labeling and one-by-one training (Fig. 2).

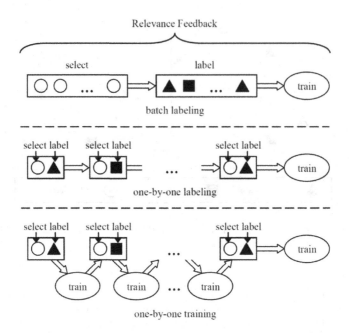

Fig. 2. Batch labeling vs. one-by-one labeling vs. one-by-one training

Now we describe our DCP scheme in detail. We use $X = \{ x_1, x_2, \ldots, x_n \} = U \cup L$ to denote the dataset, where U and L denote the unlabeled and labeled dataset respectively. For each data point $x_i \in X$ ($1 \leq i \leq n$), $y_i \in \{0, 1\}$ is its corresponding class label. If $x_i \in L$, y_i is known; while if $x_i \in U$, y_i is unknown and we use $f(x_i)$ to estimate y_i, where f denotes the current trained classifier on X.

For each unlabeled data point, we introduce the notion of *certainty* as a measurement of the confidence in its predicted label, with a sign ("$+$" or "$-$") to indicate its class label. We use the term *degree of certainty* to denote the absolute value of certainty. The lower degree of certainty an unlabeled data point has, the more informative it is. Every time, we only select one single data point with the lowest degree of certainty to label. Then we update all the rest unlabeled data's certainty according to their correlation to the last labeled data point. This procedure can be repeated until a certain number of data have been labeled.

We use C to represent the data's certainty. Initially, the certainty of each unlabeled data point x_i ($x_i \in U$) is:

$$C^{(0)}(x_i) = f(x_i) \tag{1}$$

Every time, we select only one unlabeled data point x_l with the minimum degree of certainty to label:

$$l = \arg\min_i \left| C^{(r-1)}(x_i) \right|, \tag{2}$$

where r stands for the rth selective sampling in the relevance feedback.

Our DCP scheme considers the correlation of the unlabeled data in that we treat the data's certainty as dynamically changing variable which is not only determined by the current classifier but also affected by the previous labeled data, so one data point being labeled will affect the certainty of the rest.

Firstly, we change the certainty of the last labeled data point x_l:

$$C^{(r)}(x_l) = \begin{cases} M & (y_l > 0) \\ -M & (y_l < 0) \end{cases}, \tag{3}$$

where M is a positive constant set beforehand to represent the labeled data's degree of certainty. The evaluation of M will be discussed in subsection 3.2.

Then, the change in x_l's certainty will *propagate* to the rest unlabeled data, which means it will have influence on their certainty. The intensity of this influence depends on the similarity between each unlabeled data and x_l. To depict the correlation of the data, we construct a graph $G = (V, E)$, where the node set V is exactly the dataset X, and the edge set E is weighted by a $n \times n$ matrix W representing the pairwise relationship between data points with the *heat kernel* [13]:

$$w_{ij} = \exp\left(-\frac{\| x_i - x_j \|^2}{t}\right), \tag{4}$$

where x_i and x_j ($1 \le i, j \le n$) are data points from X, and t is a parameter which controls the influential intensity of the correlated data points. It is obvious that nearby data points are assigned large weights. Using the weight matrix W as the attenuation coefficient, we propagate the change in x_l's certainty to the rest unlabeled data points:

$$\Delta C^{(r)}(x_i) = w_{il} \Delta C^{(r)}(x_l), \tag{5}$$

where

$$\Delta C^{(r)}(x_i) = C^{(r)}(x_i) - C^{(r-1)}(x_i). \tag{6}$$

It is clear that x_l will only have a great impact on the nearby data points; while for those data which are very far from x_l in the feature space, the impact is trivial.

Therefore, the new certainty of each unlabeled data point becomes:

$$C^{(r)}(x_i) = C^{(r-1)}(x_i) + w_{il}\left[C^{(r)}(x_l) - C^{(r-1)}(x_l)\right]. \tag{7}$$

Using Eq.(9), we can easily propagate the change in x_l's certainty to the rest unlabeled data points and have their certainty updated dynamically after each labeling.

Illustration. Now we can explain how the DCP scheme observes the non-redundancy principle. We still take the classification problem described in Fig. 1 for example. Suppose initially, the certainty of point A, B and C are $C(x_A)$, $C(x_B)$ and $C(x_C)$ respectively, and apparently they satisfy:

$$|C(x_A)| < |C(x_B)| < |C(x_C)|.$$

As the traditional methods do, we firstly return point A for labeling. Then different from the traditional methods, we update the certainty of A, B and C (supposing A is labeled positive):

$$C'(x_A) = M \ ,$$
$$C'(x_B) = C(x_B) + w_{BA}\left[C'(x_A) - C(x_A)\right] = C(x_B) + w_{BA}\left[M - C(x_A)\right],$$
$$C'(x_C) = C(x_C) + w_{CA}\left[C'(x_A) - C(x_A)\right] = C(x_C) + w_{CA}\left[M - C(x_A)\right].$$

In this case, the following inequality:

$$\left|C'(x_B)\right| < \left|C'(x_C)\right|$$

is not necessarily satisfied any more. Since B is very similar to A, w_{BA} is far bigger than w_{CA}. As a result, it is quite possible that C will have a relatively smaller degree of certainty, and we will label C instead of B.

Summarization. Our DCP scheme is a generic data selection method, and can be applied in machine learning algorithms where selective sampling is used. The main procedure of DCP scheme is summarized in Fig. 3.

Input: The current classifier f, the labeled training dataset L, the unlabeled dataset U, the weight matrix W, and the number of data points to be labeled N_l in a single round of relevance feedback.

Step1. Classify U with f, and initialize the certainty of unlabeled data:

$$C^{(0)}(x_i) = f(x_i) \ , \ x_i \in U \ .$$

Step2. For $r = 1$ to N_l, repeat the following procedure:

1) Select an unlabeled data point x_l with the minimum degree of certainty to label:

$$l = \arg\min_i \left|C^{(r-1)}(x_i)\right|, \ x_i \in U \ .$$

2) Add x_l to L and remove it from U:

$$L = L \cup \{x_l\}, \ U = U - \{x_l\} \ .$$

3) Change x_l's certainty:

$$C^{(r)}(x_l) = \begin{cases} M & (y_l > 0) \\ -M & (y_l < 0) \end{cases} .$$

4) Propagate the change in x_l's certainty to the rest unlabeled data:

$$C^{(r)}(x_i) = C^{(r-1)}(x_i) + w_{il}\left[C^{(r)}(x_l) - C^{(r-1)}(x_l)\right], \ x_i \in U \ .$$

Step3. Train a new classifier f' using L.

Fig. 3. The Dynamic Certainty Propagation (DCP) scheme

3.2 Parameter Evaluation

There are totally two parameters, t and M, in our DCP scheme, where t is a scale parameter controlling the propagation range of the labeled data, and M is the degree of certainty of the labeled data. In order to ensure the generalization of the DCP scheme, we decide not to attach fixed values to the parameters empirically. Instead, we evaluate them adaptively according to the distribution of the dataset itself.

As we know, the parameter t confines the influence of the labeled data to its neighborhood, so that only nearby data can be notably affected. We use the *nearest neighbor distance* to depict the neighborhood range which is adaptive to the compactness of the dataset in feature space. For each data point x_i, we calculate the distance to its nearest neighbor, represented by $d_{nn}(x_i)$, and get the arithmetic mean of the set $\{ d_{nn}(x_i) \}$ $(x_i \in X)$

$$d = \frac{1}{n} \sum_{i=1}^{n} d_{nn}(x_i) . \tag{8}$$

Then we set t as:

$$t = 2d^2 . \tag{9}$$

As for the parameter M, which depicts the strong confidence in the labeled data's class label, we evaluate it as follows. We first calculate the sample mean and sample variance of all the unlabeled data's initial degree of certainty $\{ |C^{(0)}(x_i)| \}$ $(x_i \in U)$:

$$\mu_C = \frac{1}{|U|} \sum_{x_i \in U} |C^{(0)}(x_i)| , \tag{10}$$

$$\sigma_C^2 = \frac{1}{|U|} \sum_{x_i \in U} \left[|C^{(0)}(x_i)| - \mu_C \right]^2 , \tag{11}$$

where $|U|$ denotes the size of unlabeled dataset U. Then we set M as:

$$M = \mu_C + 3\sigma_C . \tag{12}$$

It guarantees that M is a *properly large* positive number, which means on one hand, M is large enough to show the strong confidence; on the other hand, it is not excessively large and still comparable to most unlabeled data's degree of certainty.

Note that other methods can also be used to evaluate the parameters. And we find that the performance of the algorithm is not sensitive to the disturbance of parameters' value in a specific range.

4 Experiments

In this section, we give our experiments which use the DCP scheme in selective sampling for classification problems, including synthetic data classification and real-world image retrieval.

4.1 Synthetic Data Classification

We use a two-class synthetic dataset to test the effectiveness of our DCP scheme. As shown in Fig. 4(a1), the whole dataset contains 410 data points, 205 for each class, separated by a linear classification boundary. Initially, of course, we know nothing about the data's class labels and their real classification boundary. All we know is the 10 labeled training data points selected randomly from the dataset and the corresponding classification boundary trained from them (Fig. 4(a2)).

In this experiment, we compare our DCP scheme with the traditional batch labeling scheme which simply chooses the top N_l lowest confident data. We use the same

SVM classifier with linear kernel, and in each round of relevance feedback, both schemes return 10 data points which they regard as most informative for labeling.

Illustration of the experimental results is given in Fig. 4(b1) ~ (b4) and (c1) ~ (c4). We can see that using our DCP scheme, the trained classifier converges to the real classification boundary in fewer steps. For example, after only 3 rounds of relevance feedback, the trained classification boundary of the DCP scheme is almost the same as the real boundary, while it takes the traditional scheme 4 rounds to get a similarly well-performing classifier. It means that, to achieve the same performance, our DCP scheme needs fewer data labeled. In other words, the data points returned by our scheme are more informative than those by the traditional data selection scheme.

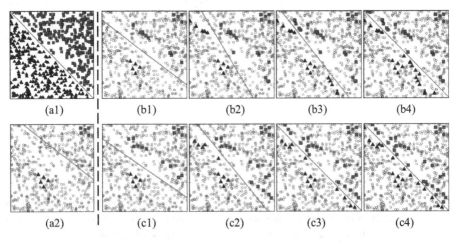

Fig. 4. The experiment on synthetic database. (a1): the data distribution and real classification boundary; (a2): the initial training data and the initial classifier. (b1) ~ (b4) vs. (c1) ~ (c4): the labeled data and corresponding classification results in 4 rounds of relevance feedback using traditional batch labeling scheme and the DCP scheme. (○: unlabeled data, ■: positive data, ▲: negative data, —: classification boundary.)

We have done the experiment repeatedly with different initial training data, and we find that although the performance of both schemes is, to some extent, dependent on the initialization, our DCP scheme always outperforms the traditional scheme steadily. Especially when the initial training data are very few and unrepresentative, our DCP scheme will perform much better than the traditional scheme. In other words, our DCP scheme seems to be more helpful when the initial situation is worse.

4.2 Image Retrieval

In order to further illustrate the effectiveness of our DCP scheme in image retrieval, we apply it in SVM$_{Active}$ and Co-SVM separately (the result of SSAIR is much the same as that of Co-SVM), and compare the performance with the original SVM$_{Active}$ and Co-SVM using the traditional batch labeling scheme. The relevance feedback algorithm using SVM, but without selective sampling, is also adopted as comparison to validate the importance of selective sampling.

Our experiments are performed on a subset selected from the Corel image CDs. In our subset, there are 50 categories with different semantic meanings, such as tiger, car, flag, etc. Each category contains 100 images, so there are altogether 5000 images. In the experiments, the first 10 images of each category, 500 in all, are picked out as query images to test the retrieval performance of different algorithms.

We employ color and texture features to represent images. The color features consist of 125-dimensional color histogram and 6-dimensional color moment in RGB. The texture features are extracted using 3-level discrete wavelet transformation, and the mean and variance averaging on each of 10 sub-bands form a 20-dimensional vector. In Co-SVM, we use the 131-dimensional color feature and the 20-dimensional texture feature as two classification views.

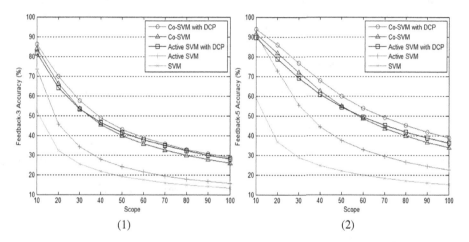

Fig. 5. The accuracy of image retrieval with 3 and 5 feedbacks. Comparisons: Co-SVM using DCP scheme, original Co-SVM, SVM$_{Active}$ using DCP scheme, original SVM$_{Active}$, and SVM.

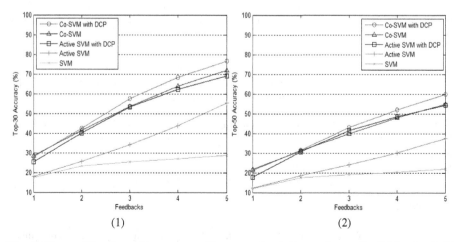

Fig. 6. The top-30 and top-50 accuracy of image retrieval. Comparisons: Co-SVM using DCP scheme, original Co-SVM, SVM$_{Active}$ using DCP scheme, original SVM$_{Active}$, and SVM.

All the SVM classifiers in our experiments use the same RBF kernel. In each round of relevance feedback, we label the same number of images selected by different algorithms. All the accuracy is the average accuracy over all the test images.

Fig. 5 shows the accuracy vs. scope curves after 3 and 5 rounds of relevance feedback, where scope $= x$ means the accuracy is calculated within the top x returned images; while Fig. 6 depicts the curves of top-30 and top-50 accuracy vs. feedback rounds.

The figures indicate that our DCP scheme outperforms the traditional data selection scheme in both SVM$_{Active}$ (curve $\square$ vs. $+$) and Co-SVM (curve $\bigcirc$ vs. $\triangle$). In SVM$_{Active}$ the advantage of our DCP scheme over the traditional scheme is quite significant; while in Co-SVM the improvement is not so dramatic, but our scheme still has constantly better result. This is probably because the utilization of multi-view learning in Co-SVM has already provided much useful information for classifier retraining. As a result, when DCP scheme is adopted, the performance can still be further improved, but less remarkably. As for the efficiency, since both DCP scheme and the traditional scheme have the same amount of training, the time complexity of them is almost the same, except that a little extra time consumption is needed in the DCP scheme for data selection.

We can also find that selective sampling is a very powerful algorithm to boost the performance of image retrieval (curve $+$ vs. $\times$), and when it is combined with multi-view learning, the result can be further improved (curve $\triangle$ vs. $+$). Although the "sole" selective sampling SVM$_{Active}$ is less effective than the multi-view selective sampling Co-SVM, after SVM$_{Active}$ has adopted our DCP scheme, however, its performance can be greatly improved and becomes even comparable to that of Co-SVM (curve $\square$ vs. $\triangle$), while its computational complexity is much lower.

5 Conclusions

In this paper, we have proposed a novel generic data selection scheme, the Dynamic Certainty Propagation (DCP) scheme, for selective sampling. We present one-by-one labeling model to combine the merits of both the traditional batch labeling model and the theoretically optimal one-by-one training model, which utilizes the information of the previous labeled data to guide the selection of next, and makes the labeled data more informative for classifier retraining. Experimental results show that after adopting our DCP scheme in the selective sampling, the classification performance can be obviously improved on both synthetic and real-world dataset, while the time consumption is still comparable with that of the traditional scheme.

Acknowledgments. This work is supported by the National Hi-Tech Research and Development Program of China (863 Program, Grant No. 2006AA01Z315), the National Natural Science Foundation of China (Grant No. 60121302, 60675003), and NSF of Beijing (Grant No. 4072025).

References

1. Smeulders, A.W.M., Worring, M., Santini, S., Gupta, A., Jain, R.: Content-based image retrieval at the end of the early years. IEEE Transactions on Pattern Analysis and Machine Intelligence 22, 1349–1380 (2000)

2. Lew, M.S., Sebe, N., Djeraba, C., Jain, R.: Content-based multimedia information retrieval: state of the art and challenges. ACM Transactions on Multimedia Computing, Communications, and Applications 2, 1–19 (2006)
3. Rui, Y., Huang, T.S., Ortega, M., Mehrotra, S.: Relevance feedback: a power tool for interactive content-based image retrieval. IEEE Transactions on Circuits and Systems for Video Technology 8, 644–655 (1998)
4. McCallum, A., Nigam, K.: Employing EM in pool-based active learning for text classification. In: Proceeding of the 15th International Conference on Machine Learning, San Francisco, pp. 350–358 (1998)
5. Tong, S., Chang, E.: Support vector machine active learning for image retrieval. In: Proceedings of the 9th ACM International Conference on Multimedia, Ottawa, Canada, pp. 107–118 (2001)
6. Zhou, Z.H., Chen, K.J., Jiang, Y.: Exploiting Unlabeled Data in Content-Based Image Retrieval. In: Boulicaut, J.-F., Esposito, F., Giannotti, F., Pedreschi, D. (eds.) ECML 2004. LNCS (LNAI), vol. 3201, pp. 525–536. Springer, Heidelberg (2004)
7. Cheng, J., Wang, K.Q.: Active learning for image retrieval with Co-SVM. Pattern Recognition 40, 330–334 (2007)
8. Muslea, I., Minton, S., Knoblock, C.A.: Active learning with multiple views. Journal of Artificial Intelligence Research 27, 203–233 (2006)
9. Blum, A., Mitchell, T.: Combining labeled and unlabeled data with co-training. In: Proceedings of the 11th Annual Conference on Computational Learning Theory, Madison, Wisconsin, United States, pp. 92–100 (1998)
10. Muslea, I., Minton, S., Knoblock, C.A.: Selective sampling with redundant views. In: Proceedings of the 17th National Conference on Artificial Intelligence, pp. 621–626 (2000)
11. Zhang, T., Oles, F.: A probability analysis on the value of unlabeled data for classification problems. In: Proceedings of the 17th International Conference on Machine Learning, pp. 1191–1198 (2000)
12. Brinker, K.: Incorporating diversity in active learning with support vector machines. In: Proceedings of the 20th International Conference on Machine Learning, pp. 59–66 (2003)
13. Belkin, M., Niyogi, P.: Laplacian eigenmaps and spectral techniques for embedding and clustering. In: Advances in Neural Information Processing Systems 14, Vancouver, British Columbia, Canada (2002)

Local Radon Transform and Earth Mover's Distances for Content-Based Image Retrieval

Wei Xiong[1], S.H. Ong[2], Weiping Lee[2], and Kelvin Foong[3]

[1] Institute for Infocomm Research, 21 Heng Mui Keng Terrace,
Singapore 119613
wxiong@i2r.a-star.edu.sg
[2] Department of ECE, National University of Singapore,
Singapore 117576
eleongsh@nus.edu.sg
[3] Department of Preventive Dentistry, National University of Singapore,
Singapore 119074
pndfwc@nus.edu.sg

Abstract. Content-based image retrieval based on feature extraction is still a highly challenging task. Traditional features are either purely statistical, thus losing spatial information, or purely spatial without statistical information. The Radon transform (RT) is a geometrical transform widely used in computer tomography. The projections transformed embed spatial relationships while integrating information in certain directions. The RT has been used to design invariant features for retrieval. Spatial resolutions in RT are inhomogeneous resulting in non-uniform feature representation across the image. We employ the local RT by aligning the centre of the RT with the centroids of the region of interest and use a sufficient number of projections. Finally the earth mover's distance method is utilized to combine local matching results. Using the proposed approach, image retrieval accuracy is maintained, while reducing computational cost.

1 Introduction

Content-based image retrieval (CBIR) is the digital image searching problem in large databases that makes use of the contents of the images themselves, rather than relying on human-input textual information such as captions or keywords. The history of CBIR can be traced back to the early 1980s [1]. The first well-known image retrieval system QBIC was reported in the early 1990s [2]. There are numerous CBIR techniques and systems published. Reviews of CBIR can be found in [3,4,5,6].

CBIR systems represent image content by making use of lower-level features such as texture, color, and shape. Most of these features are either purely statistical information without spatial information, or purely spatial information without statistical information. A typical example is the color histogram which is measured globally and loses spatial information such as the geometrical

S. Satoh, F. Nack, and M. Etoh (Eds.): MMM 2008, LNCS 4903, pp. 436–445, 2008.

relations and the distribution of regions in the image. Furthermore, complicated image segmentation procedures are normally involved in feature extraction. CBIR without complicated segmentation [7] has gained some success.

The Radon transform (RT) [8,9] is a geometrical transformation widely used in computer tomography and image reconstruction. It projects images into a parameter space of viewing angles and offsets. A collection of one-dimensional projections (i.e., signatures) is obtained to represent images, mostly for image reconstruction [9] and image matching [10]. RT has elegant properties, from which invariant feature signatures can be derived against translation, rotation and scaling [11,12]. The use of Radon signatures without a sophisticated segmentation for image retrieval [13,14] has achieved better experimental performance than well-known retrieval systems [13].

Although the RT was introduced in continuous form analytically, the viewing angles are discrete in practice. One has to sample the angular parameter and take projections at these sampling nodes. Only a finite number of projections are produced, although, theoretically, one should have an infinite number of them for perfect reconstruction [8,9]. It has been noted that, in ranking the similarity of images for image retrieval, high resolution is not required as projection data is highly correlated and there is information redundancy [13]. Thus, in [13] only two perpendicular projections are taken as signatures, causing loss of information. A follow-up paper [14] suggests taking more projections to obtain a more complete representation of the image, but it is noted that too fine a resolution of angle θ results in redundant information. It is also suggested that taking θ at equal intervals in the RT is not efficient as the information in the image may not be evenly distributed. A projection decimation method is hence proposed in [14] where the number of projections required is iteratively selected up to the point when the image is segmented into clearly defined regions, and this is done by detecting the high contrast point or clustering using the projection data derived iteratively.

From the review of past literature, it is found that current techniques that employ the RT for image matching /retrieval fail to address three problems. Firstly, as the RT is performed globally on an image and considering the discrete limitations in which the RT can be performed on a digital image, certain fine image details further away from the centre of rotation of the RT will not be represented sufficiently. A solution to circumvent this problem is to perform RT locally on objects of interest in an image. However, there is a need to segment an image into meaningful objects before performing the RT.

Secondly, there is no comprehensive method to determine the optimum number of projections to use when using the RT. The proposed solution is to then make use of the frequency characteristics of the object, along with the size of the object, to decide upon the minimum number of projections required to effectively represent the object using RT.

Lastly, there is not much work on combining local Radon signatures, though a simple feature-vector-adjoining method has been proposed in [14]. In this paper, we introduce a new method for image retrieval. We use the local RT to represent images and determine sufficient numbers of projections. Finally, the

Earth Mover's Distance (EMD) method [15] is employed to combine multiple local signatures to measure image dissimilarity.

2   Radon Transform and Sufficient Number of Projections

The Radon Transform $g(s, \theta)$ of a function $f(x, y)$ is the function's line integral along a line inclined at an angle θ and at a distance s away from the origin of the $x - y$ plane. It is given by

$$g(s, \theta) = \int_{-\infty}^{\infty} \int_{-\infty}^{\infty} f(x, y)\delta(x \cos \theta + y \sin \theta - s)dxdy, \qquad (1)$$

where $\delta()$ is the Dirac function with $-\infty < s < \infty$, $0 \leq \theta < \pi$. The function $g(s, \theta)$ is called the (Radon) sinogram of $f(x, y)$. Fig. 1(a) shows the geometry for the transform.

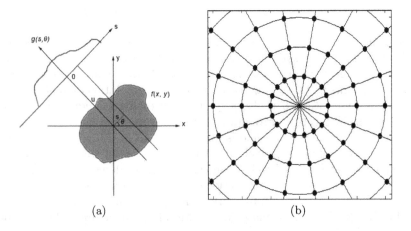

(a)   (b)

Fig. 1. Radon transform: its geometry (a) and inhomogeneous sampling grid (b)

In the rotated system (s, u), with

$$\begin{cases} x = s \cos \theta - u \sin \theta \\ y = s \sin \theta + u \cos \theta, \end{cases} \qquad (2)$$

(1) can be written as

$$g(s, \theta) = \int_{-\infty}^{\infty} f(s \cos \theta - u \sin \theta, s \sin \theta + u \cos \theta)du. \qquad (3)$$

The image function $f(x, y)$ can then be reconstructed by

$$f(x, y) = \int_{0}^{\pi} \int_{-\infty}^{\infty} g(s, \theta)dsd\theta. \qquad (4)$$

The RT has some useful properties that relates the translation, rotation and scaling of the original function $f(x, y)$ to the $g(s, \theta)$ [8]. They are tabulated in Table 1. A translation of $f(x, y)$ will result in the shift of $g(s, \theta)$ in s, a rotation of $f(x, y)$ will result in the translation of $g(s, \theta)$ in θ, and a uniform scaling of $f(x, y)$ will result in the uniform scaling of the projections. These properties are used to design features invariant to translation, rotation and scaling [13].

Table 1. Some properties of the Radon Transform

	Function $f(x, y) = f_p(r, \theta)$	Radon Transform $g(s, \theta)$
Translation	$f(x - x_0, y - y_0)$	$g(s - x_0 \cos \theta - y_0 \sin \theta, \theta)$
Rotation	$f_p(r, \theta + \theta_0)$	$g(s, \theta - \theta_0)$
Scaling	$f(ax, ay)$	$g(as, \theta)/a$

The uncertainty of x and y induced by the perturbation of θ can be derived by differentiating (5) with respective to θ respectively:

$$\begin{cases} dx = (-s \sin \theta - u \cos \theta) d\theta \\ dy = (s \cos \theta - u \sin \theta) d\theta \end{cases} \tag{5}$$

The circular uncertainty induced by the uncertainty of θ along a circle centered at the origin at radius $r = \sqrt{s^2 + u^2}$ is

$$r d\theta = (\sqrt{s^2 + u^2}) d\theta \tag{6}$$

These uncertainties are spatial resolutions of the reconstructed function. They are not homogeneous across the (s, u)-plane. For example, the circular resolution is proportional to the uncertainty of θ and the radius. Such inhomogeneity is the basis for local RT in the current work.

When finding RTs on digital images, projections are available only on a finite grid in a polar system (for an illustration, see Fig. 1(b)), i.e. [9],

$$g_n(m) \triangleq g(s_m, \theta_n), -\frac{M}{2} \le m \le \frac{M}{2} - 1, 0 \le n \le N - 1, \tag{7}$$

where $s_m = md$, $\theta_n = n\Delta$, $\Delta = \pi/N$. If ζ_0 is the highest spatial frequency in the image, then the radial sampling interval d along each projection direction should satisfy $d \le 1/(2\zeta_0)$. Assuming that the image is spatial-limited within a circle of diameter D, then $D = Md$ and $M \ge 2\zeta_0 D$.

Unlike a constant d for all projection directions, the arc interval is not constant: at offset $|s_m|$, it is $r_m = |\pi s_m/N| = |\Delta s_m| = |m| d\Delta$, $-\frac{M}{2} \le m \le \frac{M}{2} - 1$. The minimum interval is zero at the origin while the maximum $r_M = Md\Delta/2 = D\pi/(2N)$ occurs at the furthermost offset from the projection centre. Such resolution inhomogeneity is illustrated in Fig. 1(b). There is a higher concentration of points nearer the centre of rotation, and a sparser spread of points further away. For convenience, one can choose $r_M \approx d_0 = 1/(2\zeta_0)$ such that $N \ge \pi D\zeta_0$. We consider $\pi D\zeta_0$ is the sufficient number of projections for our purpose in image retrieval.

In practice, we may not take so many projections. Instead, a much smaller number of projections are used. In this case, due to this resolution inhomogeneity, some small but important objects, which are placed further away from the centre of the image, may not be effectively represented by the forward RT. High frequency components, such as variations in the boundaries of an object, may also not be represented sufficiently by the RT. Insufficient finite number of projections makes the resolution inhomogeneity ignorable. Such an effect in image reconstruction due to projections from limited angles has been extensively studied in computer tomography literature [8].

A solution is to represent an object locally, i.e., to perform the transform by putting the origin of transform at the center of the object of interest. This is the so-called local Radon transform in this work. In contrast, a transform performed on the centre of an image is refereed to a global RT. Fig. 2(b) shows the root-mean-square error of the reconstructed image against the angular intervals between projects. The ground truth is the object 2 in Fig. 2(a). It is observed that the reconstruction errors after performing local Radon transformation on the objects are lower than the reconstruction errors after performing Radon transformation globally on the entire image. This implies that by shifting the centre of rotation to the objects, the increase in the resolution of the Radon transform allows for a better reconstruction.

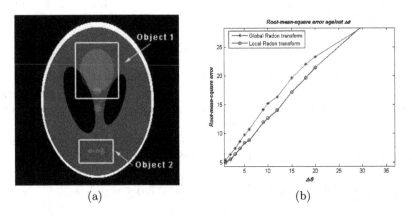

(a)   (b)

Fig. 2. Local RT represents image better than global RT when using a finite number of projections. (a): the phantom image; (b): reconstruction error vs angular intervals.

We emphasize the point here since not much attention has been paid to such a non-uniform feature representation problem in image matching and retrieval. According to the above idea, we could segment an image into meaningful clusters of objects and perform RTs locally, then combine them for final image matching and retrieval. In this short paper, we will not introduce advanced techniques in image segmentation/clustering. Instead, only simple and necessary segmentation is used.

3   Earth-Mover's Distances

After obtaining local RT projections, we utilize the Earth-Mover's-Distance method to combine them to measure dissimilarity. The EMD is used to evaluate dissimilarity between two multi-dimensional distributions in a feature space, given the ground distance between individual features. Each distribution is represented by a set of features and this representation is called the signature of the distribution. With two signatures, one of the signatures can be visualized as a mass of earth spreading out in feature space while the other can be visualized as a collection of holes which are to be filled with the earth. The EMD essentially then computes the least amount of work needed to fill the holes with earth and the amount of work, or cost needed will depend on the ground distance between the features.

Let $X = \{(x_i, w_{x,i})\}_{i=1}^{I}$ and $Y = \{(y_i, w_{y,j})\}_{j=1}^{J}$ be two signatures with I and J features and weighted by $w_{x,i}$ and $w_{y,j}$ respectively. Assume d_{ij} and f_{ij} are the ground distance and the flow between x_i and y_j. The problem is to determine the flow f_{ij} that minimizes the total cost

$$COST(X,Y) = \sum_{i=1}^{I}\sum_{j=1}^{J} f_{ij}d_{ij} \tag{8}$$

Upon finding the optimal flow that minimizes total cost, the EMD is then equal to the total cost normalized by the total flow, i.e.,

$$EMD(X,Y) = \sum_{i=1}^{I}\sum_{j=1}^{J} f_{ij}d_{ij} \bigg/ \sum_{i=1}^{I}\sum_{j=1}^{J} f_{ij} \tag{9}$$

4   The Proposed Method

Denote the query q and the target x. The images are first processed to identify interest regions and objects. Our method has four steps and is summarized as follows.

Step 1: Given two objects q_i and x_j, perform the Fourier transform and find their respective cut-off frequency $\zeta_{0,i}$ and $\zeta_{0,j}$. Set $\zeta_0 = \max\{\zeta_{0,i}, \zeta_{0,j}\}$. Find $d = 1/(2\zeta_0)$ and $\Delta = 1/(D\zeta_0)$. Perform local RTs according to (3).

Step 2: Take the summation of all absolute distances between their respective projections and use it as their dissimilarity.

Step 3: Following [13], compensate their global scaling (this can be achieved by normalizing the two images according to their object areas), remove their relative translation and rotation. Align them so that the dissimilarity is minimized. Such dissimilarity is their ground distance d_{ij}.

Step 4: Compare images using EMD as the scores and rank them. The two signatures and will be the two sets of objects from the two images that are to be compared. The weight of each feature will be assigned equally to 1.

5   Results and Discussions

We first test our method to retrieve simple images. The proposed image matching process is performed in contrast to cases when Δ is fixed to a very small interval of 5° and a very large interval of 90°, which essentially means only horizontal and vertical projections are obtained. The purpose is to show that our method can achieve better performance in terms of both accuracy and time cost. For the sake of convenience, the method using $\Delta = 5°$ will be termed method 1, the proposed method 2 and the method using $\Delta = 90°$ method 3. The performances of the processes are compared in terms of recall time and image matching accuracy over 100 binary images with translation, rotation and scaling. Retrieval precisions for the recall points of the top 10 and 19 are evaluated subjectively by looking for contextually similar images. The tests are performed on an Intel Pentium M 1.4Ghz laptop, with 768MB of RAM, using the MATLAB environment.

In Fig. 3, subfigures (a), (b) and (c) are for methods 1, 2 and 3, respectively. All the test results are displayed with the reference image shown at the top left hand corner. The rest of the images are then ranked in descending order, from right to left, top to bottom, according to their degree of similarity to the reference image, which is determined by the absolute difference between their projections. Only the top 19 matches are shown to conserve space. The recall times and matching hits for each set of results are shown in the figure labels.

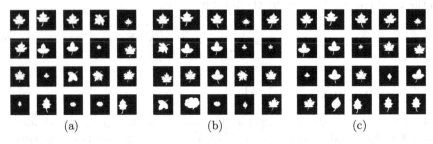

(a)   (b)   (c)

Fig. 3. Recall results using the 'leaf' image using method 1 (a), 2 (b), and 3 (c). For methods 1, 2 and 3, recall time = 195.9, 69.0 and 56.8 seconds, hits = 6, 6, and 5 in top 10; hits =12, 12, and 15 in top 19, respectively.

Comparing methods 1 and 2, our method achieves the same or better accuracy as method 1, whereas its computational time used is only about 35% to 52% (using any of 100 images alternatively) when $\Delta\theta = 5°$ is used. By using fewer projections for comparison purposes, the computational time saved is significant and vital in the construction of a good image retrieval system. Comparing the proposed method to the case $\Delta\theta = 90°$, one can find that using only horizontal and vertical projections is highly inefficient. Therefore, sufficient projections have to be taken, increasing computational times of 17% to 42% for the images. Fig. 4 shows the retrieval results of another example comparing the three methods. Again, local RT can maintain comparable accuracy with a lower time cost.

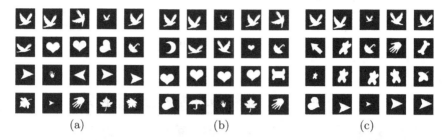

Fig. 4. Recall results using the 'bird' image using method 1 (a), 2 (b), and 3 (c). For methods 1, 2 and 3, recall time = 194.9, 88.3 and 69.1 seconds, hits = 6, 7, and 5 in top 10, respectively.

Next, we test our method in retrieving complicated images. The database (see Fig. 5) contains 100 images and each of the images has between 2 to 4 objects in them, and some of these objects can be broken down into several connected components. Most of the different types of objects can be found in various images, allowing the testing of retrieval accuracy. Each of the objects may have been subjected to flipping, translational, rotational, scaling, and shearing and other transformations.

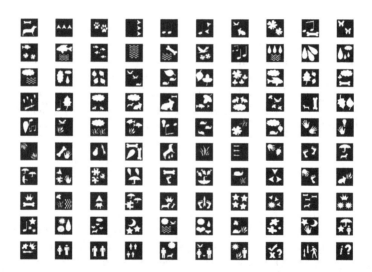

Fig. 5. Image database for multiple object matching

A query image is compared with all the other images in the database. The closest 19 matches are displayed and ranked according to their degree of similarity, with the query shown in the top left corner. Fig. 6 shows two sets of results. It is seen that by using EMD, perceptual similarity is matched reasonably well. Riding on the translation, rotation and scale invariance feature of the distance measure, the EMD algorithm manages to retrieve images which contain similar objects to the query, even though the objects have been subjected these various forms of transformations. The EMD measure also succeeds in ranking images which have objects that match more of the query's objects more closely than those that do not.

                    (a)   (b)

Fig. 6. Two retrieval results. The top-left is the query image. In (a) query contains 2 'grass' objects; in (b), the query contains a 'bone' object and a 'dog' object.

However, on the downside, the EMD measure may ascertain a degree of bias towards images which have the same number of objects as the reference image. While in most cases, this feature allows for better grouping of perceptually similar images, certain images which have the same number of objects but have objects different from those in the reference image may be ranked higher than those that have more matching objects but have a disparity in the number of objects that the image possess. One other problem is that even though an image has a few matching objects, if the image contains a vastly dissimilar object from the objects in the reference image, the image may be ranked disproportionally lower, in contrast to an observer's notion of perceptual similarity.

6   Conclusion

The Radon transform can preserve structure spatial relations and distributions. Invariant features can be designed from it for image retrieval. We have extended existing work using the RT for image retrieval. Taking into consideration the problem of inhomogeneous resolutions in RT due to the discrete nature in which projections are taken, a method is proposed to perform RT locally on individual objects by aligning the centre of rotation of the RT with the centroids of the objects. Work has also been done to determine the minimum number of projections to use to sufficiently represent an object, by analyzing the frequency characteristics of the object and its physical size, allowing for a reduction in redundancy and saving computational time and space. The RT projections of objects are then compared in a manner which maintains translational, rotational and scaling invariance. By taking into account the presence of multiple objects in images, the EMD method is utilized for matching purposes.

Experiments show that by performing local RT and using the sufficient number of projections, accurate and fast image retrieval can be performed. However, considering the high sensitivity of the image matching process, only objects which have very similar geometric structure can be recalled. Therefore, we could improve our work using a good segmentation algorithm to extract objects of interest in future projects.

References

1. Chang, N.S., Fu, K.S.: Query-by-pictorial-example. IEEE Transactions on Software Engineering SE 6(6), 519–524 (1980)
2. Flickner, M., Petkovic, D., Steele, D., Yanker, P., Sawhney, H., Niblack, W., Ashley, J., Huang, Q., Dom, B., Gorkani, M., Hafner, J., Lee, D.: Query by image and video content: The QBIC system. IEEE Computer 28(9), 23–32 (1995)
3. Smeulders, A.W.M., Worring, M., Santini, S., Gupta, A., Jain, R.: Content-based image retrieval at the end of the early years. IEEE Transactions on Pattern Analysis and Machine Intelligence 22(12), 1349–1380 (2000)
4. Rui, Y., Huang, T.S., Chang, S.F.: Image retrieval: Current techniques, promising directions, and open issues. Journal of Visual Communication and Image Representation 10, 39–62 (1999)
5. Lew, M.S., Sebe, N., Djeraba, C., Jain, R.: Content-based multimedia information retrieval: State of the art and challenges. ACM Transactions on Multimedia Computing, Communication and Applications 2(1), 1–19 (2006)
6. Liu, Y., Zhang, D., Lu, G., Ma, W.Y.: A survey of content-based image retrieval with high-level semantics. Pattern Recogn. 40(1), 262–282 (2007)
7. Rubner, Y.: Texture-based image retrieval without segmentation. In: Proceedings of the International Conference on Computer Vision, pp. 1018–1024. IEEE Computer Society, Los Alamitos (1999)
8. Deans, S.R.: The Radon Transform and Some of Its Applications. John Wiley & Sons, New York (1983)
9. Jain, A.K.: Fundamentals of Digital Image Processing. Prentice Hall, Englewood Cliffs (1989)
10. Matus, F., Flusser, J.: Image representations via finite radon transform. IEEE Transactions on Pattern Analysis and Machine Intelligence 15(10), 996–1006 (1993)
11. Al-Shaykh, O.K., Doherty, J.F.: Invariant image analysis based on radon transform and svd. IEEE Transactions on Circuits and Systems-II: Analog and Digital Signal Processing 43(2), 123–133 (1996)
12. You, J., Lu, W., Li, J., Gini, G., Liang, Z.: Image matching for translation, rotation and uniform scaling by the radon transform. In: ICIP 1998. Proceedings of 1998 International Conference on Image Processing, pp. 847–851 (1998)
13. Wang, H., Guo, F., Feng, D.D., Jin, J.S.: A signature for content-based image retrieval using a geometric transform. In: Proceedings of ACM Multimedia 1998, Bristol, UK, pp. 229–234 (1998)
14. Guo, F., Jin, J.S., Feng, D.D.: A measuring image similarity using the geometrical distribution of image contents. In: Proceedings of International Conference on Signal Processing 1998, vol. 2, pp. 1108–1112 (1998)
15. Rubner, Y., Tomasi, C., Guibas, L.J.: A metric for distributions with applications to image databases. In: Proceedings of Sixth International Conference on Computer Vision, pp. 59–66 (1998)

Content Based Querying and Searching
for 3D Human Motions

Manoj M. Pawar, Gaurav N. Pradhan, Kang Zhang, and Balakrishnan Prabhakaran

Department of Computer Science
University of Texas at Dallas, Richardson, TX 75083
{mmp051000,gaurav,kzhang,praba}@utdallas.edu

Abstract. From cartoons to medical research world, from the field of arts to scientific visualization, everyone related to these areas have been continuously using 3D motion capture data. Querying on these databases is one of the important tasks. In recent years, almost all the querying interfaces for motion databases are related to tag based search. A lot of manual work is involved in tagging each motion in a database. The focus of this research is on giving the user a freedom of expression by allowing him/her to draw queries and developing a technique to retrieve motions to find an approximate match. In our approach, we have introduced a visual query interface in which a naïve user can draw a query expressed in different human body segments. An indexing algorithm is used to produce the result for a given query format, supported by an efficient pre-processing method for large motion databases.

1 Introduction

In the last few years, lot of research has been around search and indexing on 3D human motion databases. Extracting motions from a database for customization and then using it in the application areas like cartoons, medical care and educational purpose has been a frequent task. Until now, not much importance has been given to visual and intuitive query interfaces; instead, tag based searching has been most widely used. Building a user-friendly querying interface for naïve users has been the primary objective of our research, where users can describe motion queries in visual expressions. Once a query has been translated from the interface, content-based retrieval can be performed, and the result is returned to the user. We introduce an algorithm that obtains the information from the visual query interface and then perform a content-based match with the entries in the database.

1.1 Overview

1.1.1 Query

According to our approach, a visual query consists of a graphical interface on which a set of primitive movements of five main sub-body parts can be drawn. The user will be able to graphically represent the behavior of different joints in those sub-body parts

S. Satoh, F. Nack, and M. Etoh (Eds.): MMM 2008, LNCS 4903, pp. 446–455, 2008.

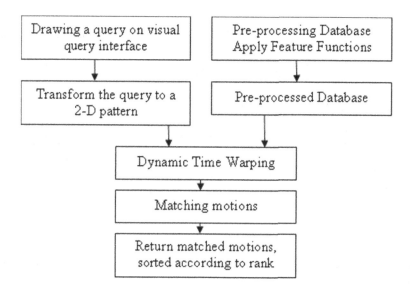

Fig. 1. Flowchart of querying and content based search algorithm

over key frames. There is a very short learning curve for the user to be able to draw a query. This interface will map between the user-drawn visual expressions and the motions of different sub-body parts in the database. The querying interface does not allow non-feasible movement of joints, and thereby reducing the overhead for repetitively running the search algorithm.

1.1.2 Pattern Representation

The visual query expressed by the user is a 2D drawing of sub-body parts, which is not the same as the actual 3D motion data. Hence, it is necessary to transform this query to a representation where actual motion information is interpreted properly. Folding-unfolding actions of sub-body parts are extracted from the querying interface by calculating angles between related joints. This extracted information pattern is simplified to two dimensions, which saves time for the pattern matching technique.

1.1.3 Body Segment Features

According to the hierarchical structure of the human body [2], there are five branches with pelvis as root, i.e. two hands, two legs and torso (head-thorax-pelvis sub body part). These sub-body parts are known as *Unit Body Parts* (UBP). The hierarchical structure implies that the human motion mainly comprises of motions related to these UBP's. In our approach, the prime importance is given to these five body segments. The motion database is pre-processed for these UBP's. Each motion data file is transformed into features related to two hands, two legs and torso. These features allow representation of angles and position of the joints with respect to body plane[1].

---

[1] A plane containing pelvis, thorax and head joints.

1.1.4 Indexing

We have created five index trees related to the above mentioned sub-body parts. Therefore, each motion data is processed and identified according to these five sub-body parts, which helps us to map individual portions of query. The UBP feature vectors defined are used as indexing keys.

1.1.5 Time and Spatial Invariance

In our approach, body segment features are defined in such a way that they store information about the angles between the joints and their positions with respect to the body plane. This fact takes care of a required spatial invariance criterion for motion search. The dynamic time warping based alignment algorithm gives time invariance since it tries to match the curves of the time series sequences.

2 Related Work

Recently, many ideas have been proposed on content based matching on motion data. Muller, Roder and Clausen [1] gave geometric features based approach for the content-based retrieval. Bruderlin and Williams [6] have given various morphing techniques for motion data. Cardle et al. [7] and Keogh [8] shows different dynamic time warping based indexing techniques for pattern matching. Keogh [4] explain dynamic time warping based matching techniques for different time length sequences. In Kover and Gleicher [5], similar motions are identified by dynamic time warping based indexing technique. Carlsson [10] describes the idea of reducing dimension of data by using geometric features instead of quantitative data. Wu et. al [9] use pose based index to find out match between query and candidate clips from database.

For query interface, Muller, Roder and Clausen [1] have proposed idea of selecting geometric features to be used while querying. Motion capture database (CMU [3]) has tag based searching technique implemented. Our approach for querying and content-based retrieval of human motion data differs from all of these previous approaches. We have proposed a simple and user-friendly query interface on which user can draw a query. Applying feature functions on this query translates it to a 2-D representation, which incorporates temporal, and spatial invariance in content based matching on motion database.

3 Visual Querying Interface

Any motion of a sub-body part consisting of a joint and two segments, called a "unit body part (UBP)," can be considered primarily on a two dimensional space. These primary two dimensions form the viewing plane, on which the motion can be qualitatively described. The inverse of the normal vector of the plane is called the *viewing direction*, in which the user views the body part when defining 2D motions. The orientation of the human body on the viewing plane is called the *reference direction*. Given a viewing direction and reference direction, different motions of any UBP can be defined.

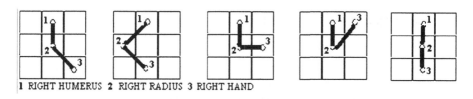

1 RIGHT HUMERUS 2 RIGHT RADIUS 3 RIGHT HAND

Fig. 2. Movement of right hand UBP (humerus-radius-hand joints segment)

A body segment is represented in 3x3 grids (Figure 2), each joint represented by a dot and a line is used to connect two consecutive joints. A sequence of 3x3 grids represents the motion of UBP over the course of time. The user can easily draw queries indicating the motions of five important sub-body parts, including left and right leg, left and right arm and pelvis-thorax-head. A single motion query comprises of key frames of these UBP's drawn separately. This simple expression of the motion in 3x3 grids is sufficient to compose a meaningful body movement. The users are able to directly construct visual expressions by creating graphical queries as partial or full body segment movements. This 3x3 grid representation provides an effective way of depicting simple motions. It would be considered the basis for more intuitive motion expressions, such as a body part image moved by a direct manipulation. All non-feasible move of joint is detected and reported to the user.

The position of left or right hand joint and foot joint can be drawn with respect to the body plane as shown in Figure 3. This positional feature is also used to find out approximate match between the query and motion entries in the database. This positional parameter is always with respect to relative body plane. This fact also helps to gain spatial invariance. According to our approach, the user can represent a position of joint in front or back or in the plane. This positional characteristic retrieved along with the movements of segments form a powerful expression, which represents the motion of body segments.

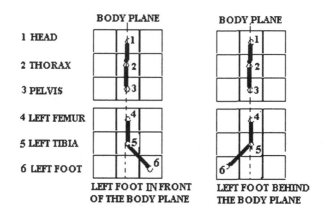

Fig. 3. Position of left foot with respect to body plane

4 Searching 3D Human Motions

This section defines metadata generation functions describing relations between joint angles and positions in the human motion. These functions transform the motion from a multi-dimensional space to two dimensions. Movements of unit body parts are captured as multiple frames that reveal relations between segments and joints. Positional features are extracted from the motion with respect to the body plane to get relative positions of joints. The functions used for extracting metadata features are described in Section 4.1. Section 4.2 presents the application of these feature function on an available database to transform them into a layer where relevant searching becomes easier for visual queries. The concept of transforming visual queries and motions in the database to the same search space is discussed in Section 4.3. Section 4.4 explains a dynamic time warping algorithm for pattern matching of query and motion database. Ranking of the resulting motions is discussed in Section 4.5.

4.1 Metadata Generation Functions

In order to extract information from a motion file, we have defined various kinds of feature functions. The movement of body segment primarily consists of contraction and relaxation of various muscles. We can interpret this phenomenon as a change in the *joint angle* between two segments. We have defined a function F^{joint} to capture changes occurring at certain joints like J1, J2 and J3. For e.g. in the Figure 4 for kick motion, setting $J1$ = *'Femur'* $J2$='Tibia' $J3$='Foot' i='Frame number'. The changes in the angle sub-stained by femur-tibia segment and tibia-foot segment around the tibia joint at i^{th} frame are captured by $F^{joint}(J1,J2,J3,i)$.

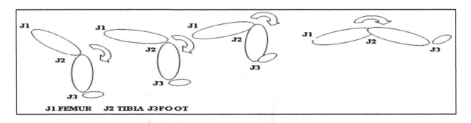

Fig. 4. Changes in the angle occurring between leg segments around knee joint during the kick motion

4.1.1 F^{joint} Function

This function describes a new notion of movement of the body segments around a given joint for each ith frame. Let J1, J2 and J3 be the three related joints.

$$F^{joint}(J1,J2,J3,i) := \begin{cases} 1 & \text{if angle between J1,J2 and J3 is increasing in } i^{th} \text{ frame} \\ -1 & \text{if angle between J1,J2 and J3 is decreasing in } i^{th} \text{ frame} \end{cases}$$

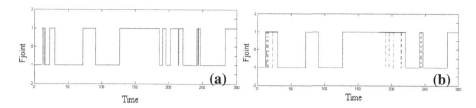

Fig. 5. Left humerus–radius–hand pattern generated after applying (a) function F^{joint} (J1= 'humerus', J2='radius', J3='hand') on the motion clip; (b) the new revised function F^{joint}

Thus applying F^{joint} on motion file, we obtain a pattern made up of 1's and -1's shown in Figure 5a.

The concept of this simple function reduces motions to two dimensions. The F^{joint} function calculates angle between the joints J1, J2 and J3 to find out folding and unfolding actions of body parts for the ith frame. Consider a specific motion of the arm segment in the above Figure 5a. For a definite amount of time, the folding and unfolding actions can prominently be seen. By modifying the above function as follows, we can remove the spikes occurring between smooth patterns of the motion as shown in Figure 5b.

$$F^{joint}(J1,J2,J3,i) := \begin{cases} 1 & \text{if angle between J1,J2 and J3 is increasing by x angle in } i^{th}\text{ frame} \\ -1 & \text{if angle between J1,J2 and J3 is decreasing by x angle in } i^{th}\text{ frame} \\ F^{joint}(J1,J2,J3,i\text{-}1) & \text{otherwise} \end{cases}$$

The threshold angle "x" in the above function can be calculated by using experimental data. It has to be selected in such way that it does not hide any meaningful behavior of body segments.

4.1.2 F^{Plane} Function

The position of body parts can be used as a significant attribute for forming metadata about the given human motion. The body plane containing three joints such as pelvis, thorax and head is used as a reference plane for position of other important joints. These positions are defined in the following format,

$$F^{Plane}(J1,J2,J3,J4,i) := \begin{cases} 1 & \text{if J4 is above or on the plane} \\ & \text{defined by J1, J2 and J3 in } i^{th}\text{ frame} \\ -1 & \text{if J4 is below the plane} \\ & \text{defined by J1, J2 and J3 in } i^{th}\text{ frame} \end{cases}$$

In Figure 6, +1 represents the position of the left hand in front of the plane and -1 represents the position when the left hand is behind the body plane. As this captured data represents the position of the left hand for a given motion, similar data can be captured for the right hand, left and right foot on the same body plane.

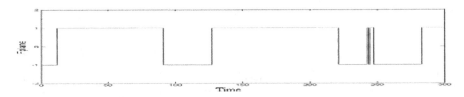

Fig. 6. Left hand position generated after applying the function $F^{Plane}(J1,J2,J2,J4,i)$ J1='Pelvis' J2='Thorax' J3='Head' J4='Left Hand'

The noise in the above square wave can be removed by modifying the function as follows.

$$
F^{Plane}(J1,J2,J3,J4,i) := \begin{cases} 1 & \text{if J4 is above by distance d or on the plane} \\ & \text{defined by J1, J2 and J3 in } i^{th} \text{ frame} \\ -1 & \text{if J4 is below by distance d or on the plane} \\ & \text{defined by J1, J2 and J3 in } i^{th} \text{ frame} \\ F^{Plane}(J1,J2,J3,J4,i-1) & \text{otherwise} \end{cases}
$$

The modified function $F^{Plane}(J1,J2,J2,J4,i)$ checks for the position of the joint that is placed at a distance "d" in the front or behind the plane. This function removes the fluctuations in the pattern by adding a threshold value "d". Similarly, the proper value of distance d is selected so that the meaningful motion information can be retained while noise is removed.

4.2 Preprocessing Database

Applying F^{joint} and F^{plane} to each motion available in the database will transform the whole motion database into a search space where searching will be much more time effective. Due to the hierarchical structure, Table 1 illustrates the features extracted from a single motion. F^{joint} and F^{Plane} on left and right leg, left and right arm. For F^{plane}, pelvis-thorax-head is used as the body plane.

Table 1. 8 features extracted from single motion by applying F^{joint} and F^{plane} over hierarchical segments

Fjoint(left foot, left tibia, left femur)	Fplane(pelvis, thorax, head, left hand)
Fjoint(right foot, right tibia, right femur)	Fplane(pelvis, thorax, head, right hand)
Fjoint(left humerus, left radius, left hand)	Fplane(pelvis, thorax, head, left foot)
Fjoint(right humerus, right radius, right hand)	Fplane(pelvis, thorax, head, right hand)

4.3 Processing Visual Queries

Changes in the angle between user-drawn body segments can be easily viewed on the visual query interface. This variation in joint angles is noted in the same pattern as F^{joint} function outputs for motions in database. The visual query contains four different rows of 3x3 grid sequences for drawing of the left-right leg and the left-right hand movement. From these sequences, we can find out F^{joint}(Query) and F^{plane}(Query) on leg and hand movements. Actual angle between the drawn joints in the query is calculated and it is used to find out F^{joint} for the query. Similarly, F^{plane} is calculated for the query by comparing position of the joint with respect to the plane drawn by the user on a querying interface.

4.4 DTW-Based Pattern Matching

In 3D human motion retrieval system, two motions are said to be similar if the movements of unit body parts are similar irrespective of their speed and direction. In order to achieve the same notion of similarity, we use the Dynamic Time Warping (DTW) technique to find a pattern match among the motions of variable lengths. DTW is an algorithm that measures similarity between two time series sequences, which may be of different time lengths. A human motion performed by different participants can result in variance of time and speed. For instance, a walking motion by two different humans will likely vary according to their speeds. Thus, motion files will have different number of frames according to the speed of an object. Applying feature functions on motion database files will generate time series sequences with different lengths. The sequences are warped non-linearly in the time dimension to determine a measure of their similarity.

4.5 Ranking

DTW algorithm runs on each segment of the motion query for each motion from the database. DTW finds the distance of body segment movement defined by F^{Joint} and F^{Plane} with respect to the query motion. All the distances for each of body segments are summed up to give the overall rank of the motion. The motion with the least distance from query motion will be considered the best match. The result obtained from summation (1) for motion files is sorted in an ascending order that provides the initial numbers of matches.

For Query Q and motion M1 from database, DTW^{Index} is defined as follows,

$$
\begin{aligned}
DTW^{Index}(Q,M1) = \; & DTW(F^{joint}Q, F^{joint}M1(left\ leg)) + DTW(F^{joint}Q, F^{joint}M1(right\ leg)) + \\
& DTW(F^{joint}Q, F^{joint}M1(left\ arm)) + DTW(F^{joint}Q, F^{joint}M1(right\ arm)) + \\
& DTW(F^{plane}Q, F^{plane}M1(left\ foot)) + DTW(F^{plane}Q, F^{plane}M1(right\ foot)) + \\
& DTW(F^{plane}Q, F^{plane}M1(left\ hand)) + DTW(F^{plane}Q, F^{plane}M1(right\ hand))
\end{aligned}
\tag{1}
$$

Sorting on DTW^{Index} for each motion M from the database against query Q will generate result in ranked order.

5   Visual Query Interface and Results

Each row of 3x3 grids represents space for a single joint. Selecting any grid from a row defines the position of joint with respect to other joints. By using this procedure, movement of sub-body part can be drawn as shown in Figure 7(a) and Figure 7(b).

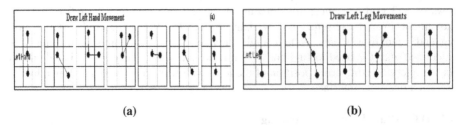

Fig. 7. Visual Query interface for drawing (**a**) left hand movements defined by humerus-radius-hand joints (**b**) left leg movements defined by femur-tibia-foot joints

Figure 8 shows the result of equation 1 for a query specified in previous Figures 7 (a) and (b). Five matching motions (motion no. 26 to 30) have $DTW^{Index}(Q,Mi)$ less than 230, while all other motions have larger summation. Figure 9 shows a motion number 26 which is one of matching motion having $DTW^{Index}(Q,M_{26}) = 110$.

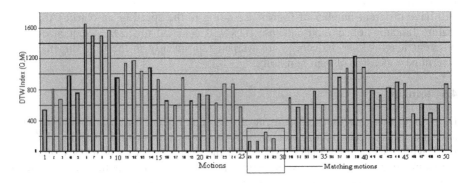

Fig. 8. Result of $DTW^{Index}(Q,Mi)$ distance based on equation 1 for a particular query and motions in database

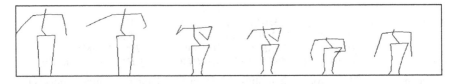

Fig. 9. One of the matching motion result for query given by user (motion no:26)

6   Conclusions and Future Work

This paper has offered a new way of looking at query interfaces and content based retrieval for search in motion databases. We proposed a visual query interface that helps us to closely understand user needs about motion databases. A visual query interface is composed of five drawing areas for unit body parts of human structure. We have introduced a concept of F^{joint} and F^{plane} feature function. By applying this feature function on motions, we transform a multidimensional data to the 2-dimensional space. Pre-processing of motion database accelerates the whole search system. Use of DTW makes motion search time invariant.

A visual query interface opens a new research problem in human computer interaction field. Modifications can be done to visual query interface to make it more user-friendly. Query validation can be extended to incorporate visual query grammar. We plan to develop a visual query language generator, which will automatically generate domain-specific query languages for applications.

References

1. Müller, M., Röder, T., Clausen, M.: Efficient content-based retrieval of motion capture data. ACM Transactions on Graphics (TOG) 24(3) (2005)
2. Pradhan, G., Li, C., Prabhakaran, B.: Hierarchical indexing structure for 3D human motions. In: MMM 2007. 13th International Multimedia Modeling Conference (January 2007)
3. CMU, Carnegie-Mellon MoCap Database (2003), http://mocap.cs.cmu.edu
4. Keogh, E.J., Palpanas, T., Zordan, V.B., Gunopolos, D., Cardle, M.: Indexing large human-motion databases. In: Proc. 30th VLDB conf., Toronto (2004)
5. Kovar, L., Gleicher, M.: Automated extraction and parameterization of motions in large data sets. ACM Transactions (2004)
6. Bruderlin, A., Williams, L.: Motion signal processing. In: Proc. ACM SIGGRAPH 1995, Computer Graphics Proc., Annual Conf. Series, pp. 97–104 (1995)
7. Cardle, M., Vlachos, S.B., Keogh, E., Gunopulos, D.: Fast motion capture matching with replicated motion editing. In: ACM SIGGRAPH 2003, Sketches and Applications (2003)
8. Keogh, E.: Exact indexing of dynamic time warping. In: Proc. 28th VLDB Conf., Hong Kong, pp. 406–417 (2002)
9. Wu, M.-Y., Chao, S., Yang, S., Lin, H.: Content-based retrieval for human motion data. In: 16th IPPR Conf. on Computer Vision, Graphics and Image Processing, pp. 605–612 (2003)
10. Carlsson, S.: Combinatorial geometry for shape representation and indexing. In: Object Representation in Computer Vision, pp. 53–78 (1996)

Bi-modal Conceptual Indexing for Medical Image Retrieval

Joo-Hwee Lim, Jean-Pierre Chevallet, Diem Thi Hoang Le, and Hanlin Goh

French-Singapore IPAL Joint Lab (UMI CNRS 2955, I2R, NUS, UJF)
Institute for Infocomm Research, 21 Heng Mui Keng Terrace, Singapore 119613
{joohwee,viscjp,studthl,hlgoh}@i2r.a-star.edu.sg

Abstract. To facilitate the automatic indexing and retrieval of large medical image databases, images and associated texts are indexed using concepts from the Unified Medical Language System (UMLS) meta-thesaurus. We propose a structured learning framework for learning medical semantics from images. Two complementary global and local visual indexing approaches are presented. Two fusion approaches are also used to improve textual retrieval using the UMLS-based image indexing: a simple post-query fusion and a visual modality filtering to remove visually aberrant images according to the query modality concepts. Using the ImageCLEFmed database, we demonstrate that our framework is superior when compared to the automatic runs evaluated in 2005 on the same Medical Image Retrieval task.

1 Introduction

Medical CBIR systems [11] can retrieve images based-on image modality (e.g. x-ray, MRI), anatomic region (e.g. skull, lung), or disease (e.g. fracture, pneumonia) [9], and are particularly useful to medical applications involving diagnosis, education, and research. Although modality, anatomy, and pathology information are normally contained in the Digital Imaging and Communications in Medicine (DICOM) header, they contain a high rate of errors [7]. Current CBIR systems [12] use low-level features such as color or texture, or logical features such as object and their relationships, and generally are not able to capture the semantic content of a medical image. This loss of information is called the semantic gap, which can be reduced by exploiting all sources of information. In particular, mixing text and image information generally increases the retrieval performance significantly. Recent evaluation of visual, textual, and mixed approaches within the Cross Language Evaluation Forum (CLEF) [1] shows that the mixed approaches outperformed the results of each single approach [5].

In this paper, we use medical concepts from National Library of Medicine's (NLM)[2] Unified Medical Language System (UMLS) meta-thesaurus to represent both image and text. This allows our system to work at a higher semantic level and standardize the semantic index of medical data, which facilitates the communication between visual and textual indexing and retrieval. We propose a structured learning framework to learn medical semantics from images. Each

S. Satoh, F. Nack, and M. Etoh (Eds.): MMM 2008, LNCS 4903, pp. 456–465, 2008.

image is represented by visual percepts and UMLS concepts. Global and local visual indexing schemas are used within this framework. It is important to extract local information from images as pathology bearing regions tend to be highly localized [6]. We also propose two fusion approaches to benefit from both images and associated text. The first is a simple fusion of the textual and visual retrieval. The other uses a visual modality filtering, designed to remove visually aberrant images according to the query modality concept(s).

The main contributions of this paper are:

1. the use of the medical meta-thesaurus UMLS to standardize the semantic indexes of the textual and visual data;
2. a structured approach for designing and learning medical semantics - that are a combination of UMLS concepts and visual percepts - from images;
3. the fusion between global and local image indexing to capture both modality, anatomy, and pathology information from images;
4. the fusion between textual and visual information: (1) through a simple late fusion between textual and visual similarities to the query, (2) through a visual filtering according to UMLS Modality concepts;
5. the superior experimental results of the UMLS-based system on the ImageCLEFmed medical image retrieval benchmark. Our proposed approach, achieves 7 more Mean Average Precision (MAP) points (23% relative improvement) over the best automatic run in ImageCLEFmed 2005.

2   Conceptual Text Indexing

Conventional text information retrieval (IR) methods extract from text, words that are directly used for indexing. Despite staying at the syntactic level and the simplicity of word extraction, this method is relatively effective and widely used. In precise technical domains such as medicine, terms are more important than words as they are forged by specialists to express diseases, treatments, etc., and indexing using terms improves precision as they denote unique meanings. However, a recall problem exists due to term variation and synonymy. Indexing at the conceptual level solves this problem as concepts are abstraction of terms. Moreover, at the conceptual level, the indexes are language independent and support multilingual IR as only one unique set of concepts is used to index a document in any language. However, setting up a conceptual indexing is challenging because we require a knowledge resource built by specialists and an automated tool to extract concepts from raw text. Concept extraction is difficult because of the inherent ambiguity and flexibility of the natural language.

UMLS has more than 5.5 million terms with different types of links. The terms are associated with concepts. UMLS is a "meta thesaurus" i.e. merger of different sources (thesaurus, term lists), and is neither complete nor consistent. To manage term variation, we use MetaMap [3] provided by NLM. This concept extraction tool does not provide any disambiguation. We partially overcome this problem by selecting concepts associated to the longest terms, and we also manually ordered them by thesaurus sources: we prefer source that strongly belong to medicine.

For example, this enables the identification of "x-ray" as radiography and not as the physical phenomenon (wave) which seldom appears in our documents. Concept extraction is limited to noun phrases. The extracted concepts are then organized in conceptual vectors, like a conventional vector space IR model, with the same weighting scheme provided by our indexing system.

3   Conceptual Image Indexing

Our aim is to associate an image or image region with a semantic label that links to a combination of UMLS concepts and visual percepts using statistical learning. In this way, we have a common language for both images and associated text. We define 3 types of UMLS concepts that could be associated to one image or one region: modality concepts, e.g. "Diagnostic Procedure"; anatomy concepts, e.g. "Body Location or Region"; pathology concepts, e.g. "Disease or Syndrome". Two complementary indexing schemes are used within this learning framework: a global indexing to access image modality (chest X-ray, gross photography of an organ, microscopy, etc.), and a local indexing to access semantic local features that are related to modality, anatomy, and pathology concepts.

In our framework, a set of disjoint UMLS-based concepts (i.e. do not share common visual instances) with visual appearance in medical images is first selected to define a Visual and Medical (VisMed) vocabulary. Secondly, low-level features are extracted from image region instances z to represent each VisMed term using color, texture, shape, etc. Thirdly, these low-level features are used as training examples to build hierarchical semantic classifiers according to the VisMed vocabulary. The classifier for the VisMed vocabulary is designed using Support Vector Machine (SVM) classifiers. The conditional probability that an example z belong to a class c given that the class belongs to its superclass $\mathcal{C}$ is computed using the softmax function:

$$P(c|z, \mathcal{C}) = \frac{\exp \mathcal{D}_c(z)}{\sum_{j \in \mathcal{C}} \exp \mathcal{D}_j(z)} \tag{1}$$

where $\mathcal{D}_c$ is the signed distance to the SVM hyperplane that separates class c from the other classes in $\mathcal{C}$. The probability of a VisMed term VMT_i for z is:

$$P(\text{VMT}_i|z) = \prod_{l=1}^{L} P(\mathcal{C}^l(\text{VMT}_i)|z, \mathcal{C}^{l-1}(\text{VMT}_i)) \tag{2}$$

where L is the number of levels, $\mathcal{C}^{l-1}(\text{VMT}_i)$ is the superclass of $\mathcal{C}^l(\text{VMT}_i)$, $\mathcal{C}^0(\text{VMT}_i)$ is the class for all VisMed terms, and $P(\mathcal{C}^l(\text{VMT}_i)|z, \mathcal{C}^{l-1}(\text{VMT}_i))$ is given by Eq. (1).

3.1   Global UMLS Indexing

The global UMLS indexing is based on a two-level classifier according to modality concepts. This modality classifier is learned from about 4000 images divided into 32 (22 grey level, 10 color) Global VisMed (GVM) index terms, with an example each being shown in Fig. 1. Each GVM term is characterized by a UMLS modality concept and, sometimes, an anatomy concept (e.g. neck, pelvis, etc.), a spatial concept (e.g. axial, frontal, etc.), or a color percept (color, grey). The training images come from the ImageCLEFmed database and elsewhere, and were selected using modality concept extracted from medical reports.

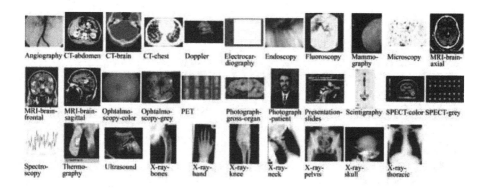

Fig. 1. Visual examples of GVM index terms

The first level of the classifier uses the first three moments in the HSV color space computed on the entire image to classify images into grey level or colored classes. The second level corresponds to the classification of UMLS Modality concepts in the grey or color class subtree. For the grey level classes, grey level histogram (32 bins), texture features (mean and variance of Gabor coefficients for 5 scales and 6 orientations), and thumbnails (grey values of 16x16 resized image), are used. For the color classes, HSV histogram (125 bins), Gabor texture features, and thumbnails, were adopted. The probability of a modality MOD_i for an image z is given by Eq. (2). More precisely, we have:

$$P(\text{MOD}_i|z) = \begin{cases} P(\text{MOD}_i|z, C)P(C|z) & \text{if } \text{MOD}_i \in C \\ P(\text{MOD}_i|z, G)P(G|z) & \text{if } \text{MOD}_i \in G \end{cases} \quad (3)$$

where C and G denote the color and the grey level classes respectively. The classifiers are first trained using SVM-Light software on half of the dataset (training set) to evaluate its performance on the other half of the dataset (validation set). The error rate on the validation set is 18%, with recall and precision rates higher than 70% for most of the classes. After learning (using the entire dataset), each database image z is indexed according to modality given its low-level features. The indexes are the probability values given by Eq. (3).

3.2   Local UMLS Indexing

Local patch classification is performed using 64 Local VisMed (LVM) terms, with each term being expressed as a combination of UMLS concepts from Modality,

Anatomy, and Pathology semantic types. Color features (first three moments in the HSV color space) and texture features (mean and variance of Gabor coefficients for 5 scales and 6 orientations) were extracted from these local patches, and classified based on SVMs and the softmax function [4] given by Eq. (1). A semantic patch-based detector, similar to the Global Visual and Modality classifers described above but now on local image patches, was designed to classify a patch according to the 64 LVM terms. Fig. 2 illustrates one visual example each for these 64 LVM index terms. We used 3631 patches extracted from 1033 images (921 from the web; 112 from the ImageCLEFmed database) for training and validation. The classification error rate on the validation set is about 30%.

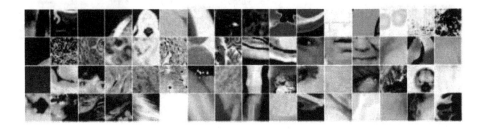

Fig. 2. Visual examples of LVM index terms

After learning, the LVM indexing terms are detected during image indexing from image patches without region segmentation to form semantic local histograms [8]. Essentially, an image is partitioned into overlapping image blocks of size 40x40 pixels after size normalization. Each patch is then classified into one of the 64 LVM terms using the SVM classifier. Thus, an image containing P overlapping patches is characterized by the set of P LVM histograms and their respective locations in the image. A histogram aggregation per block gives the final image index: $M \times N$ LVM histograms. Each bin of a given block B corresponds to the probability of a LVM term's presence in this block which is computed as:

$$P(\text{VMT}_i|B) = \frac{\sum_z area(z \cap B)\, P(\text{VMT}_i|z)}{\sum_z area(z \cap B)} \qquad (4)$$

where B and z are block and patch in an image respectively, $area(.)$ is the number of pixels common in both B and z, and $P(\text{VMT}_i|z)$ as in Eq. (2). We ensure the sampling of z is dense enough to cover the entire image so that $area(z \cap B) \neq 0$. To allow spatial aggregation and matching of image with different aspect ratios, we design 5 tiling templates, namely $M \times N = 3 \times 1, 3 \times 2, 3 \times 3, 2 \times 3$, and 1×3 grids resulting in 3, 6, 9, 6, and 3 probability vectors per image respectively [8].

4   Conceptual Image Retrieval

Considered in this section is the problem of retrieving images that are relevant to a textual query (free text) and/or to a visual query (one or several images) from a large medical database. This database consists of cases, each case containing a medical report and one or several images. We developed a retrieval system enabling three types of retrieval methods: textual retrieval for textual queries, a visual retrieval for query image(s), and a mixed retrieval that combines visual and textual indexes. This system is presented in Fig. 3 and each proposed retrieval method is described in the next subsections.

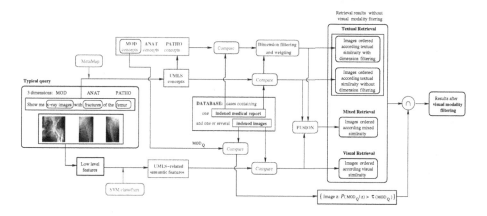

Fig. 3. Retrieval system based on UMLS-based Image and Text Indexing

4.1 Retrieval Using Text Index

We tested three text retrieval approaches based on conceptual indexing using UMLS concepts extracted. The first Conceptual Text Retrieval approach (denoted as (T_1)) uses a Vector Space Model (VSM) [10] to represent each document and a cosine similarity measure to compare the query index to the database medical report. The $tf \cdot idf$ measure is used to weight the concepts. Next, a semantic dimension filtering (DF) step was added (denoted as (T_2)), in order to explicitly taking into account the query dimension structure. This extra filtering step retains answers that incorporate at least one dimension, and discards noisy answers with respect to the dimension query semantic structure. The semantic dimension of a concept is defined by its UMLS semantic type, grouped into semantic groups: Anatomy, Pathology and Modality. Finally, answers are re-weighted according to dimensions before the DF step (denoted as (T_3)). The Relevance Status Value output from VSM is multiplied by the number of concepts matched with the query according to the dimensions, and strongly emphasizes the presence of maximum number of concepts related to semantic dimensions.

4.2 Retrieval Using Image Index

For query by example(s), three retrieval methods are proposed based on the two visual indexing approaches. The first two methods (denoted as (V_1) and (V_2)) are based on the global and local indexing scheme respectively. While the third visual retrieval method (V_3), is the fusion of (V_1) and (V_2). An images is represented by semantic histograms, with each bin corresponding to a modality probability for (V_1), or LVM probability for (V_2). For (V_1), the distance between two images is given by the Manhattan distance between the two semantic histograms. The similarity between a query image q and a database image z is then given by:

$$\lambda(q, z) = 1 - \frac{1}{2} \sum_k |P(\text{MOD}_k | q) - P(\text{MOD}_k | z)| \qquad (5)$$

where $P(\text{MOD}_k | .)$ is given by Equation (3). For (V_2), an image is represented by $M \times N$ semantic histograms. Given two images represented as different grid patterns, a flexible tiling matching scheme is used to cover all possible matches [8]. Finally in (V_3), the similarity to a query is given by the mean of the similarity to a query according to each index. When multiple images are given in the query, the similarity between a database image z with the query is given by the maximum value among the similarities between z and each query image.

4.3   Mixed Retrieval

The first fusion method, denoted as (F_1), is a late fusion of visual and textual similarity measures, obtained from (V_3) and (T_3) respectively. The similarity between a mixed query $Q = (Q_I, Q_T)$ (Q_I: image(s), Q_T: text) and a couple composed of an image and the associated medical report (I, R) is:

$$\lambda(Q, I, R) = \alpha \frac{\lambda_V(Q_I, I)}{\max\limits_{z \in \mathcal{D}_I} \lambda_V(Q_I, z)} + (1 - \alpha) \frac{\lambda_T(Q_T, R)}{\max\limits_{z \in \mathcal{D}_T} \lambda_T(Q_T, z)} \qquad (6)$$

where $\lambda_V(Q_I, I)$ denotes the maximum of the visual similarity between I and an image of Q_I, $\lambda_T(Q_T, R)$ denotes the textual similarity between the textual query Q_T and the medical report R, $\mathcal{D}_I$ denotes the image database, and $\mathcal{D}_T$ denotes the text database. After emperical tuning, we choose $\alpha = 0.7$. The second fusion paradigm (F_2) is based on a direct matching between UMLS modality concepts in a query and in the image modality index to remove all aberrant images i.e. an image I is admissible for a query modality MOD_Q only if $P(\text{MOD}_Q | I) > \tau(\text{MOD}_Q)$ where $\tau(\text{MOD}_Q)$ is a threshold defined for the modality MOD_Q extracted from query. This decision rule defines a set of admissible images for a given modality. The final result is the intersection of this set and the ordered set of images retrieved by any system. As several images of different modalities can be associated to a medical report, the ambiguity is removed with this filtering. Finally, the modality filter was also applied to the result of late fusion (F_1) as another fusion method (denoted as (F_3)).

5   Experimental Evaluation

We tested each of our proposed UMLS-based indexing and retrieval approaches on the medical image collection of the ImageCLEFmed benchmark [1]. This database consists of 50,026 medical images with the associated medical reports in three different languages. For the ImageCLEF 2005 Medical Image Retrieval task (i.e. ImageCLEFmed), 25 topics were provided, with each topic containing at least one of the following axes: anatomy, modality, pathology and abnormal visual observation (e.g. "enlarged heart" in a chest x-ray image). Each topic is also associated with one or several query images to allow for both textual and visual retrieval. An image pool was created for each topic by computing the union overlap of submissions and judged by three assessors to create several assessment sets. The relevant images are the ones judged as either relevant or partially relevant by at least two assessors. The relevant set of images is used to evaluate retrieval performance in terms of uninterpolated mean average precision (MAP) computed across all topics. We present in Table 1 the results of 9 different approaches described in this paper on these 25 queries to evaluate the benefit of using a UMLS indexing, especially in a fusion framework.

Table 1. Comparative results on ImageCLEFmed 2005

Method	Image	Text	MAP
(V_1) Global UMLS image indexing	X		10.38%
(V_2) Local UMLS image indexing	X		6.56%
(V_3) Fusion between (V_1) and (V_2)	X		12.11%
(BV) Best automatic visual run in 2005 (GIFT)	X		9.42%
(T_1) UMLS text indexing		X	16.08%
(T_2) UMLS text indexing with DF		X	18.94%
(T_3) UMLS text indexing with DWF		X	22.01%
(BT) Best automatic textual run in 2005 (DFMT)		X	20.84%
(F_1) Fusion between (V_3) and (T_3)	X	X	27.96%
(F_2) Visual modality filtering on (T_3)	X	X	29.25%
(F_3) Visual modality filtering on (F_1)	X	X	34.60%
(BM) Best automatic mixed run with DFMT in 2005	X	X	28.21%
(BM') Best automatic mixed run without DFMT in 2005	X	X	23.89%

For visual retrieval, two of our results (V_1, V_3) outperformed the best visual only result of ImageCLEFmed 2005 (BV), especially when local and global UMLS indexes are mixed (V_3). By using UMLS text indexing with DWF (T_3), we managed a slight improvement of 1% with respect to the best text only result of 2005 (BT). Using the UMLS meta-thesaurus, modality, anatomy, and pathology dimensions can be accessed, by using the semantic type associated to each UMLS concept. The fusion between image and text result in significant benefits: from 22% for (T_3) and 12% (V_3), we achieve 28% MAP with a simple fusion of the retrieval results (F_1). Also, the use of a visual filtering according to the modality concept contributes to the improvement of retrieval results (F_2). Our best result is obtained using visual filtering on the result of the fusion between text and image retrievals (F_3), leading to an improvement of 7 MAP points (i.e. from 28% to 35%) with respect to the best mixed result of 2005 (BM).

Fig. 4 illustrates the benefit of fusion between text and image retrieval methods. It shows the first 30 retrieved images for Query 13, which is intended to retrieve abdominal CT images where blood vessels are visible in the liver, and may be linked to the presence of abnormal tumors in the liver. There are 3 query

Query 13 : Show me abdominal CT images showing liver blood vessels

Visual retrieval results (V3)   Textual retrieval results (T3)
3 relevant images / 30 retrieved images 4 relevant images / 30 retrieved images

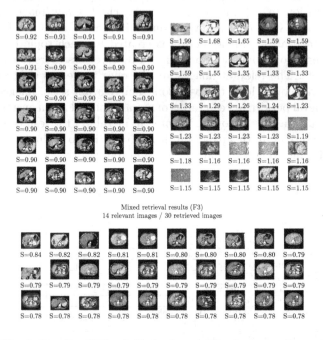

Mixed retrieval results (F3)
14 relevant images / 30 retrieved images

Fig. 4. Results of Visual, Textual, and Mixed runs on Query 13

image examples provided with this query. Detecting visible blood vessels in CT liver images is a non-trivial image analysis task and without a specialized detector for such purpose, the result of the visual retrieval method is very poor. It turned out that the text-based retrieval is poor as well. However, through image-text fusion, the number of relevant images improved to a more satisfactory level.

6   Conclusion

Medical CBIR is an emerging and challenging research area. We proposed a retrieval system that represents both texts and images at a very high semantic level using concepts from UMLS. A structured framework was proposed for designing image semantics from statistical learning. The flexible framework also allows fusion of global and local similarities to enhance image retrieval results further, as demonstrated by visual retrieval method (V_3). Two fusion approaches were developed to improve textual retrieval performance using this UMLS-based image indexes. The first uses a simple fusion of the two retrieval approaches (F_1), resulting in significant improvement the retrieval results. The other approach, performs visual modality filtering (F_2, F_3), to remove visually aberrant images.

Using the ImageCLEFmed 2005 medical database and retrieval task, the effectiveness of our framework was demonstrated.

As an extension, we plan to use LVM terms from local indexing for semantics-based retrieval and complement the similarity-based retrieval (FlexiTile matching). We are currently investigating the potential of an early fusion scheme using appropriate clustering methods. A visual filtering based on local information could also be derived from the semantic local LVM indexing. For the visual indexing, currently we only use a two-scale approach: global image-level indexes for GVM terms and local fixed-size patch-level indexes for LVM terms. A natural extension would be to embed the UMLS-based visual indexing approach into a multi-scale framework, using appropriate scales for various types of semantic features.

References

1. Cross language evaluation forum, http://www.clef-campaign.org/
2. National library of medecine, http://www.nlm.nih.gov/
3. Aronson, A.: Effective mapping of biomedical text to the UMLS metathesaurus: The MetaMap program. In: Proceedings of the Annual Symposium of the American Society for Medical Informatics, pp. 17–21 (2001)
4. Bishop, C.: Neural Networks for Pattern Recognition. Clarendon Press, Oxford (1995)
5. Clough, P., Müller, H., Desealers, T., Grubinger, M., Lehmann, T., Jensen, J., Hersh, W.: The clef 2005 automatic medical image annotation task. In: Peters, C., Gey, F.C., Gonzalo, J., Müller, H., Jones, G.J.F., Kluck, M., Magnini, B., de Rijke, M., Giampiccolo, D. (eds.) CLEF 2005. LNCS, vol. 4022, Springer, Heidelberg (2006)
6. Dy, J., Brodley, C., Kak, A., Broderick, L., Aisen, A.: Unsupervised feature selection applied to content-based retrieval of lung images. IEEE Transactions on Pattern Analysis and Machine Intelligence 25(3), 373–378 (2003)
7. Guld, M.O., Kohnen, M., Keysers, D., Schubert, H., Wein, B.B., Bredno, J., Lehmann, T.M.: Quality of dicom header information for image categorization. In: Proceedings of the International Symposium on Medical Imaging, San Diego, CA, USA, vol. 4685, pp. 280–287. SPIE (2002)
8. Lim, J., Chevallet, J.-P.: Vismed: a visual vocabulary approach for medical image indexing and retrieval. In: Proc. of AIRS 2005, pp. 84–96 (2005)
9. Muller, H., Michoux, N., Bandon, D., Geissbuhler, A.: A review of content-based image retrieval systems in medical applications - clinical benefits and future directions. International Journal of Medical Informatics 73, 1–23 (2004)
10. Salton, G., Wong, A., Yang, C.: A vector space model for automatic indexing. Communications of the ACM 18, 613–620 (1975)
11. Shyu, C.-R., Pavlopoulou, C., Kak, A.C., Brodley, C.E., Broderick, L.S.: Using human perceptual categories for content-based retrieval from a medical image database. Computer Vision and Image Understanding 88(3), 119–151 (2002)
12. Smeulders, A., et al.: Content-based image retrieval at the end of the early years. IEEE Trans. on PAMI 22(12), 1349–1380 (2000)

Audio Analysis for Multimedia Retrieval from a Ubiquitous Home

Gamhewage C. de Silva, Toshihiko Yamasaki, and Kiyoharu Aizawa

Department of Information and Communication Engineering, the University of Tokyo, 102B2, 7-1-3 Hongo, Bunkyo-ku, Tokyo 113-8656, Japan

Abstract. We present a system for video retrieval based on analyzing audio data from a large number of microphones in a home-like environment. Silence elimination on individual microphones is followed by noise reduction based on regions consisting of multiple microphones, to identify audio segments. An algorithm based on the energy distribution of sounds in the house is used to localize sound sources, thereby removing sounds heard in regions other than they are generated. A set of time domain features are used to classify these sounds for video retrieval. The algorithms were evaluated with 200 minutes of audio data from each microphone, gathered during an experiment where a family lived in the ubiquitous home. It was possible to achieve an overall accuracy of above 80% from all algorithms.

1 Introduction

Audio analysis and classification is widely used for automated video retrieval for a number of reasons. Due to the smaller size, audio data are easier and faster to process in a computer than video data. A large amount of information regarding the scene and events is contained in an audio signal acquired from the scene. An example is sports video, where there is a high correlation between sounds and actual events. In some types of video, such as news video, the audio has a much higher signal-to-noise ratio allowing higher accuracy in retrieval.

Audio analysis can facilitate more efficient video retrieval in smart and ubiquitous environments. Since most smart environments require multiple cameras for complete capture of the scene, the amount of video to be analysed is quite large. Audio data can be successfully used to reduce the search space by selecting cameras according to the results of processing audio. However, audio analysis for such environments is more difficult than that for broadcast audio. Multiple microphones are often required for capturing audio with an adequate signal-to-noise ratio. Since the coverage of a microphone is much less restricted than that of a camera, sounds from a single source are picked up by several microphones, calling for the additional task of source localization.

This paper presents a system for video retrieval from a home-like smart environment with a large number of cameras and microphones, using audio analysis.

S. Satoh, F. Nack, and M. Etoh (Eds.): MMM 2008, LNCS 4903, pp. 466–476, 2008.

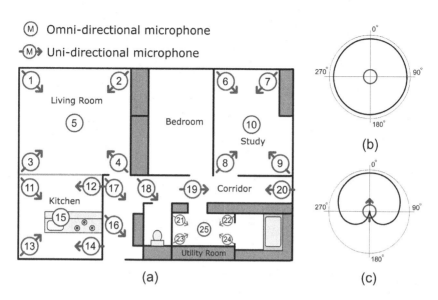

Fig. 1. Microphone positioning and orientation

Section 2 contains a brief survey of related work. Sections 3 and 4 describe the environment and the algorithms used for audio analysis respectively. We evaluate the performance of the algorithms and present the results in Section 5. Section 6 concludes the paper, suggesting possible future directions.

2   Related Work

This work is a specific application of audio analysis for video retrieval. A detailed review of the common techniques used for audio analysis in multimedia content can be found in [1], while a more recent review is available in [2]. Most of the existing researches deal with broadcast video such as news and sports video .

There are several ongoing researches on multimedia retrieval from ubiquitous environments using audio analysis. Smeaton et al. [3] demonstrate that audio data can be a significant aid for video surveillance, by achieving accurate event detection in a ubiquitous environment based on time-domain audio features. Audio feature extraction followed by Hidden Markov Models has been successfully used to extract information from audio recorded in meeting rooms [4]. Vacher et al. use audio from multiple microphones to facilitate telemonitoring of patients based on audio events [5].

A brief review of the techniques used for sound source localization can be found in [6]. The most common approaches are based on time delay of arrival (TDOA), microphone arrays [7] and beam-forming techniques [8]. However, the conditions required by these approaches are difficult to satisfy in most smart environments.

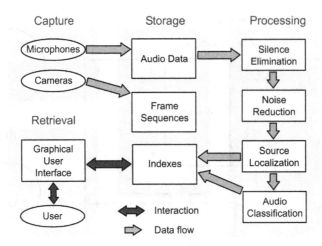

Fig. 2. System overview

3   Ubiquitous Home and Data Acquisition

This work is based on *Ubiquitous Home* [9], a two-room house equipped with 17 cameras and 25 microphones for continuous capture of audio and video. Pressure based sensors, mounted on the floor, capture data corresponding to the footsteps. Cardioid and omni-directonal microphones are mounted on the ceiling at locations shown in Figure 1a. The numbering of the microphones in Figure 1a will be used to refer to them in the coming sections of the paper. Figures 1b and 1c show the directional responses of omni directional and cardioid microphones respectively. Audio data from each microphone are captured at a sampling rate of 44.1kHz, and stored in *mp3* file format.

Our goal in research related to ubiquitous home is to create a multimedia diary [10] that the residents can use to *capture* memorable events, *recall* things they forgot, and *discover* events that they were not aware of. Our earlier work in this environment facilitated the retrieval of personalized video and key frame sets, and basic activity classification, by analyzing floor sensor data[11]. In this work, we extend the capability of the diary by incorporating audio analysis and classification. This facilitates queries related to events characterized by different types of sounds, such as voices.

A *real-life experiment* was conducted, to ensure that the data collected resemble those from life at home to the maximum possible extent. A family of three members (a married couple with their 3-year old daughter) stayed in the ubiquitous home for 12 days. They lead their normal lives during this stay. The husband went to work on weekdays; the wife did the cooking; and everybody went out at times during the weekend. The data were captured and processed offline; however, the algorithms were designed to be usable in real-time.

4 System Description

Figure 2 is an outline of the proposed system. The audio streams are partitioned into *segments* of one second each. Sets of audio segments that are captured during the same 1 s interval (hereafter referred to as *segment sets*) are processed together. After eliminating silence, the segment sets are processed further to reduce noise. Source localization is followed by audio classification to identify the location/s of the sound sources and the type of sound. The results are stored as indexes for video retrieval. The following sub-sections describe these steps in detail.

4.1 Silence Elimination and Noise Reduction

We perform silence elimination for a single audio segment by comparing its RMS power against a threshold value. The threshold for each microphone was estimated by analyzing one hour of audio data for silence for that microphone, extracted from different times of day. These were partitioned into *frames* having 300 samples. Adjacent frames had a 50% overlap. The RMS value of each frame was calculated and recorded, and the statistics obtained. The data were combined to make a probabilistic model and the threshold value was selected to be at 99% level of confidence according to its distribution.

For silence elimination, each audio segment is divided into overlapping frames in the same manner as above, and the RMS value of each frame calculated. If the calculated RMS value is larger than the threshold, the frame is considered to contain sound. Sets of contiguous sound frames that are less than 0.5 s apart are combined together to form single segments. Sets of contiguous sound frames having a duration less than 0.1 s are removed.

The second stage uses data from multiple microphones in close proximity to reduce false positives resulting due to noise. For this purpose and for use in the following stages, the microphones are grouped in to *regions* as specified in Table 1. The bedroom has no microphones installed. However, it was identified as a separate region, for use in further analysis.

Noise is random, and usually has small duration. Due to its randomness, it is less likely that noise in sound segments from different microphones occur simultaneously. Due to small duration, noise can be distinguished in most situations.

Table 1. Regions for audio segmentation

Label	Region	Microphones
LR	Living room	1–5
SR	Study room	6–10
KT	Kitchen	11–15
C1	Corridor - section 1	16,17
C2	Corridor - section 2	18–20
UR	Utility room	21–25
BR	Bedroom	–

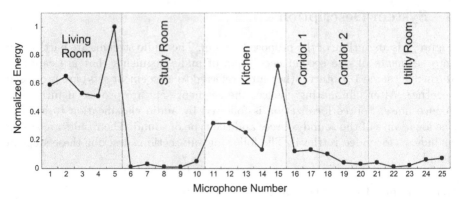

Fig. 3. Energy distribution template for the living room

A region-based voting algorithm based on the above arguments is used to reduce noise in sound segments.

Silence elimination resulted in 0% false negatives (sound misclassified as silence) and 2.2% false positives (silence misclassified as sound). The algorithm for noise reduction was able to remove 83% of the false positives that remained after silence elimination in individual audio streams.

4.2   Sound Source Localization

The sounds contained in the segments can be categorized into two types. One is *local* sounds, that is, sounds generated in the same region as the microphone belongs to. The other, *overheard* sounds, refers to the sounds that are generated in a region other than that the microphone belongs to. To prevent false retrievals, audio segments containing only overheard sounds must be removed before further processing. We refer to this task as *sound source localization*, as it identifies the regions where one or more sound sources are present.

The regions of the house are partitioned in different ways. For example, the study room is well partitioned from the rest, whereas the living room and kitchen are not so strongly partitioned. This results in different amounts of overhearing in different regions. With only a limited amount of directivity present in the setup of microphones, source localization for ubiquitous home is a difficult task.

4.3   Localization Based on Maximum Energy

A simple approach for sound source localization is to select the region with the microphone that captures the sound with the highest volume [5]. Although this approach fails when multiple sound sources are active at the same time, we investigate its performance for comparison. We use the following algorithm for *localization based on maximum energy*. For each segment set, the mean square value (which is proportional to short-term energy) of the samples in each segment is calculated. The average energy for each region is calculated by averaging mean

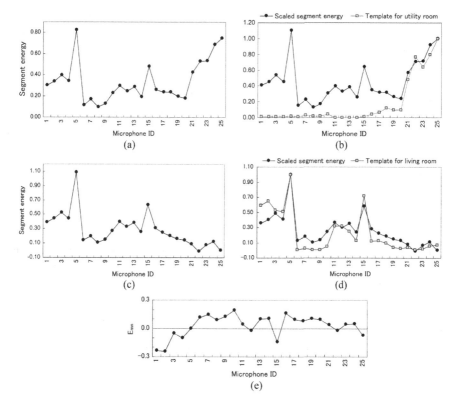

Fig. 4. Scaled template matching for source localization

square values for the segments from the microphones in that region. The region with the maximum average energy is selected as the location of the sound source.

4.4   Localization Based on Scaled Template Matching

A sound generated in one region of ubquitous home can be heard in other regions, in different levels of intensity. Based on this fact, we model local sounds in each region with the variation of energy received by each microphone. For each region r, a number of segment sets are selected for instances where sounds were generated only in that particular region. The energy distribution $E(n)$ for each segment set is determined by calculating the energy for each segment in the set. The *Energy Distribution Template*, T_r of the region r is estimated by averaging all such energy distributions and normalizing to the range [0 1]. Figure 3 shows the energy distribution template for sounds originating in the living room.

Each audio segment set is a mixture of sounds from one or more regions of the house. We hypothesize that the energy distribution of a segment set is a linear combination of one or more energy distribution templates, and attempt to identify them. We use the following *scaled template matching algorithm* for this task. The main idea behind the algorithm is to repeatedly identify the loudest sound source available, and remove its contribution. This is repeated until there is no significant sound energy left to assume the presence of another sound source.

1. Calculate the energy distribution, $E(n)$ for the current segment set
2. Find the region r in the distribution with the maximum average value
3. Scale $E(n)$ by dividing by the max value, A_m in that region
4. Subtract the template T_r corresponding to that region, and obtain $G(n)$. Multiply by A_m to obtain $E'(n)$
5. If the average value of $E'(n) \leq 0.2$ then stop.
6. Repeat steps 2-5 on $E'(n)$, for k times where k is the number of regions where sound segments are detected after noise filtering.

Figure 4 visualizes the application of this algorithm to an actual segment set. In this case, local sounds are present in the utility room and the living room. Figure 4a shows the energy distribution for the original segment set. Since the highest average energy is present in the *utility room* region (microphones 21-25), the utility room is identified as having local sounds. The energy distribution is scaled by dividing by the energy for microphone 25 (the maximum value for this region), and the template for the utility room is subtracted (Figure 4b). The result of subtraction, $E'(n)$, is shown in Figure 4c. The process is repeated using the template for the living room (Figure 4d), which records the highest average in $E'(n)$. The algorithm stops at this point as the average value becomes lower than the set threshold (Figure 4e).

4.5   Audio Classification

The results of source localization can be used directly to retrieve video for basic *audio events*, that is, instances where a sound was generated in a given region. However, retrieval by different classes of audio such as voices and music will greatly enhance the precision of retrieval. We classified the sound segments remaining after localization into eight categories, to support more detailed queries. An audio database (Table 2) was constructed using audio clips extracted from

Table 2. Description of audio database

Label	Class	No. of clips
1	Footsteps	40
2	Noise	40
3	Voices of people inside the house	112
4	Voice of a household robot	32
5	Voices from television	50
6	Other sounds from television	60
7	Vacuum cleaner	60
8	environmental sounds	86
	Total	480

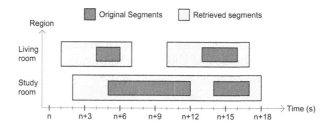

Fig. 5. Video retrieval for the detected audio events

the real-life experiment. The duration of each audio clip is between 1 and 15 seconds. The classes were selected by observing data from the real-life experiment, and aiming at detecting higher level events at a later stage. The following time domain features are extracted from each clip for audio classification:

- Mean of RMS values of the frames
- Standard deviation of RMS values of the frames
- Mean of Zero crossing ratios of the frames
- Standard deviation of Zero crossing ratios of the frames
- Silence ratio of the audio clip

All features were calculated according to the definitions in [12]. Each feature was normalized by subtracting the mean and dividing by the standard deviation for the feature in the entire database. A number of classifiers, including Multi-layer Perceptron (MLP), k-Nearest Neighbor and *Random Forest* were implemented and evaluated using 10-fold cross validation.

4.6 Video Retrieval

The method of audio-based retrieval is fairly straightforward once audio segments are localized. First, consecutive sound segments that are less than 4 seconds apart are joined together, to prevent retrieving a large number of fragmented videos for the same event. After joining, the start time for retrieving video is set to be 3 seconds earlier than that of the sound segment, to allow the

Table 3. Ratios of overheard sounds

(a) before source localization

	LR	SR	KT	C1	C2	UR	BR
LR	1.00	0.00	0.28	0.03	0.13	0.00	0.00
SR	0.00	1.00	0.00	0.01	0.39	0.07	> 0
KT	0.73	0.00	1.00	0.12	0.01	0.00	0.00
C1	0.06	0.00	0.10	1.00	0.36	0.16	> 0
C2	0.00	0.02	0.02	0.27	1.00	0.18	> 0
UR	0.00	0.00	0.00	0.02	0.27	1.00	0.00

(b) after source localization

	LR	SR	KT	C1	C2	UR	BR
LR	1.00	0.00	0.03	0.02	0.03	0.00	0.00
SR	0.00	1.00	0.00	0.00	0.04	0.00	0.00
KT	0.05	0.00	1.00	0.00	0.00	0.00	0.00
C1	0.01	0.00	0.00	1.00	0.06	0.05	0.00
C2	0.00	0.04	0.00	0.13	1.00	0.05	> 0
UR	0.00	0.00	0.00	0.02	0.06	1.00	0.00

user to prepare to receive the audio event. The end of the video clip is set to be one second later than that of the sound segment. Figure 5 is a visual representation of this process. Video clips are retrieved from all cameras in the region for the time interval determined as above. The same approach is applicable for retrieving video segments for different classes of audio.

5   Evaluation and Results

We used 5000 minutes of audio data captured from 7:45 a.m. to 11:05 a.m. on a day of the real-life experiment, for evaluation of sound source localization. The time interval was selected such that all regions of the house had been used for a considerable duration for ordinary household activities. The ground truth with regard to the sounds generated in each region was determined manually.

To present the degree of overhearing between different regions of ubiquitous home for these data, we define the *ratio of overhearing*, H_{ij}, as

$$H_{ij} = \frac{No.\ of\ sound\ segments\ coming\ from\ region\ j\ and\ heard\ in\ room\ i}{Total\ number\ of\ sound\ segments\ generated\ in\ region\ j}$$

where $i, j \in \{LR, SR, KT, C1, C2, UR, BR\}$. Table 3(a) shows the matrix $H = [H_{ij}]$ for the seleted data before sound source localization. To take an example on how to interpret the values, 73% (0.73) of the sounds coming from the living room can be heard in the kitchen. It should be noted that H is not symmetric. For example, only 28% of the sounds coming from the kitchen can be heard in the living room, compared to the 73% for the other way. This is because most sounds generated in the living room (e.g. sounds from the TV) were louder than those generated in the kitchen (e.g. preparing food). The exact values of the ratios cannot be determined for the bedroom, due to the absence of microphones.

Table 3(b) shows the ratios of overhearing after source localization using scaled template matching. The sounds coming from the bedroom are now heard only in C2. The main reason for the high accuracy is the fact that the algorithm makes use of the high partitioning present in the environment.

Table 4. Results of source localization

Region	Before Localization			Max. Energy			Temp. Matching		
	P	R	F	P	R	F	P	R	F
Living Room (LR)	0.561	1.000	0.719	0.970	0.927	0.948	0.950	0.993	0.971
Study Room (SR)	0.785	1.000	0.879	1.000	0.449	0.620	0.965	0.598	0.738
Kitchen (KT)	0.721	1.000	0.838	0.956	0.776	0.857	0.972	0.791	0.872
Corridor 1 (C1)	0.691	1.000	0.817	1.000	0.604	0.753	0.862	0.888	0.875
Corridor 2 (C2)	0.464	1.000	0.634	1.000	0.797	0.887	0.842	0.974	0.903
Utility Room (LR)	0.712	1.000	0.831	1.000	0.816	0.899	0.912	0.891	0.901

In source localization, it is important to minimize both retrieving overheard sounds as local sounds, and ignoring local sounds as overheard sounds. We define the Precision P, Recall R, and Balanced F-measure F of source localization for each region of the house, as follows:

$$P = \frac{No.\ of\ local\ segments\ retrieved\ correctly}{Total\ no.\ of\ segments\ retrieved}$$

$$R = \frac{No.\ of\ local\ segments\ retrieved\ correctly}{Actual\ no.\ of\ local\ segments}$$

$$F = 2PR/(P+R)$$

Table 4 compares the precision, recall, and F-measure for audio segments before source localization with the results obtained by maximum energy-based selection and scaled template matching. It is evident that the scaled template matching performs best, although the accuracy is relatively low for some regions. AdaBoost with MLP classifier yielded the highest overall accuracy for audio classification. Detailed results for evaluation using this classifier are presented in Table 5. The accuracy of classification using only time domain features suggest that higher accuracy can be obtained using frequency or MFCC domain features.

Table 5. Results of audio classification

Class	1	2	3	4	5	6	7	8
Precision	0.681	0.909	0.793	0.912	0.731	0.815	1.000	0.784
Recall	0.800	1.000	0.821	0.969	0.760	0.883	1.000	0.674
F-Measure	0.736	0.952	0.807	0.939	0.745	0.848	1.000	0.725

6   Conclusion and Future Work

We have proposed a set of algorithms for multimedia retrieval from a home-like ubiquitous environment by analyzing audio data from a large number of microphones. The proposed scaled template matching algorithm is able to achieve generally accurate sound source localization, despite the absence of microphone arrays or a beam-forming setup. The average accuracy of audio classification using time domain features was found to be 83.2%.

Use of frequency domain features for similarity matching is a possible approach for improving the performance of source localization. We intend to process the results of audio classification further, to identify activities at a higher symantic level, such as conversations and watching TV.

Acknowledgments

This work is supported by CREST of JST, and NICT of Japan.

References

1. Wang, Y., Liu, Z., Huang, J.: Multimedia Content Analysis Using Both Audio and Visual Cues, IEEE Signal Processing Magazine, pp. 12–36 (November 2000)
2. Cai, R., Lu, L., Hanjalic, A.: Unsupervised Content Discovery in Composite Audio. In: Proc. ACM Multimedia 2005, pp. 628–637 (2005)
3. Smeaton, A.F., McHugh, M.: Towards Event Detection in an Audio-Based Sensor Network. In: Proc. ACM VSSN 2005, pp. 87–94 (2005)
4. Gatica-Perez, D., Zhang, D., Bengio, S.: Extracting Information for Multimedia Meeting Collections. In: Proc. ACM MIR 2005, pp. 245–252 (2005)
5. Vacher, M., Istrate, D., Besacier, L., Castelli, E., Serignat, J.F.: Smart Audio Sensor for Telemedicine. In: Smart Objects Conference 2003 (2003)
6. Rui, Y., Florencio, D.: New Direct Approaches to Robust Sound Source Localization. In: Proc. IEEE ICME 2003 (2003)
7. Chen, J.F., Shue, L., Sun, H.W., Phua, K.S.: An Adaptive Microphone Array with Local Acoustic Sensitivity. In: Proc. IEEE ICME 2005 (2005)
8. Hoshuyama, O., Sugiyama, A., Hirano, A.: A Robust Adaptive Beamformer for Microphone Arrays with a Blocking Matrix using Constrained Adaptive Filters. IEEE Trans. Signal Processing 47(10), 2677–2684 (1999)
9. Yamazaki, T.: Ubiquitous Home: Real-Life Testbed for Home Context-Aware Service. In: Proc. Tridentcom2005, pp. 54–59. IEEE Press, Los Alamitos (2005)
10. de Silva, G.C., Yamasaki, T., Aizawa, K.: An Interactive Multimedia Diary for the Home, In: IEEE Computer, pp. 52–59. IEEE Press, Los Alamitos (2007)
11. de Silva, G.C., Yamasaki, T., Aizawa, K.: Interactive Experience Retrieval for Ubiquitous Home. In: Proc. ACM CARPE 2006, pp. 45–48 (2006)
12. Liu, M., Wan, C.: A Study on Content-Based Classification and Retrieval of Audio Database. In: Proc. IDEAS, pp. 339–345 (2001)

Effectiveness of Signal Segmentation for Music Content Representation

Namunu C. Maddage[1], Mohan S. Kankanhalli[2], and Haizhou Li[1]

[1] Institute for Infocomm Research, Heng Mui Keng Terrace, 119613 Singapore
{maddage,hli}@i2r.a-star.edu.sg
[2] School of Computing National University of Singapore
mohan@comp.nus.edu.sg

Abstract. In this paper we compare the effectiveness of rhythm based signal segmentation technique with the traditional fixed length segmentation for music contents representation. We consider vocal regions, instrumental regions and chords which represent the harmony as different classes of music contents to be represented. The effectiveness of segmentation for music content representation is measured based on intra class feature stability, inter class high feature deviation and class modeling accuracy. Experimental results reveal music content representation is improved with rhythm based signal segmentation than with fixed length segmentation. With rhythm based segmentation, vocal and instrumental modeling accuracy and chord modeling accuracy are improved by 12% and 8% respectively.

Keywords: Music segmentation, chord detection, vocal and instrumental regions.

1 Introduction

The fundamental step for audio content analysis is the signal segmentation where, within the segment, information can fairly be considered as quasi-stationary. After that, the feature extraction and other advanced processing steps, such as statistical information modeling, are followed for music content modeling. Higher accuracies of the above mentioned steps lead better performances in semantic music information processing such as music information indexing, retrieval, lyrics identification, polyphonic music transcription and music summarization. Fixed length segmentation has commonly been used in speech processing [2]. In the past, music research community has also employed fixed length signal segmentation technique for music content analysis research [3] [8] [9] [11] [12] [14]. However, compared to speech, music is wideband signal (> 10 kHz), structured and heterogeneous source in nature. Given the fact that music and speech have differences in terms of production and perception, it's not clear how suitable the fixed length segmentation is for music information modeling. Our focus in this paper is to analyze two signal segmentation techniques (frame level): fixed length segmentation and rhythm level segmentation for their effectiveness in modeling music chords, vocal and instrumental region information.

In our literature survey we found, the importance of time domain multi resolution signal analysis for harmonic structure detection has been discussed in [9]. For similarity analysis, timbre level signal segmentation with the understanding of music

S. Satoh, F. Nack, and M. Etoh (Eds.): MMM 2008, LNCS 4903, pp. 477–486, 2008.

structure has been discussed in [8]. Information carried by music signals can conceptually be represented or grouped as sound, tone, melody, harmony, composition performance, listening, understanding and ecstasy [10].   Similarly underlying information in music: time, harmony, acoustic events and music semantics can conceptually be represented bottom up in a pyramid [5]. From the music composition point of view, smallest note played in music can be considered as an information measuring unit. Recent studies in [4] [5] [13] [15] have also suggested tempo based signal segmentation for music content analysis. It can be seen that when research advances, more efforts have been devoted to both understand the behaviors of music signals and incorporate music knowledge for music content modeling.

In this paper we compare the effectiveness of both fixed length (30ms frames) and rhythm based music segmentations for music information representation. Music region contents (vocal and instrumental class information) and music chords are chosen as different music contents to be represented. We consider intra class lower average feature distance which implies the feature stability within the music class, inter class higher average feature distance which implies higher feature deviation between two different music classes and higher accuracy of class content modeling as the parameters to measure the effectiveness of music signal segmentation.

In section 2 we briefly explain music composition. Our rhythm based segmentation method is explained in section 3. Section 4 details modeling and analysis of different music contents. Experimental results are discussed in section 5 and we conclude the paper in section 6.

2 Music Composition and Signal Visualization

Duration of the song is measured as number of *Bars*. The steady throb to which one could clap while listening to a song is called the *Beat* and the *Accents* are the beats which are stronger than the others. In a song, the words or syllables in the sentence fall on beats in order to construct music phrase [7]. Fig. 1 shows the time alignment between music notes and the words. Since accents are placed over the important syllables, the time signature of this musical phrase is 2/4, i.e. two quarter notes per bar. Approximately 90% of sound generated during singing is voiced [3].   In the perfect singing, these voiced sounds are held longer to align with the duration of a music note. This can even be seen in Fig. 1, where the time duration of the word 'Jack' is equal to a quarter note and the length of a quarter note is defined according to the tempo (measured as number of beats per minute).

The chord knowledge has been applied to effectively detect the rhythm information [1], reveals that harmony changes are in discrete inter-beat time intervals. Common chord transitions are as follows.

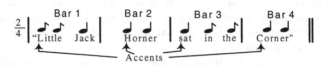

Fig. 1. Rhythmic group of words

- Chords are more likely to change on beat times than on other positions.

- Chords are more likely to change on half note times than on other positions of beat times.

- Chords are more likely to change at the beginning of the measures (bars) than at other positions of half note times.

Therefore, from the music composition point of view, progression of music chords (harmony event), and music regions i.e. pure instrumental, pure vocal, instrumental mixed vocal, and silence regions can be measured as integer multiples of music notes or inter-beat proportional units. Fig. 2 depicts time domain and frequency domain visualization of music signal with their note alignments. Fig. 2(middle) shows the normalized spectra differences. We can clearly see lower spectral difference within the music notes and higher spectral difference at the note boundaries. Therefore such time frequency visualization reveals quasi-stationary behavior of the temporal properties within music notes.

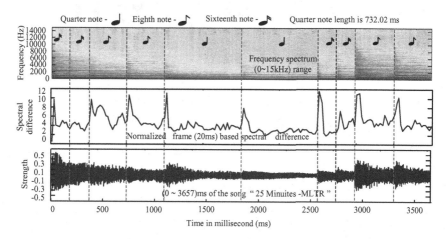

Fig. 2. Note boundaries of a 3667ms long clip from the song "Paint My Love - MLTR". Quarter note length is 736.28ms.

Thus there is a good reason for us to believe that inter-beat proportional segmentation is an effective method for music content modeling. In the next section we briefly discuss our inter-beat proportional segmentation technique which we further use for music modeling to compare the performances against fixed length signal segmentation.

3   Frame Level Music Segmentation

As mention earlier, we are interested in learning about the effectiveness of two signal segmentation techniques: fixed length segmentation and rhythm based segmentation for music content representation. In our previous work [4] [5], we detailed a rhythm extraction and an inter-beat proportional segmentation technique. In this rhythm based segmentation technique, we first decompose the signal into octave sub-band signals and detect onsets on each sub-band. Then final sub-band onsets are detected by taking weighted summation of sub-band onsets. For onset detection we followed similar approach in [14]. Fig. 3 depicts the graphical user interface (GUI) that we developed for onset detection. We then search equally spaced inter beat proportional intervals with the help of dynamic programming. Using this approach, we compute duration of smallest notes and then we segment the song into these inter-beat proportional signal frames. We called this segmentation as *Beat Space Segmentation*.

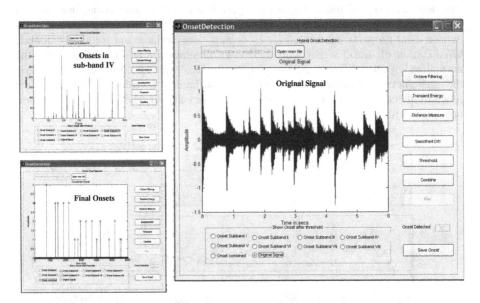

Fig. 3. GUI for onset detection

In speech processing, the sliding window technique is commonly used with two window type: hamming or rectangular. The window size varies from 20ms to 40ms. In Fig. 4 we have shown both hamming and rectangular windows of 20ms, 100ms and 200ms durations in time and frequency domains. Both hamming and rectangular windows operate as low pass filters. Hamming window has very high stop band attenuation than rectangular filter. The bandwidth of hamming window is also higher than it is of a rectangular window. However, bandwidth decreases with the length of the window (see Table in Fig. 4).

Unlike speech signals, music signals have wider bandwidth in nature. Therefore useful information in music spread beyond 10 kHz whereas in speech, useful information is well below 8 kHz. The bandwidths of both rectangular and hamming windows are significantly smaller for music signal analysis. Compared to rectangular window, hamming window has sharp stop band attenuation and suppresses useful information in the higher frequencies nearly by 3 fold over the rectangular window. In view of this, the rectangular window is better for music analysis. Simple implication of using the rectangular window is that it analyzes the signal frame as it is. Thus rectangular window is considered in the feature extraction process.

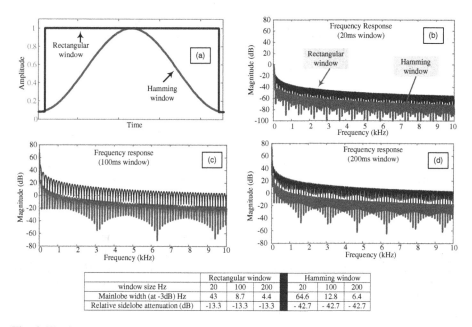

	Rectangular window			Hamming window		
window size Hz	20	100	200	20	100	200
Mainlobe width (at -3dB) Hz	43	8.7	4.4	64.6	12.8	6.4
Relative sidelobe attenuation (dB)	-13.3	-13.3	-13.3	- 42.7	- 42.7	- 42.7

Fig. 4. The frequency responses of hamming and rectangular windows when the window lengths are 20ms, 100ms and 200ms

4   Feature Analysis

When the signal is quasi-stationary, the signal prediction and feature stability are improved [2]. From the statistical analysis point of view, the feature variance within the class (intra class) is very low. For different classes (inter class) feature variance is very high. In addition, extracted feature coefficients have high un-correlation when the signal section is quasi-stationary. This can be investigated by looking into the diagonal matrix at singular value decomposition (SVD). Diagonal matrix consists of singular values. Higher singular values imply lower correlations among the coefficients of the feature vectors.

In order to analyze the features, we first extract the features from both fixed length (30ms) signal frames and proposed beat spaced signal frames using the data set described in section 5. Silence regions are removed from the music signals in the pre-processing.

4.1   Feature Analysis for Vocal Instrumental Boundary Detection

It is found in our previous experiments that the spectral domain features are better for characterizing both the instrumental and vocal music [5]. Sung vocal lines always follow the instrumental line such that both pitch and harmonic structure variations are also in octave scale. Thus we used "Octave Scale" instead of "Mel Scale" to calculate Cepstral coefficients to represent the music content. These coefficients are called Octave Scale Cepstral Coefficients (OSCC) as detailed in [5]. For feature analysis, we extract 20 OSCCs from both 30ms frames and beat space length frames. The average distances (*Avg Dis*) between feature vectors are computed according to Eq. (1), where n, V_i, and L are number of feature vectors, i^{th} feature vector and dimension of the feature vector respectively.

$$Avg\ Dis = \frac{2}{n*(n-1)}\sum_{i=1}^{n-1}\sum_{j=i}^{n}\left[norm\left|V_i - V_j\right|/L\right] \tag{1}$$

We model vocal and instrumental regions using Gaussian mixture models (GMMs) where each model consists of 64 Gaussians. We consider both pure vocal and instrumental mixed vocal regions as vocal region and pure instrumental region as instrumental region.

4.2 Feature Analysis for Chord Detection

Chord detection is important to identify the harmony event in the music. Here we extract the pitch class profile (PCP) features which are highly sensitive to fundamental frequencies (F0s) of the music note and less sensitive to timbre of the source of the note [11]. Calculation of PCP features for each chord is similar to the method described in [4]. Then we compare the distance between feature vectors extracted from same chord using Eq. (1)

For chord modeling, we consider 48 chords, each of 12 music chords belong to Major, Minor, Diminish and Augmented chord types. Each chord is then modeled using GMM which has 128 Gaussians in the model. In [5] these chord models are called single layer chord models.

5   Experiments

For the vocal and instrumental class feature analysis experiments (section 4.1), we use 120 popular English and Chinese songs sung by 12 artists; MLTR, Bryan Adams, Westlife, Shania Twain, Mariah Carey, Celine Dion, Huang Pingyuan, Wen Zheng, ADu, Liu Ruoying (Rane), Leung (Jasmine), and Li Qi . For music chord feature analysis, we constructed a chord data base which includes recorded chord samples from original instruments, synthetic instruments and chord extracted from English songs with the help of music sheets and listening tests. We have about 10 minutes of each chord sample spanning from octave C2 to B8.

All experimental data are sampled at 44.1 kHz with 16 bits per sample and mono format. Listening tests have been carried out to annotate vocal instrumental boundaries. Music signals are then framed into both beat space segments and fixed length segments to extract OSCC features. We carry out experiments; inter class and intra class feature distance measure, *Avg Dis(.)* in Eq. (1), to examine effectiveness of both beat space and fixed length segmentation for content representation. It can be seen in Fig. 5, the average intra class feature distance of vocal and instrumental regions are lower when OSCC features are computed from beat space segments than they are computed from 30ms segments. *Avg Dis(.)* is higher for inter class (Vocal - Inst) when features are extracted from beat space segmented frames.

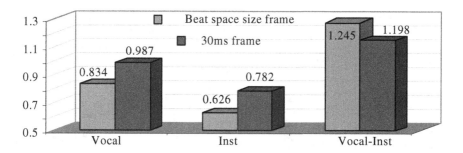

Fig. 5. Distance between both inter and intra class feature vectors

Singular value decomposition (SVD) is then applied to vocal and instrumental feature sets to find the correlation between octave scale cepstral coefficients. The plot of singular values in the diagonal matrices of SVD for both vocal and inst class feature vectors is shown in Fig. 6. Singular values are higher for features calculated from beat space frames than from fixed length frames. Thus we can conclude feature coefficients extracted from BSS are relatively lower correlated that the feature coefficients extracted from fixed length segments.

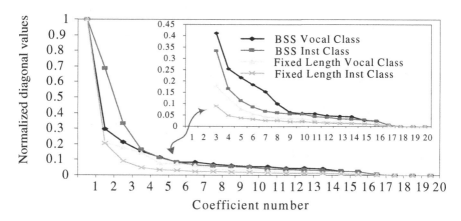

Fig. 6. Singular values in the diagonal matrix of SVD

Then we model vocal and instrumental region information using OSCC feature vectors and mixture of 64 Gaussians. In this experiment all the songs of each artist are used by cross validation where 5 songs of each artist are trained and test at each turn. We then compare the modeling effectiveness of vocal and instrumental region information with different frame sizes, beat space frames (X1.0), half beat space frames (X0.5) and fixed length frames (FIX Length). Fig. 7 depicts the frame level correct vocal and instrumental classification results. Compared to the average vocal and instrumental classification accuracy with fixed length signal frames, we managed to achieve 12% and 7% higher average classification accuracies with X1.0 and X0.5 beat space frames respectively.

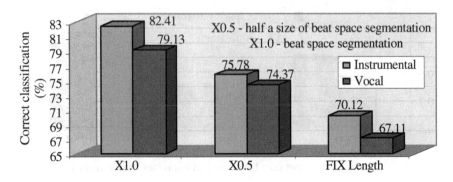

Fig. 7. Effect of classification accuracy with frame size

The results of the above experiments; inter class and intra class feature distance measure, singular value analysis and vocal instrumental content modeling accuracies, imply higher improvement of feature stability with beat space proportional frames than with fixed length signal frames. Thus signal sections within beat space segments are more stationary that the signal sections within fixed length segments.

Following experiments are focused on the analysis of signal frame size for music chord representation. Fig. 8(a), details the intra chord class average feature distance, *Avg Dis(.)*. It can be seen that *Avg Dis(.)* is lower when the frame size is beat space than it is fixed length (30ms). The average distance between chords (inter class) is 26.67% higher when feature vectors are extracted from beat space signal frames than they are extracted from fixed length frames. Fig. 8(b) shows the average distance between chord C and other chords.

We also compare the correct chord detection accuracies when they are modeled with Gaussian mixtures. It's found that 75.28% and 67.13% frame level correct chord classification accuracies are obtained with beat space frames and fixed length frames respectively.

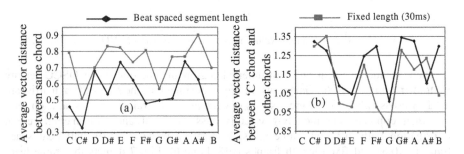

Fig. 8. (a): Average feature vector distance between the same chords. **(b):** Average feature vector distance between 'C' chords and other chords.

6   Conclusion

In this paper we compare the effectiveness of both beat space segmentation (BSS) and fixed length segmentation for characterizing and modeling music contents. Selected music contents for such analysis are vocal and instrumental region contents and music chords.

For vocal and instrumental contents, it is found that intra class average feature distances are lower with the features extracted from beat space signal segments than with the features extracted from fixed length frames. However inter class average feature distance is higher with the features extracted from beat space frames than with the feature extracted from fixed length frames. Low average distance between intra class feature vectors indicates the compactness of the feature vectors for that particular class. High average distance between features of inter classes implies the high discrimination of the features belong to different classes. Thus features extracted from beat space frames can effectively represent vocal and instrumental contents. Singular values of SVD study has also indicated that features extracted from beat space segments are lesser correlated than they are extracted from fixed length segments. Vocal and instrumental content modeling results highlight 12% accuracy improvement with beat space frames than with fixed length frames. For music chord characterization and modeling, we obtain more stable features with BSS than features with fixed length signal frames.

For music chord characterization and modeling, we obtain more stable features with BSS than with fixed length signal frames. Average chord modeling accuracy has also been improved by 8% with beat space frames compared with fixed length frames.

It can be concluded that music contents; vocal and instrumental contents and chords can more accurately be modeled using rhythm level signal segmentation (beat space segmentation) than using fixed length signal segmentation. We will continue our research in this direction to improve the accuracies of music content representation and modeling.

Acknowledgement

Authors thank Mr. Ardy Salim for his support in the development of onset detection GUI.

References

1. Goto, M.: An Audio-based Real-time Beat Tracking System for Music With or Without Drum-sounds. Journal of new Music Research 30(2), 159–171 (2001)
2. John, R.D., John, H.L., John, G.P.: Discrete-Time Processing of Speech Signals. IEEE Press, Los Alamitos (1999)
3. Kim, Y.E.: Singing Voice Analysis / Synthesis. PhD. Thesis, Massachusetts institute of Technology (September 2003)
4. Maddage, N.C., Xu, C.S., Kankanhalli, M.S., Shao, X.: Content-based Music Structure Analysis with the Applications to Music Semantic Understanding. In: ACM Multimedia Conference, New York (2004)

486 N.C. Maddage, M.S. Kankanhalli, and H. Li

5. Maddage, N.C., Li, H., Kankanhalli, M.S.: Music Structure based Vector Space Retrieval. In: Proc. ACM SIGIR Conference (August 2006)
6. Rossing, T.D., Moore, F.R., Wheeler, P.A.: Science of Sound, 3rd edn. Addison-Wesley, Reading (2001)
7. Rudiments and Theory of Music, The associated board of the royal schools of music, 14 Bedford Square, London, WC1B 3JG (1949)
8. Aucouturier, J.-J., Sandler, M.: Finding Repeated Patterns in Acoustic Musical Signals: Applications for Audio Thumbnailing. AES 22nd International Conference on Virtual, Synthetic and Entertainment Audio, Finland (2002)
9. Brown, J.C.: Calculation of a Constant Q Spectral Transform. Journal of Acoustic Society of America 89(1) (1991)
10. Jourdain, R.: Music, The Brain, and Ecstasy: How Music Captures Our Imagination. HarperCollins press (1997)
11. Yoshioka, T., et al.: Automatic Chord Transcription with Concurrent Recognition of Chord Symbols and Boundaries. In: Proc. of 5th International Conference of Music Information Retrieval (ISMIR) (2004)
12. Nwe, T.L., Wang, Y.: Automatic Detection of Vocal Segments in Popular Songs. In: Proc. of 5th International Conference of Music Information Retrieval (ISMIR) (2004)
13. Ellis, D.P.W., Poliner, G.E.: Identifying 'cover songs' with Chroma Features and Dynamic Programming Beat Tracking. In: ICASSP. Proc. International Conference on Acoustics, Speech, and Signal Processing (2006)
14. Duxburg, C., Sandler, M., Davies, M.: A Hybrid Approach to Musical Note Onset Detection. In: Proceedings of International Conference of Digital Audio Effects (DAFx), Hamburg, Germany (September 2002)
15. Wang, Y., et al.: LyricAlly: Automatic Synchronization of Acoustic Music Signals and Textual Lyrics. In: ACM Multimedia Conference, New York (2004)

Probabilistic Estimation of a Novel Music Emotion Model

Tien-Lin Wu and Shyh-Kang Jeng

Department of Electrical Engineering, National Taiwan University,
10617 Taipei, Taiwan
b90501064@ntu.edu.tw, skjeng@ew.ee.ntu.edu.tw

Abstract. An approach is proposed to estimate the emotional probability distribution of a novel music emotion model based on the updated Hevner's 8 emotion groups. Possible application includes browsing and mixing music with different emotion distributions. It is based on ground truths collected for 200 30-s clips (subdivided into 1200 segments further) chosen from soundtrack and labeled by 328 subjects online. Averagely, there are 28.2 valid emotional labeling events per clip, and constructing a probability distribution. Next, 88 musical features were extracted by 4 existing programs. The most discriminative 29 features were selected out by the pair-wise F-score comparison. The resultant 1200 segments were randomly separated into 600 training and 600 testing data, and input to SVM to estimate an 8-class probability distribution. They are finally evaluated by cosine, intersection, and quadratic similarity with the ground truth, where the quadratic metric achieves the best 87.3% ± 12.3% similarity.

Keywords: musical emotion, film music, probability distribution, SVM, similarity.

1 Introduction

This study tries to model the emotion most people perceived while listening to music. In general, there are two main approaches to study musical emotion: categorical and dimensional. Categorical approach treats emotion as distinct class from each other using descriptive terms. However, no standard taxonomy system exists. Hevner proposed [1] a checklist of 67 expressive terms and grouped them into 8 classes, including *dignified, sad, dreamy, serene, graceful, happy, exciting,* and *vigorous*. It exhausts user to reason all 67 terms, and the expressive terms often overlap semantically within class and a few of them have been out of date. In contrast, dimensional approach focuses mainly identifying emotions according to their positions on abstract dimensions, such as *valence, arousal,* and *potency* [2]. Investigators often gather data in such a continuous space but classify the data into discrete classes regardless of the semantic relationships between classes. It has very few expressive terms to describe the emotional content of music, and focuses more on the position in emotion space rather than the emotion description, although its low granularity is easier for getting high accuracies in classification problem.

S. Satoh, F. Nack, and M. Etoh (Eds.): MMM 2008, LNCS 4903, pp. 487–497, 2008.

Furthermore, the dimension *valence* is often subjective and its average over a group of people may be difficult to capture the perceived emotion.

Individual difference is obvious for a group of listeners, but as far as we know, no literature has ever modeled it. For subjects listening to the same music, if they report their perceived emotions individually using limited descriptive terms, we should obtain a distribution instead of a single label. In this paper, we call this kind of distribution as *Emotion Histogram* for each segment of music, and attempt to estimate it by learning it and its associated musical features using the probability estimation capability of the Support Vector Machine (SVM). The estimated emotion histograms are compared with the ground truth according to their similarities. The obtained similarities are then used to construct a new emotion space via the multi-dimensional scaling (MDS) technique.

The derived model can be applied when selecting music from an online music database like **AllMusic** [3], in which the 179 possible moods often confuse customers. Our musical emotion model also extracted essential descriptors and their frequencies of usage on the web, which is useful for future researches. Furthermore, terms can be visualized in our emotion space and their possible emotion distribution may help user to find songs fitting to their desired emotion categories more intuitively.

2   Proposed Methods

Three main procedures are addressed here: First, musical emotions are labeled by subjects to construct the ground truth. Then musical features are extracted and selected according to their discriminabilities. Finally, probability distribution of musical emotion is estimated by SVM through the selected musical features.

2.1   Subjective Emotion Labeling

We have constructed a database of ground truth for musical emotion classification, based on a comprehensive checklist, of descriptive terms derived in [4]. Figure 1 shows the musical emotion taxonomy obtained there and adopted in this research [4].

The emotion taxonomy adopted has a hierarchical lay-out of 8 main emotion classes, with 4 distinctly expressive terms for tagging and 1 representative categorical label included in each main class. Semantically, terms within each group have similar but distinct meaning and the meaning of neighboring groups vary in a cumulative way until reaching a contrast for groups in opposite positions. They were chosen from 1200 candidate terms (*abominable, accelerating,..., happy, hard,...,yearning, zealous*) based on mainly the Hevner's model and 9 other noted researches (including *Farnworth Paul, Lage Wedin, Russell James, Whissell Cynthia, David Huron, Alf Gabrielsson, Schubert Emery, Tao Li, and Patrik Juslin* [4]) mapped by synonymous searching from online dictionaries and their frequent linkages with 5 music-related terms (**audio, music, song, sound,** and **voice**) according to Google search outcomes. Final results are organized based on the semantics of the expressive terms and the simplified Hevner's model while retaining its semantic circle as much as possible.

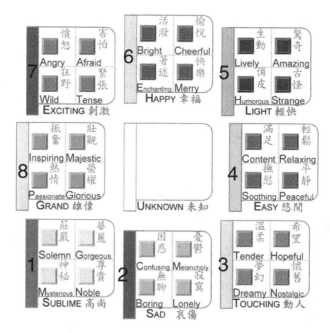

Fig. 1. Emotion Checklist

Music adds to the emotional quality of the film. There is some empirical evidence to support this: fast and loud music arouses, slow and soft music calms. Motion and emotion are often entwined [5]. In order to construct the music-eliciting emotion ground truth, the first author selected 30-s long segments (stereo-channel, wav format, sampling rate 44.1 kHz) from 200 soundtracks respectively, which are from all over the world and with extensive variation of genres (action, adventure, comedy, drama, fantasy, horror, mystery, romance, and thrillers). All segments are purely melodies without vocal cues.

Online tagging was implemented in this study. We designed the on-line tagging procedure carefully to eliminate the bias due to order-dependence and the inconsistency of re-evaluation of the same clips, as much as possible. The online tagging was conducted on our website. The subjects were asked to select a suitable emotional appraisal from a checklist shown in Fig. 1 for each of 10 random clips, which was typically a 5~10 minutes' task. While tagging, the subject can replay or stop a clip as they wish. For any clip, at most 3 tags among 32 choices (as Figure 1 shown) are permitted. The subjects may also enter any other expressive term if they can not find a suitable one from the given checklist. In addition, personal data for further research are also collected, including gender, birth year, location, interest, specialty, and handedness. In the end, 5645 valid music samples were collected by 328 people (44.8% male, and 55.2% female, whose ages are from 12 to 61, mostly located between 20~30, and in 6 different countries). The average number of participants in labeling each clip is 28.2, where the maximum and minimum numbers of labeling one clip are 59 and 16.

Figure 2 shows examples of the *emotion histogram* for 30-s excerpts of 4 soundtracks and their waveforms. The bars of the histogram correspond to relative frequencies (denoted as probability) from class 1 (**Sublime**) to class 8 (**Grand**). Take *King Kong* as an example, emotions tagged by subjects mostly are centered on **Exciting, Grand**, and **Sublime**. It reveals that the resultant emotion labeling forms a distribution rather than a single label, mainly due to individual difference. The peaks often appear in neighboring classes, which means that some semantic correlation exists between each class and it is inevitable to count them in.

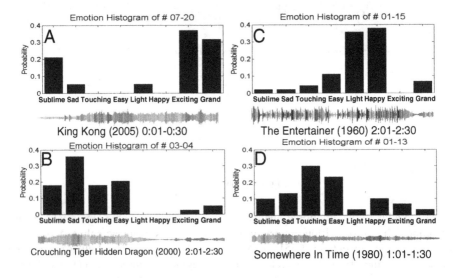

Fig. 2. Examples of Emotion Histogram

Among the 200 clips, about 44% soundtracks were familiar to the first author and they are also assumed well-known for many subjects. The possible confusion subjects may have between the emotion elicited by the music and the one elicited by the film itself. To check if the familiarity of a film may affect people's judgements due to its scenes or stories, we did a *t*-test to test if the difference of the means of the label probability is significant enough. We checked the probabilities for the 1st (primary, i.e. the majority), the 1st ~2nd, and the 1st~3rd labels, and the results are given in Table 1. From Table 1 we can see that for the primary label, we accept the null hypothesis that no difference exists, while if more labels are considered, familiarity of the films may affect people. Since we will input only the primary label information to SVM, explained later, we can assume that the familiarity of films does not matter much in our study. Further studies on the effect of previous exposure to specific soundtrack could be carried out in the future for each individual subject, and possibly be modeled by some popularity index from music database like **AllMusic**.

Table 1. *t*-test results of emotion cohesion between well-known and not-so-well-known music ($\alpha = 0.05$)

Label	1st	$1^{st} \sim 2^{nd}$	$1^{st} \sim 3^{rd}$
p-value	0.7646	1.9015	2.5396
result	*Accept*	*Reject*	*Reject*

2.2 Musical Feature Selection

In order to characterize the factors in musical signal quantitatively, we rely heavily upon the existing feature extraction methods. Four programs and algorithms once used in classifying emotion in music are utilized: MARSYAS (F1~F30) [6], PsySound (F31~F55) [7], Daubechies Wavelet Coefficient Histograms (F56~F76) [8], and Spectral Contrast (F77~F88) [9]. The resultant eighty-eight features are summarized in Table 2.

Table 2. Musical features used in this study

No.	Name	Description (number of feature)
1~6	Rhythmic Content	Relative amplitude of A0, A1 (2); Ratio of A0/A1 (1); Period of A0, A1 (2); Beat Strength (1)
7~15	Timbral Texture	Means and variances of spectral centroid, roll off, flux, zero-crossings over the texture window (8); Low energy (1)
16~25	Timbral Texture	Means and variances of the first 5 MFCC coefficients (10)
26~30	Pitch Content	Dominant pitch class (1); Octave range (1); Main pitch class (1); Main tonal interval (1); Pitch Strength (1)
31~35	Sound Level	Loudness in A-, B-, C-, and unweighted SPL (4); Loudness Level (1)
36~39	Spectral & Spatial	Power spectrum centroid (1); Level difference (1); Inter-channel cross correlation and its lag (2)
40~45	Harmony	Spectral and tonal dissonance (4); Pure and complex tonalness (2)
46	Texture	Multiplicity (1)
47~49	Tonality	24 Major and minor keys (1); Major/minor and its Correlation (2)
50~51	Loudness	Loudness (1); Short term max. loudness (1)
52~55	Timbre	Sharpness (2); Timbral width; Volume (1)
56+3k, k=0~6	DWCH1	Octave-band Daubechies Wavelet Coefficient Histogram mean (7)
57+3k, k=0~6	DWCH2	DWCH standard deviation (7)
58+3k, k=0~6	DWCH3	DWCH (sub-band Energy) (7)
77~82	SC1	Average of a percent of the lowest amplitude values in the spectrum of each sub-band (6)
83 ~ 88	SC2	Difference between the largest and lowest amplitude in each sub-band (6)

To understand the discriminability between each pair of classes (one-against-one), we exhaustively do binary classification with all features using SVM [10] and then construct the related F-score ranking. All combinations of pair-wise classes (e.g. class 1 is positive, and class 2 is negative) are calculated under the F-score criteria [11]. The results are then averaged to decide the global discrimination capability for the 8-class classification.

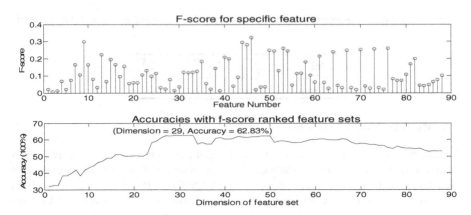

Fig. 3. (a) Averaged F-score of 88 features and (b) The relationship between 5-fold cross validation accuracy and dimension of used feature sets

To avoid the curse of dimensionality, the classifier model with the smallest dimension and the highest accuracy is pursued by greedily removing the worst feature sequentially. Figure 3 shows the averaged F-score of 88 features and the 8-class 5-fold cross validation accuracies with F-score-ranked feature sets. Among them the best 29 features are mostly related to timbre and pitch, which means that these two musical factors are dominant for discriminating 8 emotions in this study.

However, the F-score method does not provide mutual information among these 29 features, and sometimes they overlap meaningfully. For a better interpretation of our selection, factor analysis [12] is used to describe the covariance relationships among these 29 features in terms of a few underlying but unobservable factors. The result includes 6 factors explaining 90% variance. Among the first 3 factors explaining 78% variance, the first factor, interpreted as the **Timbre** (sub-band Energy) and **Dynamic** effect (DWCH3, and F35, F50~F54), has positive loadings on the first factor, and unimportant loadings on the other two factors. Similarly, the dependence on Tonalness features (F44~F46) is primarily on the second factor, interpreted as the **Pitch** and **Texture** effect.

2.3 SVM Probability Estimation

LIBSVM [10] is used to build a classifier, which not only predicts class but also estimates a posterior class probability (predicted histogram) by a sigmoid function [13], which is related to their probability distributions among the whole training set.

The label of a specific segment of ground truth should be extracted from its emotion probability distribution. However, SVM classifier currently does not allow input in probability format, and two or more labels make their distributed weights uneven. Further, if labels are with almost equal probabilities, using multi-labels does not ensure their almost identical probability distribution. A tradeoff is adopted and addressed here. As shown in Table 3, compared with the overall probabilities (prior) among all 200 emotion histograms in specific classes, the primary label with the maximal probability is used as the input for the multi-class classification, which fits the original emotion distribution well and is the most representative for each emotion class.

Table 3. Emotion distribution in ground truth (prior) and the adopted approach. (Unit: %)

Class	Sublime	Sad	Touching	Easy	Light	Happy	Exciting	Grand
Prior	12.92	11.61	16.38	18.28	9.38	12.50	7.52	11.40
Primary (1st)	14.00	12.50	14.50	22.50	7.92	10.50	7.50	10.50

Firstly, 29 features are scaled into -1 to 1 due to their variances in their respective feature ranges. Those 1200 samples are then divided into training and testing data by a random 50%-50% split. After searching for the best parameter for building a robust classifier among the grid space consisting of penalty C and RBF's kernel γ, we use these best parameters to create a model as a predictor for the rest 600 testing sets and generate 600 corresponding predicted histograms.

3 Evaluation Metrics

Semantically, eight emotions used here are correlated rather than mutually exclusive. The emotion histogram for a musical clip is constructed by counting the normalized frequency of each emotion component. The evaluation is made by comparing the similarities between the 600 predicted histograms generated by SVM and the 600 ground truths collected from subjects. Three metrics often used to compare color components between figures in image information retrieval are adopted here: cosine similarity, histogram intersection, quadratic (cross) similarity.

a. Cosine similarity
Here an emotion histogram is treated as a vector in an 8-dimensional emotion space. Thus $S_C(p,g)$ can measure if two vectors are close by the cosine value of the angle between the predicted histogram (h_p) and ground truth (h_g).

$$S_C(p,g) = \frac{h_p \cdot h_g}{|h_p \| h_g|} \tag{1}$$

b. Histogram intersection
It compares the corresponding emotion component (e from 1 to 8) between histograms. $S_I(p,g)$ chooses the intersection value and sums them all.

$$S_I(p,g) = \frac{\sum_{e=1}^{e=8} \min[h_p(e), h_g(e)]}{\min(|h_p|, |h_g|)} \tag{2}$$

c. Quadratic (Cross) similarity
The cross similarity metric $S_Q(p,g)$ considers the cross-correlation between emotion components based on their mutual perceptual similarity. It measure the weighted similarity between two histograms, which provides more desirable results "like-emotion"-only comparisons.

$$S_Q(p,g) = 1 - (h_p - h_g)^T A (h_p - h_g) \tag{3}$$

The set of all cross-correlation values are represented by a similarity matrix $\mathbf{A}$. The (i,j)-th element in the inter-emotion similarity matrix A is given by:

$$a(i, j) \equiv 1 - d(e_i, e_j) / d_{max}, \tag{4}$$

where $d(e_i, e_j)$ is the L_2 distance between emotion class i and j in the emotion similarity space, and the maximum distance (d_{max}) in this study is found to occur between 4 (**Touching**) and 7 (**Exciting**) as Fig. 4 shown.

A procedure to obtain the inter-emotion similarity matrix A is addressed in the following. The relationships between 32 expressive terms (or 8 emotions) in 5645 valid labeled data could be inspected by their sequential Pearson's correlation coefficients between their co-occurrences (any two sub-emotions appear simultaneously). A high correlation coefficient reveals that the corresponding terms are closer semantically. Take sub-emotion *Peaceful* for example, its closest sub-emotion is *Soothing* because $R_{Peaceful,Soothing} = 0.2476$ is the largest value among all 31 pair distances in *Peaceful*. Similarly, *Tense* is the farthest one where $R_{Peaceful,Tense} = -0.1242$. Therefore, these coefficients could be interpreted as their inter-emotion semantic similarities. Given similarity between any pair of terms (or emotions), the metric multi-dimensional scaling (MDS) technique [12] is adopted to

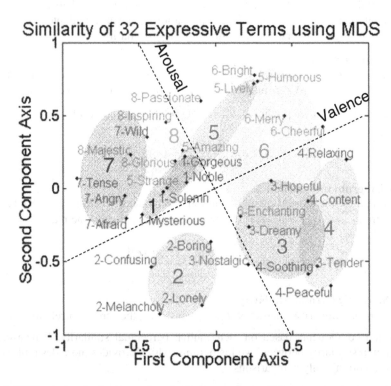

Fig. 4. MDS solution for inter-emotion similarity matrix A of 32 expressive terms and 8 main emotions with property vectors for *valence* and *arousal*

creates a configuration of terms minimizing a loss function called *stress*. It transforms the correlation similarity into a cross-product matrix and finds its eigen-decomposition providing a principal component analysis (PCA), then producing the inter-emotion similarity matrix A.

Figure 4 shows the MDS solution for inter-emotion similarity of 32 expressive terms and they are grouped according to their main emotions in the minimized colored ellipse. After comparing the positions of 4 basic emotions (*Happy*, *Angry*, *Sad*, and *Relaxing*) with their positions in Circumplex, we manually draw the *valence* and *arousal* axes orthogonally for its psychological interpretation and understanding.

4 Results and Discussions

Results of probability estimation and traditional classification are given here for discussions. Table 4 lists the final similarity results between 600 predicted histograms and corresponding ground truths which are evaluated by cosine, intersection, and quadratic similarity. From Table 4 we find that the quadratic similarity is better than the others, because it takes the cross-relation of emotions into considerations and weights the inter-emotion distance by pair-wise weighting factors.

Table 4. Similarity between 600 predicted histograms and ground truth

Metric	Similarity (Avg. ± Std.)
Cosine	0.732 ± 0.166
Intersection	0.583 ± 0.139
Quadratic	0.873 ± 0.123

Table 5 shows the confusion matrix generated by the musical emotion classifier using both the primary and secondary labels. The columns correspond to the ground truth and the rows to the predicted class. The percentages of correct classification lie in the diagonal. It points out that confusion often occurs between **Sad** and **Easy**, where they both have low arousal but only differ in *valence*. This may reflect the intrinsic subjectivity [14] in evaluating perceived emotion in music, where cause the ambiguity in tradition classification problem.

Table 5. Confusion matrix of the classification of music emotion by SVM (Unit: %)

	Sublime	Sad	Touching	Easy	Light	Happy	Exciting	Grand
Sublime	70.2	0.0	7.1	7.1	2.4	7.1	3.6	3.6
Sad	4.0	65.3	4.0	24.0	2.7	4.0	0.0	2.7
Touching	4.6	4.6	67.8	12.6	2.3	2.3	4.6	1.1
Easy	2.9	2.2	2.2	88.1	2.2	2.2	0.0	0.0
Light	12.5	0.0	0.0	8.3	68.8	6.3	0.0	0.0
Happy	3.2	3.2	3.2	1.6	1.6	85.7	0.0	1.6
Exciting	11.1	0.0	0.0	11.1	0.0	2.2	71.1	4.4
Grand	9.5	0.0	3.2	6.3	0.0	1.6	1.6	77.8

From these results, we can say that a semantic gap between musical emotion (similar to other human perceptions, understanding, expectation, and personal identity, etc.) and music signal features still exists, even though a probability model has been adopted. The semantic differentials between subjects also show that how common factors in our society is shared when people use emotion descriptive terms to interpret the abstract musical meaning.

In addition, the results also imply that "distribution" like the emotion histogram is a better representation than a single "classification label" when discussing emotional contents, due to the large variation in appreciation ability, cultural background, and musical training. Selection of expressive terms and graphical representation of emotion based on correlation similarity are also important for labeling and classification.

Another point is that in many other literatures [15] the rhythm structure is often a key factor for recognizing musical emotion, however, our features are dominated by timbral texture, dynamic and pitch. The reason could be that our rhythm features (Beat histogram) mainly focus on their relative amplitude and period of A0 and A1, which should reflect their musical level difference (regular-irregular; complex-firm; fast-slow). However, their uni-polar properties are hard to classify 8 subtle classes. In addition, the 5-s segment we used may be too short to get enough statistical information about their tempo distribution (measured in minutes in general), especially that they only have small number of notes.

Three phenomena can also be explored in our inter-emotion similarity results (Figure 4): emotional terms shown in different groups overlap semantically, and their distributions roughly fit the rotated *valence-arousal* model, i.e., the rotated Circumplex model widely used in psychology [16]. However, some aesthetical terms like *Noble, Solemn, Melancholy* never show in Circumplex model, and could possibly be separated to another dimension. Thus, this emotion similarity mostly matches the model built by Wedin [17] using multidimensional scaling to verbal response, where the three axes respectively are: (Energy vs. Relaxation), (Gaiety vs. Gloom), and (Trivial/Light vs. Serious/Solemn). Moreover, unlike the original order of Hevner's circular lay-out, our result also reveals that the order might be 1, 2, 3, 4, 6, 5, 8, and 7, and their mutual distances are not perceptually uniform.

5 Conclusion

The estimation of the probability distribution for a novel music emotion model built upon ground truths collected on line has been conducted, which has taken the individual difference of subjects into considerations. Four feature extraction algorithms have been applied and the feature combinations with the best discriminabilities were also determined. The estimated distributions have been evaluated by similarity and classification accuracy. The results seem to be satisfactory. The possible applications of this study include smoothly mixing music with different emotion distributions and selecting music intuitively with dedicated emotion categories. More refined experiments toward more accurate music emotion studies are planned and will start soon.

Acknowledgement

This paper is primarily based on the work supported by the National Science Council (NSC) under sub-project 2 of the program for promoting academic excellence of universities (phase II) (contract No. NSC95-2752-E002-006-PAE).

References

1. Hevner, K.: Experimental studies of the elements of expression in music. The American Journal of Psychology 48(2), 246–268 (1936)
2. Thayer, R.E.: The Biopsychology of Mood and Arousal. Oxford Univ. Press, Oxford (1989)
3. All Music, http://www.allmusic.com
4. Wu, T.L., Jeng, S.K.: Regrouping expressive terms for musical qualia. In: WOCMAT. Workshop on Computer Music and Audio Technology, Taiwan (2007), \url{http:// www2. ee.ntu.edu.tw/~b0501064/paper/WOCMAT_2007_TerryWu.pdf}
5. Meyer, L.: Emotion and meaning in music. University of Chicago Press, Chicago (1956)
6. Tzanetakis, G., Cook, P.: Musical genre classification of audio signals. IEEE Transactions on Speech and Audio Signal Processing 10(5) (2002)
7. Cabrera, D.: PsySound: A computer program for the psychoacoustical analysis of music. In: Proceedings of the Australian Acoustical Society Conference, Melbourne, pp. 47–54 (1999)
8. Li, T., Ogihara, M.: Toward intelligent music information retrieval. IEEE Transactions on Multimedia 8(3) (2006)
9. Lu, L., Liu, D., Zhang, H.-J.: Automatic mood detection and tracking of music audio signals. IEEE Transactions on Audio, Speech, and Language Processing 14(1), 5–18 (2006)
10. Chang, C.-C., Lin, C.-J.: LIBSVM: A library for support vector machines. (2001), Available: http://www.csie.ntu.edu.tw/ cjlin/libsvm
11. Chen, Y.-W., Lin, C.-J.: Combining SVMs with various feature selection strategies. In: Guyon, M.N.I., Gunn, S., Zadeh, L. (eds.) Feature extraction, Foundations and Applications (2005)
12. Johnson, R.A., Wichern, D.W.: Applied multivariate statistical analysis. Englewood Cliffs, NJ: Prentice-Hall (1982)
13. Wu, T.-F., Lin, C.-J., Weng, R.C.: Probability estimates for multi-class classification by pairwise coupling. Journal of Machine Learning Research 5, 975–1005 (2005)
14. Wu, T.L., Jeng, S.K.: Automatic emotion classification of musical segments. In: 9th International Conference on Music Perception and Cognition, Italy, University of Bologna, pp. 385–393 (2006)
15. Gabrielsson, A., Lindstrom, E.: The influence of musical structure on musical expression. In: Juslin, P.A., Sloboda, J.A. (eds.) Music and Emotion: Theory and research, pp. 223–248. Oxford University Press, New York (2001)
16. Russell, J.A.: A circumplex model of affect. Journal of Social Psychology 39, 1161–1178 (1980)
17. Wedin, L.: Multidimensional scaling of emotional expression in music. Svensk Tidskrift för Musikforskning 54, 115–131 (1972)

Acoustic OFDM: Embedding High Bit-Rate Data in Audio

Hosei Matsuoka, Yusuke Nakashima, Takeshi Yoshimura,
and Toshiro Kawahara

Research Laboratories, NTT DoCoMo, Inc.
3-5 Hikarinooka Yokosuka Kanagawa, Japan 239-8536
matsuoka@nttdocomo.co.jp

Abstract. This paper presents a method of aerial acoustic communication in which data is modulated using OFDM (Orthogonal Frequency Division Multiplexing) and embedded in regular audio material without significantly degrading the quality of the original sound. It can provide data transmission of several hundred bps, which is much higher than is possible with other audio data hiding tehcniques. The proposed method replaces the high frequency band of the audio signal with OFDM carriers, each of which is power-controlled according to the spectrum envelope of the original audio signal. The implemented system enables the transmission of short text messages from loudspeakers to mobile handheld devices at a distance of around 3m. This paper also provides the subjective assessment results of audio clips embedded with OFDM signal.

1 Introduction

Because of the increasing popularity of mobile handheld devices that offer high level audio functions, there is a strong possibility of using sound for data transmission from ordinary loudspeakers to the handheld devices. Although the data rates offered by sound are relatively low and the sound can be annoying, it enables no-cost solutions linking traditional media with mobile devices. For example, a commercial on TV or radio can transfer the URL of the company to user's mobile devices through the sound waves. No additional hardware infrastructure is necessary on both media and mobile devices.

However, existing acoustic communication methods that use data hiding techniques offer only very low data rates, less than 40bps. These methods take many seconds to transmit even a short message such as a simple URL or e-mail address. Higher data rates, from hundreds of bps to more than 1kbps, can be achieved by sending the modulated signal en clair, but the resulting sounds are noisy and often annoying. Ultrasound acoustic communication can achieve even higher data rates and is imperceptible to human ears, but ordinary low cost loudspeakers and microphones do not support ultrasound, which prevents the use of ordinary audio devices. Given these considerations, the goals of our work are:

- To transmit at data rates from hundreds of bps to 1kbps.
- To use the audible audio band so that ordinary low cost loudspeakers and microphones can be used.

S. Satoh, F. Nack, and M. Etoh (Eds.): MMM 2008, LNCS 4903, pp. 498–507, 2008.

– To embed information in pre-existing sound almost in a perceptually transparent fashion.

This paper proposes Acoustic OFDM; it satisfies the above requirements. Acoustic OFDM replaces the high frequency band of the audio signal with OFDM modulated data signal where each carrier is power-controlled according to the spectrum envelope of the original audio signal. In Section 2, we address the existing data hiding techniques for audio and their weakness in aerial acoustic communications. Section 3 describes the modulation and detection method of Acoustic OFDM. The implementation and performance measurements are described in Section 4. Section 5 concludes the paper.

2   Prior Works

Several audio data hiding techniques have been proposed in recent years. Most of them are designed for watermarks and so offer robustness to D/A-A/D conversion. When an audio source is transmitted as an analog signal across a clean analog line and re-sampled, the abolute signal magnitude and sample quantization change. However, acoustic communication over aerial links is more challenging, because when a signal is broadcast into the air and re-sampled with a microphone, the signal will be subjected to possibly unknown nonlinear modification resulting in phase change, amplitude change, echo, frequency drift, etc. Therefore, most existing data hiding techniques cannot be applied to aerial acoustic communications. The typical data hiding techniques for audio and their problems are described below.

Echo Hiding
Motivated by the fact that the HAS (Human Auditory System) cannot distinguish an echo from the original when delay and amplitude of the echo are appropriately controlled, this method employs two different delay times to carry binary information[1]. Unfortunately, the signal experiences damping oscillation in the loudspeaker and environmental reflection both of which result in a variety of echoes which lowers the data rate; its actual data rate becomes insufficient for practical applications.

Phase Coding
To a certain extent, modifications of the phase of a signal cannot be perceived by the HAS. By taking advantage of this fact, data can be embedded by altering the phase in a predefined manner. This can be done by using all-pass filters to modify the phase without changing the magnitude response[2]. Similar to echo hiding, this method does not suit aerial communications, because the loudspeakers used and the aerial links may cause nonlinear phase distortion which complicates signal detection and lowers the overall data rate.

Spread Spectrum
The basic spread spectrum technique is designed to encode information by spreading the signal across a wide frequency spectrum[3]. By using the masking

effect, a faint sound becomes inaudible if overlaid by a louder sound, a spread signal can be imperceptibly embedded in audio[4][5]. This technique spreads the signal by multiplying it by a PN (Pseudo-random Noise) code, which is usually a maximum length sequence called M-sequence. The decoder can retrieve the embedded information by despreading the received signal with the PN code.

The spread spectrum technique is more robust to aerial communication than the other two techniques described above. However, the spreading rate has to be high in order to offset the various distortion and noise sources common in aerial links, consequently the data transmission rate is less than 40bps. As described above, existing data hiding techniques fall well short of being able to transmit a short message, such as a simple URL or e-mail address, in a reasonable time. Different approaches for aerial communications have been proposed. They use the same modulation techniques as radio communications such as ASK and FSK[6][7]. While these methods can provide high data rates, more than hundreds of bps, their sound can be annoying and they cannot be transmitted in parallel with pre-existing sounds such as voice or music. Acoustic OFDM, proposed in this paper, offers data rates more than hundreds of bps and can coexist with pre-existing sound streams. The method uses the audible audio band and so is supported by ordinary audio devices.

3 Acoustic OFDM

Acoustic OFDM employs OFDM as its modulation shceme. OFDM is a multi-carrier modulation method that distributes the data over a large number of narrow frequency carriers. By selecting a special set of orthogonal carrier frequencies, high spectral efficiency is obtained[8]. We show in this section the basic scheme of OFDM, then detail Acoustic OFDM. One of the main characteristics of OFDM is flat fading of the individual carrier. Conventional single carrier transmission systems suffer spectrum distortion due to frequency selective fading. In multi-carrier transmission systems, however, the individual carrier experiences flat fading as depicted in Fig. 1, since each carrier has a narrow bandwidth. This simplifies the equalization process and improves the signal detection accuracy.

The second key principle is the introduction of a GI (Guard Interval) to minimize inter-frame interference under multi-path conditions[9]. Each OFDM frame has a GI and a data symbol. The GI, a copy of the last part of the data symbol, preserves the orthogonality of carriers and the independence of subsequent OFDM frames. Without the GI, the delayed signals resulting from the multi-path waves would interfere with adjacent OFDM data symbols. This implies that GI duration is simply selected to be larger than the maximum excess delay of the multi-path channel. In aerial acoustic communications, GI duration is somewhat larger than the maximum excess delay due to the presence of the damping oscillation of the loudspeaker and the delayed waves created by environmental reflection.

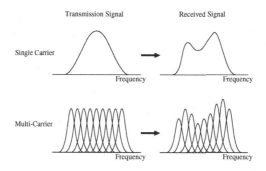

Fig. 1. Frequency Selective Fading

We apply this OFDM modulation to sound waves in consideration of audio quality for human ears. Next, we describe each component of Acoustic OFDM.

3.1 Spectrum Envelope

One of the main advances of Acoustic OFDM is that it controls the power of the carriers to mimic the spectrum envelope of the original audio stream. Fig.2 shows the encode step of the Acoustic OFDM signal in the frequency domain. First, the high frequency band of the original audio is eliminated by a low-pass filter (LPF). Next, an OFDM modulated signal is generated in the equivalent high frequency band where each carrier is modulated with PSK, and each carrier is power-controlled to match the frequency spectrum of the original audio signal. The low-band audio signal and the power-controlled OFDM signal are then combined. The resulting synthetic audio signal can then be played back by conventional loudspeakers. The sound of the native OFDM modulated signal is simply noisy just like a White Gaussian Noise. However, after power modification, the OFDM signal sounds similar to the high-band signal of the original audio, so the OFDM signal is not obtrusive or annoying.

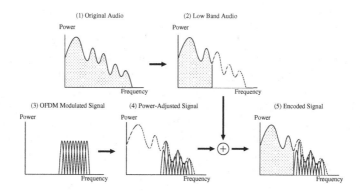

Fig. 2. Acoustic OFDM Encoding

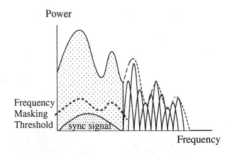

Fig. 3. Frame Synchronization Signal

3.2 Frame Synchronization

Frame synchronization is essential if the receiver is to identify the start of the OFDM frame. Acoustic OFDM embeds a synchronization signal in the low-band audio signal in the same way as the Spread Spectrum data hiding technique. The signal is spread by an M-sequence code and the spread signal is embedded below the frequency masking threshold of the low-band audio as shown in Fig3. M-sequences have good autocorrelation properties where the autocorrelation function has peaks equal to 1 at 0, N, 2N (approximately 1/N elsewhere). Because of these periodic peaks, the M-sequence is self-clocking, thus the receiver can easily identify the start of the OFDM frame. The frequency masking threshold is calculated based on the psycho-acoustic model[10]. The M-sequence code signal is power-adjusted below the masking threshold, and embedded in the low-band audio signal. At the receiver, the low-band audio signal is de-spread using the same M-sequence code, and the peak point is detected as the OFDM frame start point.

3.3 Modulation and Demodulation

Each OFDM carrier is modulated and demodulated with D-BPSK (Differential Binary Phase Shift Keying) because it requires no complicated carrier recovery circuit as does coherent detection at the receiver. For each carrier, the differential phase from the previous symbol is modulated by the binary state of the input signal. Therefore, the phase is not continuous at the boundary of OFDM frames. This discontinuity causes sidelobe leakage over a wide bandwidth which is readily perceptible to human ears. Moreover, a radical phase change at the boundary of OFDM frames also degrades the quality of audio. Windowing is a well-known technique that can reduce this sidelobe leakage. Since the applied window must not influence the signal during its effective data period, the additional cyclic prefix is inserted to the boundary between data symbol and GI, then overlap-added as shown in Fig.4.

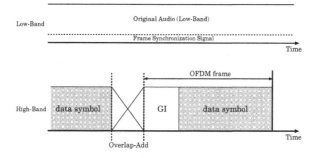

Fig. 4. Windowing

3.4 Error Recovery

Applications which transmit text data require reliable delivery with virtually no tolerance of bit errors. Since some bit errors are unavoidable on aerial acoustic links, it is essential to implement an error recovery scheme. FEC (Forward Error Correction) is an effective error recovery method that works without any feedback channel. Acoustic OFDM employs convolution codes which have good error recovery performance and work best if the errors of the incoming data are random. Therefore, to randomize the bit errors of the received data sequence, the transmission data is interleaved both frequency and time. At the receiver, the received data sequence is de-interleaved and applied to the soft-decision Viterbi decoding. The decoding in Acoustic OFDM uses

$$\lambda(1) = Re[z_n \cdot z_{n-1}]$$

$$\lambda(-1) = -Re[z_n \cdot z_{n-1}]$$

as a branch metric, where zn is a complex value x+jy that indicates an amplitude of the carrier as $(x^2 + y^2)^{0.5}$ and an arbitrary phase of the carrier as $tan^{-1}(x/y)$. The path metric is the sum of branch metrics along the candidate sequence. The most likely path which has the maximum path metric is then determined.

4 Implementation and Performance

Acoustic OFDM system can be all implemented as software because there is no need for additional hardware modules as described in the introduction. We implemented the Acoustic OFDM encoder for PC and the decoder for mobile handheld devices with Windows Mobile 5.0. Table 1 shows the detail parameters of the implemented system. Using wide frequency for OFDM signal improves data transmission performance, but degrades the quality of original audio. For this reason, the OFDM signal band is set around 6-8kHz. There are 36 OFDM carriers in this band. Since some carriers might not have enough power to transmit data, the minimum carrier power is set to the -65dB from the maximum power of the original audio signal. The carrier in which the power is lower than the minimum carrier power is power-adjusted to the minimum carrier power.

The transmission data is divided into some fixed-length data segments which are called data frames. A single data frame is composed of the code length 1116 bits (36 carrier x 31 time slot). Given the coding rate of 1/3, the effective information is 45 bytes. A single data frame can be transmitted in 1.5 seconds, so the data transmission rate is approximately 240 bps. We use this implemented system for subjective quality testing and performance measurements described below.

Table 1. Acoustic OFDM System Parameters

Sampling Frequency	44.1 kHz
OFDM Signal Band	6400 - 8000 Hz
OFDM Symbol Length	1024 samples (23ms)
Guard Interval	800 samples (18ms)
Number of OFDM Carriers	36
Chip Rate of Frame Sync	2756 cps
Coding Rate	1/3
Code Length	1116

4.1 Subjective Quality Test

Subjective listening tests were performed in order to evaluate the impact of Acoustic OFDM encoding. The MUSHRA method was used for the subjective quality test of audio clips in which OFDM signal is embedded. This is a method which compares audio clips with a hidden reference and bandwidth limited anchor signals. It has been recommended at the ITU-R under the name BS.1534[11].

For this test, we chose two band-limited anchor signals; one is limited to 3.5kHz and the other is limited to 7.0kHz. We also use MP3 encoded signal just for reference. The encoding bit rate is set to 128kbps for monaural signal. We tested two configurations; one is Acoustic OFDM encoded signal, and the other is Flat OFDM encoded signal where the OFDM signal is added in the same way as Acoustic OFDM but the power-controlling for the spectrum enveleop is not performed. The average OFDM signal power is same as that of the Acoustic OFDM encoding.

For each configuration and reference, 4 audio clips described below are tested. "Rock music" has strong power in OFDM signal band while the "pop music" and "jazz music" has moderate power and "speech only" has little power.

1. rock music
2. pop music
3. jazz music
4. speech only

Fig.5 shows the results obtained for each tested configuration and audio clip. The different configurations and audio clips are spread along the X-axis while the quality scale is along the Y-axis. The average over the 18 listeners and the confidence interval at 95% are displayed.

As expected, the hidden references are rated the highest with a small confidence interval. It is noticeable that the scores given to the Acoustic OFDM configuration considerably depend on the audio clips. For "rock music", the score is relatively high and almost same as that of the MP3 encoding configuration. For "pop music" and "jazz music", the scores are lower than the scores of MP3 encoding configuration, but still higher than the scores of the anchors. The score of "speech only" is low and almost same as the score of the 3.5kHz band-limited anchor. It is because the OFDM signal is embedded almost without power-adjusting to the spectrum envelope of the original audio. For the same reason, the Flat OFDM encoding configuration has the low scores for all the audio clips.

To conclude, we can say that on the average, the quality of Acoustic OFDM encoded signal is not significantly degraded for music materials which has a certain power in OFDM signal band.

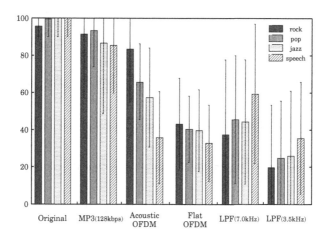

Fig. 5. Subjective Assessment Results

4.2   Aerial Transmission Performance

We tested the Acoustic OFDM performance on the implemented system. In this experiments, we used an ordinary low-cost loudspeaker and microphone whose frequency responces ran from 100Hz to more than 10kHz. We evaluated transmission distance with the same Acoustic OFDM encoded audio clips as used in the subjective quality testing.

Fig.6 shows the relation between the transmission distance and BER(Bit Error Rate). For "speech only", BER becomes high even from short transmission

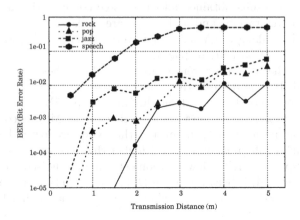

Fig. 6. BER(Bit Error Rate)

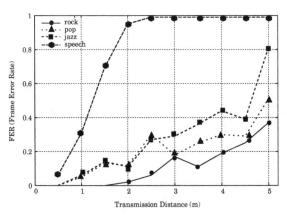

Fig. 7. FER(Frame Error Rate)

distance, while the other audio clips have moderate BER around 10^{-2} up to the transmission distance of 4m. Rock music clip has the smallest BER because it has strong power in the OFDM signal band.

Fig.7 shows the relation between the transmission distance and FER(Frame Error Rate). The frame is a data block which is a unit of error-recovery coding. In this system, a data block has code length of 1116 bits as described in Table 1. In a frame, even if only one bit is not correctly recovered, the frame is discarded.

Except for "speech only", the FER is reasonable up to around 3m, in order to transmit the data frame within a few decode trial at the receiver. From this results, the data transmission is possible at a transmission distance of around 3m when embedding data in music which has a certain power in the OFDM signal band.

5   Conclusions

In this paper, we proposed Acoustic OFDM and implemented a system. It achieves data transmission of about 240 bps simultaneously with the playback of conventional audio streams when the audio streams have a certain power in high frequency band such like rock, pop and jazz music. By adjusting the power of the OFDM carriers so that they match the spectrum envelope of the high-band component of the audio signal, the modulated data signal does not degrade the original audio quality significantly. However, for audio streams which have speech only, the quality is degraded. For that case, it might be better that BGM is added to the speech before Acoustic OFDM encoding.

The system enables applications to transmit short messages to mobile hand-held devices over aerial audio links. A typical application is embedding an URL into the audio stream of a TV or radio program. Users of mobile handsets can access the web-site via the URL without inputting the URL manually. Experiments showed that the data transmission region is acceptable for TV viewing area in the home. Since many audio devices are located in public places, aerial acoustic communication, realized by Acoustic OFDM, is considered to be an effective way of establishing ubiquitous communications.

References

1. Gruhl, D., Lu, A., Bender, W.: Echo Hiding. Information Hiding 1996, 295–315 (1996)
2. Yardimci, Y., Cetin, A.E., Ansari, R.: Data hiding in speech using phase coding. In: Eurospeech 1997, pp. 1679–1682 (September 1997)
3. Pickholtz, R.L., Schilling, D.L., Milstein, L.B.: Theory of Spread-Spectrum Communications - A Tutorial. IEEE Transactions on Communications COM-30, 855–884 (1982)
4. Boney, L., Tewfik, A.H., Hamdy, K.N.: Digital Watermarks for Audio Signals. IEEE Intl. Conf. on Multimedia Computing and Systems, 473–480 (March 1996)
5. Cox, I.J.: Spread Spectrum Watermark for Embedded Signalling. In: United States Patent 5,848,155 (December 1998)
6. Lopes, C.V., Aguiar, P.M.Q.: Aerial Acoustic Communications. IEEE Workshop on Applications of Signal Processing to Audio and Acoustics (2001)
7. Gerasimov, V., Bender, W.: Things that talk: using sound for device-to-device and device-to-human communication. In: IBM Systems Journal (2000)
8. Weinstein, S.B., Ebert, P.M.: Data Transmission by Frequency-Division Multiplexing Using the Discrete Fourier Transform. IEEE Transactions on Communications COM-19, 628–634 (1971)
9. Speth, M., et al.: Optimum Receiver Design for Wireless Broadband Systems Using OFDM-Part I. IEEE Transactions on Communications 47, 1668–1677 (1999)
10. Johnston, J.: Transform Coding of Audio Signals Using Perceptual Noise Criteria. IEEE Journal on Selected Areas in Communication 6, 314–323 (1988)
11. ITU-R Recommendation BS.1534. In: Method for the subjective assessment of intermediate quality level of coding systems (2001)

Author Index

Abe, Tsutomu   369
Aßfalg, Johannes   123
Ahlers, Dirk   101
Aizawa, Kiyoharu   466
Akiyama, Yasushi   165
Aoki, Masaki   210
Ariki, Yasuo   210

Baba, Takayuki   90
Babaguchi, Noboru   144, 253
Bailer, Werner   80
Birchfield, David   230
Boll, Susanne   101
Böszörmenyi, Laszlo   265
Boucher, Alain   307
Brémond, François   307

Chang, Wei-Lun   186
Chen, Bing-Yu   277
Chen, Chin-Han   358
Cheng, Jian   425
Chevallet, Jean-Pierre   220, 456
Chiang, Chen-Kuo   329
Chiang, Yueh-Hsuan   186
Chin, Tat-Jun   220
Chinomi, Kenta   144
Chu, Wei-Ta   186
Chua, Tat-Seng   13
Chuang, Yung-Yu   358
Coutrix, Celine   220
Cuenca, P.   413

de Silva, Gamhewage C.   466
Deliège, François   198

Fan, Jianping   1, 45
Fernando, W.A.C.   413
Foong, Kelvin   436
Fukuhara, Takahiro   380

Gao, Yuli   1, 45
Goh, Hanlin   456
Gu, Zhiwei   24

Hosaka, Kazuhisa   380
Hou, Z.   113

Hsu, Ping   277
Hua, Xian-Sheng   24, 175
Huang, Po-Chung   186
Huang, Shih-Chia   391, 402
Huang, Szu-Hao   70
Huang, Wei-Jia   186
Hung, Yi-Ping   186

Ide, Ichiro   287
Ito, Yoshimichi   144
Iyoda, Tetsuo   369

Jeng, Shyh-Kang   358, 487
Jin, Huan   230
Jin, Yohan   318
Jung, Ho-Ryong   35
Jung, Moon-Ryul   35, 348

Kameda, Yoshinari   134
Kankanhalli, Mohan S.   477
Kawahara, Toshiro   498
Kiya, Hitoshi   380
Kobayashi, Tomoyuki   134
Kriegel, Hans-Peter   123, 155
Kröger, Peer   123
Kunath, Peter   123, 155
Kuo, Sy-Yen   391, 402
Kurihara, Yousuke   253

Lai, Shang-Hong   70, 329, 338
Le, Diem Thi Hoang   456
Le, Thi-Lan   307
Lee, Felix   80
Lee, Weiping   436
Li, Haizhou   477
Li, Jintao   242
Lim, Joo-Hwee   220, 456
Liu, Rujie   90
Lu, Hanqing   425
Luo, Hangzai   1, 45

Ma, Songde   425
Maddage, Namunu C.   477
Martínez, J.L.   413
Masumoto, Daiki   90

Matsuoka, Hosei   498
Mei, Tao   24, 175
Miyahara, Masanori   210
Murase, Hiroshi   287

Na, Kyung-Gun   348
Nagata, Shigemi   90
Nakashima, Yusuke   498
Neo, Shi-Yong   13
Nigay, Laurence   220
Nitta, Naoko   144, 253

Ogawa, Akira   287
Ohta, Yuichi   134
Ong, S.H.   436
Onuki, Hiroko   369
Oore, Sageev   165

Pan, Wei-Hau   329, 338
Pawar, Manoj M.   446
Pedersen, Torben Bach   198
Peng, Wei-Ting   186
Prabhakaran, Balakrishnan   318, 446
Pradhan, Gaurav N.   446
Pryakhin, Alexey   123, 155

Qian, Gang   230
Qiu, Xianjie   242
Quiles, F.   413

Renz, Matthias   123

Sakamoto, Shoji   369
Satoh, Shin'ichi   1, 45
Schöffmann, Klaus   265
Schubert, Matthias   155
Shi, Meng   369
Shingu, Jun   369
Sun, Li-Feng   175

Takahashi, Tomokazu   287
Takiguchi, Tetsuya   210
Tang, Jinhui   24
Tang, W.   113
Thallinger, Georg   80
Than, N.L.   113
Thonnat, Monique   307
Tian, Qi   13
Tokai, Kiwame   369

Uchihashi, Shingo   369
Uehara, Yusuke   90

Wang, Kongqiao   58
Wang, Rongrong   242
Wang, Wenzhong   242
Wang, Yuehong   90
Wang, Zhaoqi   242
Weerakkody, W.A.R.J.   413
Wei, Shou-Der   338
Weng, Ming-Fang   358
Wu, Tien-Lin   487
Wu, Xiuqing   24

Xiong, Wei   436
Xu, Lei   58

Yamasaki, Toshihiko   466
Yanai, Keiji   297
Yang, Bo   175
Yang, Shi-Qiang   175
Yau, W.Y.   113
Yoshimura, Takeshi   498
You, Yilun   220

Zeng, Hui-Chi   70
Zhang, Kang   446
Zhang, Xiaoyu   425
Zheng, Yan-Tao   13

Lecture Notes in Computer Science

Sublibrary 3: Information Systems and Application, incl. Internet/Web and HCI

For information about Vols. 1– 4519
please contact your bookseller or Springer

Vol. 4903: S. Satoh, F. Nack, M. Etoh (Eds.), Advances in Multimedia Modeling. XIX, 510 pages. 2008.

Vol. 4882: T. Janowski, H. Mohanty (Eds.), Distributed Computing and Internet Technology. XIII, 346 pages. 2007.

Vol. 4881: H. Yin, P. Tino, E. Corchado, W. Byrne, X. Yao (Eds.), Intelligent Data Engineering and Automated Learning - IDEAL 2007. XX, 1174 pages. 2007.

Vol. 4877: C. Thanos, F. Borri, L. Candela (Eds.), Digital Libraries: Research and Development. XII, 350 pages. 2007.

Vol. 4872: D. Mery, L. Rueda (Eds.), Advances in Image and Video Technology. XXI, 961 pages. 2007.

Vol. 4871: M. Cavazza, S. Donikian (Eds.), Virtual Storytelling. XIII, 219 pages. 2007.

Vol. 4858: X. Deng, F.C. Graham (Eds.), Internet and Network Economics. XVI, 598 pages. 2007.

Vol. 4857: J.M. Ware, G.E. Taylor (Eds.), Web and Wireless Geographical Information Systems. XI, 293 pages. 2007.

Vol. 4853: F. Fonseca, M.A. Rodríguez, S. Levashkin (Eds.), GeoSpatial Semantics. X, 289 pages. 2007.

Vol. 4836: H. Ichikawa, W.-D. Cho, I. Satoh, H.Y. Youn (Eds.), Ubiquitous Computing Systems. XIII, 307 pages. 2007.

Vol. 4832: M. Weske, M.-S. Hacid, C. Godart (Eds.), Web Information Systems Engineering – WISE 2007 Workshops. XV, 518 pages. 2007.

Vol. 4831: B. Benatallah, F. Casati, D. Georgakopoulos, C. Bartolini, W. Sadiq, C. Godart (Eds.), Web Information Systems Engineering – WISE 2007. XVI, 675 pages. 2007.

Vol. 4825: K. Aberer, K.-S. Choi, N. Noy, D. Allemang, K.-I. Lee, L. Nixon, J. Golbeck, P. Mika, D. Maynard, R. Mizoguchi, G. Schreiber, P. Cudré-Mauroux (Eds.), The Semantic Web. XXVII, 973 pages. 2007.

Vol. 4822: D.H.-L. Goh, T.H. Cao, I.T. Sølvberg, E. Rasmussen (Eds.), Asian Digital Libraries. XVII, 519 pages. 2007.

Vol. 4816: B. Falcidieno, M. Spagnuolo, Y. Avrithis, I. Kompatsiaris, P. Buitelaar (Eds.), Semantic Multimedia. XII, 306 pages. 2007.

Vol. 4813: I. Oakley, S.A. Brewster (Eds.), Haptic and Audio Interaction Design. XIV, 145 pages. 2007.

Vol. 4810: H.H.-S. Ip, O.C. Au, H. Leung, M.-T. Sun, W.-Y. Ma, S.-M. Hu (Eds.), Advances in Multimedia Information Processing – PCM 2007. XXI, 834 pages. 2007.

Vol. 4809: M.K. Denko, C.-s. Shih, K.-C. Li, S.-L. Tsao, Q.-A. Zeng, S.H. Park, Y.-B. Ko, S.-H. Hung, J.H. Park (Eds.), Emerging Directions in Embedded and Ubiquitous Computing. XXXV, 823 pages. 2007.

Vol. 4808: T.-W. Kuo, E. Sha, M. Guo, L.T. Yang, Z. Shao (Eds.), Embedded and Ubiquitous Computing. XXI, 769 pages. 2007.

Vol. 4806: R. Meersman, Z. Tari, P. Herrero (Eds.), On the Move to Meaningful Internet Systems 2007: OTM 2007 Workshops, Part II. XXXIV, 611 pages. 2007.

Vol. 4805: R. Meersman, Z. Tari, P. Herrero (Eds.), On the Move to Meaningful Internet Systems 2007: OTM 2007 Workshops, Part I. XXXIV, 757 pages. 2007.

Vol. 4804: R. Meersman, Z. Tari (Eds.), On the Move to Meaningful Internet Systems 2007: CoopIS, DOA, ODBASE, GADA, and IS, Part II. XXIX, 683 pages. 2007.

Vol. 4803: R. Meersman, Z. Tari (Eds.), On the Move to Meaningful Internet Systems 2007: CoopIS, DOA, ODBASE, GADA, and IS, Part I. XXIX, 1173 pages. 2007.

Vol. 4802: J.-L. Hainaut, E.A. Rundensteiner, M. Kirchberg, M. Bertolotto, M. Brochhausen, Y.-P.P. Chen, S.S.-S. Cherfi, M. Doerr, H. Han, S. Hartmann, J. Parsons, G. Poels, C. Rolland, J. Trujillo, E. Yu, E. Zimányie (Eds.), Advances in Conceptual Modeling – Foundations and Applications. XIX, 420 pages. 2007.

Vol. 4801: C. Parent, K.-D. Schewe, V.C. Storey, B. Thalheim (Eds.), Conceptual Modeling - ER 2007. XVI, 616 pages. 2007.

Vol. 4797: M. Arenas, M.I. Schwartzbach (Eds.), Database Programming Languages. VIII, 261 pages. 2007.

Vol. 4796: M. Lew, N. Sebe, T.S. Huang, E.M. Bakker (Eds.), Human–Computer Interaction. X, 157 pages. 2007.

Vol. 4794: B. Schiele, A.K. Dey, H. Gellersen, B. de Ruyter, M. Tscheligi, R. Wichert, E. Aarts, A. Buchmann (Eds.), Ambient Intelligence. XV, 375 pages. 2007.

Vol. 4777: S. Bhalla (Ed.), Databases in Networked Information Systems. X, 329 pages. 2007.

Vol. 4761: R. Obermaisser, Y. Nah, P. Puschner, F.J. Rammig (Eds.), Software Technologies for Embedded and Ubiquitous Systems. XIV, 563 pages. 2007.

Vol. 4747: S. Džeroski, J. Struyf (Eds.), Knowledge Discovery in Inductive Databases. X, 301 pages. 2007.

Vol. 4744: Y. de Kort, W. IJsselsteijn, C. Midden, B. Eggen, B.J. Fogg (Eds.), Persuasive Technology. XIV, 316 pages. 2007.

Vol. 4740: L. Ma, M. Rauterberg, R. Nakatsu (Eds.), Entertainment Computing – ICEC 2007. XXX, 480 pages. 2007.

Vol. 4730: C. Peters, P. Clough, F.C. Gey, J. Karlgren, B. Magnini, D.W. Oard, M. de Rijke, M. Stempfhuber (Eds.), Evaluation of Multilingual and Multi-modal Information Retrieval. XXIV, 998 pages. 2007.

Vol. 4723: M. R. Berthold, J. Shawe-Taylor, N. Lavrač (Eds.), Advances in Intelligent Data Analysis VII. XIV, 380 pages. 2007.

Vol. 4721: W. Jonker, M. Petković (Eds.), Secure Data Management. X, 213 pages. 2007.

Vol. 4718: J. Hightower, B. Schiele, T. Strang (Eds.), Location- and Context-Awareness. X, 297 pages. 2007.

Vol. 4717: J. Krumm, G.D. Abowd, A. Seneviratne, T. Strang (Eds.), UbiComp 2007: Ubiquitous Computing. XIX, 520 pages. 2007.

Vol. 4715: J.M. Haake, S.F. Ochoa, A. Cechich (Eds.), Groupware: Design, Implementation, and Use. XIII, 355 pages. 2007.

Vol. 4714: G. Alonso, P. Dadam, M. Rosemann (Eds.), Business Process Management. XIII, 418 pages. 2007.

Vol. 4704: D. Barbosa, A. Bonifati, Z. Bellahsène, E. Hunt, R. Unland (Eds.), Database and XML Technologies. X, 141 pages. 2007.

Vol. 4690: Y. Ioannidis, B. Novikov, B. Rachev (Eds.), Advances in Databases and Information Systems. XIII, 377 pages. 2007.

Vol. 4675: L. Kovács, N. Fuhr, C. Meghini (Eds.), Research and Advanced Technology for Digital Libraries. XVII, 585 pages. 2007.

Vol. 4674: Y. Luo (Ed.), Cooperative Design, Visualization, and Engineering. XIII, 431 pages. 2007.

Vol. 4663: C. Baranauskas, P. Palanque, J. Abascal, S.D.J. Barbosa (Eds.), Human-Computer Interaction – INTERACT 2007, Part II. XXXIII, 735 pages. 2007.

Vol. 4662: C. Baranauskas, P. Palanque, J. Abascal, S.D.J. Barbosa (Eds.), Human-Computer Interaction – INTERACT 2007, Part I. XXXIII, 637 pages. 2007.

Vol. 4658: T. Enokido, L. Barolli, M. Takizawa (Eds.), Network-Based Information Systems. XIII, 544 pages. 2007.

Vol. 4656: M.A. Wimmer, J. Scholl, Å. Grönlund (Eds.), Electronic Government. XIV, 450 pages. 2007.

Vol. 4655: G. Psaila, R. Wagner (Eds.), E-Commerce and Web Technologies. VII, 229 pages. 2007.

Vol. 4654: I.-Y. Song, J. Eder, T.M. Nguyen (Eds.), Data Warehousing and Knowledge Discovery. XVI, 482 pages. 2007.

Vol. 4653: R. Wagner, N. Revell, G. Pernul (Eds.), Database and Expert Systems Applications. XXII, 907 pages. 2007.

Vol. 4636: G. Antoniou, U. Aßmann, C. Baroglio, S. Decker, N. Henze, P.-L. Patranjan, R. Tolksdorf (Eds.), Reasoning Web. IX, 345 pages. 2007.

Vol. 4611: J. Indulska, J. Ma, L.T. Yang, T. Ungerer, J. Cao (Eds.), Ubiquitous Intelligence and Computing. XXIII, 1257 pages. 2007.

Vol. 4607: L. Baresi, P. Fraternali, G.-J. Houben (Eds.), Web Engineering. XVI, 576 pages. 2007.

Vol. 4606: A. Pras, M. van Sinderen (Eds.), Dependable and Adaptable Networks and Services. XIV, 149 pages. 2007.

Vol. 4605: D. Papadias, D. Zhang, G. Kollios (Eds.), Advances in Spatial and Temporal Databases. X, 479 pages. 2007.

Vol. 4602: S. Barker, G.-J. Ahn (Eds.), Data and Applications Security XXI. X, 291 pages. 2007.

Vol. 4601: S. Spaccapietra, P. Atzeni, F. Fages, M.-S. Hacid, M. Kifer, J. Mylopoulos, B. Pernici, P. Shvaiko, J. Trujillo, I. Zaihrayeu (Eds.), Journal on Data Semantics IX. XV, 197 pages. 2007.

Vol. 4592: Z. Kedad, N. Lammari, E. Métais, F. Meziane, Y. Rezgui (Eds.), Natural Language Processing and Information Systems. XIV, 442 pages. 2007.

Vol. 4587: R. Cooper, J. Kennedy (Eds.), Data Management. XIII, 259 pages. 2007.

Vol. 4577: N. Sebe, Y. Liu, Y.-t. Zhuang, T.S. Huang (Eds.), Multimedia Content Analysis and Mining. XIII, 513 pages. 2007.

Vol. 4568: T. Ishida, S. R. Fussell, P. T. J. M. Vossen (Eds.), Intercultural Collaboration. XIII, 395 pages. 2007.

Vol. 4566: M.J. Dainoff (Ed.), Ergonomics and Health Aspects of Work with Computers. XVIII, 390 pages. 2007.

Vol. 4564: D. Schuler (Ed.), Online Communities and Social Computing. XVII, 520 pages. 2007.

Vol. 4563: R. Shumaker (Ed.), Virtual Reality. XXII, 762 pages. 2007.

Vol. 4561: V.G. Duffy (Ed.), Digital Human Modeling. XXIII, 1068 pages. 2007.

Vol. 4560: N. Aykin (Ed.), Usability and Internationalization, Part II. XVIII, 576 pages. 2007.

Vol. 4559: N. Aykin (Ed.), Usability and Internationalization, Part I. XVIII, 661 pages. 2007.

Vol. 4558: M.J. Smith, G. Salvendy (Eds.), Human Interface and the Management of Information, Part II. XXIII, 1162 pages. 2007.

Vol. 4557: M.J. Smith, G. Salvendy (Eds.), Human Interface and the Management of Information, Part I. XXII, 1030 pages. 2007.

Vol. 4541: T. Okadome, T. Yamazaki, M. Makhtari (Eds.), Pervasive Computing for Quality of Life Enhancement. IX, 248 pages. 2007.

Vol. 4537: K.C.-C. Chang, W. Wang, L. Chen, C.A. Ellis, C.-H. Hsu, A.C. Tsoi, H. Wang (Eds.), Advances in Web and Network Technologies, and Information Management. XXIII, 707 pages. 2007.

Vol. 4531: J. Indulska, K. Raymond (Eds.), Distributed Applications and Interoperable Systems. XI, 337 pages. 2007.

Vol. 4526: M. Malek, M. Reitenspieß, A. van Moorsel (Eds.), Service Availability. X, 155 pages. 2007.

Vol. 4524: M. Marchiori, J.Z. Pan, C.d.S. Marie (Eds.), Web Reasoning and Rule Systems. XI, 382 pages. 2007.